Straighten Up and Fly Right

OXFORD CULTURAL BIOGRAPHIES

Gary Giddins, Series Editor

A Generous Vision: The Creative Life of Elaine de Kooning
Cathy Curtis

Music by Max Steiner: The Epic Life of Hollywood's Most Influential Composer
Steven C. Smith

Straighten Up and Fly Right: The Life and Music of Nat King Cole
Will Friedwald

Straighten Up and Fly Right

The Life and Music of Nat King Cole

WILL FRIEDWALD

OXFORD
UNIVERSITY PRESS

OXFORD
UNIVERSITY PRESS

Oxford University Press is a department of the University of Oxford. It furthers the University's objective of excellence in research, scholarship, and education by publishing worldwide. Oxford is a registered trade mark of Oxford University Press in the UK and certain other countries.

Published in the United States of America by Oxford University Press
198 Madison Avenue, New York, NY 10016, United States of America.

Library of Congress Cataloging-in-Publication Data
Names: Friedwald, Will, 1961– author.
Title: Straighten up and fly right : the life and music of Nat King Cole / Will Friedwald.
Description: New York City : Oxford University Press, 2020. |
Series: Cultural biographies | Includes bibliographical references and index. |
Identifiers: LCCN 2019049935 (print) | LCCN 2019049936 (ebook) | ISBN 9780190882044 (cloth) |
ISBN 9780190882051 (pdf) | ISBN 9780190882068 (epub) | ISBN 9780190882075
Subjects: LCSH: Cole, Nat King, 1919–1965. | Singers—United States—Biography. |
Pianists—United States—Biography. | Jazz musicians—United States—Biography.
Classification: LCC ML420.C63 F75 2020 (print) | LCC ML420.C63 (ebook) |
DDC 782.42164092 [B]—dc23
LC record available at https://lccn.loc.gov/2019049935
LC ebook record available at https://lccn.loc.gov/2019049936

9 8 7 6 5 4 3 2 1

Printed by LSC Communications
United States of America

Dedicated to the children of Nat and Maria Cole—Natalie, Kelly, and the twins, Casey and Timolin (who were born exactly ten days after I was)—and especially to the much-missed Carole "Cookie" Cole, who loved what I wrote about "A Blossom Fell" and who encouraged me to write this book. And, not least, also to Freddy.

But most of all, as always, to Patty: my Mona Lisa, my ramblin' rose, and my ballerina.

Praise The Lord with the harp;
  make music to Him on the ten-stringed lyre.
Sing to Him a new song;
  play skillfully, and shout for joy.

—from *Psalm 33*

Old King Cole was a merry old soul,
And a merry old soul was he;
He called for his pipe, and he called for his bowl,
And he called for his fiddlers three.

Every fiddler he had a fiddle,
And a very fine fiddle had he;
Oh, there's none so rare, as can compare,
With King Cole and his fiddlers three.

—Traditional

Contents

Editor's Introduction

Will Friedwald on NKC: cognoscenti will be thrilled, but hardly surprised, to find that this seemingly inevitable book (he has been analyzing and chronicling Nat King Cole for a few decades in essays, liner notes, and his indispensable *Biographical Guide to the Great Jazz and Pop Singers*) exceeds its promise. There are other volumes on the incomparable King, but this is the one that marries the life to the art. It shows us how one of the finest pianists and most imaginative ensemble leaders of his generation became that generation's supreme crooner, swinging sublimely and setting hearts aglow with a uniquely suave candor and implacable charm. Reading this biography of Cole, you may even surmise that the postwar era in American popular music was truly the Age of Nat, rather than Frank or Elvis. Cole was everywhere, despite the restraints of bigotry. Here's a tip to get in the mood: go online and watch the TV duet of Nat Cole and Ella Fitzgerald on "It's Alright with Me." Can we agree that he was the very embodiment of aplomb?

The first two records I asked my mother to buy me for our monophonic console, back in the Autumn of 1956, were Presley's "I Want You, I Need You, I Love You" b/w "My Baby Left Me" (a 78 rpm disc because that's mostly what we had), and Cole's "That's All There Is to That" b/w "A Dream Sonata" (a purple, donut-hole 45), in part because those were two names I recognized from radio. We were in a suburban supermarket, browsing a display of new records available at three speeds. The 78, in time, slipped from my hands and shattered. The 45 lies before me, a reminder that, as Friedwald demonstrates, though Mr. Cole would not rock and roll, he did help to create rhythm and blues, without which, etc. etc. "That's All There Is to That" is now a forgotten rhythm number with triplets and male choir, but back then it got plenty of Top-40 radio play, and the B-side let you in on his cool manner with a ballad, a gift few pop singers could touch, let alone match. Ray Charles found his own style after an apprenticeship imitating Nat *and* his illustrious trio.

If Frank and Elvis divided the generations in those years, Nat never really did. Like Armstrong and Crosby, he was a musical unifier: easygoing, yes, but not easy listening in the derogatory sense. He had too much feeling for that. Friedwald offers a diverting depiction of Cole's unexpected success with "Nature Boy," a divining rod of a song in 1948, a harbinger of the beats to say nothing of the Summer of Love. It got so many radio spins that its producer pondered trying to limit them for fear that people would tire of it. People never did.

Still, many postwar jazz lovers had no idea how fully accomplished an artist he was. For me, that epiphany was cued by two comments: Dizzy Gillespie noted that there was no pianist he preferred to play with than Nat Cole; and a colleague expressed horror when I admitted I had not heard the 1957 album, *After Midnight*. (Another tip: go to that disc's "I Know That You Know" and check out the instrumental exchanges between Cole and the violinist Stuff Smith.) From then on, I had to hear everything he had done. Even so, it was not until years later that Friedwald himself told me about the 1958 album, *St. Louis Blues*, a far deeper work than Cole's biopic inspired by the life of W. C. Handy, in which the blues are miraculously transmuted into a cross between love songs and spirituals.

Cole effortlessly, or so it appeared, presided over the transitional culture of the 1950s, defining its surface optimism, beneath which a strange passivity masked a momentous daring waiting to erupt: as Marlon Brando said when asked, in *The Wild One* (1953), what he was rebelling against, "Whaddaya got?" Cole, forever natty and trim in his bespoke suits and narrow ties, brandishing a contagious confidence and self-esteem, was not above the meretricious ("Those Lazy-Hazy-Crazy Days of Summer"), but somehow it never tarnished him. Nothing could. He was the first African American to have his own network television show, though NBC could not find the sponsors for it. "Madison Avenue is afraid of the dark," Cole said, and moved forward. Though he died way too young, his art retained its undiminished satisfaction.

No one knows this better than Friedwald, who is by common consent the leading chronicler of the great American vocalists who sang and sing the great American songbook. He knows exactly where to look for the gems and the gemlike moments in Cole's oeuvre. All of his varied gifts as a researcher, a connoisseur of the evocative anecdote, and a critic of dependable discernment are brought to bear in his life of Nathaniel Adams Coles. I've known Will for many years, as friend and colleague, and I was particularly delighted when he suggested this project. I think you will agree that after some fifty-five years, the King now has a biography and critical assessment worthy of him.

Foreword

IT WAS EARLY January in 1980, as I recall it. I was playing music with my high school buddy/now college buddy Joe Francis on Monday nights at an Italian restaurant in Tappan, New York. Joe had the voice and matinee idol looks of Dick Haymes, while I was a cross between a young John Turturro and Detroit Tigers outfielder, Steve Kemp.

I would accompany Joe on my seven-string guitar as he performed a set of what we would come to learn was the Great American Songbook. Joe would occasionally ask me to sing a tune, and in those days I always had Kenny Rankin's "Haven't We Met" or James Taylor's "Don't Let Me Be Lonely Tonight" available in my musical back pocket.

One Monday night following our four-hour set, Joe's sister suggested I listen to a song called "Straighten Up and Fly Right" on the record *As Time Flies* by a singer/songwriter named Frank Weber. She said she thought it would be a good song for me. I obliged, learned it and, as always, played it for my father, jazz guitarist Bucky Pizzarelli, to have it vetted.

At what I thought would be an "I got him" moment he rolled his eyes and calmly said, "Go find the Nat Cole trio records, and you're gonna hear something..."

The "you knucklehead" was implied.

Lo and behold, Capitol Records had just re-released *The Best of the Nat King Cole Trio* (Volumes 1 and 2), and they happened to be in the bin of the local Sam Goody record store, awaiting my arrival.

I brought them back to Bucky Pizzarelli's house where my father, after perusing the track titles, instructed me to "Put on 'Paper Moon,' sit down, and listen."

As the four-speed Garrard turntable spun, it was at that moment that I heard things I'd been hearing for years on records my father had made and in the music of his drumless trio at the Café Pierre. I began to realize we'd hit father/son paydirt, an "A-ha" moment of other-worldly proportions. Things had come full circle. This fifty-four-year-old man was re-experiencing the music that had moved *him* at age twenty.

Next song—"Sentimental Reasons." "Hear how he sings that." For "Route 66"—"Hear what Oscar Moore is doing—rhythm, block chords . . . single-note solos?"

We played both records non-stop for weeks.

"You big jerk!" my father would often say, which was his own way of saying "I love you." But that's a story for another time.

It was a life-changing afternoon that stays with me to this day and brings tears to my eyes as I write about it. I had found something that wasn't "I've Got You under My Skin," "Witchcraft," or "Lush Life." This was jazz—set up by a "buzzard and a monkey" and a highway that ran through the middle of America. It was a food source to be swung and smiled at—ballads that were accessible to this youngster who had just enough sincerity but who hadn't yet visited those "come what may" places.

I learned every note of every song on those two albums. My father and I had just started working together as a duo around that time, and he began to occasionally ask for the new songs in our sets with the words, " 'Straighten Up' or 'Route 66.' "

When the opportunity arose for me to record my first vocal album in 1983, it seemed only right to include many of those same Nat Cole songs. They have since made their way into everything I have done musically. My first professional group was even piano, bass, and guitar. I have released three tribute CDs to Nat. I have been honored to work with Natalie Cole, Nat's daughter. I also met Nat's wife, Maria Cole, and have shared stages and become friends with Nat's younger brother, Freddy Cole.

I have tried to learn as much as possible about Nat Cole by collecting every record that could be found and by seeking out people who knew Nat and made music with him. The joy that man and that group brought me on that early January day in 1980 has never faded, and the musicality of his trio sides remain as fresh and as vibrant as the day they were recorded. He is the reason why I do what I do.

We are lucky to live in a world that gave us Nat Cole—the man and his music. And we are fortunate indeed to have access to an account of that man—and especially his music—that only Will Friedwald could have written.

John Pizzarelli, New York, 2019

Acknowledgments

I walk on the world, but I'm not usually in it.
—NAT KING COLE, *1964*

IN 1990, I FLIPPED A COIN. Having finished my first book about music, *Jazz Singing*, there were two other books I was anxious to write, one about Sinatra and the other about Nat King Cole. I went with Sinatra—not merely because of the coin toss but because he was very much still with us, and so were most of the people he worked with. And also, my agent (at the time), Claire Smith, encouraged me to take the Frank path—Ol' Blue Eyes seemed to be everywhere at that moment, and the long-departed Cole was much less visible. We had no way of knowing that Natalie was about to release a bestselling single and album that would rekindle the public's love affair with her father. Ironically, in the early to mid-'90s, the two major artists competing for our attention would be Sinatra and Cole—exactly as it had been forty years earlier—Sinatra in his *Duets* albums and Cole in the form of the blockbuster "duet" single with his daughter and the album that went with it.

It was while working on *Sinatra! The Song Is You* that I established a career-long relationship with the legendary (I don't mind saying) editor Robert Gottlieb. From that point on, and for the next twenty years or so, we worked on a total of four books (so far) together. Bob encouraged me to write about the big picture of American music rather than focusing on any one individual artist, and thus we produced *Stardust Melodies* (2003), *A Biographical Guide to the Great Jazz and Pop Singers* (2010), and *The Great Jazz and Pop Vocal Albums* (2017); with those three books, there's about two million words spilled about jazz and the Great American Songbook. (Along the way, I also accepted Tony Bennett's offer to work with him on his memoir, *The Good Life*.)

All of which is a roundabout way of saying that I never had the chance to work on my dream book about Nat Cole—not until now. In many ways, I'm glad I waited. I have easier access to much more information now than I did then, and besides, now I have the benefit of twenty years of steadfast research by my great friend Jordan Taylor, who has gathered information on every aspect and every detail of Cole's short-lived but copious career. Jordan has been researching Cole's music since the 1990s, and he has done a lot of the heavy lifting, including countless hours spent poring through rapidly disintegrating contracts, piecing together the specifics of Cole's extensive recording sessions. Jordan's work is the most thorough that I have ever seen done on any major vocalist or entertainer. Authors are forever saying, "This book could not have been done without so-and-so," and while this book could have been done without Jordan, that just would not have been a book that I would want to have written, or even to read myself. I remain eternally in his debt. As with *Sinatra! The Song Is You*, this book is primarily about the music and the professional career of the artist in question, but there is a lot of biographical and historical context surrounding it—as we know, even an artist on the level of Cole doesn't create in a vacuum. My goal is to lead readers and listeners through the path of Cole's career while anatomizing his output; there's one brief sidestep out of the general chronology where we talk about his non-Trio, piano "jam session" recordings made from 1942 to 1946, most done under the aegis of his best friend at the time, producer Norman Granz. Throughout, my aim is to include biographical details where they're most pertinent to a greater understanding of the work itself. Even though Cole's wasn't a long career, it was an extremely productive one, filled with no less innovation and excellence than those of Cole's closest colleagues, like Sinatra, Ella Fitzgerald, and Duke Ellington.

My acknowledgments need to start with Seth Berg of South Bay Music, who runs the estate of Nat King Cole, and who, unlike many of his peers (running the estates of certain other iconic entertainers that I could name), has proven to be extremely helpful with the writing of this book. Then, there's Norm Hirschy, who acquired and then edited this volume for Oxford University Press—here's hoping we can do many such projects together. Thanks also to my original mentor, Gary Giddins, who remains the best writer on music currently active and whose ongoing biographical epic on Bing Crosby remains a source of joy and inspiration. And thanks also to my extremely valuable literary agent, William Clark, and the love of my life, Patty Farmer.

I also wish to acknowledge Jeff Abraham, Jonathan Alexiuk, Brook Babcock, Jim Burns, Mark Cantor (the ultimate authority on the subject of jazz-and-film), Brian Chidester (biographer of eden ahbez), Eric Comstock and Barbara Fasano, Dave Dawes, Jim Davison, Anthony DiFlorio III, Patty Farmer, Zev Feldman (along with Matt Lutthans and George Klabin of Resonance Records), Michael Feinstein, Chuck Granata, Suanne Gray,

Howard Green, Chuck Haddix and the Marr Sound Archive including the Dave Dexter Collection (Kansas City), David Hajdu and Karen Oberlin, Jane Klain and Ron Simon of the Paley Center, Wayne Kline, Stephen A. Kramer, Juliette Kurtzman, David Lennick, Steven Lasker, Sylvia Maderic, James Fox Miller and Barbara Miller (whose cousin, the late Jack Segal, wrote several important songs for Cole), Beth Naji, Anais Reno, David Rosen, the late Michael B. Schnurr, Billy Vera, Holly Foster Wells, and the A Team (Andrew Poretz and Andrew J. Lederer).

Next, I need to give special thanks to four long-departed, much-missed scholars in four different countries who dedicated much of their working lives to researching the music of Nat King Cole: Ken Crawford (United States), Gord Grieveson (Canada), Roy G. Holmes (United Kingdom), and Klaus Teubig (Germany).

My final acknowledgment goes to Freddy Cole: I have known Freddy for more than twenty-five years and spoken with him dozens of times about his brother and their music. Forgive me if all the quotes and information supplied by Nat's kid brother aren't accurately footnoted: Freddy was never much of a talker, and he prefers not to give formal interviews, thus everything he told me was doled out in dribs and drabs over the years, usually before or after sets at Dizzy's, Birdland, or the Jazz Standard (alas, there's no way of documenting whether he told me something in 1997 or 2017).

Last, before we begin, I need to offer a note on a name. The artist was born Nathaniel Adams Coles, and he began leading the King Cole Trio at age eighteen. From around the time he was twenty, he was known professionally as "Nat King Cole" (although there were always a few close friends, like his pal and promoter Dick LaPalm, who addressed him affectionately with the more formal "Nathaniel"). For roughly twenty years, he was generally billed as "Nat 'King' Cole"—and occasionally also signed his name (as for his friend Claire Phillips Gordon) as "Nat (King) Cole" using parentheses. Then, around 1957, he had the name legally changed; he told one interviewer at the time, "You can take the quotes off [the name] when you print your story."[1] In this book, I refer to him as either "Cole" or "Nat," depending on the context. (In writing about his personal life, or talking about his family, I occasionally exercise the biographer's prerogative to use the so-called Christian name). In this book, just to be consistent, I refer to him throughout his adult life simply as "Nat King Cole" without any superfluous punctuation.

Will Friedwald, Harlem 2019

Straighten Up and Fly Right

Cole in the lobby, apparently, of the London Palladium, where he played from March 22 to April 3, 1954. "He who pays the minstrel calls the tune" (London Palladium, 1954). (Courtesy South Bay Music)

Introduction

OF FALLING BLOSSOMS AND PAPER MOONS

Frozen in time, I can't let it go
Nat Cole, Unforgettable
The pedestal
I'm on, I'm a end up on the Federal
Reserve note
Your money with a hip hop quote.
—From "Who Tells Your Story" (on The Hamilton Mixtape)

WHEN NAT COLE SINGS A SONG, he says what he means, clearly and distinctly, without any unnecessary complication. Yet everything in Cole's career and his life happened on at least two levels, and there is a constant duality in his art.

No other figure in American music ever succeeded so well at two entirely different pursuits. He was at once a major instrumentalist and then a major singer; there were precedents, but no one who did quite what he did—Louis Armstrong or Fats Waller, for instance, were both outstanding jazz players who doubled as equally brilliant jazz singers. But only Cole completely mastered the equivalent of two different instruments in what amounts to two different fields, being at once one of the greatest pianists in all of jazz as well as one of the most popular vocalists who ever lived. In fact, he succeeded so overwhelmingly as a pop singer that most people even forgot that he had ever played the piano. By comparison, Frank Sinatra was a popular vocalist who occasionally made a jazz album, while Ella Fitzgerald was a jazz artist who frequently added a pop dimension to her work. But only Cole was both indisputably jazz and inarguably pop at the same time—and virtually all the time.

Cole's statistics are staggering—approximately 150 chart hits, beginning in 1942, when he landed one of the first ten "number ones" on the *Billboard* rhythm-and-blues listing, and continuing at least as recently as 2019, as "The Christmas Song" continues to chart annually. He has had, so far, one of the longest spans ever on the pop charts—almost seventy-five years as of his centennial—and what makes it doubly remarkable is that he created all this music in such a relatively short time span, a career that was curtailed by his death from lung cancer at the age of forty-five.

Cole also represented completely different ideals to the jazz listener and the pop audience; Cole also stood for something very different to white listeners and black listeners. To the latter, he was both a romantic figure and a role model for Afro-American achievement, whereas the former embraced him and treated him with more respect and admiration than they ever had for a black performer, before or since. And the dichotomy of his music persists: like Sinatra and Fitzgerald, Cole excelled at singing what we refer to as the Great American Songbook, the largely theater-centric canon of Cole Porter, Irving Berlin, and their peers. Yet Cole could and did sing just about everything, having hits in every variety of the blues (from the basic traditional blues to high-powered rhythm and blues [R&B] and even the nascent rock and roll of his day), to Gospel music to Latin American music (*tangos, choros, boleros*), and, at the end of his life, country and western. He could also take the silliest novelty song and, by singing it without condescension, make it seem both funny and poignant. He could do almost anything that any other artist could do, but no one else could do what he did.

ON DECEMBER 20, 1954, Nat King Cole, accompanied by arranger-conductor Nelson Riddle, recorded "A Blossom Fell." The song would be one of Cole's big hits of 1955 (#2 in the United States and #3 in the United Kingdom); in April 1956, it would become the lead-off track of his album *Ballads of the Day*, a popular compilation of successful singles from the years 1953 to '55. Cole regarded the song as significant enough for him to re-record it in stereo in 1961 for his retrospective album *The Nat King Cole Story*.

"A Blossom Fell" was, in many ways, a typical Nat King Cole song. Like many of his hits in the '50s and '60s, it was a European import (a trait he shared with another of his heroes, Louis Armstrong, whose Eisenhower-era repertoire also consisted largely of foreign-born melodies). This song came from England, the work of three rather obscure authors named Harold Cornelius, Dominic John, and Howard Barnes.[1] And even more than any of his colleagues, Cole's audience, no less than his material, was hugely international. Around the same time that "A Blossom Fell" was released in America, Cole's disc also charted in the song's native country, climbing considerably higher than rival recordings of the song by home-grown crooners Dickie Valentine and Ronnie Hilton.

"A Blossom Fell" is also an archetypical Nat King Cole hit in that, with no disrespect intended to Mr. Valentine and Mr. Hilton, I doubt that anyone would remember this particular song—along with a great many others—were it not for Cole. Classic songs like "All the Things You Are" have a way of surviving even if they were originally written for flop shows, but we would have no reason to remember a great many songs in Cole's canon were it not for him. He not only put such songs on the map, but he was the whole map. This "Blossom" has continued to flower in performances of other artists who grew to love it through the classic Cole-Riddle version. (Filmmaker Terrence Malick tapped into its power by using it as a central element in his seminal 1973 *Badlands*, much as Richard Benjamin did with Cole's "Stardust" in his classic 1980 comedy *My Favorite Year*.)

The lyric pivots on two key points, the first being the use of plants as a metaphor. Cole would sing other songs that used variations on this idea, most notably the famous "Blue Gardenia" (1953), the obscure "Sweet William" (1952), and the classic "Autumn Leaves" (1955). The other factor in the narrative is also a time-honored conceit of songwriters: the notion that gypsies (itself a politically incorrect term these days), being fortune tellers, are a race of mystics who have the inside dope on fate. While many of the ethnic stereotypes of Tin Pan Alley had faded away by the postwar era, such preconceived ideas regarding the Romany people were apparently alive and well. In songs like "Golden Earrings," "The Gypsy," and even Cole's own, earlier "That Ain't Right," lovers assess the fidelity of their partners based on tell-tale signs that can only be read by gypsies via tea leaves and crystal balls.

The tradition presented in "A Blossom Fell" is one of those concepts that's so goofy that only Tin Pan Alley could have dreamed it up.[2] In "Golden Earrings," we are told that if your love wears the so-described jewelry, "then she belongs to you." Here, in a "A Blossom Fell," if two lovers are sitting beneath a tree, exchanging vows of affection, and a petal happens to fall off a branch and touch the lips of one of them, it means that one of them isn't telling the truth when professing love for the other.

It's an awkward idea to express in song, and make no mistake, it is very awkwardly expressed. The song opens, "A blossom fell / From off a tree / It settled softly / On the lips you turned to me." As you can see, the last two lines of the A section are particularly cumbersome. They make little sense when you read them in print, especially considering that even if this is a genuine gypsy tradition, it's certainly one that not many people would be familiar with. Sammy Cahn believed that it was a mortal sin for a lyricist to put something in a line that needs to be explained: a songwriter's job is to make his point immediately understandable. It can be deep and profound, like those ideas found in the texts of such high-level sages as Cole Porter or Alan Jay Lerner, but never obscure or incomprehensible.

The most obvious point was that only a really top-drawer vocal artist—a Cole, a Sinatra, a Clooney, a Holiday—could take a lyric like this and not only make its meaning crystal clear but turn it into a hit. As he so often did, Cole compensates for any inadequacies a text might have—he puts over exactly what the lyricist wanted to say even on those frequent occasions where the lyric is lacking. The lyric needs help, and it gets it.

Arranger-conductor Nelson Riddle does the same for the melody: he opens with a glorious string flourish that literally depicts the wind blowing leaves and branches around in a cherry orchard with blossoms falling hither and thither. The secondary voice on "Blossom Fell" is valve trombonist Juan Tizol, who appears frequently on Cole's sessions in the mid-'50s, most prominently on the 1956 album *After Midnight*. (In the 1961 stereo remake, Cole takes the chart slightly slower and replaces the valve trombone with the customary slide instrument.)

One of Cole's key strengths as a vocalist was his unique capacity to improve any melody, for emphasizing the parts of the tune that worked and minimizing its shortcomings. It's no insult to Sinatra to say that, for all his musical strengths (including a remarkable sense of timing), he had to take a backseat to Cole in the realm of pure melody. The only major singers who compete with Cole in this respect were Ella Fitzgerald and Sarah Vaughan, and neither of those grand divas was the lyric interpreter that Cole was.

Bing Crosby or, say, Carmen McRae could have sung "A Blossom Fell" and made us understand, but Cole does something that no other singer could have possibly done with it: he makes us believe it. Cole sings it as if he was imparting wisdom gained from actual experience, and he makes the words and music sound unique to his idiom. Even though Frank Sinatra did more than anyone to perfect the art of lyric interpretation, he would have a hard time convincing anyone that he actually exists in this particular stylistic universe—where prevaricators can be readily identified by the blossoms sticking to their lying lips. This is not meant symbolically; Cole makes you believe it in the most concrete way: there never would have been any Watergate scandal in this world, because Nixon would have had blossoms all over his face.

Such an approach is perhaps hard to fully fathom in the world of 21st-century popular culture—where precious little actually means what it's supposed to mean. Everything in the millennial era is ironic or sarcastic, a series of codes where the truth is hidden, and nothing is obvious. Yet Cole is precisely the opposite: Cole doesn't mean things metaphorically, he means exactly what he says, literally. We could only accept this from Cole at all because he is so imminently believable and never tells us anything but the absolute truth; there are no blossoms on his lips.

And that is the central tenet of Cole's music. Sinatra, contrastingly, was about singing great songs with multiple levels of meaning—songs with deep gray areas between black and white, like "Glad to Be Unhappy." Even when Sinatra sings something simple, he makes it deeper and more complicated and adds in gradations of feeling—Johnny Hodges–like microtones and emotional glissandos in between points A and B. Cole, on the other hand, is more direct. Sinatra can take a simple song and make it profound; Cole takes a complex song and makes its meaning abundantly clear.

As Peggy Lee, a close colleague of both men, put it, "Nat had the advantage of phrasing very well, and phrasing beautifully, and the taste of a fine musician. Perhaps it was the simple honesty and the really sincere depth of feeling that he had, he understood every lyric that he sang."[3] Another factor was his enunciation: he came from an era when the African Americans worked hard to assimilate into white culture by speaking as properly as possible, when the black bourgeoisie disdained blues shouters but praised black classical violinists and tenors. The black male singers whom Cole heard when he was growing up, like Pha Terrell with Andy Kirk and Bill Kenny of the Ink Spots, tended to enunciate almost exceedingly correctly; and in his own generation, singers like himself (as in, "are you *wahm*, are you *rill*, Mona Lisa . . ."), and even more so those like Al Hibbler and Della Reese, carried it to such an extreme that they often sounded like students of Professor Henry Higgins.

The driving force behind Cole's career was neither his keyboard artistry, which was evident from the beginning, nor his vocal virtuosity, which matured later, but rather the superlative musical intelligence that powered both. Cole had started his career leading a big band in Chicago, for which he wrote all the arrangements; thus, in later years, rather like Quincy Jones, he didn't need to write all of his own orchestral arrangements, but it was his own ability as an arranger that allowed him to work with such giants of pop music orchestration as Nelson Riddle, Billy May, and Gordon Jenkins, even before Sinatra. Likewise, he knew how to write a song—all three of the numbers that propelled him to the top of the "race records" charts were his own: "Gone with the Draft," "That Ain't Right," and "Straighten Up and Fly Right." This became a virtual superpower that enabled him to find good songs (and, in some cases, help hone them into shape, as he would do with "Unforgettable"), songs that the public would love, well before his friends and rivals.

This power was absolutely essential to Cole, not least because he had less access to the other media that his white colleagues did, specifically film and television. He didn't just stumble across good songs; he knew how to find them, in part by cultivating songwriters. He sang "It is Better to Be by Yourself" by Bob Wells before the same writer came back to him with "The Christmas Song," and he performed "Calico Sal" by Irving Gordon, who returned to him with "Unforgettable." His long hours playing piano in small clubs, six hours a night, six nights a week, helped him learn how to predict which songs would be beloved by the public; as a result, he introduced more new standard songs than anyone after Fred Astaire and Bing Crosby. "Working in those clubs for years, I learned that you have to reach audiences." As he later told Ralph Gleason, "You have to get across the footlights to the crowd. If you don't—you're sunk."[4]

That's partially why Cole is so closely identified with individual songs—and had so many hit singles—whereas Sinatra was better suited, in the long run, to create his masterpieces in the album format. Cole could put over a song and make his point in three minutes; Sinatra did better when he could put a story together point by point. And in his career, Cole would introduce many more classic songs than anyone of his generation, even Sinatra, whose brilliance lay more in celebrating the great songs of the past—although, Cole, as we know, did that as well. Sinatra created more classic albums in the long run, but Cole's best albums—*Nat King Cole Sings for Two in Love* (1953), *After Midnight* (1956), *Love Is the Thing* (1956), *Just One of Those Things* (1957), *St. Louis Blues* (1958), *The Very Thought of You* (1958), *Wild Is Love* (1960), *The Touch of Your Lips* (1960), and *Nat King Cole Sings / George Shearing Plays* (1961), *Let's Face the Music* (1961), *Where Did Everyone Go?* (1962)—are second to none.

Cole was markedly different from his contemporaries in other ways; for roughly ten to twenty years after the war, the majority of hitmakers on the pop charts were veterans of the big band experience, from Sinatra on down. This applied to the white artists as well as the small number of black performers, led by Cole and Billy Eckstine, who were beginning to break through to the "mainstream" audience. Cole was the only jazz musician to ever make the transition, with the exception of Louis Armstrong—and even to the end of his life, no one ever forgot Armstrong was a trumpet player. Cole went so far into the world of mainstream pop that virtually everyone forgot he had ever played the piano.

The larger truth is that Cole was a key player in the era when multiple artists, a female singer, a male singer, a big band, frequently were in competition on the charts with different—sometimes very different—versions of the same song. But Cole's signature hits were so unique that no one could have done them anywhere nearly as effectively. In that way, Cole's relationship with his material foreshadows the pop of a decade later; when there was, essentially, only one artist per song, and by that point, so called "covers" were anathema.

In the second half of his career, Cole was both amused and confused to be confronted by fans who wanted him to revive the Trio or just play more piano—as the older Richard Rodgers was when fans would remind him of his earlier work with Lorenz Hart. He had actually thought of himself, from the beginning, as an entertainer rather than a pianist or singer, and the medium with which he entertained was secondary. (And it's also a myth that he stopped playing the piano; virtually every live performance we know of has at least a few numbers where he plays.)

His relationship with other singers was different too. Said Sammy Davis Jr., "When he had a big hit, other singers paid him a particular compliment. They didn't rush out to copy him on the same song. I've heard singers, including me, say 'Forget it. Nat's done it already.' "[5] Usually singers had the opposite effect on Sinatra: when he heard an artist he admired, like Bing Crosby, or Ella Fitzgerald, or Judy Garland, or Tony Bennett, introduce him to a song, he felt compelled to sing it as well, to add his own imprimatur to it. Nat Cole seems to be the only artist who scared him away from doing a song—most famously "Lush Life," which Sinatra made the mistake of attempting, but wisely aborted halfway through, and it was obviously because of Cole that Sinatra never left us with a definitive "Stardust."

"UNDER THE MOON THE BACKLOT was thirty acres of fairyland—not because the locations really looked like African jungles and French *chateaux* and schooners at anchor and Broadway by night, but because they looked like the torn picture books of childhood, like fragments of stories dancing in an open fire." In other words, a Barnum and Bailey world of paper moons and muslin trees.

That line, from *The Last Tycoon* always makes me think of "It's Only a Paper Moon," a 1932 song that the King Cole Trio recorded at their second session for Capitol Records on December 15, 1943. This had been one of the first songs written by the new team of composer Harold Arlen (then ensconced at the Cotton Club regularly writing songs for with Ted Kohler) and lyricist E. Y. Harburg. In addition to Arlen and Harburg, one other collaborator receives credit for the song, Billy Rose, best known as a Broadway producer and later an influential columnist. In 1932, Rose was producing a play called

The Great Magoo, a story about con men and hustlers on a carnival midway, and even though it wasn't a musical, he had the idea to include a single song that spoke to the discrepancy, the cognitive distance as it were, between reality and illusion. Armed with that inspiration, they proceeded to write the song—Harburg had actually thought of the "Paper Moon" title a few years earlier, and now he had the excuse to use it.[6]

The Great Magoo opened on December 2, 1932, and closed eleven performances later. However, Rose was nothing if not street smart and knew he had a valuable copyright on his hands. He arranged for the song to be featured in *Take a Chance*, a 1933 Paramount Pictures musical filmed at the Kaufman Astoria Studios in Queens. Here, "Paper Moon" is the basis for an elaborate production number in which the leading man and leading lady project themselves into a *Three Musketeers*–like romantic fantasy. Early on, "Paper Moon" was recorded famously by Paul Whiteman's Orchestra with a vocal by Irene Taylor, and also by the pioneering jazz and pop singer-instrumentalist Cliff "Ukulele Ike" Edwards, who sang the verse. Both of these 1933 recordings have more than a slight edge of melancholy, focusing on the song's minor-key aspects. (After Cole brought the song back to everyone's attention, Warner Bros., who by then owned the publishing rights, used it again in a 1945 picture titled *Too Young to Know*.)

Cole recorded his version of "Paper Moon" at the same session as another all-time career signature song, "Sweet Lorraine." The Trio treatment is sleek and swinging, more upbeat than bittersweet. Its most salient feature is the harmonic interweaving of Cole's keyboard and Oscar Moore's guitar, a combination that utilizes elements of block chords as well as octave playing, added to doubling and tripling of notes between piano and guitar. The idea of block chords is generally attributed to Milt Buckner,[7] one-time pianist with Lionel Hampton, but Cole and the Trio refined it considerably, and, it later became the sonic signature for the George Shearing Quintet.

The remarkable sound of the piano and guitar playing so closely, you literally can't tell where one ends and the other begins, also helps to bring out the inner lyric: the main instrument playing the Arlen melody isn't a piano or a guitar but something completely new, a single hybrid instrument created by a merger of the two, being operated by two amazing musicians functioning as one. A two-headed giant with four arms, a fabulous creature that fully belongs in a song about blurring the boundaries between fantasy and reality.

If a bittersweet love song was appropriate in the depths of the depression in 1932–33, what was called for during the wartime era was a cheerful, optimistic, and swinging song about unreality: men were thousands of miles away in foxholes and trenches, women were wearing overalls and working in assembly lines straight through the night. It was an age of paper moons and cardboard seas—and the news arriving constantly from Europe, about entire populations being obliterated, seemed even more unbelievable. And for all of its brash chutzpah, Harburg's lyric can still be interpreted as a World War II–era song of separation: "Without your love / It's a honky tonk parade. . . . It's a melody played on a penny arcade." Cole's only lyric alteration is slight but significant: the lyric originally opened with a throwaway syllable, "*Say* it's only a paper moon . . . " That was cute, but so 1933. Cole adjusts it by re-expanding the contraction in a way that seems much more swingingly up-to-date: "*It is* only a paper moon . . ." "It is" is much more formal than "it's," but the extra beat also makes it much more swinging and syncopated.

All the more remarkably, "It's Only a Paper Moon" was a major hit when it was first issued, even though it was not actually released as a single, but only one of eight songs on Cole's first album, *The King Cole Trio*, released in October 1944. Yet it reached the #5 spot on the Harlem Hit Parade (then the term for the *Billboard* Rhythm-and-Blues chart) and became one of the career perennials that he would perform almost every night for the rest of his life. At least fourteen different recordings exist, both live and studio, including (as with "Sweet Lorraine") two hi-fi album remakes—on *After Midnight* (1956) and *The Nat King Cole Story* (1961). There's also an excellent full-on arrangement that combines big band with piano and trio-style interplay (the best document of this version was taped live at the Latin Quarter in Tokyo in 1963).

In taking a melancholy song and transforming it into a joyful and optimistic—not to mention thoroughly irresistible—swinger, Cole was directly foreshadowing what Sinatra would achieve a decade later in classic albums like *Songs for Swingin' Lovers*. Yet "Paper Moon" was primarily a song for the late wartime and early postwar era, overflowing as it is with brash peacetime optimism. The joy Cole radiates in his vocal, as well as that amazing instrumental combination of piano and guitar, expresses a euphoria that both supports and undercuts the lyric. In the end, the final message is that it doesn't matter whether the world is real or not, whether it's "a melody played in a penny arcade" or something more substantial. It only matters that *you* believe in *me*. Love is the thing, he is telling us, it is the only thing that matters, even in a world where reality itself is up for grabs.

HOW WAS COLE ABLE TO ACHIEVE so much, so many albums and innumerable singles in the middle of a constant schedule of touring, combined with radio and then television appearances? And somehow do it all in a span that was much shorter than the careers of any of his peers? For one thing, Cole kept constantly changing what he was doing—even more so in the second act of his career than the first. Every period was different from the previous one, and every era was a time of transition. During the years 1948 to 1951, when he very gradually shifted from trio to orchestral accompaniments, virtually every session brought something new, something he had never tried before.

"You have to be bold," he said in 1961; "you gotta keep changing. You need to do it for *you*—to keep growing. You also need to do it for the public." He continued, drawing on an analogy from baseball, his favorite non-musical pastime, "You gotta keep 'em loose—you know, like a ballplayer. Keep the public loose at the plate. You gotta cross 'em up, throw something different at their head."[8]

In Cole's short life, he simply hadn't time to repeat himself. In 1953, he made *Nat King Cole Sings for Two in Love*, a classic album of vocals on standards with stellar arrangements by Nelson Riddle, and though it was widely accepted as a masterpiece, he never did another set quite like it—the same for *After Midnight* (1956), his brilliant set of small group jazz with vocals. It was only closer to the end of his career, when *Cole Español* (1958) became such a huge hit that more Spanish albums were clearly called for, and then even later, when *Ramblin' Rose* was such an overwhelming success that he had to fill the demand for more country-centric albums. But, for the most part, his classic albums were sui generis. As he said at the time of what was then announced as his twenty-fifth anniversary in show business in 1962, in the wake of his smash "Ramblin' Rose," "Sure, I want another hit record, and I'll be trying hard with 'Dear Lonely Hearts' and 'Who's Next in Line?' But you'll notice that neither one of them is a copy of 'Ramblin' Rose.' I never tried to follow 'Nature Boy' with a copy either. If an artist thinks he's found the right formula with one hit, he's mistaken. Copying is such a blind alley. You've got to be fresh and new each time out."[9]

The Latin albums, which started with *Cole Español* (1958), were, no less than the country albums, another highly rewarding detour that none of his friends and fans saw coming—especially since Cole, unlike his close friend Sammy Davis Jr., didn't actually speak Spanish. Davis was the grandchild of Cuban immigrants, and he grew up speaking Spanish to his mother, the Latina dancer Elvera Sanchez. At the height of the popularity of the three *Español* albums, Sammy would constantly kid Nat about his diction on Spanish and French songs. "He learned the songs phonetically, and they sure sounded like it. But when I went to South America, everybody asked me, 'Why don't you sing in Spanish like Nat?' I stopped teasing him."[10]

To the end of his short life, he never stopped experimenting, he never stopped varying the mixture; even his final work, the *L-O-V-E* album, released even while he was in the hospital with just a few weeks to live, was a whole new concept, a set of Eurocentric swing numbers unlike anything anyone had ever done before. As we've seen already, Cole could do many things: he could play the piano, he could sing, he could lead a band and write arrangements for it, he could write songs, he could run a business empire that included production and publishing firms. He could do virtually everything except stand still.

"You gotta keep moving," as he put it; "you know the public can curl up on you and go to sleep if you don't watch it."[11] In 1962, he elaborated, "I guess some people would sit back and rest on their laurels after having a successful career. Not me! I want to keep building. If you don't give yourself plenty to do, you go stale."[12] As we are about to see, he constantly kept moving and never sat back. Like Lin-Manuel Miranda's "Hamilton," Nat King Cole "got a lot farther / By working a lot harder / By being a lot smarter / By being a self-starter."

Prelude: Paris, 1930

In the summer of 1930, Noble Sissle and his Sizzling Syncopators were on top of the world—or, at the very least, at the top of the food chain of black show business. Sissle (1889–1975) already had distinguished himself on multiple fronts, the first of which was, literally an actual front of warfare; during the big one, he had served with honor as a member of Jim Europe's New York 369th Infantry "Hellfighters" Regiment. He distinguished himself on the cultural battlefield as well, as part of the band that helped introduce American jazz to Europe and the world. A songwriter, singer, violinist, bandleader, producer, and talent scout, Sissle had been one of the creators of *Shuffle Along*, a show that, again quite literally, changed the face of Broadway. Then, as the leader of his own hugely popular orchestra, Sissle was, at the start of the Great Depression in 1930, considerably more famous than Duke Ellington or Fats Waller, especially internationally.

In a lesson he would indirectly impart to Nat Cole, Sissle had already outgrown the racist constraints placed around black musicians in the United States and spent much of the post–*Shuffle Along* period, in the late 1920s, touring Europe; his was one of the first African American bands to play Paris and London. At the time of his forty-first birthday in July 1930, the

Sizzling Syncopators were ensconced in one of the most celebrated venues in the world. Les Ambassadeurs on the Champs-Elysées was described as "the prize job of the continent," and the Sizzling Syncopators had beaten out many a competing orchestra, domestic or American, black or white, to claim that prize.

Back home, "the Negro press," as it was known, didn't generally have a budget for foreign correspondents, but a journalist bylined as J. A. Rogers was in town and interviewed Sissle for the *Philadelphia Tribune* (then, as now, the oldest established black paper in the United States). Not surprisingly, Sissle had a lot to say about the state of jazz and popular music. First things first, he told Rogers, "The Negro was the real inventor of jazz music. Immediately after the war, the world was sad, it wanted noisy music to cheer it up." He added, "Soon after the war, no society leader would have thought of having an affair without a Negro orchestra."[13]

"Later, however, that was superseded by soft, symphonic music still of jazz origin, and here was where most of our Negro musicians fell down, and just where the white ones came in. ... when the time for softer music came in, then came more than ever the time for the use of brains. The white musicians, who had been imitating Negroes, used their brains, while the Negroes continued to rely on their natural talent. Entertaining calls for brains and real cleverness these days."

He continued, "The Negro can make people laugh. That is his gift. But he is afraid to do it, thinking he is being undignified. Why, there is no greater gift than that of being able to create laughter. It is an art, and nothing wins friends easier."

That was roughly the way Sissle saw it from the perspective of 1930, the start of the Depression and the age of radio, five years before what we now call the Swing Era, when Jelly Roll Morton and Bix Beiderbecke were still active, and the game-changing innovations of Louis Armstrong and Earl Hines were still fresh in everyone's ears. As Sissle saw it, Negroes invented the music, but clever white men, using their brains and not merely relying on natural talent, had managed to take the play away from the originators.

But Sissle was optimistic. "But some new men are entering the field, and if this keeps up, the Negro will soon be coming back into his own, for the public really likes the colored musician, but he must be able to deliver the goods." Doubtless by the term "new men," he meant Armstrong, Hines, Ellington, Waller, and a few others, all of whom were a generation younger than he. Obviously, we can debate the finer points of his summation of jazz history up to that point, but there's no arguing his assertion that these "new men" were indeed in the process of putting the spotlight back on black musicians and delivering the goods.

As a rather generous footnote to history, the *Tribune* story gives us a complete list of the current personnel of the Sizzling Syncopators.[14] Playing "bass tuba" in the band is a young man from Montgomery, Alabama, by way of Chicago, Illinois, the twenty-one-year-old Edward Coles. His kid brother, Nathaniel, was only eleven at the time, making him the very newest of the "new men." But although still just a boy, Nat was about to make his first public and professional performance. Maybe even then, Nathaniel somehow knew that he had to get started as early as possible, as if he somehow knew that he would not live to be an old man. But in his relatively short time on earth, Nat King Cole would not only change the meaning and the sound of both jazz and popular music several times over, but he would also significantly alter the public perception of what it meant to be black.

Sissle concluded, "In some quarters, there is a definite propaganda against the colored musicians, entertainers, and we need all such good men as we can get." The story ended with the optimistic pronouncement that "The Noble Sissle Ambassadeur's Revue will remain until the close of the season."

Origin Story (1919–1937)

> My father didn't like my being a musician at all, in fact, he disapproved of it entirely. But my mother thought it was a good idea and eventually talked him 'round. Now he goes out and buys all my records as they are released and says it's for my two kid brothers.
>
> —Nat King Cole, 1945

In my younger and more vulnerable years, I read a famous line by F. Scott Fitzgerald that I've been turning over in my mind ever since, especially as it applies to Nat King Cole. Of all the hundreds of thousands of words written by Fitzgerald in his four finished novels and 164 short stories, it's ironic that one of the most quoted phrases in his canon never even made it into one of his actual works. You know the one I'm talking about: "There are no second acts in American lives." Seven words strung together into a very powerful thought. Yet we'll never know exactly what Fitzgerald meant, since the line originates in the rough notes for his unfinished final novel, *The Last Tycoon*. Was this meant to be an observation by the narrator? Was it a line of dialogue? Does it reflect the author's own personal philosophy? If he had lived to complete the book, would that line have even made it into the final draft? We'll never know. But for me, at least, it's impossible to hear those words without thinking of Cole, whose life divides almost perfectly into two highly symmetrical acts, each a fourteen-year period, from 1937 to 1951 and then from 1951 to 1965.

Francis Scott Fitzgerald died at age forty-four in 1940, largely in the aftermath of his longtime addiction to alcohol; Nathaniel Adams Cole (originally "Coles") died at age forty-five in 1965, the direct result of his lifelong addiction to tobacco and cigarettes. There are actually several points in their biographies when they were roughly in the same place at the same time. Fitzgerald's wife, Zelda Sayre (who, in the 21st century, is perhaps an even greater cultural icon than her husband), was the daughter of one of the more prominent families of Montgomery, Alabama, the same city where Nat's father, the future Reverend Edward Coles, was then working as a grocer and a butcher.

In 1918, momentous changes were concurrently occurring in both families, even as they were for millions of other families in the United States and Europe during this final year of the Great War. In the more upscale part of town, the young Private Fitzgerald was courting a judge's daughter; meanwhile, a few miles away in the "colored" section, at 1524 St. John's Street, Mrs. Coles, the former Perlina Adams, was carrying her fourth child. The two families could have hardly been aware of each other; the distance between them wasn't so much geographic as it was social, ethnic, and economic.

Yet, twenty years later, that divide had begun to erode. At the end of the 1930s, it's far more likely to imagine that the paths of Cole and Fitzgerald might have crossed in Los Angeles. By then, Cole would have surely heard of Fitzgerald, one of the major American writers of his era. And it's altogether possible that Fitzgerald had heard the King Cole Trio: they were the talk of Los Angeles at precisely the period when Fitzgerald was writing for Hollywood. Who's to say that Scott and his lover, Sheilah Graham, didn't find their way into the Swanee Inn or the Radio Room, or any of the other Los Angeles night spots, to hear this sensational new trio that the whole movie colony was buzzing about? But the most obvious point that these two cultural icons had in common is this matter of "second acts." Both were able to transition through many distinct phases of their artistry in very brief careers; the Fitzgerald of the Hollywood years is different from the brash young writer who so vividly detailed the doings of flappers and philosophers fifteen years earlier.

The career of Nat King Cole encompasses two very distinct phases, and the customary way to distinguish them is between Cole the pianist and Cole the singer. This is obviously an oversimplification: Cole sang on the great majority of his recordings during the early Trio period, and he also kept playing the piano right up to the end of his life. It's better to think of these two acts as those of Cole the bandleader versus Cole the star. In his early phase, keeping the Trio going was just as much of a focus for him as his own playing and singing, the emphasis was always on the ensemble, the Trio as a whole. In the second act, his key collaborators were his arranger-conductors: Nelson Riddle, Gordon Jenkins, Billy May, and Ralph Carmichael. In the first act, he regarded (and paid) his bassist and guitarist as equals. In the second phase, his collaborators were tasked with putting the focus exclusively on him, making him sound good, while being largely invisible themselves.

This pattern of duality occurs over and over again in Cole's career: jazz versus pop, solo versus trio, piano versus voice, wife number one (Nadine) versus wife number two (Maria), the good songs versus the less-than-good songs, the rhythm numbers versus the ballads, the funny songs and novelties versus the "serious" songs of love and loss, Cole as an advocate for the Great American Songbook versus Cole the intrepid explorer of other options: world music, rhythm and blues, country and western.

There are many worthy figures in American music who were able to achieve only one glorious act, like Louis Jordan and Dick Haymes, both of whom were selling hit records alongside Cole in the 1940s but whose stay on the charts was largely finished by the Eisenhower era. There are also major artists whose careers very neatly divide into first and second acts, with a noticeable break in between the two, like Frank Sinatra, Count Basie, and Duke Ellington. Cole, conversely, paralleled Louis Armstrong, who kept going from one phase to another with absolutely no entr'acte; in the words of Stephen Sondheim, they both simply "careered" "from career to career."

THE RESIDENTS OF MONTGOMERY, ALABAMA, can point to four residents who have changed the world. As we've seen, there was Zelda Sayre Fitzgerald, born in 1900, whose life became the stuff of literary legend and whose courtship served as the basis for what many regard as the Great American Novel. Apart from Nat King Cole, born in 1919, there was also Hank Williams, a great American songwriter and a founding father of an entire genre of American music, in 1923. Then, there was Rosa Parks, born in Tuskegee in 1913, but whose actions in Montgomery would spark the civil rights movement.

Fittingly, three out of these four Montgomerians have local museums, and other civic landmarks, celebrating their achievements, in current day Montgomery. There is an imposing Rosa Parks Museum on Montgomery Street, just a few blocks away from an independently operated but very charming Hank Williams Museum on Commerce Street. Then there's the house at 919 Felder Avenue, where Scott and Zelda lived in 1931 and 1932, when he was writing his fourth novel *Tender Is the Night*. This too has also been preserved as a museum.

The only major cultural icon from Montgomery not celebrated in a local museum is Nat King Cole. Most likely, the absence of a Cole museum is because the family moved from Montgomery to Chicago when Nathaniel was about four.

Nathaniel was the middle child, of the five siblings who survived to adulthood, between two older and two younger. He was born on March 17, 1919, and both the day and the year are important. For most of his life, he didn't know what his actual birth year was; he grew up thinking it was 1917. Hence, virtually everything written about Cole up to about his thirty-first birthday makes him out to be at least two years older. He learned the truth in 1950, at the time of his first overseas tour, when he applied for a passport. He asked his mother for his birth certificate, and so she "rummaged around. There were other children and several birth certificates—the one she found with the name 'Nathaniel' had the birth date of March 1919."[15]

As he grew older, the St. Patrick's Day birthday gave Nat a whimsical penchant for all things Irish, a fascination that was later encouraged by one of his best friends, the great Irish poet of a lyricist, Johnny Burke. But even as early as 1947, when he was celebrating what he thought was his thirtieth birthday, he told the *New York Amsterdam News* that he went everywhere with a shamrock in his pocket.[16] Both African American and Caucasian fans alike were amused by the idea of a black entertainer who identified with the Irish.

In leaving Alabama for Illinois, the Coles joined the movement known to history as "The Great Migration," describing the path for millions of mostly African American families from the agrarian South to the industrialized North. Upon reaching Chicago, they settled at 4200 South Prairie Avenue. Tragedy struck within roughly two years of their arrival in the North, when the eldest child, the daughter Eddie Mae, died of pneumonia at fifteen or sixteen in 1925. However, to their surprise, two more children then arrived over the next few years, both boys. Thus, the age range, from the first to the last, was twenty-two years, from Eddie Mae (1908), Eddie Jr. (1909–1925), and Evelyn (1912) to Nathaniel (1919), Isaac (known as "Ike," 1927), and Lionel Frederick (known as "Freddy," 1931). By the time Freddy arrived, the oldest surviving child, big brother Eddie Jr., had already been working for a while as a professional musician.[17]

The Coles family soon learned that there were all kinds of opportunities in the new land of the Urban North: professional, musical, and even spiritual. All four of the Cole brothers grew up to become musicians, but the overwhelming ambition of Edward Coles Sr. was to preach The Holy Word. He had done so at every opportunity at the local church back in Alabama, but now the layfolk were planting in the New Land even faster than God could keep up with them. Within a short while of their arrival on South Prairie, Edward was doing The Lord's work full-time; the 1930 census lists his occupation as "Baptist Minister." He was originally called to work with the Second Progressive Baptist Church and the True Light Baptist Church.[18] Perlina Coles was in charge of the music in her husband's church; even with five surviving children to take care of (and no eldest daughter to help) she found time to lead the choir and play organ on Sundays and other services.

Now fully ordained as a minister, Edward Sr. was particularly zealous about his work in God's newer houses, and The Almighty was much on everyone's mind. One of the earliest memories that anyone has of Nathaniel was later shared by Ike. "There's one cute little story, about when Nat was small. We were in Chicago at the time, but I wasn't born yet. My daddy and mama used to tell it. My daddy was a Baptist Minister, and we had this big potbellied stove that was in the living room, and it was red hot, and Dad noticed Nat looking at it, and he said, 'Son, what's the matter?,' and Nat said, 'Daddy, can God do anything?' and Dad said, 'Yes, of course, he can do anything,' and Nat said, 'Are you sure?' and Dad said, Yes, of course He can!' And Nat said, 'I betcha He can't sit on that hot stove!' They talked about that for years."[19]

Thus, the two biggest influences in Nat's formative years were the church, specifically the African American Protestant Church, and the city of Chicago. Cole's most successful original song—and his first major hit, "Straighten Up and Fly Right" (1943), was inspired by his father's folkloric sermons. In 1958, he recorded an album of Gospel music titled *Every Time I Feel the Spirit*. Although this wasn't one of his better efforts, its existence illustrates the depth of the impact of the church on Cole's music, and, indeed, on his soul. The mere fact that he chose to express himself using the two instruments that are most frequently found in worship everywhere, the keyboard and the human voice, is additional proof of that.

Some of the early biographies of the pianist report that "he had six years of formal piano instruction, and used to play in his father's Chicago church, where his mother directed the choir ('I'd let loose sometimes')."[20] Milt Hinton, one of jazz's all-time great bassists, later claimed that his mother, Hinda Gertrude Robinson, had been one of Nat's teachers,[21] but Cole himself insisted, "Mom was the only music teacher I ever had."[22] "My church work was a constant worry to dad," Nat remembered in 1941; "I was inclined to play the accompaniments too much on the hot side, which often resulted in a familiar raising of his eyebrows. That meant, 'Tone it down, son, or take the consequences later.' "[23]

In the 1930 census, the family's address is given as "South Parkway in Chicago." Three children, Nat, Evelyn, and Isaac, were currently living with their parents, along with an older cousin, one William Robinson, who is described as working in a shoe-shine parlor. Conspicuously absent is the big brother, Eddie Jr.

If the Reverend Coles had wanted his four boys to become something other than musicians, then he made the worst possible decision in moving the family to Chicago. He could have had no idea that he was placing his sons right in the absolute eye of the cultural hurricane that Fitzgerald christened "The Jazz Age," at precisely the right place and the right moment when the twenties were beginning to roar. Possibly more than any other city—even New Orleans, Kansas City, Harlem or the whole of New York—the South Side of Chicago was the epicenter of jazz in the years of Prohibition. There was glamour, gambling, gangsters, and good times, and the soundtrack of it all was the new music created by African Americans and other people of color in New Orleans.

Nine years older than Nathaniel, Eddie was both a big brother and a second father to him—as well as a musical role model. By his late teens in the mid-1920s, Eddie had grown into an in-demand tuba player, and, as the music evolved and the Jazz Age began to evolve into the Swing Era, Eddie switched from tuba (i.e., the brass bass) to the string bass. Soon, he was playing with jazz and dance bands all over the South Side—and, surprisingly soon, all over Europe. He joined a band led by one Vernie Robinson,[24] around 1927 or '28, which took him to Madrid, and then probably around 1929, he moved up the hierarchical ladder to Noble Sissle and His Sizzling Syncopators.[25] He was playing tuba with the band during their summer 1930 engagement in Paris, as we've seen, as well as their December 1930 run at the equally swanky Ciro's in London. During that period, the band recorded for Columbia Records' British branch, and also made an early sound film.

This is a Pathé short subject filmed in Ciro's, which captures the Sizzling Syncopaters in a medley of two current American hits, "Little White Lies" and "Happy Feet." The leader sings the first, and then, without missing a beat, the band jumps into the second, wherein the drummer, Jack Carter, stands up from his kit, moves forward, and starts to sing, even while Eddie puts down his tuba. After one chorus, we hear Sissle saying quickly (and somewhat off-mic), "Eddie's got happy feet!" The tempo then goes into double time, and, surprise, surprise, Eddie flies into a lightning-fast tap dance.

AS IT HAPPENED, Eddie was out on the road just at the moment when Nat could have benefited from his guidance; a few years later, Nat had left for California just when Ike and Freddy needed him. Cole, however, had long since discovered the man who would be his number one inspiration as a musician, the legendary pianist Earl "Fatha" Hines (1903–1983). As Nat said in 1962: "He was my idol."[26]

Hines's inner essence is captured not only in the copious recordings he made over a sixty-year period but also in two famous photographs: one seen on the cover of his 1966 album *Once upon a Time* and the other on the cover of Stanley Dance's 1977 book, *The World of Earl Hines*. The first shows Hines's beaming face and a radiant smile with the piano keyboard reflected in his spectacles; the second shows Hines's face itself reflected in the mirrored paneling above the keyboard of the piano. In one, Hines seems to be inside the piano; in the other, the piano seems to be inside him. In both, Hines and the piano are miraculously merging into the same entity, a combination of instrument and man, so much so that we can't tell where one ends and the other begins.

It's impossible to imagine the evolution of jazz piano without the influence of Earl Hines. Before Hines, there was stride piano, ragtime piano, and blues piano, but Hines was among the first to play in a style that resonates in contemporary ears as unhyphenated jazz piano: no subgenre necessary, just pure jazz. Earlier masters like Jelly Roll Morton conceived of the piano as a microcosm for an entire jazz orchestra, and they replicated a whole set of brass, reeds, and rhythm with their fingertips. This was also largely true of the stride piano masters, like James P. Johnson, Willie "The Lion" Smith, and Thomas "Fats" Waller. Hines, contrastingly, figured out how the piano would fit in with the other instruments in the jazz ensemble and developed an approach with which the keyboard could hold its own against any horn soloist. He called it "trumpet style piano," and when we listen to Hines today, he sounds less like his predecessors, like Morton, and more like his successors, like Teddy Wilson or Art Tatum.

Over and over, Hines is the musician that Cole most consistently cites as his major influence. In 1944, he referred to himself as a "Hines man" and also praised the emotional aspect of the Fatha's playing, explaining "he's got a soul."[27] In 1957, Cole described Hines's playing as a welcome improvement upon the earlier, more orchestral style of the Harlem stride pianists. Cole later recorded several Fats Waller songs ("Honeysuckle Rose" and "Ain't Misbehavin'"), but when it came to the piano, there was no contest for Nat.[28] "It was his driving force that appealed to me. I first heard Hines in Chicago when I was a kid." He continued, "His was a new, revolutionary kind of playing because he broke away from the Eastern style, where the left hand kept up a steady, striding pattern. Of course, I was just a kid coming up, but I latched onto that new Hines style. Guess I still show that influence today."[29]

Hines would spend most of his career in Chicago, and in the '20s he established his reputation by working with two pioneers from New Orleans, clarinetist Jimmie Noone and trumpeter Louis Armstrong. Both collaborations would exert a profound influence on the young Nathaniel Coles. Hines's recordings with Armstrong begin with a session under the nominal leadership of clarinetist Johnny Dodds in 1927 and continue through the iconic Armstrong Hot Seven sessions (among them perhaps the number one masterpiece of the jazz idiom, "West End Blues"). The twenty or so sides made by Armstrong and Hines literally changed the course of civilization; it's these sides that did more than any other to establish the primacy of the improvising soloist in jazz.

And that's the other reason Cole loved Hines so much, because in loving the best of Hines, he was also loving the best of Armstrong—who not only inspired him as a musician and an entertainer but also provided a role model as to how a black artist might comport himself in a white world. Talking about one inevitably led back to the other: Fatha is to the piano "like Louis is to the trumpet" (1944) and "He was regarded as the Louis Armstrong of piano players" (1957). In comparing Hines to Armstrong, Cole was paying him the ultimate compliment.

It's hardly a surprise that Cole was influenced greatly by the Hines-Armstrong sessions—so was every musician ever to work in jazz. But it was Hines's next professional experience that made an even greater and more personal impact on Nathaniel: the band at Chicago's Apex Club was billed as "Jimmie Noone's Apex Club Orchestra," but it was more properly a quintet, consisting of two clarinets (Noone and "Doc" Poston, the latter doubling on alto saxophone), plus Hines, guitarist Bud Scott (another Armstrong associate), and drummer Johnny Wells. This was the group that really captured Nat's imagination. He would religiously listen to their broadcasts on local Chicago radio, and on nights when they weren't on the air, he would hang around outside the club; he was too young to enter legally, and he didn't have the price of a cover charge or a drink in any case. He would stand in front, in the side alley, by the backdoor, listening to the music, soaking it all in, memorizing every detail.

Cole wasn't alone in his love for Noone and Hines; among the other major figures in jazz they profoundly influenced were future bandleaders Benny Goodman and Stan Kenton. Cole also fell in love with the band's theme song, "Sweet Lorraine" by the pianist Clifford Burwell, then (1928) playing with Rudy Vallée and his Connecticut Yankees. Cole would make four distinct recordings of the song even before he turned twenty-five. You never forget your first love; no less than with the song "Sweet Lorraine," Cole remained infatuated with both Hines and Noone for the rest of his life.

Hines was a vain man and eventually became virtually the only person ever disparaged by Louis Armstrong—who, famously, had something good to say about (practically) everybody. According to the back-alley talk bruited about by musicians, the nickname "Fatha" was a boast of his romantic prowess with the ladies. This was an age, apparently, when many pianists were homosexual, and Hines wanted to make sure there was no doubt regarding his sexual preferences. It may be telling, however, that the major time Hines mentioned Cole in an interview—rather than the other way around—he had plenty of praise for the younger man, but only as a singer. "Among the singers, I especially liked Nat Cole—just as natural and smooth as could be."[30] It wasn't recorded what he thought of Cole as a piano player. Hines famously did have an affinity for great singers; his big band launched the careers of Herb Jeffries, Billy Eckstine, Sarah Vaughan, and Johnny Hartman. (Hines did make a testimonial speech at Cole's "Twenty-fifth Anniversary" celebration in 1962; alas, exactly what he said was not documented.)

Cole's love for Hines went beyond any specific aspect of the older man's style or his prodigious technique. When he discovered Earl Hines, he didn't just fall in love with this Fatha and his music but the instrument itself—it was Hines who made Nathaniel Coles want to play the piano to begin with. Hines's work with Armstrong and Noone was more or less unique, sui generis. But it was the big band Hines launched at the Grand Terrace Ballroom on Hines's twenty-fifth birthday, December 28, 1928, that provided Cole with his greatest inspiration. A jazz orchestra led by a dazzling superstar of a virtuoso pianist; in the parlance of the 21st century, here was a business model that was both sustainable and scalable. Throughout the Jazz Age and into the Swing Era, the great black bands would be led overwhelmingly by piano players—there were more of them than all other instruments combined—Duke Ellington, Earl Hines, Fletcher Henderson, Count Basie, Claude Hopkins, Cliff Jackson,

Eubie Blake, Fats Waller, Bennie Moten—thus, playing the piano was more than an end unto itself; it was also a path to bandleading.

By the time he was ten or eleven, Cole was obsessed with music, practicing constantly and playing at every opportunity. At the moment while Eddie Jr was playing with Sissle in London, Nathaniel was winning honors of his own, thanks to the "Bud Billikens" Club. This was a special organization for black children in Chicago that centered on a unique kids' column in the *Chicago Defender*, the country's leading black newspaper. On Sunday, November 22, 1930, the Billikens mounted their most elaborate affair yet. It began with a massive parade of at least 10,000 people (including 6,000 children) marching up South Parkway leading to the Regal Theater. At that point, 3,000 kids managed to cram their way into the theater (thankfully, including Nathaniel) while another "3,000 Billkins [were] still in the streets and they remained there like little soldiers until the Billiken show was over."[31]

Inside, there was a huge party, in which one of Chicago's most prominent bands, led by Dave Peyton (still another pianist), performed, along with an entertainer named "Sweet Papa Garbage," described by the *Defender* as "Chicago's favorite comedian" (a picture of "Garbage" shows him looking like a turn of the century minstrel, with an elaborate top hat, burnt cork face, and exaggerated white lips). The entire day culminated in an elaborate talent show, in which hundreds of youngsters competed. "Nathaniel Cole," in his first ever press notice (and photo), was one of ten winners who came home with the top prize, "a freshly killed and dry-picked turkey."

He won again for three successive years. "Every year they used to give a turkey away," brother Ike remembered, "and he won the turkey. And we could almost depend on Nat bringing a turkey home every year."[32] The November 1931 contest was an especially memorable one; the final Cole child, Lionel Frederick, had been born on October 15, 1931, and the prize was welcomed by the rest of the family, even though the new arrival, nicknamed "Freddy," wouldn't be eating any turkey for at least a few years. More important for Nathaniel, as part of the 1931 festivities, Earl Hines and his Grand Terrace Orchestra were playing on stage. Not only was this a rare opportunity to hear them in person without sneaking around the Grand Terrace, but there was always a chance that the Fatha might stick around and listen to Nathaniel.

Shortly after winning for the third year in a row, in November 1932, the thirteen-year-old prodigy wrote a letter to the column. "Dear Bud Billiken: Just a line telling you how much I enjoyed the turkey I won for Thanksgiving. This makes the third turkey I have won at your parties. Here's hoping I shall win the fourth. From Nathaniel Coles, 4034 Prairie Ave., Chicago."[33] This was the last time, however, that Cole competed against other kids; suddenly, he was grown up and professional, and was playing for stakes considerably larger than a turkey.

IN SEPTEMBER 1933, Nathaniel Cole, now fourteen, entered Wendell Phillips High School, and it was there that his musical dreams began to take shape. This was where the self-confidence of the Fatha began to rub off on him: he decided, very early on, that he could never be a sideman. He had to be the leader of whatever ensemble he was playing in. "I kind of thrive on responsibility," he told Edward R. Murrow in 1957. "When I started out with a high school band in Chicago, I wanted to be the leader, and I guess I've stuck my neck out all these years."[34] It's tempting to speculate how history might have changed if Cole had instead tried out for the piano chair in, say, McKinney's Cotton Pickers, Cab Calloway's Orchestra, or Don Redman's Orchestra. (His own favorite band, after Ellington and Hines, was easily Jimmie Lunceford's Orchestra; in an interview from three years after Lunceford's death, Cole lamented that there were about five Glenn Miller clone bands going strong, but that no one was keeping alive the great Lunceford sound.)[35] But even more than Hines, who served as a sideman for a few years on arriving in Chicago, Cole knew that the musical vision he would follow would have to be his own.

He put together his first band at Wendell Phillips. Located at 244 East Pershing Road in the city's "Bronzeville" section, Wendell Phillips Academy High School was the perfect place for Cole to study, at least for a year or so. Eddie Jr. had attended there, and so had many soon-to-be famous black musicians and entertainers: bandleader Lucius "Lucky" Millinder, bassist Milt Hinton (who was probably in the same class as Eddie), and later Dinah Washington, Sam Cooke, and Herbie Hancock. Music students at Wendell Phillips were fortunate enough to train under one of the country's most imposing musical educators, Captain Walter Henri Dyett (1901–1969), a strict taskmaster who suffered no fools gladly and made sure that his charges were well versed in the musical rudiments; they all became first rate "readers." By the time he was fifteen, Cole could not only read music as well as any classical or studio musician but was also an ace improviser, with a gift for devising ingenious "head arrangements" right on the spot. Nathaniel played in the school ensembles led by Captain Dyett, and it's there that he met other aspiring young black musicians who, like him, were bitten by the jazz bug and determined to find their place in this new music. He was playing every night around the South Side, and somehow also making it to classes in the morning. For most of the 1933–34 school year, he was apparently also working regularly around town as a sideman in the evenings but diligently assembling like-minded players both night and day for his own bands.

Around this time, Nathaniel met Malcolm B. Smith, who would later claim, with some justification, to have "discovered" Cole and launched his career. Smith is described in the press clippings at the time as a "newspaper-business man."[36] His actual job description blurred the boundaries between journalist (for the *Pittsburgh Courier*), publicist, and manager.[37] He encouraged Cole to put together a dance band, eight pieces at first, and hired them to play for other teenagers on Sunday afternoons at the Warwick Hall, 543 East 47th Street. Cole got the job when the ballroom abruptly fired its current band as, he later remembered, they "tried to put the squeeze on the management for a boost in wages." At the last minute, Cole was offered the gig if he could get a band together in time.[38] It's probably because of Smith's promotional skills that Cole's name, photo, and band were in the *Courier* and the *Defender* fairly regularly for the two-year period during which he was a professional musician in Chicago, 1934 to 1936. In early October, the *Defender* ran a photo of Nathaniel and described him as "the leader of one of the hottest bands in the Middle West."[39]

By November, the Nat Cole Orchestra at the Warwick had expanded to ten pieces, including himself and a male vocalist.[40] They were then alternating with another young orchestra, led by Tony Fambro, whom the paper described, with considerable hyperbole, as Chicago's answer to Duke Ellington. The promoters played up this two-band engagement as a "battle of jazz." Said battle was still raging at the Warwick into December. "The orchestra of youngsters plays a style of syncopation that seems to express the pent-up emotions of the Race as interpreted by the younger set," the *Pittsburgh Courier* reported. Cole's band "won a trophy in a local battle of jazz. Out of a total vote of 274, Nat Cole won 271."[41]

Cole was still attending classes, but by now Sunday was the busiest day of the week. He would start early in the morning playing the organ for his father's service, then play an afternoon Tea Dance at the Warwick, and follow that with a second church service on Sunday evening. When an interviewer later asked him, "When did you get your homework done?" he reluctantly answered, "Well, I guess it didn't get done."[42] When Cole entered his second year of high school, he was fully a professional musician, as confirmed by his membership in the local union. At this point, after fluctuating between "Coles" and "Cole" for a few years, he now settled on "Cole" as a permanent, professional name.

His first working band was billed as "Nat Cole and His Royal Dukes." What's significant is that even a few years before Nat began referencing the "Old King Cole" nursery rhyme, he was already participating in the long tradition of monarchical hierarchy in jazz nomenclature. Famously, there had been a King Oliver and a Duke Ellington, and Bessie Smith was officially billed "The Empress of the Blues"; Ferdinand Morton had even written a song to designate himself "Mr. Jelly Lord." For a highly democratic music, jazz had a notable preoccupation with royalty: around this time, there would emerge both a Count Basie and a King of Swing. Even down in the Caribbean, perhaps as a holdover from British rule, the top Calypso singers were known as Lord Invader, Lord Flea, and the Duke of Iron. Hines later realized that his given name admitted him into the pantheon; in 1941, Mel Powell wrote a dedicatory piece to Hines's prowess, titled "The Earl," for Benny Goodman's Orchestra.

All of which gives credence to the story that it was bassist Wesley Prince who thought up the "King Cole" name in 1937. Surely, if Nat had thought of it earlier, he would have used it; "King Cole and His Royal Dukes" would have been a great band name.[43] In a profile from December, the *Courier* also states, "All members of the orchestra are students at Wendell Phillips High."[44] By Thanksgiving that was no longer true; the grind of full-time musician and full-time student was too much for Nat, so he had stopped showing up for classes at Wendell Phillips. It wasn't that Captain Dyett had run out of things to teach him, but there was much more that he could learn—and earn—in the world of professional music. However, he was still living at his parents' house on South Prairie Avenue. This was only appropriate. After all, he was only fifteen.

NINETEEN THIRTY-FIVE WOULD be the year that Benny Goodman ignited the explosion known as the swing era; essentially, this meant taking the music of the black bands on the South Side of Chicago, from Harlem, and Kansas City, and sharing it with the larger audience of white Americans—and the rest of the world. As the year began, Nat Cole was working regularly with his ten-piece band, Sundays at the Warwick and elsewhere. Mal Smith later told the *Chicago Defender* that the Warwick tea dances were a losing proposition for him, that he paid for the band and the venue out of his pocket, but in 1934 and '35, the papers were full of stories, undoubtedly placed by Smith, about how popular Cole and his band were. The year started out with a well-placed portrait of Cole in the *Defender* on January 19, looking very serious and somewhat mysterious. If the idea was to make him look older than fifteen, then it worked. The caption read, "Nat Cole, one of Chicago's most popular band leaders, who dishes music for dancers at Warwick Hall Sundays, is considering an offer to tour in the East. He has one of the finest orchestras in the city."[45]

Their popularity began to expand beyond the Warwick. On Friday, March 1, 1935, they played for an adult crowd at the Madison Street Casino ballroom, "one of the largest on the west side"; supposedly a thousand people showed up to dance. "According to the management, young Cole brought the house down with his latest dance hit, 'Blue Moon.' "[46] Announced the *Defender*, "Nat Cole's Band Is New Sensation."

Edward Sr. and Perlina were still somewhat suspicious of the sinful atmosphere of the Chicago dance halls, so, for at least a few Sundays, they sent along Nat's sister Evelyn, seven years older, as an unofficial chaperone. She later remembered that Nat was so shy at this point that the throngs of young girls who would cluster around the bandstand were actually a problem; Nat managed to dodge them by claiming, "I have to take my sister home." Apparently, he was already so tall and mature-looking that no one questioned why a twenty-two-year-old woman needed a fifteen-year-old boy to escort her home.[47]

On Sunday, February 7, Cole took a kind of a sideways look into the future when he presided over an event at the Warwick that was a combination of master vocal class and talent show. "Students Learn to Sing with Nat Cole," the *Defender* proclaimed.[48] This is the first indication we have that Cole was interested in singing—at a time when his own band carried a male vocalist (the otherwise unknown Arthur Hicks)—and well before we have any indication that he ever sang in public, or even in private. Regarding the talent shows, Cole said, "I shall continue them" and on June 7, he participated in a bigger competition at the Regal Theater, where he had won a turkey three years in a row. Now serving as the professional band opening for an amateur show, "the Warwick Ballroom Orchestra burnt up the stage in their playing of [Jimmie Lunceford's] 'Rhythm Is Our Business,' [his own future classic] 'Stardust', and [the jazz standard] 'Dinah.' "[49]

Meanwhile, the band was growing; on the day before he turned sixteen, he received a present in the form of a glowing write-up from the *Courier*. "He's only 17 [*sic*] but what manner of man is this Nate [*sic*] Cole, who swings piano along the Duke Ellington approved style, yet with refreshing originality of his own.... Dapper Nat Cole is the talk of the town. A good pianist par excellence, young Cole's band is composed of eleven [rather than ten] teenage boys."[50] Smith—or someone—also heavily promoted a Friday night dance, "The Aces' Confetti-Kiss Frolic," on March 29: "Come and Dance to the Beautiful and Tantalizing Music of Nat Cole and his Royal Dukes at the Beautiful Warwick Hall." The event started at 10:00 p.m. and promised "dancing until the Wee Hours."[51]

On May 5, 1935, Smith took out a large ad in the *Defender*, promoting the band's Sunday dance on Mother's Day (May 12) and billing himself above Nat. "Malcolm B. Smith presents to the World—God's Little Chillun of Rhythm'—'Nat' Cole and his Band." Now the band is clearly twelve pieces; as the leader, Nat is in a white suit and towers over most of the others, who are shorter and wearing dark suits.[52] He's wearing the same suit in a *Courier* item on the same day, which describes the band's "monster Easter concert at the beautiful Warwick Ballroom in Chicago," in which they were joined by singer Pearl Baines, who usually worked at the Grand Terrace, and one Euclid L. Taylor, who is described as Cole's attorney. "He's Marvelous," Miss Baines said of Cole. "According to his manager, Malcolm B. Smith, the occasion was Nat's greatest triumph. Throngs of people were turned away."[53]

Even allowing for all the promotional hype, Cole himself was clearly becoming a fixture on the South Side "nite life" scene. He was undoubtedly present when columnist Jack Ellis opened his own establishment, "The Clef Club" (in the Harlem Hotel on Michigan Avenue). The premiere attraction was his hero Louis Armstrong, joined by his second wife, Lil Hardin, and Cole's band was announced to follow.[54]

In the summer of 1935, Cole experienced his first important gig outside of Chicago, as well as his first personal tragedy since the death of his oldest sister. He seems to have stopped working with Smith around this time, apparently under the belief that "he could make better progress under white management." He then began working with a Caucasian impresario named Earl Taylor. Taylor set up a "show tour" for the band, which also led to Nathaniel's first experience playing for singers and dancers in a revue.

The Royal Dukes were booked in Kankakee, Illinois, about sixty miles outside of Chicago, on Sunday, August 4. Some of the musicians went swimming in a rock quarry between shows, and, unfortunately, seventeen-year-old trumpeter Charles Murphy developed a cramp and suddenly disappeared. When the *Defender* asked Smith about the incident, he responded that "he did not know that the band was out of town."[55] "Expert swimmers" were recruited to search for the body, at the request of Illinois Governor Henry Horner, but came up empty handed. The next step was to drain the rock quarry,[56] but it's not known if the corpse was ever found.

NAT WAS, NOT SURPRISINGLY, greatly disturbed by the tragedy, but he found some comfort, at least briefly, in a renewed relationship with his prodigal, wandering big brother, Eddie Jr. The Sissle orchestra returned to Chicago in the summer of 1935, and this time, Eddie made a point to bring his fellow Sizzling Syncopators to hear Nat's band. "Edwin [*sic*] Cole, Noble Sissle's bass player, took his mates over to hear young Nat Cole [on] Memorial Day, and, after seeing the boys smile in appreciation, asked 'How you like me kid brudder?' "[57] This *wisenheimer* verbiage is consistent with the Eddie we know, always a cut-up and a comedian. It's been said that with Nat's success as a bandleader, Eddie was already somewhat jealous of the success of "the kid brudder." Still, if Eddie had wanted to be a superstar leader, he never would have chosen the tuba or bass—there simply were no marquee-name jazz bassists at that time.[58]

Was Eddie thinking of joining forces with Nat at this point? If so, his mind was made up for him after the events of September 7, 1935. It's not known how it came to pass, but on that night Nat Cole and his fledgling orchestra, less than a year old and with a sixteen-year-old leader, played a battle of the bands with the most celebrated pianist-bandleader in Chicago, Earl Hines and His Orchestra, at Chicago's Savoy Ballroom. The news made the top item in Jack Ellis's column. "Hello, gang. Earl 'Father' Hines and Nat Cole's cats swung down to a low gravy at the Savoy. No, Nat didn't wash Earl, but he was in his collar all night. You gotta give it to these kittens, they rehearse every day from 11 to 5 at the union and when he turns that five-part brass loose, the bricks in the wall begin to jump around." But, Ellis concluded, "Father Hines dished the jazz in a big way."[59] "That was a tough band Nat faced," as *Metronome* reported nine years later, probably relying on Cole's own account, "Nat rehearsed as many of Earl's arrangements as possible—Hines was and still is his piano idol—but those, together with his own originals, still totaled only fifteen. Nonetheless, the enthusiasm of the crowd was with Nat Cole and the Rogues of Rhythm, and Hines was thoroughly cut in that battle."[60]

It was a David-and-Goliath battle of the piano, but Nat realized that he didn't actually have to beat the Fatha to win. Cole was like one of those nervous amateur boxers that you see in old movies, where the promoter advertises "$100 to anybody who can stay in the ring with the Killer!" All Cole had to do was to "beat the spread" and show that he could stay alive in the ring. If he could avoid being knocked out completely, that would count as a victory—and this he did. Everyone agreed that Cole and company had acquitted themselves adequately, and it was at this time that Cole began billing his band as "The Rogues of Rhythm" or "The Rhythm Rogues." Dempsey

Travis, a neighbor of Nat's, put it this way: "They were 'rogues,' because they stole from Earl Hines."[61] Whether or not they won the battle, they won the prize: they were now hired as the regular Sunday afternoon band at the Savoy Ballroom on 47th and South Parkway.[62] On September 22, 1935, they played by themselves, and on September 29 they shared the gig with a group led by trumpeter (and violinist and vocalist) Ray Nance, who would go on to jazz immortality with Duke Ellington's Orchestra.[63]

This seems to have been the final inducement for Eddie Jr. He had spent the last six or seven years on the road and was now ready to return to the town that he called home. "Jelly Coles," as he was referred to in the papers,[64] officially left Sissle's employ in Rochester, New York, and joined his brother in late October 1935. His first move was to cut the band down to six pieces.[65] Eddie was much more of a promoter than Nat, much more given to exaggeration and promotion, and when they first began working together, he loudly announced, "The Coles brothers band will start a tour early next week that will keep them on the road for several months. They will tour Oklahoma, Arkansas, and other points in the Southland and then set sail for the east. The band is booked to appear in New York in early December." Big talk, but there's no evidence that any of this was more than a pipe dream on the part of "Jelly" Coles.[66]

Around March 1936, they went to work for Chicago nightclub entrepreneur, Benny Skoller, who brought them into the Panama Cafe at 307 East 58th Street,[67] opened the previous June by Skoller, who already owned the Swingland Cafe. The Panama was another valuable experience for Cole in playing for dance acts and entertainers rather than strictly for social dancing. At the Panama, there was an evening's worth of entertainment put together by producer Jimmie White, which also included the "clever dance team of Robert Bell and Katherine Walker. Dorcelle Chapman and Blanche Cole are the stars of the revue."[68]

A *Courier* write-up from April describes the Cole band as "the best small combination in the entire city" and tells us that their theme song is "Blue Paradise." The group includes Kenneth Johnson, doubling violin and trumpet (*à la* Ray Nance); two reed players, Tommy Moore and William Wright; and drummer Johnny Adams, in addition to the Cole brothers. This essentially was Nat's band, but now Eddie was positioning himself as the leader and star, doing some of the same kind of song-and-dance routines he had done with Sissle, "assisted by his brother Nat."[69] Nat was still the musical director and arranger[70]—clearly he can't have been happy doing all the work while someone else took the bows.

Eddie wasn't the only dancer working at the Panama; this was the moment when the brothers crossed paths with Nadine Robinson. She was the daughter of Charles Robinson and the former Emma Oliver, born in East St. Louis, Illinois, on June 10 1909, making her a year older than Eddie and a decade older than Nat.[71] As the *Negro Who's Who in California* reported in 1948, "She was educated in the public schools of East St. Louis and Chicago. Soon after her graduation from high school, she began her career as a dancer, becoming quite famous in her chosen art."[72] Robinson was working in Chicago and being noticed by the black press as early as 1934. She was, indeed, quickly famous in the windy city for both her dancing skills and her remarkable beauty, her lovely face, and long legs. Apparently, both brothers were smitten, but then, so was much of the male population of the South Side. Despite the difference in their ages, by the summer of 1936, Nat and Nadine were, as Walter Winchell would have said, an "item." This is the first romance of his that we know about.

On June 17, 1936, the Panama opened a new revue, titled "Rhapsody in Rhythm," the *Defender* proclaiming that the cafe enjoyed "turnaway crowds"—"even during the hot spell."[73] The new show, again produced by White, starred Babe Matthews, "golden voiced siren, direct from the Ubangi club in Harlem" and Mae (a.k.a. May) Alix, a vocalist (of sorts) who had famously recorded with Louis Armstrong in 1926. The comedy star was "Lovin' Sam" Theard, remembered as a novelty songwriter who wrote signature numbers for both Louis Armstrong ("(I'll Be Glad When You're Dead) You Rascal You") and Louis Jordan ("Let the Good Times Roll"). "Eddie Cole's swinging music men, with Nat Cole at the piano, supplied the music. The chorus has been augmented to eight girls."[74] On July 25, Jimmy White changed the lineup again, adding a crooner (Lawrence Steele), a female dancer ("dainty-toed Maurice Mitchell"), and a comedy team ("Slick & Slack"). The *Defender*'s review closed with a sentence that must have stopped the brothers dead in their tracks when they read it: "Few bands in the middle west can compare with Ed Cole's outfit, considering its size. Nat Cole at the piano would give Earl Hines the jitters."[75]

It does sound like the show was a success—even with the columnist's exaggeration—and the Panama was indeed a jumping, "happening" spot. One man paying attention was J. Mayo Williams (1894–1980), a veteran record producer and music publisher, who had been making "race" records ever since a few ambitious entrepreneurs discovered, in the early 1920s, that black people would actually buy records by black artists. Williams had been appointed head of the race division for the new Decca label at the time of its inception in 1934. Williams and Eddie had both been present when Sissle recorded in Chicago two years earlier, and now Williams was obviously reading the black papers. The consistently positive notices regarding the Coles were as good a reason as any to take a chance on a new band.

The band that convened in Decca's Chicago facility on July 28, 1936, was largely the same as reported a month earlier at the Panama. Kenneth Johnson had been replaced by trumpeter Kenneth Roane, who later played with Sidney Bechet and Louis Jordan; saxophonist Tommy Moore had been replaced by Tommy Thompson,[76] but the other reed player, Bill Wright, and drummer Jimmy Adams were still there, along with Nat and Eddie. The six men recorded four original selections, all of which were by Nat, and Decca released the titles as "Eddie Cole's Solid Swingers." Nat can't have been thrilled that Eddie's was the name on the label—not his—but he must have been delighted to be making his recording debut at age seventeen. The records don't seem to have been noticed by anybody at the time; the Chicago papers don't mention them, but most mainstream newspapers weren't doing record reviews and the jazz press barely existed at all.

Metronome's Barry Ulanov, writing about the four sides in 1944, described them, as "hard to come by now, [and] more interesting as a picture of Nat's development as a pianist than anything else. The ensemble is fairly rough and the arrangements not especially interesting, but Nat plays some good Hines-style piano."[77] The inspiration of Hines's Grand Terrace Orchestra does indeed loom large. All four are piano-centric numbers for social dancing, especially "Stompin' at the Panama (Skoller's Shuffle)," an obvious bow to the club and owner Benny Skoller. Here, Cole's piano connects everything together and links the horn solos and the ensembles in a manner much informed by Hines's big band. "Bedtime" (issued also as "Sleep, Baby Sleep" and "Sleepy Moan") is more of a number for slow dancing than a lullaby, with vaguely Ellingtonian aspirations.

"Thunder" is even more of a riff number for lindy hopping, embellished by diatonic riffs reminiscent of Lunceford's "Raggin' the Scale." Cole's piano solo is the main attraction here, and it comes in three sections, starting with a catchy, deliberately repetitive triplet pattern that reminded some listeners of Fats Waller up at the top end of the treble. The last section, which sounds the most like Hines, is a call-and-response with the band. Taken as a whole, the solo seems disjointed, as if these were three separate piano breaks on three unconnected records—maybe even by three different pianists—and a far cry from such brilliantly constructed, masterpiece solos as Cole's 1944 version of "Body and Soul." As Dick Katz later observed, "Nat was only 17 years old, but he had already mastered the essentials of Hines's style. The lightning-fast octave passages and the syncopated left-hand runs were fully assimilated. But in the manner of most youngsters, he tried to show all of his 'stuff' at once."

The first tune recorded, "Honey Hush" (which survives in two takes) represents Cole's first known interest in songwriting; clearly, his ongoing obsession with the beautiful Nadine inspired him to write words for the first time, as well as music. (Eddie, the alleged leader, takes the vocal.) More specifically, "Honey Hush" is a first cousin of "Babs," a 1935 song by Fred Ahlert and Joe Young that Cole learned from Lunceford. Both songs fall into a well-established category of genre novelty songs written by and for black artists, excitingly recounting the considerable charms of a better-than-average woman. In the tradition of "Sweet Georgia Brown," "Louisville Lou," "Hard-Hearted Hannah," "Miss Brown to You," and "Streamlined Greta Green," here we have a femme fatale, who, though it's rarely stated explicitly, is understood to be African American. As all these "Brown" and "Green" women may suggest, these women are highly prized for their skin color; the girl in "Honey Hush," one "Miss Sadie Green," is described as a "high yellow," a thankfully now-archaic term referring to the light-skinned girls, who were valued more highly than your basic black women. "In those days, there was a lot of intra-racism—prejudice by blacks against blacks," as Cole's daughter, Natalie, would later write. "And dark [skin] was considered socially inferior to pale. My mother called it 'a matter of breeding.' "[78]

This would be the first and last recording session for the band. In September 1936, they left Chicago for the second time and misfortune struck again. They were now signed to an agency called the Graham Artists' Bureau, Inc., and they announced "an extensive tour beginning the week of September first" for the band, which now consisted of "14 expert musicians, with his younger brother, Nat Cole, at the Steinway Grand."[79] But then, two weeks later, Earl J. Morris, Senior Theatrical Correspondent of the *Pittsburgh Courier*, reported that the Cole brothers' band was somehow "stranded." He doesn't say where, he doesn't say why, but it sounded fishy to him. Morris thus went to the Graham agency to investigate, and he reported, "A visit to the pretentious offices of Mr. Graham will cause one to think that it is a million dollar set-up. His offices are in the South Center Building and [occupy] a large suite with office girls and visitors by the score."[80] The splendiferousness of the Graham offices is relevant; not only were the Cole brothers broke, but the Graham agency also claimed to be busted as well, so much so that they were unable, they claimed, to send any money to the brothers.

Fortunately, their boss at the Panama, good old Benny Skoller, described as a "good Samaritan," wired them the funds needed to get back home.

It was obviously a highly embarrassing moment for the Cole(s) family, especially since, right around this time, Edward Sr. had graduated to a higher-level position at a more prominent house of worship, the First Baptist Church, in North Chicago.[81] So why were the brothers broke? Did some local promoter refuse to pay them? Did someone steal their payroll? It became part of Cole's early mythology that his band was stranded in Jackson, Tennessee, and they had to bum their way back to Chicago by persuading a bus driver to accept their instruments as collateral.[82] There's one likely reason they were stuck without a cent: "Jelly Coles," as the press referred to him, was long known to have a gambling problem.[83] Yet even if the "big brudder" had lost the band's "kitty" shooting crap, that still wouldn't account for the agency refusing to help them. Said Morris, "It just doesn't sound kosher to me."[84]

SEPTEMBER 1936 WAS an extremely busy month for the Cole brothers. On September 4, they announced they were, at long last, going on tour. Then, on September 19, they suffered a rather public humiliation when the news broke that the band was stranded and had to be bailed out before they could come back to Chicago. But by September 25, they were on the road again, this time serving as the pit band for a touring musical revue. This was the new 1936 edition of the venerable *Shuffle Along*. Premiering in 1921, *Shuffle Along* is, to this day, easily the most successful and important black Broadway show of all time (though not the first) and established a presence for African Americans in the mainstream musical theater.

Created by two teams, librettists and star comedians Flourney Miller and Aubrey Lyles, and songwriters Noble Sissle and Eubie Blake, *Shuffle* launched the careers of Adelaide Hall, Josephine Baker, Paul Robeson, Florence Mills, and Fredi Washington; it introduced any number of hit songs and standards, like "Love Will Find a Way" and "I'm Just Wild about Harry." Virtually all the black shows of the 1920s and '30s, including *Hot Chocolates* (1929) by Fats Waller and Andy Razaf and Lew Leslie's *Blackbirds* revues, were children of *Shuffle Along*. The 1921 show launched a vogue for black entertainment that was part and parcel of both the Roaring Twenties and the Great Depression, and extended to black night spots, like the Cotton Club, as well as full-scale theatrical productions.

Unfortunately, as the 2016 show-about-the-show, titled *Shuffle Along, or, the Making of the Musical Sensation of 1921 and All That Followed*, made clear, the four original partners could never get their act together to create a suitable follow-up. As late as 1932, Miller and Lyles were still planning a new edition of *Shuffle Along*, but Lyles, aged forty-eight, died in July of that year. By that time, Sissle was touring the world with his "Sizzling Syncopators," and Blake, who also briefly led his own big band, was writing songs with Andy Razaf. In 1936, Miller planned a new touring production of *Shuffle Along*, costarring his new partner, Mantan Moreland (later of *Charlie Chan* movie fame) which would start in Chicago and gradually head west. Where the original *Shuffle* had something of an actual book (it was hardly Eugene O'Neill), the 1936 production was strictly a revue—a fifty-five-minute "tab show" that could play movie theaters as well as "legit" houses. It was obviously Sissle who recommended his former sideman, Eddie Cole, and his piano wizard kid brother, as the guys to lead the pit orchestra.

Miller reached out to other black stars to shuffle along with them, but the best he could do was close relatives of two headliners, Louis Armstrong's wife and Cab Calloway's sister. Lil Hardin Armstrong was extremely popular in the black community at the time; alas, when *Shuffle Along* opened at the Orpheum Theater in Lincoln, Nebraska, on September 25, her name was on the marquee, but she was nowhere to be found. Likewise, Jean Calloway, who was billed as "Cab's little sister," was apparently an out-and-out fraud.[85] *Variety*'s review was especially harsh on her and not very positive overall. The reviewer wasn't too fond of the headliners, Miller and Mantan ("just fair") but he had more positive words for the dancing, the "ten-gal chorus line," and for Ollivette Miller, a jazz harp virtuoso who was also the producer's daughter. *Variety* also mentioned that Eddie Cole led the band nearly all the way through, and "biz" was "fine" in spite of the higher-than-usual ticket price—all of 40 cents—which also included the movie, a 20th Century Fox B-picture titled *Back to Nature* starring Jed Prouty and Dixie Dunbar.[86]

Not exactly an auspicious beginning. But if there had been no actual book in this *Shuffle Along*, there was plenty of drama backstage, much of it concerning the Cole Brothers. One dancer not mentioned in the initial review of the revue is Nadine Robinson, who was now one of the ten gals in the chorus line, thanks to Nat. The story that has come down to us is that, by now, the brothers were constantly fighting over Nadine; Eddie didn't want to see the "kid brudder" involved with a woman, a dancer no less, who was even older than he himself was. Nat thought that Eddie, who already had one divorce, was in no position to give him advice and even less so to order him around. It was later reported that "Nat and Eddie fought so hard . . . that their parents had to hold them apart" and, in the aftermath, "the brothers didn't speak for a year."[87] What seems clear is that Eddie, who had traveled the whole world between 1929 and 1935, no longer "had eyes for" the road, as Lester Young would say; even though he made announcements about taking the band on tour, he seems to have wanted to stay in Chicago. Nat, on the other hand, was thrilled to be immersed in show business—that's one reason he eventually became something more than a musician. And he also liked being around those ten gorgeous girls, especially Nadine. It's also obvious that Nat, who had welcomed the idea of working with his big brother a year earlier, now realized that he had outgrown Eddie. The reasons for the two of them to split up, even as the Dorsey Brothers band had in 1935, come even more sharply into focus if it was, as seems highly possible, Eddie's misdeeds that had caused the band to be stranded in the middle of nowhere just a few weeks earlier. So, if Nat had to choose between staying with Eddie and remaining a sideman in Chicago and being on the road with Nadine where he was now, once again, the leader and conductor, then this was one of the easier decisions he would ever make. By early December, when the tour started in earnest, Nat was now conducting for *Shuffle* alone, and Eddie was leading a new band at Chicago's 5100 Club.[88]

The tour was now under way, and Nat got his first taste of the constant traveling that he would do for the rest of his life. After Lincoln and then a few shows in Chicago,[89] they began crisscrossing the Midwest: La Cross (Wisconsin),[90] Fort Wayne (Indiana),[91] Ann Arbor.[92] They received some positive press in Grand Rapids, while playing a five-day run at Keith's Theater: "The show was exceedingly good and drew large and enthusiastic crowds." While there, on January 19, the owner of a local black night spot, the Club Indigo, invited the cast to come as his guests, and many were happy to perform spontaneously. The evening was described as "a show of shows featuring the entire *Shuffle Along* company and Nat Cole's band." Between the traveling thespians and his regular local patrons, the club owner reported he drew his biggest crowd of the year.[93]

The company was in the mood to celebrate in Michigan, for reasons that had nothing to do with the show itself. The revelry in the Grand Rapids Club Indigo doubled as a wedding party: Nadine Robinson, age twenty-seven, and Nat Cole, seventeen, would be married on Friday, January 29. The ceremony was held at midnight, after the final show, at the home of one Thomas Harris in Ypsilanti. The *Defender* ran a formal portrait of the happy couple, the "well known young band leader" and the "lovely young favorite of the theater." They look made for each other; he seems older and she, younger. If they're not the most attractive couple ever pictured in the pages of that paper, it's impossible to imagine who would be.[94] The groom, listed as "Nathaniel Coles" on the marriage certificate, gave his age as twenty-one (no one checked for a driver's license or a birth certificate), so his parents' permission wouldn't be necessary, even though he wouldn't even be eighteen for another two months. In fact, there's no evidence at all that Edward Sr. and Perlina had even met Nadine before the ceremony; the God-fearing reverend and his wife could hardly have been pleased with the news that Nat had essentially eloped with a showgirl a decade his senior.

As remembered by Claire Phillips Gordon, one of Nat's few friends to be close to both of his wives, "Nadine was a small, slender woman with a dancer's grace and figure. It was said that she was older than Nat, but it wasn't something you'd notice."[95]

THE PROGRESSION OF EARLY 1937 was hardly a straight line: Cole's big band worked extensively both with and without the *Shuffle Along* company. In February they played RKO houses in Chicago, on their own,[96] then rejoined the troupe for an exceedingly busy March that included at least twenty-one days of shows (in many cases doing multiple shows per day) in some twelve different theaters and cities,[97] among them Minnesota, Wisconsin, back to Minnesota, South Dakota, Montana, and Washington. In early April, the band was set to "hit Hollywood [on] April 5, where they will swing a two week's stand at the Golden Gate"[98] and then rejoin the show once again in northern California for the rest of April; "the big collection of stars and chorines [has] been playing up and down the coast."[99]

In the first week of May, the full company arrived in Los Angeles, and then opened on Saturday, May 8, for a five-day run, including a "special midnight show added on the opening night." The *Los Angeles Sentinel* previewed the opening by proclaiming that *Shuffle Along*, at the Lincoln Theater on Central Avenue, was "packed with ebony dynamite." Said "dynamite" referred to a new dancer named Helene Phillips, described as a "female Bill Robinson," along with "the rhythmical Brown Spots" plus "a chorus of bronze Creole beauties, and Nat Cole's swing band."[100] The *Defender*, which had a Los Angeles column written by Harry Levette, also gave the production a definite thumbs up and posted a report of good business. "Flournoy's Shuffle Along, 1937, packed them in at the Lincoln all week," Levette wrote. He had positive things to say about "Jean Calloway, dynamic queen of swing," and even more about the orchestra. "Nat Cole's hot band brought many new arrangements that have set the town whistling."[101]

There was something of an upset during the five-night run at the Lincoln, however. The *Pittsburgh Courier* reported that Jean Calloway was "so mad at the crude management of the Lincoln Theater and she is literally biting nails."

The paper suggested that the cast was badly treated by the assistant manager, whom they referred to as "Mr. Right" and identified as "Negro"; but they also pointed out that the primary manager, Jules Wolf, who was white, "has always been very generous to colored enterprises." In other words, no black act had ever complained of ill treatment before. The *Courier* concluded that the assistant manager was "the cause of all the disturbance" and added, "Although the show was a rip-roaring smash hit, it refuses to run a second week."[102] This seems odd, since it was announced only as a five-day run to begin with, and they had another booking to get to.

The next stop was fairly near to Los Angeles, at the New Strand Theater in Long Beach, California. Since arriving in the area, the newlyweds, Nat and Nadine, had been staying with one of the bride's aunts, who lived in Long Beach; obviously the New Strand Theater was a much easier commute for them. According to one source, "In Long Beach, the revue got its biggest audience of the tour."[103] Flournoy Miller had more stops scheduled; after Long Beach, *Shuffle Along* was booked to play Denver and Salt Lake City.[104]

They never made it past Long Beach. The next thing we hear about the production is a rather ominous notice from the end of May. "For some reason not disclosed to the press, the famous *Shuffle* revue closed without notice following their last date [about May 25] in Long Beach," the *Defender* reported, "The revue has busted up."[105] Nat offered his own explanation as to what happened, saying in 1954, "After the show"—which suggests that the production only played one performance in Long Beach—"it was discovered that one of the company had vanished with the box-office receipts. 'We guessed that he got maybe $800,' says Cole. 'None of us have ever seen the light-footed rascal since.' "[106]

Cole is being surprisingly light-hearted about a major crime—almost $15,000 adjusted for inflation to 2019 dollars—which put a whole company of forty players and musicians out of work and left them stranded thousands of miles from home. We'll never know what actually happened or if it had anything to do with the incident at the Lincoln. When Cole talked about such events in his life, he was invariably trying to tell the most entertaining story, not trying to seriously document what actually happened for the benefit of future historians and biographers. Still, no matter how it had gone down, without that payroll, the company couldn't keep going. The show was indeed, as the *Defender* reported, "Busted Up."[107]

FLOURNOY MILLER, HOWEVER, was a man of his word. He couldn't continue with his full-scale revue, but he wasn't about to let his cast, including his daughter, Olivette, and the band, who were all depending on him, go hungry. With Nat's support, he looked around for more opportunities; he made every effort for the company to stay together and to find work more or less as a unit. Alas, he had to let his "ten chorus girls" go; he knew that it was unlikely that he would find a venue big enough to accommodate a full-scale chorus line; presumably, he at least was able to give them train fare home. "The chorus was sent back to New York, as this concluded the cross country tour."[108]

On June 3, Nat and Nadine and about seven members of the band, plus Olivette Miller, were all present at a birthday party.[109] At least two of the musicians, saxophonist George Skinner and bassist Henry Fort, had been with Nat since the forming of his very first band in fall 1934. Even if they weren't being paid to play at the party, at least they took the opportunity to eat. But it wasn't long before Miller found something.

On Thursday, May 6, a new club, the Ubangi, opened on Atlantic Boulevard; as the name suggests, it was a showcase for "Race" talent. Like Frank Sebastian's Cotton Club, the primary audience was "ofay" (white) but "Race profession and press are always welcome." (In other words, other black singers and dancers, especially celebrities, and black journalists, could come in, but not your basic rank-and-file black folks.) Around mid-June, a much-truncated edition of *Shuffle Along* opened at the Ubangi, described in the *California Eagle* simply as "Flennoy [*sic*] Miller's Stage Show."[110] They played at the Ubangi for about a month, long enough for the *Chicago Defender* to run an item, showing a smiling picture of Nat, and proclaiming him a "hit on coast."[111] "Youthful maestro and pride of Bronzeville with his young tunesmiths are spreading white heat rhythm for dance patrons at the swanky Ubangi club in Los Angeles." But that was all; the club ended the engagement around July 15, "closing out the all-colored band and company and replacing them with whites." So much for the Ubangi; needless to say, the Flournoy Miller crew was not pleased, and neither was the local black press.

Now in need of work, Cole was sending out feelers to his old friends back in the Midwest. It was announced that he and his band would participate in one of the year's major events, "The Swing Parade," an all-star spectacular event to be mounted at his old stomping ground, the Chicago Savoy Ballroom, and set to feature no fewer than seventeen big bands. Following this all-star event, the band would play several other unnamed Chicago venues for about two weeks, before then moving on to an unnamed venue in Detroit, beginning on August 1.[112] But it wasn't to be. Despite these optimistic projections, Cole wouldn't make it back to Chicago until 1941.

Instead, Miller found them a gig at another new-ish nightclub spotlighting African American talent, the Century Club, also known as the Cafe Century, on Beverly Boulevard, near Fairfax Avenue. During these weeks (roughly July 28 to August 18), the final holdouts from the *Shuffle Along* company were members of Miller's immediate showbiz family: Miller himself, Mantan Moreland, and Olivette Miller (the hot harpist). But Cole was also beginning to make long-lasting professional and personal connections with other talent that he met at the club. There was Marie Bryant, later a well-known Hollywood dancer (and longtime girlfriend of Nat's future buddy and partner, Norman Granz); she would enjoy a long association with Cole and served as choreographer for his 1956–57 NBC TV series.

And there was also Dorothy Dandridge, a fourteen-year-old aspiring singer from Cleveland, then part of the Dandridge Sisters Trio. For the last year and a half, ever since the Panama Café back in Chicago, Cole had primarily been in the business of accompanying singers and entertainers. The girls' mother, Ruby Dandridge, commissioned him to write some arrangements for the group, which launched a lifelong, apparently platonic friendship between Cole and the future movie star and pioneering black actress. Twenty years later, Nat and Dorothy would daydream together about starring in their own TV sitcom—a family show about an orchestra leader and his wife. (In the vague outline, it suggests a black *I Love Lucy*.)[113]

The engagement at the Century ended before Labor Day.[114] This was not quite the end of the line for Cole's association with Flournoy Miller; remarkably, there would be yet another new *Shuffle Along* in July 1938. But the August 1937 booking at the Century would be important to history for one major reason: this was the last known gig for Nat Cole before the formation of the King Cole Trio.

ACT ONE

The King Cole Trio

1

The Birth of the Trio

1937–1943

We were playing maybe even better then [in 1941] than we did later on.
— NAT KING COLE, *1951*

YOU KNOW, IT'S A STRANGE THING that everything that brought me success was an accident," Nat Cole said in 1945. "For instance, I always wanted to have a big band, never thought of a trio, particularly as there were no small groups playing on the Coast. It was Bob Lewis of the Swanee Inn who suggested that I add guitar and bass and bring the trio into his place. I figured it would be just another job for a few weeks and look what happened! It still amazes me."[1]

Nat King Cole was a great believer in luck. Or, at least, he made himself out to be so in the personality that he projected to the media—especially to the interviewers and feature writers who profiled him in newspapers and magazines. Rather than giving himself any of the credit for his own success, he was much more likely to claim it all had happened because he had "the luck o' the Irish"—after all, he had been born on St. Patrick's Day and he carried a shamrock in his pocket.[2] To hear Cole tell it, everything that helped to push his career from one level up to the next was invariably a lucky accident. There was the formation of the trio: the idea of putting together a band consisting of piano, guitar, and bass was so out-of-the-box in 1937 that it almost had to be a mistake, albeit one that almost immediately righted itself. Surely no one could have come up with such a combination deliberately.

Then there was idea of Cole singing, which, as he always claimed, he had never set out to do, but something that he just tried, more or less on a whim, during long sets when they were mostly playing background music in noisy cafés, and something which the audience, to his surprise, responded to. "That was another accident," he explained (in 1945). "A trio is so limited by lack of instruments that I sort of had to sing to add to the group. All of a sudden, people decided they liked my voice. It was quite a surprise to me to be placed on so many polls as a singer."[3]

Virtually every journalist who ever wrote about Cole was, in a very real way, his willing co-conspirator. They were all partners and participants in the artist's highly ingenious myth-making. Yet the more one looks at the facts, and the closer one examines the documented evidence, the more undeniably apparent it becomes that Cole knew exactly what he was doing—at every step of the way. Luck had nothing to do with it, although good timing certainly did.

The biggest accident and the luckiest break that he liked to talk about was how he just happened to wind up in Los Angeles. He never actually planned to relocate to the West Coast, or so he claimed. No, that was just where he happened to be when *Shuffle Along* folded, and where he was stranded, along with the rest of the company. He had just turned eighteen at the time and, a few weeks before that birthday, had gotten married. In some accounts, Nadine was the one who wanted to remain—she had family there; they were currently bunking with her Aunt in Long Beach. The way that Nat later told it, when they were stranded in Los Angeles, they had no means of returning home.

But Cole had multiple reasons for staying on the West Coast. Barely nine months earlier, when he and Eddie had been stranded on the road, the Reverend Cole undoubtedly gave both of his prodigals a stern talking-to on their eventual return. Now, if he were to come back once again like a whipped dog "with his tail between his legs," he would not only have to face his father but worse, would have to admit that Eddie was right in not leaving Chicago to begin with. And now he had to think about Nadine as well as the other twelve or so musicians in his band. He didn't want to admit to anybody, especially himself, that he had simply made a bad decision and hitched his wagon to the wrong star.

But as we've seen, as recently as February, he had been working with his big band in Chicago, and he could have easily put in a call to Benny Skoller, or any other club owner on the South Side, and gotten some kind of booking. It seems obvious that Cole wanted to start his marriage and a new phase of his life with a new beginning in a whole new part of the world—even as his parents had done less than fifteen years earlier.

"California jazz echoes the spirit of California," as Cole wrote ten years later. "It's progressive, daring, individual stuff. It's cocky, corny, great stuff, with the flash of flash bulbs in its sound, the excitement of a class-A 'whodunnit' in its originality. California jazz may not be the greatest in the world, but it certainly has guts and originality."[4]

When Cole landed on the Left Coast, he immediately realized that Los Angeles was becoming a new black mecca, and Central Avenue, where *Shuffle Along* was about to open, was its epicenter. Red Callender, who played bass with Cole in 1942, remembered, "The town was full of jazz. All the bands were coming through and all the movie stars went slumming on Central, because that's where the jazz was happening. You'd see Mercedes-Benzes, Cadillacs, Bentleys; people like Mae West, John Barrymore, John Steinbeck. All the stars, black and white, came to Central Avenue. We might arrive there at two or three in the morning, hang out until ten or twelve o'clock the next day. We rarely got tired, it was too much fun. Jack's Basket Room, Milamo's on Western, Last Word, the Turban Room, the Brown Bomber, Brothers . . ."[5] Even the *Chicago Defender*, which had, to mix a metaphor, no axe to grind and no particular reason to beat the drums for Los Angeles, observed, "Central Avenue has been transformed into Seventh Avenue and East Los Angeles into Harlem."[6]

COLE'S EARLY MONTHS IN CALIFORNIA were generally described later as his "last temptation of Christ" period, his time in the wilderness, not knowing what to do next or where to turn. "It was really tough then," as he later put it; "I played piano in almost every beer joint from San Diego to Bakersfield."[7] Like so much else in his personal mythology, he deliberately exaggerated the hardship to make his genuine rags-to-riches story seem more dramatic. In actuality, there doesn't seem to be any point at which Cole was really up against it. He may have been earning only $5 a night in 1937, according to many of his own accounts (roughly $90 or $100 adjusted for inflation to 2019 dollars). But how many eighteen-year-old musicians do you know of in the 21st century who are making the equivalent of $3,000 a month playing the piano? It's important to remember that even though he was already supporting a wife, he was still just a kid. It's hardly unusual that a teenager, even one as mature as Cole, would have to serve an apprenticeship, to work hard and scuffle to find both his style and his career opportunities.

Yet it might not have been even a month between his last gig with the remnants of the *Shuffle Along* company at the Century Club and the debut of the King Cole Trio. Bob Lewis, the owner of a club called the Swanee Inn (at 133 North La Brea Avenue, one block South of Beverly Boulevard),[8] had heard Cole at the Century and invited him to put together a group.[9] As with virtually everything else in Cole's career, there are multiple stories as to how he got together with guitarist Oscar Moore and bassist Wesley Prince around August or September of 1937 to form the original edition of the King

Cole Trio. As usual, Cole chalked it up to lady luck, but the opposite seems true: that Cole's musical vision was so clear and his ambition so overarching that he would have found a completely new format for the jazz piano no matter what, along with brilliant collaborators to join him on his journey.

Within a few months of his arrival on the coast, Cole had already become close with two percussionists, Lee Young and Lionel Hampton, who were connected to everything that was happening within the burgeoning community of jazz and black musicians in the greater Los Angeles area. Young was the kid brother of the tenor saxophone colossus Lester Young, and over the years, both brothers would make musical history with Cole. Hampton was a whole generation older than Cole but had followed a similar geographical and musical trajectory: he had been born in the South (Louisville, Kentucky, in 1908), coming of musical age in Chicago where he learned to play drums and later vibraphone, and then, at about twenty, relocating to Los Angeles. By the mid-1930s, he was a true star of California jazz, including some notable appearances with Louis Armstrong. In 1935–36, he led his own band, which featured trumpeter Teddy Buckner and bassist Wesley Prince.[10] Hamp's band was a hit with the local black community, but he was willing to give it up to join Benny Goodman, after the legendary clarinetist heard him at the Paradise in summer 1936.

Hamp later remembered[11] that he first met Cole at the Paradise; this would have been in the summer of 1937, while he and the Goodman band were doing record dates, a radio series, and the movie *Hollywood Hotel*. While Hampton was working with Goodman, Cole, as we've seen, was playing at the Ubangi and then the Century Club. But after their paying work was through, the two would join forces at the Paradise, just for the thrill of working with each other. "Nat hadn't been on the coast from Chicago long," the percussionist later remembered. "He didn't even have a steady gig."[12] Hampton added, "He and I used to jam every day, and I was going around town trying to hip people to him."[13]

Hampton also remembered distinctly that the first time he encountered Cole, the pianist was already in the middle of a partnership with the outstanding guitarist Oscar Moore. Because he had been born on Christmas Day in Austin, 1916, Moore's friends sometimes addressed him as "Jesus Boy."[14] Like Nat, Oscar had grown up in the shadow of a significantly older brother, Johnny Moore, who was also a guitarist. Oscar landed in Los Angeles in 1936, a few months before his future partner, and like him, he was quickly accepted by musicians on the local scene.[15] "The first time I laid eyes on Nat," Moore chuckled in 1957, "he looked like a real mean guy—his eyes almost closed, glintin' out at you, diggin' what was goin' on. After I met him, I found out how wrong I was."[16]

So, whatever group Cole would bring in to the Swanee Inn, it was already bound to feature Oscar Moore. Other musicians were up for grabs. Bob Lewis and Cole both knew that the twelve-piece band was too ambitious for his small club; with no other work around for the full contingent, Cole reluctantly had to disband. "The manager of the Swanee had told Nat that if he could get a [group] together, he had a job," Hampton remembered. "So Nat got Oscar, and then they started looking for a bassist."[17] Cole's first choice was Wesley Prince, who had formerly played in Hampton's own band at the Paradise, and he was now available ever since Hamp had broken up that band to go on the road with Goodman.[18]

For a drummer, Cole reached out to Lee Young, and there are multiple accounts of why that didn't happen—either because three musicians was the maximum number that could fit on the Swanee bandstand, or, equally likely, Young just never showed up. Thus, whether by accident or design, the group that began playing at the Swanee Inn in September 1937 featured Nat Cole, piano; Oscar Moore, guitar; and Wesley Prince, bass. At that point, said Moore, "We just thought that the Trio was going to be a good thing. We had faith in it."[19]

One major inspiration for the new group came not from Cole himself but rather from his new bassist. As Prince later remembered, "I thought of the name of the trio, and put two and two together, I thought of 'Old King Cole was a merry old soul,' you know, and that's what gave me the idea of calling him Nat King Cole."[20] Nat had fluctuated between Coles and Cole for years, but somehow, he had never thought about using that old nursery rhyme, again in millennial parlance, for marketing and "branding" purposes. As we've seen, he had already named his first band, in Chicago in fall 1934, "The Royal Dukes." And this is clearly why the band had to be a trio; the nursery rhyme, which goes back at least to 1708, states explicitly that Old King Cole "called for fiddlers three." The very first mention of the Trio in print is an ad in the *Los Angeles Times*, announcing "Chicago's Sensational Trio, King Cole's Swingsters Three appearing at the Swanee Inn."[21]

A trio of piano, guitar, and bass—where did such an idea come from? The dominant keyboard sound of the 1930s was stride piano, and the greatest exponent was Thomas "Fats" Waller. Waller's band, the "Rhythm," utilized bass, drums, and guitar (along with trumpet and sax), but none of his sidemen were essential, either harmonically or rhythmically—stride was foremost an approach for unaccompanied solo piano. The other musicians in the "Rhythm" added to the impact, but they weren't essential.

"Why did I go twelve years without a drummer?" Cole explained in 1950, "Because with one we'd have looked just like a rhythm section. And when we came on stage, people would wait for the rest of the band to appear."[22] He might have just said that he wanted something different. As we've seen, the vast majority of black bands were directed by pianists. Between the reference to the nursery rhyme character and the use of a formal term from chamber music—not many swing era groups billed themselves as "Trio" or "Quartet" (that was undoubtedly inspired by Benny Goodman)—the King Cole Trio established themselves as a blend of the jivey and the serious, even though he didn't permanently settle on that name for a few years.

So why this particular trio? Cole's piano would be at the center of any of his groups, but guitar and bass were relatively new instruments in the jazz pantheon. In early New Orleans bands and up through the 1920s, the primary rhythm instruments were banjo and tuba, not least because those instruments were easier to capture in the primitive, acoustic recording process. As the rhythm and the technology both grew more sophisticated, the banjo gave way to the more graceful guitar and the tuba ceded to the more fluid and flexible string bass, and the two "new" instruments immediately helped to give birth to the 4/4 swing beat of the big band era. These newcomers found their first virtuosi in a parallel pair of short-lived innovators who would work briefly but spectacularly with the two leading bands of the period, Charlie Christian with Benny Goodman and Jimmy Blanton with Duke Ellington.

Earlier in the 1930s, the precedent was set for the unity between vocal harmony groups and the guitar, especially those that featured African American males. There were, most famously, the Mills Brothers (billed as "Four Boys and a guitar"), The Ink Spots, and the Spirits of Rhythm, which featured the manic scat vocal genius Leo Watson. There was also Slim and Slam, a duo of guitar and bass, who specialized in jivey novelty songs, usually accompanied by piano and drums. The closest precursors to the Trio are the Three Keys, a vocal-instrumental trio that recorded in New York in 1932–33 and featured piano, guitar, and bass along with harmony vocals.

But precedent can take us only so far. There can be only one answer to the question: why a trio of piano, guitar, and bass? Because it sounded awesome; once again, Cole knew exactly what he was doing. Like King Oliver's band with two cornets, Benny Goodman's quartet of clarinet, piano, drums, and vibes, or Gerry Mulligan's later quartet of baritone saxophone, trumpet, bass, and drums, and other legendary but, at the time, unconventional jazz ensembles, Cole wasn't thinking of the instrumentation. Rather, he was thinking in terms of the men themselves. He had heard Prince and Moore and he wanted to play with them. He knew they were the perfect partners to help him take his music up to the next level—or, in this case, to the first level.

THE ONLY DETAILED DESCRIPTION of the Swanee Inn—birthplace of the King Cole Trio—comes from friend and fan Claire Phillips (later Gordon). As she tells it, the place was decidedly not a dump: "It was all black and silver, considered very chic at the time." It's worth noting that, even though in Cole's own account he was playing "beer joints," the truth seems to be that from their first gig onward, the Trio was only playing relatively classy establishments. "We passed a short bar, and threaded our way among cocktail tables and chairs to the back of the room, where we thought we'd be inconspicuous." Claire and her brother Bob walked in, sat down, and proceeded to have their minds blown by what they were hearing. This was fall 1939, at the time of the Trio's return to the Swanee, when they had already been playing together for two years. "Oscar seemed to read Nat's mind," said Phillips. "Even when Nat played a new improvisation, Oscar followed along with the correct chords."[23]

The Trio opened at the Swanee in September 1937 and were an immediate success: the first gig lasted seven months. This set a pattern for the early part of the Trio's development: long runs and low money. Where Cole had been making $5 a night as a single, or so he said, the Swanee started the Trio off at $75 a week, presumably for five nights. But there was an upside to the long runs: the men didn't need to spend any time traveling, so they could concentrate more fully on the music; and then, seeing the same local faces in the house night after night obviously inspired them to keep expanding their repertoire as well as their stylistic vocabulary. On the personal side, Cole was feeling secure enough to encourage his parents to come visit in October; this may have been the first time they got to experience Nat and Nadine as a married couple.[24]

The earliest reference to the group in print that has been found is an ad from the *Los Angeles Times* from November 25, 1937: "For your Thanksgiving Party, Enjoy Chicago's Sensational Trio, King Cole's Swingsters Three, appearing at the Swanee Inn. Cocktails, 25 cents. No Cover. 133 La Brea, South of Beverly."[25] Lewis ran another ad on December 23: "Merry Christmas and a 'Swinging' New Year from King Cole and his Swingsters Three, The Swanee Club—Hollywood." It's significant that Lewis chose to advertise in the mainstream *Times* (as well as the *California Eagle*, one of the city's two black papers); from the beginning, the Trio attracted a white audience as much as a black one.

In April, the *Chicago Defender* dropped Nat a line for the first time in about nine months, "The Swanee has Nat Cole's trio with Nat at the piano, Wesley Prince, the bass, and Oscar Moore, guitar."[26] This seems to have been in the final weeks of their long first run at the Swanee. Fortunately, a *Down Beat* scribe was able to catch them there and gave them their first write-up in what would become an important publication. Describing the Swanee as a "little night spot," he explains that "the entertainment is very intimate in keeping with the size of the place. Three Colored musicians do plenty with piano, guitar, and bass and the local musicians have been coming around to get a load of it on their night off." He added, "Piano man is the finest heard in these parts for a long time. Has a fine voice too."[27]

In Spring 1938, they left the Swanee and began branching out to other venues in the general area, such as Shep Kelley's in Hollywood, the Club Circle in Beverly Hills[28] and the steakhouse, Jim Otto's. But local clubs, even if they were not "joints" or "dives," paid only so much, and Cole knew the bigger money was to be found playing in the stage shows in movie theaters. Even while the Trio was less than a year old, he had such ambitions, and in June, after two week's at Jim Otto's, he announced that they would be soon playing at Vogue theater on Hollywood Boulevard. The plan was that the Trio would share the stage with a local dance orchestra led by one Ken Baker, and that they would alternate with the big band much the same way that the Benny Goodman Trio did with the clarinetist's full orchestra. This was going to be a big deal, "with a National Network tie-in and big money behind it." Alas, the gig lasted only one night: "They opened on a Thursday and folded the same night. It seems that that the gent behind the scenes absconded with the evenings 'take.'" The Trio would not get another opportunity to do a high-paying theater gig until 1944.[29]

They quickly rebounded and found work at a "swank spot" called Fox Hills, so named because it was nearby 20th Century Fox studios; there, they were caught by Earl J. Morris of the *Pittsburgh Courier*, who described the leader as "Nat King Cole, that guy who plays a lot of piano" and added, "His fingers run over a keyboard like Henry Armstrong's fist ran over Barney Ross" (the latter being a reference to a prizefight that had occurred a few weeks earlier).[30]

In June, Morris informed readers that "these mellow cats will swing out over a national hook-up." This was true, in more ways than Morris realized at the time. In October, not long after their first anniversary, Cole, Moore, and Prince began regularly broadcasting Monday evenings on NBC affiliate KECA Los Angeles.[31]

But Cole would soon be heard over the airwaves via several different approaches. Our earliest extant documents of the King Cole Trio are from what was known at the time as "commercial transcriptions." In the days before disc jockey programming, the majority of music heard over the airwaves was live, but still there was a need for pre-recorded music. There were whole programs made up of music from transcriptions, usually during the afternoon, in the same way that syndicated programming dominated non-primetime hours later in the television era. (It was not considered fair game to play commercial recordings on the air; both the record companies and the musician's union pooh-poohed the practice.) Thus, even as mainstream, big-market broadcasting was growing up, independent transcription firms were supplying "canned" programming to stations on a subscription basis. Some of these firms were loosely affiliated with existing record labels (Thesaurus with RCA Victor and NBC, World with Decca) but others, like MacGregor and Standard, were independent. And although there were few commercial record labels based in California, a disproportionate number of these transcription services were located there.

In early 1936, *Variety*[32] listed roughly thirty commercial transcription services operating in New York, Chicago, San Francisco, Hollywood, and Los Angeles. Standard Radio Advertising, as it was officially known, had been in business at least since 1933 and we know that Standard recorded the group for the first time around late September 1938, about the same point when they first began broadcasting over KECA. Other dates followed in October and November, resulting in a total of twenty songs cut over three months. The pay was decent; as of 1940, musicians were receiving "eighteen dollars for each quarter hour" to make these commercial transcriptions, plus six dollars for each five minutes of overtime. Seventy-two dollars an hour was very decent money for musicians at the time; it is not quite what the full-scale commercial labels paid per the American Federation of Musicians.[33] Transcription work was also more plentiful, especially in California.

The transcription services—not only Standard, but soon Davis & Schwegler, Keystone, MacGregor (beginning in 1941), and finally Capitol Records' own transcription service—loved the King Cole Trio. The group had already spent night after night for a whole year working up material in clubs. In these early years especially, the live gigs essentially became woodshedding sessions where the Trio not only perfected its unique inner dynamics but also worked up an astonishing range of material, including new songs, jazz standards, current swing band favorites, and "hot" treatments of familiar nursery rhymes and other traditional melodies.

The Standard Transcriptions, the first recordings of any kind of the King Cole Trio, show that in the very beginning the group was a lot more like the Spirits of Rhythm or the Three Keys, a combination of vocal harmony and instrumental virtuosity, than the "chamber jazz" style group that they later became. And, despite all the stories Cole dreamed up over the years, he was singing from the beginning, mostly in harmony with Moore and Prince but also occasionally solo.

In one of his more credible accounts of how he first started singing, Cole said, "When I organized the King Cole Trio back in 1937, we were strictly what you would call an instrumental group. To break the monotony, I would sing a few songs here and there between the playing. I sang things I had known over the years. I wasn't trying to give it any special treatment, just singing. I noticed thereafter people started requesting more singing, and it was just one of those things."[34] Thus not exactly an accident, and not exactly deliberate.

Cole sings on virtually all of the early transcriptions, even as he would continue to do on the Trio's commercial sides for Decca and then Capitol—in fact, there are many more vocals in the earlier Standard titles, from 1938 and '39, than in the later ones, in 1940 and '41. There's a lot more harmony singing on the earliest titles, and the solos by Cole and Moore are much more firmly rooted in the swing era, with Cole still displaying his Hines influence. Overall, though, they do sound like the same King Cole Trio that we know from its later commercial recordings. In its prime, the King Cole Trio would launch many musical trends, but at the beginning, they were content to follow them.

In 1937, Maxine Sullivan launched the vogue for swinging traditional songs and folk songs with her hit "Loch Lomond"; then in May 1938, Ella Fitzgerald and Chick Webb's Orchestra opened the floodgates by swinging a familiar nursery rhyme with "A-Tisket, a-Tasket," easily the biggest seller of her long career. The very first Trio session includes swing treatments of Johann Strauss's waltz "The Blue Danube" (they play it in 4/4 rather than 3/4), the nursery rhyme "Button, Button," and "Swanee River" (from Stephen Foster's "Old Folks at Home," and possibly a dedication to the venue that birthed them). After hearing their 1938 transcription of "Three Blind Mice," which quotes liberally from "A-Tisket," you begin to wonder if it's just a coincidence that the Trio took its name from a nursery rhyme.

It's on the very first number of the very first transcription disc by the King Cole Trio that we finally encounter what has to be a genuine coincidence: song number one is "Mutiny in the Nursery," a brand-new number by Johnny Mercer, whom the Trio would meet in person around this time and who would play a key role in their story starting a few years later. (His first move, upon hearing the group, was to return to the Swanee with no less than Bing Crosby himself in tow.) "Mutiny" was a new song by Mercer and Hollywood veteran Harry Warren, written for two major black entertainers, Maxine Sullivan and Louis Armstrong, in the Warner Bros. musical feature *Going Places*. In the lyrics to "Mutiny," Mercer, who himself was only twenty-eight, is keenly aware that he's writing for the "Loch Lomond" lady, Maxine Sullivan herself, in that the song encapsulates a miniature medley of traditional nursery rhymes (including "Little Boy Blue," "Three Little Kittens," and "Lazy Mary"), all rendered in 4/4 swingtime.[35]

The twenty tracks from fall 1938 cover all the diverse styles and sources that the King Cole Trio was working in during their first year. In addition to "Mutiny in the Nursery," there's another Warren song, "With Plenty of Money and You," a late depression bromide from *Gold Diggers of 1937*, as well as, coincidentally, an older, pre-Hollywood Warren song, the 1931 "By the River St. Marie." The latter would become an early King Cole Trio (KC3) signature, which they would record on a commercial 78 in 1940 and then perform again in the 1944 movie *Swing in the Saddle*. Cole's first-ever show tune was "F. D. R. Jones," by Broadway tunesmith Harold Rome for the topical revue *Sing Out the News*, a Broadway number that was immediately adapted by black entertainers and the swing community (Ella Fitzgerald, the Mills Brothers); seventy years before Barack Obama, the closest we would come to having a black president was for a black family to name their baby after the thirty-second president.[36] These new show and film songs were the ones most heavily "plugged" (promoted) by publishers, who were looking to get as many recordings and radio plays as possible, not only to encourage record sales but to push the still-important sheet music market. Cole was already aware that to own the publishing rights to songs, even more than writing music or words, was to be able to make money both coming and going.

These early sessions also address jazz standards written by musicians themselves, such as two numbers by arranger Edgar Sampson co-credited to Benny Goodman, "Dark Rapture" and "Lullaby in Rhythm," and "Caravan" by Juan Tizol and Duke Ellington, which Cole would return to, famously, in 1956. They play two older songs that were already jazz standards, Dorothy Fields and Jimmy McHugh's "Don't Blame Me" (another future Cole classic) and the 1921 Dixieland standard "The Sheik of Araby," along with other songs that would have been familiar to radio audiences: Irving Berlin's "Blue Skies" and George Gershwin's "Liza." But the swinging folk songs and nursery rhymes predominate, such as "Three Blind Mice," and "Patty Cake, Patty Cake," the latter inspired by an adaptation by Fats Waller. There are also two new songs, "Flea Hop" and "Wiggly Walk," written for a local theatrical presentation, titled *The Hollywood Revue Production 1938–39,* which are very much in the nonsensical, unabashedly juvenile style of the swinging nursery rhymes.[37]

Also heard in the fall 1938 Standard Transcriptions sessions is Cole's first-ever Christmas recording, a swing-style adaptation of the traditional 1857 air "Jingle Bells." It starts with a graceful acoustic guitar intro by Moore before the three voices launch into a high octane, incessantly jived-up yet still tasteful reworking of the familiar melody. Moore plays an eight bar solo, and then Cole sings the verse ("Dashing through the snow . . .") in solo, before the other two rejoin him. Just as "Three Blind Mice" quotes "A-Tisket, a-Tasket," "Jingle Bells" becomes a paraphrase of the 1935 big-band classic "Ride, Red, Ride" (by The Mills Blue Rhythm Band featuring trumpeter "Red" Allen). At this point, the threesome launch into numerous tempo changes, going from achingly slow to horse-race fast, a device virtually unknown among swing bands, mainly because to play around in such a fashion with the beat makes the music impossible to dance to.

By November, the black press, at least, was buzzing about the Trio's broadcasts on NBC. "When the theme song 'I Lost Control of Myself,' is ushered onto the airwaves, the King Cole Jesters are on the air," the *Defender* proudly announced. "Nat Cole, leader and pianist for the trio, describes their inimitable style as 'descriptive swing.' Many of the tunes they feature are original compositions by Cole." Their program was weekly, fifteen minutes each Monday at 5:00 PM, which was prime time (8:00 PM) in New York and the rest of the country. This was a major step; even though they had yet to make a commercially issued recording, they were, in a sense, leapfrogging over other, more well-established bands by moving into the promised land of big time, national network radio. "The King Cole Jesters first started on NBC less than a month ago and have already met with great success."[38]

IN NOVEMBER 1938, the group, this time called "King Cole and His Sepia Swingsters," settled back into a long run (at least seven months) at Jim Otto's Steak House, where they were heard not only by Mercer and Crosby but by future manager Carlos Gastel.[39] Long before Gastel stepped in, however, the Trio was briefly managed by one Irwin "Hap" Kaufman, described by Claire Gordon as "a good-looking, Melvin Douglas-lookalike in his mid-twenties, with a cat-ate-the-canary smile on his face. We could count on seeing him at least once a week when it was payday—he would be at the club to collect his

10 percent." Between the weekly series on NBC, the nightly sets at Jim Otto's, and the Trio's ongoing recording dates for the transcription services, it's hard to believe that they had time for anything else, but apparently Cole was also part of yet another new edition of the venerable *Shuffle Along*.

Shuffle Along of 1939 (a title that would prove to be overly optimistic) officially opened on about Thursday November 10,[40] 1938, at the Criterion Theater.[41] Apart from the headliners, Miller and Mantan, the biggest name was Ruby Elzy, who had been "borrowed" from another black show (*Run Little Chillun*) that was concurrently running in the city. The newcomer who attracted the most attention was a young baritone billed as "Herbie Jeffries," then also starring in a series of pioneering all-black westerns and who would find major success a few years hence with Duke Ellington's Orchestra. The other recognizable name was Juanita Moore, who later gave the performance of a lifetime in Douglas Sirk's epic weepie *Imitation of Life* (a picture with some Nat King Cole relevance, as we shall later see).

The white press (*Los Angeles Times*) was kinder than the black papers (*Pittsburgh Courier*) or the showbiz industry press (*Billboard*), and the show quickly closed. Still, the *Courier* was quick to absolve the legendary Flournoy Miller from the blame: "The great F. E. Miller, who is famous as a playwright also, didn't have anything to do with this butchery on the part of his brother, Quintard Miller."[42] So what, exactly, did Nat Cole have to with this production? His wife, billed as Nadine Coles, was either a chorus girl or a featured dancer, and one write-up[43] mentions that Cole himself was in the cast, at least on opening night. But all the notices list him as the composer: "The songs were composed by Sammy Scott and Nat 'King' Cole with arrangements by Phil Moore"[44]

In fact, Cole seems to have been putting in a lot of effort toward writing songs in late 1938 and early 1939, more than at any other point in his career, partly due to the encouragement of a new music firm called "Davis & Schwegler." In the early years of commercial radio, the American Society of Composers, Authors and Publishers (ASCAP) had a literal monopoly on popular music; they controlled the rights to every song that anybody wanted to hear. And they acted like robber barons: over the course of the 1930s, ASCAP raised rates to radio stations some 448 percent;[45] eventually, in 1941, stations would try to ban ASCAP music altogether. The new company (Davis & Schwegler [D&S]), founded by a "former Seattle attorney" named Kenneth C. Davis and Paul Schwegler, a "former football star" was open for business in June 1938.[46] Their mission statement, said Davis, was to "amass some 50,000 songs, which he claimed was twice the number controlled by

ASCAP, and to give radio 'a perpetual license to use our music at no charge whatsoever.' " Even while gathering the rights to this huge pool of songs, the firm was simultaneously producing "some 3,000 programs, musical and dramatic, upon transcriptions and phonograph records. These would be sold or rented to stations as a complete library service." In other words, one single company, D&S, would be both producing the content and controlling—or, in this case, giving away—the publishing and performance rights.

The Trio recorded some twelve songs for the D&S transcription service, the bulk of which were credited to some combination of the three members, and others were clearly written for the 1938 edition of *Shuffle Along*. At least one tune, "Riffin' at the Bar-B-Q," was published and released like a proper piece of mass-market sheet music: the cover shows a photo of the three young men, billed as "King Cole and his NBC Swing Trio." The twelve tracks that the Trio cut for the firm are a distinct step down from the generally excellent twenty songs that they had already recorded for Standard Transcriptions a few months earlier (and the others that they would do later on). They're also less interesting than the Standard titles in that too many tracks feature rather nondescript female vocalists, Juanelda Carter and Bonnie Lake. (Lake, the sister of actress Ann Sothern, would have more success as a songwriter.) Both the *Defender* and the *Courier* praised Cole's songs after he played them on his NBC series, especially "I Lost Control of Myself" (music by Cole, words by agent Hap Kaufman), the theme song for the show, and "Riffin' at the Bar-B-Q." "Give yourself a treat and listen to him tickle the ivories."[47]

The most notable D&S title is the first track on the first 16" disc to be issued (not necessarily the first recorded), titled "There's No Anesthetic for Love," words and music by one Marshall Walker. It's not a great song, but what is surprising is the degree to which it features both Oscar Moore and Nat Cole in solo vocals. In the song's scenario, Moore plays one of Cupid's victims, struck down and immobilized by love, and he sings, in jivey double time, "Cupid let fly a dart / And it went straight to my heart / The doctors looked at my chart / And wound up right where they start." (The grammar isn't perfect, no.) Cole, essaying the role of the doctor, answers, first speaking the words, "I'm sorry son," and then singing, "There's no anesthetic for love." Most of the piece is a unison scat solo by the threesome, but this opening chorus is notable as an early attempt by the trio to tell a full-scale story in the framework of a 32-bar popular song and a three-minute track.

The twelve D&S titles had much more of an afterlife than most of the Trio's transcriptions; they were not only reissued on Keystone transcriptions but also briefly pressed as commercial 78s. The twelve mostly original songs in the Davis & Schwegler transcriptions (and subsequent 78s) were an interesting detour but nothing more. Of the hundred or so titles that Cole transcribed in the years 1938 to 1941 these are probably the least interesting overall. Even though Cole was clearly pleased with "Riffin' at the Bar-B-Q" and "I Lost Control of Myself" at the time, I don't think they'll be heard on any Nat King Cole tribute albums anytime soon.[48]

FOR AT LEAST SIX MONTHS, from January to June 1939, Cole was upgraded by NBC to what appears to have a been a nightly, national half hour series, *Swing Soiree,* which he shared with the network's own "Swing Staff Orchestra" conducted by his future collaborator, Gordon Jenkins.[49] Meanwhile, the Trio continued to hold forth at Jim Otto's Steak House, and in February they resumed recording transcriptions for Standard. In April and August, Standard increased the Trio's workload, and presumably their bottom line if not necessarily their visibility, by assigning them to accompany two vocal groups "Pauline and Her Perils" (led by Pauline Byrne) and the Dreamers. The first group is a pseudonym for the better known "Six Hits and a Miss" and their eight highly polished titles with the Trio sound like the best white vocal groups of the day. Conversely, the Dreamers are a black group with a high tenor lead in the tradition of the Ink Spots or the Delta Rhythm Boys.

Apart from these two vocal groups, the Trio cut no fewer than thirty-eight generally excellent titles for Standard in 1939. Between February and August, there were more nursery rhymes ("Georgie Porgie"), swinging treatments of iconic European classics (Franz Liszt's "Liebestraum"), and many Trio adaptations of famous swing band flag-wavers ("Undecided," "Tain't What You Do," "Do You Wanna Jump, Children?," "Blue Lou"), plus many first-rate songs of the kind that would later be characterized as part of the Great American Songbook ("My Blue Heaven," "Russian Lullaby," "Crazy Rhythm," "Moonglow").

By apparent coincidence, the April 1939 Standard transcriptions include three songs with lyrics by Frank Loesser, all of which were heard in upcoming Paramount pictures: "Some Like It Hot," the title song from the 1939 Bob Hope comedy of the same name, "Snug as a Bug in a Rug" from *The Gracie Allen Murder Case,* one of the Trio's all-time most charming harmony vocals, and "Fidgety Joe" from *Man about Town.* The last finds the Trio alternating back and forth between three-beat and two-beat phrases, which afford the song a suitably jumpy, staccato quality of the sort described in Loesser's lyrics. This track not only swings, as virtually all the King Cole Trio numbers do, but it also fidgets.

In addition, there's an increasing number of solid originals composed by the Trio members, both vocal and instrumental, including a lot of riffing. "Riffin' in F Minor" boasts an impressive early bass solo by Prince with allusions to "I Got Rhythm," while "I Like to Riff" is another winning Trio vocal number. Many of the 1939 titles stand out: on a May date, Cole recorded two titles that, as a personal point of pride, offer homage to his idol, Earl Hines. The first is the Fatha's most famous composition, "Rosetta," which Cole decorates with alternating sustained notes and a dancing keyboard touch; we would expect his treatment of Hines's most famous composition to reveal his filial allegiance, and indeed it does, but it also shows Cole becoming his own man.

Then there's "Sweet Lorraine," the Earl Hines perennial that Cole was already making his own, particularly in the vocal, which Cole sings mostly in solo (his most extended vocal solo yet) but with harmonic background singing by Moore and Prince. Cole is also moving ever closer to something like a ballad feel here. The May titles also include a lovely arrangement of the 1932 standard "Moon Song (That Wasn't Meant For Me)," and another vintage jazz classic, Clarence Williams's 1919 "Baby Won't You Please Come Home."

Also, in May, the Trio introduced another remarkable original, "Black Spider Stomp," Cole's most fully realized instrumental yet. The inspiration here is a combination of Django Reinhardt (essayed by Moore) and Art Tatum (played by Cole), at a breakneck tempo that's possibly even faster than tempos of either of the two originals, in a way that suggests both collaboration and competition, as if Moore and Cole were trying to outrun each other. Here and elsewhere, the Trio sustains rhythmic interest within the 4/4 time signature not merely by phrasing each measure as four distinct beats, but by thinking in terms of two-measure units, each of which is phrased as something more like 3 + 3 + 2 rather than the expected 4 + 4.[50] Most jazz groups would play for a lifetime before they ever achieved such a high level of synergy, and yet the King Cole Trio was just getting started—they still had not made an actual commercial recording.

DURING SUMMER 1939, the Trio worked at "Shep Kelly's night spot in Hollywood" in June and then "Jimmy Turner's Circle Club in Beverly Hills,"[51] before Bob Lewis brought them back to the Swanee Inn.[52] They stayed at least as long as November 8—sharing a bill, remarkably, with the great Art Tatum himself.[53] It was during this second Swanee run that Claire Phillips Gordon got to know Wes, Oscar, and, eventually Nat. She saw Wes, the bassist, as the most outgoing; he "had an easy manner and a warm smile and in spite of his stammer, he was ready to get into a conversation." Oscar "was the hippest of the three, the first musician we ever saw wearing dark glasses at night. Oscar was about 5' 10", medium build, light skinned"—as opposed to the leader, who was much taller, much younger, and much darker. Nat was the hardest to get to know, the one who seemed to be suspicious as to why these white kids were hanging around; he went off to the side, as always, "smoking his mentholated cigarette."[54] One Saturday afternoon, the two Phillips siblings, Claire and Bob, went to visit Oscar at his home; his wife and baby greeted them, and Mrs. Moore tried to be polite, even as they gradually realized Oscar wasn't there. He eventually showed up and told everyone he had just come from an all-night jam session; still, his wife seemed furious at him. Phillips gradually realized that Oscar had been out all night at a different kind of a session.

Phillips was one of Cole's few musical associates who made a point to get to know Nadine. "The Coles lived in a court, a California residential type of multiple housing. Usually there were four or five small, one-story homes attached to one another built along the depth of the lot."[55] This was their home at 2910 South St. Andrews Place, a short drive away from Central Avenue,[56] where they lived for most of their marriage, from 1939 on. The couple was closest during these early years, when the Trio was enjoying long residencies in Los Angeles clubs, but they started drifting apart when Cole began leaving home for long periods—as he did for most of 1941. (Even so, only one of his friends, Norman Granz, has even briefly mentioned Cole indulging in any extracurricular activity.)

The Trio was gradually attracting notice in the show business and music trade. Lindley "Spike" Jones, a well-established studio percussionist (not yet a famous bandleader), was then briefly serving as artists and repertoire (A&R) director for a short-lived jukebox-style service called Cinematone, which recorded several songs with the Trio that fall. (The titles were registered with the Los Angeles colored musicians' local, meaning that the men were paid, but thus far only one, a jive number called "Trompin' " has surfaced.)[57] After the Swanee, the Trio finished out 1939 back at Shep Kelly's, where they did "swell business."[58]

AT THE START OF THE NEW YEAR and the new decade, the Trio quickly entered a whole new phase. The bookings from 1937 to 1939 seem somewhat chaotic and random, but from 1940 until their major breakthrough in the spring of 1944, more consistent patterns and more long runs start to emerge. From this point on, there were, generally speaking, three different kinds of venues wherein the Trio worked. The rarest gigs were in ballrooms; these were generally the exclusive province of the big swing and dance orchestras. Even at the height of their popularity, the Trio played these only occasionally, as on an event advertised as "concert dance" at the Dorie Miller Auditorium in Austin, Texas, in July 1949.[59] Then there were theater dates; they had done their first, as we have seen, one night in June 1938 at the Vogue, but, as far as we know, they didn't play another movie house until spring 1944, when "Straighten Up and Fly Right" hit. From that point on, for the next fifteen years or so, stage shows in picture palaces would be Cole's virtual lifeblood—just as they were for the name big bands.

But from 1940 to 1944, when they had gotten their act together and were deemed good enough to get work outside of the Los Angeles area, their main employment came from what Cole and others referred to as "Cocktail Lounges." They were much larger than the intimate jazz clubs on New York's 52nd Street, for instance, with a capacity on the average of roughly 250 people. People came to drink and talk and not incidentally to listen (if they weren't interested in the music, there were plenty of nearby saloons without any). These lounges were springing up all over major cities in the immediate prewar era, and Cole played them in Los Angeles (the Radio Room), Chicago (the Capitol Lounge), Cleveland (the Sky Bar), and elsewhere. As far as we can tell, these rooms were usually rather inclusive, both musically and racially. Hap Kaufman seems to have no longer been in the picture; now they were working more extensively with agent Berle Adams, particularly in the Midwest and Chicago.

After finishing at Shep Kelly's, it turned out that the steadfast Bob Lewis had other plans for the Trio. He brought them into the Radio Room on Vine Street, where they launched one of their most significant long runs, which lasted for most of 1940.[60] The club was so named because it was right across the street from NBC's Los Angeles studios, and the engagement there helped to cement Cole's lifelong, highly productive relationship with NBC. This was a pivotal gig for the Trio, Cole later said. "We made lots of friends. We were the first group of any kind to break in cocktail lounges out there. Hollywood had never been the place for them. But Bob Lewis took a chance—gave us our chance—and the breaks were right, we did all right."[61] Everybody remembers that there was a bowling alley in the back; the Trio didn't actually perform in said bowling alley, but, later on, Cole liked to joke about it. On the *Hollywood Palace* in 1964, he quoted an apocryphal early review that supposedly claimed, "When Nat Cole sang in the bowling alley last night, you could hear a pin drop."

The other news of early 1940 turned out to be more important in the long run than it might have seemed at the time.[62] They were hired to record a session of four titles for jukebox use by a short-lived operation called Ammor (Automatic

Music Machine Operators Recording) Records, founded by one Jack Gutshall, a well-known player in the coin-operated music business.[63] To actually produce the recordings. Gutshall recruited he songwriter Leon Rene, who, with his brother, Otis, had been among the more successful black entrepreneurs in Los Angeles. The two had co-written Louis Armstrong's theme song "When It's Sleepy Time Down South,"[64] but unlike most songwriters, they also ran their own publishing firm. "I started scouting for new talent," said Rene. "I recorded Nat at the old Melrose Studio. In those days, they were still cutting masters on wax cylinders. I played the masters for Jack. He liked the hot numbers, but turned down 'Sweet Lorraine,' which became one of Nat's biggest hits."[65]

Cole seems to have taken the occasion very seriously, picking three numbers they had been playing for a while: "I Like to Riff" (which the label names as "I Like *The* Riff"), "Black Spider" (leaving out the word "stomp" this time), and "By the River St. Marie." The fourth tune was a new treatment of a venerated standard that also had the potential to become a King Cole classic, "On the Sunny Side of the Street." This pivots around a jivey, double-talk routine heavily inspired by Don Redman on his 1937 recording of the Fields-McHugh classic. So far so good. But here's what went wrong: somebody, either Cole or, equally likely, Rene, decided to bring in a drummer. When the tracks were later issued on Savoy, the 78 labels gave credit to "King Cole Trio, vocal with Lee Young, drums." But otherwise, I wouldn't have guessed it was him, even though he told me, many decades later, "Any time you hear drums on a King Cole record, it's me."[66] It doesn't sound like Young's playing, in spite of the label credit—either that or he had grown into a much better drummer by the time he played with Cole on the classic *After Midnight* album sixteen years later.

The idea, perhaps, was to make the group sound more like a conventional swing quartet. Alas, the drummer takes away much more than he adds—especially when he plays a full break on "I Like to Riff." The odd man is especially superfluous, on "On the Sunny Side of the Street." The original concern with the Trio had been that the piano and guitar would potentially step on each other's toes, since the two instruments were both accustomed to being the sole harmonic support; when guitar did play with piano, especially in swing band rhythm sections, the guitar supplied the necessary rhythmic support. The most famous guitarist was Freddie Green with Count Basie, continually supplying that solid four afterbeat that propels the ensemble along. Here the drummer seems to exist in his own space, so much so that in some pressings of these tracks, it sounds as if the drums were dubbed in after the fact. Perhaps it's unfair to blame the percussionist himself; he was brought in to play drum parts on arrangements that were already perfect without a drum part, and things could have hardly turned out otherwise.

The titles were originally issued on Ammor 108 and 109—for jukebox use only, not for sale to the public (which is why the original 78s are so rare today)—with the artist credit as simply "King Cole." The Ammor relationship was a one-session deal, and the company soon went out of business in any case. The masters were summarily acquired by industry veteran Eli Oberstein, then running his own independent label, Varsity; since the Ammor releases had been distributed only to juke joints, Oberstein immediately issued the four Cole titles on Varsity in August 1940. Cole was already important enough that the jazz press took notice. *Down Beat* wrote, "Oscar Moore's dynamic, technically astounding guitar work is enough recommendation."[67] And *Metronome* praised "I Like to Riff," "with Cole and Moore turning in brilliant performances. 'On the Sunny Side' has [vocal] chorus effects [that] Don Redman might investigate."[68] (In 1945, the four masters passed into the corporate hands of Savoy Records, who issued and reissued them many times over, into the LP and CD eras.)

IT WAS A REMARKABLY INAUSPICIOUS BEGINNING for the Trio on records, but more copasetic platters lay ahead. In May and then November, the Trio cut more sides for Standard, six in spring and ten in fall (and then finally, ten more in February 1941). Less notably, in July 1940 they also cut twelve tracks for a firm called Keystone Transcriptions, which had become the successor to Davis & Schwegler in terms of providing radio stations with copyright-free music. The Keystone sides are, in the main, just as dispensable as the 1939 D&S sides—all the songs are eminently forgettable.

But the later Standard transcription titles (sixteen from 1940, another ten from 1941) are an entirely different matter; these contain some of the finest playing ever by the group and capture the Cole-Moore-Prince combination better than any other audio documents (including the sixteen Decca titles of 1940–41). Compared to these, the 1938–39 sessions with their emphasis on jivey vocal group harmony, seem relatively simplistic. There were still a few group vocals here and there (such as "Crazy 'bout Rhythm," 1940), but they were gradually declining in favor of solo vocals and instrumentals.

We don't have definitive composer credits on many of the Trio's transcription recordings of this early period, which matters primarily because some of the titles are undoubtedly the work of Cole or Moore. Cole himself would be a fairly persistent songwriter for most of his career, and he himself composed the three songs that did the most to elevate the Trio to stardom: "Gone with the Draft," "That Ain't Right," and "Straighten Up and Fly Right." The Trio's later Standard transcription tracks, the twenty-six titles from 1940 and

'41 (which include two different versions of "Gone with the Draft") are exceptional. The arc of the ninety titles the Trio recorded for Standard reveals a remarkable transition, one that travels in precisely the opposite direction from what we expect. Our preconceived ideas about Cole's career tell us that he gradually transitioned from jazz to pop, but in this period, the trajectory is reversed: the 1938 Standard titles are mostly jivey pop-oriented trio vocals, like "Jingle Bells," but the 1940–41 titles are some of the most sophisticated jazz yet recorded by anybody.

One of the most remarkable pure jazz numbers is "Early Morning Blues." At twenty, Cole is already one of the finest blues pianists in history: few of the piano giants he revered could touch him as far as the blues were concerned, not Tatum, not Wilson, not Waller, and not even his original hero, Earl Hines; the only blues players in his league were the Midwest and Kansas City boogie-woogie specialists like Albert Ammons, Pete Johnson, and Meade Lux Lewis, and they had nothing like Cole's technical proficiency or his harmonic and melodic invention. Cole had grown up more deeply immersed in church music than most of them (Waller's father was also a minister, but Cole's experience was in the more intensely soulful, rural church music of Alabama and the Deep South), and the proximity of the black church to the blues clearly had an influence on his mastery of the blues form and the blues ideal. Later, we'll take a closer look into the ways that Cole played and sang the blues, but for now, we'll take note of how he specialized in the "themeless" variety of the form, those blues in which the melody, the embellishments, and the improvisation all seem to be the same thing. It's almost as if he doesn't want to waste time in any of these three-minute tracks by indulging in something as banal as a theme; he just wants to take a deep dive into the meaning of the blues.

"Early Morning Blues" begins and ends with Cole playing a repeated figure in the bass clef, followed by a thunderous bass pattern from Prince; when first we hear it, we think he's setting us up to hear a boogie-woogie riff on top of it. Like many later King Cole Trio classics, "Early Morning Blues" makes brilliant use of contrast, once Cole and then Prince have established the deep darkness, Moore enters on the opposite end of the sonic spectrum, plucking his way in with bright and high notes—they're putting the frequency range of the 1940 transcription equipment to a rather extreme test. To sustain rhythmic interest, Cole employs a "Scrontch" pattern, of the kind established in Ellington's 1938 composition of that name, in which the fourth beat of every two bars is dramatically emphasized—sometimes Nat is playing the scrontch, sometimes it's Oscar. The piece builds to an intense climax of activity, and it's in his use of repetitive patterns that Cole shows his mastery of the blues as a concept—one riff that he plays for a few seconds anticipates the line that Charlie Parker would later call "Now's the Time" and which eventually became an R&B hit as "The Hucklebuck." Then, having reached that peak, it gradually falls apart. "Early Morning Blues" starts to deconstruct itself in a manner that implies Cole was familiar with Haydn's "Joke" Quartet (op. 33), a piece of music that seems to deliberately fall apart and makes a point of not ending where you think it's going to end.[69]

"Early Morning Blues" briefly contains one of Cole's very few nods to the boogie-woogie style, which, much like Waller, he seems to have dismissed as a kind of a cheap thrill. There are relatively few examples of Cole playing in the form, such as "Windy City Boogie Woogie," from the November 1940 Standard sessions, and "Boogie a la King" (a 1944 MacGregor transcriptions title), which are both mere throwaways.

Yet "Early Morning Blues" is merely one of twenty-six tracks that the Trio cut for Standard in this period, a track that was only heard randomly on the radio in selected markets. It's proof that the group had already attained a highly rarefied status. The best of the King Cole Trio tracks, as experts acknowledged both at the time and since, places them in the same lofty pantheon as the best of Goodman (particularly the legendary sextet he was then leading with Charlie Christian), Ellington, Basie, and Lester Young, or even the Louis Armstrong Hot Fives and Sevens series. And yet Nat King Cole was hardly finished with jazz greatness as far as 1940 was concerned. (And neither was he finished with the blues.)

DURING COLE'S 1954 TOUR of England, a local journalist and jazz buff asked him about the eight remarkable sides he cut with Lionel Hampton in 1940. "Golly, you remember those? This was while Hamp was still with Goodman. He heard the Trio one night on a club date, and thought he'd like to cut some records with us as his rhythm section."[70]

In September 1939, *Down Beat* had reported that while the Goodman orchestra was in Los Angeles, Hampton, as we know, "was out every night playing two-finger piano with King and his boys" at the Swanee Inn.[71] This makes sense: Hampton was rushing out after the Goodman gigs, and rather than dealing with the vibraphone or drums (there was no room for them on the Swanee bandstand in any case) he just sat next to Nat and played the piano as if it were a vibraphone and his fingers were mallets, two notes at a time. He told *Down Beat* at the time that he was already planning to "use the Trio on some records soon."[72]

In April 1940, the Goodman Orchestra was back in LA, playing the Palomar and recording for Columbia. On Thursday, April 10, Hampton played on a famous session with Goodman and Fred Astaire in the afternoon, but a few hours later, he was part of an equally auspicious team-up, when he guest starred with the Trio, for the only time in front of a general paying audience (as opposed to jamming after hours at the Paradise and at the Swanee). That evening, some enterprising producer was staging a "fast-moving, all-colored revue" done in the style of a Harlem nightclub at Los Angeles City College. "The King Cole Swing Trio" was on the bill, along with a roster of singers, dancers, and a big band.[73] To the surprise and delight of the crowd, however, the biggest hit of the program was scored by Lionel Hampton, making a surprise appearance. "A program of jam and jive, [featuring] the guest appearance of the one and only Lionel Hampton, had the ancient L. A. City College Auditorium in an uproar last Thursday," the *California Eagle* reported. "It remained for 'Popsie' Hampton, sitting in with the King Cole Trio, Nat Cole, Wesley Prince and Oscar Moore, to break up the show. His jamming the vibes on 'Flying Home' and 'Moonglow,' piano solo and drumming, had the campus agog for the rest of the day."[74]

The combination of Hampton and the King Cole Trio was too good not to be recorded. Hampton was currently making a series of all-star sessions for RCA Victor, using different musicians from various bands (including Ellington and Basie) as they happened to be in town. In May and July they would record eight titles total, using the Cole Trio as the core group, adding Hampton (mostly on vibraphone), and drummer Al Spieldock. Most of the eight numbers are Hampton originals, and six are instrumentals—Helen Forrest, one of the leading "canaries" of the big band era, then working with Goodman, sings on two, "I'd Be Lost without You"[75] and the standard "Ghost of a Chance." Claire Phillips was on hand as a timekeeper to make sure that none of these free-wheeling jam sessions exceeded the standard 78 RPM single playing time of three minutes.[76]

Unlike the mystery drummer on the Ammor-Varsity titles, Hampton and Spieldock know enough not to try playing in the middle of the Cole-Moore-Prince sonic equation but rather to play around it. In fact, they balance each other, with Hampton's vibes on the top of the sonic spectrum and Spieldock's bass drum on the low end. The two guest players frame the three regulars, rather like a pair of parentheses, and, unlike the Ammor drummer, never get in their way. Ever the showman, Hamp also takes solos on piano and drums.

Spieldock is, at best, a footnote to jazz history, known for two things: his work on these sessions and being married at the time to Helen Forrest. His playing, mostly on brushes, is superb here, and Hampton's is even more so. And even though Hampton already had a reputation as a show-boating, scene-stealing kind of a player—and he is, after all, the dominant instrumental voice—he's frequently generous enough to cede the spotlight to Cole as well as the general direction of the ensemble.

There's a lot of blues here, at nicely varied tempos. The opener, "House of Morgan," is a pun on the famous banking family and a dedication to the leader's uncle, Prohibition liquor-entrepreneur Richard Morgan, who had introduced his not-yet-famous nephew to his famous paramour, Bessie Smith. "House of Morgan" is medium fast, but "Jack the Bellboy" is much faster, climaxing in a full-on solo by Hampton. "Central Avenue Breakdown" is a spotlight for Hampton's famous two-finger style keyboard soloing, a highly entertaining device that he used to goose audiences for many generations, only this time we can hear Cole playing more full-fingered piano accompaniment in the background.

Conversely, "Blue" isn't a blues at all, but a rather lyrical pop song from the book of Earl Hines. "House of Morgan" and "Jack the Bellboy" come off like the Trio guesting on a Hampton date, but the two harmony vocals, "Dough-Rey-Mi" and "Jivin' with Jarvis,"[77] sound like King Cole Trio records with Hampton making a guest appearance. They were billed on the original RCA labels as the "Hampton Rhythm Boys"—the vocal on the latter is just chanting the title at the start of each A section (and introducing a scat break by Hampton), but that's all that's necessary.

The group also plays beautifully behind Forrest on her two ballad vocals—she is easily the best female singer they would accompany, at least up to Anita O'Day in 1944. Which brings up another point: Hampton later wrote of Cole, "I liked his style of piano playing, but even more I liked his singing. I was the one who kept telling him, 'Man, you sing, you sing.' I knew he could sell the public on his singing."[78] Which naturally enough begs the question: Hampton being the leader, why didn't he ask Cole to sing on "I'd Be Lost without You" and "Ghost of a Chance"—or even "Blue (Because of You?)"

The eight titles are overall superb, so much so that one of Cole's favorite bandleaders, the great Jimmie Lunceford, paid him the honor of commissioning a big band orchestration of "Jivin' with Jarvis." Hampton and Cole also continued to "jam" together at the Casa Manana "Monday Night Jamboree," one Monday in August, in the middle of Lunceford's gig there.[79]

The recordings were so well received that some people started getting ideas. Journalist Leonard Feather, writing in *Down Beat*, reported that Hampton was organizing his own orchestra and "The King Cole Trio, famed nightery unit, will be incorporated in the new combination."[80] Hampton later denied that this was ever his idea and suggested instead that Feather was the one who was lobbying for a permanent Hampton-Cole combination. "I had plans for a new band that did not include Nat's kind of sound. Besides, I wasn't planning on a featured singer, and I knew that's where Nat's real popularity was going to come."[81] However, Nat himself remembered that it was indeed Hamp's idea that they should keep on working together. "Then Hamp formed his own band and wanted us to join *en bloc*. Well, sir, we'd just got the Trio going, and I just didn't know. I dickered with the idea, and finally asked Count Basie for some advice. Bill said I'd be damn silly, all those fine things we were starting to do within the group would be blasted out by Hamp's powerhouse stuff. So we didn't join."[82] He was right, the Trio's kind of "chamber jazz," which they were featuring on the November 1940 sessions for Standard, was just not Hampton's "kind of sound"; the vibraphonist and showman's big band would be much louder, much less subtle, and highly oriented toward raucous R&B-centric dance music.

To give Hamp credit, he later did much to help "discover" such essential vocalists as Dinah Washington and Joe Williams. But, in his rather dubious memoir, he made all kinds of audacious claims: by his account, he was not only the one who encouraged Nat to sing, but he was also responsible for getting Capitol Records to record Nat doing "Straighten Up and Fly Right"; Capitol, he said, only did so as a personal favor to him. This is likely more than a bit of an exaggeration. But then again, perhaps it's not a coincidence that between the two Hampton sessions, in June 1940, the Trio played at the opening of a new music store on Sunset and Vine; "Music City," as it was called, was owned and operated by Glenn Wallichs (and his father Oscar). It's altogether likely that Johnny and Ginger Mercer were there for the opening. As Dave Dexter Jr. later remembered, "Glenn Wallichs was running this music shop at Sunset and Vine, in Hollywood, called 'Music City.' It was without a doubt the most successful retailing venture in the record business west of Chicago. Johnny Mercer used to come in, buy his records [presumably meaning records of his songs], sit around and play records he wanted to hear."[83]

Whatever Lionel Hampton's actual role in the King Cole Story—beyond the great sessions of 1940—and apart from whatever Hamp wanted to take credit for, as it happened, Cole did make his first contact with Wallichs at the very moment he was working with Hamp.

MEANWHILE, THE LONG RUN at the Radio Room continued, largely uninterrupted. "The King Cole Trio, Hollywood's most sensational small musical combination, [has] thrilled such artists as the Andrews Sisters, John Boles, Wally Vernon, and Harold Lloyd, of the films, nightly at the Radio Room for a solid year."[84] Cole gained another fan, and a lifelong friend and future collaborator, when the twenty-two-year-old pianist Jimmy Rowles walked into the Radio Room and heard him for the first time.[85] Later, Rowles would become Cole's number one keyboard deputy on pop sessions and other record dates when Cole elected not to play himself.

Other opportunities were coming Cole's way. In fall 1940, the radio comedian and entrepreneur Edgar Bergen hired him to put together a band to accompany the singer-pianist-entertainer Rose Murphy in a series of short films that were to be used in an early movie-jukebox program that presaged the more famous Soundies operation of a few years later. Cole didn't personally perform on the screen or the soundtrack of these films, although Moore and Prince were both present. Though the project didn't lead to other similar work for Cole (as a band contractor), the Bergen-Murphy films (some of which still exist) are a fascinating footnote to his early career—and, in a way, are a prelude to the Soundies that he would make in 1943 and '45.[86]

Around the same time, Cole was apparently involved in what might have been his first motion picture feature, *No, No, Nanette* (1940), Hollywood's second (of three, eventually) films of the classic 1924 Broadway musical by Vincent Youmans and Irving Caesar. There's no trace of Cole or the Trio anywhere in the finished film, but it seems possible that producer Herbert Wilcox at one point considered hiring a black group for one of the musical numbers. Cole himself mentions the project in a 1941 profile, which claims, "King Cole made the recordings and sound track for the film, *No, No, Nanette*, starring Anna Nagle [*sic*]." The story added, "Despite the fact that he was one of the busiest sepia musicians in Hollywood, he has never appeared before the camera."[87] Whatever Cole's involvement in the film might have been, it did have a long term impact on his music: for the rest of his career, long beyond the Trio, three of the most-played songs in his repertoire were from the score: "I Want to Be Happy," "I Know That You Know"[88] (which he famously played as a flag-waver instrumental in multiple tempos and sang on *After Midnight*, 1956) and even more, "Tea for Two."[89]

Cole may or may not have had anything to do with the 1940 film of *No, No, Nanette*, but just around the time that it was being released, the Trio made its first extant radio performance. We only know the date—December

1, 1940—we don't know the show or the circumstances, but the location was presumably Hollywood. The tune is Trummy Young's jive number "What'Cha Know Joe," which opens with an elaborate fanfare then is primarily a solo vocal for Cole abetted by Moore and Prince chanting the title riff (and words) behind him. The group races through two signature quotes, "Rhapsody in Blue" (as he would later in his famous coda to "I Know That You Know") and the folk air known as "The British Grenadiers" (at the time more popularly known as "American Patrol," but quoted here by Moore rather than Cole). The threesome would return to the tune in support of singer Anita Boyer (on a MacGregor transcription) a few months later, but this slightly longer live version (included on the Resonance package) has all the charm and the energy.

In a way that set the pattern for his life, Cole's musical purview was continually growing and expanding, and in the early 1940s in particular, the Trio was getting tighter, more swinging, and more expressive with every month, every new session; even the ninety or so Standard Transcription tracks never become repetitive or redundant. Then in December 1940, we get the confirmation—in a big public way—that the King Cole Trio had reached a new plateau. For the first time, a real record label was taking notice—and it was high time, too.

War wouldn't be declared by President Roosevelt and Congress until the attack on Pearl Harbor at the end of 1941, but most Americans, a few radical isolationists and anti-Semites aside, knew that America was going to get involved with the war in Europe at some point or another—it was just a question of when. The popular arts were already taking notice: Irving Berlin was even then devoting most of his energies toward songs in support of the Allied war effort, Warner Bros. had released *Confessions of a Nazi Spy* in 1939, and Captain America was already fighting Nazi bad guys in the funny books. In September, President Roosevelt signed into law the Selective Training and Service Act of 1940, which required all men between twenty-one and thirty-five to register with the draft, beginning in October.

In his Standard Transcription date of November 1940, the Trio introduced a new novelty song, credited to Cole, Prince, and someone named Earl Dramin. This was "Gone with the Draft," a topical political cartoon in song form that riffed on the selective service act. The title derives from Margaret Mitchell's 1936 literary phenomenon, *Gone with the Wind*—in fact, the 1937 song "Gone with the Wind" is quoted instrumentally. The vocal is sung by Cole mostly in solo, with Moore and Prince joining in on the title phrase.

When skinny me went out with my honey,
The boys all started to laugh.
But now it's not so funny,
They're all gone with the draft![90]

Basically, the message of the song is that since time immemorial, rugged, masculine he-men have been poking fun at frail, skinny, wimpy guys. However, now that "Franklyn D" has signed the draft into law, all the real manly men are being conscripted, so it's the ninety-nine-pound weaklings who now have the pick of all the hot chicks. Cole continues, "They now realize that skinny me / Was the luckiest one of all." This was the first of many occasions on which Cole would catch the national *zeitgeist* and deliver precisely the right message at the most perfect moment. There was only a short window after the signing of the Draft bill when it was still okay to derive humor from it. After Pearl Harbor, it would have been considered grossly unpatriotic to suggest that the skinny guys who were too frail to be drafted were better off than the macho men who were "Gone with the Draft." Even in the second verse to the song, Cole seems to be backtracking on his original message, consoling draftees with the bromide that they're only going to be taken out of circulation for a "year of drill," but when it's over, they can get discharged in order to "come back home and freshen up."

It wasn't exactly Cole Porter (the second chorus sounds like Nat actually wrote the words while driving to the recording date), but it caught the ear of Decca Records and they wanted it. The decision to sign the Trio for at least one session was probably made by J. Mayo Williams, who had produced the Cole brothers band date in 1936 and was then in his final months running what Decca now called their "Sepia Series."[91] It was a year and a day before the attack on Pearl Harbor, on Friday, December 6, that Nat Cole, Oscar Moore, and Wesley Prince had entered the Melrose Avenue recording studio for what is generally regarded as their actual first record session. Cole continued to experiment: on the 1940 Ammor date, he added drums, which turned out to be a terrible idea, and on the first Decca date, he added a second guitarist, heard very faintly playing rhythm behind Moore on three of the four titles.[92]

This all-important "premiere" Decca date begins with "Sweet Lorraine," the tune that Cole had been working on for years, ever since he heard Earl Hines and Jimmie Noone play it while he was standing outside the Onyx Club as a very young man in Chicago. This was the song that he would practice incessantly at Kelly's Stable and which he first transcribed for Standard in May 1939. Each of the previous versions finds Cole coming closer to the

Capitol version of 1943: the 1939 Standard has Cole singing solo with vocal backing from Moore and Prince and the signature "oh-ho-ho . . ." is already there; the 1940 Decca version has Cole completely in solo, but the tempo is still faster and less ballad-y than we're accustomed to. Still, it's hardly surprising that of all Cole's myriad skills, the one that would take the longest to develop is his ability to sing ballads.

"Sweet Lorraine" was only the first of four titles that they cut on what would be the first of four dates (in three cities: Los Angeles, Chicago, and New York) yielding a total of sixteen that they would record for Decca in four sessions between then and October 1941. One major change that would take place at Capitol was that Decca had consigned the Trio to their "Sepia Series," meaning that they were manufactured only for the "race" market—you could pretty much find them only in music shops in black neighborhoods. Jazz fans knew about them, *Down Beat* and *Metronome* reviewed and praised them, and some specialty stores like the Commodore Music Shop carried them. But by and large, they were marketed toward minority audiences, referring to minorities of taste (hardcore jazz fans) as well as genetics (African Americans). It wouldn't be until 1943 that Cole would connect with a musical operation that, like him, had its eyes on the big picture.

This first commercial session featured two new compositions by Cole, the novelty vocal "Gone with the Draft" and the blues instrumental "This Side Up," along with two thoroughly re-imagined jazz standards, both with a piano lineage: the Earl Hines-associated "Sweet Lorraine," and Fats Waller's 1929 "Honeysuckle Rose." In fact, these two standards are no less harbingers of the future than the new Cole originals.

"Honeysuckle Rose" is a piano showcase in which Cole seems to be serving notice to Fats Waller, the major jazz pianist of the 1930s (or at least side by side with Art Tatum), that a new keyboard voice had arrived, and he spins webs around Waller's classic tune—including several classical tempo changes, that even the Fat One himself had never imagined. Cole, as we've seen, viewed stride as an old-fashioned and limited form; he was determined to move beyond it. In fact, the Trio's "Honeysuckle Rose" is especially keyed to the future; on a blindfold test, most listeners would have guessed that it comes from the Trio's high Capitol years, 1943–1948 rather than from their very first session for Decca in 1940. Cole's own solo, where he darts pointillistic-style on top of Prince's solid support, sounds much later than 1940—it remains hard to believe that the pianist is still only twenty-one here. Even more impressive is what follows: this is one of many examples showing that Cole's heart was in the great big bands—Henderson, Goodman, Ellington, Basie, Lunceford.

After the guitar and piano solos, we get what classical composers would call a *tutti*, the opposite of a solo, that moment when all the instruments of the ensemble come back together. Cole structures his tutti more like what swing band arrangers call a "shout chorus," the last chorus of a big band number, following the solos or the vocal, where the ensemble plays the melody one last time, but louder and jazzier and more aggressively than before; it's one of many big band devices and traditions that Cole transmuted into the trio format. The last chorus of "Honeysuckle Rose" shouts highly aggressively, with no shortage of energy and imagination. These "flagwavers" numbers, almost all based on jazz and popular song standards, would form another key part of the mature Trio's output.

The fourth number is an original blues, "This Side Up," which is almost as good as "Early Morning Blues," which itself was about to be remade for Decca in the second session. "This Side Up" has something closer to a theme, although it's really just a riff that Cole rushes through, barely worth the twelve bars of attention he gives it, at the very start, on his way to the meat of the matter, and at greater length at the conclusion. There's a stop-time exchange near the end, but our ears are more drawn to Cole's brief quote from "In the Hall of the Mountain King," which would become one of his pianistic signatures, notably in his classic version of "Body and Soul." (This movement from Edvard Grieg's *Peer Gynt Suite* was a public domain classical theme that would be rendered in 4/4 swing time by numerous big bands during the ASCAP ban of 1941, including Will Bradley and Jan Savitt.) *Down Beat* was enthusiastic: "A blues, 'This Side Up' [and] the grand old 'Sweet Lorraine' show this LA unit at its best. Nat Cole's piano with Wesley Prince's bass and Oscar Moore's guitar jell okay. A promising debut for this group."[93]

But the tune that was most "promising" to Decca was "Gone with the Draft"; the label wanted it so badly that they made sure they had at least two perfectly good takes. We don't know exactly how well the record sold, since *Billboard* was not yet reporting the sales of "race records" (that wouldn't start until October 1942), but we have other evidence that it was a hit. In January 1941, the *Pittsburgh Courier* reported that after a year at the Radio Room, "the popularity of King Cole's new composition 'Gone with the Draft'" was inspiring "their agency" to start booking them on an Eastern tour.[94] This was General Artists Corp, or GAC for short, through whom, thanks to the success of the Decca sides in general and "Gone with the Draft" in particular, the Trio would soon be sent in early 1941 to Chicago; Philadelphia; Washington, DC; and back to New York.

The paper added, "The new hit tune may be sung by Bob Hope in his [forthcoming] film, based upon conscription, now in production at Paramount Studios, if negotiations can be completed."[95] A month later, the *Courier* reported that the idea was still in play, "His 'Gone with the Draft,' because of its timeliness, is being sought for the film comedian, Bob Hope, who is working in a picture of this nature."[96] That movie would be titled *Caught in the Draft* and released later in 1941, but the song placement never happened.

However, before 1940 was through, Nat King Cole received validation from two even higher authorities than Bob Hope, one of whom, coincidentally, was Bing Crosby, who had just launched a lifelong sub-career as Hope's sparring partner with *The Road to Singapore*. Even as the Radio Room gig continued, the Trio took the night off to play at a party for a local school, the African American Ascot Avenue Elementary School, where he shared the spotlight with several old friends: Mantan Moreland and Dorothy Dandridge, as well as Crosby himself. A lifelong political conservative and unswerving Republican, Crosby was nonetheless decades ahead of his time in his lifelong support of black causes and black artists. The Trio seems to have accompanied Crosby on several songs, and one attendee, described the Crosby-Cole performance as "just the greatest thing that ever happened around here."[97] Four years later, the Trio would guest star with Crosby on his long-running *Kraft Music Hall* series on NBC.

The Trio also received the stamp of approval from the King of Swing, Benny Goodman himself. Less than two weeks after the recording of "Gone with the Draft," Goodman's Sextet, co-starring the legendary guitarist Charlie Christian, recorded their response to Cole's tune, titled "Gone with *What* Draft."[98] Thus the year 1940 finished with a clear-cut case of noblesse oblige: The King of Swing was officially acknowledging King Cole as new jazz royalty—the King is alive, long live the King.

THERE WAS ONE MORE POSITIVE UPSHOT of the first Decca session in December 1940. From the beginning of the Trio in 1937 to that date, the name of the group seems to have never been fixed; there's at least one notice from 1938 that refers to Cole, Moore, and Prince, as "The King Cole Trio,"[99] but they are variously billed as "The King Cole Swingsters," "The King Cole Swingsters Three," "The King Cole Swing Trio"[100] and apparently were billed on their first NBC radio appearances as "King Cole's Jesters." The credit on their first commercially issued recordings (the Ammor session) was simply "King Cole." By 1939, Cole had adopted his stage name as Nat "King" Cole, although even then, he was listed as "Nat Coles" in his early songwriting credits. But from the Decca date onward, the group is officially and permanently known as "The King Cole Trio"—at least until 1949, when, for the last two years of the group's official existence, the billing was changed to "King Cole and His Trio."

For Cole, especially in 1941, the allusions to monarchy were both ironic and playful: much of the treatment he received was anything but royal; 1941 would find the Trio bouncing back and forth among six different clubs in that many cities. This was nothing, of course, compared to the extensive touring Cole would do at the height of his fame, and many of these gigs were at supper clubs, which tended to be longer runs than movie theaters, although theaters paid a lot more. But from 1944 going forward, the Trio could afford to hit the road in style; in the early days they were just scuffling from one town to the next, trying to stick to northern cities where they hoped they were less likely to encounter racist attitudes. At that time, a big star like Fats Waller was making at least a thousand a week[101] for his six-piece band; the top bandleaders, like Benny Goodman, could dependably pull in $7,000 on a good week. As for the Trio, they were lucky to get $140 a week at Kelly's Stable in New York. As Kelly's owner Ralph Watkins remembered, "They arrived in a broken-down car, bedraggled and without any clothes to perform in."[102]

After roughly twelve upbeat and relatively non-stressful months at the Radio Room in 1940, the big news of 1941 was that they were taking to the road at last, starting with Cole's first trip back to his home town, Chicago, since 1937. "The Trio, for several years a prime favorite with Californians, is slated to head East sometime in 1941," *Down Beat* reported in February, adding, "Moore is reputed to be Charlie Christian's equal on electric guitar." Before they left, however, there was still work to be done in Los Angeles, including a week at "The Cinema Sports Center on Hollywood Boulevard."[103]

More important, in February the Trio had to finish their obligation to Standard Transcriptions, with ten tracks, all jive numbers and/or Trio originals. These ten final Standard cuts are all excellent, and although no new ground is broken, they maintain a very high level of slangy jive. There are three blues numbers: "Windy City Boogie Woogie," the most notable example of Cole playing boogie woogie; "Fudge Wudge," a dark and compelling minor key blues with Prince holding down a solid, steady foundation; and "This Side Up," reprised from the first Decca session. And there's yet another version of "Gone with the Draft"—it was so popular that Standard wanted another master that they could send out to the stations, making it the only tune that Cole cut twice for the company. There's also "Scotchin' with the Soda" (and the similarly titled "Jumpin' with the Mop"), which they would recut for Decca in a month. "Let's Try Again," a ballad recorded a few months earlier by Jimmie Lunceford and His Orchestra, is slower and more tranquil, and begins to point toward the style of "custom ballads" that Cole would fully develop in the high Capitol years.

Within a week or so, Cole launched into a new relationship with another transcription service, officially known as "The MacGregor Company and Studio." Founded by C. P. "Chip" MacGregor, the company not only supplied pre-recorded music to radio stations but also maintained a state-of-the-art recording facility that they rented out to other producers. When Cole walked into the MacGregor studios, on 729 Western Avenue in Hollywood, it would be a momentous occasion—this is where he would later record the majority of his early Capitol sessions and also cut fifty excellent tracks with the Trio for the MacGregor corporation itself.

But Cole's first recordings for MacGregor were hardly as auspicious: in February 1941, the Trio was hired to accompany Anita Boyer, a big band singer who had already toured extensively with Tommy Dorsey and was currently with Artie Shaw. (Later, she would work with Harry James, Jimmy Dorsey, Red Nichols, and other name bandleaders.) Boyer was a first-rate band singer but not quite one of the immortals—not on the same level as Helen Forrest, Kay Starr, Anita O'Day, or Jo Stafford (all of whom would be accompanied by Cole at some point). The thirty-three tracks, originally released as by "Anita Boyer and her Tomboyers," are certainly pleasant but not world-beating or game-changing; the most interesting for us are two in which we hear Cole's voice, "What'cha Know Joe," a hit for the Pied Pipers with Tommy Dorsey, wherein the Trio sings in harmony behind and with Boyer, and "Blues in the Night," Harold Arlen and Johnny Mercer's venerable blues-inspired film song and future standard, which is more of a true duo between Boyer and Cole. That in itself is somewhat remarkable in the racial context of the period, a white woman and a black man singing together, even though "Blues in the Night" is hardly a love duo. (What's also unusual is that the majority of the titles were ASCAP copyrights, meaning that none of them could have been played on the air until after the ASCAP boycott was over in November 1941.)[104]

Then it was on to Chicago. They were booked to play the Panther Room of the Hotel Sherman, one of the city's number-one jazz spots, and the black press was delighted: "It's the old story of 'local boy makes good.' "[105] He shared at least part of the run with Bob Crosby and His Orchestra, perhaps not coincidentally one of Decca's top artists—and another notable instance of a "mixed bill" with both black and white groups. They seem to have opened on Friday, March 7 and played for about a month.[106]

The Friday after the opening, the Trio cut their second session for Decca, which opens with two rhythm-and-jive numbers emphasizing harmony vocals by the whole Trio: "Babs" and "Scotchin' with the Soda." The KC3 had already cut the latter for Standard, and, in a sense, "Babs" was also a remake—of sorts. In 1936, Cole's band had already recorded "Honey Hush," which was more or less his take on "Babs," which had famously been recorded by Lunceford in 1935; the bridges to the two songs are practically identical. (And to confuse matters further, the Trio had remade "Honey Hush" for Standard in 1940.) Both "Babs" and "Scotchin' with the Soda" sound much more like where the Trio had already been than where they were going. There would be more of these rhythm-and-jive numbers going into the Capitol period, but clearly Cole wanted to move beyond, both into more serious ballads and more intense jazz instrumentals and blues. And there had already been dozens of jivey jump tunes in the same mold as "Scotchin' with the Soda," cut by dozens of black groups, both large and small, on both a national and local level—"Scotchin' with the Soda" is no better or worse than "Jumpin' with the Mop."

Still, it's hard to deny the fun of both "Babs" and "Scotchin' with the Soda"—the only one who was possibly beginning to tire of what wasn't yet a formula was Cole himself. The Decca "Early Morning Blues" is possibly even better than the 1940 Standard version, but "Slow Down" is more of a harbinger of the future. Set in a medium tempo, it's closer to a ballad than anything Cole had recorded previously, other than "Sweet Lorraine."

"The Frim Fram Sauce" actually has something in common, in terms of subject matter, with "Scotchin' with the Soda"—in fact, a lot of early R&B (rhythm and blues) was directly inspired by F&B (food and beverages). This dish would, in fact, become the main course for another increasingly popular African American "combo" of the period, Louis Jordan and His Tympany Five; Jordan would spend the better part of his career telling listeners all about chicken, beans, cornbread, fried fish, salt pork, and boogie-woogie blue plates, and questioning the wisdom of achieving sobriety when the long-term plan was to get drunk again. But as we'll see, by the end of the war, after serving up the "Soda" and "Fram Fram Sauce," Cole was content to leave the tall tales of gastronomy and gluttony to Mr. Jordan while he went on to sing about other things. Love, actually.

As it happened, the King Cole Trio was about to cross paths with the Tympany Five. Both bands were being booked by Berle Adams of GAC, and in spring 1941, he brought both to Chicago. The agent had become friendly with Ernest Byfield, owner of the Sherman Hotel, who asked him for a fresh act for the Sherman's Dome Room; one of the senior agents, Art Weems (brother of the famous Chicago bandleader Ted Weems), suggested that Adams call the firm's Los Angeles office, and someone recommended the King Cole Trio. Berle fell in love with the group immediately, but Byfield thought they were too subtle for the room that he booked them into. "The Dome Room was a popular hangout for dames waiting to be picked up. They wanted a noisier band, something more in keeping with the tempo of the clientele." This wouldn't be the only time that the Trio was described as being too subtle for certain venues. "Nat is so polite, such a nice man; I won't fire him," instructed Byfield, "You'll have to find him another job."[107]

Fortunately, there was another such room in Chicago that GAC was also booking, the Capitol Lounge. *Billboard* described the venue as "long and narrow and always crowded. Entertainment starts early in the afternoon and continues until dawn. Suitable attractions are torrid musical combinations, with colored outfits for the evening hours preferred."[108] Adams had already put together an all-star triple bill of emerging black talent: the Tympany Five, the blues-driven pianist and singer Maurice Rocco (roughly the Little Richard of the 1940s, and a far less subtle pianist than Cole) and the Mills Brothers. This long-running vocal group was consistently among the most popular acts in the country, black or otherwise, and their popularity would be re-infused with a succession of major hits during the wartime and early postwar era. However, when Adams had initially approached Jordan with the idea of sharing a bill with the Brothers in the Capitol Lounge, he hesitated. "They came and asked me if I could play with the Mills Brothers in Chicago," the saxophonist remembered. "The Capitol Lounge was for white folks. It was across the alley from the Capitol Theatre. Not many Negroes came because they felt they weren't welcome. They wanted me to play intermission for the Mills Brothers."[109] He added, "I started not to go—but that [would have been] a big mistake."

It really was a mistake because, after Jordan changed his mind and took the gig in Chicago, the Capitol Lounge quickly became one of the top rooms in the city to spotlight black artists, with as many as 280 customers, both seated and standing, cramming into the place. When the Mills Brothers had to move on, Adams decided to bring in the King Cole Trio, and join the ongoing bill with Jordan and Rocco.[110]

Moving on from Chicago, the Trio next played Philadelphia, at the Rendezvous Club, located in the Douglass Hotel (for the first two weeks of April), and then traveled to Paul Young's Romany Room, in Washington, DC. When the proprietor's wife gave birth to a baby boy, the Trio went into a local studio and made a private recording to commemorate the occasion with an original song (based, not surprisingly on "I Got Rhythm"):

The Romany Room is jumpin'!
The Romany Room is jumpin'!
The Romany Room is jumpin'!
Let it jump, let it jump, let it jump, let it jump!

And then for a bridge, we hear Cole in solo,

Paul Young is the father
Of a seven-pound baby boy.
He's so glad about it,
He's jumpin' up and down with joy! [111]

Coincidentally, Al Spieldock, the drummer who had played so well with the Trio on the Hampton sessions a year earlier, was sharing the bill as the leader of his own band and informally joined the Trio on several occasions. That moment was captured in images: William Gottlieb, then a twenty-four-year-old aspiring journalist, covered the show for the *Washington Post*; he took some brilliant, justifiably famous shots of the group, including at least one image that clearly shows Spieldock playing drums with them.

Gottlieb gave the Trio a sentence in his column, "Swing Sessions: "A lot of swing in a small package comes from the King Cole Trio on their coupling of 'Honeysuckle Rose' and 'Gone with the Draft.' That's the outfit that's packing them in at Paul Young's, by the way." He captured the group much more eloquently with his camera. Most of the earlier extant shots of the Trio have them posing in a photographer's studio; Gottlieb was probably the first photographer to nail them in the heat of performance.[112] There are at least two shots taken from the lower house right angle of the bandstand, looking up at Cole, who is making do with an upright piano. In one shot, Prince is looking at Spieldock, whose drum kit is perched on a higher platform than the other three, while Moore and the drummer are looking at Cole. The pianist has his eyes closed and his mouth open, probably not singing, probably just opening his chops as a reflex option as he hits some particularly delicious chord change.

Whereas in 1940, the Trio hardly left Los Angeles at all, he was now barely able to spend a single night with his wife in the house they were renting at 2910 South St. Andrews Place.[113] After Philadelphia and DC, the Trio finally made it to New York and into the very heart of the jazz scene, where they infiltrated both of the city's jazziest neighborhoods (south of Harlem, at least), the West Village and Swing Street in midtown. They first played a week or so at Nick's Steakhouse, then and for decades to come, the main hangout of guitarist-bandleader Eddie Condon and his "Mob." Then, on Wednesday, June 12,[114] they settled in for a longer gig at Kelly's Stable, at 137 West 52nd Street. "I found Nat through a Lionel Hampton record," Ralph Watkins said. "It was called 'Jack the Bellboy' and there were sixteen bars by an unknown trio. I tried my darndest to find out who handled them." Watkins later remembered, "Nat Cole worked for me for about nine months," from summer 1941 to spring 1942.[115]

Their memorable stay on Swing Street was only interrupted by a six-week return to the Capitol Lounge in Chicago in September and October, where they again shared the bill with the Tympany Five and then jazz violin giant Eddie South and His Orchestra. When *Billboard* covered this booking, they made it clear that Jordan was the headliner and the King Cole Trio were only supplying intermission music.[116] But *Down Beat* took notice. In September 1941, the magazine's resident piano scholar, a gentleman named Sharon A. Pease, came into the Capitol Lounge and realized at once what he was hearing. After listening to the Trio at length, he wrote one of the first feature articles on Cole, including a transcription of part of his solo on "Early Morning Blues."[117]

In October, the Trio resumed the run at Kelly's in New York, where they shared the bill with any number of jazz legends, the most impressive, to Cole, being Art Tatum. Watkins related, "Nat used to sit in a corner and listen to Tatum. He'd be so upset. He was a fine jazz pianist, but he couldn't play like Tatum. But I remember one night when [composer and pianist] Alec Templeton came in. He and Tatum—both were blind—sat in a corner, staring up at the lights and listening to Cole."[118] Indeed Tatum was listening closely: the day after the Trio's summer opening, June 13, Oscar Moore participated in a Tatum recording session for Decca. "Art has said many times how much he'd like to have Oscar on guitar."[119]

Tatum was hardly the last jazz icon to work with Cole at Kelly's in 1941–42: the parade of jazz giants who shared the spotlight with the Trio started, in July, with two extravagant instrumentalist-vocalist-entertainers with colorful nicknames, violinist Stuff Smith and trumpeter Hot Lips Page, plus two full-time singers named Billy: cabaret singer-entertainer Billy Daniels and the legendary Billie Holiday.[120] In September, it was trumpeter Red Allen's band featuring J. C. Higginbotham on trombone, plus Art Tatum,[121] and in October, Benny Carter and His Orchestra were the featured band along with the blues singer Miss Rhapsody (Viola Gertrude Wells), with Daniels and Tatum both staying on.[122]

During fall 1941, a young, and, by his own account, penniless, jazz fan named Norman Granz somehow scraped together enough small change to get into Kelly's Stable, where he encountered the music of Nat King Cole for the first time, and he forgot the line-up of alto saxophonist Pete Brown's band, Art Tatum, and the King Cole Trio.[123]One student who was walking by was so young that he wasn't allowed to stay. "I was going home from my violin lesson and I went out of my way to walk down Swing Street," said Alan Bergman, then about thirteen, "and I heard the most amazing piano playing coming out of Kelly's Stable. I nervously went in, and the bartender said I had to leave, but when he saw I was carrying a violin and that I really was loving the music, he let me listen for a few minutes." Fifteen years later, Bergman would write a theme for Cole's TV show.[124]

"In those days, the Trio only did unison songs" or so remembered Adams. "The only solo I remember Nat doing was 'Sweet Lorraine.' "[125] Billy Daniels also remembered that Cole didn't sing at all at the time "because he had a speech problem. It was only after he had gotten help from a speech therapist that he acquired the confidence to sing publicly."[126] Songwriter Don George claimed to have been present at Kelly's in the company of Duke Ellington, Billy Strayhorn, and Lena Horne on one particularly fateful night. "Billie, with her many problems, wasn't always able to make it to the club," George later wrote; "Ralph Watkins, the proprietor, faced with a large crowd and no Billie, said to Nat, 'Either you sing or you're fired,' thus starting Nat on his illustrious career."[127]

It's a good story, but clearly apocryphal—we have copious recorded evidence of Cole's singing going back to 1937. Nobody else remembers Watkins as being quite that brusque. The impresario's own account was that "I didn't know that Nat could sing when I booked him, but one day my sister, who was the bookkeeper at the Stable, phoned me and said, 'My God, you've got to come here. Nat's been rehearsing this one number all day. He's sung it so many times I'm going out of my mind. I told her that she must be mistaken, Nat didn't sing. That's how we found out and got Nat to sing once or twice."[128] Watkins's niece, Phoebe Jacobs, then nineteen, was working in "The Stable" as a hat-check girl. Jacobs, who later went on to run the Louis Armstrong Educational Foundation, had her own tall tale to tell about a legendary night that Holiday failed to show up and the reluctant Nat Cole was pressed into singing for her.[129] "Did that really happen?" I asked Phoebe, who was about ninety at the time. "You better believe it," she answered; "I was there, baby!"

Cole's singing was steadily improving during the Kelly's run, as heard on the Trio's final two dates for Decca, both of which were done in New York (on July 16 and October 22, 1941) and supervised by Milt Gabler. The opening tune of the July session is a true breakthrough: "This Will Make You Laugh" is the first of what we might call the "custom ballads" of the King Cole Trio; they would record dozens of these in the pinnacle Capitol years (1943–1948), some of which would become major hits and eventually standards. The words and music of "Laugh" are brilliantly suited to Cole; as Gunther Schuller has pointed out, Cole's playing reveals "any number of remarkable harmonic/melodic felicities that, moreover, do not appear to be brought in as some unusual reaching-out effect, but are clearly a natural, spontaneous and inseparable part of the whole."[130] What's most remarkable about "This Will Make You Laugh" is that of the sixteen Decca titles from 1940 to 1941, this is the sole vocal number that sounds as if it might have come from a few years later.

The other tracks from the New York Decca dates are considerably more retro. We get one instrumental blues, "Hit the Ramp," first rate but not really exceptional, and more vocal group harmony singing on "Stop, the Red Light's On," which was enough of a song to also be recorded effectively by Gene Krupa and Anita O'Day; "Call the Police" is catchy and memorable, and is the first of several Cole numbers (especially in the later Trio years) to use sound effects. "Are You Fer it?" is fairly indistinguishable from the dozens of slangy catchphrase numbers that the KC3 had recorded and transcribed up to now—by 1941, the Andrews Sisters were also recording this kind of number by the carload.

While "This Will Make You Laugh" points most clearly to the Trio's future, three other numbers connect to the past in meaningful ways. Cole's original "I Like to Riff" is, conceptually, identical to "Are You Fer It": it's another combo vocal, with the three voices in harmony, combining conventional lyrics, slang, and out-and-out scat nonsense, riffing non-verbally like a three-piece trumpet section for most of the piece. But it's just better: somehow this piece nails it in a way that most of the earlier numbers do not. The Trio had already cut it for Standard and for Ammor, but this third version for Decca brought it to the attention of the world beyond the Central Avenue scene and the race market. When, in April 1942, Charlie Barnet and His Orchestra recorded it for Decca with a chart by Andy Gibson, "I Like to Riff" became the first Cole composition to be adapted into a big band arrangement. Barnet's version, which featured both a suitably scatty vocal and a high note trumpet solo by Peanuts Holland, became much better known at the time than the original Trio recording.

The same is true of "Hit That Jive, Jack," as composed by the North Carolina–born saxophonist Campbell Aurelius Tolbert, who, as the leader of "Skeets Tolbert and His Gentlemen of Swing," recorded for the Decca Sepia Series. When the Gentlemen of Swing cut "Hit That Jive, Jack," another variation on "I Got Rhythm" (particularly in the bridge) in December 1941, it was a surprisingly languid affair, but when Cole and company recorded it in October 1941, they totally re-infused it with new energy, kicking the tempo up considerably and also streamlining the nonsensical lyric. Although Cole didn't write it, when the tune caught on, all subsequent versions—the Loumell Morgan Trio, Erskine Butterfield, Stan Kenton, Slim Gailliard, and even middle-of-the-road bandleader Art Mooney,[131] used the Cole version as a template. (The Trio would continue to refine their treatment, and later, performed it in the 1944 Columbia Pictures feature, *Stars on Parade*, in a chart that's far superior to the Decca.)

The next-to-last of sixteen titles cut by the Trio for Decca was "That Ain't Right," which would be a major number in Cole's development, even though there's no other recording (live or transcribed) of him performing it. To describe "That Ain't Right" as a basic blues is to put it mildly; it's just about the bluesiest blues that Cole ever played, sang, or wrote. It's essentially two different strains of melody, both in the fundamental 12-bar mold, one strain presents the repeated title motif of the blues theme ("That ain't right, Baby, that ain't right at all . . .) and the other is a series of comic one-liners using a stop-time pattern to emphasize the punchline, as follows,

I went to a fortune teller,
And had my fortune told.
He said, you didn't love me,
All you wanted was my gold.

"That Ain't Right" forges a vital connection between the past and the future; the overall form goes back to the vaudeville blues of Bessie Smith or Ethel Waters fifteen or more years earlier, and it is also the kind of comedy blues that Louis Jordan and others were having a huge success with in the wartime era—things like "I'm Gonna Move to the Outskirts of Town." Yet at the same time, Cole's harmonic voicings are amazingly modern, and so, for that matter, is the playing of Oscar Moore, who ends his solo here on the flatted fifth, the harmonic trademark of the nascent modern jazz movement.

"That Ain't Right" points to the near future in other ways as well. It's the first time we see the name Irving Mills in connection with Cole. The veteran publisher and manager, as was his custom, both published the song and put his name on it as co-author. Largely because of Mills's skills as a promoter and wheeler-dealer, the song caught on to a much greater extent than any previous number either written or introduced by the Trio, although it seems to have taken a while. In 1943, Mills maneuvered to get the song into *Stormy Weather*, the spectacular all-black musical produced by 20th Century Fox; the majority of the songs in the score came from his catalog. For Mills more than anyone, *Stormy Weather* was a significant windfall.

In the movie, "That Ain't Right" is performed as a rather bodacious duet between Ada Brown, a highly theatrical blues singer, and Fats Waller, making one of his final appearances, alas, but not about to be overshadowed. Waller would be dead by the end of 1943, at the very time Cole was making his breakthrough sessions; it's not hard to see Waller's last major moment in the spotlight as a symbolic passing of the torch from the greatest singer-pianist-entertainer of one era to that of the next.

In January 1943, six months before *Stormy Weather* was released in July 1943, Cole's record of "That Ain't Right" reached the number one spot on *Billboard*'s race records chart, then less than a year old and called "The Harlem Hit Parade." It would later be interpreted by such well-known artists as Mildred Bailey, Frankie Laine, and Slim Gailliard. Indeed, the song was so popular that several singers would record a second set of variations on the "New That Ain't Right." Everyone in the music business knew the way that Mills worked; it's almost certain that Cole would have sold the song outright to him, which meant he got a flat fee (usually $50) and no royalties. Adding insult to injury, Mills also listed himself as a co-author; it was grotesquely unfair, but it shows that Cole, once again, knew exactly what he was doing when he brought his next noteworthy original song to Mills roughly eighteen months later.

DECEMBER 1941: AT the end of what was already a momentous week in the history of the world, the past and the future collided on stage in the very epicenter of African American culture. Beginning in 1937, the *Amsterdam News*, the leading black newspaper of New York, had produced an annual series of Midnight Benefits at the Apollo Theater. "Proceeds from the affair will, as usual, go to buy Christmas baskets for the deserving needy of Harlem." In the paper of Saturday, December 6, it was announced that the fifth such annual benefit would take place on the upcoming Friday, December 12. Between the 6th and the 12th, the world shifted after the events of Sunday, December 7, and the resulting declaration of war on Monday. Now the need for the benefit was greater than ever, and it went on, as announced, both live at the Apollo and broadcast by WMCA at midnight on December 12. Virtually all the contemporary music world present in New York was there, be they black (Noble Sissle, Lionel Hampton, Willie Bryant, Hazel Scott, Bill "Bojangles" Robinson, Sister Rosetta Tharpe, Billie Holiday, Savannah Churchill, John Kirby) or white (Benny Goodman, Harry James, Gene Krupa, Glenn Miller). There were also stars of showbiz (Ed Sullivan, Lucille Ball, Desi Arnaz), and, most important for Nat, at least four piano giants were there in the flesh: Count Basie, Art Tatum, Teddy Wilson, and Fats Waller.

Surely Nat, Oscar, and Wes were flying high and thrilled to be part of the concert. But there were also realities to face: all three of them now had to worry, as they had recently (and rather whimsically) put it, about being "gone with the draft." The Apollo gala benefit may have made them feel as if they had gone as far as a black combo could in prewar America: in making "race" records and playing in small clubs on 52nd Street, there was only so much potential for earnings and advancement. To get any bigger, they would need to reach the white market: to sell hit records in huge quantities to a mainstream audience, one needed network radio, one needed exposure in films and coverage in major national magazines. Such things were well beyond the dreams of virtually every African American musician at the start of World War II. There were a few who had done it: Ethel Waters, Louis Armstrong, Duke Ellington, Cab Calloway—you could count them on the fingers of one hand, and, unless you counted Fats Waller (the case could be made), you would run out of artists before you ran out of fingers. Cole, Moore, and Prince and their wives were comfortable but hardly rich, and they were far from financially or even socially secure.

A few weeks earlier, after the October Decca date, the Baltimore *Afro American*[132] reported that the KC3 had "clicked solidly at Kelly's Stable" and was about to record a new song for Decca by Walter Bishop, titled "The Devil Sat Down and Cried." The tune was recorded by Harry James and His Orchestra for Columbia and then by pianist-vocalist-bandleader Erskine Butterfield for Decca, but not by Cole. Sometime in November, the Trio had received a blow to their career which set them back a few rungs down the ladder: Milt Gabler had decided not to renew their contract with Decca. "I had been doing great things with Louis Jordan, his records were really taking off at the time," Gabler told me fifty years later, "so the bosses told me that I could keep one top-flight 'race' act, Louis or Nat. Since Jordan was already becoming a major star, it was an easy—but regrettable—decision." The war was on, shellac was increasingly difficult to obtain, and belts had to be tightened.

Milt, and I knew him fairly well, was at least slightly exaggerating. Clearly there was room for more than two black acts on Decca, but the one major thing that Cole and Jordan had in common was that, more than any of the artists on their roster, Jordan's Tympany Five (the T5) and the KC3 had the most potential to "cross over" to the big mainstream (i.e., white) audience. Milt admitted that if Cole had stayed with Decca, they might never have done for the Trio what Johnny Mercer and Capitol Records were able to do, and the group might never have become as big as it did. The decision was painful for Milt as well as for Nat because he loved Nat's playing and loved to feature him in the jam sessions he was hosting at Nick's in the Village and other clubs. (Cole obviously did not hold a grudge; he later recorded several of Gabler's songs, and enjoyed his last hit with "L-O-V-E," which featured Gabler's English lyrics to Bert Kaempfert's German melody.)

The King Cole Trio wouldn't make any records for a year. But even if Decca had renewed their contract, there was more trouble looming: the American Federation of Musicians was about to put a ban on all recording and render all such contracts null and void. As of July 31, 1942, when the ban actually began, the KC3 couldn't make a record even if a label wanted them to. It was a big deal when on January 7, 1942, they appeared on NBC's long running series *The Chamber Music Society of Lower Basin Street*. The program satirized the so-called longhair music radio programming of the day by having its announcers introduce jazz and blues numbers as if they were operas and symphonies. It seems dreadfully unfunny and wrong-minded today, but the *Chamber Music Society* was so popular in January 1942 that news of the Trio's appearance was carried in at least three different African American newspapers.[133]

THE KING COLE TRIO was in the papers again three months later, for very curious reasons, and we will probably never know the full details. In early April 1942, after many months at Kelly's Stable, the group left New York and headed west for Cleveland, where Adams had booked them at Lindsay's Sky Bar. "After driving at least 350 miles, they found the place padlocked. The piano player in the group that had preceded them had been accused of raping a woman, and the bar's liquor license had been suspended."[134] Contemporaneous accounts, however, tell a slightly different and considerably stranger story; it's actually one of the more disturbing incidents connected to Cole. For once, he had good reason to thank those lucky stars of his that he was not directly implicated.

The Cleveland incident, as we might call it, was a local scandal in a cocktail lounge that *Variety*[135] covered on a national level—and put on their front page, no less. Piercing together details from both *Variety* and local Cleveland papers, this seems to be the general outline of what actually happened: three or four white girls (most of them underage and several from wealthy families) had their "morals corrupted" by fraternizing on an intimate level with Negro men at the Sky Bar, a prominent Cleveland club that primarily featured black talent. On the bill at the moment of the scandal were a local singer, Harold Simpson, and his pianist, Ray Raynor, and also a national, touring act: the King Cole Trio. Simpson and Raynor were arrested at the time—along with five other black men and one white guy—fortunately, Cole, Moore, and Prince were not.

The local African American paper, the *Cleveland Call and Post*, had a different take on the situation: it described a group of thrill-seeking, upper-middle-class Caucasian young women who were already of loose morals. According to this account, they had long since taken to overnight visits with all sorts of gentlemen, both for kicks and for pay, and also had begun to lift "mail and pouches" from the various buildings they frequented. What's more, the *Call* reported, several of the girls had already contracted a "social disease" from a college student who was the sole white man among the total of eight (in some accounts nine) who were arrested.[136] *Variety* also reported that the girls had "intimately consorted with over a dozen policemen, as well as a hotel bellhop, a blacksmith, and a cab driver."[137]

The incident nearly provoked a lynch mob and a race riot. "Several Negroes working in private families have overheard white comment that 'they are out to lynch those n-----s.'" In another case, "a white foundry worker quit his job as a crane operator rather than work with a Negro." He said he would rather quit than work besides a "n----r," and the foreman, to his credit, told him he could just go right ahead and quit, which he did.[138]

Earon Rein, the owner of the Sky Bar ("favorite jitterbug rendezvous"), was apparently accused in the local white papers of running a cover-up for a "white slave ring." He demanded a retraction and apology, saying that he "bars high school students by making the prices too high and forbidding drinks to them."[139] This was well before young people had to show proof of age before they could order a drink. "'I guess we'll have to start asking them for birth certificates,' said one nightclub operator ruefully." None of the girls was named in the papers, but all the men were. This is one time that Nat King Cole was happy *not* to get his name in the papers.

Only *Variety* mentioned the group as being on the bill at the time and did not connect them to "the vice case."[140] Not surprisingly, it was the black community that had to suffer the consequences; as *Variety* reported, "Rein is dropping Harlem acts at his Lindsay's Sky Bar and switching to white-skinned entertainment."[141] Ironically, the white entertainer whom Rein then brought in to headline was the singer and pianist Nan Blakstone, an infamously risqué diva who specialized in naughty material, songs like "The Horse with a Buggy Behind" and "Little Richard's Getting Bigger." She was probably the least suitable entertainer imaginable for a venue trying to clean up its act and rid itself of "vice."

HOWEVER LONG THE CLEVELAND GIG lasted, one thing is certain: it ended very, *very* abruptly, and the Trio were, as black musicians used to say back in the day, "SOL," or "sh*t out of luck." It wasn't as if they had some cash in reserve or any kind of emergency fund, so they needed to get back to work immediately. Cole was frantically on the phone with Adams, looking for a replacement booking. Then Adams started no less frantically calling every booker and every club he could think of. When he did find something, it was all the way back East in New York. "The rub was that they had to be there by Friday—the weekend was important. Nat and the boys had to drive day and night to cover the [500] miles."[142] Cole, Moore, and Prince worked several spots in Manhattan for most of April, May, and into early June in 1942, starting in the West Village, where they played at a spot called Jimmy Kelly's near Washington Square Park.[143] Around this time, they also played the venerable Onyx Club, one of the more celebrated spots on Swing Street.

Finally, after nearly eighteen months on the road, the Trio made it back to Los Angeles, where, on or about June 13, they opened at Herb Rose's 331 Club at 3336 West Eighth Street ("Corner Ardmore"). Except for a sojourn of about two months in Omaha at the Beachcomber's Night Club (which, as we'll see, became important for a different reason), they would spend most of the next two years in residence at the 331. A surviving matchbook from the 331 at the time shows that the club had more to offer than merely music, namely, that the bill of fare included "Charcoal Broiled Eastern Cornfed [*sic*] Steaks & Chops" as well as "MAN-SIZE cocktails. The local black community welcomed them home.[144]

By summer 1942, however, the Trio's main worry was, increasingly, the draft—that institution that they had so successfully poked fun at about a year and a half earlier. After five years with the group, Wesley Prince, by far the oldest member, was apparently feeling a combination of road weariness and an onslaught of patriotism. He gave his notice in August, first to work in a war plant, and then, two months later, to enter military service. It's said that Prince helped pick his own replacement in Johnny Miller, but there was a significant detour first, in terms of the major bassist in Cole's musical life.

There was good news, however, in July and August 1942. Not only was Cole now back in the city he called home, but so too were old friends and new. At this time, Cole reconnected with a newish but increasingly close friend, the aspiring jazz producer and promoter Norman Granz, a native Angelino who had first heard the Trio in Kelly's Stable a year or so earlier. Even better: the Young brothers, Lester and Lee, were also now working in town. It was kismet that all these characters should come together to create something special: a highly successful series of Sunday jam sessions at the Club Trouville (where Cole had last played five years earlier), which, often as not, featured Lester Young on tenor and Lee on drums. We'll take a closer look at these sessions in another chapter, but for now it's important to note that Granz was the one handling the details and making sure everyone got paid (and also that there was no discrimination both in terms of who was on the bandstand and who was in the audience), but he always gave credit to Cole as a de facto co-producer and co-conspirator and overall general inspiration for his first regular series of jam sessions. This Sunday series lasted only five or six weeks before Granz too went into the service, but it would be he who, in the mid-1940s, would steer Cole to his most celebrated work as a jazz pianist.

The first of Cole's actual recordings with Granz and Lester Young—and one of the most magical sessions of all time—occurred on July 15, 1942. Again, we'll talk about that in greater detail later, but one of the ramifications for the Trio was that the third musician on the first Young-Cole date (July 15, 1942) was the bassist with the Young Brothers band, Red Callender, who was already a well-known exponent of his instrument. And for a brief moment, probably more like weeks than months, Callender also took over the bass chair with the Trio. Also, not coincidentally, the Young-Cole date was held rather informally at Music City, the store that Cole had helped christen in summer 1940 and which itself had helped give birth to the company that had become Capitol Records a few months earlier.

By September 1942, two men close to Cole, Prince and Granz, were both officially gone with the draft, and Nat himself was very nervously checking his mail every day, looking for the inevitable "Greetings" letter from Uncle Sam. But the recording ban, put into action by the American Federation of Musicians (AFM) beginning on July 31, 1942, was no less an obstacle to Cole's ambitions. The ban was a calculated move on the part of union boss Caesar

Petrillo to throw a spanner in the works of the music industry. The whole record industry had been down in the dumps during the Great Depression; you could probably have purchased the entire business for less than the annual gross of just one movie studio or even a few local radio stations. But by the eve of the second world war, the situation was changing, especially with such blockbusters as Tommy Dorsey's "I'll Never Smile Again" (1940), Glenn Miller's "Chattanooga Choo Choo" (recognized at the time as the first record since the 1920s to go "gold" and sell a million copies, in 1942), and then "White Christmas" and the other blockbuster hits by Bing Crosby.

Records were becoming a force again, and Petrillo knew it. But as of August 1, no one could officially make a record. This was a major obstacle that Cole and an unlikely group of colleagues were determined to find a way around. Among them were two highly successful African American songwriters, Rene Brothers, Leon and Otis; a younger aspiring songwriter, Robert Scherman; the jukebox mogul, Jack Gutshall; two veteran music business entrepreneurs, Glenn Wallichs and his father, Oscar; and a young man named Hughie Claudin, who was then working for Glenn at Music City.[145] In the late summer of 1942, they all came together to form a new company titled "Excelsior Records." Somehow or other, this outfit made records during the AFM ban; it's not known if they had come to an agreement of some kind with the Los Angeles local or more likely, just operating under the radar. *Metronome* reported that the new label's aim was to "put out swing records of small bands heretofore unheard on discs."[146]

The King Cole Trio would record ten titles under the aegis of Otis Rene and Robert Scherman, over roughly a year between October 1942 and November 1943, and on all of these, the producers not only steered clear of the musicians' union but also avoided dealing with the equally powerful music publishers: all ten numbers were originals, either by Rene, Scherman, Cole, or Oscar Moore. It seemed a little suspicious to *Metronome* at the time that "Oscar Wallichs will be one of the active directors of the new company."[147] The magazine deemed it an "odd situation" that Oscar was actively involved in Excelsior Records just a few months after his son Glenn had founded the more ambitious Capitol Records. As it turned out, it wasn't the least bit "odd"; rather, it was prophetic.

The first Excelsior session, in summer 1942, featured crooner Herb Jeffries (who had worked with Cole in the 1938 *Shuffle Along*),[148] and the second which took place on October 11, spotlighted the King Cole Trio—Cole, Moore, and Red Callender. The new bassist later remembered what it was like to make a record with the King Cole Trio: "Nat Cole was a very organized pianist, concise in his introductions. He'd say, 'okay I got four bars.' And it would be four bars; he had a way of letting you know exactly when to enter. Nat was a thorough musician—that's why everything he did came off so well." He added, "Nat was the kind of guy who would do anything he said he would do—even if he had to break his butt to do it."

The October 11, 1942, date consisted of two songs: "Vom, Vim, Veedle" and "All for You." The first was the latest of dozens of jive numbers/harmony trio vocals that the Trio had been doing since 1937. Its most surprising component is a verse: "Songs of every nation/are filled with some creation/of a lyrical sensation"—as if this scatty nonsense required some kind of logical setup. Like dozens of Cole novelties, both later and earlier, Cole solos on the bridge, which yet again is based on "I Got Rhythm." The actual meaning of the phrase "Vom, Vim, Veedle" is never revealed, but it's got that swing, and therefore it must mean something. "All for You" is another step forward in Cole's developing skills as a balladeer, though his diction isn't as perfect as it would be later (he would never sing anything like the opening line here, "when you raise yo' eyes . . . ," ten years later). Even so, Cole makes both songs into something better than they actually are, but neither is bad to begin with.

Excelsior was light-footed enough to get fresh product into the music stores at a moment when none of the established labels, even Capitol, were able to offer any. The company "pulled a Houdini last week and signed the celebrated King Cole Trio for a series of waxings,"[149] referring to the sleight of hand necessary to circumnavigate the musician's union. The two songs were described in the black press as "chock full of harmony and melody" and said the recording was "a cinch to become a bestseller." Roughly a week later, they informed readers, "Attesting the overnight popularity of Excelsior Record Company's new waxing by the King Cole Trio, 'All for You,' Mrs. Ruth Sampson, comely proprietress of Ruth's Record Shop here, last week purchased 1,000 of the waxings to satisfy the immediate demands of her customers. 'I plan to order several hundred in the near future, as once I play the record, it is a cinch seller,' she told reporters."[150]

People were paying attention, including Dave Dexter Jr., only recently hired by the new firm now known as Capitol Records, and the Armed Forces Radio Service (AFRS). Beginning in fall 1942, the Trio was regularly invited by the AFRS to appear on radio shows including *Mail Call* (the flagship variety show of the AFRS), *Personal Album*, and *Jubilee* (for black servicemen). Roughly a half dozen tracks have turned up and been issued from AFRS programs from late 1942 and '43, including red hot flagwaver versions of the standards "Honeysuckle Rose" and "I Know That You Know," Trio signatures (and "Rhythm" variations), "Hit That Jive, Jack," "Solid Potato Salad," and "I'm an Errand Boy for Rhythm," and several topical wartime era songs, "Hip Hip Hooray" ("We're living in the USA") and Louis Jordan's hit, "Slender, Tender, and Tall." (The AFRS may have also been the first to document Nat's new song, "Straighten Up and Fly Right," composed in Omaha a few months earlier, but more on that presently.)

Meanwhile, they continued to hold forth nightly at the 331. One of the earliest live radio recordings of the Trio that's known to exist is also possibly the first that's believed to include the new bass player, Johnny Miller, the second and most important of three bassists who came to Cole by way of Hampton. This is an excerpt from a location broadcast from the 331 Club, probably from fall 1942. Over a few notes of the now familiar sound of the KC3 in the background, we hear a typically effusive-sounding announcer of the period:

> Mutual again brings you music by the famed King Cole Trio from the 331 Club in Los Angeles, California. Music with swing, jive, and the solid stuff! Up and coming with brother King Cole and the outfit.

Mutual was an independent network, but it was a step up the ladder. The Trio plays Louis Jordan's hit "I'm Gonna Move to the Outskirts of Town," with Cole authoritatively singing the blues in solo, in much the same mold as his own "That Ain't Right." It does these very fundamental 12-bar comedy blues riffs with style and elan: they may be hoary blues cliches but they don't sound that way when Cole, Moore, and Miller play them—likewise the familiar punchlines about questioning the paternity of one's own offspring.

At the same time, singing the blues was proving to be the luckiest break that Cole had had up to that point. In November, the two-year-old Decca master of "That Ain't Right" marked Cole's debut on the *Billboard* record charts, this being the brand-new "Harlem Hit Parade" chart, launched only a few months earlier. It hit number one in January and then in July was heard in the highly successful *Stormy Weather*. This left the King Cole Trio in a highly curious position: a hot combo lands a number one hit record, a song plugged in a major motion picture no less, but they don't have a record contract. On the other hand, no one was making records anyhow.

AT THE START OF 1943, the popularity of the Trio at the 331 Club showed no sign of abating. They took a night off to play the Calship Welders Dance for war workers, hosted by the Los Angeles Elks Club, on February 13.[151] A few weeks later, they appeared on a CBS variety program, *Hollywood Showcase*, hosted by film actress Mary Astor.[152] As they wound up the "first act" (June 1942 to March 1943) of the long, long run at the 331, *Billboard* went in to give them a review, noting that "few people know the leader of the colored King Cole Trio, Nate Cole [*sic*], by his real name" but they know that he indeed deserves "the monarch title." "The leader is known in composing circles and the evening's work includes a number of originals that hit the bull's-eye like an archer's arrow. Cole vocalizes on his own songs." The review concluded, "The boys have plenty of tricks, so if one wants to stay from 8 to 12, there's sufficient change to keep him entertained."[153] For a trade paper reviewer, accustomed to seeing multiple acts in a night and probably overwhelmed by the sameness of it all, this was high praise indeed.

A lot was happening at once in March 1943. The Trio prepared to depart the 331 Club and Los Angeles in general for the first time since the previous spring, for a gig in Omaha.[154] (Trumpeter Red Allen and trombonist J. C. Higginbotham came west from Kelly's Stable to replace them at the 331.) And the month began with their second session for Excelsior.

But all of that paled in comparison with the scary news that also arrived in early March: Cole's long-dreaded induction notice finally showed up, prompting the *New York Amsterdam News* to remember a certain record he had made a few years earlier, the one about being "Gone with the Draft." "He was wanted—flat feet and all."[155] Cole was instructed to report for his physical, and, somehow, miraculously, was rejected. *Down Beat* reported that "Nat Cole drew a 4-F when he was called for army duty, due to nervous hypertension. Oscar Moore and Johnny Miller are family men and do not expect to be called."[156] Cole's second wife, Maria offered a different explanation, saying that she used to kid her husband about those so-called flat feet. She would tell him, "Honey, if I had seen your feet first, I never would have married you." She later continued, "Those same feet were bad enough to have kept Nat out of military service during World War II."[157] Cole told her that he was so ecstatic to have dodged this particular bullet that he jumped into his clothes and bolted from the building. He only realized later that he had been in such a hurry to get out of there—before the doctor changed his mind—that he had forgotten to put his drawers on. On March 20, the *Amsterdam News* let its readers know that "Cole reported to the army but was rejected."[158]

The March 1 Excelsior date consists of four songs—two novelties ("Let's Spring One" and "Pitchin' Up a Boogie," both with trio harmony vocals) and two solo ballads ("I'm Lost" and "Beautiful Moons Ago"). None of these numbers had the same impact as the previous Excelsior sides, but Cole thought enough of Moore's love song, "Beautiful Moons Ago," to re-record it in 1946. A lively dance number, "Let's Spring One," makes a clever pun on the idea of the word "spring" as both a season and a verb or a dance move. Cole's own "Pitchin' Up a Boogie" is only the second Cole track to contain any kind of allusion to boogie woogie, but there's no eight-to-the-bar piano in it whatsoever; the only "boogie" content is in the song title. The two ballads indicate the slow but undeniable progress of Cole the balladeer, although he was barely twenty-four, and this is a characteristic that is generally slow to develop in a musician. The quality of his crooning was keeping pace with the quality of the songs he was recording. (He wouldn't be ready for "Stardust" for a while.) "Beautiful Moons" ends with Cole humming wistfully over Moore's guitar accompaniment, a device that we haven't heard the last of.

The Trio arrived in Omaha at the end of February and proved to be a "solid" hit at the Beachcomber.[159] During this period, they moonlighted at a dance, also in downtown Omaha, "for a mixed crowd" at the nearby Dreamland Ballroom. By the end of April (or early May), they were back at Herb Rose's 331 Club. This second act of a two-year run proceeded uninterrupted for another year, up until spring 1944. "While out Los Angeles way, there's a report that the sensational King Cole Trio goes into 331 Club for the duration, depending on [Uncle Sam]."[160]

Cole was already working at the 331 six nights a week, but when Norman Granz was mustered out of the service, the two of them launched a new series of Sunday night jam sessions. So now Nat was playing there *every* night, both with and without the Trio. In early July, he participated in a publicity event to launch a new radio program by his old friend and supporter, Al Jarvis, in which he was photographed at the piano flanked by a group of bandleaders who were at the time far more famous than he—but not for long: Freddy Martin, Count Basie, Woody Herman, and Phil Harris, an event covered in the black and music press.[161] (At this point, Jarvis was doing Nat a favor by including him in the same shot as these widely celebrated maestros.) The Trio would also play several extracurricular dance dates at the newly opened Los Angeles Savoy Ballroom, which must have made Nat think about his months at the Chicago Savoy, eight years earlier.

In July 1943, the Trio made its first documented appearance in a feature-length film; even though there is evidence that points them working in *Too Had to Hot to Handle, No, No, Nanette* and *Citizen Kane*, this is the earliest full-on Hollywood movie role that we can actually verify. On July 10, Cole, Moore, and "John Miller" were hired by the actor and choral director Ben Carter to record a backing instrumental for the Universal musical

Top Man, starring Donald O'Connor. In the finished movie, they are heard accompanying a quartet of four young black male singers, led by falsetto Bobby Brooks, emulating the Ink Spots. Even though we see Count Basie playing the piano for a few seconds, it is unquestionably Nat's piano and Oscar's guitar that we hear.[162]

Also in July, it was announced that the King Cole Trio was going to appear several times on the *Romo Wine Program*, a mainstream Hollywood-based radio series hosted by Mary Astor.[163] On Labor Day, they played for dancers as part of a "Youth Jamboree," in an echo of the "Bud Billiken Club" experience a decade earlier in Chicago, held at the Alpha Bowling Social Club. [164] Suffice it to say that soon enough, Nat King Cole would no longer need to work in bowling alleys.

Cole would end this era with one last session for a startup micro-label. Robert Scherman had obviously witnessed the success of his song "All for You" on Excelsior and concluded that he would have stood to profit more if he had owned the company as well as the songs. Thus, he started his own label, which he called Premier Records, officially based in St. Louis[165] but operating in Los Angeles. Scherman produced the Trio's last date of the pre-Capitol period at the NBC Studio in Hollywood on Tuesday, November 2. He had the group record three of his own songs—two ballads "My Lips Remember Your Kisses" and "Let's Pretend," and a novelty, "Got a Penny," and one Cole instrumental original. Neither of the ballads had the impact of Scherman's "All for You" a year earlier, but both are worthy vehicles of Cole's ever-maturing romantic "crooning" style. At this point, as Moore later remembered, "I didn't even think of Nat as a singer. We always did the vocal things, of course, but I never thought Nat would become important as a singer. To me, the cat was always a crazy piano player."[166]

"Got a Penny" is a chanted trio number with Cole singing parts in solo, including the bridge (more "I Got Rhythm"). This might be described as the first of Cole's "lowlife novelties"; he would sing at least a dozen of these in the mature Trio period. There's something like a poignant underpinning, as Cole portrays a low-rent Romeo ("I've just got four cents to my name") who needs one more cent to make a phone call to his girlfriend.[167]

For the fourth tune, Scherman threw Cole a bone in allowing him to record one of his own compositions, "F.S.T. (Fine, Sweet and Tasty)." This is interesting only in that it's rather uninteresting: it's just a mild vamp used to set up solos, yet it had already been established as Cole's radio theme. Perhaps he thought there might be a demand for the song since listeners had already been hearing it on the air. But in retrospect we can see that choosing to record

““F.S.T.” at this session is further proof that he knew exactly what he was doing. As it turned out, he was at that very moment sitting on a great song, the best that he would ever write, and he was not about to throw it away by recording it for a little podunk outfit like Premier or Excelsior. Nat had always had his eye on the main chance, and that chance was to come very soon.

Cole's ballad style would be the final element of his music to take shape, but he was ready, as Cole Porter might say, to attain the upper brackets by fall 1943. All the ingredients were in place, including the about-to-be launched relationship with Capitol Records. As we've seen, Cole and the Trio had been going around in circles with the founders of Capitol since he met Johnny Mercer in 1938 and Glenn Wallichs in 1940.[168]

More than the sixteen Decca titles of 1940 and 1941, the ten tracks recorded for Excelsior and Premier during 1942 and 1943 are a very direct prelude to the Capitol era. The material is hardly as good as he would get to work with slightly later, but two sides were about to be directly absorbed into the Capitol catalog.[169]

Thus, everything was already in place for a career that would exceed everyone's wildest expectations. This was abundantly clear to everyone who heard them, even well before the King Cole Trio did their first date for Capitol Records on November 30, 1943. As Cole later put it, “For seven years we knocked around, until something happened.”[170] In November 1943, that “something” was about to happen.

2

The Rise of the Trio

1943–1946

There's a lot to be said for making people laugh. Do you know that's all some people have? It's not much, but it's something—in this cockeyed caravan.
—"JOHN L. SULLIVAN," *Sullivan's Travels* (written by Preston Sturges, 1941)

There's a guy up at the Apollo. No one knows him, but he's going to be the biggest star in the world.
—STAN KENTON TO MARVIN FISHER, 1945

WHEN THE KING COLE TRIO cut its premiere session for Capitol Records, on the Tuesday after Thanksgiving, 1943, everyone involved, most especially the artist himself, seemed very much aware that this was going to be a historic occasion. It almost was predestined that this, to quote the last line of the most recent Oscar-winning best picture, was going to be "the beginning of a beautiful friendship." With this in mind, Capitol commissioned a photographer, one Rolland Shreves, to document the date.[1] The session took place on November 30 at the C. P. MacGregor Studios at 729 South Western Avenue, Hollywood, where Capitol customarily rented the facilities before they had the resources to acquire their own.

The session started with the "money" song, Cole's own original, "Straighten Up and Fly Right," which was followed by three other numbers, all of which became instant classics as soon as they were released. Yet what Shreves captured with his camera was no less fascinating than the music itself. In the most famous photo from the session, Cole is the only one looking at the camera. Guitarist Oscar Moore and bassist Johnny Miller are concentrating on their instruments and the music. Producer and Capitol co-founder Johnny Mercer is standing behind the piano, his hands in his pockets, his famous gap-toothed smile beaming very widely even as his eyes gaze down on Cole; he clearly knows that he is looking at a million dollars' worth of talent. At twenty-four, Cole looks young and handsome, but most of all fully *aware*. He is playing—his hands are on the keyboard—but clearly his mind is on something more than the notes; he's playing to ~~it~~ the camera and is engaged with it, as if it were an actual audience.

There are several posters on the wall that make the studio like a conference room in a World War II munitions plant, with mottos like "courtesy is not unpatriotic" and "serve in silence." There is also a sign over the door that clearly reads, "Positively No Smoking." In utter defiance of this, resting on the piano, is an ashtray overflowing with cigarette butts. Alas, this too is an indicator of things to come.

VIEWED FROM THE PERSPECTIVE of history, that is to say, backward, it was almost a foregone conclusion that the King Cole Trio was destined to become the most popular "combo" of its era. There were three major trends in black popular music in the mid-1940s: bebop, rhythm and blues, and star vocalists—and the Trio incorporated all three of these developments, not just partially or lightly, but aggressively and completely. Fans of modern jazz (like Dizzy Gillespie), fans of blues and riff dance numbers and novelties (like Louis Jordan), and fans of superstar singers (like Frank Sinatra and Billy Eckstine) could all equally enjoy the King Cole Trio. More than any other musical act of the postwar era, the Trio perfectly captured the zeitgeist of the time and offered something for everyone. In millennial parlance, they checked every box.

"One night at the 331 Club, in late 1943 it was, Johnny Mercer and Glenn Wallichs came in and told me they were forming a record company, Capitol Records," Cole said in a 1957 profile. They asked me if I'd be interested in recording for them. Well, that sounded groovy to me. Of course, I had been with Decca, but I wasn't too happy there. So, I decided to go with Mercer and Wallichs and just see what happened."[2] As always, Cole was trying to make it seem as though everything about his career was highly casual, if not completely random. It was just pure luck that Johnny and Glenn just happened to stroll in to the 331. In actuality, Cole, Mercer, and Wallichs had all been dancing around each other for more than three years by the time of their first Capitol date.

As we've seen, the Trio's first ever recording (a 1938 Standard Transcription), was a Johnny Mercer song, and Mercer himself apparently had heard the Trio in person around that same time. "I was with Bing Crosby the first time I saw him," said Mercer, "in a steakhouse on La Cienga Boulevard called Jimmy Otto's. He looked about eighteen and underfed, and I didn't catch his name, but he was very, very good on piano. The Trio had a nice sound."[3]

Cole probably met Wallichs in spring 1940 when the Trio was ensconced at the Radio Room on Vine Street, across from the NBC Studios. "He spent many days and evenings with me in the bar in the bowling alley next to Music City," said Wallichs. Wallichs, described as "a genial heavy set fellow,"[4] was preparing to launch his ambitious new store, Music City, that summer; he and his father, Oscar, were already so impressed with Cole that they hired the Trio to play at the opening.[5] The Wallichses were from Nebraska, where Oscar (like the father of Peggy Lee in North Dakota), for most of his career, had been a railroad man, who was transferred to Los Angeles in 1926. Glenn Wallichs's original trade was selling and repairing radios, and he first met Mercer at some point around this time when the songwriter's wife, Ginger, hired him to install a radio in Johnny's car as a present for his birthday.[6] Encouraged by Mercer and other celebrity clients, in 1940, Glenn and Oscar marshaled their resources to open their own permanent retail outlet. Music City, located "in the heart of the Hollywood Radio District on Sunset and Vine,"[7] quickly became the go-to emporium for records and sheet music in the Los Angeles area, especially because it also contained listening rooms and a rudimentary recording booth.

Thus, both Cole and Mercer were part of the Music City scene from the beginning, and throughout the first year of the store's existence, Mercer not only increasingly admired Wallich's technical ability but also began to get a sense of his business acumen and his understanding of the music industry. There they were, two young men (Mercer was only thirty in 1940) with invaluable experience on different sides of that business: Mercer in creating songs, Wallichs in selling them. They both had new ideas about how things should be done: "Mercer complained about bad arrangements, sloppy recordings, and the sloughing off of new talent. Wallichs thought that selling and distribution of the [established labels] was completely out of date."[8] In the words of Dave Dexter, soon to become one of the first employees of the new firm, "One day, Johnny said 'Gee! You know, we ought to make records of our own.' "[9] Apparently it was as simple as that.

At the time, the two biggest labels, Columbia and RCA Victor, were affiliated with major radio networks, CBS and NBC, while Decca, launched in 1934, started as the American wing of a powerful British corporation. Mercer and Wallichs launched Capitol Records with just their own experience, chutzpah, and, in 21st-century parlance, "sweat equity." They also enjoyed the resources, financial and otherwise, of an invaluable third and silent partner, George "Buddy" DeSylva. In 1942, DeSylva was best known as a successful and wealthy producer at Paramount Pictures; earlier, he had been a prominent lyricist, as one-third of the highly successful three-man songwriting team of the 1920s, DeSylva, Lew Brown, and Ray Henderson, who had written many hit shows and early talking picture musicals and dozens of standard songs. The three went their separate ways in the early thirties, and DeSylva climbed the Hollywood ladder, where he gradually assumed his place among the top Tinseltown moguls. He was not, however, a particularly long-lived one; he died at age fifty-five in 1950. Around 1941–42, both lyricists, Mercer, forever a working songwriter, and DeSylva, now one of the guys in charge, were talking at Paramount about the idea for a new label and the older man said, "Great! I'll give you $10,000 to start it."[10]

But what to name the new venture? Their first choice was "Liberty Records." However, they were well aware that there was already a famous store on Madison Avenue in Midtown Manhattan called Liberty Music Shop, which also operated its own "boutique" record label.[11] Undaunted, Mercer and Wallichs went ahead and incorporated their new company in March 1942 as Liberty Records, hoping that they could acquire the use of the name from the Liberty Music Shop. On April 6, the new firm produced its first session, and the four titles had Liberty master numbers: LIB-1 and LIB-2 (Martha Tilton) and LIB-3 and LIB-4 (Johnny Mercer).

Alas, the company name "Liberty" was apparently the only thing that was not for sale at the Liberty Music Shop. "They were reluctant to let us have it and seemed steamed at the suggestion," said Mercer. It was his long-suffering wife, Ginger, who came up with the second choice: "Capitol Records."[12] By May, the new name—and everything else—was in place, and none too soon. The American Federation of Musicians (AFM) was just about to announce a ban on all recordings, and there was just enough time for the partners to squeeze in about a dozen sessions before the ban officially put an end to new recording as of July 31. Capitol had its first releases in their hands by June; their earliest hits included "Travelin' Light," by Paul Whiteman's Orchestra with a vocal by an incognito Billie Holiday, and a wartime blockbuster, "Cow-Cow Boogie" by Freddie Slack's Orchestra with Ella Mae Morse. Mercer himself was in a unique position: two of Capitol's earliest hits were "Strip Polka" and "G.I. Jive," both of which offered words, music, and vocals by Mercer, who also served as producer and label co-founder.

The AFM strike went into effect on August first, which normally would have been a disaster for a fledgling operation like Capitol, but the twin leaders were quick to see the upside. "The war and even the musicians' strike made our little company better known and more quickly recognized," as Mercer later wrote. "Due to the shortage of other labels, we got heard a lot. We could do nothing wrong. Everything that should have held us back worked for us."[13] Wallichs concurred, "When [AFM head] Petrillo slapped his ban on all recordings shortly after our first release, we again thought we were licked. But it turned out to be our biggest piece of good fortune. Before the ban, we worked night and day turning out such tunes as 'Cow Cow Boogie' and 'G. I. Jive.' When those tunes became popular, we were the only company that had recorded them and dealers all over the country began to buy from us."[14]

In early 1943, the label hired its first public relations man, Dave Dexter Jr., a longtime music journalist and reviewer from Kansas City. Dexter's primary job was to turn out press releases and write and edit the label's "house organ" publication, the *Capitol News*, but as a committed jazz and blues advocate, he also took it upon himself to help steer Capitol in that direction. Even with only three months of "runway," Capitol somehow managed to release twenty-five singles in its first (partial) year. Because they couldn't record anything new after July 31, Dexter scouted around for worthwhile existing masters that the company could acquire. "In 1943 I was instrumental in signing Nat Cole for Capitol," as he put it. "The year before there was a record he made where he sang all by himself. All his previous records had been ensemble singing with Oscar Moore and the old bass player, Wesley Prince. I used to hear this ballad 'All for You,' late at night on the record shows broadcast. One day, I had a chance to buy this master. This was the summer of 1943, and the Petrillo strike was still on. We couldn't make any new records and we were beginning to run low."[15]

Dexter gave other accounts of this over the years but never contradicted himself. "We were waiting for the first Petrillo record ban to end," he said in 1977, "and one day on lunch hour when I was over in Music City, Hughie Claudin, who ran this place for Glenn Wallichs, told me that Bob Scherman had a record that had been getting a lot of airplay. And I said, 'Is it "All for You?"' And he says, 'That's it!' And he said, 'Scherman wants to peddle it to another company.'"[16]

What Dexter doesn't say, and what everyone seems to have forgotten, was that Excelsior Records, the independent "race" label that had originally released these two sides, had direct ties to Capitol from its inception. At least two of the men running Excelsior, Hughie Claudin and Oscar Wallichs, were directly connected to Glenn Wallichs: Claudin was apparently continuing to work at Music City (even while moonlighting at Excelsior) and Oscar, as we know, was his father.[17] In retrospect, it seems probable that the Wallichses had planned this from the beginning; if the ban were to go on long enough (say, more than six months), with the help of Rene and Scherman, they now had the option to use Excelsior as a feeder label, a means by which Capitol could acquire issuable masters without having to deal with Petrillo.

Finally, Dexter said, "So we put out this record and it was a big, big seller. Of course, in those days, two hundred thousand copies of a single was a big hit and made the top ten chart."[18] "All for You," backed with "Vom, Vim, Veedle," was released during the last week of October 1943,[19] as Capitol 139, the label's thirty-ninth single. It was an immediate success, reaching number one on the race chart and number nineteen on the mainstream pop chart. This was only about eight months after "That Ain't Right" on Decca had reached number one; within one year, Cole had reached the top of the Harlem Hit Parade twice, and now even cracked the white charts for the first time as well.

When Decca declined to renew the Trio's contract at the end of 1941, it must have appeared to be the end of the world, but by summer 1943, it was starting to seem like a lucky break. Now they were at liberty to negotiate with an ambitious new startup label that could, potentially, do a lot more for them. Throughout 1943, King Cole had a remarkable trick up his sleeve—an ace in the hole; he was armed with a song that was, effectively, the Manhattan Project in 32 bars. Despite what Cole wanted us to think, the overwhelming success of "Straighten Up and Fly Right" was no accident. Rather, Cole planned his next move with the tactical skill and ingenuity of the scientists at Los Alamos and proved that he was the Robert Oppenheimer of pop music.

IN 1957, NAT KING COLE reprised his most famous original song, "Straighten Up and Fly Right," on his NBC TV series. He says in his introduction, "[In] the early forties I was playing piano in a little cafe in Omaha, Nebraska, when I wrote a song based on an old joke that my father used to tell." After singing a chorus, he adds, "This song was the real beginning for me."[20] This was a folk tale that the ~~right~~ Reverend Edwin Coles Sr. sometimes worked into his sermons; in fact, the tradition of light humor and comedy mixed with a more serious message is probably also something that Nat Cole learned in church.

Cole had imparted a compatible account of the origin story in 1946. "The elder Cole, a Baptist minister, had preached many sermons, but it was one sermon in particular that Nat remembered. He remembered it for a long time. Years after he left Chicago and was touring the country with the then-little-known King Cole Trio, Nat recalled this particular sermon," the (Baltimore) *African American*[21] wrote. "It was an allegorical tale of a buzzard who picked up a monkey. As the bird carried the small simian creature off to its nest in a craggy mountain, the monkey admonished the bird to straighten up and fly right." (In yet another variation on the "Straighten Up" origin story, Cole says that he did hear about the buzzard and the monkey in a sermon, but not from his father. "It comes from an old joke we used to tell when we were kids, which runs along the same lines as the song. In fact, my wife's uncle, who is also a minister, once preached a sermon with that as a text. You know what happened with that record.")[22] By the time of that story in 1946, the *African American* tells us, "Straighten Up and Fly Right" had sold two million records.

It was an Aesopian fable about power and trust; the buzzard can drop the monkey at any point, or so he thinks, but the monkey has its hands around the buzzard's neck and can strangle it whenever he wishes—but to do so would be to also ensure his own downfall. It was a perfect moral lesson for the United States at the height of World War II: Who do you trust? After the world watched two super-forces, represented by Hitler and Stalin, turn on each other, it seemed like the entire war was made up of buzzards and monkeys; will they take us for a joyride and do as they promised, or will they turn on us and dash us to bits on the jagged rocks below? Will the monkey choke the buzzard, or will the buzzard drop the monkey? Or can we all, somehow, in the face of universal annihilation, learn to live together? The message was clear: straighten up and fly right.

(At least one listener had a very different interpretation of the song, and the larger meaning of the fable of the monkey and the buzzard. Lee Young recalled, "There was an audition for Nat and the Trio, and it was for a movie with Lucille Ball, she was very big at MGM at the time. The musical conductor was Georgie Stoll, who was crazy about Nat's trio, and he said to her, 'I want you to really hear this song. This song is really something.' She listened to it and she said, 'That's the dirtiest song I ever heard in my life!' ")[23]

As we've seen, for most of two years, 1942 to 1944, the King Cole Trio was in residence at the 331 Club at 3361 West 8th Street in Los Angeles, with the exception of about six or seven weeks from March to April of 1943 when they played the Beachcombers Club in Omaha.[24] Owned by one Ralph Goldberg, the Beachcombers was apparently ironically named—whoever heard of a beach in Omaha, Nebraska? In fact, not only was there no beach, but there was also nothing at all to do in Omaha for two months in 1943. So, as Berle Adams, who booked the gig, later remembered, with all this "time on his hands,"[25] Cole took the opportunity to work out a song that had been germinating in his mind.

This was "Straighten Up and Fly Right." The tune was catchy, and the harmonies were solid—after all, it was based, like hundreds of other jazz originals, on the chord changes of "I Got Rhythm."[26] The lyrics were memorable, and the message was precisely the right one that America and its Allies needed to hear in the second half of the war. Much like "Gone with the Draft" in the early aftermath of Selective Service Act, and then, later, "Nature Boy" in the immediate postwar period, it was the right song at the right moment. Even having just turned twenty-four, Cole had enough experience playing in front of the public to know that he had a potential hit on his hands. The problem was exactly how to get his song out there: in spring 1943 the Trio was still without a recording contract, and even if they had one, the dreaded AFM ban, like the war itself, still showed no sign of ending.

Every move that he made from this point going forward illustrates how Cole already knew how the music business worked and was looking for a trick, a turnaround, to make things happen to his advantage. During the summer and early fall of 1943, Cole and Capitol Records continued to dance around each other, even as the Trio did one final date for a non-Capitol independent operation in early November. But Cole had the street smarts to know that Capitol was the label that could take him, his Trio, and his song to a whole new level—with the help of one other man.

The publishing on "Straighten Up and Fly Right" went to Irving Mills, who had already published "That Ain't Right" and had done more than anyone, especially Decca Records, to make a hit out of it. Cole essentially gave Mills "Straighten Up" for bupkis, as Mills would have said; he was paid all of $50 with no prospect of participating in future royalties. In a 1959 radio interview, he put it this way, "In 1943, things were pretty rough. So, I took some songs I had written to the music publishers to see if I could sell one. I sold 'Straighten Up and Fly Right' for fifty dollars, outright, no royalties."[27] In 1949, he told a reporter that he had sold it "for a paltry $50 in order to secure money to pay his hotel bill," and they added, "the buyer, who will remain anonymous to this day, hasn't given Nat so much as a necktie."[28]

Yet it won't do to portray Cole as an innocent fish who was swallowed whole by a greedy shark. The more likely truth is that Cole was well aware of what Mills could do for the song—and, by extension for the Trio—and what Mills would demand in return. Up to this point, by far the most successful song in Cole's career was "That Ain't Right": Mills put his name on it as co-composer and gave Cole only a token fee, but he promoted the song like crazy and got it placed in a major motion picture. Mills had at least left Cole's name on the covers of both songs so that the credits read, "Words and Music by Nat 'King' Cole and Irving Mills." This was Nat's deal with the devil: Mills could make a song a hit, but what he asked in return was at least 50 percent of the credit and darn near 100 percent of the ownership and future proceeds.

This was standard practice for Mills, most famously on roughly 13 percent of the songs composed by his longtime star client, Duke Ellington (with whom he had parted company in 1940).[29] Did Mills ever write so much as a single note of a melody or a word of a lyric? I once put that question to Mitchell Parish, lyricist of "Sweet Lorraine" and "Stardust," two of Cole's signature songs, among dozens of other songbook standards. The veteran songwriter responded by forming his thumb and forefinger into a big zero and saying "Nada!"

"Straighten Up and Fly Right" was officially published by one of Mills's firms, American Academy of Music, and the publisher was working his wizardry on it as early as summer 1943. Mills almost immediately got the song placed on perhaps the most popular radio program in the country, *The Kraft Music Hall*, starring Bing Crosby, where it was performed by Crosby's resident African American quartet, the Charioteers. Not only did the Charioteers sing it twice that summer, on June 24 (marking the song's debut on the airwaves) and July 22, but Mills also made sure that the newspapers gave it coverage, and indeed both the *Chicago Defender* and the *New York Amsterdam News* ran an identical item, obviously submitted by the publisher's publicity flack: "'Straighten Up and Fly Right' is the title of a very catchy number recently composed by Nat Cole, head of the King Cole Trio, that is fast catching on. Recently Bing Crosby featured the number on the *Kraft Music Hall* radio program."[30] The groundswell around the song had already begun; the Trio themselves played it on several Armed Forces Radio Service (AFRS) broadcasts (*Personal Album* and *Jubilee*) well before the first Capitol session.

And then Mills pulled the ultimate rabbit of his hat. Once again, he placed Cole's song in a feature motion picture—now this was big-time stuff. Alas, it wasn't a grade A production like *Stormy Weather*, but the consolation prize was that he not only got the song in the movie, but he got the Trio in it as well. One "exploitation" technique begat another—the news that the KC3 was appearing in a movie was also widely reported in the black press.[31] The movie was called *Here Comes Elmer*. Despite the regrettable title, it was a typically spirited and solidly crafted production of Republic Pictures; it may not have been 20th Century Fox, but it was a major step in helping the song to get heard. *Here Comes Elmer* was one of dozens of wartime B-level comedies and musicals that pivoted around popular radio shows. Al Pearce, at the time, was widely loved for his portrayal of the bashful door-to-door salesman "Elmer Blunt," and also for the cast of comedians he surrounded himself with on *Al Pearce and His Gang*—among them Artie Auerbach as "Mr. Kitzel," later on the *Jack Benny Show*. (Pearce was one of those famous figures of an earlier era whose vast popular success seems incomprehensible today. You might call it "The Arthur Godfrey Syndrome.")

Elmer utilized a variety of famous radio attractions, revolving around the Pearce gang: Jan Garber and his band, the Sportsmen (also better known from the *Jack Benny Show*), announcer Wendell Niles, and country-ish singer-entertainer-songwriter Pinky Tomlin, in addition to the King Cole Trio. Here, Cole, Moore, and Miller are cast as Pullman porters who just happen to be jazz virtuosi. Pearce and the gang are heading east on the night train. We're in a bar car, and we hear a small band playing, in the background. We see a porter yelling, "Telegram for Mr. Pearce, telegram for Mr. Pearce" and it takes us a few seconds to realize that here is Nat King Cole, making a rather inauspicious motion picture debut. Cole, Moore (dressed like a bartender with a smock), and Miller then take their places on piano, guitar, and bass, and they play what is our earliest known document of what will soon become Cole's breakthrough song. The soon-to-be famous arrangement, with its distinctive intro, is already in place, as is the balance between Cole's solo vocals and the Trio's harmony, and what is perhaps Cole's first truly iconic piano solo, with its crossed hands darting, as well Moore's brief but zingy guitar interlude.

Thanks to Mills, "Straighten Up and Fly Right" was well on its way to becoming a hit even before Cole could record it, thanks to its placement on the radio and even in a movie. In years to come, it seemed to observers that Cole, no less than Alexander Hamilton, was deliberately throwing away his shot, but it worked out much better for Cole than it did for the first secretary of the treasury. He would reap all the benefits of landing a major hit—except, regrettably, the specific royalties from the song itself. Yet to him at the time, this was an acceptable bargain.

At the end of 1944, when the song was being heard everywhere, Cole filed a civil suit to reclaim the rights, citing a technicality, claiming that Mills "attempted to take possession of the tune by maintaining that it was written under an old contract which gave the publisher ownership of any Cole compositions."[32] This seems like, at best, a half-hearted attempt. Everyone knew that when you sold a song, you never got it back.[33] Let it be said that this would be the last time anyone would take advantage of Nat King Cole. Especially when he had Carlos Gastel on his team, Cole would make himself into a Jedi master of the music business, no less than he was of the piano or singing. And even in 1943, he was no naïf—it had clearly been a calculated risk for Cole to throw himself under a bus. Unlike most deals with most devils, Mills made good on his promise: it was his wheeling and dealing that placed the song on *The Kraft Music Hall* and in a major motion picture. When the

King Cole Trio record finally came out in April 1944, everything was already in place for "Straighten Up and Fly Right" to become a major, across-the-board national hit. Say what you like about Irving Mills, but he was a devil who delivered.[34]

THE RECORD FINALLY GOT MADE in November 1943. Decca had been the first major label to come to an agreement with the AFM, and their number one artist, Bing Crosby, was making proper records with a union-sanctioned orchestra beginning at the end of September, with one of the biggest hits of the era, "Pistol Packin' Mama." Capitol soon followed suit, signing with the AFM on or about October 9. Less than one week later, on October 15, Mercer would record his huge wartime hit, "G.I. Jive."[35] There already would be over a dozen Capitol sessions between that date and November 30, when Nat King Cole, Oscar Moore, and Johnny Miller faced the microphone for Capitol for the first time.

The first date was indeed a prophetic one, which set the tone for most of their sessions going forward: "Straighten Up and Fly Right," classified as a novelty trio vocal and soon to become a groundbreaking hit, was followed by Don Redman's "Gee, Baby Ain't I Good to You." This blues-centric ballad had been introduced by the composer-arranger-bandleader-vocalist on a 1929 session with McKinney's Cotton Pickers, but hardly heard from since. Cole not only made "Gee Baby" into a standard but into one of the virtual templates for the soul ballads that became so important in rhythm and blues, anticipating "Since I Fell for You" and "Please Send Me Someone to Love" and many others. Like few before him, Cole shows how it's possible to croon the blues.

The third tune of this pivotal first session is an instrumental jazz tour de force, a dedication to the new label and the group's new affiliation, "Jumpin' at Capitol," which is one of many songs composed by Cole but published under his wife's name, Nadine Robinson. (Never released as a single, Capitol included "Jumpin' at Capitol" in their 1945 album, *The History of Jazz, Vol. 4: This Modern Age.*) This riff number reveals the extent to which Moore and Cole had been listening to Charlie Christian, the electric guitar virtuoso who achieved immortality with Benny Goodman. There are important similarities between "Jumpin'" and "Shivers" (credited to Christian and Lionel Hampton), most famously recorded by the Goodman Sextet in 1939. The KC3 number is many times faster, but it becomes more "Shivers"-y after the opening ensemble melody statement and then a modulation from D minor to B-flat minor. At this point, we hear a chase chorus between piano and guitar that parallels the one between guitar and clarinet on the

Goodman disc. "Jumpin' at Capitol" offers both improvisation (including Johnny Miller's first important bass solo) and ensemble playing at the group's most intricate and exciting; the piece eventually explodes in a series of coda cadenzas, then slows down, like a dancer strutting her stuff in half time. It's hard to imagine any other group of any size playing this fast, this accurately, and this excitingly.

We end the date with a semi-comic, semi-romantic song, this one a solo vocal for Cole: "If You Can't Smile and Say Yes (Please Don't Cry and Say No)," the work of Timmie Rogers, a triple threat comedian, singer, and songwriter who appeared on radio and TV shows into the 1970s, inevitably uttering his catchphrase, "Oh yeah!" "If You Can't Smile" is precisely the kind of distinctly self-deprecating novelty that Cole would record dozens of over the next ten years; in fact, this pivotal date presents us with virtually every kind of tune the Trio would play during the peak Capitol years—the period between the two AFM bans—a jazz standard, a pop hit, a riff instrumental, and the blues.

Yet the big news of the session was clearly "Straighten Up and Fly Right." Cole had tapped into something that was deep and significant, and yet, obviously, also frivolous and fun. In 1947, both Count Basie, with a vocal by Jimmy Rushing, and Cab Calloway, would record a song titled "The Jungle King," and Basie would observe that this song was "about the same signifying monkey that 'Straighten Up and Fly Right' was about.[36] Oscar Brown, a veteran scholar of African American folklore, would later write a song called "Signifyin' Monkey." Such simians are all over the tree of African American music: Harry Belafonte, Clarence Williams, Dave Bartholomew, and Chuck Berry would all do songs about monkeys, usually outsmarting predatory animals—including human beings—who are bigger and more powerful. The monkey is the eternal symbol of the underdog.

Even though "Straighten Up and Fly Right" derived from African American folklore, Capitol Records deserves credit for not shunting it into the ghetto. If the Trio had still been on Decca, it would have doubtless been issued on the label's Sepia Series. But Capitol, to their credit, from the beginning kept Cole in their musical mainstream—he was never on anything like a "race records" imprint. There was no race-driven ghetto here.[37]

Thanks to the combination of Capitol and Mills, Cole's song became a late swing-era anthem. Big-band arrangements were commissioned by Jimmy Dorsey, Les Brown, Charlie Barnet, Woody Herman, Vaughn Monroe, Erskine Hawkins, Will Osborne, and, most famously, the Andrews Sisters.

it's hard to think of another song of the era that received so much coverage in spite of the recording ban, which was still ongoing for the two biggest labels, Columbia and RCA Victor. In Maysville, Kentucky, the teen-aged Clooney Sisters, Rosemary and Betty, went into a coin-operated recording booth and made a demo recording in which they mimicked Cole's accent and his pronunciation of the line "release your *holt* and I will set you free" in the bridge. Among Cole's supporters, there were already a few, like Dave Dexter and Lionel Hampton, who were correctly foreseeing that Cole's long-term success would be as a solo singer (or so they both later wrote); "Straighten Up," his first epic hit, was foremostly a trio vocal with solo portions, and thus a key interim step in Cole's vocal evolution.

The runaway success of "Straighten Up and Fly Right" accelerated the Trio's ascent into the stratosphere; by the end of the war, they were well on their way, holding onto the buzzard and steadily heading skyward.

THOSE FIRST YEARS OR SO at Capitol, a period that I would argue extends up through the departure of Oscar Moore and then the coming of the second AFM ban, were something of a golden age for the King Cole Trio; as Gunther Schuller and others have remarked, nearly every tune that they cut at these first sessions was a kind of a classic.

The key reason that their output was so high, apart from their superior abilities and Cole's visionary foresight, was that Cole and Moore had been playing continually, without any kind of a let-up, virtually uninterrupted for nearly seven years. Even the switching of bassists in 1942 wasn't enough to slow them down, and by now Johnny Miller had fit into the group perfectly, becoming, unquestionably, the most perfect bassist Cole ever worked with. Then too, they had been stockpiling repertoire at least since 1941.

Ever since the final Decca session, the only opportunities they had had to make records were for a couple of specialty outfits, Excelsior and Premier, whose main interest was to serve the needs of their owners, who were exclusively interested in pushing songs that they owned. When they got to Capitol, the situation was just the opposite: Mercer and Wallichs aggressively encouraged Cole to record whatever he wanted, and they shared a common goal of wanting to make great music and sell a lot of records in the process. Capitol was equally receptive whether the song he wanted to record was a Cole original, something by a friend of his (or a friend of a friend), or a vintage standard that the Trio could transform into something utterly new and fantastic. Thus, the Trio was sitting on a treasure trove of amazing material that was already good to go; most of their arrangements of standards, for instance, had already been tested in front of live audiences at the 331 Club. For Capitol to get it down on wax was essentially as simple as turning on a faucet.

"You must remember, though, that when the Trio joined Capitol, we'd been together seven years. Why, I had a jazz repertoire from here [Chicago] downtown," as the artist remembered in 1957. "Matter of fact, when our first album was released, it was just the repertoire we'd been playing for years. The simple fact was we had a foundation. We were ready. The desire was there, all right. But more important, the material was there too." What Cole says next in this interview is especially important. "Here's what I'd like to say to jazz groups who want recording contracts today: don't go in cold; have a repertoire to offer. In spite of the fact that the record business is riding the crest, it's still not enough just to go into a studio and play the first thing that the A&R man suggests."[38] This is virtually the only example of Cole allowing himself to take credit for his own smart decisions, even though, characteristically, he's presenting it in the form of advice to young artists rather than self-congratulation.

Cole learned very early that it wasn't only new songs that, in his words, reached across the footlights and grabbed the public; he was also a pioneer in the discovery and long-term acceptance of what gradually became classics. Songs like "You Call It Madness" and "It's Only a Paper Moon" were a major factor in Cole's longevity, a reason he outlasted most of his colleagues and contemporaries. With the important exception of Frank Sinatra, Cole was the only recording star (black or white, jazz or pop) of the period to invest so much time and energy in playing and singing standards, the body of music that later became collectively known as the Great American Songbook.

Jazz musicians, who habitually jammed on old favorites like "On the Sunny Side of the Street" and "After You've Gone," were probably the first population group to regularly revisit the more vintage standards. Cole was playing them from the beginning, and dozens of them are scattered, for example, among his early Standard Transcriptions (1938–1941). His love for this body of music was obviously encouraged by Johnny Mercer, a great songwriter himself, who keenly appreciated the work of his predecessors and colleagues.

As we've seen, the classic song that came to be most closely associated with Cole was a hand-me-down from two of his heroes, Earl Hines and Jimmy Noone. On a 1957 episode[39] of *The Nat King Cole Show*, we hear a clarinetist play the opening notes of "Sweet Lorraine." "You hear that?" the star asks us. "That's the spirit of Jimmie Noone, Chicago's late great clarinet stylist. His theme was a thing called 'Sweet Lorraine.' And Jimmie called my attention to it early in my early days here in Chicago, for which I'll be eternally grateful."

"Sweet Lorraine" goes back to 1928. Fittingly, it was composed by a pianist, Cliff Burwell, who had played for a number of dance bands, including Paul Whiteman's, but he is remembered mainly as Rudy Vallee's accompanist for roughly fifteen years. The lyric was the work of Mitchell Parrish, an Irving Mills contract writer, best known for "Stardust" and "Deep Purple," among dozens of others. Vallee had introduced "Sweet Lorraine" on radio and recorded it in June 1928,[40] well before anyone else, and he probably would have had a hit with it, but for some reason, the Victor company chose not to issue that version. The most famous early recording was done in August by Nat's heroes, Jimmie Noone and Earl Hines. Thanks to Hines, it was largely associated with pianists, including two who were among Nat's favorites, Teddy Wilson (in 1935 and 1939), and Art Tatum (in 1940, plus numerous live and transcription versions). Cole would have been familiar with all of these performances.

Cole's first version, transcribed for Standard in May 1939, contains his famous routine in embryo; over the next few years, he wouldn't so much add to this arrangement as refine it. Here Oscar Moore and Wesley Prince sing harmony behind Cole, whose scatty embellishments are much friskier than they would be in 1943. Further, the tempo is much faster, enough that Cole can sing two full choruses. Over the next four years, he continually pared down those ornamentations that he deemed to be superfluous and brought out the deeper meaning of the song. He next recorded "Sweet Lorraine" in 1940 for Decca, a performance that is at least a few degrees closer to the familiar version; the vocal harmony by the trio is gone, but the tempo still seems rushed, and Cole is, again, more agitated.[41]

"Sweet Lorraine" was recorded at the second Capitol session, December 15, 1943, and by now the routine is perfect: he sings the melody essentially straight, with much less embellishment than in either of the previous versions, but all the most important additives are retained: he starts with what soon became a famous piano intro. On the first line, he enters very late—as if he's waited till the last possible moment when he can make his entrance; you might call it fashionably late. This serves to make him sound extremely "cool," in the sense that we later came to understand that word in the 1950s and '60s. He incorporates vocally the same kind of repeats-for-emphasis that he might make on the keyboard: "I'm as happy as a baby boy, *baby boy*" and "when I met my sweet Lorraine, *Lorraine, Lorraine* . . ." The vocal is highly informed by his vocal-instrumental predecessors, especially Louis Armstrong and Fats Waller, most obviously on his signature mispronunciation of "choo choo toy" as "choo choo *choy*." This in itself is unique in Cole's canon; he consistently strove for the utmost in clarity, and "choo choo choy" is virtually a lone example of Cole the singer inserting a deliberate distortion into one of his vocals.

The bridge is much more on the beat and *legato* ("Now when it's raining..."), and he punctuates it with a semi-scatted *"oh ho oh ho"* (following "lead her down the aisle"). The piano solo is remarkably brief, especially considering the legacy of the song as a keyboard showpiece; Cole isn't trying to outplay Hines, Tatum, or Wilson, but darned if he doesn't out-*cool* them. He comes back at the bridge, which now has more "Oh ho"s than the first time around, and the coda includes a scatted cadenza that points to both Louis Armstrong and Billie Holiday. This is three minutes and ten seconds of pure hipness.

If you wanted to distill the essential essence of Nat King Cole down to one track, "Sweet Lorraine" is as good as any. Nobody ever got hipper and cooler than this, except possibly Cole himself on his later versions: famously, he recorded the song again on two classic albums, rejoined with Sweets Edison on *After Midnight* (1956) and remaking the classic trio track in stereo on *The Nat King Cole Story* (1961). He also cut an instrumental revision of the classic Trio arrangement for MacGregor transcriptions in 1944, and later, during his European tour of 1960, Cole left us an even sweeter "Lorraine," a six-minute instrumental version in which he plays breathtaking variations on his own variations. Then there's Cole's only recorded meeting with Frank Sinatra, from the 1946 Metronome All Stars session, in which he sets up the singer's entrance with a tasty intro and a brief exchange with bassist Eddie Safranski and drummer Buddy Rich. Sinatra's vocal on Cole's signature song is very groovy in its own way—but even Frank is no Nat.

And "Sweet Lorraine" may not have even been the most remarkable song that the Trio gave us at the second Capitol date. The session on December 15, 1943, started with "Sweet Lorraine," followed by two more standards, "Embraceable You" and "It's Only a Paper Moon" (which we discuss in the intro), then by one of his early tailor-fitted blues-ballad hybrids, his own "I Can't See for Lookin'" (the latter issued as the flip side of "Straighten Up and Fly Right"). Clearly, Cole was testing the limits of how many masterpieces it was possible to create in a single day.

"Embraceable You" also became a Cole classic, which he returned to in 1961 for the *Story* album. Cole's treatment of the 1930 Gershwin Brothers standard (from *Girl Crazy*) is still another absolute masterpiece. The vocal, the piano, the guitar, and the bass are all remarkably laid back—Cole isn't so much cool here as mellow; he only gets comparatively frisky at the end of the bridge when singing of how his embraceable one brings out the gypsy in him. The vocal on "Embraceable You" is perfect, but the instrumental break is one of Cole's most dazzling. Here, the pianist liberally paraphrases a French classical piano work titled *Le Secret (Intermezzo Pizzicato No. 276)* by Léonard Gautier. Published in 1916, *Le Secret* is fairly obscure a century later, but it was much better known in Cole's time. The piece was considered less challenging for piano students because of its even eighth-note rhythms, but Cole plays it in a more expansive, less staccato fashion, making it seem more like Ravel or Debussy. He merges Gershwin and Gautier together and creates something entirely new out of the two of them, something deeply impressionistic and unmistakably modern. Something Cole.

IN SPRING 1944, the Trio and its new label were faced with what we might call a "quality problem"—meaning, a desirable problem, the kind that one wants to have.[42] The first Capitol release, 154, was a huge hit, both sides appearing in all three charts that *Billboard* was then running. ("Straighten Up and Fly Right" was #9 pop, #1 R&B, and #1 country, while "I Can't See for Lookin'" was #24 pop, #2 country, and #2 R&B.) But this was still wartime, there were shortages of material, Capitol's distribution system was still limited, and Cole was, after all, a new name to most listeners. The company was able to release only two singles by the Trio in 1944; the second, featuring the new ballad "I Realize Now" backed with the bluesy "Gee, Baby, Ain't I Good to You?" (Capitol 169), hit the stores in early September. The next year, 1945, was only slightly better; Capitol was able to get all of three singles by the King Cole Trio out; only with postwar prosperity did the new Cole singles start arriving in sufficient abundance.

But as we've seen, even as early as 1944, Capitol already had a sizable backlog of classic material by the Trio and the standard channels of release, stand-alone 10" 78 RPM singles, were not able to keep pace. That fall, Mercer and Wallichs made an extraordinary decision: to gather eight sides by the Trio and release them in an album. Albums were, at the time, a relatively new format, much like the photo albums, in which individual discs were gathered into a cardboard-and-paper holder with a cover and descriptive notes on the back. In 1944, Decca Records, which had just released the first important original Broadway cast album, *Oklahoma!*, was the industry leader as far as albums went, but now, Capitol also wanted to keep up. No one had done an all-original pop album by 1944, not even Bing Crosby or the new guy, Sinatra.[43] The latter would make history by recording *The Voice* in 1945 (Columbia Records would release it a few months later in early 1946), but

Cole and Capitol had, in a sense, already beaten him to the punch with *The King Cole Trio*, released in October 1944. In the August 1944 *Metronome*, Barry Ulanov enthused, "There's an album to come on Capitol in which such time-honored favorites as 'Embraceable You,' 'The Man I Love,' 'It's Only a Paper Moon,' will vie with an original or two, such as 'Jumping at Capitol.' "[44]

Was *The King Cole Trio* a true concept album, like *The Voice?* It meets one important criterion: all eight songs were being released for the first time.[45] But unfortunately we can't answer the one remaining essential question: we don't know whether Cole had any idea these tracks were going to be part of an album when the Trio recorded them in late 1943 and early 1944. Most likely not. Probably, Cole just wanted the Trio to get them down on wax while they had the opportunity and figured that they would wait until later to decide what to do with them. They were all, in a sense, "King Cole Classics" at that point; all were time-tested standards and arrangements thereof. There were no new novelties or love songs of the sort that might get on the Harlem Hit Parade.

Even so, *The King Cole Trio* album was an overwhelming hit; within a few months, 50,000 copies had been sold—and remember, this was at a time when virtually no one was buying those bulky 78 RPM albums. The esteemed critic (later a close friend of the Coles) Leonard Feather proclaimed it "far and away the most exciting album of the year."[46] Hearing all eight tracks in a row, albeit interrupted by having to change sides with every track, must have been a rather overwhelming experience in 1944: it must have made everyone's hair stand on end to hear "Paper Moon," "Sweet Lorraine," or "Body and Soul" for the first time. *The King Cole Trio*—which was followed by *King Cole Trio, Vol. II* in 1946 and *King Cole Trio, Vol. III* in 1948, both also consisting of eight previously unreleased tracks—surely counts as one of the first and greatest jazz albums ever. It also shows that Cole was breaking new ground in terms of technology—not to mention marketing—no less than in terms of music.

CAPITOL DESERVES CREDIT not only for letting Cole record what he wanted but making sure that everything sounded so good. Dave Dexter described MacGregor as having "the best studios west of Chicago." As we've seen, the Trio had already recorded there in 1941, in support of former band canary Anita Boyer, and by this time, MacGregor was both recording and distributing its own commercial transcriptions as well as leasing its studios to other producers. C. P. MacGregor (1897–1968), known variously as "Chip" or "Chick," began his career in San Francisco as a manager for Brunswick Records. He founded his first company, MacGregor & Ingram Recording

Laboratories, in 1929 in San Francisco, and then, in 1932, he reformed as MacGregor & Solly Recording Laboratories.[47] By the end of the 1930s, the MacGregor Company and Studio, as it was now known (the various partners were gone), was based at 729 South Western Avenue, in Hollywood. The outstanding audio was the work of chief executive Paul Quon and his brother, Vic Quon, the primary recording engineer. Stan Kenton recorded for MacGregor at the same time as Cole, and his aide-de-camp (and later wife) Audree Coke, remembered, "We recorded in a very small studio, using the standard microphone set-up for those days. But Vic Quon had great technical expertise and had developed a system whereby everything sounded live when he recorded it, a sort of early echo chamber idea."[48] Not only were other independent producers using the MacGregor facilities, like Norman Granz and Ross Russell (of Dial Records), but so was the United States government, in the form of the Armed Forces Radio Service.

The King Cole Trio renewed their association with MacGregor at the end of 1943, around the time of the Trio's first Capitol sessions; at this point, MacGregor once again had Cole, Moore, and Miller accompany female singers: Ida James, late of the Erskine Hawkins and Earl Hines bands (they also worked with her on two 1943 Soundies films), and also four superb titles with the brilliant Anita O'Day, late of the Kenton and Gene Krupa bands. The least likely pairing was to combine the King Cole Trio with the Barrie Sisters, a duo of popular entertainers (born Minnie and Clara Bagelman) who were widely known as "The Jewish Andrews Sisters."

But the creme-de-la creme of Cole's relationship with MacGregor is a series of fifty outstanding titles that the Trio made on its own between late 1943 and early 1945—more than twice the number of tracks they cut for Capitol in the same period.[49] The MacGregor titles, the majority of which were recorded only for transcriptions, are possibly even more animated and full of joy than the contemporaneous Capitols; one gets a feeling that every tune was cut in one take, no more, giving them a greater feeling of spontaneity than the 78 RPM masters; minor lyric flubs can be heard, of the kind that would never be tolerated on a Capitol master (as on "The Old Music Master").

The addition of so many new titles to the King Cole canon shows both how deep and how diverse the Trio's repertoire was; for instance, there are three on the MacGregor Transcription series by Johnny Mercer, which is two more than Cole recorded commercially in these years: "Too Marvelous for Words" anticipates the classic Capitol version by at least a year; "Laura" is one of Cole's first great solo ballads, while "The Old Music Master" is a treasure of a Mercer lyric most famously cut by the lyricist himself in a duet with Jack

Teagarden. Cole essays both parts here: that of the Old Music Master himself, a 19th-century composer (a close friend, we are told, of "Beethoven and Mr. Reginald de Koven"), and "a little colored boy," who visits him from the future to tell him that if he wants his music to be heard in the 20th century, then "You got to jump it, music master / you got to play that rhythm faster!" Mercer's text is a primo example of his ability to tell a complete and, in this case, rather fanciful story in a mere 32 bars, and Cole's ability to bring it to life. He achieves this not only with his singing but also with an ingenious arrangement that contrasts classical piano figures with Basie-style riff patterns; so much work went into this track—and the results shine as brightly as any Capitol master—that it's hard to believe it was heard nowhere except on a radio-only transcription.

The MacGregor series is filled with such gems, including some contemporary novelties that sound like they could have been written for Cole and the KC3, like "'Tain't Me," Phil Moore's "Shoo Shoo Baby," and "D-Day," a war-theme rhythm tune ("there never was a finer sight / than when our boys were picked to fight / on D-Day . . .") that amounts to the first important song by the young composer Lew Spence. There are also many standards Cole never recorded elsewhere, like an instrumental of "I May Be Wrong" and a real barn-burner arrangement of "After You've Gone" in the general mold of his "Sweet Georgia Brown" and "Honeysuckle Rose." There are very substantially different versions of tunes he would also cut commercially, like a treatment of Offenbach's "Barcarolle" that's a whole minute longer than the 1945 Capitol version, and finally, a satisfying run-through of "On the Sunny Side of the Street" much better than the 1940 Ammor recording.

Some of the all-time great MacGregors are based on classic songs, like Cole's darkly swinging, hypnotic treatment of the iconic Mexican song "Besame Mucho," and a romping, gleeful rendition of Clarence Williams's 1919 blues standard, "Baby Won't You Please Come Home," both sung beautifully by Cole. Some are otherwise completely unknown, like "I Wanna Turn Out My Light" and "Keep Knockin' on Wood," two unique charmers that, in some issues, were both credited to Cole himself as composer. There are some major new songs that he should have, by all rights, done for Capitol, like "Do Nothing till You Hear from Me," which he intertwines with an intriguing, original countermelody and vamp that would have surely impressed composer Duke Ellington. He also crafted a beautiful little subset of inspired instrumentals associated with the Count Basie band: "Miss Thing," "Swingin' the Blues" and "Lester Leaps In." Cole even showed his love for the Casa

Loma Orchestra by playing "Wild Goose Chase," a 1933 hot stomp by the band's pioneering arranger Gene Gifford.

Capitol Records and MacGregor transcriptions were not the only organizations to record the King Cole Trio during the war years. Since 1942, they were regularly presented by the Armed Forces Radio Network and the V-Disc program, two organizations dedicated to bringing the latest American music to GIs in all branches of the service. The Trio appeared at least a dozen times on the AFRS show *Jubilee*, which, at the time, was a literal who's who of black talent. The AFRS programs and the V-Discs had a profound impact on two Italian-Americans from the East Coast, John Paul (Bucky) Pizzarelli of Paterson, New Jersey, and Anthony Dominick Benedetto (later professionally known as Tony Bennett) of Astoria, Queens, who were both born in 1926. As young infantrymen with big musical dreams, they both give thanks to Uncle Sam for letting them hear a group that would have a profound impact on their lives and careers. Both men would work with Cole in subsequent years: Pizzarelli, who became a swing guitar virtuoso and (and who would play with Nat in 1958), and Bennett, who would co-star on Nat's NBC TV series in 1957. Bucky, naturally, was blown away by the interplay of piano and guitar and became a major disciple of Oscar Moore; and Tony declared that the Trio was possibly the most perfect musical ensemble that ever existed and was inspired by their intimacy and simplicity when he made his classic collaboration with Bill Evans thirty years later.

THE FINAL TUNE of the first Capitol session, as we have seen, was "If You Can't Smile and Say Yes (Please Don't Cry and Say No)," by comedian-composer Timmie Rogers, who said[50] that he wrote the song for Cole. This seems highly unlikely, since, on Cole's original 78 (Capitol 192) the credited co-author is Louis Jordan, who, played the song extensively during the war years (many airchecks exist) but never recorded it, probably because of the AFM ban. As we've seen, the Cole Trio and the Tympany Five were crossing the other's paths fairly often during the years when "race" music had yet to be re-christened "rhythm and blues." Generally, the KC3 and Jordan's Tympany Five went a long way around to avoid doing each other's repertoire[51]—stepping on each other's musical toes as it were—and they stayed out of each other's way in other areas as well.[52]

For a brief time around 1941, both Cole and Jordan were being booked by Berle Adams, of GAC (General Artists Corp.). But even then, Cole knew the man he wanted to work with: a giant, Hispanic bear of a manager named Carlos Gastel. The two had their sights on each other from 1938 on, when Gastel first heard the Trio at Jim Otto's. Nat and Carlos could literally see eye-to-eye; they were roughly the same height, about 6' 1", although Gastel, being chronically overweight, was many pounds heavier.

Gastel's father, so it's said, had been a diplomat from Honduras, and his mother was from Germany. He was born on March 21, 1914, in San Pedro Sula.[53] He grew up mostly in Honduras, occasionally joining his parents in trips around Europe, and then, when he reached high school age, he was sent to the La Jolla Military Academy in California. Anyone who knew of Gastel's insatiable appetite for liquor, food, tobacco, and general carousing—which helped put him in the grave at the age of fifty-six—would have had a hard time envisioning him lasting very long at a military boarding school. But at least it brought him to California, where he got his first prolonged taste of American music and showbiz. From the time he heard his first North American swing band, he knew this was a world that he had to be part of. He started by managing dance orchestras, although neither of his first two clients exactly set the world on fire: Sonny Dunham, ace trumpet soloist from the Casa Loma, a brilliant musician who had little actual star quality or skill as a bandleader, and Max Baer, the heavyweight boxing champion. In an era when even Chico Marx, who at least was a musician, could lead his own swing band, this might have seemed like a good idea. (Needless to say, it wasn't.)

Cole also might have liked the idea of working with the affable Gastel, who was an outsider, an immigrant and somewhat "swarthy" as he was often described at the time, in an age when nearly everyone in the music business was white or Jewish, even those booking, recording, and publishing the work of African American talent. Louis Armstrong, one of Cole's own mentors, had a career-long mantra about how a black artist needed a white man or a Jew to intercede for him in the showbiz world. Cole had said as far back as 1935 that he felt "he could make better progress under white management,"[54] and by the start of the Capitol contract, he decided on a representative who was literally halfway between him and the white world.

When the Trio's first manager, "Hap" Kaufman, was drafted, probably in late 1941, Cole turned to his friend Claire Phillips, who at that point had a talent booker's license and was cautiously considering a career path as a personal agent. But she wisely declined; she knew she didn't have the firepower and chutzpah to get Cole to the next level.[55] In 1940, *Down Beat* had announced that the William Morris Agency was interested in the trio (that would have changed the course of history—they might have gotten famous much earlier) but that never happened.[56] The Trio was affiliated with General Artists Corp. at least as far back as 1941; when Ralph Watkins booked them at Kelly's Stable, he had gone through Frank Henshaw of GAC, based in Atlanta.[57] In 1943, one Gene Andes insisted to *Down Beat* that he was, in fact, the present manager of the King Cole Trio.[58]

But well before then, Gastel had already worked with the Trio at General Artists Corp., and in 1943 they were ready to commit to each other as manager and client in a permanent relationship. Yet Adams was still in the picture; he had been very helpful in the past and had gotten the Trio some of its best bookings, helping them conquer the well-paying world of cocktail lounges. Adams had recently left GAC to manage Louis Jordan full time, and he wanted to add Cole to his roster as well. As Adams later told the story,[59] he suggested the idea sometime in 1943, and Nat agreed. Then, a week later, to Adams's surprise, Carlos Gastel, who like Cole was based in Los Angeles, showed up on his doorstep in Chicago. Gastel proposed that they work together: Adams knew every room in Chicago and the Midwest, whereas Gastel's strength was everything west of that. Between the two of them, they covered the vast majority of the venues where the Trio would work, so they could share the management of the group. Although slightly suspicious, Adams had to agree that it was a great idea.[60]

But then, all of a sudden, absolutely nothing happened. Berle never heard another peep from either Nat or Carlos. Upon investigating, Adams soon learned that Gastel had simply gone ahead and cut him out, and he was outraged. "Gastel snookered me and stole my client," Adams thundered, but he realized that there was nothing he could do about it. "I treasured Nat's friendship, so I decided not to press the issue. For years I puzzled over Nat's decision." He continued to hold a grudge against Gastel: in 1950, when Adams was working for the Music Corporation of America (MCA), he ran into the Honduran at Lucey's Restaurant on Melrose Avenue, and the two agents literally had to be held back from a fistfight. (It wouldn't have been much of a contest; Adams, as he described himself, was a "little shrimp" while Gastel was very literally a heavyweight.) Finally, about twenty years later, at a Christmas celebration, Adams finally came out and put the question to Cole directly.[61] The answer was obvious to everybody but him. "You know why I didn't sign with you?" Cole responded, "Carlos told me that your first love was Louis Jordan and that I would always be second fiddle. That was it."

Clearly, Gastel was correct, and Cole was doing the right thing to sign with him. It's the same reason that Cole was better off going with the new Capitol Records rather than the older and more established Decca, where he also would have played second fiddle to Jordan. Another point in Gastel's favor was that, like Cole himself, he was based in Los Angeles, and he already had a good relationship with Wallichs and Mercer—and it was constantly getting better. Before long, Gastel would represent the majority of the key artists of the early days at Capitol Records, including bandleaders Stan Kenton, Benny Carter, Billy May, and Nelson Riddle, plus singers Peggy Lee, June Christy, Mel Tormé, Nellie Lutcher, and Jeri Southern, to name a few.

Pianist Jimmy Rowles, who had met Cole in 1940 at the Radio Room, remembered hanging out with the Trio at Herb Rose's 331 Club, when Gastel—whom he referred to without the least trace of irony as "The Brain"—came in. "We got to talking with this guy, and the first thing you know, Herb Rose says, 'I'd sell his contract for ten dollars.' 'Oh yeah? Right now?' Gastel asked. So, he whips out the ten dollars and says, 'Give me the contract.' And from that moment, Carlos Gastel owned Nat Cole."[62] But it was nothing like ownership; for nineteen years, Nat and Carlos were a team, best buds as well as business partners.

Cole and Gastel formalized their relationship in spring 1944. Rather than being super-aggressive with each other, as client and agent, Maria Cole later remembered that they were almost overly sensitive to each other's feelings. Nat at first felt the Trio was making too little money to justify any kind of professional representation; in other words, he doubted that they were worth Carlos's time. But Carlos persisted, and they reached an early agreement when Nat insisted that Carlos be paid and Carlos refused to accept any money at all. Finally, they agreed that Carlos would take a cut of their earnings if and when the Trio's fee reached $800 a week.[63]

That happened almost instantaneously with the release of "Straighten Up and Fly Right," Capitol 154, at the end of March 1944. Cole later remembered, "I'll never forget it. One night we closed at the 331 Club in Los Angeles at about four hundred dollars a week"—thus ending a two year run—"and the next day we were making one thousand dollars per at the Orpheum Theatre [Los Angeles]."[64] They opened on April 10, marking their first theater date (at least since 1937), for a one-week stand.[65] "One record seems to be enough, these days, to establish a band," *Metronome* claimed a few months later. "King Cole has that record in 'Straighten Up and Fly Right' (backed with 'I Can't See for Lookin'") both sides of which are currently pulling in thousands of nickels in jukeboxes from coast to coast. And so, finally, a trio that lots of us have been raving about has won public approval, acclaim, and the plentiful gold that goes with same."[66] One thousand dollars a week was a huge leap over the $75 a week they had made at the Swanee in 1937 and the $140 (which had to cover travel and accommodations) they had made in 1941 at Kelly's Stable.

"Carlos and I thought generally the same way," Cole said in 1957. "This is really unusual in an artist-manager relationship. Generally, an artist signs with a manager because he thinks the manager can do him some good and leaves it at that. Often the manager has very different ideas from those of the artist—basically different, I mean. This wasn't the case here, though. I knew the direction I wanted to travel and realized Carlos could help me. Actually, he was thinking on something very different from his past associations. He'd managed the Stan Kenton band and other groups that were nowhere near our Trio in format. It was a gamble for him, but he was willing to give it a try. I can honestly say that much of the success I enjoy today I owe to Carlos. Our association was—and is—a good one, and it worked out the way I wanted it to."[67]

It's hard to imagine that anybody, including Adams, could have done a better job in guiding Cole's career. Between Gastel and Capitol Records, Cole now had a platform from which he could be heard; a launching pad from which he could take off, straighten up, and fly right. As we have seen, throughout the 1940s, Cole's chief rival, or point of comparison, was Louis Jordan; by the 1950s, the only artists Cole could rightfully be compared to were Frank Sinatra and Ella Fitzgerald, in terms of musical visionaries who were equally gifted in terms of raw talent and street smarts and who parlayed their virtuosity into mass-market success.

Cole also embraced the idea of experimentation and tinkering with his own formulas. He eagerly tried out ten different new ideas to find the one that worked, and he also didn't mind working his way through dozens of songs, new songs and old songs, great songs and, as he once called them, "dog songs" to find the ones that the audiences most responded to. He constantly tinkered with his sound and his music, even when everyone else thought that it was already perfect. Although there is a continuity throughout his career, the Trio of 1943 sounds very different from the Decca years (1940–41) and the earlier transcription recordings (1938–40). And the Trio of 1949–1951—even before Jack Costanzo made it a quartet—sounds completely different from that.

The relationship between Cole and Gastel lasted almost twenty years, at the end of which Cole was more popular than ever; the relationship between Jordan and Adams lasted nine years, and at its end, Jordan was undeniably in decline. This wasn't entirely the fault of either Adams or Jordan; many of the major hitmakers of the war years would have a hard time transitioning into the next decade, including the Andrews Sisters, Dick Haymes, most of the big bands, and even Sinatra. Yet even as Jordan and the others faded, Cole went from strength to strength.

When we compare the output of the two groups, something else becomes apparent. Almost every one of the Tympany Five's hits is an upbeat novelty—something you would play at a party, conducive to dancing and drinking. Both combos also played the occasional slow, comic blues (Cole's "That Ain't Right," Jordan's "I'm Gonna Move to the Outskirts of Town").[68] But on the whole, it's impossible to miss the diversity in Cole's output. Cole played no shortage of upbeat novelties, especially after the success of "Straighten Up and Fly Right," but nearly every entry on the charts shows him growing musically and exploring a new direction. From the beginning, there are ballads, like "All for You," "I Realize Now," and "I'm Lost," all of which charted in 1943–44; these are very different from even slightly later love songs, starting with "For Sentimental Reasons" (1946). By contrast, Jordan's later hits, like the 1949 "Saturday Night Fish Fry," aren't that different from his wartime hits, like "Deacon Jones" and "Somebody Done Changed the Lock on My Door."

Nineteen forty-four was the year that both Cole and Jordan landed their breakthrough numbers, "Straighten Up and Fly Right" and "Is You Is or Is You Ain't My Baby"—those two recordings became cornerstones for what later became known as rhythm and blues. (As if in a symbol of mainstream acceptance, the Andrews Sisters, by far the most popular vocal group of the war years, sang both songs in a 1945 Universal Pictures musical titled *Her Lucky Night*.) The two basic components of a novelty song are a happy dance-able tempo, at least medium fast (slow tempos are emotionally associated with ballads, love songs, and sad songs), and some sort of jivey, humorous lyrical component. Novelty songs were also called "rhythm songs" during the swing era, not only because they tended to be more rhythmic than ballads and love songs but also because a disproportionate number of them were also based on the original "rhythm song," George Gershwin's "I Got Rhythm." Cole performed almost too many of these "Rhythm" variations to count, some of the most famous being "Hit That Jive, Jack" (1941) and "I'm an Errand Boy for Rhythm" (1945)—not to mention "Straighten Up and Fly Right."[69]

A great many rhythm songs and novelties are built around topical expressions of the day. Some were inspired by existing catchphrases, like "Now He Tells Me" (1947), and others are examples when the song itself would inspire such an expression, as was the case with "Straighten Up and Fly Right." The idea of using familiar phrases as song titles goes well beyond 1940s novelties—especially in the great standards of Ira and George Gershwin ("How Long Has This Been Going On?" "Nice Work If You Can Get It")—but the Trio perfected the art of employing these expressions as if they were the punchlines of a joke. The 1940s were the great years of radio comedy, a medium that was highly dependent on repeated catchphrases, from Abbott and Costello ("I'm a bad boy!") to the many characters played weekly by Red Skelton ("He don't know me vewy well, do he?"), and every cast member on *The Jack Benny Show*—including Artie Auerbach (who costarred with the Trio in *Here Comes Elmer*) as "Mr. Kitzel" chortling "Hmmm . . . could be!" But it was *The Fred Allen Show*, hosted by Benny's longtime sparring partner, that became ground zero for classic catchphrases—most famously, "That's a joke son," coined by Kenny Delmar as "Senator Claghorn" on a regular segment of the program titled "Allen's Alley." All of these were precisely the kind of thing that the King Cole Trio would turn into a song.

In Cole's music, rhythm and comedy are very closely interconnected, and so is harmony. Humor is also an integral part of the blues, which immediately gives it a specific harmonic relevance, but more obviously, there's the KC3's tradition of distinguishing between what might be called the setup lines of the joke, which Cole typically sings in solo, and the punchline, which the trio sings in harmony. Typically the setup lines lead to the punchline, but occasionally the song starts with the three-part harmony punchline (usually the song title) and the solo lines come after that, as in "It Is Better to Be by Yourself" (1945). After years of experimentation, Cole had realized that alternating between solo and trio vocals was more effective than a whole chorus of the trio singing together.

The Trio's timing—what pianist-scholar Dick Katz has identified as the KC3's distinctive "lope"—is a great assistance in helping the narrative to be understood and thereby heightening the humor. Roughly fifty songs recorded by the trio in the inter-ban period (1943–47) alone might be considered novelties. Among the many that have the three-part harmony punchlines are "Got a Penny" (1943) and "Oh, But I Do" (a song co-credited to Ella Fitzgerald) which shows that the trio vocal punchline idea was still valid as late as 1946.

"(I Call My Papa) Fla-Ga-La-Pa" (1945), is a real charmer: it starts with the trio vocal on the title (punchline) and Cole sings the setup afterward in solo. This is the first of many numbers that Cole would record by the songwriter Roy Alfred, here collaborating with Doris Fisher and Allan Roberts. Fisher's brother, Marvin (who would become one of Cole's favorite composers and closest friends) recalled that the unusual title originated with a postcard that Alfred received from his friend, the arranger Frank Comstock (then on staff with bandleader Les Brown). "He got a card saying, 'We miss you in FLA, GA, LA and PA,'" meaning Florida, Georgia, Louisiana, and Pennsylvania, "so they wrote a song based on that."[70]

The Trio's biggest novelty of 1945 would be "The Frim Fram Sauce"—strictly a solo vocal, no harmony punchline here—written by another of the pianist's very close songwriter friends, Redd Evans (already responsible for their 1941 "Slow Down"). The general idea also derives from the vaudeville tradition of double-talk. The most famous exponent at the time was comedian Cliff Nazarro, who showed, in a humorous way, that it wasn't the content of what someone said that was important but the tone with which he said it. The idea was to deliver nonsense with a straight face, as if it was supposed to mean something; in this case it was an absurd dinner order given to a waiter: "I want the *frim fram sauce* with the *ausen fay* / With *chafafa* on the side."

The song reached #19 on the mainstream charts (although, surprisingly, it didn't turn up at all on the race chart), and proved popular enough for Cole to choose it as one of his seven songs that were filmed by Soundies corporation; the resulting "Soundie" shows him desperately trying to get the attention of an otherwise preoccupied waitstaff. He also sang it on Frank Sinatra's radio show, his first official meeting with the rapidly rising crooner who would become one of his lifelong friends and colleagues, in November 1945.[71] In the mid-1940s, the African American columnist Dolores Calvin hosted elaborate dinner parties for Cole and other black celebrities that became known as meetings of the "Frim Fram Society."[72]

In later years, *New York Times* columnist William Safire devoted an entire column to decoding the hidden meaning of "Frim Fram Sauce," and Dave Frishberg worked it into his own song "Who's on First?" The song was so popular that in 1946 a report said that "a nationally known food products manufacturer is bidding for the rights to use the name on a new meat sauce. The piece of nonsense aroused a bit of a stir in radio circles. There was so much talk of double-entendre that CBS banned it briefly" and Carlos Gastel "offered $5,000 to anyone who could translate the lyrics. There were no takers."[73] There's plenty of meat in both Cole's and Moore's solos, tactfully cramming lots of notes in small spaces where the vocal had been comparatively spare. The meat sauce deal, however, ultimately didn't go through; oh well, as Cole states in the coda of the song, "Now if you don't have it, you can just bring me a check for the water."

"Frim Fram Sauce" and the other novelties of the Capitol years seem particularly funny because Cole was constantly working to improve his enunciation—to make it keep pace with his already perfect intonation—so that every word could be understood, even when all the words were unmitigated nonsense. Even veterans like Cab Calloway noted, "He never said 'dat,' he always said 'that.' "[74] By the 1950s, Cole was no longer demanding to know "is you is or is you ain't ma baby?" but rather he was expressing the same sentiments—lamenting a lost love—in the form of a coded request to a servant, "Dinner for One, Please, James."

One definition of nonsense songs, like "Frim Fram Sauce," "Fla-Ga-La-Pa," and the 1947 "Kee-Mo Ky-Mo (The Magic Song)" is that they play with the sounds of words rather than any meaning. They also illuminate how Cole's brand of humor was distinct from anyone else's—even though on "Frim Fram" he employed a recipe that sampled the menu of both Louis Jordan and Slim Gaillard. From a distance, it might have seemed that Cole and Jordan had much in common: both were singing instrumentalists who led fantastically popular small groups at roughly the same time. The wacko antics of Slim Gaillard had an influence on both artists, as did the deeply soulful playing and singing—and also the comedy—of Louis Armstrong.

The all-important difference between the Cole and Jordan approaches was that Cole's comedy was comically understated and subtle, in direct contrast to Jordan's, whose humor was, to an even greater degree, comically exaggerated. "If You Can't Smile and Say Yes (Please Don't Cry and Say No)" is much more of a Jordan tune than a Cole tune: it's easy to imagine Jordan mouthing off to some gullible female that she shouldn't miss her chance to get together with him; not only is he a great guy, he boasts, but he tells her repeatedly that this being the war, "men are scarce as nylons." Cole's musical persona was, this one song aside, much more self-deprecating. He invariably presents himself as the patsy, the fall guy, in everything he tries, whether it's romance or some other endeavor.

Just as "If You Can't Smile and Say Yes" concluded the first Capitol session, the second session (December 15, 1943) ended with another catchphrase-driven song, Nat's own "I Can't See for Lookin'," which gained immortality as the flip side of "Straighten Up." The mood is downbeat, the tempo slow, but the central line is another contemporary slang expression that serves to leaven the mood. In "Bring Another Drink" (1944), another very early Capitol-era novelty, Cole tells us that he and his buddy entered a "gin mill down the street" where they plied a couple of local "chicks" with alcohol in hopes of securing some romantic action. But no dice: even after the ladies had consumed plenty, at considerable expense, "we whispered love words in their ears" and "the chicks got rough . . . awful stuff!"

On "I'm a Shy Guy" (1945), Cole tells us that he yearns to be "a fly guy" but, alas, he's only a "'fraid-to-try guy": "There's a gal I idolize / But I can't get my words to hypnotize." Likewise, "(Everyone Has Someone) But All I've Got Is

Me" (1947) is a list song set in a 12-bar blues pattern with a stop-time bridge, in which he tells us "Cornbeef has its cabbage / Mother has Machree" and "Sulfur has molasses / Simon has Legree" leading him to conclude "Everyone has someone / But all I've got is me." The majority of these songs were composed at least partly by Cole himself.[75]

All of these lyrics are steeped in self-deprecating humor, which is diametrically opposed to the ethos of Louis Jordan. None of these situations would ever happen to Mr. Jordan—he was precisely the opposite of a "'fraid-to-try" guy. Jordan's songs were all about comically-exaggerated self-glorification. No shy guy he; Jordan informs his listeners that the chicks that he picks are "Slender, Tender, and All." ("They come at my beck and call / And give me no trouble at all.") He has so many women chasing after him that he feels morally obligated to provide pointers for his brother males as to how to dodge the bullet of commitment, in "Beware, Brother, Beware." Jordan not only admits to being a lowlife but he is resolutely unashamed of it. In 1954, he sang a Jon Hendricks lyric in which he proclaimed loudly and proudly, "I'm a whiskey taster / And a money waster / But I'll die happy!" Jordan is like *Don Giovanni* at the end of Act II of Mozart's opera: he is going to keep on being himself, even if he knows all too well that eventually there will be a high price to pay for it.

Cole, conversely, yearns for self-improvement and moral redemption—to straighten up and fly right. He sings song after song about how his foibles come back to bite him in the butt. He's continually having one misadventure after another, romantic and otherwise; in one 1945 lyric, he meets a gal that "knocks me out," "But She's My Buddy's Chick." A year later, in "The Best Man," he's once again in competition for a gal; she tells him he's the best man of the two, but in the punchline, he serves as the best man when she marries his best friend. In the 1947 "I've Got a Way with Women," also by Roy Alfred, he describes himself as "a Casanova in disguise." You can easily see the concluding pun coming; this one hardly requires a spoiler alert—"I've got a way with women / But someone got away with mine"—but he makes it hysterically funny just the same, even without the benefit of surprise. In both songs, he allows himself just enough self-aggrandization to heighten the comedy and to set himself up for the pratfall, and to make it that much funnier when his ego is inevitably deflated.

Cole is not only a lowlife in these novelties, but he's also a low-rent Lothario. In Robert Scherman's "Got a Penny," he's frantically begging for one cent more to add to the four he's got in his pocket, so he can call a girl; he has the girl's name and number but not the nickel with which to phone her. Conversely, in "Give Me Twenty Nickels for a Dollar," he knows only the last name of the girl he's looking for, so he's desperately dropping five-cent pieces in the slot while he diligently places calls to every "Jones" in the phone book. It isn't always about love, either: the lead character of "Loan Me Two till Tuesday" (from 1945, and composed by "Taps" Miller, a dancer who inspired a Count Basie instrumental) is just mooching pocket change without any higher motive.

In "Now He Tells Me" (1947) the hero is just a plain old schlemiel, a putz who dives into a swimming pool only to learn the hard way (hard in the sense of concrete) that it won't be filled with water "till the middle of May"; these are all old vaudeville antics, or the kind you might see in a silent slapstick comedy. "Now He Tells Me" also offers an insight into Cole's working methods, in the form of an early take that was released in 1991. This first version (July 3, 1947) is very slow, almost like a comedy monologue set to a bass line; the issued take (August 28, 1947) is set in the familiar KC3 loping dance tempo. The faster tempo actually enhances the comedy, and as an added bonus, there's another one of Cole's distinctive riff intros. The original take also makes an early, innovative use of radio-style sound effects, like an auto horn and crash noise in the first A section. (He would employ sound effects and speeded up voices in some of his later sides, notably on children's songs.) In the issued take, Oscar Moore simulates the crash more effectively with a zingy note on his guitar. The guitarist, however, played a larger role in the early take, wherein he warns Cole (a rare document of Moore's spoken voice), after the fact, about a tack on a chair; the issued take replaces all that with a funnier gag about finding a four-leaf clover in a poison ivy bed.

As a general strategy, this path of comic self-deprecation served Cole quite well at the time. He was tall, handsome, and never had a problem attracting women. Cole's choices regarding his image and musical persona parallel those of Sinatra: already the ultimate Hollywood fly lothario, Sinatra won over movie audiences by playing counter to type and portraying a romantic underdog in movies like *Anchors Aweigh*. (According to Benny Carter, the multi-instrumentalist bandleader-composer who toured frequently with the KC3 at this time, Cole was even then being known as the "Sepia Sinatra.")[76]

These lowlife numbers were a staple of early rhythm and blues; virtually all of the R&B stars of the 1940s (among them Amos Milburn, Wynonie Harris, "Stick" McGhee, and Dinah Washington) followed the Jordan template and sang of themselves as lowlifes, preoccupied with the three G's: gin, gambling, and girl-chasing (or guys, in Washington's case). Ray Charles, deeply inspired by both Cole and Jordan, kept the lowlife spirit alive with "Greenbacks" and

"Hit the Road, Jack." It was this particular subject matter that, early on, led the black middle class to dissociate itself from the blues; Lil Hardin (later Mrs. Louis Armstrong) remembered that her mother dismissed the blues as "worthless immoral music played by worthless immoral people."[77] The blues didn't become completely respectable until a generation later, when R&B merged with Gospel to become soul music. This was the turning point: you wouldn't hear Aretha Franklin or The Supremes sing of themselves as juice-head lowlifes. Soul music was not only more inspirational than R&B; it was aspirational as well.

During the high Trio years, Cole sang other kinds of novelties as well. Take, for instance, "Could 'Ja" (1946) by Carl Fischer.[78] There's no alcohol or immoral activity here: "Could 'ja, for an ice cream sundae? ... Could 'ja, for a tootsie roll?" There are also no blues inflections here (it's also one of the few new songs of the era recorded by both Cole and Sinatra); instead, Cole's voice sounds rather cute, as does the trio arrangement.

But if "Could 'Ja" is just plain adorable, and I say that without any irony, then "Flo and Jo" (by Milton Leeds)[79] can only be described as "skanky." We begin in *medias res*: a lowlife Lochinvar named "Joe" is in Mexico, trying to get away from "Flo," whom, we are told, is also in Mexico, "to get her hands on Joe." It is soon revealed that Joe has seduced and abandoned Flo, fleecing her of her savings in the process, and then fled South of the Border, with the spurned woman hot on his trail. The song is extremely un-PC, I don't expect we'll ever hear it in any Cole tributes: Flo, we are told was "fat and over 40" and therefore she should have realized that Joe only "loved" her for "her dough." But in spite of this, it's funny, funny, funny, a broad caricature of male-female relations that Cole makes even funnier with his swinging beat (this is much faster than the customary lope) and with percussive pan-American rhythmic effects. This tale of a lovelorn, weight-challenged quadragenarian losing her loot to a mustache-twirling gigolo, is as toe-tapping as it is knee-slapping and boasts a rare and ingenious 8-bar scat solo as well. One of the last tunes he recorded for Capitol before the second ban went into effect at the start of 1948, it was still popular enough for Cole to continue performing into 1949 (with Costanzo).

Clearly, what Cole was looking for was a rhythm song that would appeal to everybody, well beyond the Harlem Hit Parade, and he found it in 1945 when a young songwriter named Bobby Troup walked into his dressing room at the Trocadero supper club on Sunset Boulevard. Troup later remembered, "They had the big showroom, and then they had a very intimate, room in the back just for Nat, called The King Cole room." Troup was six months older than Cole, but he referred to him as "my idol." Troup was far from unknown; he had already written for Tommy Dorsey ("Snooty Little Cutie") and also a jivey bauble titled "Rhythm Sam" that the Trio had cut for MacGregor the previous year. He had just arrived in Los Angeles, and it was the industry factotum George "Bullets" Durgom who took him backstage at the Troc to meet Cole.

"After the set was over, Bullets introduced me to him. He said, 'Nat, would you mind listening to a few songs of Bobby's?' "[80] The main objective was to entice Cole to consider a blues-ballad hybrid titled "Baby, Baby All the Time" that he had published a few months earlier. Nat heard it and loved it. But there was one other tune Troup wanted to audition for Cole, even though it was far from finished. Newly discharged from the Marines, Troup and his wife, the former Cynthia Hare, had just driven across the country, 2,000 miles from Missouri to California. Along the way, Mrs. Troup had begun humming the names of the towns they passed in a little sing-song rhythm, and she might have even been the one who came up with the phrase "get your kicks on Route 66." It was her husband, however, who had started turning it into a song even before they reached the end of the highway. He started to demonstrate it for Cole, but with an apology. " 'Nat, I wrote half a song about my trip out here. I haven't even played this on the piano yet. I don't even know what key I do it in.' So, I played this 'Route 66' and he fell in love with that, too, and he sat down at the piano and played it." (This was also a likely instance, like "Unforgettable" in 1951, of Cole helping a composer finish a song and make it viable, but not cutting himself in on any of the credit or royalties.)

Both songs were exceptional: "Baby All the Time" would become a jazz standard, especially among such knowledgeable song cognoscenti as June Christy and Shirley Horn. "Route 66," however, as Cole had intended, was embraced by everybody. Like "San Fernando Valley" and "I'll Buy That Dream," it was one of those songs of the moment that precisely captured the short-lived but vital spirit of the first few months of immediate postwar optimism. "Route 66" was about more than a highway, and also about more than either a journey or a destination; the driving idea was the notion of relocation as a metaphor for self-reinvention: move to a new place, build a new home, find a new job, make yourself into something new. Besides that, it swung like crazy, especially when Cole outfitted it with a stunning trio arrangement and an introductory vamp that became as much a part of the song as Troup's melody.

At the same session, March 15, 1946, Cole also recorded "Everyone Is Saying Hello Again (Why Must We Say Goodbye?)," a contemporary ballad that also had postwar relevance. It was a lovely song, but not a hit—the narrative describes a couple breaking up at the same time that everyone is coming back together; it was easy to jump to the conclusion that it was about a soldier coming home just as his wife or sweetheart decides to leave him. It was precisely the flip side, literally (on Capitol 256) and conceptually of "Route 66." Alas, "Everyone Is Saying Hello" was precisely the sort of thing that no one wanted to hear in 1946. Again, Cole is taking chances, and not all risks pay off. But for one song on a record to be a hit was success enough. "Route 66" like "Straighten Up," was so popular it was picked up by the big bands—even London's Ted Heath, whose listeners could have had no idea where Route 66 itself was—and the song continued to be popular long after the highway was decommissioned in 1985. Route 66 may be gone, but Cole's record is still taking listeners on a journey.

Still, even for Cole, there were some hits that got away. In November 1944, Cole had first crack at a song by his close friend Redd Evans titled "There I've Said It Again." Capitol executive Jim Conkling remembered, "He asked two or three times, 'That's a terrific song, can't you get it out?' and I listened to it, or maybe Johnny Mercer did, or maybe Paul Weston. We kept listening to it and we didn't like Oscar's guitar solo, because it was out of tune, and we said 'Nat, we don't think you want that released.'" While Capitol hesitated, RCA released a record of the song by Vaughan Monroe, which became a career-making hit for the bombastic crooner-bandleader. As Conkling concluded, "It was a smash and Nat, really, for a while, never forgave us because his record would have been *the* big one."[81]

WE HAVE PROVIDENCE to thank, as well as the shamrock in Nat's back pocket—which is another way of saying Cole's own visionary intelligence—that the King Cole Trio came to Capitol just as the timing was perfect, and that Cole, Moore, and Miller stayed together for five incredibly productive, well-documented years. In 1944, Barry Ulanov was the first outsider to observe and document a Trio rehearsal, describing the process as "a sure-fingered, smooth, inevitable production of good music. They take a tune, they learn the melody. Then the three boys sit around and figure out the harmonic complement thereof and Nat writes down the notes."[82] Cole, as the leader, would offer some ideas that Miller and particularly Moore might play, and the other two men would refine and personalize them. "In half a day, a Cole Trio arrangement is established and made permanent in their repertoire."

A few months later, the *Cleveland Call and Post* elaborated, "The procedure is strictly Nat Cole. They take over a song and learn the melody and in the harmonic complement of the melodic variations, Nat does the writing down of the notes." Cole also works out who solos and who sings ("and all this is written down") and then "the boys put the song together the way it will be played on location," concluding, "And brother, when they play it, it is played."[83] These observations were justified not only by the Trio's Capitol releases (of which there were only two original singles by the end of 1944) and the MacGregor and Capitol Transcriptions, but in a small quantity of live performances that have survived. (These include some rather astounding remote broadcasts from the Circle Room at the Hotel LaSalle in Milwaukee from 1946, that were first issued in 1999).[84] Here, the connection between Cole and Moore was even more telepathic. "Oscar knows what I'm going to do before I do," said Nat.

That unity was threatened, when, to everyone's surprise in March 1944, Oscar, who was nobody's idea of a soldier, was actually drafted. *Down Beat* published a curious report that for three weeks, Moore's spot in the King Cole Trio was filled by clarinetist Heinie Beau, formerly with Tommy Dorsey and later a key deputy for Billy May. This almost has to be a mistake or even a typo: it seems impossible to imagine that Cole would have replaced Moore with a reed player and even less likely with a Caucasian one, something almost unimaginable in the dark days of the war. *Metronome* suggested that Cole would replace Moore with Ernest Ashley, a former schoolmate of the pianist's from Chicago. [85]. Whatever happened in that interval, thankfully, it was brief. Oscar lasted less than a month in the service, after which time he was given a medical discharge and returned to Cole's unit. The *California Eagle* trumpeted: "Let's all greet Oscar Moore who is back with the King Cole Trio!"[86]

Even so, the sea changes of spring 1944 would become something of a point of no return for the guitarist. He seems to have been most comfortable during the years 1940–44, at which point the money was certainly better than it had been in the very early days, the work was steady, and the gigs were long; while remaining in one place, there was nothing to do but concentrate on making the music better and better. From the start of the Capitol/Gastel era, the fees were proportionately higher, but the traveling was constant. Nat thrived on it; he seems to have relished every little step that he carefully planned in his steady, gradual conquest of the music world, but Oscar did not. From 1944 to his departure in 1947, Moore's attendance record would be increasingly sporadic, even if his performance record was anything but.

Clearly there was both tension and love between the two men; Moore was the first guy who "got" the basic idea that Cole was going for and then did more than anyone else to help him make it concrete. Where Cole himself was the dominant force behind the Trio and its guiding musical mind, Moore was much more than a secondary voice. As we've seen, he started on acoustic guitar, an instrument that must have driven transcription engineers crazy in the earliest days of the group as they tried to get a balance with this unfamiliar combination, but by the Decca sessions he had switched to electric. In fact, with the death of Charlie Christian and the ascendency of the King Cole Trio, Moore was, for a few key years, the preeminent guitarist in all of jazz—during an especially crucial period in which the swing era transitioned into bebop. He was already pioneering the use of such bop devices as the flatted fifth, heard most famously in "That Ain't Right" (1941) but also in "Got a Penny, Benny?" (1943). Moore's playing was coveted well beyond the Trio, by such diverse cultural icons as Art Tatum, Frankie Laine (who recruited Oscar for several early sessions), and Mickey Rooney. (The latter personally hired Moore to dub his on-screen guitar playing in the 1943 MGM musical *Girl Crazy*.)

Just as Cole started with his own influences, primarily Hines and Tatum, and then moved beyond them, so Moore started with Eddie Lang. (The only influences on the instrument he ever named were Lang and Charlie Christian, even though he couldn't have heard the latter until well after the KC3 had already been recording, and, as is obvious from "Black Spider Stomp," Django Reinhardt.) Like Christian, Moore tended toward single notes, and in this he and Cole were also highly compatible. On most classic Trio numbers, the opening melodic "heads" are primarily chordal, to give the group a fuller, more orchestral sound, but the solo improvisations on both piano and guitar were often expressed in single notes, not least to heighten the contrast between the ensemble parts and the individual solos.

Most guitarists of the big-band era—Count Basie's Freddie Greene was the archetype—restricted themselves to a solid four-to-the-beat approach in which the guitarist's role was almost strictly supportive and limited to rhythm. Moore, however, expanded the guitarist's options to providing very specific chordal underpinnings to what Cole was playing; and in doing so, he helped distinguish the Trio from a simple jam session group to something more like a true chamber music ensemble, and he explored many possibilities of expression that only became possible with the perfection of the electric instrument—they would have been all but inaudible on the acoustic guitar, especially if another instrument had been playing. Moore was the first guitarist to delve so deeply into this brave new world of harmonic possibilities, the first to explore chords, deconstruct and then reconstruct them with the same acuity as Coleman Hawkins, Tatum, or Cole.[87]

Moore was also extensively experimenting with chordal substitutions in a way that not only paralleled Cole but also such nascent beboppers as Dizzy Gillespie and Charlie Parker. Moore constructed groups of multiple tones that are perhaps better described as note clusters rather than full-blown chords, and he played with the placements of the traditional root, third, and fifth—replacing them with three notes that might only be a secondary interval apart rather than the traditional third. It may not sound like much on paper, but in the actual listening, the difference is significant, especially in the context of what is happening in the overall arrangement, as on the ending of "Vim Vom Veedle" (1942); what he's playing is an absolutely perfect match for what Cole is doing at the piano.

The move from swing to modernism is often perceived as a departure from melodic to harmonic improvisation, but nearly everything that Cole and Moore played was at the service of the melody, to exalt it rather than move beyond it. Moore uses the guitar in a way that would be impossible on the piano; he dents notes, bends them, and looks for hidden tones—like a blue third between B and B flat (in the key of G)—and more important, he connects the notes, striking one and then bending it so that it, in effect becomes a whole other note. Some of their best playing is on "Gee Baby, Ain't I Good to You" (1943) and "Body and Soul" (1944). On the first 16 bars of his solo on "Gee Baby," Moore uses a tremolo glissando to bridge notes together on a larger and more ambitious scale. The second half of his solo contains a soon-to-be-familiar pet phrase that stresses the 13th and 9th notes against the C7th chord (in the key of E flat).

Cole would play "Body and Soul" many times, but the 1944 Trio version is a masterpiece for both himself and Moore, consisting, simply of two exquisite choruses, one apiece on guitar and piano. In a reversal of their usual roles, it's Moore who opens and states the melody, and their mutual use of modernist chords makes the piece sound refreshing and new even seventy-five years later. Moore starts by playing the Johnny Green tune in a romantic ballad manner such as no string player had ever previously done, brilliantly setting up Cole's own solo. In the first few hearings, the most salient features of the iconic piano solo are the two famous quotes—from Grieg's "In the Hall of the Mountain King" in the second eight bars, then Benny Goodman's "Lullaby in Rhythm" closer to the coda; in fact, when we hear Johnny Green's actual "Body and Soul" melody, it lies on our ears rather like a quote. But in his improvisation, Cole plays around the melody in a way that makes you hear it in your head, even if it's only hinted at on the actual keyboard itself.

Sleek, solid, and supportive, Johnny Miller, for his part, was more than merely the third man. Miller was among the first bassists to reflect the pioneering work of Jimmy Blanton, and he was at his peak at the moment the bass emerged from the background and began to share the spotlight as a soloing instrument. Barry Ulanov wrote that Miller had much more presence in person than on the recordings: "You don't realize how fine Johnny is until you hear the Trio live"; "on location, he certainly stands out."[88] Miller was also described, rather gnomically, as the Trio's "one-man rhythm section": the two "horns," Cole and Moore, could go as far out as they wished in terms of harmonic adventuring or rhythmic daring because they knew Miller's sensitive-yet-strong support would never let them fall.

Miller is all over the map of the Trio's peak years and consistently plays in a way that allows him to express himself while at the same time underscoring the group's central narrative, as in "Come to Baby, Do" and the perfectly-capped coda to "No Moon at All." Entire generations of bassists would glean much from his example of supporting an ensemble while singularly swinging, as on "Jumpin' at Capitol," "I'm in the Mood for Love," "It Only Happens Once," "This Way Out," "I Want to Be Happy," and "Rhumba Azul." He solos more prominently on the spectacular "flag-waver" "I Know that You Know" and on some of the Trio's Basie-inspired titles (done mostly for transcriptions), like "Swingin' the Blues" and "One O'Clock Jump." During Miller's last year in the group, Cole gave him a feature in "Breezy and the Bass" (in the 1948 feature film *Killer Diller*), one of their least disguised variations on "I Got Rhythm," in which Cole makes a grand show out of not playing the piano and letting Miller have the spotlight to himself.

Cole later said, "You have no idea how much satisfaction I got from the acceptance of the Trio, because we opened the way for countless other small groups, units that before were strictly for cocktail lounges."[89] Indeed, the Trio was so influential that such ensembles as blues master Willie Dixon's Big Three and vibraphone virtuoso Red Norvo's Trio, with guitarist Tal Farlow and bassist Charlie Mingus, as well as groups led by pianists Page Cavanaugh and Phil Moore, were created in the KC3's image, as were still later groups led by Oscar Peterson and Ahmad Jamal. "They fit hand-in-glove like three guys who have been together a long time and like it. And that's exactly the way things are," an anonymous newspaperman observed in 1947, "although the King Cole Trio is probably the most valuable—per man—musical organization in the world, they have worked all these many years without a contract."[90]

Indeed, this Trio was so perfect that when the edges began to fray, after Moore left in 1947 (he waited until the tenth anniversary of the group's original formation) and then Miller a year later (both leaving after the arrival of Nat's second wife, Maria), it was inevitable that Cole would be motivated to go into a whole new direction. He had already created the perfect blend of jazz, pop, blues, and even classical music with Moore and Miller, and to try to scale those particular heights again would have been, at worst, impossible, and at best, both pointless and redundant.

OSCAR HAD SPENT ONLY THREE WEEKS in the army in March 1944, but when he returned, the changes were happening so fast that it must have given him whiplash. As we've seen, the Trio took to the road, starting in April with the Orpheum (Los Angeles) and the Golden Gate Theater (San Francisco), and then, over summer and fall 1944, they hit at least eighteen theaters (that we know of) in an extended tour with Benny Carter's Orchestra. In the fall, they made a triumphant return to New York, where they played the mecca for African American music, the Apollo Theater on West 125th Street. The black press noted with irony that New York had "snubbed" them when they played 52nd Street three years earlier (not exactly true), but now, "Frank Schiffman, managing director of the Apollo, has asked for extra police guards to hold the expected crowds in line."[91] By early December, as predicted, the papers were proclaiming that the combination of the Trio and Carter's Orchestra had "smashed every known house record and drew the biggest gross in the history of the Apollo." They were attracting "long queues of fans daily with lines assembling as early as 9:30 in the morning."[92]

It was at the Apollo that they were approached by an aspiring composer named Marvin Fisher. Fisher later remembered, "I was an arranger for a lot of the big bands, and I played some things, that I had written, for Stan Kenton. Stan said, 'I don't know if they're so great for the band, but there's a guy up at the Apollo. No one knows him, but he's going to be the biggest star in the world.' So, I went up and introduced myself."[93]

By that, Kenton meant that few in the white world were yet aware of him—in the mainstream music business, Fisher's own family was probably better known at this point. The Fishers were among the most abundantly prolific brood of songwriters ever: twenty years earlier, their father Fred Fisher was responsible for several of the more familiar standards of the jazz age, like "Chicago" and "Dardanella"; little brother Dan Fisher had received a co-credit on the Billie Holiday classic, "Good Morning Heartache" and sister Doris was one of the authors of "Whispering Grass"—not to mention "Fla-Ga-La-Pa."

Among the earliest songs that Fisher brought to Cole was "How Does It Feel?," which the Trio recorded on December 4, 1945.[94] It would be the first of about twenty songs by Marvin Fisher that Cole would perform over the next two decades. "How Does It Feel?" had everything Cole looked for in a song: a simple title that spun off a familiar expression, and in the form of a question, which gave it a tentative, yearning quality. The lyrics (by Roy Alfred) are straightforward, setting up a comparatively gentle narrative of retribution, vaguely along the same lines as "Goody, Goody" and "Cry Me a River," but considerably more compassionate: "How does it feel, when you find that your dreams are through? / How does it feel, when you know that the laugh's on you?" The melody is set in an ABAB pattern, slightly unusual for the time, but it is both memorable and straightforward, and the chords are attractive and inspired, the kind that Cole could work with. Over the years, the songs Fisher brought to Cole would be primarily beautiful ballads (none more so than "When Sunny Gets Blue"), but also swingers like "Destination Moon" and a few outright novelties, like "When Rock and Roll Come to Trinidad."

"How Does It Feel?" was one of the many unique love songs that Cole performed in the peak Trio years; we might deem them "custom ballads," since for the most part they seem to have been written either specifically for Cole or by him directly. With some exceptions, Cole wasn't relying on Capitol to bring him songs; he was generating them himself by cultivating a select group of songwriters and publishers whom he had acclimated to giving him first crack at their material. In the early days at Capitol, Cole's sessions were produced by Johnny Mercer for the first year or two, then arranger and friend Paul Weston and future label president Jim Conkling, while veteran guitarist Carl Kress and Walter Rivers (who happened to be Mercer's cousin) supervised some of the sessions in New York. Later, around 1951, he began a full-time artist-producer relationship with Lee Gillette, and this would last until the end of both of their careers.

Most big bands and more traditional pop singers worked with artists and repertoire (A&R) men, who, among other things, steered them toward a steady stream of new songs that were called, in the parlance of the day, "plug" tunes. These generally included many new songs by well-established composers, your Richard Rodgerses, your Harry Warrens, your Johnny Mercers and Irving Berlins, from new Broadway shows and Hollywood movie musicals. Capitol artists like Peggy Lee and Jo Stafford recorded plenty of these, but Cole virtually never recorded a new song from a show or film in all of the Trio period—even those by Mercer. For whatever reason, black artists (the same was largely true for Louis Armstrong and Ella Fitzgerald) were excluded from this pecking order.

Incredibly, Cole seems to have recorded only two new film or show songs in all of the 1943–47 period, and they were both written by the team of Johnny Burke and Jimmy Van Heusen for Bing Crosby, "If You Stub Your Toe on the Moon," from *A Connecticut Yankee in King Arthur's Court* (released in 1949) and "Harmony," from *Variety Girl* (1947). Cole was growing especially close to these two songwriters and would follow their lead as publishing moguls: in 1947, he and Gastel would launch a music publishing company administered by Burke-Van Heusen Music, and Nat and Johnny would be especially close friends for the rest of their lives.

Yet even though Cole was cut off from a major source of potential hits, his output hardly suffered. By the mid-1940s, he had gathered around him a first-rate coterie of composers, of whom Marvin Fisher was merely the most remarkable. He was turning so many of their songs into successful recordings, and even chart hits, that all of them were eager to give him first refusal on anything they wrote.

Ruth Poll is typical of the composers whom Cole supported and recorded. Little is known about her other than a mention in Maria Cole's book that she was a guest at the wedding of Maria and Nat in 1948 and presented the bride with "an exquisitely beautiful handkerchief that had been part of her daughter's trousseau at her own wedding."[95] Nat had been recording her songs since at least 1945, a year before he even met Maria. Poll wrote several sentimental ballads for him, namely, "If Yesterday Could Only Be Tomorrow" (1945) and "It Was So Good While It Lasted" (1949), as well two more bouncy numbers, "I'd Love to Make Love to You" (1945) and "Those Things Money Can't Buy" (1947). Of the four, the gem is "I'd Love to Make Love to You," one of many extremely catchy Trio songs in which Cole manages to be extremely sweet and irresistibly rhythmic at the same time. It didn't make the charts, but even seventy years later one can sense the song's hit potential. I know of only one Poll song recorded by another artist ("A New Shade of Blue" by Ella Fitzgerald in 1949); still, trying to make an objective judgment regarding the quality of Poll's songs is difficult because Cole brings so much to them and makes them sound so good.

"I'd Love to Make Love to You" is delightful, and made even more so by Cole's unique talent for dreaming up distinctive introductions, of which "Straighten Up and Fly Right" is merely the most famous. Nearly every KC3 number from the glory years has an intro riff that's at the very least as good as the central melody that follows it. Clearly Cole inspired his future collaborator, Nelson Riddle, as well as the younger pianist Erroll Garner, in this technique of starting all songs, both new and classic, with a distinctive, original intro.

In addition to Fisher and Poll, there were also Roy Alfred, who wrote the words to "Fla-Ga-La-Pa" and most of Fisher's songs of this period, including "How Does It Feel?," and Redd Evans, the man whom Anita O'Day credited with teaching her the importance of swinging riffs (and who wrote "Let Me Off Uptown" for her and Gene Krupa). Evans wrote the ballads, "There I've Said it Again," "You Should Have Told Me," and "I've Only Myself to Blame," for Cole as well as the riff numbers, "Slow Down," "The Frim Fram Sauce," and "No Moon at All." Jack Segal wrote the words to "A Boy from Texas, a Girl from Tennessee," the aforementioned lovely (if miscalculated), "Everyone Is Saying Hello Again," and "That's the Kind of Girl I Dream Of" in the Trio era, and later, when he teamed with Fisher, "Something Happens to Me," "When Sunny Gets Blue," and "I Keep Goin' Back to Joe's," all of which are mature Cole masterpieces. Another was Lorenzo Pack, a former prizefighter, who wrote "You Must Be Blind"[96] and years later, "Cherchez La Femme." And then there was lyricist Don George, who collaborated on several important songs with both Cole and Duke Ellington.

Some of these "custom ballads" are happier or sadder than others, but they're all relatively down tempo and pivot around very direct and simple ideas, especially melodically and lyrically; there's nothing like "Begin the Beguine" or "Lush Life" here. Ultimately, it's a minor flip of a switch between happy and sad. All these songs are a mix of emotions, in which Cole is empowered by the simplicity of the texts rather than constricted by them—a fancier lyric or a more profound metaphor might just get in his way. These songs aren't necessarily sentimental but they're all ineffably romantic, and a disproportionate number of them went on to become favorites of musicians and singers close to Cole, like Tony Bennett, Buddy Greco, and Cole's brother Freddy.

As early as 1944, Cole was charting with ballads like these—his own "I Can't See for Lookin'," "I Realize Now," and "I'm Lost" all landed in the top ten of the "Race" (R&B) charts in 1944. There was one other advantage to concentrating on songs like these; when a new Cole Porter or Irving Berlin song came out, usually one from a new show, the other bandleaders and singers were lining up to do it. When Cole did a song by one of the writers in his own personal posse, he pretty much had an exclusive. Other artists on other labels could pounce on it, but by the time Cole's record got on the charts, it was hard to catch up with him. Through all these circumstances, it was rare that the Trio would be competing with other artists on the same song.[97] In the philosophy of 21st-century business avatar Peter Thiel, Cole was not "competing"; rather, he was establishing a monopoly (or a series of monopolies), and, as Thiele would concur, this is an example of how a monopoly can be a good thing.

Ballads were increasingly important to Cole, and even though he sang some very substantial ones in the early to mid-1940s—"This Will Make You Laugh," "Embraceable You," and "Sweet Lorraine," to name a few—he would take the idea up a substantial notch in 1946. This itself was a risky path at the time. "They weren't ready for black singers singing love songs," Cole's contemporary, Billy Eckstine, recalled in 1984. "It sounds ridiculous, but it's true. We weren't supposed to sing about love, we were supposed to sing about work or blues or some dumb crap."[98]

Cole realized early on that singing romantic and mature love songs would take him further than the jive numbers ever could. As we'll soon see, 1946 would be an even bigger breakthrough year for the Trio on the mainstream pop charts, with six discs in the top twenty, including "Route 66" at #11 in June, and then, in November, he landed his two most successful singles yet, "For Sentimental Reasons" and "The Christmas Song." Again, they both came to Cole through a highly personal path rather than the customary channels (publisher-to-song plugger-to-label-to-A&R man-to-artist) and they both would amount to very serious game-changers in Cole's career.

IN ADDITION TO RECORDING "commercial" 78s for Capitol, starting in 1943, and radio-only transcriptions for MacGregor in 1944 and '45, the King Cole Trio also dispensed some of its magic to a number of Hollywood (and other) movie producers, of which Republic Pictures was merely the first. Cole was, apparently, so grateful to get his first shot in a motion picture that he allowed Hollywood to dress him, Oscar, and Johnny as porters and bartenders. As soon as they've finished playing "Straighten Up and Fly Right," star Al Pearce hands Cole his card and tells him, "Say, that was swell, boys, I may be able to use an act like that on my radio program. Why don't you look me up sometime. Here's my card." Cole brushes him off, saying, "Thanks just the same, Mr. Pearce, but somebody's got to run these railroads." Everybody laughs.

This might just be the single most humiliating moment in all of Cole's film career; the implication is twofold: these colored folks are too simple to realize the opportunity that they're being given, and this particular porter is so naïve that he actually thinks his job is important to the railroad company. It's a truly cringe-inducing moment, for all the magnificence of the music that we have just heard. Pearce's smile is particularly condescending; he seems to be saying, "Why, they're just like children."

From what we know of Cole's feelings on the subject, he too was clearly cringing but was willing to suck it up to get this first real shot in a major motion picture, and especially to have his song heard. We know this not least from an anecdote from Dave Dexter: "Nat burst angrily into my office one day in 1944. He was shouting, waving his arms wildly, and was obviously overwrought emotionally." Cole was upset over a piece of promotional art that had gone out to record stores advertising the Trio's latest single. "It looks like an old-fashioned pickaninny," he said; "that drawing is an insult, man. You ought to be as ashamed of it as I am." Like many jazz fans, Dexter was an early advocate for integration and racial equality, and while he couldn't see what Cole found so offensive, he conceded that "offending Nat had wounded me deeply."[99]

Cole had no reservations about clowning, but he refused to be presented like a clown—as distinct from Louis Armstrong and Louis Jordan, who indulged in out-and-out vaudeville, with costumes and props. Contrastingly, Cole could sing the most nonsensical songs, but he would never take the stage in anything less formal than a business suit or a tuxedo. In that sense, he had it both ways—essentially dignified but with a keen sense of fun. It must have deeply wounded Cole to be expected to dress up like a menial while a patronizing white man addressed him repeatedly as "boy," much the same way that we know that it hurt him to be forced to play for segregated houses. But at least he could do something about his film roles, and he would never submit himself to such a demeaning depiction again. In all of their successive on-screen appearances, the Trio is presented with considerably more dignity.

Before the war was over, the Trio would appear in four more features, all low-budget musicals: *Pistol Packin' Mama* (also 1943, Republic Pictures), *Stars on Parade* and *Swing in the Saddle* (both released in 1944 by Columbia Pictures), and *See My Lawyer* (1945, Universal Pictures). In nearly all of their cinematic appearances, the Trio is allowed to perform in the same well-tailored business suits that they traditionally wore at club appearances—that is, with two exceptions. In *See My Lawyer*, they're wearing chef's outfits; however, the Trio segment ("The Man on the Little White Keys" and "Fuzzy Wuzzy") transpires in the middle of a larger sequence of numbers in the middle of a circus number in a supper club, and everyone is wearing something silly. The group is introduced by a clown, and a featured female dancer is wearing what might be called a sexy chicken costume. Thus, the Trio doesn't look any more ridiculous than the rest of the cast; the goofiness of the garb can hardly be described as racially motivated. Likewise, *Swing in the Saddle* is a grade B musical western, and here the men are wearing comparatively high-class shiny-satin Western shirts—anticipating Cleavon Little in *Blazing Saddles* (1974). The costumes may be a bit silly, but they are not at all undignified; the major question is why Columbia had them reprise their vintage 1940 arrangement of Harry Warren's "By the River St. Marie" instead of some kind of a western song.

In general, the Trio's performances in these early features are all excellent. *Stars on Parade* (recorded and filmed in early 1944), for instance, has the Trio playing "Hit that Jive, Jack," but in an arrangement that had been much updated and evolved from 1941 (when they recorded it). "Hit that Jive, Jack" begins with a characteristically distinctive intro, Cole playing a repeated note on top of a repeated riff pattern from Moore, before they lunge into the tune, playing it at several tempos, frequently changing speeds, like gears shifting in an automobile. At one point they reduce the song to one line, "Hit that jive, Jack . . . put it in your pocket," which they repeat over and over, and then they stop time entirely, allowing Cole to talk-sing the bridge in solo. The lyrics are pure scatty nonsense, almost like something a little girl would chant while skipping rope ("I'm going downtown to a see a man / And I ain't got time to shake your hand") but it becomes a tour-de-force of rhythmic virtuosity and musical invention. Cole, Moore, and Miller even make adroit use of the cinematic medium, with several visual cues—at one point while telling us to put it in our pocket, Cole opens his suit jacket and shows us the interior pocket; near the coda, at the last mention of hitting that jive, the music stops again, just long enough for the three men to high-five each other. (It's also wonderfully filmed by director Lew Landers, framed by an interaction with a drunken Larry Parks.) The 1941 Decca version seems like a meager stepchild by comparison, one that only hints at the fully realized exuberance of this 1944 film performance.

Pistol Packin' Mama features the Trio in another "I Got Rhythm" variation, Cole's own "I'm an Errand Boy for Rhythm." It's only 1:40 minutes long, but that's all that Cole, Moore, and Prince need to blow us away. The Trio rips through at an even faster clip than on the Capitol version, and here the three men look especially good: Cole's piano has a mirrored surface, so he appears to be playing with four hands—and sounds as if he is, as well. Again, there are brief but welcome interludes by Miller and Moore. In *See My Lawyer*, a Universal picture starring the inspired, anarchic, and highly manic comedy duo of Ole Olsen and Chick Johnson, they somehow squeeze two quick numbers into a sequence that lasts all of 2:42 minutes, "The Man on the Little

White Keys" and "Fuzzy Wuzzy." The majority of the songs that the Trio performed in these early films are what might be described as advertisements for themselves: they're not necessarily "about" anything; "Errand Boy" is about how dedicated Cole and his Trio-mates are to the higher concept of rhythm, and most of these numbers are saying little more than that. And although one feels silly describing something as intellectually lightweight as "The Man on the Little White Keys" as "self-reflective," it is just that, a man playing the piano and singing,telling us about a man playing the piano and singing. "Fuzzy Wuzzy" is another dark-skinned diva in the Cole Trio tradition of "Honey Hush" and "Babs"; in "Fuzzy Wuzzy—she's just a fly little hussy," the lyric (presumably by Cole) enumerates the girl's talents: she can do "the flat foot floogie and the Susie-Q."

The Trio isn't given nearly as good a visual presentation in the seven Soundies that they made in 1943 and 1945. The Soundies company was the most successful producer of three-minute films for viewing in bars and restaurants on a jukebox-like device—for a dime a throw—called a "Panoram." The company (actually a network of producers and acquired companies) officially started in 1940, when the technology was ready, thrived during World War II, and then lasted until 1946–47, when television began to make inroads. The Soundies were particularly notable in that every genre of popular music was extensively covered—thousands of the three-minute, one-song films were made—and African American performers were especially well represented.

Cole made his first two Soundies during an interesting stop-gap moment in his career: in December 1943, when the Trio was about to become a huge hit, but nobody knew it yet. These two titles were a direct outgrowth of the commercial transcriptions he was cutting at the time for the MacGregor company, specifically backing up vocalist Ida James. Although only twenty-three at the time, she had already worked and toured extensively with both Erskine Hawkins and Cole's mentor, Earl "Fatha" Hines. James has a high-pitched singing voice that reminded some of a bird, and it was a sound very much in keeping with the nascent rhythm-and-blues era. Both her sound and her look also anticipate Eartha Kitt, though without the latter's high style, but overall she is both coy and appealing.[100] With the Trio, she sings "Is You Is or Is You Ain't (Ma Baby)" with Cole, who, one imagines, was less than thrilled at being asked to cover a Louis Jordan hit. Their other number is the Trio's latest nursery rhyme variation, "Who's Been Eating My Porridge?," and she livens it up with the request, "you better tell her to straighten up and fly right." It was mighty sporting of Miss James to throw that in, considering that the record was then months away from being released.

The 1943 Soundies with Ida James were filmed in Los Angeles and look like they could have been made by a poverty row studio—not exactly luxurious but at least legitimate. At this point, the Trio had already recorded their first dates for Capitol, and the tracks were about to be released. Two years later, in November 1945, their status had been considerably upgraded, not least as a result of their steady stream of hits from Capitol. In fall 1945, they were part of a touring package playing movie theaters with Andy Kirk's Orchestra across the East Coast, when a last-minute offer came in from the Copacabana (possibly some other act had canceled). So the Trio begged off the final week or so of the theater tour[101] and began a three-week run at the 60th Street "nite spot" that was already the most famous in the country, as indeed it had been almost since the day of its opening almost exactly five years earlier. It was only the Copa Cocktail Lounge (the legendary Joe E. Lewis was headlining in the main room), but still, it was the Copa. This would be the first of dozens of engagements of Cole at the Copa going up to the last year of his life.

During that first Copa run in November 1945, the Trio also shot five titles for the Soundies Corporation at the FilmCraft Studios in the Bronx. Considering that the Trio was now by far the most popular jazz or black act in the country, it's shocking how shoddy these productions look—much more so than the 1943 entries filmed in Hollywood. Not only are the production values distinctly inferior, but too much of the visual action is taken up by some rather unnecessary and none-too-attractive chorus girls.[102] "Come to Baby Do" and "I'm a Shy Guy" are both set in what looks like a hunting lodge; "Errand Boy for Rhythm" (which, visually, is much inferior to the way the song was filmed in the Republic *Pistol Packin' Mama*) and "Got a Penny, Benny" transpire in a something like a small club set, on a bandstand in the first and in front of stage curtains in the second—although Lord only knows why Cole chose to bring back the forgettable "Penny Benny" at this point, especially when such Trio masterpieces as "Sweet Lorraine" and "Paper Moon" had yet to be filmed.

The most interesting—and the most "meta"—of the five is "Frim Fram Sauce." Here, Nat is "discovered" singing the 1945 novelty hit while seated in a cafe, trying to catch the attention of a distracted waitress. During the instrumental break, Cole turns his head and gazes into a Soundies Panoram player on the other side of the venue, and after seeing himself and the Trio on the screen, the two Coles have some interaction with each other. As I say, it's all very meta. In the last shot, as per Cole's spoken tag, the waiter actually does present him with a "check for the water."

IN SPRING 1946, Cole gave a curiously defensive interview that ran in *The Capitol*, the label's own internal house organ.[103] Frank Stacy, at that time the New York editor of *Down Beat* magazine, seems to have caught him with his guard down, and for one of the only times in his career, Nat rather severely criticizes his own work. "Don't you guys think I ever get sick of playing those dog tunes every night?" he asks Stacy. However, in looking over what the Trio recorded for Capitol and what we know they were playing on the radio and in personal appearances, we have to wonder what in the world he was talking about.

Not everything the Trio recorded in these pinnacle years is as good as everything else, but there's nothing that could be described as a "dog tune." Virtually nothing seems to have been foisted on Cole by a song-plugging publisher or an A&R man; almost everything is from a source close to the artist—many are from Cole's developing circle of songwriters and a few are by the pianist-singer himself.

In tallying up the numbers, we see that Cole recorded roughly forty upbeat novelties in 1943–48 and a roughly equivalent number of Great American Standards, like "I'm in the Mood for Love" by Jimmy McHugh and Dorothy Fields; "I Don't Know Why (I Just Do)," another vintage Russ Columbo number; "Smoke Gets in Your Eyes," Jerome Kern's classic; and "You're the Cream in My Coffee," by Capitol co-founder Buddy DeSylva, among other standards. This was far from a personal indulgence on the part of the pianist; these songs were loved by his audience almost as much as the new songs, and some, like "It's Only a Paper Moon" and "You Call It Madness," actually charted.

Among other irreplaceable standards he played in these amazing years, there's also "The Man I Love" (1944) done in the same rough mold as "Embraceable You" but strictly as an instrumental, and an amazing tour-de-force treatment of "What Is This Thing Called Love" (1944). Here, he plays possum with Moore, allowing the guitarist to dazzle us with some breathtaking runs, but then he plays an even more spectacular piano solo himself; the ending "head" and the coda are more satisfying still. (There's also a more expansive Capitol Transcription of the Porter song from 1946.) Cole essayed four Irving Berlin tunes: "How Deep Is the Ocean" (1946), "What'll I Do?" (1947), "I Never Had a Chance" (1947), and "After You Get What You Want, You Don't Want It" (1944 and 1946). (The last two tunes never quite attained standard status, even though Marilyn Monroe herself revived the second one ten years later in *There's No Business Like Show Business*.) No wonder Irving Berlin loved him, and the two were already on a first-name basis by 1947, when the legendary songwriter tried to buy the publishing rights to "Nature Boy" from Cole.

Classic songbook standards proliferate all over Cole's canon, at every stage of his career, but especially at the very time of that somewhat suspicious 1946 interview. That was also the year that Capitol launched its own commercial transcription service, and Cole recorded yet more standards for Capitol Transcriptions. Among other unique numbers he cut for Capitol's ET (electrical transcription) line was Harold Arlen and Ted Koehler's "I've Got the World on a String," well before it became a standard of any kind, anticipating Sinatra's groundbreaking 1953 version by half a generation. Other songs sounded so good on Capitol Transcriptions that he remade them for commercial release, like "Too Marvelous for Words," virtually the only song he recorded in this period with words by Mercer (and the famous melody by Richard Whiting).

As the war ended, there were less than a handful of major pop music stars who had expressed a notable interest in what were then considered older songs—essentially it boiled down to Artie Shaw, Sinatra, and Cole. It may have seemed to some that they were immersed in nostalgia by investing so much of their energy in songs that were a generation old, and thus less likely to get on Lucky Strike's *Your Hit Parade* or the *Billboard* charts. But instead, these performers turned out to be remarkably prescient; in the coming decades, much of both jazz and popular music would be even more intertwined with these classic songs. In fact, these songs would provide the perfect content for new entertainment mediums that were emerging at this time, specifically long-playing records and television. In dwelling on this aspect of the past, Nat Cole was helping to invent the future.

The move into those new technologies was only one of many changes that took effect starting in 1946. It's probably not a coincidence that he was making changes in his music just at the same time he was making them in his personal and romantic life. As we have seen and will continue to see again, Cole's life and music were pretty much in constant flux, but in 1946 the rate of change began to accelerate. As new doors opened, others didn't exactly slam shut; it's just that Nat went through them a lot less frequently than he had in his earlier days. Beginning in 1946, Cole would experiment with many new ways, in his own words, to expand the scope of the Trio.

In the April 1946 interview, Cole also takes the opportunity to express his continuing commitment to jazz. In response to critics who were even then accusing him of "fluffing off jazz," Cole states, rather vehemently, "I'm even more interested in it now than I ever was. And the trio is going to play plenty of it." The ironic thing about this conversation is that Cole had been actively and aggressively making jazz records from 1942 to 1946, but because of various factors, few of his fans—or anyone else—were even aware of it. The tale of Cole's "other" career, as a gigging jazz pianist rather than the leader and star of his own group, is a story unto itself.

3

Interlude

NAT AND NORMAN: THE "JAM SESSIONS," 1942–1946

"And Now a Little Piano": "Shorty Nadine," "Sam Schmaltz," "Lord Calvert," and "Aye Guy."

Nat was primarily a pianist, you know, first. He never got away from that, really. Inside of him, he was a pianist.
—JOHN COLLINS, 1990

WHO KNEW GARRY MOORE was such a knowledgeable jazz buff? Unlike, say, Jack Benny or Sid Caesar (who both played host to Nat Cole on their long-running variety shows), Moore is not one of the more celebrated comedians from the golden age of television. Today, Moore (1915–1993) is best remembered for the company he kept, including such undisputed comedy legends as Jimmy Durante and Carol Burnett. Yet in his time, the various series that he hosted, almost continually from 1950 to 1967, were some of the highest-rated shows of the era.

On April 4, 1961, the primary guest on *The Garry Moore Show* (CBS) was Nat King Cole. In addition to singing "Wild Is Love" and "Illusion," Cole chats with the comedian-host in a manner that's meant to be at least semi-extemporaneous—and uncomfortable. Garry starts quizzing Nat about a series of recordings he made many years earlier, released under what Moore calls "fake names." Nat expresses surprise that Garry knows about this part of his career at all, and he also acts as though he'd just as soon not talk about it—especially on national television. ("I don't remember anything—I wasn't supposed to do it!")

But Garry persists, and together they reveal to the world that Nat made "instrumental" recordings (as a non-singing jazz piano player) for a variety of different labels because he was under an exclusive contract to one unmentioned record company as a singer—an oversimplification, but essentially true. Moore extracts maximum comic mileage out of the silliness of just two of these fake names: "Sam Schmaltz" and "Lord Calvert." ("I know that label well," says Moore, referring to the famous brand of whiskey.) For a punchline, Nat tells Garry he's still ill at ease discussing any of this, so he asks the host to announce him under a pseudonym: "Harry Belafonte." Big laugh.

Viewed today, it's a very funny two minutes of patter, perhaps the most real and authentic moment in all of Cole's variety show appearances. But to audiences in 1961, it must have opened up a major mystery without coming close to solving it. Why was the most popular singer of his generation, the man with the most easily identifiable voice, making records under the name "Sam Schmaltz?" "That's a real true story," says Moore. " 'Sam Schmaltz!' You know what 'schmaltz' means in Jewish? Chicken fat! 'The romantic voice of Sam Chicken Fat.' "[1]

TO ANSWER THAT QUESTION, we have to go back to a photograph published almost twenty years earlier in New York's major Negro newspaper, the *Amsterdam News*. In May 1942, the paper informed readers about a series of informal, Sunday afternoon jam sessions at the Village Vanguard on New York's Lower West Side. The dates were produced by the aspiring impresario Harry Lim, described as "a diminutive Javanese swing pundit," and the musicians include drummer J. C. Heard, tenor saxophonist Joe Thomas, clarinetist Albert Nicholas, bassist Billy Taylor, guitarist Al Casey, saxophonist Gene Sedric, not to mention a pianist identified in the caption only as "King Cole." In looking at this picture, it's easy to see that the two men who seem happiest to be part of it are the youngest, namely, Lim and Cole.[2]

The photo—alas, no recordings of these sessions are known to exist—tells us two things. First, it shows the degree to which Cole was accepted by his peers as a leading jazz musician: these are all hardcore players with years of experience in major bands, and both Cole and Lim look delighted to be in their company. For these venerated veterans to accept Cole, who had never done what they had done, or paid those particular kinds of dues, as one of their own, was remarkable.

Second, we also know that the Trio was working like crazy at this point, at various clubs both in the Village (Jimmy Kelly's) and Swing Street in Midtown (the Onyx Club). He was easily playing six nights a week, and, as we know, practicing for several hours every day. For him to participate in jam sessions, to work for nothing or next to it, shows us, yet again, that he just couldn't get enough of the piano. In addition to which, the jam sessions gave him something that he couldn't get from the King Cole Trio, the chance to blow off a different kind of steam. For the most part, the Trio's music was about pleasing the audience, but the extra-curricular sessions he played in, partially documented on a series of recordings made from 1942 to 1946, gave him the chance to play when he only had to worry about pleasing himself.

As a pianist, he fully embodied what might be the greatest moment in all of jazz: that transitional period when the swing era evolved into bebop and modern jazz. Cole's playing inhabits both worlds at once—the melodic pleasure of the first combined with the harmonic profundity of the second, and the joys common to both, an outstanding sense of rhythm, well beyond the call of duty, and a propensity for the blues.

Cole's use of advanced harmonies places him firmly in the pantheon of the beboppers; in fact, some of his recordings contain the earliest examples of musical devices that later became standard tropes of modern jazz piano. For example, the 1944 "Easy Listening Blues," as Dick Katz pointed out, utilizes the "B-flat major seventh and C minor seventh suspension" (bar 3) as well as the "descending minor seventh" (bar 8).[3] This is harmonic sophistication on a level with say, Bud Powell, who was probably the archetypical modern jazz pianist (the one most widely imitated at the time). Yet Cole never plays with the same degree of abstraction as Powell; the beboppers were very melodic players, but it was almost always their own original melodies that they were improvising on familiar chord changes. Cole, conversely, was always driven by the idea of exalting the written melody—"selling the tune"—sometimes refurbishing the original chord changes in the process.

Cole's biggest piano influences were Earl Hines and then Art Tatum, and like all jazz musicians, he was deeply moved by Louis Armstrong; gradually, as a vocalist, he absorbed a lot from Frank Sinatra, an influence that went both ways. But as an overall musician, one of his key role models was obviously the saxophone colossus Lester Young; Cole would have been familiar with Young's work even before he began working with the saxophonist's younger brother, drummer Lee Young. It wasn't only Lester's subtle, understated, and yet sublimely swinging approach to a tune that so inspired Cole; it was the saxophonist's overwhelming, abundant lyricism. Young famously said that he couldn't play a song without knowing the lyrics to it, and so, in effect, he was playing the words as well as the music; this could have also been Cole's mantra, and in much of the best of his music, with and without the Trio, he is constantly doing both at the same time; he is singing even when his mouth is closed, and he is playing even when he's not so much as touching the keyboard.

As historian Loren Schoenberg has said, if you want to know all about Nat Cole as a pure jazz piano player, you don't have to go any further than the two studio sessions that he and Young did together, in 1942 and 1946. Their *sympatico* styles were fully in evidence as early as the summer of 1942, a date that opens with the 1917 jazz standard, "(Back Home Again in) Indiana." Other musicians would ransack the tune for its chord changes (Miles Davis transformed it into the bebop standard "Donna Lee"), but when Young plays it, he's not focusing on the harmonic progressions; he's dreaming about the moonlight on the Wabash. And so is Cole. They're longing for their Indiana home, and, moreover, they're doing so in a way that causes us to long for it too.

Just as Cole created two distinct overall identities, pianist-leader and singer-star, his piano work also falls into two categories: Cole the master arranger-composer, represented in the classic Trio set pieces, which had been carefully honed to perfection in live performance by the time they were recorded, and Cole the freewheeling improviser, as heard in the jam sessions and most especially the live recording of the first Jazz at the Philharmonic (JATP) concert in July 1944.

Cole's piano playing with the Trio is intrinsically different from his playing in the jam sessions, yet there's never any doubt that the artist in both of these settings is the same musician. In all cases, Cole plays with a crystalline touch that makes the melodies never less than exquisitely clear. It was also the extremely vocalized line; you can always hear the songwriter's original tune, yet Cole completely makes it his own, in both the Trio and the jam session contexts. His singing and his piano work were direct counterparts of each other; in fact, when he sings one of his great mature ballads like "The Very Thought of You" and "But Beautiful," it's a use of space that only a great artist has—the notes never seem crowded or distorted, and the meaning of the text is never ambiguous, except when it's supposed to be as a dramatic device. Cole shows us that melody and meaning are the key components, forever enhancing each other.

Whether playing or singing, Cole is a musical Albert Einstein, who proved again and again that time and space are the same thing.

AS WE'VE SEEN, in his primary career, Cole was always the leader, the star, and the focal point of whatever musical situation he was in; he was never a sideman. Even during his decade-long collaboration with the brilliant Oscar Moore, there was never any doubt as to who was in charge. That's the other unique aspect of his non-trio sessions of the mid-1940s: these are the only documents of Cole playing with his peers in the jazz world; the very idea of a dominant leader was inapposite to the setting; everybody gets an equal part of the action. The amazing thing is that Cole was so busy with the Trio, particularly during the peak Capitol years (1943–1947), it's a wonder he had time to do anything else, between constantly touring, recording, and broadcasting. Yet the purely jazz sessions he made in these same years, though not nearly as numerous, are an invaluable part of his legacy.

It would be Carlos Gastel and then Nat's second wife, Maria, who would encourage the so-called commercial side of Cole's music; but even before then, it was Norman Granz who helped Cole to realize this other side of his musical mind, the purely jazz side. In turn, it was Nat who helped Norman realize his ambition to become one of the most successful concert and record producers of all time, that rare impresario who would do much to transform the shape of the music itself. Bassist Red Callender, who worked with Cole on several occasions, remembered that he was playing at the Capri club, at Pico and La Cienga, the first time that he noticed Norman. "A young college student used to come in frequently. He always wore sneakers, dressed casually, was of medium height and build, and had light sandy hair. By day he worked as a film cutter at MGM, by night he was a fixture on the jazz scene, particularly at the 331 Club. This unassuming young man was to have a profound effect on the world of jazz."[4]

Half a year older than Cole, Granz was born and raised in California, where he was attracted to jazz (and to what later became known as the Great American Songbook) from an early age. He was frequenting clubs around Los Angeles in 1938–39, at the same time the King Cole Trio was working in the same area, but, for whatever reason, they never encountered each other until fall 1941, when both were in New York. Granz was then between two hitches with the armed forces and the Trio was playing Kelly's Stable on Swing Street, sharing a bill with saxophonist Pete Brown's band and the legendary Art Tatum, playing solo.

By June 1942, Nat and Norman were both back in Los Angeles, and over the next four years or so, the two became very close. "In the beginning of my jazz career, the man most responsible for my success was, without question, Nat Cole." As Granz later remembered, "Not only was he inextricably tied in my professional mode, but he became my best friend and mentor into the black musician's way of life: its vicissitudes, its dangers, and its victories."[5] He added, "When he would hit with his Trio at the 331 Club [beginning in May 1942], I was there practically every night and between sets, we'd meet outside—there wasn't any dressing room, of course. In short, we hung out."[6]

Their friendship extended well beyond music: Granz also added, "We became, in the parlance of the day, 'asshole buddies' "—by which Norman meant that they were so close that they could "talk trash" to each other about anything or anyone, and let their deepest, least attractive feelings and opinions show, warts and all, without each having to worry what the other one would think. Granz wrote, "Nat would use my modest little pad (apartment) when he wanted privacy with a girlfriend and even shared a girlfriend with me." In 1947, Granz would even give Cole the money to cover the legal fees from his divorce from his first wife.[7]

Granz was also very frank about how Cole opened up the world of black musicians for him, and the larger implications of their friendship, as Callender observed, had an overwhelming impact on the subsequent history of jazz, and, to an extent, civil rights. Norman was Nat's first close white friend. Granz, it must be said, was a credit to his race, one of the first white men Nat had ever met who immediately accepted darker-skinned people as equals and who would become a lifelong crusader for the cause of civil rights and social justice.

At the same time Milt Gabler and Harry Lim were organizing jam sessions in New York, Lee Young was doing the same in Los Angeles, most often at the Capri. The drummer was also co-leading a band with his older brother, Lester, who had already become a huge star in the jazz world. The jam sessions became a regularly recurring event, indirectly thanks to a ruling by the musicians' union. When the American Federation of Musicians (AFM) decreed that bands had to take one night a week off, Granz remembered, "obviously the nightclub owner would choose the day that was his worst day and in most cases, it was a Sunday."[8] Granz was also inspired to action by Billie Holiday, who had recently performed in LA, where she was disturbed to learn that most clubs on the West Coast (even more so than those in New York) had a "whites only" policy.

Granz would follow the example set by Barney Josephson, whose Café Society, in Manhattan's West Village had already implemented a policy of welcoming all races, both in the house and on stage. His first "enabler," as it were, was Billy Berg, a nightclub entrepreneur who started with the Capri and then moved on to the Trouville, on the corner of Beverly and Fairfax.[9] The Capri "was a very small club," Granz noted, so "it was practically impossible"[10] for him to do what he wanted there, but the Trouville was a higher class venue that better suited Granz's ambitions.

Already developing his remarkable skills of persuasion, Granz talked Berg into letting him do his integrated jam sessions on Sunday afternoons, and there was no question who he wanted on piano. "When I started my little jam sessions, Nat was virtually my house pianist."[11] Though not the "leader" per se, Cole was the point man who kept everything running, and Norman's de facto co-producer. "Norman Granz was just a jazz fan who used to listen to me working, and we became good friends," Cole said in a 1954 interview. "So, one day we got together and decided to run Sunday afternoon club sessions with any of the boys who happened to be in town. I was the leader and fixer and contacted any fellows from the big bands. I picked the tunes, fixed the routines, and directed the groups. Norman sat at the door and collected the money."[12]

Nat took this role very seriously, "Once, we were going to one of the Norman Granz Sunday sessions," Callender remembered. "Nat came by our house on 20th Street in a Studebaker with one side of the car completely crushed. There had been a big storm and a tree had fallen over his car. Something like that would never deter Nat Cole. I climbed in the car from the driver's side, hanging on my bass all the way to the gig. That was the Nat Cole I knew, a funny, beautiful guy."[13]

Granz later described a house party at this time in which the guests included no less than four of the all-time great piano players: Jimmy Rowles, Art Tatum, Count Basie, and Cole, along with guitarist Dave Barbour. Over the course of the evening, everyone played but the Count, who instead hung out in the kitchen, just listening. "I said to Basie, 'Aren't you going out to play?' and he answered, 'After Nat Cole and Art Tatum? You're asking me to play? I would die first!' "[14]

By July 1942, everything was jumping: the Trio had begun its long residence at the 331 Club, and the Young Brothers band was headlining at the Trouville (along with Leo Watson and the Spirits of Rhythm, blues singer Joe Turner, and singer-dancer Marie Bryant, soon to be Granz's girlfriend). That was for six nights a week. Then, from 4 p.m. to 7 p.m.on Sunday afternoons, members of both groups, including bassist Callender and Rowles, would get together to jam at the Trouville. The first line-up included both Lester and Lee, the King Cole Trio (including Wesley Prince, then in his last weeks with Cole), as well as trumpeters Red Mack and Taft Jordan, trombonist Joe Ewing, and Eddie Barefield on clarinet and sax. *Down Beat* made a point to tell its industry readers, "Affairs differ from the the many regular and impromptu sessions . . . in that the musicians are paid regular union scale ($9 for three hours) and patrons are charged admission.[15]

The *California Eagle* was enthusiastic when it covered the action both on the regular nights and the Sunday sessions, noting the presence of Ben Webster, Trummy Young, Willie Smith, Joe Thomas, Callender, and "King Cole": "The whole thing is solid kicks, knocking us to our knees." The columnist, Freddie Doyle, happily informed his African American readership,

"Nice thing about the Trouville, you and I are welcome there."[16] Norman Granz wouldn't have it any other way, and neither would Cole.

This initial run of Sunday afternoon jam sessions only lasted two or three months, before Granz was re-inducted into military service on August 4. But before then, he made sure that the Young/Cole combination wouldn't be lost to history, and on July 15, they convened at Music City (the emporium Cole had helped christen two years earlier). The idea was to combine two players from the Young band, Lester and Red (who was soon to start working with the Trio as well) with Nat and Oscar. "One Friday afternoon, we all got together at Glen Wallich's little studio on the corner of Sunset and Vine," the bassist remembered. "All of us, that is, but Oscar Moore. We waited for hours, but Oscar never showed. 'Let's go ahead and do it,' I said, since I was the rhythm section. So, we got a balance and played, having no notion it would be for posterity."[17]

Indeed, the results were truly "for posterity." Lester Young was a musician for the ages, in the opinion of many (including myself) the greatest saxophonist of all time, and an innovator whose laid back yet driving style cast a giant shadow over multiple generations of musicians on all instruments, well beyond jazz, going up to the present day. And over the course of roughly fifteen tracks that Young and Cole made together (including two studio dates, the second in 1946, and one live radio appearance), Cole establishes himself as perhaps the all-time greatest piano partner of the man that Billie Holiday dubbed "The President" or simply "Pres."

Young had become a jazz legend primarily through his work with Count Basie—surely one of the most vital collaborations in all of American music—and he also made a series of classic sessions with his musical soulmate Billie Holiday, recorded under the loose direction of Teddy Wilson. No pianist ever swung harder than Basie, and none had more of a sophisticated touch than Wilson, but still Cole was Young's most perfect accompanist, a virtual Pres of the piano.

Cole had also grown listening to Basie and Wilson, and, like Young himself, they were key influences on his playing; the musical synergy of the Pres and the King was wondrous to behold. Cole seemed to know long before he had ever met Young exactly what he would play with him should he ever be lucky enough to have that opportunity. More than any of Young's other piano partners, Cole plays with the same remarkable sense of quiet, restrained urgency that was Lester Young's trademark. Where most of Young's other collaborators are swinging lindyhoppers, Cole, like Young himself, is more like a jazz ballet dancer. I don't believe that Cole ever fully fathomed his own worth as a pianist (even less so as a singer) but he truly appreciated Lester Young, and he considered it a badge of honor that they were able to create these fifteen miraculous tracks together.

For the July 1942 session, they chose four vintage popular songs that were already jazz standards and jam session favorites. (Surprisingly, there wasn't a blues among them, though they would make up for that later on.) "Indiana" opens with remarkable tranquility—from what we know about the Trouville jam sessions, and the recorded evidence of the Jazz at the Philharmonic concerts (that began two years later), we expect something much louder than this. Cole later returned to "Indiana" with the Trio (for MacGregor transcriptions, in 1944), and that version is more like the "flagwaver" we expect: fast, even frantic, and exciting—as if they were trying to race across the entire state of Indiana in the two minutes it takes them to play the song. If the 1944 "Indiana" is a race, the 1942 "Indiana" is less Jesse Owens and more Alvin Ailey; with Cole as more like a male ballerino whose job is not only to dance with the star female prima donnas but support them and lift them into the air. Cole's solo is a full two choruses, something without precedent in his catalog, but even more notable than the piano solo is the equivalent of a "chase" chorus afterward, in which Cole and Young trade phrases, essentially just shooting very brief bursts of notes back and forth at each other: bop-bop, bop; beep-beep, and so on. Something about it reminds me of a little kid playing with sock puppets, one on each hand, and Young's final chorus is an especially vivid example of how to swing at a laconic tempo.

"I Can't Get Started" is superior balladry. Young has less in common with any previous interpreter, like trumpeter Bunny Berigan, who played it with a sense of ironic braggadocio, and more like great later singers—especially Sinatra. Where Young's melody chorus is spare, Cole's piano passage is more fully two-handed. Young had previously played this Vernon Duke-Ira Gershwin standard, back when it was new, with Teddy Wilson and Billie Holiday (and it marks one of the most radical examples of her ability to bend a melody, and even words, into something almost completely different from what the composer wrote). Even without the actual, literal words, Young captures the multiple meanings of Ira Gershwin's lyric better than any vocalist other than Sinatra, and "sings" the tune better than it would ever be sung.

"Tea for Two" and "Body and Soul" are the first of many extant versions of these songs by Cole. Even the title of "Tea for Two" is an apt metaphor for the Young-Cole pas-de-deux, wherein Young takes two choruses at the start, the first of melody, the second of pure improvisation. The piano solo is unlike any that Cole would return to later, although surprisingly the twosome that the title might suggest is the exchange between Young and Calendar. In his last chorus, Young breaks down the tune into a series of short, elegant phrases. (As we'll see, Cole had a lifelong fascination with several standards by Vincent Youmans; he would record "Tea for Two" and "I Want to Be Happy" many times.)

Even by 1942, "Body and Soul" was well known as a gauntlet thrown down for aspiring titans of the tenor saxophone, as established by Chu Berry and especially Coleman Hawkins. This performance also introduces what would become one of Cole's signature piano solos; he never played it exactly the same way twice, but he did return to the idea of using the Johnny Green melody as a framework to hang a series of quotes on, the most famous of which was a reference to "In the Hall of the Mountain King" (which he had already quoted in "This Side Up"); here he sets up the "Mountain King" quote with a phrase from the 1929 standard "My Kind of Love." Callender gets more to play here, backed by Cole; although all four tracks are about five minutes long, this is the only one where they find time for a bass solo, and it's only about 16 bars. The last chorus is mostly Young, with Cole taking the bridge (and negotiating all those key changes) before Young takes it out.

As mentioned, these four tracks are all five minutes each, meaning that they could only be issued as 12" 78s, and even that was pushing the limits of the available technology. This was one of Granz's final projects as a civilian before he was officially inducted into the Army Air Corps on August 4, 1942. Well before the sides were released, everyone was buzzing about them: "Those who have heard them say they are strictly terrific," enthused *Down Beat*; "He hopes a commercial firm will take them over for marketing."[18]

Indeed, this happened; Granz sold the masters to the brothers Leo and Edward Mesner, owners of the Philharmonic Record Shop in Hollywood,[19] who issued them in 1945 on their newly rechristened label, Aladdin Records. This was virtually the only time Granz sold a session outright, and also virtually the only time one of Cole's non-Trio sessions was issued with his actual name on the labels—not "Sam Schmaltz"—since the session took place well over a year before Cole's exclusive contract with Capitol.

While Granz was back in the army, from August 1942 to May 1943, Billy Berg, "operator of the Trouville," officially took over the sessions, though it's not known whether Nat was still involved while Norman was gone.[20] Granz returned to California in June 1943 and almost immediately went to see Cole, who was working with the Trio in what was the second leg of their long run at the 331 Club. Granz and Cole convened with owner Herb Rose and relaunched the jam sessions at the 331, now on Monday evenings. For the first session, they were able to boast an extra special band consisting mostly of current sidemen with the Count Basie Orchestra: trumpeters Snooky Young and Sweets Edison, tenor saxophonist Buddy Tate, drummer Joe Jones, plus Cole and Callender. *Down Beat*, which referred to the Trio as "the house combo," noted that the club was packed "not with jitterbugs and zoot suiters, but with movie celebs and folk prominent in the show world."[21]

For the second time, Granz took the opportunity to document the action on recordings, again producing a session of four extra-long five-minute tracks. But where the 1942 date was a meeting of the titans, this summer 1943 session is more like a regulation jam session. Indeed, the last number, the well-titled "I Blowed and Gone," is an archetypical 1940s jam blues. Cole was clearly in charge, since the other three numbers all come from his own "songbook" and that of Earl Hines: "Sweet Lorraine" and the Fatha's own "Rosetta" are numbers that we know he was playing with the Trio and in other contexts as well.

This time, Granz and Cole lined up a fully developed quintet, with Harry "Sweets" Edison from the Basie band, Johnny Miller on bass, an otherwise unknown drummer named "Juicy" Owens. For the other half of the frontline, they reached out to an outstanding tenor saxophonist who was then rising in more ways than one: twenty-year-old Dexter Gordon, then with Lionel Hampton's orchestra, was not only a future star of the modern jazz movement but quite possibly the only musician Cole ever played with who was taller than he was. (Since Cole, Gordon, and Callender were all well over six feet, the band could have been called "The Giants of Jazz.")

While the 1942 Cole-Young date produced masterpieces, the 1943 session is just plain fun and almost certainly captures the jamming spirit of the 331 Club sessions. Throughout, the tenor solos by the very young Long Tall Dexter are so much under the influence of Lester that almost anyone would mistake them for the Pres himself in a blindfold test. "Sweet Lorraine" is the closest thing to a ballad here, giving the melody to Edison (who plays mostly muted on the entire date), while the rest are more purely jam vehicles. Gordon is impressive, if not particularly original on "I Found a New Baby," the 1926 jazz standard often used for blowing sessions by the original Basie-ites. "Rosetta" was also a long-venerated jam vehicle, and while Cole can't help but sound a little like his favorite "Fatha," I don't think anyone would ever confuse him for Hines—Cole's distinctive crystalline touch is, as always, unmistakable. "I Blowed and Gone," credited to Edison (who would re-record the same title in 1945), anticipates the climactic title track in *Jammin' the Blues*, a masterpiece movie short subject that Granz would help produce in 1944 for Warner Bros., which featured Edison and Young himself.[22] For this session, Granz astutely held on to the masters, releasing them in 1948, as by "The Dexter Gordon Quintet," with only the two horn players credited, "and rhythm section."

By February 1944, the Trio's long residency at the 331 Club began to wind down, "Straighten Up and Fly Right" was about to hit the charts, and Granz was taking steps to bring his jam sessions out of the nightclubs and into the concert halls. They found a venue called Music Town on the corner of Jefferson and Normandie, which *Down Beat* described as a "southside rehearsal hall."[23] At less than 200 seats, it held fewer people than the larger cocktail lounges, but the important thing was that it was a sit-down auditorium, not a nightclub—there was no drinking or dancing.

That month, Cab Calloway and His Orchestra were in Hollywood, filming a sequence in the United Artists musical *Sensations of 1945*. Granz took advantage of the opportunity to book three star players from that band: the tenor saxophonist Illinois Jacquet, trumpeter Lester "Shad" Collins, and drummer J. C. Heard. For the first Music Town event, on Sunday, February 6, he also hired bassist Gene Englund from the Stan Kenton band, alto saxophonist Kirk Bradford from Jimmie Lunceford's orchestra, and the nineteen-year-old guitar savant Barney Kessel.

The pianist, leader, and star was Nat King Cole: in all of the advertising and listings, Cole was listed first and most prominently.[24] "Have you heard about the series of jazz concerts being given each Sunday at Music Town by Norman Granz?" proclaimed an ad, placed in the form of a review. "The first was held last Sunday, and the place certainly did jump." Among those who came to sit in and observe were Ted Alexander, pianist, with crooner Tony Martin,[25] and dancer Marie Bryant (then Granz's girlfriend and soon to appear with Jacquet in *Jammin' the Blues*), and "heaps more from the Walt Disney Studio. ... They suggest that you arrive early next Sunday. That smooth, mellow jive is too good to miss."[26] "Guided by Cole's piano, the jazz really came on and never let down," *Down Beat* added.[27]

Nat and Norman were continually kicking it up a notch and once again commemorated the occasion with a recording session. Sometime early in February, the three Calloway men, Jacquet, Collins, and Heard, convened in an unknown studio with Cole and Englund for a third series of extra-long jam numbers. This time there were two fairly spontaneous blues, "Heads" and "Pro-Sky" (the meaning of the second title has been lost to history—it has nothing to do with "Proschai," a traditional Russian folk song recorded earlier by Artie Shaw), and two standards, "It Had to Be You" and "I Can't Give You Anything but Love."

Alas, it's obvious that Cole's attention is elsewhere; there's far less magic here than either of the two previous Cole-Granz sessions. This is the weakest session of all his non-KC3 dates; the rhythmic feeling is rather different for him, and he never quite jells with the drummer, J. C. Heard. Were it not for some familiar introductory figures at the start of "Pro-Sky," which are somewhat reminiscent of "F. S. T." and "Jumpin' at Capitol," I would have never guessed (on a blindfold test or elsewhere) that it was actually Cole playing. Cole had a lot on his mind at this moment; he was also worrying about the draft (both for himself and Oscar).[28] Jacquet is his usual exuberant self, growling on the blues and evoking Lester Young on "It Had to Be You," but there are no standout moments from the piano player.

Music Town was but a temporary stop for Granz and Cole. "Nat Cole, I think, got a little tired of being the house pianist," said Norman, "He suggested to me that it might be a good idea if I kind of laid off for a while. I could see that it was a no-growth proposition."[29] In April, Cole had a big opening coming up—the Trio's first important theater engagement, at the Orpheum—and probably wanted to concentrate on that; immediately after, he had a gig in San Francisco (and, of course, would spend most of the rest of his life on the road). It was clear that he could no longer keep on being the house pianist and de facto leader of Granz's ongoing weekly sessions

In February, the month that the Music Town concerts were launched, Cole signed formally with Carlos Gastel, who already represented Stan Kenton, which possibly explains how they connected with Gene Englund. Playing in public, as they did at Music Town, with a white musician on the stand was a risky business—even illegal in most of the country—but Granz and Cole were both motivated by social and political as well as musical ambitions. In fact, as Granz planned his next move, he had humanitarian issues on his mind; the heinous "Sleepy Lagoon Murder" of 1942 and the "Zoot Suit" riots of 1943 were two shameful examples of violence perpetrated against minority groups. Granz decided to stage an event as a fundraiser for the Sleepy Lagoon case Defense Committee, thus ensuring that he and his nascent concert series would be on the right side of history. As Cole later said, Granz was firm in his convictions on every level. "Even in those days Norman wouldn't knuckle down to anybody. A lot of people disliked him, but I understood his attitude. He knew just what he wanted and exactly how he was going to get it."[30]

Now Granz was ready to realize his grandest ambition yet: to bring a jam session, for the first time, into a large-scale concert setting—and at the same time, to use the event to promote a worthwhile social cause. He rented Philharmonic Hall (for what seems like the absurdly low price of $175) for

Sunday afternoon, July 2, 1944, and hired ten musicians—the entire budget was given as $750.[31] Most of the players had worked with Granz in his earlier sessions: trombonist J. J. Johnson, then in Benny Carter's orchestra and later to become the primary exponent of modern jazz on his horn; trumpeter Shorty Sherock, best known as a Roy Eldridge disciple who played in several major swing bands; two highly extroverted tenor saxophonists, Illinois Jacquet and Jack McVea, the latter better known as an R&B star; and Cole's longtime associates, bassist Red Callender and drummer Lee Young.

In an ad for the concert, the first name on the list of the artists appearing was "King Cole Trio"; obviously Nat was in, and so was Johnny Miller, but Oscar Moore was, once again, a no-show. As it happened, the last-minute substitute for Moore turned out to be nothing less than a historic choice. Early Sunday morning, guitarist Les Paul received a call from Cole urging him to appear at the concert, then just about three or four hours away. "Les, can you come to the Philharmonic and play with us today? Oscar's been shacking up in a room with a chick for three days, and we can't get him out. We're shoving pizzas under the door. So, come and play."[32] Les was thrilled to get the call; he had already played quite a bit with Cole (presumably at the 331 jam sessions). As he put it, "Nat and I had already been playing together so much for so long. I had jammed at every place he ever played."

Les Paul, born Lester William Polfuss (1915–2009) was a brilliant guitarist and technical innovator, who, in the overall arch of his career, would be equally celebrated for his virtuoso playing in at least three different genres: pop, country, and jazz. Still, he is much better known to history as the foremost creator of the electric guitar—he did more than anyone else to conceive the instrument as we know it today. He also made an invaluable contribution to many other groundbreaking developments in recorded sound, such as multi-tracking, reverberation, and overdubbing.

The original plan for the July concert was to have two extended jam sessions with the players mentioned above as well as two female singers, Marie Bryant and Carolyn Richards, and two separate other bands playing their own segments: the King Cole Trio and an all-star group playing traditional jazz led by pianist Joe Sullivan of the Chicago school and clarinetist Barney Bigard from New Orleans (and many years with Duke Ellington). With Oscar in *absentia*, Nat and Johnny didn't attempt to play any of the Trio favorites, except for "Sweet Lorraine," for which they retained some of Cole's familiar vocal and piano embellishments but no other aspects of the classic Trio arrangement.

Granz made an arrangement for the performance to be recorded by the Armed Forces Radio Service, and he stipulated that the discs and the rights later be returned to him. It was an especially far-sighted move, as no one then had any notion that nine- and ten-minute jam session tracks, recorded live in concert (with audience noise and applause) numbers, could ever be released commercially. (None of Granz's earlier five-minute, 12-inch studio sessions had yet been issued.) "You know how the JATP recordings started?" Cole recalled. "We were approached by the Armed Forces Radio Service to tape some of our sessions for overseas transmission and V-Disc coverage. That was okay as far as the AFM was concerned and didn't cost anything extra in the musicians' fees. Then a couple of years later, when Norman had more money, he got the tapes back from AFRS and decided to issue them commercially. By this time, he was in position to pay the men for the session, and so we all got a nice bonus."[33]

The majority of the July 2, 1944, concert was released for the first time in 1946 (as part of a 78 RPM album on a label called "Disc," and later on Mercury, Verve, and many other labels). At the actual concert, Les Paul had to originally be billed under a pseudonym ("Paul Leslie"), since he was officially enlisted in the military at that moment, and civilian gigs were prohibited; but the King Cole Trio was officially advertised. It turned out, however, that Capitol Records was even harder to get around than the army: when the recordings were issued, Les Paul was listed under his actual name, but Cole was billed under the *nom-de-matrimony* "Shorty Nadine," one of his pet names for his wife.[34] His vocal on "Sweet Lorraine," however, wouldn't be heard again until almost fifty-five years later.

Although two other pianists were present, Joe Sullivan and Buddy Cole (best known as a vocal accompanist, who would later serve in that capacity for Nat Cole, although the two were not related), it seems to be Nat on all of the surviving, issued recordings—even playing behind singer Carolyn Richards on "The Man I Love," which roughly follows the Trio instrumental versions he had already recorded for Capitol and MacGregor. In general, though a jam session is by definition without a leader, and even though it was the tenor saxophone pyrotechnics of Illinois Jacquet that attracted the most attention on this and many subsequent Jazz at the Philharmonic shows, the dominant voice and musical mind governing the proceedings is Cole's. Nearly all of the repertoire derives from his own personal history, tunes that he would play again and again, and indeed help make into jazz and pop standards: "Tea for Two," "Body and Soul," "I've Found a New Baby," "Rosetta."

There are Trio versions of most of these numbers, and Cole plays almost exactly the same way here as he does in the familiar piano-guitar-bass context (drummer Lee Young here stays out of his way). In fact, he sounds so much like the leader of the King Cole Trio, even without singing, that it's a wonder Capitol let Granz release these at all—the "Shorty Nadine" pseudonym wasn't fooling anybody. (During his solo on "Tea for Two," you hear someone off in the distance shouting, "Yeah, go, Nat!") "Lester Leaps In" is a dedication to the tenor star (who would later participate in many future JATP shows) and is of a piece with the many "I Got Rhythm" versions Cole would compose and perform. "Tea for Two," already a signature for the pianist, has the horn ensemble following Cole's jaunty tempo, while he plays some of the licks and variations he would later include in later performances with Nelson Riddle's Orchestra, on his 1955 album *The Piano Style of Nat King Cole* and his 1957 NBC TV show—not to mention a quote from "The Donkey Serenade."

"Body and Soul" opens with McVea and his big tenor tone referencing Coleman Hawkins's groundbreaking 1939 recording, while Cole adheres to his own tradition of using the Johnny Green melody as a delivery system for a series of quotes, including his signature lick from "Mountain King," followed by a Gershwin-y phrase that suggests both "The Man I Love" and *Rhapsody in Blue* simultaneously, a bit of "Donkey Serenade" (echoing an earlier quote from the same tune that he played on "Tea for Two"), and "Lullaby in Rhythm." Then Cole leads the ensemble into a tempo change reminiscent of the Chu Berry-Roy Eldridge "Body and Soul." Near the end, he solos again, briefly in the faster tempo, with a familiar sounding cascading run.

On "New Baby," Cole dances aggressively around the melody and sets up a passage by both bassists, Callender and Miller, soloing together. Remarkably he doesn't solo on Earl Hines's "Rosetta," a tune that really was his meat, but he's all over "Bugle Call Rag," and more important than his solos here is the way the pianist sets up the stop time breaks for Jacquet, who's at his loudest and most exciting here. Cole provides the springboard from which Jacquet propels himself into a pool of sonic euphoria.

D-Day, which launched the Allied invasion of Normandy and signified the turning point of World War II, had occurred only a month earlier on June 6, 1944; the King Cole Trio had already marked that occasion with the song (by the young songwriter Lew Spence) titled "D-Day."[35] Just as the Trio's "Gone with the Draft" caught the mood of the nation as it was gearing up for war (and later, "The Christmas Song" and "Nature Boy" depicted a world ready for Heavenly Peace), the Jazz at the Philharmonic shows served as a barometer of the mood in the final phase of the long conflict. Wearied by so many years of combat, Americans were now ready for a new kind of jazz, one that was almost violently transgressive. While Cole is a sharpshooter and a musical sniper, Illinois Jacquet's solos sound like a whole platoon of tanks descending on a German battalion.

The July 2, 1944, concert was a particular highpoint in the relationship between Cole and Granz. But perhaps they eventually stopped working together because the artistic differences between them paralleled those between Cole and Lionel Hampton. The King Cole Trio, for all of its excitement and exuberance, had little in common with a typical Illinois Jaquet tenor solo, all high notes and screams. Therein, in fact, lies the essential paradox of Norman Granz's Jazz at the Philharmonic series; he did more than any other impresario to move jazz out of smoky nightclubs and give it the respect it deserved, in concert halls alongside the European classics. Yet the signature sound of JATP was nothing like what anybody thought of as concert music—indeed, for all the battles and duels in his concert productions, many thought that a football game, or even an ancient Roman gladiatorial contest, was a more apt point of comparison. Yet there's no denying that Granz's concerts were irresistible, even addictive. Jean Bach, who was then married to Sherock (and later a radio producer and filmmaker), said that Jacquet's high note solos gave her a headache, but even she couldn't deny that it was a "milestone in jazz history."[36]

If the two battling tenors, Jacquet and McVea, could be likened to open, mechanized warfare, the most memorable moment of that premiere JATP concert was more akin to a covert military operation carried out by two spies, stationed behind enemy lines, exchanging coded messages with each other. Les Paul, until the very end of his life (and he lived to be ninety-four), was an extremely frisky and playful improvisor, sometimes to the point of being downright perverse. At the July 2 concert, he decided he was going to challenge Nat King Cole to what he called a game of "cat and mouse." The exchange occurs near the end, about seven minutes into a ten-minute track, after Cole and Paul have both already soloed. Paul ends his solo with a repeating figure, somewhat balletic (and vaguely inspired by the multiple references to "Donkey Serenade" in previous tunes), and Cole catches his cue, so he repeats Paul's guitar figure on piano. They repeat the process, trading and repeating increasingly bluesy phrases back and forth, for almost three minutes. This sequence could have been one side of a 1944 10" 78 RPM single disc all by itself, but it climaxed in a moment that was beyond the power of the microphones to capture. "When I threw that one [phrase] at him, he just slapped his hands down on the piano, took his hat off, and threw it out in the audience. The audience threw their hats all up on the stage, and the place went crazy."[37] It wasn't that the pianist couldn't play what the guitarist had thrown at him; rather he realized that the time had come to finish this exchange and he chose to do so with a visual rather than an auditory move. If JATP teaches us anything, it's that music is as much showmanship as it is musical skill, and this was sheer showmanship. As Paul described it, "People were standing in their seats, screaming."[38]

Granz and Cole quickly followed up with a repeat concert in the same venue on July 30. This was planned as a more Basie-centric event, and originally three stars of the Basie organization were set to headline: Lester Young, Sweets Edison, and drummer Jo Jones. However, they were prohibited from appearing by a lawsuit served on Granz by the Orpheum Theater on Central Avenue. The full Basie band was booked to open there two days later, and the Orpheum didn't want to take any chances that Granz's concert might draw some business away from that engagement by featuring three of Basie's biggest stars. All that survives from this second JATP concert is two incomplete fragments (issued in 1998), "One O'Clock Jump" and "Oh Lady Be Good," both featuring Jacquet and Cole. *Down Beat* noted that "for the second time, guitarist Oscar Moore failed to appear, but Cole and Miller played a duet." Les Paul was also present, this time playing under his own name rather than a pseudonym.[39]

The first two JATP concerts were the last time Cole would play on a live show for Granz, although as we shall see, the producer and the pianist would work together on one more all-time classic project in 1946. The first Jazz at the Philharmonic concert was also the one and only recorded collaboration between Nat Cole and Les Paul; it's hard to imagine how they could have possibly improved on it. "Everybody gets keyed up about the Jacquet solo with all the screaming and everything." Even Granz had to admit, "The exchange between Nat and Les Paul was more interesting, in that the give and take of what a jam session could accomplish was there in its purity." Ten years later, both Cole and Paul were on the top of the pop music charts and had moved well beyond their early lives as jazz musicians. But there's no doubt that they both well remembered that summer afternoon in 1944, when two guys with the improbable names of "Paul Leslie" and "Shorty Nadine" changed everything.

THE LAST MAJOR PROJECT that Cole and Granz would work on together was the pioneering album, *The Jazz Scene*, in 1946, but before then, in 1945 and early 1946, Cole would also participate in three major recording dates outside of the King Cole Trio—all of which can be safely described as all-star jam sessions: the Capitol International Jazzmen (March 30, 1945), the Sunset All-Stars, also called the Herbie Haymer Quintet (June 9, 1945), and the Keynoters (February 16, 1946). (The first two were done while the Trio was in the middle of an extended run, from March to June 1945, at the Trocadero in Hollywood.) Just as with the Granz sessions, he made all these dates purely for his own enjoyment, the fun and the thrills of working with his peers in the jazz world.

For all the hundreds of masters and songs that Nat King Cole recorded for Capitol from 1943 to the end of his career in 1964, it seems rather improbable that, in retrospect, he only participated in one out-and-out purely jazz jam session for the label. This was the brainchild of Dave Dexter, early in his long tenure at Capitol Records, when he conceived of a highly ambitious project that would eventually be released in 1945 as *The History of Jazz*. Promoted by Capitol as the most comprehensive word on the subject yet, the project took the form of four 78 albums of five discs each, for a total of twenty discs and forty sides.

Whereas any of the other major labels could have used vintage, historical recordings to compile a history of jazz, Capitol faced the challenge of recording everything anew. There would be some spillover between sessions specifically recorded for the project and Capitol's regular releases, but Dexter would travel to Chicago, Kansas City, San Francisco, and New York to get everything done as well as the many sessions in Los Angeles. *Metronome* reported, "Despite Capitol's inability to record certain giants as Armstrong and Ellington," who were under contract to other labels, "as well as sundry pioneers who have long since passed on, Dexter and Capitol succeeded in recording more than 100 great and near-great jazzmen. The list of participants is easily the most impressive ever assembled for a single album series." All forty tracks were being released for the first time, even though some had been recorded back in 1942 and 1943. *Metronome* added, "Capitol's investment is said to be well over $100,000."[40]

The project covered not only the history but also all of the various permutations of the music, from the African American "roots" musician Lead Belly, up to, well, Nat King Cole, who at twenty-five, was probably the youngest bandleader in the package. Cole was heard on two volumes. *Volume Four*, which was "concerned only with 1945 jazz,"[41] included the first release of a now-classic King Cole Trio instrumental, "Jumpin' at Capitol," recorded at their very first Capitol date in November 1943. And on *Volume Three*, which covered "the "zany Swing Era," [42] Cole played with the Capitol International Jazzmen.

Seventy-five years later, the group's name (apparently they were billed as "Dave Dexter's International Jazzmen" in the original album)[43] seems somewhat curious—these were all black Americans, but Dexter came up with "International Jazzmen" because three of the four horn men in the front line, the legendary saxophonists Benny Carter (alto) and Coleman Hawkins (tenor), and trumpeter Bill Coleman, had spent much of the immediate prewar years living and playing in Europe. (Carter's orchestra had also toured extensively with the King Cole Trio in 1944–45.) Everybody present was a veteran player with a considerable reputation among jazz fans: clarinetist Buster Bailey from Fletcher Henderson and John Kirby's bands; bassist John Kirby himself, one of the standout small bandleaders of the 52nd Street era; and none other than Oscar Moore (at long last) on guitar. The least-known musician at the time was drummer Max Roach, currently part of Carter's rhythm section and soon to become the best-known drummer-bandleader of the Modern Jazz era.

There was also a vocalist. Dexter later wrote, "I didn't tell the musicians, but I had also invited a young, busty, big-throated girl singer to participate in two of the four planned masters. She was Kay Starr, a confident, ebullient, part-Cherokee brunette who I had met when she worked for a time with Joe Venuti. She sang great."[44] Although this was her Capitol debut, the twenty-two-year-old from Dougherty, Oklahoma, was already somewhat known for her exceptional jazz chops, having already toured with Glenn Miller, Wingy Manone, and Charlie Barnet, in addition to Venuti.

As Starr, who sings on "If I Could Be with You" and "Stormy Weather," told me in 1990,

> Originally, I started recording for Capitol just as sort of a guest star on Dave Dexter's jazz albums. When I went down to the studio to do the first one, Dave hadn't told me who was going to be there. He just said that he did all-star jazz sessions and he kind of told me some of the musicians, but it never occurred to me that I'd actually be singing with them. And when I went into that studio, they had these two big sets of doors there, and you go through one door and then you just gently pushed open the second door which actually went into the studio, because it was blinking but not red, I knew that I needed to be in there because it was the time Dave had said. But I just looked in and I saw Nat Cole on piano and John Kirby on bass and Coleman Hawkins, I opened up the door a little more just to be sure of what I was seeing, and in the same breath I thought "This can't be the right

> studio!" I wanted to dissolve; I didn't want to make any noise so that anybody would know I was there. I must have made a mistake. I started to do what I call a crawdaddy out that door, to walk backwards like the crawdads do when they're afraid, but I heard Dave's voice saying, "Get in here, Okie, you're in the right place!"[45]

Carter's biographer, Ed Berger, felt that "considering the magnitude of talent, the results are less than spectacular."[46] That is possibly true, but the results are certainly wonderful, even if they don't quite reach the level of "spectacular"—and, from Cole's perspective, this is a gem of a session that serves to considerably enrich his discography. As Dexter put it, "Because Nat was being castigated by the eastern critics in *Down Beat, Metronome* and lesser publications for deserting jazz to become a pop singer"—this as early as 1945—"I asked Nat if he would join us. 'Say when and where,' he answered."[47]

The date consists of three standards, "You Can Depend on Me," "If I Could Be with You" and "Stormy Weather," plus a blues, Carter's "Riffmarole." The late Ed Berger was particularly critical of this date because he feels Carter's solos aren't up to his best work. However, Hawkins is the alpha horn soloist here; he's the one that you remember on the two instrumentals, "You Can Depend on Me" and "Riffmarole" (even though the Hawk was never a blues specialist), and Starr makes the most of her opportunity: she steps up to the plate on both "If I Could Be with You" and "Stormy Weather," and fairly knocks both of them out of the park.

"Stormy Weather" was the song that Starr later remembered for a special, personal reason. Somehow, she had the idea that Cole had made a record for Capitol in which he sang that Harold Arlen-Ted Koehler classic. This was wrong; as far we know, Cole never sang it,[48]nd that makes what happened even funnier. "I was supposed to do 'Stormy Weather,' and I [thought that] Nat Cole had done a vocal record of that for Capitol. I was so nervous I thought I had to ask permission, I asked him if it was okay and he laughed and said, 'Of course!' And Nat later used to kid me about that when we got to be friends. He said, 'You know, she can't sing 'Stormy Weather' without my permission.' "[49]

However, even with Hawkins and Starr at their best, no one is operating at a more consistently brilliant level here than Cole, whose every solo is an unabashed gem. It seems likely he helped Dexter pick the tunes, since the first two are by piano giants that he admired, Fatha Hines's "You Can Depend on Me," and James P. Johnson's "If I Could Be with You." These are songs that every aspiring jazz pianist coming up in the 1930s would have known backward and forward. He also sets the mood and the tempo, especially on the first two. Cole sets up "You Can Depend on Me," working with Moore to create a Trio-like interlude (Kirby is cooperative, and Roach is barely noticeable) for 16 bars, until Bailey comes in at the bridge. "If I Could Be with You" opens with even more of a Cole-Moore Trio "lope," even though he seems delighted to hand the melody over to Starr after playing his intro.

Coleman opens "Stormy Weather" with a plaintive moan on his muted trumpet, and Starr and Cole catch that dark, rainy mood perfectly, the piano's notes splattering like so many raindrops all around her. "Riffmarole," which survives in two takes, is another fast and snappy jam session blues, from the period just when swing was morphing into bop; Cole solos eloquently but shines even more brightly when he plays a back-and-forth call-and-response pattern with the three horns. On every track—even though he doesn't take a full-on solo on "Stormy Weather"—Cole sounds like he's delighted to be there. After the session was finished, Cole supposedly said to Dexter (again, this seems a tad premature for 1945), "Now I'm going back and be a singer again, but today was one I'll never forget."[50] It's as if he knew then that this would be his only out-and-out, non-Trio jam session for Capitol, the rare occasion when he could be credited under himself, without the ruse of a phony name, and be recognized, fully out in the open, as the great jazz keyboardist that he was.

ON MAY 8, 1945, the Allies declared "Victory in Europe Day," abbreviated ever since as "VE Day"; this was actually a day before the final unconditional surrender of the German forces on May 9. There were celebrations and parades everywhere, but military leaders advised caution: there still was the matter of Japan to be dealt with. Shortly thereafter, Capitol Records, in their house organ, the *Capitol News*, took an informal poll of their recording artists, sort of the equivalent of an office pool, as to when they thought the war would actually be over. Nat King Cole was one of the more pessimistic: "Put me down for September 24, 1946, and let's pray it will come sooner." The most optimistic—and thankfully, the most accurate prediction—was that international jazzman Benny Carter, who picked August 8, 1945 (which fell precisely in between the two atomic bombings of Japan, on August 6 and 9).[51]

But in June and July, caution was still the watchword; on Sunday, June 9, in Los Angeles, two American commanders, General George S. Patton and Lieutenant General James H. Doolittle, were honored in a huge parade, leading to a celebration at City Hall. An ecstatic crowd (estimated at somewhere between 750,000 and a million) gathered to hear the two war heroes speak, but Patton, in particular, was in no mood for a party. "In the midst of all this joy, there is a very serious note. This war is only half over. It could damn well be lost."[52] Yet it was in the midst of "all this joy," rather than the "serious note," on that very Sunday, that Nat King Cole and four colleagues created one of the most remarkable jam sessions in the history of jazz.

Dexter, then the editor of the *Capitol News*, later observed, "Jazz was selling briskly in the mid-1940s, so much that more than a hundred labels specializing in that idiom sprang up. Few survived."[53] Cole did some of his best pure-jazz work for two such labels that never made it beyond the immediate postwar era, Sunset Records and Keynote, both run by jazz-loving entrepreneurs. Sunset Records was owned by a gentleman with the improbable name of Eddie Laguna, a name surely more distinguished than "Sunset," especially since there already had been several other record labels so-titled.

The other focal point for the Sunset date was the talented tenor saxophonist, Herbie Haymer (1916–1949[54]), who had already played with a half dozen major white bands. Haymer had first distinguished himself with Red Norvo's remarkable group of the late 1930s, and he also had achieved the commendable task of helping to transform Kay Kyser's orchestra, at one point thought of as a novelty or Mickey Mouse band, into a full-blown swing outfit with his booting tenor solo on "Bell Bottom Trousers." Haymer would soon become a favorite player in Sinatra's general circle, and obviously Cole admired him as well. In the opinion of the legendary drummer Buddy Rich, who played on the date, Haymer was a "great tenor saxophone player." [55] It's telling that Rich recorded alongside Cole with both Lester Young and Charlie Parker, but Haymer was the saxophonist he remembered.

For the second half of the frontline, Laguna's first choice was trumpeter Harry Edison,[56] but Sweets was back on the East Coast with Basie. Fortunately, two other major bands were then in Los Angeles, Tommy Dorsey and His Orchestra and pianist Eddie Heywood's Sextet. From Heywood, Laguna got bassist John Simmons, born in Oklahoma but mostly based in New York. His second choice for a trumpeter paid off doubly: the remarkable Charlie Shavers, who brought along Rich, then Dorsey's drummer. We don't know how, in particular, Laguna was lucky enough to land Nat Cole, but the pianist, then still ensconced with the Trio at the Trocadero, was in a real playing mood. The only caveat was that Nat wanted the date to end in time to catch some of the big to-do at City Hall.

Like the International Jazzmen date, these four titles straddle the cutting edge between swing and bebop, but repertory-wise, the equation is reversed. Instead of three standards and a blues, we get mostly blues originals and one standard melody. Shavers is wonderful throughout; you can see why the trumpeter's reputation has grown steadily since his untimely death at the age of fifty in 1971 (not much older than Cole); Wynton Marsalis is one of many contemporary brassmen who sings Shavers's praises. Buddy Rich plays with taste and subtlety, and, as always, incredible power and technique. Last, the main man, Haymer, is a tenor player worthy of Cole's company—remember this is the pianist who in the last three years alone had made memorable music with Lester Young, Coleman Hawkins, Illinois Jaquet, and Dexter Gordon.

Catching the euphoric mood that came with the end of the war in sight, all five master musicians are absolutely exploding with excitement. The main order of business is four tunes, a pair of fast-as-a-bastard, boppish originals, "Laguna Leap" and "Swingin' on Central," alternating with the slightly slower "Black Market Stuff" and the 1932 ballad "I'll Never Be the Same." We are extremely fortunate with two by-products of the date: first, that virtually the whole recording session was preserved and later issued, a total of twelve takes, forty-one minutes of music and some studio chatter (making it perhaps the most thoroughly documented session of Cole's jazz career); and second, that there was time left over at the end for a "bonus track."

"Black Market Stuff" (the title refers to wartime rationing) is an elegantly loping medium-tempo dance number, with a memorable bridge, and overall mood reminiscent of an Ellington-Johnny Hodges small group; three takes survive, each with Cole playing a notably different piano solo. Shavers plays muted in the opening and closing head, but solos with an open bell. They charge into "Laguna Leap" (in E flat, a voice tells us, probably that of Laguna himself), at a horse race tempo, a blues so fast that all stumble in a false start. Cole plays a breathtakingly decorative run, all the more remarkable for its speed, with some Fats Waller–style embellishments—a thoroughly satisfying solo (with a brief allusion to Jesse Stone's "Iowa" in the first take).

Next up is the only standard, "I'll Never Be the Same," another tune in the King Cole repertoire composed by one of his piano predecessors, the jazz age keyboard master Frank Signorelli (he probably learned it from the classic 1937 recording by Teddy Wilson, Billie Holiday, and Lester Young). Shavers plays the tune in his unsentimental ballad style, then Haymer also gets mellow for 16 bars, lagging behind the beat in a Lestorian mode. Cole takes the bridge and says all that needs to be said in eight glorious bars, before Shavers and the ensemble return for the final eight. "Swingin' on Central"[57] is another fast, basic 12-bar blues that borrows Count Basie's opening "head" from "Swingin' the Blues" (earlier heard as Don Redman's "Hot and Anxious"). Here, Simmons finally gets a 12-bar chorus that he can call his own. Cole's piano literally sparkles on both takes; once again, the variations that he spins on the basic blues are apparently endless—ending in a few brief notes that sound like he's heard Dizzy Gillespie's "Salt Peanuts."

The main work is now finished, there are excellent, highly issuable takes on all four tunes. Some time is still left on the clock. What to do next? Shavers makes a suggestion by playing the opening lines of "All the Things You Are." We also hear the familiar voice of Nat declaring, more than once, "I want to see the parade." He underscores his point with a few bars of a jaunty parade march, a lick most of us know as "The Campbells Are Coming." But then, quite spontaneously, they start into a very loose but amazing jam on "Honeysuckle Rose," still another familiar tune by a great jazz pianist, with Waller's melody undisguised. The quintet leaves us with but one six-minute take, and, as they used to say, it's ragged but right. The pianist, as the kids say today, is all over this thing: he starts with the "Honeysuckle" melody, leading into a vigorous jam with Shavers taking the tune and Haymer playing sustained notes behind him. Then Haymer takes the first improvised solo, an exceptional chorus that shows why Laguna, Sinatra, and Cole, all held him in such high regard.

Nat solos next, and his playing is absolutely quintessential King Cole: he detours through Dvorak's "Humoresque" (which he had already recorded as "Mabel, Mabel" with lyrics by Ervin Drake), that brings him to the very top of the keyboard approaching high A; he then dances back down to earth with one of his signature cascading runs. Near the end, Shavers engages Cole in what Les Paul would call "cat-and-mousing": the trumpeter plays one figure then another, and Cole responds to them all. Cole sets up a solo by Simmons, but he can't hold back, and he starts playing all around the bass, with Basie-esque economy. By the end of the chorus, he's dancing all around the bass, and Shavers, also unable to resist joining back in, starts challenging him with another back-and-forth exchange; they both quote Tony Jackson's "Pretty Baby" and reference "The Campbells."

Haymer then introduces Buddy Rich's most glorious moment of the whole date. Best remembered for his bombastic playing and strident personality, Rich was also a remarkably subtle player when the occasion demanded. Haymer takes the last chorus, with even more energy and enthusiasm. They could have possibly done even better with a second take, as the playing is comparatively unfocused in the first minute or so, but they could have never topped this one as a glorious example of spontaneous, intimate creation. It's one of the great moments of Cole's jazz career.

Within a few moments, he was off to see the parade.

This was the infamous date in which the pianist was credited by the most undignified pseudonym of them all—"Sam Shmaltz." The four main titles were only briefly available on Sunset Records, but they had a remarkable afterlife in Europe. In England, the tracks were issued on Parlophone, where everyone was aware of the real identity of the pianist (credited as "E. Laguna") and "Honeysuckle Rose" was even issued on the Swing label in France, as a two-sided 78, as "Nat's Kicks, parts one & two," with the band credited as "King Cole Quintet."

Reviewing the records in 1948, the British critic Denis Preston was full of backhanded compliments: he describes Shavers's trumpeting as "tasteless as ever, but such is his technical accomplishment that at the hectic tempo of 'Laguna Leap,' he carries all before him" and Cole as "scatting to right and left the inhibitions of ten years' work with a slick novelty trio" (ouch!)—yet he loved the records: "Uninhibited, exciting," he called them.[58] Alun Morgan, writing roughly twenty years later, had fewer reservations, "I have, over the years, literally worn the surface away from a Parlophone 78 coupling of 'Laguna Leap and 'Black Market Stuff.' "[59]

Cole, Shavers, and Haymer all died tragically young—the saxophonist was killed in an auto accident following a Sinatra session at Columbia's Hollywood studios, on April 11, 1949. Simmons was hit by a different kind of disaster: roughly a month after the Sunset date, he was arrested by the Los Angeles Police Department for possession of marijuana.[60] But the Herbie Haymer Quintet session would become perhaps the most celebrated of all of Cole's pure jazz recordings, especially in the United Kingdom, where the entire forty-one-minute date was issued on LP (and later, CD) on multiple occasions.

Nearly a lifetime later, Buddy Rich himself recalled the date in an interview: "Nat Cole—nobody remembers that I recorded with Nat Cole, when he was one of the best jazz piano players. And hardly anybody ever realised how great a piano player he was. Not only his technique - also his time thing; he was a real percussive player. I loved him." [61] [INSERT FOOTNOTE]

IN TERMS OF QUANTITY, Cole probably recorded less in pure jazz settings (apart from the Trio) than any other pianist of his stature; his jam session recordings are especially valuable, not only because of their scarcity but also because he seemed to be making history with every session. Keynote Records had been founded in 1940 as a politically driven operation that swung hard to the left (recording folk and anti-war protest songs), and was eventually re-focused as a jazz label by Harry Lim, the self-same "diminutive Javanese swing pundit" who had produced the live jam sessions with Cole and company at the Village Vanguard in 1942. Lim recorded two all-star sessions under the group name, "The Keynoters," a sextet in New York 1944 with Charlie Shavers up front, and then a quartet in Los Angeles on Saturday, February 16, 1946, while the Trio was enjoying another run at the venue named after them, the King Cole Room, at the Trocadero. Cole's co-star was the alto sax star William McLeish "Willie" Smith, already famous for his earlier work with the beloved Jimmie Lunceford Orchestra, and, at this time, with Harry James, and later, Duke Ellington. Two dependable Angelinos made the rhythm section, bassist Red Callender and drummer Jackie Mills.

This date is all standards and no blues, although first-time listeners might not recognize "Airiness a la Nat," the latest but hardly the last of Cole's many contrafacts on the durable "I Got Rhythm" chord changes. Gershwin's tune is disguised, and, once again, so is the pianist, this being the session in which he was billed as "Lord Calvert." The name was given in quotes, as a kind of tip-off to the royal presence of the monarch who was actually playing.

The date is much more mellow than the Sunset or the Capitol International sessions, but no less wonderful. The absence of a strict 12-bar blues is no detriment to Smith, who invests "The Way You Look Tonight" with such a profound blues feeling that even Jerome Kern (no hot music fan he) would have had to approve. By the time Smith has played 16 bars, it's no less satisfying than a whole chorus, allowing Cole to take over in the bridge for the rest of the chorus, which feels like a complete solo unto itself. After this amazing single chorus, Smith returns and plays a 4-bar tag, ending with a lovely coda. "Airiness a la Nat" is very subdued jamming, but no less exciting—even though Cole was billed under a pseudonym, surely someone noticed that his name is in the song title. He plays a lot of signature phrases, and there's a lively trade at the end wherein Mills references "Salt Peanuts," another "Rhythm" variation.

"I Can't Believe That You're in Love with Me" is a traditional jazz favorite from 1926 that Cole almost certainly learned as an aspiring musician in Chicago, rendered here in a highly copacetic mid-tempo. This date also includes several alternate takes, and here the second take, the one actually issued in 1946, is superior to the first, not issued until many years later. Sam Coslow's "My Old Flame," a ballad loved by alto players (there's a famous version by Charlie Parker) is another slow love song, which captures Cole and Smith both in a reminiscent mood. As with Young, the two principals are not thinking of the chords or even the melody; they're thinking about their old flames. Still, "The Way You Look Tonight" may be the standout here, for both

Cole and Smith; as Dan Morgenstern observes, there's a "unique little glissando run" that Cole might have learned from Mary Lou Williams, while, at the same time, his playing here shows precisely what, in turn, Oscar Peterson learned from him.[62]

Spring 1946 saw a renewed burst of jazz activity by Cole, some of which was actually done in full public view: for the only time, the actual Trio backed up several living legends of jazz. They had been making regular appearances on AFRS *Jubilee* since early in the war, and in April 1946, they appeared on one episode playing with Lester Young (*Jubilee* #184) and another playing for three award-winning alto sax stars, old friends Benny Carter and Willie Smith and the nascent bebop genius, Charlie Parker (*Jubilee* #186). The one occasion when the King and the Bird played together was on this special broadcast for black servicemen, and it's also the only time that Cole ever played the jazz standard "Cherokee." Both of these shows feature some numbers where Buddy Rich joins in, and they were possibly both recorded on the same day—though that must have been an incredible occasion, when Cole, Parker, Smith, Carter, Rich, and Young were all in the NBC studio being used by the AFRS.

Around the same time, Cole made one final project with Norman Granz, a reunion studio date with Lester Young, and a pair of solo piano tracks, both of which were related to *The Jazz Scene*, a pioneering jazz anthology album eventually released in December 1949. Granz seems to have pulled the session together (we don't know the exact date, but it was probably early April) when the two principals were in town at the same time and so, once again, was Buddy Rich. Usually, union regulations called for four sides per session, but on this occasion, as everybody was playing so well—and would likely never get together again—Granz recorded eight tunes in one shot. The 1942 Pres-King date was a trio of tenor, piano, and bass, and here it was a slightly different trio of tenor, piano, and drums.

The 1946 repertoire consists of seven standards and a blues; some are fast, some are slow, but what's more notable than that is the way Young and Cole mix moods while sticking to specific tempos. Most of the faster numbers, like "I Want to Be Happy" (the one track by this group that was issued on the original *Jazz Scene* in 1949), "I've Found a New Baby," and "I Want to Be Happy" (the latter compliments "Tea for Two" from the 1942 date; both are from *No, No, Nanette*) have an undercurrent of melancholy even while swinging mightily. Likewise, the slower numbers, like the ancient ballad "Peg O' My Heart" and "The Man I Love," are never purely sad (and even less sentimental) but always have an element of whimsy. Young is simultaneously happy and sad, and his mid-tempo solos, like "Somebody Loves Me" and "Mean to Me," are even more accurately concocted cocktails of mixed moods.

"Back to the Land" (the title apparently refers to the earthiness of the blues) is a highly eloquent blues, laconic and laid back, that also makes you want to laugh and cry at the same time—what Young might call "laughin' to keep from cryin'." "I Cover the Waterfront," the only track to survive in two takes, is the ballad masterpiece; Young's solo has a probing, searching quality that suggests he is indeed combing each and every dive along the waterfront, looking for the one he loves. Throughout, the King matches the Pres mood for mood, even in the majority of these numbers that fall in the emotional cracks between moods. "Somebody Loves Me" is also about searching, though in this case, Young and Cole are somewhat more optimistic, as if they fully expect to find that someone that they're both looking for. On the whole, the session includes some of Cole's freshest and most inspired playing; Pres motivates him to keep away from his signature licks, and we only hear faint hints of them here and there—he seems to hint at a few familiar phrases particularly on fast tempos and on tunes he has played many times before, like "New Baby." Even so, his playing is immediately identifiable as no one else but King Cole.

We don't know the actual order that the tracks were recorded in, but the date probably started with "Peg O' My Heart," since Rich isn't present—Nat later remembered that Buddy showed up late, so the two of them got going without him. That the song is so far outside of Cole's wheelhouse apparently necessitated an especially unique ballad performance from the pianist. This may have been a sentimental selection by Cole in honor of his friend Marvin Fisher, whose father, Fred Fisher, composed "Peg" in 1913. In the early postwar era, the hepcats and bopsters would have certainly considered this old-time cornball stuff, the title of a 1912 play that inspired a song the following year. But Cole and Young, not having anything like a familiar riff to fall back on, make it work on its own terms and seem gloriously believable—much like Sinatra later did with the prehistoric waltzes of his 1962 album *All Alone*.

"I Want to Be Happy" was originally issued on *The Jazz Scene* 78 album (and then a 10" LP) in 1949, with Cole credited as "Aye Guy" (apparently pronounced "A Guy"); other tracks were issued on Mercury and then Clef singles, and eventually Clef, Verve, and Norgran LPs, although Cole wouldn't be credited under his own name almost until the CD era. Even on the fast and swinging numbers, this is hardly a jam session; this is two master storytellers spinning yarns on the tenor saxophone and piano. Every note is loaded with meaning and melody, and the spaces between the notes are hardly empty but loaded with even more meaning than the notes themselves.

As a postscript, there are two unaccompanied piano solos that were first heard in 1994 when *The Jazz Scene* was released on CD. Neither the song titles and nor the pianist were identified on the masters; it was presumed they were by Billy Strayhorn, who was believed to have done a session of his own for the album (in addition to having arranged a session with baritone saxophonist Harry Carney and a string section). Strayhorn's biographer, David Hajdu (who hadn't yet heard the recordings), volunteered two Strayhorn-style titles, and the tracks were released as "Halfway to Dawn" and "Tailspin" by Strayhorn on the finished CD package. Yet it was clear from the instant the set was released that this mystery pianist wasn't Strayhorn, as Hajdu agreed when he actually heard the tracks for the first time.

If one listens to "Halfway to Dawn" and "Tailspin" immediately after the eight Lester Young-Nat Cole titles from 1946, there's little doubt that the pianist here is Cole; he has Cole's general presence, Cole's crystalline touch, Cole's sense of timing. Of course, there's no absolutely perfect point of comparison, since Cole never recorded unaccompanied piano anywhere else. The pieces are stately and elegiac, with a pronounced Tatum influence; Professor Edward Green opined that "Halfway" sounds like a high-speed Tatum tour-de-force slowed down to something more like a tone poem.[63]

Cole made one other jazz date, apart from the Trio, on March 26, 1946, under the approving eye of Capitol Records. Here he served as a guest star with two of his favorite people: the superlative pop and jazz vocalist Jo Stafford, and her musical director and future husband Paul Weston. Both Cole and Herbie Haymer are prominent guests throughout: Cole opens the jazz and blues standard "Baby, Won't You Please Come Home" with an unmistakable piano intro, and he also makes substantial contributions to "Cindy," which sounds kind of like big-band bluegrass—it might be considered his first country and western (C&W) record, fifteen or so years before "Ramblin' Rose." "Riding on the Gravy Train" and "(I'll Be Home with You in) Apple Blossom Time," a 1920 oldie that was revived by the Andrews Sisters in 1941 as a major hit of the World War II era, are also worthy vehicles for the combination.

Stafford, Cole, and Haymer are all so marvelously in sync with each other that one wishes they'd done a whole album together, but we're lucky to have these four tracks. (One also wishes that Cole had sung a duet with Stafford on one of these tracks, although a black man and a white woman singing together was rarely if ever done at this point.) We don't know whose idea it was for Stafford to include Cole and the two other guest stars on the session, except that it encouraged Capitol's artists to think of themselves as a family. As with the International Jazzmen, Cole's presence wasn't any kind of a secret; he was clearly credited on the original 78 labels. (And when the records were sold in music shops in black neighborhoods, Cole's participation was actually advertised.)[64] Stafford would return the favor seven months later when she became the first guest star on the premiere episode of the Trio's new NBC radio series, *King Cole Trio Time* (sponsored by Wildroot Cream Oil), on October 19, 1946.[65]

This was less than two months before Nat met Maria, at which point forces were then set in motion that dictated that there would be no more jam sessions in his life, no more playing for scale, or whatever it was Harry Lim and Eddie Laguna were paying. It might be ironic that Granz gave Cole the money to obtain his divorce from Nadine—neither of them probably realized that this would be the end of their association (with the exception of a reunion on Cole's NBC TV show in 1957 and a European tour in 1960), and that the woman who would replace Nadine in Nat's life would push him in a direction far removed from Norman.

There are just a couple of jazz leftovers from 1946 and '47. Throughout the peak years of the Trio at Capitol, 1943–1948, they routinely won the *Metronome* magazine poll for best small combo, and Cole participated in the annual "Metronome All-Stars" sessions, two years in a row, in December 1946 and 1947. The 1946 date is mostly swing players, including old friends Charlie Shavers, Coleman Hawkins, and Buddy Rich, plus Lawrence Brown, Johnny Hodges, and Harry Carney, all from the Ellington band. One side of the issued disc features none other than Sinatra singing one of Cole's own most familiar numbers, "Sweet Lorraine," with prominent piano accompaniment (and intro) by Cole, the only time they officially worked together on a commercial recording. The flip side is a blues titled "Nat meets June," on which Cole sings a duet with June Christy of the Kenton band; it starts slow but goes into swingtime after the vocal. The 1947 date is mostly more modern-oriented players, such as Dizzy Gillespie, Bill Harris, Flip Phillips, and Buddy DeFranco, in an octet setting on "Leap Here" and then the same soloists with the full Stan Kenton Orchestra on the flip side, "Metronome Riff." Cole doesn't sing on either but makes his presence known just the same.

"Nat Meets June" had, apparently, come together at the last minute. "That was kind of a fluke experience," said June Christy.

> Up until that particular date, the Metronome All-Stars had always been just instrumentalists. I just happened to be in the theater when they

> were recording and somebody didn't show, one of the stars who was to have been on the recording date, and since I was available, someone suggested, "Why don't we have Nat and June do something together?" To me it was such a supreme pleasure because I had only been with the [Kenton] band for about a year, but I had been a fan of Nat for a long, long time before that. Naturally, we didn't have any music or anything and Nat says, "Well, let's just sing some blues." And I don't know if I can do it. And he says, "Sure you can!" He just made up the lyrics and I had such fun doing it. I just sat on the piano stool with him.[66]

Perhaps the last recorded jam session that Cole officially took part in occurred in June 1947, and it was produced by another jazz impresario named "Norman." This was Gene Norman, who started a series of jazz concerts in southern California titled "Just Jazz," although unlike Granz, Norman was a much smoother, less abrasive character who also enjoyed a long career as a deejay and radio and TV host. Like Granz, he gradually transitioned into record production, launching the successful label GNP Crescendo, which celebrated its sixty-fifth birthday in 2019, and, unlike Granz's Verve Records, is still independent. Unlike Granz, Norman never took his "Just Jazz" concert on the road beyond the general Los Angeles area, but he did open his own club, the famous Crescendo on Sunset Strip. Cole participated in two known *Just Jazz* concerts that were recorded and distributed via the AFRS, one in 1947 in Pasadena, in which they share the bill with a JATP-like group of swing all-stars, and another at the Shrine in LA in 1949, part of the Trio's concert tour with Woody Herman's Second Herd.

The June 23, 1947, show at the Pasadena Concert opened with a set by the Trio, alas never issued commercially, followed by an all-star jam session wherein Cole, Moore, and Miller work with Charlie Shavers, Willie Smith, vibes pioneer Red Norvo, and, for the only time, future tenor star Stan Getz. Even more than Getz, the rarest soloist in this context is Oscar Moore, in his final months with the Trio.[67] Three tunes have circulated, and they're all Cole perennials: "Body and Soul" opens with Shavers playing the melody in his usual expressive, plaintive fashion, giving the bridge (and its numerous key changes) over to Cole, before Smith then takes the last eight. Norvo solos first, revealing a much more contemplative approach than Hampton, and then Getz, who we might expect to sound more like Lester Young at this early stage but actually already sounds like Stan Getz. Then it's Cole's turn to solo, and while he uses block chords, there are none of his familiar quotes: no "Mountain King" here, for once.

There's an epic thirteen-minute "How High the Moon" that, at one point, was issued on four 78 RPM single sides, wherein everybody gets a few choruses, starting with Shavers, who builds gradually and logically to high notes at the very top end of the trumpet's range. Cole's solo fades away and comes back, indicating some missing program, but it is a fully coherent statement, different from anything else he ever played on "Moon." Though he seems to be avoiding his quote technique, near the end he can't resist the urge to dance around the melody to "London Bridge." Shavers then leads the group on the ensemble "shout" chorus, which never quite states the famous "Moon" melody, but which sets up a chorus of drum breaks from Louis Bellson. In "I Got Rhythm," Cole and Miller solo together in a true duet, with both getting equal attention (this is essentially the routine they would develop into "Breezy and the Bass"); Shavers again heads for the stratosphere before the two saxes, Getz and Smith, solo like they're trying to tie the tune into knots, and we build a longer, bigger climactic break from Bellson. What Cole probably liked most about this show was that the horn men, in particular Shavers, all solo in an exuberant extroverted fashion but never resort to the flashy grandstanding that many observers, including Cole himself, found distasteful in the later JATP concerts.

Cole would continue to play piano (as we shall soon see, no less than four of his first albums were all piano-centric) but virtually never again in one of these jam session settings. It was perfectly appropriate that this part of his career should both begin and end with Norman Granz. The producer was, in fact, the opposite of Lionel Hampton in this one regard: where Hamp took credit for encouraging Cole to sing, Granz stated plainly, "Oddly, I never dug his singing, because I was so overwhelmed by his piano playing."[68]

Now that's obviously an exaggeration. More likely, it was the overall excellent of Nat's singing—so easy to "dig"—that made Norman realize that this was the thing that would eventually take Nat away from being purely a jazz pianist—and eventually away from him. In a way, it was inevitable that Cole would part company with Granz, even as early as his first hits on Capitol. But if Norman professed not to like Nat's later music, Cole likewise expressed his misgivings with the direction that the Jazz at the Philharmonic concerts were increasingly taking. "It started out alright. We had really good men on the early sessions. I got sound musicians like Lester Young, Buck Clayton, Charlie Parker, Lee Young, Willie Smith, and they all knew what they were doing. I used to insist on musicianship and good jazz. But later the hotheads took over and found they could get even better audience reaction by honking, high notes, and turning somersaults while playing."[69]

It's significant that Cole blames (and declines to name) these "hothead" musicians for the excesses of JATP (he was hardly the only one to feel this way) rather than pointing the finger at Granz himself; he was still grateful to Norman. And Granz would continually acknowledge how Cole had helped launch his career as a producer, both of recordings and concerts, in which he became one of the few promoters to actually get rich from jazz—and without ripping anybody off along the way. In return, Granz gave Cole the chance to express an aspect of his artistry that might otherwise never have been documented, and his own legacy, along with that of the art of jazz piano in general, would have been so much poorer.

4

Expanding the Canvas

1946–1947

A lot of notes lying around that old piano. I just pick out the ones I like.
—NAT KING COLE

IN 1941, AS WE HAVE SEEN, the King Cole Trio played Kelly's Stable on "Swing Street" in New York, where they worked with the already legendary Billie Holiday. This was also the moment when Cole met the songwriter Don George, who would later work with him on several important numbers, most importantly the 1949 "Calypso Blues." When George later wrote about the occasion, he described Cole strictly as Holiday's accompanist, nothing more. Like the good storyteller that he was, George played up the drama between Cole and Ralph Watkins, the former bootlegger who owned Kelly's. "Watkins got upset because Nat continually came in and rehearsed and practiced on the piano. He complained, 'What does this guy think he's going to do, play in Carnegie Hall? He's hired to accompany Billie—if she shows up. But he comes in and practices three or four hours every day!'"[1]

The mind races to two questions: first, how would Watkins have responded if someone had told him that Cole would indeed play Carnegie Hall (the first time would be just six years later in 1947) and that, soon after, Cole would become so successful and popular that even Carnegie Hall couldn't book him? Second, what would Nat Cole, who was then practicing piano four hours a day (and then playing another four hours in nightly gigs) have thought if you had told him that the greatest success of his career wouldn't come from the piano at all?

COLE'S OWN PERSONAL and professional lives were relatively stable at the start of 1946, but there were contradictory signals. He spent much of the year in New York, which served as the temporary home base for his recording, broadcasting, and personal appearances, and if he wasn't there, he was on the road.

One place where he was not was home in Los Angeles with Nadine; but although she didn't travel with him, few if any stories have surfaced about Nat being involved with anyone else. In January, he took a major step forward to symbolically demonstrate his marital commitment to Nadine when he purchased a luxurious house for the two of them. It was located at 1917 West 21st Street, in what was then known as the "Blueberry Hill" neighborhood of Los Angeles.

When, in May, the sale was complete, all of a sudden it became clear that much more was at stake than their marriage. When the Coles' new neighbors in the all-white area realized just exactly who was coming to dinner, they were aghast. Local white homeowners took him to court, and, citing "race covenants designed to prevent non-whites from occupying certain pieces of property," obtained a temporary restraining order prohibiting the Coles from entering the house they now owned.[2] The black press reported, "The eyes of the nation are shifting to California, where momentous decisions are being awaited by the State Supreme Court body."[3] Thankfully, by mid-June, Nat and Nadine were "adjudged victors" when an out-of-court agreement enabled them "to move into their swank Blueberry Hill home."[4]

Yet here was a case of fate enjoying a big belly laugh at Cole's expense: in the very month that the sale went through, May 1946, Cole would meet the woman who soon became the love of his life. Maria Hawkins Ellington was a former band singer (most famously, albeit briefly, with Duke Ellington, although the name was a coincidence) and daughter of a highly upscale Boston family—members of what was then called the "Black Bourgeoisie." She was also the widow of a flyer, an Army Air Force lieutenant, named Spurgeon Neal Ellington, who had been killed in a plane crash in December 1945, roughly two years after they were married. At the time she toured with Ellington, she was living with Duke's lead saxophone player, Otto "Toby" Hardwick, one of the veterans in the band and eighteen years her senior.[5] As Maria and Nat's daughter, Natalie, later wrote, "She was a beautiful, light-skinned woman of elegance and refinement, and he was a dark-skinned man without a lot of education who could sing and play the piano. Despite his wealth and fame, Dad was the one who had married above his station—and my mother's family never let him forget it."[6]. But that was mostly in the future—and no doubt contributed to the rift between Nat and Maria fifteen years later.

At the moment Maria and Nat met, the King Cole Trio was headlining on a stellar bill of black talent at the Zanzibar, a hip and happening club on West 49th Street at the top of Times Square that was, briefly, one of the major presenters of jazz and black talent south of Harlem. Co-starring with Cole was the comedy legend Eddie Anderson, known to many generations as

"Rochester Van Jones" on *The Jack Benny Show*, and Maria Hawkins, who was billed simply as "Marie" during the months when she toured with Ellington, was also on the bill. Maria was singing a new song titled "Personality"[7] when Nat heard her for the first time; by the summer, they were an item. Thus, even before the legal action in Blueberry Hill was completed and the Coles were able to move in, Nat was already at least vaguely aware that his marriage to Nadine was about to come to an end. After all that fuss, Cole himself would never actually live in the Blueberry Hill home (which cost him $19,000);[8] instead, it would go to Nadine as part of the divorce settlement.

It can hardly be a coincidence that even as the stakes were increasing in his personal and romantic life, he was about to enjoy unprecedented success as a singer of love songs. In early fall, Cole became the first solo black vocalist to land a number one hit on the pop chart—and with a love song, no less: "For Sentimental Reasons." Ever since the launch of the record sales chart in *Billboard* magazine in 1940,[9] the only artists of color to reach the top spot were vocal groups, specifically the Mills Brothers and the Ink Spots. "For Sentimental Reasons" was written by two men who were better known as harmony singers than composers, Ivory "Deek" Watson of the Ink Spots and William "Pat" Best, of the Four Tunes. In later years, each challenged the other's contention about who wrote what: Best claimed that he wrote the whole thing, both words and music, but Watson insisted that he wrote the lyrics. [10] And that's not all: it might be said that the veteran songwriter Jimmy McHugh also deserved part of the credit, since the bridge is taken almost note-for-note from his 1943 song "A Lovely Way to Spend an Evening." Likewise, the title of "For Sentimental Reasons" had been used before, on a successful 1936 song by Abner Silver, Al Sherman, and Edward Heyman, which had been recorded by Tommy Dorsey, Mildred Bailey, Kay Kyser, and others.

Yet no matter who wrote what, the 1946 "For Sentimental Reasons" was a beautiful song; Cole's 1946 recording of it was a stunning disc and inarguably a vocal record, rather than a combo record. We hear Cole's voice almost immediately; after a very brief piano flourish, he sings and plays with absolute clarity. After the vocal, the song goes back to the bridge, which is divided into four bars of Cole's piano, as usual playing mostly highly personalized melody, and then four bars of Oscar Moore, playing mostly improv. Even more than "Route 66," this is a song of postwar optimism—after four years of loud, brassy patriotic numbers, here's a love song imbued with pure simplicity and absolute tranquility. The Trio was almost ten years old by 1946, and it had taken all this time, a decade of constant work, to reach this point of perfection.

By August 1946, when he recorded the song, the very air was abounding in sentimental reasons. It was clear that Nat and Maria were inseparable, a relationship only slightly inconvenienced by the fact of his current marriage. There would be occasional fits, starts, interruptions, and distractions, and near the end they almost broke up, but Maria would remain the "queen" to his "king," as the papers were fond of calling them, the mother of his children, and, much too soon, the keeper of his flame, the custodian of his legacy.

Exactly three days before the "Sentimental Reasons" session, Cole tackled another new song that would have equally important ramifications for his long-term career. "The Christmas Song" had come to him from Robert Wells Levinson, another young songwriter whom he was encouraging. A year earlier, in summer 1945, Cole had recorded two songs by Levinson, the charming "I Wanna Turn Out My Light" (for MacGregor) and the lowlife novelty number, "It Is Better to Be by Yourself" (which the Trio also performed in their only feature film of 1946, *Breakfast in Hollywood* (released by United Artists). Based on another popular radio program, this was one of the Trio's better features, and they're exceptionally well photographed and presented in a four-minute sequence that also includes another novelty, the purely nonsensical "Solid Potato Salad." (The movie performance of "Better" is even more intense than the unissued Capitol master, incorporating several exciting tempo changes, as well as an instrumental section that incorporates the material from "Jumpin' at Capitol" and "I Found a New Baby." Director Harold D. Schuster affords them considerable dignity even while they're singing about "potato salad" and telling us that "a man's best friend is his dog.")

Thus, Cole was receptive when, around the same time, the songwriter—now known professionally as "Bob Wells"—came to him with something called "The Christmas Song" that he had written with his new songwriting partner, singer and composer Mel Tormé. Both collaborators told the story many times about how "The Christmas Song" came to be written; in fact, the story itself even became iconic—a kind of a creation myth.[11] At this time, Tormé, who had started his career first as a singer with a big band (the orchestra briefly led by comedian and gambler Chico Marx), then formed his own vocal group (The Mel-Tones), had recently gone out on his own as a solo vocalist. He was also one of the few singers of the day, along with Cole and Peggy Lee (all three of whom were managed by Carlos Gastel), who pursued a side career as a songwriter: Mel, then twenty, wrote the music, and Bob, then twenty-three, the words.

The commercial Christmas song was a new innovation, an indirect byproduct of the war. There had barely been a handful of these in the 1930s (the most notable example being "Santa Claus Is Coming to Town"), but then it was "White Christmas," first heard around the time of the attack on Pearl Harbor, with which Irving Berlin and Bing Crosby launched the idea of the new-fangled, secular Christmas song. Introduced in the movie *Holiday Inn*, "White Christmas" was an overwhelming hit, but it was perceived as such a unique occurrence that it was only tentatively followed by others: "I'll Be Home for Christmas" in 1943 and then "Have Yourself a Merry Little Christmas," from *Meet Me in St. Louis*, in 1944. (Which may explain why Cole waited a whole year to record the Wells–Tormé song; likewise, no black artist had recorded a holiday song prior to this.) These were all songs of the wartime era and thus imbued with a built-in emotional resonance that they might not have otherwise had; as Crosby famously observed of "White Christmas," it became something like a hymn for peace, a kind of secular prayer.

"The Christmas Song" was born in late spring 1945, while the war was still raging in the Pacific and a sweltering heat wave was engulfing Los Angeles. Tormé had gone over to Wells's house in the San Fernando Valley, which, as Mel noted, was always "at least ten degrees warmer than the rest of the town, blistered in the July sun."[12] The door was unlocked (not uncommon in the days before Charles Manson), Mel walked in, shouted for Bob, and, on not getting any answer, sat down at the piano. He found four lines written on a piece of paper, beginning with the soon-to-be familiar phrase, "Chestnuts roasting on an open fire." Soon, Bob materialized, and explained, "It was so damn hot today I thought I'd write something to cool off. All I could think of was Christmas and cold weather." Apparently, these were just lines of verse; Wells hadn't even realized that he was setting down the basic idea for a song, but Tormé did. It then took the two of them all of forty-five minutes to write the rest of it.

After finishing what they very simply titled "The Christmas Song," their first move was to play it for Gastel and then lyricist and publisher Johnny Burke, who published it through Burke & Van Heusen Music. "Mel Tormé brought it to me while I was working at the Trocadero," Cole remembered in 1961.[13] "It was in the middle of a heat wave in June, when so many Christmas songs seem to be recorded. I told him it was beautiful, but I didn't feel it would be right to do it with just a Trio. Carlos suggested that we add a few strings just for this one song." It's often assumed that it was Capitol Records who pressured Cole to go into a more pop direction, to add strings and work with orchestras, but Nat and Carlos were the ones who had to pressure the label to let him add a few violins. In fact, Cole added, "Capitol was adamant against the idea, so I cut it with [just] the Trio."

That first recording, from June 1946,[14] sounds more like a blueprint, a rough sketch. On the same date, he also recorded a take of "You Should Have

Told Me," one of his "custom ballads," by Redd Evans, and here, as on most of his slower love songs, the open spaces surrounding his vocals and piano melody notes sound just right. But on the Trio-only take of "The Christmas Song" these become huge sonic caverns, fairly begging to be filled in. "As soon as they played it back," Cole added, "I knew it was wrong, and I finally convinced them to let me remake it with the string section added."

In August, when Cole went ahead with the string section, the Trio was still lingering around New York; on August 16, they took part in a benefit for wounded veterans at the famous Lewisohn Stadium. For most of the summer they were broadcasting regularly for NBC, most frequently on *The Kraft Music Hall* in a summer replacement run for Bing Crosby, which co-starred comedian Edward Everett Horton and pianist-society bandleader Eddy Duchin; they were also performing with Perry Como on the *Chesterfield Supper Club*.[15] The Trio cut all of its sessions from May to December in Manhattan, not least because Maria was in New York and Nadine was back home on Blueberry Hill. When Cole began to think about adding strings to "The Christmas Song," the first arranger that he reached out to was Russ Case, a staff conductor for NBC. Case, however, didn't want to violate his exclusive contract with RCA Victor records, and so he recommended his assistant, Charlie Grean.[16]

The remake (the issued take) of "The Christmas Song," with Charlie Grean conducting a string section, took place on August 19 (three days before "For Sentimental Reasons").[17] When you listen to the June and the August versions of "The Christmas Song," you can hear how most of the heavy lifting was already done by Cole; all that Grean had to do was fill in the sonic blanks remaining in the existing Trio arrangement with a few well-placed violins. Not a huge string section, mind you, but just enough; throughout, the most prominent instrument behind Cole's voice is never the strings but, as always, his piano—the notes descending down from the heavens like so many snowflakes. "The Christmas Song" also includes eight bars of instrumental, divided between Cole and Moore. Cole returns to sing the last eight bars, but Moore gets the last word, playing a coda that quotes brilliantly from "Jingle Bells," which would remain part of the song for as long as Cole (and his disciples) continue to sing it.

On the same date, Cole recorded his latest lowlife novelty by Roy Alfred, "The Best Man," for which he again tinkered with the Trio format by adding drummer Jack "The Bear" Parker. Thus, somehow in two sessions over four days in August 1946, Cole created three significant chart hits: "The Best Man" (#14), "The Christmas Song" (#3), and "For Sentimental Reasons" (#1). In the long run of Cole's career, "The Christmas Song" would be the most important.

Mel liked to boast, "It was unquestionably the most successful thing that Nat ever sang," and while that was at least a slight exaggeration—"Nature Boy" and "Mona Lisa," coming up in the next few years, were also blockbusters—in statistical terms, "Christmas Song" possibly surpasses even "Nature Boy" as probably the most "covered" of any song that Cole introduced.

Pittsburgh Courier columnist Billy Rowe noted, "The King Cole Trio's 'Christmas Song' is expected to push 'White Christmas' off the jukeboxes. Capitol is so sure of it [that] the company made 130,000 for its first pressing, more than it has for any other artist. With nine strings backing the ever-popular group, the tune is one of the best we've heard. It's chock full of the Yuletide Spirit for kids from one to ninety-two, and Nat's intimate voice is at its best, to say nothing of the intoxicating rhythm of Oscar Moore and Johnny Miller."[18]

Now with two formidable hits under their belt, the Trio rose another rung on the show business ladder when they played the world famous Paramount Theater in Times Square (sharing the bill with fellow Gastel client Stan Kenton and His Orchestra) starting in October 1946—and then were extended. The *New York Amsterdam News* agreed: "That wonderful guy, King Cole tells me that his Trio is being held over for four more weeks at the [New York] Paramount, and his sensational recording of 'Christmas Song' has already sold 350,000 in just two weeks."[19] *Seventeen* correctly predicted at the time, "Now it looks as though 'The Christmas Song,' that the Trio plays against a background of twelve strings, will vie with 'White Christmas' as a seasonal standard."[20] Cole himself would re-record it on several occasions, including a full-orchestral version with Nelson Riddle in 1953 and a stereo version of that Riddle arrangement in 1961.[21]

As we've seen, the most recent "secular" Christmas songs, "White Christmas," "I'll Be Home for Christmas," and "Have Yourself a Merry Little Christmas" all pivot around a shared notion of wartime separation: I'm dreaming of a Christmas when I can see my loved ones again—when I can see *you* again—if only in my dreams; the best we can do for now is dream about a white Christmas just like the ones we used to know—before the war.

Thus, the timing for "The Christmas Song" worked out perfectly: by 1946, we were ready to experience a new kind of contemporary urban Christmas. Unlike the wartime Christmas songs, "The Christmas Song" is hardly a song of nostalgia; it is a song very much of Christmas present. Note how Wells's lyric is all written explicitly in the present tense, those chestnuts are roasting on that open fire right this very moment, and Jack Frost is nipping at one's nose even as we speak. When I hear "White Christmas" I visualize a snow-covered New England countryside, like the one depicted in *Holiday Inn*;

when I hear "The Christmas Song," I picture all those "folks dressed up like Eskimos" trudging through the slush in a contemporary urban setting, down city streets, strolling past department stores and sidewalk Santas. There's no mention of a separation, nor any hint that the old time Christmases were somehow better; no, thank you very much, the Christmas that we are enjoying right now is just perfect. Christmas is a holiday with a great tradition, but it's right now that we're celebrating, not some old ghost of Christmas past.

THE FORTUNES OF THE TRIO were now rising in direct parallel to those of Capitol Records; as we've seen, throughout the war, the label was using the recording studios of the MacGregor transcription operation even while MacGregor recorded and released pre-recorded music by most of Capitol's leading artists. Then, around the time the war ended, the two companies ceased working together. Both sides cited their own reasons for the split: MacGregor claimed it was now "too busy" to devote so much time to a single client,[22] and Capitol claimed that MacGregor had sabotaged the sound of its studio by painting the walls.[23] The real issue, however, seems to be that MacGregor and Capitol both now wanted a piece of each other's action: MacGregor asked Capitol to give them a royalty of a penny for every disc sold of every master recorded in the facility, which would have meant Capitol would have had to pay out a fortune on blockbuster hits like "Nature Boy" and "Manana." Capitol, in turn was tired of letting MacGregor make money by issuing radio transcriptions of Capitol artists like Cole, Kenton, and Lee.

Capitol launched its Transcription Library Service in 1946, and both Cole and Peggy Lee made their first recordings for the new wing in March, which is when the service was announced in the label's house organ, the *Capitol News*. "Capitol Records has formed the Capitol Transcription Service, a division of Capitol Records, with program service for radio stations throughout the nation." The three key men running the operation were Don Otis, program director; Walter Davidson, head of national sales and general manager; and Lee Gillette, head of programming production. Nat King Cole and Gillette first began their long relationship as artist and producer on the 1946 Capitol ET dates, which began in March with two versions of the King Cole Trio theme, "F. S. T." ("Fine, Sweet, and Tasty"). The recordings themselves began to be heard around the country in July.

The Golden Age of Radio was already entering its final phase in the postwar era, but Capitol Transcription's service was highly profitable for a few years at least and recorded much invaluable music, including many sessions by artists then not commercially recording for Capitol, like Duke Ellington and Gene

Krupa and their orchestras. Cole would record sixty songs for the service, produced over four years (until 1950), roughly half of which were also done for conventional Capitol 78 RPM singles. For example, Cole recorded his only version of the Harold Arlen standard "I've Got the World on a String" at his second session for the Capitol ET (electrical transcriptions) service, in 1946. The label was determined that the audio quality of their own ET releases should be at least as good as MacGregor's, and, if anything, these 16" discs sound even better; the surfaces are as quiet as recording tape, and the Trio sounds bright and vibrant.

The pinnacle of success for the division was probably about 1947–48, when the service had as roughly 300 subscribing radio stations, drawing from a library of 2,000 (later 3,000) individual selections.[24] Capitol got in late but managed to be profitable. By 1950, what we now know of as deejay radio had taken over, and local hosts were playing actual commercial singles and albums; with the market share of energy in broadcasting shifted over to television, the idea of creating special original music for airplay was soon a thing of the past. (Although, as we'll see, in 1950, a new firm called Snader Telescriptions had the idea of doing the same thing with pre-filmed musical performances for television.)

ADDING STRINGS—FOR "THE Christmas Song" only—was just one of the many new ideas that Cole introduced around this time. One such notion went back to the beginnings of the King Cole Trio in 1937 and 1938, although it resurfaced with a vengeance in the early postwar period. In the mid to late 1940s, the Trio recorded almost a dozen piano-centric works that took Cole's playing into a whole new area, a kind of music that virtually no one had played before—a unique approach that combined elements of jazz, popular, and classical music and which remains sui generis to him.

At the same time the original Trio was being formed, first Maxine Sullivan and then Ella Fitzgerald, as we've noted, launched a vogue for taking traditional songs, folk airs, and nursery rhymes and swinging them, starting with "Loch Lomond" and "A Tisket, A Tasket." In the very early days, the King Cole Trio likewise found traditional and classical melodies to be a ready source of new material, and their first radio transcriptions include swing treatments of "Three Blind Mice," "Swanee River" (the latter also inspired by the Swanee Inn), and "Button, Button." Cole also devised jive arrangements of Johann Strauss's 1866 "The Blue Danube" (1938) and Franz Liszt's 1850 "Liebesträume" (1939). Cole really makes a point to jive up Strauss: he constantly changes the tempo, in a way that shows off the Trio's developing stop-and-start technique, and for the most part renders Strauss in 4/4—a most unusual way to play a waltz. On "Liebesträume," however, the Trio approaches Liszt's iconic melody with a more serious intent. Only a year later, they're trying to enhance a classical piece by means of modern rhythmic techniques and harmonic voicings, not necessarily just swinging it for the sake of swinging it. This is a highly thoughtful rendition, with Cole laying out the tune in long piano tremolos, playing it with wit and humor but never making fun of it. But better was to come.

In 1944, Cole introduced his remarkable interpretation of *Prelude in C Sharp Minor* (1944), the 1892 keyboard tour-de-force by Sergei Rachmaninoff, which he followed a year later with "Barcarolle" (from Jacques Offenbach's opera, *Tales of Hoffmann*). Both of these pieces already had a history in the world of jazz and swing; in fact, both were frequently heard on the air during the ASCAP boycott of 1941. Thus, there already was a long tradition of "swinging the classics" (which Cole would continue in later years with "Madrid" and "Ebony Rhapsody"); however, that's not what the Trio is doing here with Rachmaninoff and Offenbach. Rather, Cole is inventing a whole new kind of chamber music that draws on all of these genres. The *Prelude* is especially intense and dramatic, and Cole plays it with great pianistic energy. Although he can't help but swing it—at least a little bit—it's not about the swinging; it's about the melodic invention, and the transformation of a classic into something wholly new. There's a run at the end of the *Prelude* where Cole, Moore, and Miller all solo briefly, as if they were playing "Honeysuckle Rose" or "Sweet Georgia Brown," and these additions serve to make Rachmaninoff sound more like Basie. "Barcarolle," which the Trio first recorded in a longer, four-minute arrangement for MacGregor transcriptions, is lighter and more romantic, appropriate for the song as a ballad from Act Three of Offenbach's opera, set in Venice and eternally associated with singing gondoliers.

In 1945, Cole pushed even further into this new area with "To a Wild Rose," the first of ten pieces in *Ten Woodland Sketches* (1896) by Edward MacDowell, an early American composer who had a profound influence on both the jazz and classical fields; Eastwood Lane and Bix Beiderbecke were among his devotees.[25] Cole invested a lot of thought and energy in his treatment of "To a Wild Rose," first attempting it in a Capitol session in May 1945, rejecting that version and then trying again almost a year later, in two takes from April 1946, one of which was issued at the time. Cole sets up MacDowell's tranquil theme, which depicts a peaceful woodland scene, and there is space for all three of the Trio to solo, in individual improvisations that remain true to the mood of MacDowell's music.

What remained for Cole was to develop his own original compositions in this idiom, whatever it was, semi-classical/semi-jazz chamber music. And that's precisely what he did: over the next two years, Cole wrote and recorded five such pieces: "Rex Rhumba," "In the Cool of Evening," "Rhumba Azul," "Laguna Mood," and "Lament in Chords" (the last credited to Oscar Moore), all recorded in 1946 and '47. At the very beginning of 1946—this is not even two years after the release of "Straighten Up and Fly Right"—Cole announced that he was going to play Carnegie Hall on January 16. He was taking the forthcoming concert very seriously, fully aware, he told the press, that several jazz orchestras (Goodman, Ellington, Lionel Hampton) had already played Carnegie, but as of 1946, no jazz small group had yet done so. What would he play? Some of his hits, naturally, but he also dropped tantalizing hints about a new kind of concert-type music for the Trio. "To those [hits] he expects to add originals by himself and the members of his unit, thus giving him an overall program of a certain number of songs which will be developed in theme to concert pitch."[26] Cole added that he would feature both of his partners, Moore and Miller, in extended solo features, and even more ambitiously, he was planning to use "additional musicians for background purposes," meaning classical-style strings and woodwinds. (This was well before "The Christmas Song" and "Nature Boy.")

Cole did participate in a major concert on January 16, 1946,[27] but it was as part of the Third Annual *Esquire* All Star Jazz Concert, at the Ritz Theater (on West 48th Street). Three award-winning groups were featured, Duke Ellington and his Famous Orchestra, Woody Herman and his Thundering Herd, and the King Cole Trio. One hour of the overall concert was broadcast over the relatively new ABC network, hosted by no less an eminence than Orson Welles. The Trio played two of their specialties, "After You've Gone" (a treatment and tempo much inspired by the Benny Goodman Quartet, with Cole playing homage to Teddy Wilson) and "Sweet Lorraine."[28]

The 1946 *Esquire* concert anticipates the KC3's two major appearances at Carnegie Hall, and even though they played their usual material, there was a concerted effort to brand the King Cole Trio as chamber music. Welles introduces the Trio in highly effusive terms, expounding on the notion of "chamber jazz" as a new form of the music designed for concert-style listening rather than dancing: "The next time your son asks you, 'Pop, what is 'chamber music?' Do not flub and fluster around and give the little fellow an evasive answer. Chamber music began a long time ago as works written for small groups. . . . Chamber music is still the best method of showing off the virtuosity of individual musicians, whether their hair be long or short. . . . The King Cole Trio has caused music lovers of infinite variety to sit quietly by and listen attentively too, and to pause and to ponder at the wonderful sounds three men can make together." At least one newspaper ran a photo from the concert, of Welles and Ellington watching as Leonard Feather presented Cole and Moore with the "Esky" award, with the caption, "Chamber Music Champs Receive Esquire All American Awards."[29]

Cole continued to talk about this new "serious" music he wanted to create: "Our popularity probably will put us in a better position to play a more serious type of music, especially in the jazz idiom. Then I hope to be able to perform the kind of music we tried so hard to make the public listen to and accept before." He added, "I'm in the middle of writing my concerto and hope to have it finished soon. I'd like to use new music by other composers too."[30] In various interviews, he mentioned forthcoming works from the songwriter Marvin Fisher, the arranger Frank Comstock,[31] and also his friend, the singer (and occasional songwriter) Frankie Laine, who had written a work titled "Swampland Nocturne." "Much of the work will be modern music . . . experimentation . . . three or four changes in tempo in a number . . . maybe a little like Debussy or Gershwin's serious compositions. There'll be lots of rhythm tunes too, of course, and some jazz rhumbas."[32] In a July 1946 interview, Cole informed journalist-photographer William Gottlieb that he had already recorded two original compositions intended for this concert, "Rhumba a la King" (aka "Rex Rhumba") and "Chant of the Blues." "I'll keep listening for what I want to play on the concert tour. Maybe this is a happy dream, and maybe it won't work—but I'm going to try, and hard, and you can't blame me for trying."[33]

When the group played the Chicago Opera House on September 16, 1947, which would be Moore's last major appearance with the Trio, *Down Beat* noted that they played, among others, "Rhumba Azul," "Laguna Mood," and "Lament in Chords" in addition to the hits, novelty songs, and ballads. The Trio made their debut as a "solo" act at Carnegie in October 1947, and while no recording or broadcast survives, according to one review, the Trio played an original by the new guitarist, Irving Ashby, titled "'Allegro-Suite,' which featured a pretty waltz bit."[34]

For the most part, Cole's five original chamber works follow the basic outline of most jazz discs in that they start with a theme, develop it over a chorus or two, give brief solos, usually to Cole and Moore, and then return to a new iteration of the original theme at the end. But other than that, they're not like any other jazz ever; there are no familiar standard chord progressions of any kind (no "Rhythm" changes) and no blues format. Overall, they have a lot in common with the two "mystery" piano solos from the *Jazz Scene* project, "Tailspin" and "Halfway to Dawn."

These titles represent the final culmination of, by 1946, nearly ten years of a close-as-brothers collaboration between Cole and Moore. They're so on the same page in terms of melody, harmony, rhythm, and, here especially, dynamics, that not only is one man's "very soft" exactly the same as the other man's, but they are as mirror images of each other, only on different instruments. On one level, they knew each other so well by this point that it was easier to play with each other, but it was also harder in that Cole was never satisfied; he kept kicking the music up a notch, and what should have gotten easier was getting harder and harder. Throughout, Nat and Oscar are remarkably *Sympatico*, even by their own standards; there seem to be at least six things happening at once, though the playing is tightly focused.

There are two lightly Latin-influenced works, "Rex Rhumba" (also called "Rhumba a la King"), which was first waxed for a Capitol Transcription in a slightly slower version (and at points seems like an outgrowth of the 1939 "Rhythm Serenade"), and "Rhumba Azul." Having stated the melody, the two principals start to chase each other, alternating between chordal and single-note solos, flowing in and out of each to blur the distinction. The Latin quotient remains understated—after all, this isn't just another *rhumba*, this is the *rhumba à la* King. "Rhumba Azul" ("Blue Rhumba") is more aggressive than "Rex Rhumba" but has less of a distinct melody. "Azul" is more like a series of Latinate phrases, played in close unison by Cole and Moore over a booming, rock-steady vamp by Miller. There's also more than a touch of a Latinate blues that anticipates Horace Silver's "Senor Blues."

"In the Cool of Evening" is more of a song-like melody than the two rhumbas, and one can more readily imagine lyrics being added at some point. That melody is heard as a recurring motif, mostly framing statements by Miller, and then Cole himself, leading to an especially elegant, graceful solo by Moore, reminding us that there were other great guitarists—Les Paul for one; but none of them had what Oscar had. They had plenty to offer, but he had Moore. Just as the piece threatens to meander into the realm of the semi-abstract, Cole pulls it back together by restating that main motif. The way Cole brings the theme back to us—until it's like an old friend in the last chorus—suggests that this is Cole's answer to Debussy's "Reverie" and Ellington's "Reminiscing in Tempo."

"Laguna Mood" is presumably named for the beach rather than producer Eddie Laguna of Sunset Records. The most tranquil of all, it could be titled "Sleepy Laguna," since it's an elegiac, restful tone poem for trio. The gentle washes of the piano and the guitar suggest limpid pools, or waves upon a tropical shore. This is programmatic and descriptive chamber music at its finest.

With both "Cool of the Evening" and "Laguna Mood," Cole has gotten as far away as he can from the standard format of jazz: theme-solos-theme and the concept of improvisations that run the cycle of chords and choruses; like few other works in jazz, these two rather remarkable instrumentals are thoroughly "through-composed." Taken collectively, the nine chamber works—three adaptations and six originals—are some of the most arrestingly lovely music in all the King Cole canon.

Throughout 1946 and '47, Cole continued to talk about the music he was going to play at these concerts. In summer 1946, in multiple interviews he mentions a forthcoming work titled "Concerto for Three."[35] This could have been another name for any of these pieces or possibly some umbrella title for combining two or more of them into an extended, suite-like work. At the Chicago Civic Opera House concert (September 1947), there were extended features for both Oscar and Johnny, respectively, "Lament in Chords" and "Breezy and the Bass." Neither was officially recorded for Capitol, but both survive in other ways. The first (preserved by Capitol Transcriptions), one of only three songs credited to Moore, is as the title promises, a feature for the guitar, though emphasizing single-string playing rather than chords, while "Breezy" (played by the Trio in the 1947 film *Killer Diller*) is an extended bass feature on "Rhythm" changes. Either one of these could have been part of the proposed "Concerto for Three." Cole described the piece as "completely unlike anything we have ever attempted before. It runs 10 minutes, some of it is out of tempo, and there is no vocal. It isn't the kind of music that lands atop the Hit Parade, but we feel it has lots of merits and that it shows the Trio in another light."[36] Presumably Cole performed the work at his premiere headlining concert at Carnegie Hall, October 18, 1947.

Cole's interest in this so-called chamber music reached its apogee just as Moore was getting ready to leave the group. Even though the Trio performed what was apparently a concert work ("Allegro Suite") by Ashby at Carnegie, the departure of Moore spelled the end of the Chamber series. It had taken so much work for Cole to get to this point with Moore and Miller that when they started leaving, he couldn't invest the energy to start all over again with Ashby and then Joe Comfort. The Chamber series was a direction that he saw the Trio going in 1945 and '46, but by 1947 and '48 he was starting to be pulled in other directions. There would be only one more semi-classical work, the 1949 "Laugh, Cool Clown," which shows how *Pagliacci* would sound with bongos.

Perhaps it's disappointing that Cole never continued the chamber series, but by this point, the days of the Trio itself were numbered. This is some of the most extraordinary music that Cole ever created: when he plays "To a Wild Rose," he's not so much hitting the notes on the keys of the piano but summoning up the sound of the rose itself, the actual melody of the petals as they fall. Likewise, on "Laguna Mood," he translates the sound of the rippling waves into tangible musical form. Cole had taken his music to a place where it had become so intimate, so personal, and so uniquely reflective of his own personality and soul that virtually no one, except for his very closest musical associates, could follow. This is some of the most dazzling and yet, at the same time, most exquisitely personal music of his entire career, and even seventy years after it was created, we still haven't fully caught up with it.

COLE WAS, ESSENTIALLY, moving beyond a strict definition of jazz on two fronts at once. "Laguna Mood" and "Rex Rhumba" amount to a rather thoughtful and sensitive assault on the bastions of classical and "serious" music even while such chart-topping ballads as "For Sentimental Reasons" and "The Christmas Song" represent the true beginning of his conquest of pop music. Cole may have been the most consistently creative musician-entertainer of the mid- to late 1940s—and well beyond; he was ceaselessly working to increase the artistic "scope" of his music (his preferred term) just as, say, Charlie Parker or Dizzy Gillespie were doing for theirs. We find much more experimentation in Cole's output than that of Jordan, Fitzgerald, or, at this particular moment, even Sinatra. By the late 1940s, the rest of the industry was trying to catch up to him—there were already numerous groups patterned after the Trio, both black and white, such as the Three (later Four) Blazers, the Page Cavanaugh Trio, and the Phil Moore Four, who frequently worked with singers like Doris Day, Mel Tormé, and even Sinatra, who wanted a little of Cole's magic in their own music. But Cole, as he would be for the rest of his career, was always at least a few steps ahead of the competition.

In the summer of 1946—not long after Maria entered Nat's life—at the same moment as the joint breakthrough of "For Sentimental Reasons" and "The Christmas Song," his stock was rapidly advancing on network radio as well. NBC had supported Cole from the beginning: the Trio was on the air for the National Broadcasting Corp. as early as 1938 (and then with *Swing Soiree* in 1939), and then he began to make inroads into *The Kraft Music Hall* in 1943, first alongside superstar Bing Crosby, then as part of the cast that essentially replaced him. *Down Beat* enthused, "Thursday is a top dialing night for good music. The *Kraft Music Hall* (NBC 8PM) continues as musically interesting as when Bing Crosby was in charge. Now the King Cole Trio, Eddie [*sic*] Duchin, songstress Milena Miller, and Russ Case's excellent band make up the menu."[37]

Finally, NBC gave the Trio their own series, *King Cole Trio Time*, sponsored by Wildroot Cream Oil (hair tonic); it was just fifteen minutes on a Saturday afternoon, but it was a breakthrough at the time: no other African American entertainers of that era had their own "regular," sponsored network series. For a brief time, the two shows overlapped, on Saturday, October 19, *King Cole Trio Time* premiered, with special guest Jo Stafford; then on Thursday, October 24, the Trio played *The Kraft Music Hall* for the last time (at least until the TV years), and on October 26, they did the second Wildroot show, with June Christy as guest.

Within a few weeks, the black press was proclaiming the show a hit: "Playing a record-breaking engagement at the [New York] Paramount, they will be held over until December. At the same time they are starring on their own, and the only, Negro commercial [meaning formally sponsored series], via the national outlet of NBC, while holding down another job on the *Kraft Music Hall*."[38] This quickly became a cause célèbre for the "race" intelligentsia; and, in fact, if the mainstream media didn't give the KC3 its props, readers were encouraged to give 'em hell. Columnist Billy Rowe complained, "The *New York Daily News* still refuses to list the King Cole Trio's 5:45 radio show via WNBC every Saturday evening. Some of you guys and gals out there ought to write 'em a letter and kick 'em around a bit." He not only provided readers with the name and address to write to at the *Daily News* but even the phone number, and suggested, "If you haven't got a nickel, get one from the NAACP."[39]

IN THE YEAR 1947, Nat King Cole would say goodbye to both of the two people he had been closest with in the early years of the Trio: Oscar Moore, his professional partner, and Nadine, his personal one. Now that the Trio was doing a regular radio show, in addition to constant touring, Moore, who had already been growing increasingly unreliable, was starting to crack under the strain. And early in the year, Cole officially parted with his first wife, Nadine Robinson Cole.

A few friends and industry people feigned shock at the split, but the larger truth was that the Coles had been essentially living apart for some years. Sometime around December 1946, while the Trio was playing the Paramount (an unprecedented nine-week run that lasted from October to the end of the year), Nat invited Nadine to join him in New York. Nadine's first thought was to book a day coach, but no, Nat assured her that he was making enough for her to take a much more expensive Pullman car. (The difference is important: Maria would have never given a second thought to traveling in any fashion other than first class.). Nadine and Nat were set to stay with Mary Kirk, wife of Cole's friend, bandleader Andy Kirk. She later recounted the incident in a highly dramatized account published in *Tan*, the black equivalent of *True Confessions*. "As it turned out, she would have been better off if she had elected to stay at home. For when she arrived in New York, it was then that she learned that Nat no longer wanted her as a wife. There was no mincing of words. . . . [H]e told her in precise language that he wanted a divorce, that he no longer loved her."[40]

By January, the press was reporting, "Nadine Cole has started her proceedings in New York. Named in the divorce action was Marie Ellington, at one time with Duke Ellington's band."[41] Once proceedings were initiated, it would take a year for the divorce decree to come through—and by that time Oscar would be gone as well. Ironically, the man who for years had been Nat's best friend and major musical partner wouldn't even be present at his wedding on Easter Sunday, 1948.

While waiting for the divorce to be finalized, Nat and the Trio—probably with Maria—spent most of the winter and spring of 1947 on the road. First, they played up and down the East Coast (Baltimore, Philly, DC, Boston, Secaucus, NJ, and Brooklyn, NY) and then gradually headed west (first passing through Detroit, three cities in Ohio, and a month in Chicago), then making it to Texas in May. By the end of the month, Cole and company were back home again in Los Angeles, where he played a week at the Lincoln Theater, one of the major venues for black audiences and black talent (he shared a bill with Benny Carter), at 2300 South Central Avenue. In 1945 and '46, Cole had played long runs at the Trocadero, where a room had been named after him, but the "Troc" had closed earlier in 1947. So the Trio switched to another swanky upscale "nitery" called the Bocage, at 5927 Sunset Boulevard, and stayed there for most of the summer[42]—a run that was only interrupted by a week at the Million Dollar Theater in downtown Los Angeles.

Nat was essentially off the road for at least two months, which gave him ample time to go into the studios and try out some other ideas. He would do roughly a dozen sessions for Capitol in August 1947, dates that were filled with experimentation and new ideas. According to friend Sammy Davis Jr., this was the moment when Cole stood up to sing for the first time, and this may have been partly due to an actual accident. "He was playing piano at the Million Dollar Theater and singing a little on a gooseneck mic." Davis remembered. "Nobody was paying attention, and then the mic broke off in his hands. He had to stand up and sing and they started listening."[43]

At the same time that Nat and Nadine—and then Nat and Oscar—were breaking up, relationships were likewise also disintegrating, once again, between the record companies and the American Federation of Musicians. By summer, it was increasingly clear that the AFM was going to call a second strike, but because of the Taft-Hartley Bill, the union had to give the record companies considerable notice. Finally, in the fall it was announced that the second ban was set to take effect beginning on January 1, 1948. In 1942, the labels had been caught with their pants down; this time they wanted to be sure they had enough music to last out a strike. No one knew what the long-range ramifications would be, but in the short term, it turned into a bonanza for AFM members: the major labels, now including Capitol, began to stockpile a huge inventory of issuable masters. Anybody who could even hold an instrument was put to work in a long session-a-thon that heated up especially in October and November.

It was, quite possibly, the threat of the oncoming strike that motivated Cole to put some of his newest ideas into action sooner rather than later. His innovations from this period were more than specifically musical—the first experiment with strings, the jazz-classical chamber works; they were also technological. As we've seen, in 1944, Capitol had released *The King Cole Trio*, one of the first-ever albums of new jazz by a single contemporary artist. The original album was so overwhelmingly successful that the label issued three more volumes of *The King Cole Trio*, all consisting of previously unreleased material (as opposed to a collection of greatest hits), between 1946 and 1949. Among other benefactions, the multitude of sessions in August 1947 provided him with the opportunity to record two entirely new "concept albums," among the world's first: *King Cole at the Piano* on August 13 and *King Cole for Kids* starting on August 15. And then, on August 20, he cut his most important single of the year, his first duet with another major recording star.

EVEN AS COLE WAS WINDING DOWN both the jam sessions and the chamber works, he was constantly looking for new things he could do with the piano, new applications for his keyboard skills. Three years earlier, in 1944, he had experimented with the blueprint for an idea that led to a series of all-original, piano-centric albums, the first of which was *King Cole at the Piano*, recorded in August 1947 and released in early 1949.[44] Essentially, Cole recorded two full collections of piano-centric Trio instrumentals: in 1944 he cut twelve titles for MacGregor transcriptions (as with all the MacGregor material, for radio use only) and the 1947 set of eight titles, released by Capitol as *King Cole at the Piano*.

Both the 1944 and the 1947 "piano" sessions had certain things in common: the tracks were of standard 78 RPM singles length, and Cole clearly intended both sets to be played continually, one track after another without interruption, a fairly advanced idea for the time, both technologically and musically. Both sets were purely piano showcases in which Cole plays continually all the way through; there's none of the amazing ensemble playing of the kind we've heard in "Paper Moon," for instance, and no solos by either Moore or Miller. There's also nothing like a tour de force of the kind we hear in the Trio's big-band-style razzle-dazzle flag-wavers like "What Is This Thing Called Love" or "Honeysuckle Rose," or the no-less-dazzling classical technique heard at ballad tempo in "Embraceable You." Yet these are far from easy listening or mood music. Cole does more than state the melody; he improvises at least briefly on all these tracks and interprets the melodies with startling originality—in a way that's even more impressive considering all the ground rules he set for himself.

Four songs are repeated from the 1944 date in 1947: "Poor Butterfly," "How High the Moon," "These Foolish Things," and "I Got Rhythm," which is herewith repurposed into the new original "Cole Capers." And in both projects, he recorded everything on a single date.[45] A year earlier, he had tinkered with the Trio format by adding drums to "The Best Man" and strings to "The Christmas Song," and here he was experimenting by paring down the Trio format rather than expanding it. In terms of the overall arch of Cole's career, the 1947 *Piano* album marks the first occasion in which King Cole is presented strictly as a star and not as a leader or soloist, even though it's as a pianist and not a singer; the billing for these releases was not "The King Cole Trio" as was customary, but rather "King Cole with rhythm."

You might think that the basic concept behind the project—that every track is piano all the way—may inadvertently make the music sound somewhat formal. But no, these are among the most pop-oriented of all the Trio's recordings: unfailingly light and dancing, his improvisations are more melodic than harmonic in nature, and you can tell the familiar songs are on his mind even as he's dancing around them. These were the kinds of instrumentals that we imagine the Trio featured when they played for dancers in a ballroom gig, such as at the Dreamland Ballroom in Omaha in 1943 or the Renaissance Casino and Ballroom in Harlem on Christmas Eve, 1948.

King Cole at the Piano consists of six standards plus one original blues and one new "I Got Rhythm" variation; all eight can be described as *jazz concerti* for solo piano, with Moore and Miller both being more felt than heard. The opener "Three Little Words" has Cole spinning variation after intriguing variation, steadily increasing both the rhythmic and melodic interest as he goes along, ever supported by barely audible but essential rhythmic support from the guitar and bass. The ballads include the newest tune in the lineup, "Moonlight in Vermont" (rendered in a way that anticipates the spirit of the 1955 *Piano Style* album), and "I'll Never Be the Same." The second was a much more familiar tune to listeners in 1947, thus Cole takes the liberty of interpreting it here with virtually no melody at all; he merely drops hints only to the six notes of the title when he reaches the appropriate spots in the first 16 bars. Of the eight tunes, only "These Foolish Things" follows the accepted jazz trajectory from melody to improvisation.

"Poor Butterfly" gets a multi-tempo treatment; Cole starts out of time, effectively pre-cycling the last eight bars as a rubato intro. He zings into a bouncy gait for the central refrain and returns to ballad time for the coda. "How High the Moon" is cocktail piano like *The Searchers* is a western, meeting all the requirements of the genre yet completely transcending them. To hear piano playing this expert in a saloon would instantly render the act of drinking both redundant and irrelevant. The "Rhythm" variant, "Cole Capers," has a head that suggests many a contemporaneous bebop band, into which Cole weaves a complex pattern of fast-moving original lines.

In its review, *Billboard* wrote that Cole's playing was "unfailingly tasty, but he rises to no great heights of invention. Best of the six sides is one of his originals, 'Cole Capers'—and he really justifies the title with some fly capers in bebop."[46] Today, however, I would give the nod to "Blues in My Shower" as the most creative and fascinating track on the album. The last of the Trio's great instrumental blues numbers, "Shower" (like the 1946 "Chant of the Blues") finds Cole spinning an intricate web of variations, yet he keeps his lines so crystal clear you can hear him singing at any given point—occasionally breaking up a highly involved pattern to go into a highly vocalized stop-time sequence.

Even at its height, the Trio had worked in cocktail lounges, from the Sky Bar in Cleveland to the Copa Cocktail Lounge in New York. Yet they never played what later became known as "cocktail piano"—a style we associate with such players as Cy Walters and Irving Fields. Cole's music was always something to listen to; it was never merely a background for cocktails and alcohol-infused conversation. It's one thing to showcase a familiar melody like "Poor Butterfly" or "Moonlight in Vermont," but to use this approach on a themeless blues is singularly brilliant; this is as gloriously sophisticated an interpretation of the basic blues as anyone has ever played. With both "Cole Capers" and "Blues in My Shower," Cole is taking the basic building blocks of jazz, "I Got Rhythm" and the blues, and building toward new heights with them. *Down Beat* was among the first to appreciate its value: "There are no vocals and not so much as eight bars of anything else but piano, although the other members of the Trio come along for the sake of the beat. Most of this is about halfway between jazz and cocktail music, but even the slightly commercial edge can't dull the excellence of the King's playing."[47]

THAT WAS ON AUGUST 13, 1947. Two days later, the Trio would do the first of several dates for the *King Cole for Kids* album, and then, a week later, on August 20, Cole "consummated" what had already been a ten-year personal and professional relationship with songwriter, singer, and impresario-entrepreneur Johnny Mercer.[48] While these would be Cole's first true duets on records, Mercer had virtually invented the genre; over the years he would cross many a memorable cadenza with Bing Crosby, Ginger Rogers, Benny Goodman, Wingy Manone, Jack Teagarden, Jo Stafford, Margaret Whiting, Bobby Darin, and his own onetime lover, Judy Garland. He was supremely endowed as a duet partner, not only because of his distinctive voice and ready wit, but because his skills as a wordsmith empowered him to write brilliant, one-of-a-kind libretti for these team-ups.

Appropriately for a team that first met in a steakhouse, when the monarch from Montgomery and the savant from Savannah got together in the studio, the main item on the menu was a food-driven novelty from New Orleans. Songs about food—which fall under the category of what Billy Eckstine would have described as "some dumb crap"—were, as we have seen, a dietary staple of the of early R&B pioneers like Louis Jordan and Slim Gaillard, and the King Cole Trio had also enjoyed a little taste with "The Frim Fram Sauce" (1945). The name "Henry Jones" had labeled a stock character in black vaudeville and minstrelsy, as in songs like the 1920 "Henry Jones (Your Honeymoon Is Over)."[49] This new "Henry Jones" originated in the imagination of Danny Barker, a guitar and banjo player from New Orleans who spent the swing era in Cab Calloway's rhythm section (and who would enjoy a late-life career as an educator and mentor of many a young Crescent City jazz player, among them Wynton Marsalis and his brothers).

"Save the Bones for Henry Jones ('Cause Henry Don't Eat No Meat)" would be Cole's biggest hit of 1947, reaching #1 (R&B) in October. In some ways, "Save the Bones" was ahead of its time in that it roasts and skewers the concept of vegetarianism—yet it was a perfect meal for its day, a well-remembered comedy dish that, in later years, Dr. John and the team of Ray Charles and Lou Rawls revived in tribute to Mercer and Cole. Cole and Mercer deliver the fast and pun-y rhymes with the intensity of a well-trained comedy team, a kind of musical Abbott and Costello. Surprisingly, there's even room at this rather crowded table for a juicy solo from Mr. Moore.

None of the four titles from the date were by Mercer, although he deftly customized all of them. "My Baby Likes to Bebop" is the work of the Jamaican-born songwriter Walter Bishop Sr.[50] The funniest ingredient of the Cole-Mercer duet on "Bebop" is the out-of-key whining that both partners do, which, along with the copious scatting, is clearly meant to be their satirical take on the "far out" harmonies of modern jazz—all those flatted fifths. They get even further out in "Harmony," by Burke and Van Heusen, introduced by the team of Bob Hope and Bing Crosby and then virtually the entire cast of Paramount Pictures' all-star vehicle *Variety Girl* (1947). Where "Bebop" uses off-key whining in a send-up of flatted fifths and other bop devices, "Harmony" uses flat notes and musical discord as a metaphor for people who can't get along, with a lyric full of comic exaggerations and a kind of hillbilly mise-en-scène inherited from Cole Porter's "Friendship." Throughout, Cole makes a joke of hitting all kinds of clinkers on the piano and quickly apologizing under his breath; this specific use of musical humor directly anticipates what Jo Stafford and Paul Weston would achieve under the guise of "Jonathan and Darlene Edwards" a few years later, with the major difference being that here, the song itself is meant to be funny (rather than a hilariously amateurish version of a "straight" song). While "Henry Jones" hit #1, "Harmony" made it to #12.

"You Can't Make Money Dreamin'," by Terry Shand, a pianist, occasional vocalist (who had worked with many big bands), and successful songwriter, is in ballad time but offers more comedy, this time not in flat notes or piano clinkers but in the form of rhyming dialogue between the two principals, which one suspects was written by Mercer rather than Shand. Where "Henry Jones" riffs on veganism, "You Can't Make Money Dreamin'" anticipates the market for bottled water many decades later. Who says that you can't make money dreamin'?

JUST AS "FOR SENTIMENTAL REASONS" reflected the start of the relationship with Maria, *King Cole for Kids* seems to have been inspired by Cole's decision to start a family. Of all of Maria's relatives, Nat was only really close to her sister Charlotte, but he was also growing increasingly fond of Carole, the toddler daughter of Maria's other sister, Carol. Bing Crosby had already done a children's album in 1941, a collection of previously released tracks titled *Small*

Fry: A Collection of Songs about Small Fry. The six songs in *King Cole for Kids* would be recorded over three dates (both before and after the Mercer session) and would be released a year later in August 1948—well before *King Cole at the Piano*, recorded slightly earlier. It was, coincidentally, in the middle of the *Kids* sessions that Cole recorded a very special bonus track, a song that would change his life and, not unimportantly, help him to earn enough money to put all of his future children through private school and even college.

For the *Kids* album, Cole sought to expand the Trio for specific purposes; on various songs, he added extra instruments, a full orchestra, and even a specialist in vocal and sound effects. The latter idea was a natural since Capitol now had a children's records division, which featured among other licensed properties, Pinto Colvig as "Bozo the Clown."

Alan Livingston, later president of Capitol Records, got his first job at the label producing the children's series, which wildly successful in the wake of the postwar baby boom. "I was king of the children's record business," he told me. "The *Saturday Evening Post* did a story on me. *Billboard* finally decided to publish the best-selling children's records, and the first time they published them, nine of the top ten were mine, which shook up the whole industry. So, everybody started to get into it."[51]

Livingston's musical director of choice (already a friend of Nat Cole) was the formidable Billy May. "I went to work for Capitol, and Capitol was expanding, and they got into the children's records," May explained. Having learned how to underscore dramatic and comedy scenes on the *Ozzie and Harriet* radio show, he continued, "I used my training from radio, and I started writing shit for Bozo the clown. We made a lot of money. And slowly I got to doing everything. We got really busy with those kiddie things, because this was before television in Los Angeles. Jesus, every grandparent in the world bought those things! But then TV came in and knocked the bottom right out."[52]

Cole himself came up with the idea, transmitted to Livingston via Gastel. For the first date, August 15, the trio tackled three "kids" songs, all adapted from traditional sources, and the only change in instrumentation from the familiar trio format is that Cole plays celesta in addition to piano. "I Wanna Be a Friend of Yours" is an old-time nursery song adapted into the verse and (AABA) chorus form of a mid-20th century popular song. This is Cole's most pronounced use of the celesta, although he had experimented with it as far back as "Moon Song" (1939) and "Two against One" (1941). As Cole intended, this smaller and more tinkly-sounding keyboard does indeed give the proceedings a distinctly child-like quality. Cole sings all six songs with remarkable sweetness, as if he's singing lullabies to his yet unborn children.

"Ke-Mo Ky-Mo (the Magic Song)" starts with a spoken introduction by Cole, backed lightly with his own celesta. This new number by Cole regular Roy Alfred is loosely inspired by a traditional song that goes back to the beginnings of minstrelsy in the 1840s, recorded circa 1916 by vaudevillian and banjo soloist Harry C. Browne as "Keemo Kimo."[53] In the earlier version, the title phrase is just pure nonsense, but here "Ke-Mo Ky-Mo" is chanted like the words of a magic spell—real Harry Potter stuff. Cole makes *"soup-bang-nip-cat-polly-mitch-a-cameo"* sound incredibly profound, especially in the last chorus where he recites the phrase ad lib rubato, as if its meaning were the most obvious thing in the world.

In 1938, the KC3 transcribed a swing arrangement of "Three Blind Mice" that was very much in the same vein as Ella Fitzgerald's "A Tisket, A Tasket," with a trio harmony vocal. This 1947 version is much more mellow, Cole seems to be crooning it toward kiddies rather than teen or adult jitterbugs. He also includes some technological tinkering by including "the farmer's wife" herself, as essayed by Nat in a speeded-up chipmunk-style voice.

Skipping ahead to the third date (August 27), the Trio puts down more nursery rhymes, starting with a charming medley of "Mary Had a Little Lamb," "London Bridge Is Falling Down," "Go In and Out the Window," and "Pop Goes the Weasel." There's also a highly entertaining treatment of "Old MacDonald Had a Farm," and both are enhanced via sound effects performed by Pinto Colvig (who not only played "Bozo" for Capitol but "Goofy" and "Bluto" for animated cartoon soundtracks), who mimics ducks, chickens, pigs, mules, a gasping Ford, and furiously-gobbling "turks."

"The Three Trees" is a spoken word performance, narrated by Cole with musical accompaniment. It was written and introduced by Tom McNaughton, who performed it in two Broadway productions, *The Spring Maid* (1910) and *The Magic Melody* (1919),[54] and also recorded it for Victor in 1911.[55] Cole narrates the story of a woodland scene, wherein a "pretty little rabbit" stops to take a drink from a "beautiful bubbling spring," "surrounded by three trees, there . . ., there . . ., and there." The rabbit is represented by a Brahms-like mazurka figure played by Cole in the treble clef, one tree is depicted by Miller bowing his bass arco, while Moore manipulates his strings to emulate a bow-and-arrow. Colvig also helps illuminate the story with various sound effects. It's another very effective and unique musical narrative; no one else in the worlds of either jazz or pop music was doing anything like this.

It's the middle date that yielded the biggest bonanza—and completely unexpectedly. Cole had decided, with the support of producer Jim Conking, to include a few lullabies and for the second occasion (this was almost exactly a year after "The Christmas Song"), Cole requested a string orchestra, this time under the baton of a thirty-five-year-old, West Coast–based arranger-conductor named Frank De Vol. He was, at that time, one of the more established brand names on the label, having conducted for singers and also done three albums under his own name (*Concert of Waltzes, Waltzing on Air,* and *Classics in Modern*). Many listeners also knew him from a popular radio series called *California Melodies*, which, for a time, also featured Capitol's own guitar star, Les Paul.

For this date, there were three lullabies, plus a couple of odds and ends. The main order of business was two new children's songs; ever since well before "Little Man You've Had a Busy Day," songs about kids falling off to sleep were a standard trope of Tin Pan Alley. "There's a Train Out for Dreamland" and "(Go to Sleep) My Sleepy Head" were two very lovely lullabies, the first credited to Carl Kress, the pioneering jazz guitarist who then worked as a producer for Capitol in New York. De Vol's arrangements are resplendently lush and are made even more dreamlike by the inclusion of a theremin as well as a second keyboardist, Buddy Cole (a prominent white studio musician, no relation to Nat). Both Coles can be heard playing various keyboards at different points. "Dreamland," in particular, feels like a Disney "Silly Symphony" of the mid-1930s, with rich and vivid storybook imagery, a nursery equivalent of "The Christmas Song" in which unrelated images add up to a narrative.[56]

The six key tracks were released by Capitol in August 1948 as *King Cole for Kids*, with a brilliantly imaginative cover that showed a cut-out cartoon of the three kingsmen playing candy instruments: "Oscar," strumming a lollypop like a banjo, "Johnny" enthusiastically slapping a stand-up candy cane, and "Nat," the King himself, wearing a crown and seated at a piano made out of an ice cream sandwich. *Billboard*[57] wrote enthusiastically: "Cole employs his soft, velvety tonsils to good advantage" and noted that the two issued lullabies with strings "are soothing for sleep-bound youngsters. . . . Retailers should find the King Cole name a lure for the adults who buy disks for their kiddies." The record was a success, but, disappointingly, neither this nor *King Cole at the Piano* (released in 1949) were kept in print in the 12" LP era. By that time, Cole was giving Capitol so much amazing new material, and most of it was so overwhelmingly successful, that these two pioneering early albums simply fell by the wayside.

As successful and well-received as the *King Cole for Kids* album was, it was that bonus track, waxed at the string session (the one with the three lullabies, on August 22, 1947), that would catch everyone's attention. "Nature Boy" was recorded more or less as an afterthought, but it would eclipse everything on that package. In fact, it would overshadow every other song sung by anyone in 1947 or 1948. It would also be the last hit that Oscar Moore would record with Nat King Cole.

COLE FINALLY MADE HIS MUCH-ANTICIPATED Carnegie Hall debut in the middle of the fall recording marathon, on Saturday, October 18, 1947.[58] This wasn't a standard full concert but rather an early evening opening set, starting at about 6:30 p.m. and then finishing by 7:45 so that the "regular" main event could begin at 8:00. (The Trio also did their usual fifteen-minute show for NBC and Wildroot Cream Oil that same night.) A *Down Beat* scribe was there, and his only complaint was that the short program was so rushed that Cole didn't have the chance to play as many piano solos as the reviewer would have liked. Still, the Carnegie concert was a big deal; nine years after Benny Goodman, and four years after Duke Ellington launched his annual series there, it was still a major event when a jazz artist played in this most prestigious of classical music venues. Cole took pride in that the Trio was, as far as anyone knew, the first jazz small group to give a Carnegie recital all by itself, albeit an abbreviated one.

As he anticipated earlier, the formal concert bookings were coming more frequently. The Trio had given an important full-length concert in a major concert hall a month earlier, on September 16 at the Civic Opera House in Chicago.[59] This had turned out to be the last big night for Moore. The guitarist had agreed to stay until the second week of October, at which point the Trio could celebrate its tenth anniversary even as its second most vital member was departing. The Carnegie concert (October 18) would also serve as the launch event for the new guitarist, Irving Ashby, occurring less than a week after he joined the group.

Why did Moore leave after ten years with the Trio? Clearly, the thrill was gone for him, partly because the Trio was less and less the completely cooperative unit that it had been in the beginning. It certainly wasn't the money. Early on, they split all the "take" equally—which wasn't fair to Cole, since he was putting in the bulk of the labor necessary to get the Trio booked regularly and working steadily. After Carlos Gastel took over as manager in spring 1944, they gradually adjusted the ratio. "Carlos arranged for all expenses to be deducted from earnings first, then Nat received 50 percent of the remainder, with the final

50 percent being split 60-40 between Oscar and Johnny." As Maria Cole, who was paying careful attention to where Nat's money was coming from and where it was going, later wrote, "Even so, when Nat's fame as a singer began to spread, there were weeks when Oscar was earning as much as $1,600 to $1,800."[60]

Yet by 1946, Moore was starting to miss some important dates. One of the biggest was a full-scale concert that the Trio gave for 5,400 fans at the USO Arena on Granby Street in Norfolk, Virginia, in July 1946. ("The local hepcats were 'knocked out' and everybody went away happy in spite of the relatively steep $2.50 ante.") [61] Moore was too sick to play, so Cole recruited a guitarist named Harry Polk from Philadelphia, to substitute for him, and also added a drummer named Jackie Hobbs to further compensate for Oscar's absence.[62] Moore missed some other dates in August '46, for which Cole used his "Best Man" drummer, Jack Parker.[63]

Now with the weekly radio series and the abundance of pre-ban Capitol sessions, the workload, already staggering, became even more impossible for Moore to keep up with; by now, it was all he could do to make all the radio and recording dates, even while he kept missing more and more road gigs. Then too, the road was not an easy place to be; traveling was mostly by car on antiquated roads, with both air travel and the comparatively smooth infrastructure of superhighways very much a thing of the future. It was hard enough for white musicians, and even worse for African Americans, who, on top of everything else, had to depend on the famous *Green Book* to help them navigate the travails of segregation and racism on the road. In spite of such treatment, Nat was motivated, and literally driven to keep up the relentless pace of one-nighters and other dates. But Oscar, as much as he loved Nat, was beginning to wonder why he was still doing it, ten years later. He may have been one of the highest-paid sidemen in the world, but it wasn't his star that was rising.

Moore had already given notice when, on October 7, when the Trio was due to give a concert at still another "local home of long-hair music,"[64] the Syria Mosque in Pittsburgh. Cole, traveling with his fiancée, Maria, and Miller got there on time, but Oscar never made it. The promoter threatened to cancel, but the road manager, Mort Ruby, talked him into letting the show go on without Oscar. Cole explained to the crowd that Moore "had disappeared somewhere and that the management would refund ticket money to those who did not care to listen to just the twosome. Only a scattered few in the packed house asked for refunds; the rest listened to two hours of music as played by the short trio."[65] Maria later remembered, "Nat played for one hour and twenty-five minutes without stopping for anything but applause. Then he took an intermission and played the second half. Two or three times during the performance, he got up and sang *a capella*, then went back to the piano."[66] By this point, Carlos—and, more recently, Maria—had been trying for a while to convince Nat that Oscar and Johnny were only sidemen, not full-blown co-stars. When Cole saw how well he went over without his guitarist, it started to dawn on him that they might be right.

Moore's explanation was that he left the Trio because he was tired of the road, yet immediately after, he went back on the same road, this time as a star sideman with "Johnny Moore's Three Blazers," a trio led by his older brother, Johnny, also a guitarist. Lee Young, the rather outspoken drummer, dismissed Johnny Moore as a "nobody,"[67] which isn't quite true. The Three Blazers, which now consisted of two guitars and a pianist, were consistently on the *Billboard* "Race" (R&B) charts in the mid-1940s, although, unlike the King Cole Trio, there was never any attempt to push the group into the mainstream market, that is, to sell their records to white people. Ironically, the Blazers' success, such as it was, was due to the presence of another star singer-pianist, the R&B legend Charles Brown, who could be considered the missing link between Nat King Cole and Ray Charles. After his years with this combo, Moore eventually wound up doing non-musical work; he had said that he always wanted to open a music shop, but instead, in his later years, had a business dealing in fishing equipment. He died in 1981.

Moore's last known performance with the Trio was the Wildroot program of October 11. Cole had already sent a telegram to guitarist Irving Ashby: "Save me—Oscar Moore quitting."[68] Born in Summerville, Massachusetts, in 1920, Ashby played a variety of members of the guitar family including ukulele, tipple, and Spanish guitar, before gravitating to the familiar electric instrument. His first major job was at age nineteen with one of Lionel Hampton's early bands, where he stayed for two years, then, remaining in Hollywood, became one of the first black musicians to work on staff for a major movie studio. That position only lasted a few weeks before, he said, "the draft board got me," but in that time, he was able to play with Fats Waller in *Stormy Weather* (1943) on "That Ain't Right," a composition by Nat Cole. After the war, Ashby freelanced on dozens of studio sessions with various Central Avenue combos, including many that were inspired by the King Cole Trio: Les Paul, André Previn, Phil Moore, Eddie Beal.

Only a few years younger than Moore, Ashby seemed to come from a much later generation, one in which formal music education was more prevalent. It was noted that he had "written a technical text book on guitar which is used by the [New] England Conservatory of Music and has recently completed a course in harmony at the University of Chicago."[69] Ashby was actually teaching at the Westlake College of Music when the telegram arrived from Cole. Appropriately, one of Ashby's first contributions to the group was a composition titled *Allegro Suite*, heard at Carnegie Hall.[70] This was highly ambitious, especially considering that Ashby had been in the group only a few days. He wrote two instrumentals that the KC3 recorded for Capitol, which might have been part of the suite, including "Return Trip" and the more modernistic "Top Hat Bop," both recorded in 1949. "Return Trip" was possibly so-named because it was the Trio's final variation on "I Got Rhythm"; when Leonard Feather played it for Cole in a *Down Beat* blindfold test five years afterward, Cole praised Ashby's contribution but played down his own: "This tune was something that Irving Ashby made up himself, I don't even remember the name of it [but] he took a wonderful solo here."[71] (The Trio played one other number by Ashby, titled "Nothing to Fret About," at their 1950 concert in Zurich.) In a 1950 interview, Cole compared the two guitarists, saying "Oscar was a technical musician, [but] Ashby has more of a rhythm feeling."[72]

Ashby was even more comfortable than Moore at faster, boppish tempos and was especially adept at long lines of eighth notes; but the point, at first anyhow, was for the new man to fit into the contexts and arrangements that his predecessor had worked out for the Trio. Like Cole himself, his playing didn't suggest just one era or one style. Ashby's work on his own "Return Trip" is mostly chordal and much more firmly rooted in the big-band era, like that of Al Casey or Allan Reuss. On the blues "My Mother Told Me," Ashby plays in an R&B style, employing double stop bends and sliding triads. On the 1950 ballad, "Baby Won't You Say That You Love Me?," he plays very traditionally indeed—using an acoustic guitar and strumming in an even four, like Freddie Greene with Count Basie. Yet his specialties with the Trio were the modern jazz-style instrumentals, like "Etymology" and his own "Top Hat Bop"—that were a notable feature of the last four great years of the trio, 1947–1951.

Ashby's baptism of fire with the Trio was not only the Carnegie debut but the pre-ban recording land rush. While working primarily at the Times Square Paramount Theater in November[73] they laid down a total of ninety-one tracks for Capitol, a combination of commercial singles and transcriptions, which were waxed over thirteen sessions at the RKO Pathé Studios, 1443 Park Ave. Clearly the AFM situation was much on their mind; at Carnegie, Cole treated the music industry insiders to a pair of hilarious in-jokes in a comic list song titled "Baby I Need You": one line goes, "Like Capitol Records needs Johnny Mercer, but Mercer needs them worser." (According to *Down Beat*, this line produced a "trade howl" from the crowd at Carnegie.) There's an even more inside baseball line at the conclusion, after Cole sings "Like a bed needs a pillow," the music stops, and all three chant, a capella and in a highly declamatory fashion, "We all need Petrillo!" By October 1947, you hardly had to be a member of the American Federation of Musicians to know who James Caesar Petrillo was.

FOLLOWING THE PARAMOUNT, they were off for a two-week run at the Latin Quarter in Newport, Kentucky (they broadcast the Wildroot show from Cincinnati), and then headed back east and north to Buffalo, just the place to spend Christmas week. Along the way they stopped in New York, not for an actual gig but for some business both personal and professional. Around December 20, Nat and Maria attended a Town Hall concert by Billy Eckstine, and then joined the after-party in his honor hosted by songwriter Ruth Poll, at which Nat played for both Eckstine and Mel Tormé.[74]

At this time, Cole, Ashby, and Miller also headed for a low-rent soundstage in the Bronx (Pathé Studios on East 166th Street), where they filmed a sequence for an all-black feature movie titled *Killer Diller*, thereby gifting us with the only footage of the 1947–48 line-up with Ashby and Miller.[75] Like the 1945 Soundies (also shot in the Bronx), *Killer Diller* was an all-black feature with a total budget that must have been less than what Paramount Pictures spent on lunch on any given day, yet it's quite possibly the single best visual document of the King Cole Trio in action. The band is positioned the way they were in theaters, with Cole staring straight into the camera (the audience) and playing at the piano at a forty-five-degree angle, with Ashby directly behind him and Miller slightly off to stage right. Unlike the Soundies, there are no distracting dancers or dumb sets. The most valuable aspect of the sequence is that it seems to have been filmed with the Trio performing "live," not, like the Soundies (and the Hollywood features and shorts), lip-synching or sidelining to pre-recorded tracks.

This seven-minute sequence is perfect, a remarkable one-reeler unto itself. Making the audience wait a whole number to hear him sing, Cole opens with the instrumental "Breezy and the Bass." This was Cole's latest and most minimally disguised version of "I Got Rhythm," in which he seems to have been throwing a bone to Johnny, who, unlike Oscar, was sticking with him for the foreseeable future. This is, in fact, Miller's major moment in the spotlight, culminating what would be five very full years with the Trio. It's no less revealing to watch what Cole is doing while Miller takes an extended solo. Without trying to pull focus, the pianist makes a point to communicate to the crowd, "This is Johnny's number, folks. Me? I'm not even playing." To underscore the point, he even closes the lid of the piano for a few moments. Surprisingly, there isn't a ballad. The remaining two numbers are both novelties: one is slow, self-deprecating, and funny (another "lowlife" number, "Now He Tells Me"), and the other is fast and swinging and funny (the nonsensical "Ooh, Kickarooney").[76]

Killer Diller, which also featured Cole's frequent touring partner, bandleader Andy Kirk, and two legendary black comedians, Clinton "Dusty" Fletcher and Jackie "Moms" Mabley, was released as a theatrical feature in early 1948, and subsequently recycled and chopped up for use in Soundies machines. Who needs actual production values when you can have the King Cole Trio at the pinnacle of its magic?

THE OSCAR PROBLEM WAS SOLVED, as had been the Nadine problem. Maria was now a permanent part of the entourage; Cole introduced her to his mother when the Trio played the Cleveland Music Hall in October and Perlina made the trip over from Chicago.[77] But as 1947 came to a close, Cole could anticipate many more changes on the horizon. He was looking forward to being able to spend more time with Maria, even to starting a family (which would happen sooner than they expected). And he was dreading the coming of the second recording ban; he knew that was going to shake things up. but he could have had no idea that this would turn out to be a blessing rather than a curse for his recording career. At the start of 1948, even as Cole prepared for his next run at the Apollo, he was also trying like crazy to convince Capitol to release a certain master of a certain song that they were sitting on, namely, "Nature Boy." He knew it would be a very important record, but even he couldn't anticipate what a game-changer it would be.

5

Entr'acte

TRIO TO QUARTET TO SOLO, 1948–1951

Nat is one of two guys who took a style and made a voice out of it. The other is Louis.
—BILLY ECKSTINE

TO THE END of her life (at sixty-four in 2009), Carole Cole, Nat and Maria's oldest child, remembered eden ahbez[1] very vividly. Whenever the songwriter would come into their home in Hancock Park, the young Carole would think, "Jesus Christ is paying us a visit. My Daddy knows Jesus personally!"[2]

Based on the way "Cookie" and others described him to me, in my mind's eye I imagine eden ahbez walking around early postwar Los Angeles, dressed like the very picture of an Old Testament prophet, trudging past the La Brea Tar Pits in flowing robes and sandals (except that at 5' 2" or so, he was hardly the imposing Jesus of Renaissance paintings). In photographs from the period, ahbez is dressed like a 1950s beatnik or even a 1960s hippy—dungarees and a sweater. Not many photos show his feet, but he did, apparently, wear the shoes of the fisherman.

"We were playing in the Orpheum Theater in Los Angeles when I first met ahbez," Cole remembered in 1954. "He was a strange looking guy and every day I arrived at the theater, there he was, waiting at the stage door. Finally, in self-defense, I took him into the dressing room and listened to his song. It was the luckiest break in my whole life."[3]

That, at least, was how Cole recalled those events of late spring 1947 from the perspective of seven years later. But it almost certainly didn't happen that way. Almost from the moment "Nature Boy" was released, around the last week of March 1948, interested parties were already trying to create a mythology around the song, to serve their own ends—none more so than Capitol Records, which. in May 1948, took out oversized advertisements in newspapers across the country, that proclaimed the following:

> Eden Ahbez [*sic*], a man of faith who worshiped in the great cathedral of nature, brought to Capitol a simple song, that told of a searching soul who found the truth. There had seemed no place for his simple song in a complex world. But Johnny Mercer of Capitol Records, saw in this strange music great beauty and sincerity. He sent Ahbez [*sic*] to Nat Cole, a Capitol artist, with the suggestion that Nat consider recording his music.[4]

There's no part of this statement that's remotely true. Capitol Records was anything but anxious to record the song and then, once it had been recorded, Cole had to twist their metaphoric arm to get them to release it. When "Nature Boy" became the song of the year, the greatest thing that ahbez learned was the veracity of that old aphorism about how success has many wannabe fathers. In terms of its long-term implications for Cole's career, "Nature Boy" was perhaps the most significant song that Cole ever recorded, and it's also the one with the most confusing and conflicting backstory.

eden ahbez—he insisted that mere mortals didn't deserve anything better than lower-case letters—was a man of many names. He had been born George Alexander Aberle in Brooklyn in 1908; his mother was from England (of Scottish-Irish heritage) and his father was "an American of Jewish descent," but neither actually raised him.[5] He spent his childhood in a Jewish orphanage, and, as a teenager, he was adopted by a family in Kansas, at which time he was known as George McGrew. Having experienced both an urban and a rural upbringing, he became one of the first converts to—and proselytizers for—what would later be called a naturalistic lifestyle, as a proponent of vegetarianism, health food, and raw food. From the beginning, he was drawn to both music and spirituality, conceiving of the two as conduits for each other.

Now known as eden ahbez, he made his way to Los Angeles about 1940, around the same time that some very alien ideas from far-flung lands were also washing up on the shores of California. In 1923, *The Prophet*, a book of life lessons in the form of poetry by Kahlil Gibran, a Maronite from what is current-day Lebanon, and, likewise, the teachings of Paramahansa Yogananda, who advocated yoga and meditation, also began to catch on in the West in the immediate prewar era. In 1944, W. Somerset Maugham's bestselling novel, *The Razor's Edge* (filmed by Hollywood in 1946)[8] did much to introduce these ideas into American popular culture.

Gibran and Yogananda were Eastern mystics, while Maugham and ahbez were Westerners writing about eastern spirituality from their own perspectives, although ahbez was a true believer and a sincere convert to the cause. By the mid-1940s, ahbez was writing songs in Los Angeles, and he was working toward a song cycle, or suite, inspired by the glories of nature.[9] He later claimed that he was, in fact, meditating in a cave when the melody that later became "Nature Boy" suddenly came to him. Later, several attorneys concluded otherwise: when the song became a runaway hit, ahbez was hit by a plagiarism suit and was ordered to pay a hefty penalty. At the time, everyone who knew the composer believed that the borrowing was accidental and that the evidence of the alleged plagiarism was strictly circumstantial. At worst, if he had realized he was utilizing an existing melody, he might have assumed it was a traditional air and therefore in the public domain. His motivations were genuine; he wanted to create a successful song to spread a message of love and peace. Ahbez was a legitimate prophet who was also writing for profit.

No one questioned that the lyrics were his own. As Frank De Vol,[10] who arranged the original recording for Cole and Capitol, told me, "It was such a wonderful lyric that I don't think the melody would have meant anything without the words." Ahbez not only caught the ideas but the texture and feel of Muslim and Hindu poetry; phrases like "a little shy and sad of eye" and "we spoke of many things, fools and kings" sound like they could have been written by Rumi or Omar Khayyam. De Vol continued, "In sorting through some music recently, I went through clippings and so forth, I ran across some of the reviews of the record, and I couldn't believe the kind of reviews they were. They analyzed the lyric and the melody and the arrangement in such a way that they felt it was a standard immediately. It had religious overtones—though not of any one particular religion."[11]

De Vol is speaking of the classic, final text of the song. In 1946, ahbez had published an earlier version of "Nature Boy" (on his own imprint "Goldenheart Press") with quite a different set of words:

There was a boy,
And they called him nature boy.
For he used to greet the dawn all alone,
By a mountain stream.
He loved to watch
The clouds go by
And he would sing and dream.[12]

The 1946 edition credits the author as "EDEN AHBE," all in uppercase letters, and with no "Z." The cover of this first edition is an artist's rendering of the long-haired songwriter himself, from the back, barefoot and shirtless, like a prophet wandering past cactus plants in the Judaean Desert.[13]

One of the major points of contention regarding "Nature Boy" is how ahbez actually got the song into Cole's hands. But regardless of how that happened, ahbez deserves props for having anointed Cole as the one to bring his song and his message to the world; if he were paying attention to the world of pop music, he would have heard Cole's two 1946 hit ballads, "For Sentimental Reasons" and "The Christmas Song." But still, in 1947, Cole was still regarded as a jazz musician and a pianist much more than a singer, and we ultimately have no idea why ahbez picked Cole—other than the notion that he felt that his words were best brought to the world by an African American artist, someone who was, like the songwriter himself, outside the social and cultural mainstream.

In late May and early June 1947, the King Cole Trio was playing the Lincoln Theater on South Central Avenue, Los Angeles. For some time before then, Cole had long been an inevitable target for songwriters and their emissaries—the song pluggers. Cole was, in fact, far more accessible than most entertainers at his level of success; one aspiring composer even cornered him in the men's room at the Paramount Theater and chose that moment to shove a lead sheet in his face.[14] (Try to imagine how Sinatra would have reacted in that situation.) Ahbez, who was described in one early clipping as "a peculiar-looking character, complete with beard and weird eyes,"[15] showed up at the stage door of the Lincoln but was prevented by one (or possibly both) of Cole's lieutenants, who were put off by his appearance. Depending on whose story you believe, it was either Cole's road manager, Mort Ruby, or his valet, Otis Pollard.

In Ruby's telling, "The Trio had just come in from eight weeks at the Paramount Theater and believe me, we were beat!"[16] This was one of many occasions when Gastel and Cole were producing the entire stage show themselves, collecting the receipts and paying the other entertainers and musicians out of their profits. "We had bought the show. We own the band and the acts and now I'm trying to time the show and put the thing together so that it would run down. And the doorman came over to me and said, 'There's a crazy, goofy-looking guy at the door who wants to talk to you.' Well, I said, 'I might just to face the music, have him come in.' He walked in and he said, 'I have written a song, especially for Nat Cole.' And I thought to myself, Holy Mackerel, how many times have I heard this? He handed me a dirty manuscript. It was filthy. And he said, 'Now please deliver this to Nat King Cole.'"

In the conflicting story, ahbez approached Pollard, the valet, and offered him a percentage of the song if he could get his boss to record it. I'm inclined to at least partially believe Pollard on the strength of the evidence that after "Nature Boy" was a hit, Pollard demanded a 25 percent share, and then that he was subsequently fired by Cole for such shenanigans. Pollard claimed that he promised to find both a publisher for the song and an artist to record it (not necessarily Cole) in return for that piece of the action. Various publishers and singers were approached, but they all "nixed the tune as too classical and ahbez took a powder."[17]

But eventually, Cole tried out the song himself, according to virtually every account, by playing it from a beat-up and dirty-looking piece of manuscript paper. This latter detail is in direct contrast with the findings of ahbez biographer Brian Chidester, who has found that the composer's musical handwriting was immaculate, the paper would have been clean and the notes and lyrics very easy to read. Either way, Cole found it intriguing enough to try it and, as soon as he heard it, he was converted. Nat, according to Maria, thought the melody sounded ineffably "Jewish" to him.[18] Not a bad thing, considering the Jewish saturation of popular music, especially in 1947, when one of the big hits of the year was "The Anniversary Song," a key track in the revitalized career of Al Jolson. (Based on a Romanian waltz from 1880, this was about as Hebraic as you could get.) In spring 1948, the eventual release of "Nature Boy" just happened to coincide with the founding of the state of Israel. If there ever was a moment when it was hip to be Hebrew, this was it.

After the Lincoln Theater, the Trio played for a month at the Bocage, an upscale "nighterie" at 5927 Sunset Boulevard, where they were now making $3,000 per week.[19] When Irving Berlin (then working on *Easter Parade* at MGM) came into the Bocage one night in June 1947, Cole decided to try it out for him. Berlin not only liked the song but he wanted to publish it. This was a moot point, since at that moment no one had the slightest idea who the author was or where to find him. Cole was already convinced of the song's worth, and, he and Gastel then decided that they would form their own publishing house so they could participate in the profits at a whole new level. (This was one potential hit that the music publishing sharks would not get their greedy fins on.) The new firm, titled "Crestview Music," was administered by the larger publishing house owned by their friends, the veteran songwriters and publishers, Johnny Burke and Jimmy Van Heusen.[20] Unlike Cole's own experiences with Irving Mills, however, they were giving ahbez both full credit and his fair author's share of the proceeds—in other words, profits with honor.

But still, they had to find the songwriter first. Maria later claimed that Mr. and Mrs. ahbez were then living al fresco, camped out under the "L" in the Hollywood sign. (More likely, ahbez and his wife were bunking in sleeping bags in the backyard of a friend.) Having found him, Cole and Gastel were able to go ahead with their plans for publishing and recording the song and set a session date for August 22, 1947. Then there was one other deal breaker: as with "The Christmas Song" a year earlier, Cole now once again had to convince the label that the song demanded a string orchestra; yet even after the huge success of the Tormé-Wells song, Capitol was again reluctant. As Nat told Leonard Feather in 1961, they were afraid he would be "losing the identity of the trio."[21] "Finally," Cole continued, "with tongues in their cheeks, and rocks in their jaws, they let me try a session using Frank De Vol, and that was how we made 'Nature Boy.'" Indeed, as we have seen, they slipped it into the *King Cole for Kids* session of August 22, right after the three lullabies, but thankfully before the union-covered string players went home.

The genius of the song was in the simplicity: only 16 bars of melody and eight lines of lyric. Cole was so committed to getting the lyric and his vocal exactly right that he stood at the microphone the whole time and let Buddy Cole play the piano solo. De Vol's own ramp-up to "Nature Boy" was a song he had arranged for Peggy Lee a short while earlier, titled "A Nightingale Can Sing the Blues." De Vol wasn't that preoccupied with the instrumentation or other such details; his main concern was the overall texture of the recording. As with "Nightingale," he wanted it to sound like Cole wasn't in a recording studio or nightclub; he wanted the acoustics of the track to put the image in the listener's mind that the singer was standing in a forest somewhere—as DeVol put it, "a feeling of being outside."

When I interviewed Frank De Vol about "Nature Boy," around 1990, he did one thing that surprised me: he hummed the melody in waltz time. "Nat was playing at a club upstairs over a restaurant (probably the Bocage)," De Vol explained. Capitol producer Jim Conkling

> and I went up there and set the key, because in those days, the artist didn't have anything to do with the arrangement. You just set the key with them, and then you brought the arrangement in. So, when we brought it in it was a waltz, and we played it down, and Nat said . . . I'm sure it was Nat, because I don't think that Jim would have made this move on his own. Nat said, "Why don't we do this out of tempo?" So, what we did, then, is I did the introduction, and then, instead of going into tempo, we did it rubato. But it was very interesting, and it didn't go into tempo until Buddy Cole's piano solo. Nat did not play that. It was a very simple, one-finger thing, I think. And that is where we went into tempo, the rhythm. Then later on, why, he sang it out rubato again. . . . I think that the combination of doing it rubato plus with the

lyrics was what made it a hit. I don't think it would have been a hit as a waltz.[22]

By now, Cole, Gastel, and Conkling were all convinced that the song was going to be a huge hit, but the higher-ups at Capitol somehow weren't so sure. They had the finished master but made no plans to release it. The earliest known live performance is at the Civic Opera Hall in Chicago, on September 16, 1947, and *Down Beat* specifically noted the new song. "The most impressive number of the entire concert [was], strangely enough, a vocal. It was titled 'Nature's Boy' [*sic*] and is more than anything, the beautifully simple philosophy of its yogi composer, eden ahbez, set effectively to music. Here it should have been obvious that musically excellent as the Trio is, it's Nat Cole's vocals that are their most effective single thing."[23] Cole continued to sing the song on live gigs, but he deferred from including it on his ongoing NBC radio series, *Wildroot Presents King Cole Trio Time*. Even so, a groundswell started around the song. "It all started last November," the *Chicago Defender* wrote, "when rumors started circulating around the [music] trade that the King Cole Trio had cut one of the greatest discs of all time. But what this disc was remained a secret."[24]

Then, in November, Cole was asked to record what would be the first of dozens of Cole movie themes, a ballad from *The Bishop's Wife,* a rather pious and somewhat heavy-handed comedy with spiritual overtones, starring Cary Grant as an angel named "Dudley." This was "Lost April" by Emil Newman (of Hollywood's most famous family of film composers) and Edgar Leslie (the veteran lyricist and ASCAP co-founder). In what was becoming a familiar story, the unadorned trio cut "Lost April" on November 29; but then the decision was made, once again, that the song needed strings, so it was recorded a second time on December 20, this time in New York.

"Lost April" was cut with strings just a few days before the 1948 American Federation of Musicians (AFM) ban was to go into effect and *The Bishop's Wife* was about to be released. Now they had "Lost April" with strings for the A-side, and there was only one other compatible master, that is, a ballad with strings, to put on the flip side, and that was "Nature Boy." The three conspirators, Cole, Gastel, and Conkling, seem to have very cagily planned this move; thanks to the Taft-Hartley Act, everyone in the record business knew that the AFM ban was coming. Capitol had the disc ready to go, and Cole, in his role as publisher, deliberately did *not* encourage other labels to record their own versions. This was completely counter to the way the business worked at that time, but it was a calculated risk.

Everyone knew they were going to have a hit on their hands after Monday, March 22, 1948, the date that "Nature Boy" was first heard on the air. "Al Trilling, custodian of the hundred-thousand record library at WNEW, handed the record over to Jerry Marshall to play over the latter's disc show at 2:15 p.m. Four minutes later, according to Marshall, "we were swamped with telephone calls—people wanting to know the name of the haunting melody."[25] Trilling was quoted: " 'Nature Boy' is very beautiful, almost a tone poem, the words and music answer the longing in everyone's heart." On Easter Sunday, March 28, Nat and Maria were married, and the next day they flew to Mexico for their honeymoon. The record was finally in the stores in the first week of April 1948.[26] *Billboard* proclaimed it one of their picks of the week: "Melody here is haunting, rich and compelling, and could well be broadened into a magnificent piano concerto by its penner [composer], Eden Ahbez [*sic*], who might well have the makings of another 'Warsaw Concerto.' " Another write-up, in the same issue, went, "Fragile tone poem ... set in a pastoral mood by soft voiced vocal and semi-classic arrangement in a minor key. Spellbinding."[27]

Within days, and certainly by the end of April, the entire music industry was going nuts, what *Down Beat* vividly described in slangy jargon as a "Mad Discery Whirl."[28] Every label wanted a piece of the "Nature Boy" action, but because of their strategic release, Cole had virtually the whole market to himself. The AFM had somehow become the unlikely accomplice of Capitol Records: they were effectively preventing any other label from releasing their own competing "cover" of "Nature Boy." Frank Sinatra recorded a rather anemic version for Columbia Records, using an a capella choir rather than a union orchestra, and Sarah Vaughan had also cut it for Musicraft Records. *Billboard*, raving about the song's "surprise ... immediate success," noted that RCA Victor had pressured Perry Como to record the song and Decca likewise wanted Bing Crosby to do it. Both declined for different reasons: Como, because he believed he was too late to the party, and Crosby, because he didn't want to buck the union.[29]

"Nature Boy" was such a huge upset that the industry started doing things it had never done before or since. Burke and Van Heusen, who were ecstatic to be involved in the publishing, actually asked radio stations to stop playing the song so much, they were afraid audiences might grow tired of it "if the public is fed an overdose of the song too quickly. This is a complete reversal of the publisher's usual attitude."[30] By this point, Capitol had sold a million and a half copies, and they were holding off on releasing the next scheduled Cole single, a blues-infused novelty titled "Money Is Honey," until they felt that "Nature Boy" had been sufficiently milked. While they waited, Leeds Music, publishers of "Money Is Honey" grumbled and pressured Capitol to release their song while the Trio was still so incredibly steaming hot.

Meanwhile, ahbez was going through tribulations of his own: even before the plagiarism suit began, everybody started coming out of the woodwork and claiming that the composer had promised them a percentage of the profits. Ahbez admitted he had promised 25 percent to a certain Mrs. Hi Kanter, the former Lorraine Tatum, "for assisting him with the lyrics." But the biggest troublemaker was Cole's former valet, Otis Pollard, who continued hounding ahbez for a piece, even after Cole had fired him.[31] Pollard then made things even more complicated by selling half of his alleged cut to "Bullets" Durgom (the same music industry tout who had brought Bobby Troup and "Route 66" to Cole).[32] Pollard, for his part, denied all these charges. He claimed that he had actually known ahbez for years and that they were "very thick friends" well before "Nature Boy" was even written: "I loaned eden money to take out his girl one night in California, the girl he married." Pollard also claimed to have written two of the song's eight lines, and therefore was morally entitled to receive a 25 percent share.[33] Still, no one believed him; methinks he doth protest too much.

But then in May, a plagiarism suit was brought forth by attorney A. Edward Masters, representing J. & A. Kammen Music Co., publishers of "Schweig, Mein Hartz"[34] written by Herman Yablakoff for a 1935 show called *Papirossen* (Cigarettes). That song was probably never heard by anyone outside of the lower East Side or the more orthodox neighborhoods in Brooklyn, but the ultimate decision was that possibly, although not necessarily probably, ahbez could have chanced upon it during a trip back to New York sometime in the late 1930s. When we compare the two, "Schweig, Mein Hartz" is in C minor and in 2/4 or cut time; "Nature Boy," as published in 1947 by Crestview, is in E minor and in 3/4 or waltz time. "Nature Boy" is 16 bars, while "Schweig," is much longer, containing a verse and a bridge, and the portion that inspired "Nature Boy" is a fast tango. Yet even if abhez's account was true, that the tune came to him while he was meditating in a cave, the melodies are nonetheless similar enough that the plaintiff undeniably had a legitimate case.

So ahbez lost the suit, but even after having to make what seems to have been a one-time payment of $25,000[35], there still was plenty of moolah in the till; one publication "estimated that ahbez will make $20,000 on his song this year."[36] That figure was soon rounded upward. "Meanwhile, it looks like the tune is far from its limit. RKO two weeks ago paid $10,000 for the right to use 'Nature Boy' as theme music in its [film *The*] *Boy with Green Hair,* now in production."[37] In the long run, that $25,000 payment was the bargain of the century, considering the millions that were eventually made on the song. (In 2001, for instance, David Bowie sang it, many times throughout the soundtrack of Baz Luhrmann's hit movie musical *Moulin Rouge!*)

"Nature Boy" was another example of Cole's ability to light on the right song at the right moment—even more so than "Gone with the Draft," "Straighten Up and Fly Right," "Route 66," "For Sentimental Reasons," and "The Christmas Song"—and to create a classic in the process. No one would have wanted to hear "Nature Boy" four years earlier in 1944, as the D-Day invasion went forward; its message wouldn't have been particularly comforting to the men on the front lines or the women at home waiting for them. Nor would it have worked four years later at the height of the Cold War and the Red Scare; the lyrics, which talk of "fools and kings"—that is, world leaders—and describe them as rough equivalents, would have almost certainly prompted Senator McCarthy to brand both Cole and ahbez as pinkos. Nineteen forty-eight was the perfect year for the song; it was the perfect moment in the political and social climate, and the AFM ban served to help it obliterate any possible competition.

Nineteen forty-eight would be a banner year for Capitol Records; the second AFM ban marked the moment when the youngest of the major "disceries" came into its own as an industry leader, with Cole leading the charge. "Nature Boy" followed on the heels of another major blockbuster, "Manana" by Peggy Lee. (That song, coincidentally, had also been "exhibit A" in a plagiarism suit; Miss Lee, however, won hers.) Those two megahits dominated the charts straight from mid-March to the end of June. Then, in the same year, Capitol also had "Twelfth Street Rag" by Pee Wee Hunt and "A Tree in the Meadow" by Margaret Whiting, two other "smash, socko" hits in the trade jargon of the time. "While other companies are beating their corporate breasts about the state of the recording business, youngest of the big firms, Capitol Records, has quietly been making gains. So far in 1948, Capitol announces, its business is up 18 percent. Sales are so strong that the firm's Scranton, PA, plant is working double shifts and overtime, and its Hollywood production has been augmented by the entire output of the Duraflex plant in Long Beach, CA." This was reported not in a black paper, not in an industry sheet, but in the very mainstream *Washington Post*.[38]

For King Cole, new success meant new vistas; on April 10, he wound up his successful two-year run on NBC's *King Cole Trio Time* with a special broadcast wherein the Trio played "Nature Boy" for the first time live on the air, backed by a string orchestra. Six weeks later, Capitol flew both

Cole and ahbez across the country to New York (ahbez from Los Angeles, Cole from Chicago, where the Trio was playing at the Rag Doll) to appear on NBC's *We the People* on June 1. This talk and variety show was making its first simultaneous broadcast on TV and radio. Although it seems like the television portion was an afterthought, this was Cole's highly auspicious television debut. In 1948, the idea of a black man taking an airplane to appear on television would have seemed like science fiction—what in the 21st century would be called "Afro-Futurism." In a surviving kinescope, ahbez drives his bicycle onto the stage, is interviewed about the background of the song, what he intends to do with the money (buy a jeep "that will get me back to nature quicker") and then, we are told, he is introduced to Cole in person for the first time.[39] All the participants carry around big, clunky, and heavily wired handheld microphones—this being way before boom mics were used in broadcasting.[40] Ahbez looks like a vertically challenged beatnik Jesus and speaks rather awkwardly from a prepared script, especially compared to the statuesque Cole, looking very dignified in a formal tuxedo, singing the immortal song, accompanied by an offscreen string orchestra.

Capitol 15054, "Nature Boy" (backed with "Lost April") was a record that not only pushed Cole further along on his career transition from jazz pianist to popular singer but one that truly changed the world. Ahbez's lyrics and his message anticipate much of the pop music of two decades later and seem much more like something written during the summer of love, the age of flower children, sit-ins, and be-ins, rather than twenty years earlier at the start of the Cold War. "Nature Boy" was number one on the pop singles chart for seven weeks,[41] sold two million copies in that time, and, much more than songs of that era or this, expressed sentiments that the whole world embraced, or at least wanted you to think they did. The Grammy Awards wouldn't exist for another decade, but "Nature Boy" unquestionably would have been the song of the year for 1948. "Nature Boy," has been recorded hundreds if not thousands of times, by jazz colossi like Miles Davis, Django Reinhardt, and John Coltrane, and deep into the rock era, by Grace Slick, David Bowie, and Lady Gaga. All have been drawn to its universal sentiment, especially the iconic closing lines, "The greatest thing you'll ever learn / Is just to love and be loved in return."

Rapidly, Cole was proving himself not only one of the greatest musicians in the history of the American idiom but also one of the smartest players in the game of career advancement in the entertainment industry—a man who, at every turn, from his choice of managers, to his choice of labels, to his pick of musicians and collaborators, to his selection of songs, consistently made all the right decisions; and he climbed, step by step, up a ladder where none of "his race"—indeed precious few of any race—had ever gone before. He emerged at a moment when opportunities for African Americans were severely limited, but rather than being restrained by boundaries, walls, and ceilings, he repeatedly broke through them, one after another. And in consistently pushing upward and outward, both by design and otherwise, he carried the cause of humanity with him. Surely, it's no coincidence that eden ahbez wanted his message to be transmitted to the world by Nat King Cole; he was a rising tide that lifted all boats.

FALL 1947 HAD BEEN THE TRIO'S busiest season ever, especially in terms of recording sessions, but then the ban kept Cole, Miller, and Ashby out of the studios for almost the whole of 1948. They made only one date, on December 21, immediately after the strike was settled. Yet the ban year hardly amounted to a vacation for Cole. The *King Cole Trio Time* radio series was still going strong the end of spring. In March, Cole's divorce from Nadine was set to be finalized, and plans were being made for Nat to marry Maria as soon as possible. The wedding date was set for Easter Sunday; for the April 3 episode of the Wildroot show, another married couple, Peggy Lee and Dave Barbour, took over as hosts—as Nat and Maria jetted to Mexico for their honeymoon.

On the big day, March 28, the cream of black nobility were all there—the ceremony was held at the most celebrated house of worship in all of the African American community, the Abyssinian Baptist Church on 138th Street in Harlem, and the presiding minister was none other than the Reverend (and Congressman) Adam Clayton Powell. There were also numerous figures from the music world, white as well as black, such as pianist-entertainer Hazel Scott (Mrs. Adam Clayton Powell), Buddy Rich, and Leonard Feather. Duke Ellington, Maria's former employer, Nat's hero, and a close friend of the couple, was then playing the Howard Theater in Washington, doing multiple shows even on Easter Sunday, so he sent his deputy, Billy Strayhorn, in his place. The event went down in the annals of African American history as the most elaborate wedding in Harlem in at least twenty-five years. Eddie Cole served as best man; Ike and Evelyn were also there, and so were the Reverend Edward Sr. and Perlina (but not Freddy, then sixteen years old). The honeymoon couple then flew off to Mexico City and next to Acapulco. At precisely the moment when "Nature Boy" broke, and while the entire music industry was fighting over a piece of the action of this blockbuster hit, Cole was like the Nature Boy himself, far from the madding crowd, relaxing on a beach in the Mexican Riviera.

Maria recalled that they received a telegram on the trip, saying "What a wedding gift," referring to the biggest song of the year.

By the time Cole returned to the United States, and especially by the end of the ban in December, his self-driven makeover was complete: a new wife, then a new home, and soon enough, a new family; and by the time he resumed recording again in December, there was essentially a whole new King Cole Trio. There also would be a "new" Capitol Records, in at least one sense: Johnny Mercer chose this moment to officially retreat from active involvement in his company. He would no longer be a producer and entrepreneur but strictly a songwriter and occasional singer; his biggest hit as a performer had been "Save the Bones for Henry Jones" with the Trio. He and Nat would remain friends, even though they argued over one major issue. Like Norman Granz, Mercer was opposed to Cole's transition into pop singing and pop music. As Nat remembered in 1956, jazz fans "said that I was playing for the squares to make some loot," and that Mercer "lost interest" when he "went commercial." "I told him, 'Everybody else is making money, how come you don't want me to make any?' "[42] This didn't cause any long-term rift to their friendship; they would sing together, and gloriously at that, on Cole's 1957 NBC TV series.

In August, Cole moved into his new home in Hancock Park with his new wife just at the time that the new bassist, Joe Comfort (more about whom presently), joined the Trio at the Coona Club in El Cerrito. The house, at 401 South Muirfield Road, was a major step forward in Cole's personal life and his career as well. Cole and his new wife already knew well that the Deep South hardly had a monopoly on racism; as Martin Luther King himself later charged, the bigotry that he encountered in Chicago, for instance, was even more prevalent and disturbing than that in Alabama. As Maria later remembered, when the Trio played through Tennessee or Georgia, they would know never even to try to book rooms in a regular hotel. However, when they worked through Pennsylvania or even Chicago, sometimes the rooms would be booked but the reservations would mysteriously disappear as soon as they walked through the door.[43] During the period when percussionist Jack Costanzo toured with the Trio, he would usually enter the hotel first and ask for the rooms; then all would hope that when the other members of the group, which often (especially in the early years) included Maria, arrived, there would be no further incident.[44]

Geri Branton, wife of the Coles' lawyer Leo Branton Jr., had this to say about Hancock Park: "It was *the* posh area, the last WASP enclave."[45] But Cole knew exactly what he was letting himself in for; as we have seen, two years earlier Cole had bought a house for himself and Nadine in the white neighborhood known as "Blueberry Hill." He and Maria both knew that it would never be as easy as putting down a deposit and signing their names on a lease. Yet they both fell in love with the house in Hancock Park, and there's no doubt that Maria's fortitude was a major factor that empowered Nat to acquire it. The new Mrs. Cole had had a substantially greater sense of self-worth and entitlement than her husband, who, like most children of poor families from the South, were so acclimated to second-class treatment or worse that it rarely occurred to them to do something about it.

Nat and Maria bought the house through a black realtor named Joe Bradfield;[46] he, in turn, had used a very fair-skinned African American woman named Camille Laflotte as a "purchasing agent."[47] She paid the $6,000 deposit (the total cost was $85,000—that would be many millions in millennial dollars) and soon after transferred the property to the Coles. "There was bedlam everywhere, when I think back on it, it's amusing, because we were, thank God, so young that I was just angry," as Maria said in one of her last interviews; "I never felt any fear or anything like that."[48] In her book as well as in subsequent interviews, Maria, for reasons known only to herself, tended to downplay the danger of the situation and the fortitude that she and her husband had to have to get through it.

The local white homeowners immediately began what, essentially, amounted to a campaign of terror by threatening the previous owner and his real estate agent for not being aware they were selling to a black family. Then they started in on the Coles: they quickly formed an organization called the Hancock Park Property Owners Association and tried to explore any means that could be used to force the Coles out using the courts and the law. "All the people in the neighborhood," as George Benson pointed out the hypocrisy of racism, "they all had his records in their homes, but they signed a petition to get him out."[49]

On the less-than-legal side, they harassed the family in various ways: they posted a sign with the words "*N-word* Heaven" on the front lawn[50] and they poisoned the family dog. And then they burned in the *"N-Word"* in the same front lawn; as Nat's oldest child, Carole Cole remembered, "The shadow of that word was just always there"—and she meant that literally, not symbolically. When Maria later said she "never felt any fear or or anything like that," she was either being exceptionally brave or forgetful. On November 18, 1948, a would-be assassin fired a shot through a window of the Hancock Park house; thankfully the Coles were in Toledo, Ohio, where the Trio was opening at the Rivoli Theater.[51] (Only caretaker Chauncey Shaw was home, and he wasn't hurt, but he did report the incident to the police.)[52]

So far, the AFM ban year, 1948, had been the height of Cole's celebrity: in the early part of the year, all the black papers (and at least a few of the mainstream white ones) carried announcements about the wedding. Then, almost to the day when Nat and Maria were married, every media outlet in the country was buzzing over the unexpected success of "Nature Boy," and that kept the papers busy until the summer. And then, throughout July and August, papers as far afield as the *Irish Times* were carrying the news of the confrontation in Hancock Park. The latter quoted Cole explaining, "I have always been a good citizen and I wish I could meet all my new neighbours and explain this situation to them. This is not an act of defiance—my bride and I like this house and we would like to make it our home."[53]

As the Coles well knew, the restrictive clauses that the Hancock Park extremists were hoping would keep them out of the neighborhood turned out to be a kind of unwritten code—and not a legally enforceable one. All of the harassment by the neighbors (the threats of death and violence aside) was just so much wailing and gnashing of teeth; the long arch of the moral universe was indeed bending toward justice. The law was on the side of the Righteous: the Hancock Park Property Owners Association pointed to "covenants" designed to prevent non-Caucasians from owning property in the neighborhood, but the United States Supreme Court had recently decided the landmark case of *Shelley v. Kraemer*, which established that such covenants were not constitutional. Nat was aware that this decision had become the law of the land on May 3, 1948. Racial discrimination and segregated housing were now illegal in California as well as the rest of the United States, and the Coles were allowed to keep their house. "You either have to think of it as something like, 'how stupid can people be?' or a real tragedy," said Maria, "but being as young as we were, I think we were able to handle it."[54]

After her husband's death, Maria eventually sold the house and moved back to Massachusetts—her three younger children hadn't reached their teens yet. But they all agreed that despite an unpleasant beginning, the years in Hancock Park were happy ones. This can clearly be seen in several on-site television interviews, including a famous profile of the Coles by Edward R. Murrow on the widely watched show *Person to Person* in 1957. "Marie [*sic*] brought in Tom Douglas, the best decorator around, and they lived in grand style," said friend Bobby Short, "Nat's old friends thought that he was putting on the ritz, but he had simply found a new way of life, because of commercial success. He was living up to that image and enjoying it, and I can understand that. You can't hang on to the old gang forever."[55]

IF, IN 1927 OR '28, you had asked Nathaniel Adams Cole to name the two most important people in his young life, he would have cited his father and his older brother: Edward Sr. and Eddie Jr. In 1937 and '38, and many years to come, he would have named the two other members of his trio, Oscar Moore and Wesley Prince. During the war years, Cole had grown close to his jazz-loving buddy—and "partner in crime"—Norman Granz. By 1948 and for about fifteen years going forward, most of the remainder of his life, the two most important people in his world were his wife, Maria, and his manager, Carlos Gastel. Cole was so close to his manager that another woman would have been jealous of the time they spent together, but for the time being at least, Maria loved Carlos just as much as her husband did. Not that their relationship was entirely free from tension, even in the early days, as Irving Ashby noticed: "Carlos, I think, gritted his teeth every time he saw Maria coming."[56] But Carlos and Maria saw in each other an ally in terms of their vision of Nat's career; for the time being at least, they were both on the same page.

When Carlos Gastel died at the age of fifty-six ("following a heart seizure"), his obituary in *Variety*[57] described him as "one of the first successful managers for music personalities." There had been "music personalities" for many decades before Gastel went into the talent business in the late 1930s, but the postwar period amounted to a whole new world. Most of the new stars, including many of Gastel's clients, like Peggy Lee and Mel Tormé, were emerging out of the worlds of bands and vocal groups. The record industry had been virtually negligible for over a generation. Sales were practically nil during the Great Depression; only Crosby and Glenn Miller really sold anything worth a darn, at least through World War II. But by 1946–47, the market for records was expanding along with national prosperity; it was now increasingly possible to get rich from hit singles. As late as the war, most singers only worked with big bands in ballrooms, but now nightclubs and theaters were starting to open up, even as taxes levied on dancing venues made it more profitable for club owners to hire singers and smaller groups rather than big bands. In June 1948, Columbia Records would introduce the long-playing disc, and at the same time, another new medium, this one known as "television," was also on the horizon. It all amounted to a whole new ballgame with new rules, and whole new vistas for "music personalities."

When Mel Tormé first started working with Gastel, he was the leader and star of the Mel-Tones, a five-voice singing group that had made some impressive recordings, both on their own and with Artie Shaw's band. Gastel convinced Tormé that it made no sense for him to stay with the group when it was so clear to Carlos that Mel's individual star power outshone that of the group as a whole. In both cases, Gastel was convinced that the singer could go further on his own, like, earlier, Jimmy Durante without Eddie Clayton or Lou Jackson, or later, like Sammy Davis Jr. without the Will Mastin Trio. In the eyes of Gastel, these extra, "unnecessary" partners amounted to toxic assets.[58]

With "Nature Boy" now one of the biggest hits in the history of the record industry, Carlos and Maria were exerting ever more pressure on Nat to focus less on the piano and more on his singing. He had been leading the Trio since he was eighteen, after all, and they now regarded it as a childish thing that must be put aside. Still, Nat himself couldn't quite see their point, not just yet. "There are still too many potential possibilities in trio playing to think of anything else,"[59] he said in 1948. And then, in 1949, rather than scale back the King Cole Trio, he actually enlarged it.

AFTER NAT AND MARIA HAD MOVED into their new home, fall 1948 was the time to launch a new tour with the new Trio including the new bassist, with the new Mrs. Cole tagging along. Wisely, they avoided the South; they started on the West Coast in September, going as far north as Vancouver, and then gradually headed east—Ohio, Wisconsin, and then Chicago—during October and November. They were heading for New York, where they had a special gig booked on Christmas Eve.[60]

When Johnny Miller had given his notice, Cole, as was by now his tradition, once again turned to two virtuoso bassists who had both proven their mettle in Lionel Hampton's Orchestra. The first was Charles Mingus, who would go on to become one of the most legendary figures in all of jazz, although he was already infamous for something else. "I was supposed to go into the King Cole Trio, but I think my reputation stopped him," the bassist, composer, and bandleader said years later. "I think somebody must have told him I was a bad character or something. I went as far as to go to the tailor and get my suits cut down."[61] Mingus would however, soon become part of one of the best jazz groups inspired by the KC3, the exceptional trio led by vibraharpist Red Norvo and co-starring guitar wizard Tal Farlow.

Thus, the offer went to Joe Comfort (1917–1988),[62] who had actually been one of Mingus's mentors. He had started on a series of different string instruments and also played both trumpet and trombone with his high school band. He first became attracted to the bass, he said, when he heard it being played in a white group, British bandleader-composer Ray Noble and His

Orchestra—which might have further endeared him to Cole, who was also an admirer of Noble, both as a composer and a bandleader.[63] Like Ashby, Comfort had had a formal music education. His mother taught piano and his father was a professor of music at Alcorn College; Comfort himself graduated from Compton College.[64] Cole had first invited Comfort to join the Trio in 1942, to replace Wesley Prince, and Comfort would have accepted, except that, as they said at the time, Uncle Sam had other plans for him. He served in army bands until 1946, at which point he too joined Lionel Hampton for roughly a year, and then went freelance. At this point, like Ashby, he was a persistent presence in all sorts of Central Avenue groups during the pinnacle years of that scene, working and recording with singers, vocal groups, hot combos, big bands, jazz, R&B, whatever.

Miller had a big sound; it seemed like he could lift and carry the other two players on his back and give them all the support they needed for their harmonic and melodic flights of fancy. Comfort, however, was the perfect counterpart for Ashby; he was fast and nimble-fingered, and he had chops enough to handle the added melodic responsibilities and challenges of bassists during the modern jazz era. This was truer than ever in the King Cole Trio, where, like Prince and Miller before him, Comfort essentially had to serve as bassist and drummer at the same time.

After leaving the Trio in 1951, Comfort became one of the first wave of African American musicians—along with Benny Carter, Buddy Collette, and Sweets Edison—to graduate into the mainstream studios for movie, TV, and record dates. He played several standout solos during his three years or so with Cole, being very prominent on the studio recordings of "Peaches," "Don't Shove, I'm Leaving," and "'Deed I Do," among others, and is featured in a brilliant extended improvisation on "Tea for Two" at the 1949 Carnegie Hall concert. However, in the overall arc of his career, Joe Comfort may be best remembered for the most famous bass solo ever to be heard on a Sinatra record—the Jimmy Blanton-inspired bass break on Nelson Riddle's arrangement of "Too Marvelous for Words" on *Songs for Swingin' Lovers*—a solo that has been studied and imitated by contemporary bassists like Christian McBride.

Comfort later said of Cole, "He could play anything and drive the average piano player crazy. I loved him. I knew just about every song he ever played, had all his records. I just loved his sound. It made me mad when he stopped playing and started singing. He was a musician's musician."[65]

The first significant performance of the new Trio with Comfort and Ashby is actually a Hollywood feature film, *Make Believe Ballroom*, a 1949 Columbia

Pictures production (filmed and recorded in early October 1948).[66] This was Cole's third movie to be inspired by a radio program, following *Here Comes Elmer* and *Breakfast in Hollywood*. The visual is up to Hollywood standard on "The Trouble with Me Is You," a swingy, catchy novelty; this time Cole threw a bone to Roy Alfred and Marvin Fisher, two of the songwriters he was closest to from the beginning, who must have been delighted at landing one of their songs in a major motion picture. It would be the Trio's official last appearance in a Hollywood feature and the first footage of the group with the new bassist.

They arrived in New York for a special one-nighter on Christmas Eve, at the Renaissance Ballroom on 138th Street and Seventh Avenue—right down from the Abyssinian Baptist Church, where Nat and Maria had been married just a few months earlier. (This was apparently the only time Cole ever performed in Harlem, other than at the Apollo Theater.) The Trio was the headliner, but there was also a local band playing for dancing, led by one Buddy Valentino, which included the nineteen-year-old pianist Bill Evans in its rhythm section. Evans later cited Cole as one of the primary influences on his own playing, describing him as "one of the tastiest and just swingin'est and beautifully melodic improvisors that jazz has ever known, and he was one of the first that grabbed me hard." When it came the big band's turn to play, Evans sat at the piano, and, for what seemed like the longest time, just stared at it, unable to force himself to touch the keys that his idol had touched, to play the same piano that Nat had just played. "It was reverential," he said. [67] On arriving in Manhattan, the Trio learned that there was a big Christmas gift in store for them, and for the music industry entire: the AFM had at last settled with the record companies, and the second recording ban was now officially over. The new Trio did its first studio session on December 21, at the WMGM Studio on 5th Avenue, which amounted to a sort of test date; none of the specific takes they cut on that date were issued at the time, but all four songs were summarily remade. There was a lovely "custom ballad," "It Only Happens Once," words and music by friend Frankie Laine, and also two numbers aimed squarely at the race market: a slow and sexy semi-comic blues by Cole and Don George titled "My Mother Told Me" and the fast and swinging "Bang, Bang Boogie," co-written by Sid Kuller.[68] Both represent the blues at its bluesiest.

But the most important number at this first post-ban date was "Portrait of Jennie," the latest in what was now an ongoing series of ballads with strings; for the first time, Capitol didn't balk when Cole requested a string quartet. "Portrait of Jennie" was also the latest of Cole's movie ballads, deriving from a high-profile fantasy drama produced by David Selznick (a cinematic expression of his obsession with his new bride, Jennifer Jones, co-starring Joseph Cotton). Like a lot of Hollywood epics, *Portrait of Jennie* is somehow both simultaneously pretentious and moving.[69] There's no main title theme in the actual movie; this number was apparently written as what was once called "an exploitation song." It's the work of J. Russell Robinson, formerly of the Original Dixieland Jazz Band (and the writer of the Trio's 1947 hit, "Meet Me at No Special Place"), although it doesn't sound like anything else he's known to have written.[70] "Jennie" is a lovely melody, with a lyric concerning an unforgettable woman with a kind of a beauty that's almost mythic, but, alas, she is only visible in a painting. "Portrait of Jennie" was not a hit, either as a film or a song, but the subject matter would soon re-appear rather significantly in Cole's career.[71]

As we have seen already, and will again (many times), every period in Cole's life was a transitional one; he never did anything by rote or by formula. But the final years of the Trio, 1948 to 1951, are especially experimental. The journey from jazz pianist to pop star and from pianist to vocalist was never a direct path; there were all kinds of unpredictable stops along the way. The next date occurred on January 14, 1949, also in New York—the entourage had just come up from The Click in Philadelphia. It includes the perceptively different remake of "Portrait of Jennie" (famously later on the *Unforgettable* album); another special ballad, "Don't Cry, Cry Baby"; another blues song by Don George, "An Old Piano Plays the Blues" (co-written by future TV superstar Steve Allen, also a close friend and supporter of Cole); and an unknown song by an unknown author, like so many others, distinguished and enhanced considerably by Cole's keyboard enhancements, titled "How Lonely Can You Get."[72] (Neither "Old Piano" nor "Lonely" were issued at the time, although the first would have been worthy.)

"'Tis Autumn," recorded at the March 29 session, may be the single most perfect example of a ballad by the "pure" 1949 King Cole Trio—Cole, Ashby, Comfort—with no additives. This was a 1941 song by Henry Nemo that came with a considerable pedigree (Benny Goodman, Woody Herman, Les Brown). The laid back, relaxed track opens with lush chords from Ashby, and prodding single notes from Cole. The tune is a natural for Cole's voice, especially with several very warm wordless sections, wherein he hums and scats, written right into the libretto. Overall the mood is more like a slow deep summer rather than a busy autumn in New York.

As charming as "'Tis Autumn" still sounds today, Cole was nonetheless determined to add something new to the Trio. That something new is first heard on the March 22 date, done immediately after their latest opening at the

New York Paramount. Here, the new Trio is unveiled, and, mathematically speaking, it is a trio no more (and also no Moore). They start with a classical adaptation ("Laugh, Cool Clown," ingeniously based on "Vesti la giubba" from *Pagliacci*) and then a very hot modern jazz number, "Bop Kick," and last, an all-time classic ballad, "For All We Know." This is the kind of diversity we have grown to expect from Cole, but the group dynamics have fundamentally changed. We are now hearing a whole other sound, something almost completely different, from the classic Trio of 1943–1947.

The presence of percussionist Jack Costanzo is unmistakable, even on the first few seconds of the first track on which he plays, "Laugh, Cool Clown." As ever, Cole was excited to try new ideas, and Afro-Latin jazz was very much in the wind as the 1940s became the 1950s. It was the intertwined lineage of Afro-Cuban music and modern jazz that Cole addressed in an interview with *Metronome*'s Barbara Hodgkins, in which one gets a very clear sense of the artist's refusal to stand still. He talks about how crooners were once the new thing, but now all pop singers sound alike. The same with combos and even trios; "Now all trios sound the same."[73] Big bands too: "Now all bands sound practically the same except Dizzy and Kenton." Cole continued, "Everybody who has a creative mind should try something different, that's why I give Stan credit, he's going his own way. You can't cling to the past. Too many different things are coming into the world. I took a chance on 'Nature Boy,' though I think 'Lost April' is a much better song. . . . [T]he public liked 'Nature Boy' because it was something different."

It was, in fact, the bands of both "Dizzy and Kenton" that directly inspired the use of Latin percussion in the Trio. Gillespie had broken new ground when he incorporated Afro-Cuban rhythms in his big band, in the person of Chano Pozo, the legendary *conguero* imported straight from Havana. At the time, Gillespie described working with the new rhythms as being "akin to the joy of the man who realizes he has discovered fire." The next musical figure, after Gillespie, to try to catch the spark of that Afro-Cuban rhythmic fire was Stan Kenton, who hired Jack Costanzo in 1947. Costanzo (1919–2018) was an American musician of Cuban descent, who like, Cole, was raised in Chicago but spent most of his career in California. He started as a professional dancer at the age of fourteen, and within a short while he was giving dance lessons at the Merry Gardens in Chicago, where he heard his first set of bongos in 1938, from a rhumba band out of Puerto Rico.

Costanzo became determined to establish himself as a musician, at a time when pan-American rhythms were all but unknown beyond Xavier Cugat and Carmen Miranda—and to that end he made repeated pilgrimages to

Havana to study the rhythms of his people at their source. Like Ashby and Comfort, Costanzo too was drafted—and even then apparently managed to get onscreen work dancing in several movie musicals while still in the service.[74] By war's end, however, he was a full-time player and worked with two giants of Cuban music, the famous composer Ernesto Lecuona and his Lecuona Cuban Boys and the singer-actor-bandleader Desi Arnaz and His Orchestra. By 1947, Costanzo was one of the first Latin percussionists to be working regularly in mainstream show business and performed and recorded with a wide range of stars, in addition to touring with Kenton. Dark and good-looking, he was the very picture of a Latin lothario, and for years, his number was always the first that any producer or star would call when he wanted to "go Latin." Costanzo's first important gig with a *gringo* orchestra was that of Stan Kenton, who, like Cole and everyone else in the American Federation of Musicians, was banned from recording in 1948, and it was Gastel who introduced him to Cole. It was no secret that the agent's machinations had helped Kenton reach the top of the band business, but, unlike Nat, Stan and Carlos were in a state of perpetual disagreement. Gastel kept pushing Kenton to play more pop music and crowd-pleasers whereas Kenton incessantly wanted to play only the most far out "progressive jazz" works that he could commission. Finally, in June 1949, they parted company.[75] Continuing without the benefit of Gastel's management savvy and street smarts soon became just too overwhelming for Kenton; six months after the split, the exhausted bandleader announced that he was disbanding. Thus, in December 1948, even as the ban was ending, Kenton temporarily retired, leaving both Jack Costanzo and arranger Pete Rugolo (1915–2011) free to work with Cole.

As Costanzo recalled much later, "Nat wanted to make a change, he wanted to get more into, as then we would have said, 'today's music,' so he decided he wanted to add a bongo player. Musically, we had Joe Comfort and Irving Ashby, I was on the congas more than the bongos and Nat was the star."[76] Afro-Latin music was still so new to mainstream audiences that the *California Eagle* actually ran a story headlined, "King Cole Adds Banjo Player to Trio."[77]

When Kenton disbanded, he left behind a market for both Afro-Cuban music and "progressive jazz." Thus Cole and Gastel soon announced that the Trio would tour with Woody Herman and His Orchestra (known to history as "The Thundering Herd," and this particular line-up as "The Second Herd"). With Kenton out of commission and Gillespie going through a lull, it was Herman who now had the most modern big band around. Originally the percussionist was set to work with Cole for only this two-week period: "Although

[Costanzo is] just joining up with the King Cole Trio for the duration of the tour, Nat has already stated that if the venture is successful, he would like to keep Jack with the group permanently."[78]

In discussing these changes, Cole was remarkably consistent: he told the *Melody Maker*, "After all these years, I wanted to develop our sound without too drastic a change, and I felt a bongo player would make out fine. I realized too, the growing interest in Afro-Cuban rhythms."[79] "As a trio, we'd gone as far as we could," Cole told John S. Wilson in *Down Beat*; "We've done everything except imitations."[80] He continued, in *Melody Maker*, "Of course, the change met with a lot of opposition as well. They said we'd lose our individual sound and asked why, after all those years of success, we had to make the Trio a quartet. My answer was that Jack's drumming would add interest to our beat numbers." Cole used the same phrase in three different interviews (*Melody Maker*, *Metronome*, and *Down Beat*): "Now the bongos give us more scope." He added, in *Metronome*, "The change gives us that progressive feeling. Jack relaxes the guys. A lot of the tension that the bass and I used to feel is gone now because the bongo and conga drums give the rhythm we were supposed to give. That leaves us free to do much more."[81]

One issue immediately presented itself: with four men now on the bandstand, what should they call the group? Ivan Mogull, music publisher and lifelong friend of the Coles, had a suggestion. "They were saying, 'What are you going to call the group now that you have another musician?' They said, 'Call it the King Cole Quartet.'" That did not fly; it was a branding imperative, though that term wasn't being used yet, to keep the word "Trio" in the group's name—to continue the reference to "Old King Cole and his Fiddlers Three." Mogull continued, "I said, 'Well everybody knows that Nat is the piano player and that Nat now is doing the singing. So, I said he's the star, call it 'Nat King Cole *and His* Trio.' Well, they were very upset that I put my two cents into it, and they read the riot act to me. But that's what it became."[82]

Randy Weston, the Afrocentric jazz piano giant from Brooklyn (who could be considered a Cole disciple), best articulated what Cole was going for with Costanzo. "Whenever I work with a trap drummer"—in other words, a conventional jazz drummer who uses sticks—"I can never hear myself." He told me once, "That's why I always prefer to work with hand drummers." Cole wanted to alter the rhythm and the texture of the group without having to increase the volume and to be able to maintain the amazing inter-group dynamics that were always a trademark of the KC3.

Cole recorded comparatively few pan-American-style numbers at this point, those that use an actual *clave* rhythm. It wasn't as if he wanted to go completely Latin," but he wanted to use the new percussion to enhance what he was already doing. Judiciously applied, he surely does. The exotic feeling that Costanzo instills on "Laugh, Cool Clown" transforms the iconic aria into something more like a Mohammedan chant rather than Italian opera. (At Carnegie Hall, November 4, 1949, Cole introduces it "as a song from a very great play, *Pagliacci*.") Costanzo is especially useful behind Cole and then Ashby, making their solos seem like dances for two of the seven veils. In its use of Middle Eastern exoticism, "Cool Clown" anticipates later piano travelogues like Lennie Tristano's "Turkish Mambo."

Costanzo's finest hour is on the original instrumentals; as we've seen, there had been elements of modern jazz in the Trio's music for a decade already, but Cole didn't dive head first into the bebop pool until the arrival of Costanzo. The four-piece King Cole Trio is instantly a smooth and beautifully functioning contemporary jazz combo, heralding the start of an era of modern jazz–era piano superstars. Earlier, we have compared Cole to his predecessors, especially Earl Hines, Teddy Wilson, and Art Tatum, but now we find Cole helping to usher in a new age of piano headliners: Oscar Peterson, Erroll Garner, Ahmad Jamal, Dave Brubeck, Bill Evans, and, most of all, George Shearing.

"Bop Kick" is a different melody, but in many ways it's a follow-up to "Jumpin' at Capitol," from the first Capitol date in 1943, announcing a new era with a hot and jumping instrumental. Both of these Cole originals were accurately labeled: one jumps and the other kicks, boppishly. In most bop groups, the drums are all important—the horns, strings, and keys increasingly stressed the higher intervals of the chords, which drummers like Max Roach emphasized by spending more time on the high-hat cymbals. Fully aware of that, Cole picked a percussion option that would deliberately not follow the path of most other modernist groups; once again, he found his own way.

Which isn't to say he didn't make use of existing tropes: "Go Bongo," credited to Cole and Costanzo, is a percussion-centric feature inspired by "Cubana Be, Cubana Bop," Dizzy Gillespie's classic feature for Chano Pozo, and similarly follows the percussion solo with a chanting episode by the entire group. "Top Hat Bop" (by Ashby) and "Rhumba Blues" (by Cole) both astutely combine three elements: modern jazz, Afro-Latin rhythms, and the blues. Terry Gibbs, one of the first modern era vibraphonists (then with Woody Herman), wrote two excellent bop instrumentals for the group, "Peaches" and "Last but Not Least." The latter seems to have derived from an old vaudeville conceit—milking applause by being the last one to leave the stage—and posits the idea of Cole and Ashby playing in competition as well as collaboration; the tempo changes, the slow-downs and speed-ups, also seem to come out of a vaudeville tradition. "Etymology (The Language of Love)," by Roy Alfred, is a bop novelty, more thoroughly modern in conception than "My Baby Likes to Bebop" from two years earlier. (Alas, Capitol chose not to issue it at the time.)

Despite Costanzo's valid contributions to these numbers, not everyone was thrilled with his addition to the group—both inside and outside Cole's immediate entourage. As the combo played through the South that spring and summer, it was anyone's guess in exactly what venues the percussionist would be legally allowed on the same stage as the rest of the Trio. Although Hispanic, according to the institutionalized racist laws of the day, he was still technically considered Caucasian, and this officially made the Trio a "mixed race" band, which was illegal in most of the United States. At this time, racial segregation applied to both performers and audiences, and wherever they traveled below the Mason-Dixon line, they either played to a house divided (one side for blacks and the other for whites) or gave two separate shows, inevitably with the white audience getting the prime time. During Cole's 1949 spring tour, Costanzo was not permitted to appear onstage at all in at least four cities: Shreveport, Little Rock, Memphis, and Cole's own hometown, Montgomery.[83] In some cities, the good news was that Costanzo was permitted to perform with Cole, Ashby, and Comfort, but the bad news was that white people were completely barred from attending at all.[84]

Cole almost always presented a positive face to the press; this is one of the first instances when he let his anger and dissatisfaction with the racial status quo be known: "In an exclusive interview with Nat and Jack, what this department was told must be off the record—as it isn't possible to write such things in a family newspaper."[85] Still, he couldn't afford to boycott the South. Southern audiences both black and white were clamoring for the Trio, with or without percussion. Five nights in the Atlanta area (some of which costarred tenor honker Hal "Cornbread" Singer and his R&B combo) in July broke local box-office records: $3,720 in Atlanta and $2,350 for a one-nighter in Norfolk. "Reports from promoters say that the Nation's number one Trio and his package are averaging better than most big bands booked for dance engagements."[86] In August, they did four concerts in northern California, costarring with Woody Herman, that netted a gigantic total of $15,000.[87]

Yet to Ashby and Comfort, Costanzo was frequently prohibited from performing for all the wrong reasons. Presumably, they kept their opinions to themselves at the time, but toward the end of their lives, they were both highly critical of the percussionist. The coming of Costanzo "was the beginning of the end of my happiness with the King Cole Trio," said the guitarist. "Can you imagine conga drums on 'Sweet Lorraine?' That just turned my stomach! But what could I say? I wasn't paying him. I just did the job."[88] "I just didn't like it, and Irving didn't like it," said the bassist. "We both didn't like it because it just didn't fit. A conga drum with a bass and guitar and piano." (Notice the order in which Comfort lists the instruments). It's too lopey. If you play 'Sweet Lorraine' with a conga drum, it would sound like a horse clopping its feet." Ashby described the sound of the conga as "*ker-plak, ker-plak, ker-plak!*" and Comfort described it as "*clack-a-lack, clack-a-lack, clack-a-lack.*"

Still, their reasons for objecting were not completely musical. In fact, Cole responds to their charges very definitively in his 1950 *Melody Maker* interview: "As for the ballads, they're still Trio numbers, Jack doesn't play on them." That wasn't the end of Ashby's complaints: "We'd be on the train riding someplace and instead of being with us, talking or playing cards with the guys, or having a sip or something, he'd be sitting with the boss's wife, yakking about the latest things from the perfume world. So, you can imagine what kind of impression that made on us."[89]

Thus, the gripes against Jack were probably more of a personality conflict. Just listen to the way that Costanzo enhances and supports Comfort's already brilliant solo on "Tea for Two" in the 1949 Carnegie concert. The 1948 (unissued) version of "Bang, Bang Boogie," another semi-comic R&B number, is classic Trio, but there's no denying that the 1949 remake, with Costanzo, is much more exciting. In Sid Kuller's lyric, a family patriarch (identifying himself as "Daddy") expresses his eagerness to perform his husbandly duties, even as the KC3 builds up a rope-skipping beat (the same loping rhythm that the guitarist and bassist professed to despise) into a rhythmically righteous forerunner of what, in the 1950s, became known as coffeehouse cool. Yes, it was bongos that were soon to put the beat in beatnik.

Perhaps the real issue, for Ashby and Comfort, was that the addition of a fourth musician meant that they had to divide up whatever diminishing glory was left for them into ever smaller portions. It was a further step in the Trio's receding into the background; Ashby and Comfort had thought of themselves as co-stars, even as Moore and Miller had been, not mere sidemen. When they became "King Cole and his Trio," it set Nat further apart from the rest of the group; now he even started dressing in a slightly different colored suit from the other three. This was almost certainly Maria's idea, supported by Carlos, but Nat went along with it.

Despite Ashby and Comfort's specific charges, Costanzo does not play on any known version of "Sweet Lorraine" from this period, or any of the other ballads they recorded at the time, such as "'Tis Autumn" and "What Have You Got in Those Eyes." However, Costanzo's playing was highly appropriate on standards of faster, more dance-oriented tempos. Costanzo contributes much to one of the KC3's great records of the year, "Yes Sir, That's My Baby," and especially so on the final coda, where Cole and company play with the tempo (and even more so on the live versions), slowing down and speeding up.

Both with and without Costanzo, the Trio was turning in some amazing work in 1949, as witnessed by two tracks originally recorded for Capitol Transcriptions. "Boulevard of Broken Dreams" is a perfectly appropriate dramatic ballad, wherein the Latin percussion certainly makes sense, not least because this 1933 movie song (from *Moulin Rouge*) was originally written as a tango. "Exactly Like You" is a gem, with Ashby and Costanzo riffing behind Cole's vocal in a way that's irresistibly hip. (Nearly fifty years later, Diana Krall played homage to the Trio with a note-for-note, beat-for-beat recreation of this lesser-known Cole classic on her 2006 album *From This Moment On*.)

Then too, Joe and Irving could have been jealous because there was one number wherein Cole spotlighted Jack more extensively than any other member of the group had been featured before: "Calypso Blues," by Don George and Cole. Several of Cole's contemporaries had already enjoyed hits in the Trinidadian style, most famously "Stone Cold Dead in the Market," the blockbuster duet by Louis Jordan and Ella Fitzgerald. The melody of "Calypso Blues" was memorable, though not remarkable, and the lyrics were similar to dozens of punchline-centric novelties the Trio had already recorded. The amazing thing about the record was the instrumentation: just voice and conga, with Cole singing in a cool, understated fashion, practically *a capella*, and opening and closing with a low sensual moan. Nat renders a series of comic complaints in a mock West Indian *patois*, some of which are quite funny: describing "Yankee girls," he tells us, "her eyelash false, her face is paint / And pads are where the girl she ain't." "Calypso Blues" didn't chart, but it was a notable song that Cole included on personal appearances and on Ed Sullivan's *Toast of the Town* (on November 5, 1950), accompanied by a dance troupe dressed in West Indian drag. Throughout the three minutes, Cole stays remarkably in tune, completely bereft of any harmonic or melodic support—proof that his intonation was now among the best of anyone in popular music or jazz.

"THIS TIME WE'D LIKE TO DO a great song, written by a young man, by the name of Mr. Billy Strayhorn, a tune that we think is very wonderful. It's quite abstract, and that means it's a very noncommercial tune, but we think it's a very wonderful song, and it's called 'Lush Life.'" That was how Cole introduced the song at Carnegie Hall in November 1949. The composer himself described "Lush Life" as, "a song most persons have to listen to twice before they understand it, and lots of them still don't know what it's about."[90]

By 1949, listeners had learned to expect the unexpected from Cole; every one of his significant songs thus far sounded completely different from the one that had preceded it. That was certainly the case with "Lush Life," which Don George was also involved in, indirectly. George knew Strayhorn through Duke Ellington: George had written a few songs with the Maestro and Strayhorn spent most of his career as Ellington's musical partner. The lyricist was having breakfast with Nat and Maria, around the time of "Calypso Blues," when the mailman delivered a large manila envelope that Cole was obviously eagerly anticipating. "Come on Don, I want you to hear something."[91] "He played and sang a song called 'Lush Life,' that I was hearing for the first time. He turned to me and said, 'What do you think?' I loved the song. I said, 'It's just great.' He nodded enthusiastically. 'I'm going to record it on my next date.'"

"'Lush Life' wasn't the first tune of mine that Duke heard," Strayhorn said in 1949. "In fact, he didn't hear it until just a little while ago. I wrote it in 1936, when I was clerking at the Pennfield Drugstore at the corner of Washington and Penn in Pittsburgh."[92] He added, "I called it 'Life Is Lonely,' but when anyone wanted me to play it, they'd ask for 'that thing about lush life.'" "Swee' Pea," as his friends called him, was the opposite of the pushy songwriter who cornered Nat in the men's room; he had no ambition for the song that he regarded as his own personal statement. "It was just something that I did and I had written that I liked for myself, and I just did it at parties."

So how did "Lush Life" exit the closet and transition from a private party piece for its composer to become one of the most celebrated of all jazz ballads? The backstory here is almost as complex, confusing, and self-contradictory as "Nature Boy." Cole himself told Leonard Feather that Strayhorn gave it to him personally in 1940 while the Ellington band was in Los Angeles,[93] but he also apparently told George that he had never met Strayhorn up to the time he recorded the song.[94]

As Strayhorn said, he played and sang the song himself at parties, and one of these was at dancer Marie Bryant's house, where her boyfriend, Norman Granz, heard it. Then, at some point, Norman, Nat, and Billy were all in the midst of production on *The Jazz Scene*, Nat playing on his final session with Lester Young and Strayhorn arranging and conducting a session of Harry Carney, Ellington's brilliant baritone saxophonist, with strings. Strayhorn remembered that Norman asked him to record "Lush Life" for *The Jazz Scene*, but if he did, no trace of this recording has ever surfaced. "I made a record of ['Lush Life'] for an album of modern arrangers' works Norman Granz was putting together," he said in 1949, "but it wasn't used."[95]

In a 1962 interview,[96] the composer added that Granz had offered to give him a full orchestra, but he demurred, saying, "There's only one way to do 'Lush Life,' and that's with piano [only]." The composer had decided that he didn't want the song to be on the album in any case. "I didn't particularly like the idea of doing an isolated [song] in a collection of things," he said; the album "didn't seem to have any kind of form."[97] But it was because he had played it for Granz that Cole heard it. "Cole happened to be cutting some instrumentals at Capitol the day we were recording the Granz album."[98] Strayhorn casually demonstrated the tune for Cole, and "he asked me for the lead sheet." The composer later elaborated, "So I recorded it, and as we finished the date, Nat came in, because he had to do some retakes on a piano album he was doing, and he came in a little early. He said, 'What's that?' I said, 'Well, a song of mine.' So, he said, 'I'd like to do that.'[99] After Cole asked about the song, Strayhorn went to the trouble of writing it down, which he had never done previously.

How could Cole not love it? He was happy enough doing blues and novelties or anything that sold, but he was constantly on the lookout for anything that was new and different. A sophisticated song like this, and especially from an African American composer in the Ellington fold, was a Godsend. "Lush Life," to use Sinatra's favorite expression, is a "saloon song," theoretically similar to "One for My Baby (And One More for the Road)." Both lyrics begin in the immediate aftermath of a breakup; but where Johnny Mercer's protagonist can barely bring himself to stumble into the nearest saloon, Strayhorn's jaded *distingue* lover has both the wherewithal and the resources to head off for "a week in Paris to ease the bite of it." Maria, with her connections to Ellington and Strayhorn, as well as her relentless ambition to elevate the two of them into a higher class, musically and socially, undoubtedly encouraged him to sing it as well. "Lush Life" is a very literal boost up the social ladder; this was still the age of Nick and Nora Charles, at a moment when "jazz and cocktails" were considered sophisticated and worldly.

Thus, in this third and most likely account (which contradicts both Don George and Leonard Feather), Strayhorn played the song for Ellington around the same time he gave it to Cole. The composer explained, "One night I remembered it and played it for Duke. He liked it and we've used it occasionally, with Kay Davis singing and myself on piano."[100] In the summer of 1948, Strayhorn was part of an Ellington tour of Europe, and Duke had soprano Kay Davis introduce it, with Strayhorn's accompaniment, during a concert in Paris. On November 13, Davis and Strayhorn performed the song for the second time in public, at Ellington's annual Carnegie Hall concert.

So by the end of the 1948 AFM ban, "Lush Life" had been performed in concert but not yet recorded.On March 29, 1949, again in New York, Cole did his third session after the ban, and the primary order of business was a follow-up to "Nature Boy," another unconventional tone poem by eden ahbez titled "Land of Love (Come My Love and Live with Me)," somewhat inspired by Christopher Marlowe's 1599 poem, "The Passionate Shepherd to His Love" (and its famous opening line, "Come live with me and be my love").

Up to now, all the previous sessions by the "Trio-plus-orchestra" had been one-shot deals with various musical directors with whom Cole was only barely acquainted. However, for the arrangement for "Land of Love," Cole and Gastel chose Pete Rugolo. "I go back with Nat to about 1945 when I first joined Stan [Kenton]," remembered the arranger-conductor.[101] "We did a lot of theaters together around, and so Nat wanted to do some songs with the orchestra. Since Nat already had done 'The Christmas Song' with strings, he asked me to add some [band] parts to it." There were other informal collaborations in these years between the Cole Trio and the Kenton Orchestra. "Nat loved playing with the big band," Rugolo added. "I took a lot of his Trio arrangements and added the big band stuff. I guess he liked the stuff that I did then, so much maybe it helped me get on his record dates."

"When we came back into town one day," Rugolo continued, "Carlos said, 'Nat would like you to make some records with him,' and I said, 'Gee, I'd love to.' Like Stan, Nat was another wonderful man to work for, he was just so nice. I'd go to his house and he'd give me some tunes, we'd talk about them, and I'd take them home and write whatever I thought they should be. Of course, I just admired Nat so much."

Job one was "Land of Love." As a song, it's both more complex and less satisfying overall than "Nature Boy." Rugolo embellishes it with an exceptionally resplendent orchestration, effectively using an angular string background and exotic woodwinds, oboes, and bongos in place of brass and reeds, as well as terrific singing and a brief piano solo by Cole. It would be the first of many quasi-Middle Eastern/Asian numbers recorded by Cole throughout the 1950s, many of which were film theme songs, most famously (or even infamously) "Hajji Baba (Persian Lament)," from the motion picture of the same name in 1954.

The money was on "Land of Love" to be the next big hit; but, now that he had access to Rugolo and a full orchestra, Cole decided to cut "Lush Life" on the same date, more or less as an afterthought. Said Rugolo, "Nat handed 'Lush Life' to me, and said 'See what you can do with this.' I'd never heard it before, but I liked it, and I created [an orchestration]. I added bars at the beginning and made sort of a tone poem out of it. I just studied the words and thought I'd make a little tone poem out of it, I tried to catch all the lyrics in there."

Rugolo continues, "Even after we recorded it, I had no idea what would happen because Capitol didn't know what to do with it, it was so unusual. At least six months to a year later they put it in back of a terrible commercial thing 'Lillian,' they just put 'Lush Life' on the B side. However, the jockeys started playing it and it sort of caught on. When I went to M-G-M Pictures in the '50s, I found out that all the movie stars loved it, especially Ava Gardner. Lana Turner said it was her favorite song, she told me, 'God, I love that 'Lush Life.' Word about it just went around."

One dissenter, however, was Strayhorn himself. The composer had viewed the song as an intimate piece for voice and piano rather than an orchestra and strings, and wasn't happy with the changes that had been made. "The verse wasn't written that way," said Rugolo; "I just went on bar by bar, and I added bars, like on the words 'jazz and cocktails,' where I added a few extra bars in between." This meant the "interstitial" phrases that he adds after certain key lines, which do, in fact, anticipate, the jazz settings for poetry recitations that would be heard in coffeehouses across the nation in the next generation or two.

Perhaps even more significantly, Strayhorn had written the song in two distinct sections, with the first in minor, the second in major; Rugolo, however, put both in minor. "It turned out really great," said Rugolo. But Strayhorn was so angry that he said he preferred "Lillian" (which, as David Hajdu points out, rhymes his mother's name, Lillian, with his own, William) to his own song. "That was the first time I ever heard Billy so upset," said Aaron Bridgers, the composer's life partner; "I had never heard him talk like that. He was screaming, 'Why the fuck didn't they leave it alone?' "[102]

Then there was the matter of Cole's delivery of the lyrics: in 1949, when the song was new, no one would have noticed the lyric flubs, but today, after Chris Connor, Johnny Hartman, Billy Eckstine, and many others, we all know the words by heart, and Cole's faux-pas are painfully obvious: "siren of song" instead of "siren song," "strifling" instead of "stifling," and "those who lives are lonely too" instead of "those whose lives." Even more curiously, when

Cole recorded a new stereo version of the song in 1961, he still failed to correct all of these mistakes.

Thanks to Cole and Rugolo, "Lush Life" became an instant jazz standard, not to mention a cause celébrè of all sorts of showbiz industry insiders. Though never a hit single,[103] the public that got to hear it loved it. In 1951, *Down Beat*'s Don Freeman was interviewing Nat between sets at Tops in San Diego, and their conversation was "periodically interrupted by a woman requesting 'Lush Life.'" This prompted Cole to give voice to his continued enthusiasm for the song. "'Lush Life' is jazz. Some so-called music experts and fans think music must be fast and loud like Illinois Jacquet or else it isn't jazz. But after all, Billy Strayhorn gave me 'Lush Life' and Billy's no square. Besides, the song has some nice changes and real jazz feel to it." He continued, "Now there's a song, 'Lush Life.' You know why I did that? Not to make money, for sure, it's too subtle for any wide appeal. I mean, it's not like 'Too Young' or "Mona Lisa.' But 'Lush Life' is, well, a kind of contribution. I'd like people to say, 'Lush Life?' Sure, that's the song Nat Cole does. That's all I ask."[104]

IN 1946, COLE HAD SAID, "Don't think that we're fluffing off jazz. We're only waiting until we've reached a firm enough point where we can start mixing the real stuff with the popular and still have an audience. And I think we're just about at that point now. I'm already planning to make more and more jazz records." He concluded, "Let's get it straight: I love jazz and I'm going to play more of it all the time!"[105] Then, in 1949, he re-energized the jazz aspect of the Trio's music with Costanzo, and the four-piece edition of the KC3 became at once the hottest and the coolest ensemble of his career. But while there's no shortage of "the real stuff" in the last great years of the Trio, Cole was, by this point, much too restless a soul to remain content to confine himself to any one category of music. It's said that in these years he transitioned from jazz to pop, but that's much too reductive a way of looking at it. He was starting from a jazz background and endlessly covering the waterfront in search of different ways to reach the mass audience, a market well beyond the jazz audience or the black audience.

Thus, relentless experimentation was a necessity. Most pop hitmakers found a formula and stuck with it, but Cole, as we have seen, was directly opposed to the very concept of a formula, a repeatable practice, and instead was continually searching for something new. Some have speculated, rather incorrectly, that as Cole got a taste of the good life—and especially in the early 1950s, when he was being pilloried by the IRS and needed to come up with a lot of cash very quickly—he became less determined to take chances with unusual songs or instrumental formats. In reality, precisely the opposite was true. He already knew that it was impossible to clone and then replicate his own success—in 20th-century speak, his work was neither "scalable" nor "sustainable." For Cole, the shortest path to the biggest payout was to avoid formula, to keep coming up with new ideas—Bang! Bang! Bang!—faster than his rivals could copy them.

Even "Lillian" had something new to offer; Pete Rugolo, who arranged it, dismissed the song as a "horrible commercial thing," but it's actually delightfully boppish. That is, it's hardly the same old same old; the vocal group sounds very hip and contemporary. It's no "Lush Life," but one can see why Strayhorn dug it. This would be the first of a series of titles wherein Cole and company are backed by a vocal group, led by Alyce King, of the King Sisters, and billed as "The Alyce King Vokettes." Jazz purists at the time viewed this as one more step in the mass-marketing of Cole—another nail in the commercial coffin—but in fact, these are lovely sides, beautifully arranged by Rugolo.

The Trio-plus-Vokettes series climaxed with "I Get Sentimental over Nothing," the latest of Cole's unique ballads. Such love songs were clearly suited for the vocal group accompaniment, as were two numbers from screen and stage (at a time when such things were still rare on Cole's sessions), "Baby Won't You Say That You Love Me" (by Mack Gordon and Joseph Myrow, from the Fox Film *Wabash Avenue*) and "You Can't Lose a Broken Heart" (by stride piano giant James P. Johnson, from *Sugar Hill*).[106]

Other numbers in this format are in something more like dance tempo, *à la* "Lillian." "Who Do You Know in Heaven (That Made You the Angel That You Are)," by veteran composer Peter DeRose and newcomer Al Stillman, has an early swing era kind of a feel, all jaunty and bouncy. The slightly slower "A Little Bit Independent" (which playfully accelerates and decelerates in the second chorus) and the sprightly "I'll Never Say 'Never Again' Again" are both from the mid-1930s and testify to Cole's exquisite taste in vintage songs. He gets "Never Again" in precisely the right romping tempo. (Good thing, too; this was, famously, the song that broke up the Dorsey Brothers band in 1935.) The most famous of the Trio + vocal group numbers would be the children's song "All I Want for Christmas (Is My Two Front Teeth)." It's certainly cute, but Cole and company refuse to treat it as mere kiddie fodder and instead they render it with a solid beat. For once, Santa Swings.[107]

On all of these numbers, the voices intermingle beautifully with the piano, guitar, and bass. (Costanzo sits most of them out.) And Alyce King and her singers deserve as much of the credit as Ashby and Comfort. Diehard jazz listeners and critics were already starting to wear blinders—or earplugs—as far as Cole's music goes, but it's hard to imagine that anybody could have heard these tracks and not considered them first-class music; whether they were jazz or pop didn't matter. Remarkably, the swinging numbers are just as "lovely" as the slow love songs.

The trio-plus-voices series turned out to be a worthy investment for Capitol, but no one could have predicted that the most successful would be "I Almost Lost My Mind" (#7 R&B, #26 Pop), a "cover," as some might say, of an R&B hit written, played, and sung by blues singer-pianist Ivory Joe Hunter. Who would have thought that the use of these rather white-sounding voices on an R&B number would make it so successful with the race market? The other R&B number in this format, "Twisted Stockin's," was the work of Joe Greene, who seemed to specialize in novelty songs (most recorded successfully by Stan Kenton) that tend to seem overtly misogynistic and politically incorrect today, like "And Her Tears Flowed Like Wine" and "Across the Alley from the Alamo." In "Twisted Stockin's," a rather unsympathetic male chauvinist gripes about his girlfriend because the seams of her hosiery aren't straight. No jury would convict her for plugging him one in the forehead, which she does. Heard today, it produces nervous giggles and guilt in equal quantities.

Cole seems to have been willing to try anything. At the same date as "Calypso Blues" (September 9, 1949) he recorded "(Here Is My Heart) Nalani," his only Hawaiian song, done with the Trio plus what sounds like a full-sized choir of hula girls. A few weeks earlier, the Trio had performed its first notable engagement outside of the North American continent, a two-week run at McKinsey Auditorium in Honolulu. While in Hawaii, they also played a private party for Doris Duke, the tobacco heiress, who presented him with this song by a friend of hers.[108] "Nalani" is totally out of left field, but beautiful, especially Cole's tranquil keyboard solo, reminiscent of Claude Thornhill, over the uncredited background voices. Though it didn't chart, it's hardly a waste of Capitol's resources: as with Calypsos, Hawaiian songs were definitely worth a shot.

The track immediately following on the date was "The Horse Told Me," a kind of follow-up to the 1947 "Harmony" and another comedy song written by Burke and Van Heusen for a Crosby movie (*Riding High*). "Horse" uses a deliberately non-swinging, clunky rhythm for comic effect. Costanzo is probably playing, but the percussion sounds like a bag of pots and pans falling down the stairs. Cole seems to be playing the piano with one hand while holding a stein of beer in the other.[109]

"Your Voice," recorded in May (while the Trio was headlining at Ralph Watkins's ambitious new club, Bop City in New York), was also a worthy experiment. Like many a radio sitcom, this comic complaint (by Sid Lippman, whose "Too Young" was just around the corner) has a belittled husband griping about his wife's constant chattering: "Oh boy, how good it feels / When you pause just long enough to eat your meals." That sound is made concrete in the form of a speeded up, double-time female voice, provided by Maria Cole and heard at the start and the windup. Yet if you listen closely, you'll hear her reciting a list of King Cole Trio song titles arranged into something like a coherent sentence.[110]

"Nalani," "The Horse Told Me," and "Your Voice" are three completely different songs in very different formats, yet each is successful in its own way. In 1949–50, no less than the rest of his career, there's virtually nothing that's not worth hearing today. (A rare exception is "A Little Yellow Ribbon (In Her Hair)," a 1949 track that's one of the very few that qualifies as a true dog tune, thankfully not issued at the time.)

AS WE'VE SEEN, Cole made his television debut on NBC's *We the People* in June 1948, and then, for the next half decade or so, was most frequently seen on the new medium courtesy of Ed Sullivan on CBS. Cole first appeared on Sullivan's *Toast of the Town* during his first of twenty-two seasons, on March 27, 1949. The Trio played "A Portrait of Jennie," probably with strings; "Flo and Jo," which showed off Costanzo, then in his first week with the Trio; and the up-tempo "Little Girl." Even by 1949, Sullivan was well on his way to becoming the most essential host in the history of the variety show. Sullivan's name has become a permanent synonym for that kind of programming, with his patented mix of pop stars, comics, singers, bands, acrobats and plate-spinners, sopranos and tenors, dance acts and ballet companies—not to mention "something for the youngsters," be it the Beatles or the Muppets.

Sullivan was also a particularly enthusiastic though historically under-appreciated supporter of African American talent. He had started as a sports columnist and gradually made a lateral move to covering entertainment. To his considerable credit, he consistently advocated racial equality and even integration in both fields at a time when that was hardly the norm in either athletics or showbiz. In 1951, Sullivan announced boldly that he intended to use the new medium of television to help "the Negro in his fight . . . to win the guarantees [of] his birthright [by taking the civil rights battle] into the living rooms of America's homes where public opinion is formed."[111] Cole would return to Sullivan's stage roughly twice a year until 1961.

In early 1950, Cole entered into a highly productive, long-term relationship with Universal International (UI) Pictures, which would eventually lead to no less than four theatrical featurettes and a supporting acting role in a feature film. Of all his projects for Universal, the first, titled *King Cole and His Trio*, is the most valuable today. By 1950, Universal was probably the last studio in Hollywood to still be producing musical short subjects, and their series of big band–driven two-reelers would run for almost twenty years from the late '30s to the late '50s. *King Cole* would be pre-recorded on January 4 and then filmed on January 18;[112] it's the only one of the UI shorts to feature the working trio (by then in its quartet phase, with Ashby, Comfort, and percussionist Jack Costanzo) and also the only one to place the Trio in the context of an inspired roster of all black talent.

Apart from the Trio, the short co-stars Cole's old friend (and touring partner) Benny Carter, who opens with his big band playing "Harlequin Bounce"; we also see the brilliant tap dancer Bunny Briggs, whose routine to "Stupendous" (the bop head to "S'Wonderful") is truly that; "Scat Man" Crothers, the singer and comic, does a jive routine based on Irving Berlin's "Blue Skies"; femme fatale Dolores Parker, previously with Earl Hines and Duke Ellington, struts out in a tight but tasteful grown and high heels, looking the very picture of one of Cole's man-eating vamps (as described in "Babs" or "Honey Hush"), and sings a flirty novelty called "That Ain't It."

They're all excellent, but Cole and the Trio are the featured attraction, and you know why from the first notes of their first number. Two older Trio works, "Ooh, Kickerooney," and "Route 66," both sound even better thanks to Costanzo, whose percussion makes those "kicks" even kickier. For the finale, the Trio joins forces with the full orchestra for a mashup of two hot instrumentals by the two leaders. It starts with a tight close-up on the bongos, then pulls back to the full Trio, emphasis on the leader's piano, stating the main riff, Cole's "All Aboard." Then the orchestra joins in to play a secondary theme, Carter's "Congeroo" and the two ensembles complement each other beautifully. Carter takes an alto solo, and there's a further piano interlude before the brass and bongos take it out.[113] None of Cole's three later featurettes for UI would be this good, but they all have outstanding moments.

IN GENERAL, THE FINAL YEARS of the Trio, 1948 to 1951, are among the most rewarding of Cole's entire career. In the early years, 1936 to 1947, Cole is essentially playing jazz, but with persistent pop elements; in the last decade of his career, 1953 to 1964, he is mostly making pop music but with a great deal of jazz content. It's in the middle years, however, that he is most consistently creating both jazz and pop at the same time. He had already picked the perfect collaborator for this process. Pete Rugolo would arrange and conduct on roughly forty different titles with Cole, mostly from 1949 and 1950. "I don't know if I came up with anything special," Rugolo told me; "I just wrote what I thought would be good for each song."

Cole was so overwhelmingly successful so much of the time that he made it impossible to realize how much work went into this transitional process. Even the most so-called commercial sides were hardly a sure thing. Take "Red Sails in the Sunset" (1951). It's a lovely ballad, which utilizes the classic trio elements solidly at its center, the voice and piano of Cole, plus the guitar and bass. That's the foundation: yet the voice is augmented with a vocal group and the trio is enhanced with woodwinds. Today, it sounds beautiful and rather like a foregone conclusion, one that conceals the risk and experimentation that went into it: an African American pianist singing a long forgotten, sentimental old British song (which had been scarcely if ever heard anywhere in the world since 1935), with a white choir (actually the King Sisters). "Commercial" as it seems in retrospective, everything about it was a new idea at the time, and nothing was done by rote. Even the instrumental backing was far from your typical big band or string group, but a reed section of five saxes and woodwinds, plus one brass (Buddy Childers of the Kenton trumpet section) and a drummer (the famous Louis Bellson) joining the other three members of the trio.

The Cole-Rugolo combination was especially successful in terms of ballads, like "It Was So Good While It Lasted" (1949) by the Coles' old friend Ruth Poll, while "Home (When Shadows Fall)" (1950) was a lovely old song—one that Cole probably learned from Louis Armstrong and Paul McCartney later learned from Cole.

"Roses and Wine" was even more of a gamble; here's another ambitious song, just as completely unprecedented as both "Nature Boy" and "Lush Life" had been. The 1949 track opens with the speaking voice of Nat King Cole, telling us, "This is the story of a man who was passing on in years, who met and fell in love with a young girl. Some say that youth and maturity have no chance for successful love. Some disagree. Others say that youth and maturity can be happy together because" . . . he pauses here, momentarily, and then continues . . . "they complement each other. His maturity was as wine to her, while her youth was as roses to him." It's too easy to take the notion of older men pursuing younger women at face value, but the song must have had special meaning to Cole, whose first wife was eleven years older than he was—and he sings it with real emotional investment. It's hardly surprising that Pete

Rugolo remembered the song fondly forty years later, even though he hadn't heard it in all that time, since it wouldn't be issued until 1993.[114]

Another art song, "Jet" and the up-tempo, "Destination Moon," both from December 11, 1950, were precisely the kinds of songs that Cole would have had Rugolo orchestrate for him, but Pete must have been unavailable for this session. "Jet" was composed by Harry Revel (best known for his many movie musical songs of the 1930s) as one of six movements of *Perfume Set to Music*, a suite recorded as an early 10" LP (conducted by Les Baxter for RCA) that stands as a pioneering example of the musical genre known as "space age bachelor pad music." The work combined a European string orchestra (the melody and the string writing sound more liked David Rose than anybody, with generous use of *pizzicato*), a wordless vocal chorus, and a theremin—not to mention celesta. Cole was able to record it thanks to lyrics by Bennie Benjamin and George Weiss, and a chart by swing era veteran Joe Lipman. Like "Lush Life," "Jet" wasn't a hit, but it became an important part of the Cole songbook, an American *lied*.[115] "Destination Moon" was a highly topical and highly memorable swinger, inspired by a current sci-fi film, with words and music by Roy Alfred and Marvin Fisher, and a unique arrangement by Herman Herd veteran Neal Hefti.

Another new angle that Cole was exploring in these highly transitional years was duets with other vocalists. Capitol's vice president Jim Conkling explained that they were directly inspired by Jack Kapp of Decca Records, who, starting in the mid-1930s, had the brilliant idea to team his star baritone, Bing Crosby, with a series of different musical partners. "That was the same idea we were trying," he said, "to team up top artists in different ideas."[116]

Following the 1947 session in which Johnny Mercer and the Trio produced the #1 R&B hit "Save the Bones for Henry Jones," the next big Cole duet would also be a comic novelty. "Mule Train" came about as a result of the Trio's 1949 tour with Woody Herman and His Orchestra, which also produced two extant live-in-concert recordings: at the Shrine Auditorium, Los Angeles, July 29, and Carnegie Hall, November 4.[117] Herman (1913–1987) was a true brother to both Cole and Dizzy Gillespie in that he was an innovative musician, with modernist leanings, who also doubled as a master entertainer and musical comedian. It may have happened slightly later than Cole had promised in 1946, but these concerts (from the evidence of the two that have survived) are pure jazz performances all the way through—the quality of the music, from a jazz perspective or any other, is as good as any of the jazz recordings he made at any point of his career. On both of these shows, the group plays only jazz standards and jazz originals: there are none of the novelties, ballads, or hits.

"Mule Train," contrastingly, is pure goofiness. "We had both been listening to the radio while traveling every day in the car or whatever," Herman said in 1977. "Frankie Laine had another big smash going with a thing called 'Mule Train.' He did a very heavy performance with it. And Nat and I got to chuckling about it, and then thought about the possibilities of satirizing the thing and doing it in our fashion—or, as we thought, the song was really written to be done. And so, he hurriedly called some of the Capitol executives and arranged to do a date. We'd be in New York within a day or so. And we started up and got a lead sheet on the tune. Then we went into the studio and you know the result."[118]

"Mule Train" released as by "Woody Herman, Nat 'King' Cole and the Muleskinners," is a fun, silly record, more comedy than country.[119] Herman and Cole do some singing but mostly banter back and forth about the various ways to motivate a pack of stubborn mules, surrounded by the noise of whip-cracking and other sound effects. Instead of berating the uncooperative beasts, Woodrow encourages Nathaniel to use the "new sounds . . . the progressive way," prompting King Cole to croon to them softly and sweetly—and get a sort of an inside joke dig in to Stan Kenton (whose buzzword was "progressive") and much of their shared fan base. The flipside, "My Baby Just Cares for Me," was credited to "Woody Herman, Nat 'King' Cole and the Trio." If "Mule Train" was a goof, "My Baby Just Cares for Me," is classic KC3. Like "Exactly Like You" and "Yes Sir, That's My Baby," this is another jazz age standard beautifully reinvigorated by the Ashby-Comfort-Costanzo combination.

The Cole-Herman disc wasn't a particular hit, but it was a swell bonus for the two stars to offer to their fans. But then Capitol struck real pay dirt with Cole's next duet disc, in which he teamed with another extroverted entertainer, Nellie Lutcher, also a client of Carlos Gastel. Although both artists sang and played piano, they had very different styles that complemented each other well. "Carlos approached, me about doing it," she remembered in 1977. "He suggested that Nat and I would do a thing together. But anyway, it was a real fun session."[120] "For You My Love" had already been an R&B hit, written by Paul Gayten and sung by Larry Darnell. The Cole-Lutcher disc (which itself became a #8 R&B hit) features swing-era saxophonist Charlie Barnet wailing away like Illinois Jacquet or any of a number of honking-and-wailing tenor men. Said Lutcher, "Charlie Barnet sort of surprised us—and surprised everybody—because when many people hear this record, they can't believe that it's Charlie."

The flip side was "Can I Come In for a Second?," a cute boy-girl duet in the mold of "Baby It's Cold Outside," with both music and words by Sammy Cahn. Four years later, as we shall see, and very much in the same spirit, Cole teamed up with Dean Martin for two bro-mantic duos, "Open Up the Doghouse" and "Long, Long Ago." These are also wonderful, shticky fun, like the best TV variety show duets of the period. All of these duet projects—Cole with Woody Herman, Nellie Lutcher, and Dean Martin—were a worthy investment of Cole's time and Capitol's capital, especially when "For You My Love" reached the R&B top ten.

All of the duets Cole recorded in this approximate period, with Johnny Mercer, Woody Herman, Nellie Lutcher, and Dean Martin, succeed on a musical level, and the team-ups with Mercer and Lutcher produced chart hits as well. But there are also five duet tracks he cut in these years that weren't quite as worthwhile. In a 1949 interview, Maria Cole stated that she hoped that someday her husband would invite her to sing with him. "I don't know," she whispered engagingly, with a little girl look in her sparkling eyes, "but maybe he will. Oh, I hope so!"[121] Three months after the birth of their second child, Natalie, Nat and Maria went into the studio together and gave birth to some very curious music. Rugolo later talked about the two of them being such a cute couple and very much in love; they loved working with each other, and the feeling between the two of them was palpable, and he felt privileged to be there, sharing the moment. It was all very enjoyable and very loving—at least if you happened to be in the studio with them.

All well and good, but none of the charm that Pete experienced comes through in the actual recordings. Personal chemistry between a man and a woman alone does not a great record make. Maria had a lovely voice and was a competent singer, but chemistry is not the same as magic, and there's none of that on any of their duets. Indeed, Maria's entire career as a vocalist is decidedly bereft of magic.

The single nastiest moment in all of Maria Cole's memoir is a long anecdote regarding Nellie Lutcher; it's so mean-spirited that the pianist considered taking legal action.[122] However, the anecdote had a reverse effect and makes Mrs. Cole, not Lutcher, look bad; her co-author, *Ebony* writer Louie Robinson, should have pressured her to leave it out, but Mrs. Cole obviously had a score to settle. In retrospect, it's very obvious that Maria resented Lutcher because "For You My Love" was a big hit while the five sides that Maria cut with her husband failed to attract any attention whatsoever. Paul Gayten, the R&B bandleader who composed "For You My Love," later told singer and historian Billy Vera that, "Whenever Nat and Maria had a tiff, he would storm out and come stay at my place for few nights." Which offers another explanation as why Mrs. Cole might have resented the record of Gayten's song.

Nat and Maria tried old songs, "Get Out and Get Under the Moon" (1928) and "Ev'ry Day"[123] (1934), as well as two new ones written for them by Cole's longtime standby Roy Alfred (with Marvin Fisher on the second). Both "Hey, Not Now! (I'll Tell You When" and "It's a Man Every Time" were filled with battle-of-the-sexes type routines and one-liners. All had excellent arrangements by Rugolo. But all of them fall flat, in stark contrast to the two sides with Lutcher as well as the 1954 Dean Martin session, which also featured two songs by Alfred and Fisher. Despite her obvious talent and movie-star looks (although, as the *Pittsburgh Courier* profile admitted, "She's engagingly pretty [but] doesn't take particularly good photos"),[124] she was too smart not to realize that her true calling was to be the role-model wife of the first African American superstar. (She would, however, attempt to revive her musical career at several points, while her husband was alive and afterward, with mixed results.)

As a couple, however, Mr. and Mrs. Cole were a resounding success. In 1949, they adopted their first child, who had been born Carol Lane, on October 17, 1944; she later changed the spelling to "Carole," but her actual name didn't matter, since she was always known as "Cookie." Not long after the death of her biological father, Cookie had been a flower girl at Nat and Maria's wedding; her birth mother, Maria's younger sister, Carol Hawkins Lane, had been a bridesmaid. Her mother died of consumption on May 7, 1949, at which point Nat and Maria immediately took steps to formally adopt Cookie. As early as June, Nat announced the news to the black press. "There's a little miss who is going to have nearly everything in life she wants as soon as her aunt and uncle complete plans for adopting her. She's four-year-old Carol Lane, niece of Mrs. Nat King Cole."[125]

Nat and Maria still continued to pursue the idea of conceiving their own child, something which had never happened with his first wife. After consulting a fertility specialist, Nat began receiving hormone injections. These achieved the desired effect—Maria was pregnant by the summer of 1949—and several others as well. He would start to grow facial hair—a first for him; he had, apparently, never even needed to shave before that.[126] And his vocal range began to widen, which became more apparent by 1951, at which point he was being almost increasingly featured as a popular singer who occasionally played jazz piano. Nat and Maria, and the two girls, Carole ("Cookie") and Natalie ("Sweetie," born in February 1950) would constitute his family for most of the rest of his life.

IN SUMMER 1950, even as his difficulties with the IRS (covered in Chapter 6) were starting to worsen, Cole and Rugolo gave us one of the most ecstatically upbeat songs of his career. "Orange Colored Sky" was by far the most successful, sales-wise, of the forty or so arrangements written for him by Rugolo and was also the track that reunited both men with Stan Kenton. By early 1950, the visionary bandleader, after a year-long sabbatical, was back in business, although "business" may not have been the right word. He was trying to create Artistry in Rhythm on an epic scale with the most enormous jazz ensemble ever to hit the road. The staggeringly huge "Innovations" orchestra was precisely the sort of project that Gastel would have talked Kenton out of. Even with the bandleader's legions of fans, there was no way he could help but lose money with this elephantine ensemble that fully required two buses to transport all forty musicians men from one gig to the next. After losing his shirt with this experiment, Kenton then went back on tour with a more reasonably sized big band, and that is the group that joined with King Cole and His Trio in the Capitol Studio on August 16, 1950.

Milton DeLugg, who died in 2015 at the age of ninety-six, was best known as a musical director for early television. Before that, he conducted on the radio, and after that, for many generations, on the annual Macy's Thanksgiving Parade; and all the while he doubled as a jazz accordion virtuoso. He also composed a number of successful songs, mostly bouncy novelties: "Hoop De Doo," "Shanghai," "Be My Life's Companion," and "Just Another Polka." He was probably the last songwriter you'd expect to write something for the very serious Mr. Stan Kenton—who wasn't about to release an album titled *Artistry in Polka!* But then, Kenton's most popular singles had been upbeat comedy numbers like "And Her Tears Flowed Like Wine" and "Tampico," which featured lots of jolly singing by the band.

DeLugg had an idea for a song and brought it to Frank Loesser, then hard at work on what would be his greatest triumph, *Guys and Dolls*. The songwriter and publisher helped DeLugg finish his song—he wrote the final sixteen bars, the "flash, bam, alakazam," section, which was precisely the sort of thing that he had been writing for years for Betty Hutton at Paramount Pictures: jaunty, lively songs that combined rhythm and zany comedy. Hutton specialized in a unique blend of musical schizophrenia; she could be both completely serious and totally ridiculous, especially in the right type of number which allowed her to be both. When DeLugg's song was finished, Loesser published it and brought it to his friends at Capitol Records.

"Frank brought it in and said, 'Have you got two artists, one of whom is loud and one of whom is soft, that you could team up? If you've got the right team, this would be a great idea.'" Jim Conking remembered,

> So, I said, "Well, if you want something really loud that would be Stan Kenton." So, he said, "That's great. Now who would be good to do the soft part?" And our first thought was girl singers, starting with Peggy Lee, but that didn't gel. And finally, we said, "Nat!" and boy, that was it! Because they had never done anything together [on recordings] and they were both hot and they were both acceptable to the college age, and young kids, and also to everybody else. That was the reason it was major, because we were looking for two artists and it happened to fit the two of them perfectly. It was fun making that, because Stan plays as loud as you can play anyway. But he got his guys playing extra loud that day! He had Maynard Ferguson with him and everybody was screaming as loud as they could go. And Nat was singing as soft as he could possibly sing. And it was really great.[127]

It was a brilliant fit for the two artists, especially with Rugolo doing the fitting. More than a star singer backed by a name band, it's a brilliant juxtaposition of two very different but surprisingly compatible ensembles. The track starts with a classic romping, loping Trio intro—surely devised by Cole, who then sings, "I was walking along, minding my business / When out of an orange-colored sky . . ." At this point we not only hear the whole band playing but collectively chanting "Flash! Bam! Alakazam"—and all rather loudly—and then back to Cole's voice in solo (over just the Trio), "wonderful you came by." It was apparently Rugolo's idea to continually alternate between four bars of the Trio followed by four bars of the Orchestra: the subtle, understated sound of Cole's swinging sunshine, dramatically contrasted by Kenton's flaming brass and flying glass.

"Orange Colored Sky" is one of a few major works in jazz, or anywhere in the American idiom, that follows the form of a concerto grosso, in which a chamber group and a symphony orchestra interact with each other. The flipside, "Jam-Bo" (the Swahili word for "hello"), by trumpeter Shorty Rogers, might be better described as a more conventional concerto for solo piano and orchestra, utilizing that familiar classical form in the context of an Afro-Latin jazz setting. In "Orange Colored Sky," Kenton sounds more like Kenton and

Cole sounds more like Cole than they do anywhere else, and the fun is in the contrast. In "Jam-Bo," both men sound like they're trying to meet each other in the middle; the Orchestra sounds more like Machito, and the piano is a four-handed duet by Cole and Kenton together, Afro-Cuban style, *en clave*.

"Jam-Bo" is marvelous, but it was never heard again; "Orange Colored Sky" was, literally, the money song. It not only suited the Kenton aggregation in its use of band chanting, but the melody calls for Kenton's angular and dissonant sound—this wasn't Glenn Miller here—which is also paralleled in the lyrics. "Orange" reached #5 on the *Billboard* chart, making it Kenton's second-biggest ever hit and eventually a major milestone for Cole as well. He sang it on his third appearance on Ed Sullivan's *Toast of the Town* in November 1950, in one of his first visual performances apart from the piano as a standup singer. He looks very regal in a formal morning suit, with proper tail coat (why, it could even be the very suit that he had been married in, two years earlier) and a cane (clearly, he needed something to do with his hands). He's accompanied by two dancers that Sullivan informs us are on loan to him courtesy of the Apollo Theater. We have no evidence that Cole ever sang it on live appearances (although he did remake it in 1961 with Kenton); still it became one of his most iconic numbers, included on dozens of posthumous Cole tribute projects. "Orange Colored Sky" is a song that everybody loves, and also like "Smile," you can't help but smile when you hear it.

"ORANGE COLORED SKY" represented the climax, but not the conclusion, of the collaboration between Nat Cole and Pete Rugolo, both artistically and commercially. They would still make a dozen or so additional titles as a team, going into January 1952. By now, the focus of Cole's work was starting to shift in a different direction, but the two men would still make some marvelous music together. There was a spiffy holiday song, "The Little Christmas Tree," a ballad composed by movie star Mickey Rooney (and published by Gastel's firm, Bradshaw Music, BMI), which failed to sell as well as the gimmicky but delightful seasonal novelty "Frosty the Snowman"; the latter had been arranged by Lou Busch, pianist and producer then married to Margaret Whiting, and utilized a choir of speeded-up voices billed as "The Singing Pussycats."

There also were more ballads, both old and new, all lovely, by Cole and Rugolo: "I'll Always Remember You" (utilizing the template of Sinatra and the Pied Pipers, with celesta and very tight, slow harmony with the choir), "Time Out for Tears," all making beautiful use of background singers. "I Wish I Were Somebody Else" by Cole's close friends and publishing partners,

Johnny Burke and Jimmy Van Heusen (the rare song by the partnership not from a film), is kind of a wry downer with a good use of female voices.

There were more swingers, the aforementioned R&B-styled, "Get to Gettin,'" and two more punchline-driven novelties from old friends, "You Can't Make Me Love You" (more gags and one-liners from Don George) and "Where Were You" (Leonard Feather), both good numbers significantly improved by Cole and Rugolo. Likewise, "It's Crazy" is the best of the songs that another old buddy, Timmie Rogers, wrote for Cole; it's an enduring up-tempo (and future favorite of Freddy Cole) that Cole brought into a whole new medium when he sang it in a 3D short subject in 1953.

With "That's My Girl" (1951), however, Cole and Rugolo created another classic. This was a British song by Ray Ellington (no relation to Duke or Maria), a multi-faceted drummer-vocalist, best known as a bandleader and occasional comedian on the legendary *Goon Show*, who was somehow black, Jewish, and British all at the same time. Ellington's own 1950 version was already deeply inspired by the King Cole Trio, and the song was a natural for Nat. "That's My Girl" is possibly Rugolo's most successful job of expanding the Cole canvas, taking the fundamental Trio sound and making it work with a full-sized big band; it has the same loping beat we know from the 1949 sessions with Costanzo, expertly translated to brass and reeds. There's a full-scale Trio interlude, wherein the horns drop out and we hear the classic combination of piano, guitar, and bass; the brass is loud and swinging, but it never overwhelms the three men at the center. In the last eight bars, Cole borrows an interjection from Ray Ellington, and shouts, "You hear me?" but even when doing someone else's shtick, Cole sounds hipper than the originator.

There's one line of "That's My Girl," however, that Cole was importuned to change: at the end of the lyric, Ellington sings, "She's all mine, every curve and line, and even each golden curl." Cole, however, sings, "even those dark brown curls." Apparently on This Sceptered Isle, it was acceptable for a dark-skinned man to sing about his love for a blond woman, but not in the Land of the Free, the Home of the Brave.[128]

In general, Cole and Rugolo enjoyed a sainted partnership: nearly everything they did together is sublimely sui generis and doesn't sound like anything else in Cole's canon. In the exotica department, there's "Make Believe Land" (1950) which could almost be a bonus track from the 1947 *King Cole for Kids* album, a make-believe land that sounds like a fantasy world where everything is warm and fuzzy and "the dreams that you dream all come true." Rugolo's arrangement uses female background voices, woodwinds, and strings, and lovely pastel colors (not to mention a celesta solo). "Poor Jenny Is A-Weepin'" and "Summer Is a Comin' In" are modernist updates of traditional English folk songs; the second (by Alec Wilder, pop music's token intellectual) has a charming lyric by Marshall Barer (of *Once Upon a Mattress* fame). Rugolo's brass section effectively conveys the balmy mood of impending seasonal change with arousingly growling trumpets and trombones inspired by Duke Ellington's "jungle band" sound of the Jazz Age.

Cole and Rugolo parted ways with two final milestones. "Funny (Not Much)" has a convoluted history: it had originally been copyrighted as simply "Not Much" in 1948[129] before being revamped in 1952. At some point, the name of Bob Merrill (then writing a lot of jukebox pop, and later a major success on Broadway) became attached to the song. Whoever wrote the words, they're emblematic of the kind of "direct irony" that makes for successful pop lyrics, as in Hoagy Carmichael and Jane Brown Thompson's "I Get Along Without You Very Well." Here, the speaker is telling us one thing, "I get along without you," or "funny how I've stopped loving you." But, at the same time, the details that they provide make us aware that precisely the opposite is true: she *doesn't* get along without him very well; he *hasn't* stopped loving her. Cole has long since reached the point where he can easily convey those ironies and contradictions—they, in fact, are the stuff of great pop music.

Rugolo makes an even more brilliant contribution to "You Stepped Out of a Dream," an exceptional movie song composed by Nacio Herb Brown (from the 1941 *Ziegfeld Girl*), whose exceptional harmonies would inspire legions of jazz musicians. (Chick Corea recorded it as "Chick's Tune.") Cole's vocal is direct and straightforward, "honest and truly," as Gus Kahn's lyric goes, but Rugolo's horns surround him with lines that are at once swinging and dreamlike. Rugolo invests it with a series of different countermelodies, which suggest dreams running parallel, and there's a brief Trio-ish interlude with a notable guitar solo by John Collins. Appropriately, this would be one of the most-heard of all Rugolo arrangements included on the highly successful album, *Nat King Cole Sings for Two in Love* (the expanded 12-inch edition from 1955).

Between 1949 and 1952, Cole and Rugolo had created a consistently high level of music together. And yet, it was only a foreshadowing of what was to come. Rugolo was a kind of John the Baptist in Nat King Cole's life and career, the prophet whose calling is primarily to prophesy the coming of another, even greater prophet. Rugolo had helped Cole move up several important rungs on the ladder, but with his next collaborator, that ladder became an elevator, even a rocket ship, that would carry the two of them further than they had ever dreamed, to the very mountaintop of success.

THROUGHOUT 1950, COLE was all over the place musically, but everything he was doing was exceptionally good. Two sessions in early March, the 9th and the 11th, serve as signposts of the state of his art at that moment. Both dates consist of what was by then, a typical but still unpredictable mix of past and future, pop and jazz, Trio and orchestra, seriousness and silliness. They also signify what might be considered the last hurrah of the King Cole Trio.

The March 11 session includes five songs, ending with the lively Trio novelty "Who's Who," by Nat's dear friend (and steady source of good new songs), Marvin Fisher. This track is one hundred eighty-two seconds of pure delight, beginning with a rubato verse that sets up the story. The proceedings then rev up into tempo, and our hero laments in tempo of how he can't tell his girlfriend from her twin sister. ("I can't tell Sue from Emma / . . . I think they switched, to add to my dilemma.") The song isn't "All the Things You Are" or "So in Love," but it's a superbly crafted and catchy novelty, full of ingenious topical references. Cole's articulation by now is perfect, and the Trio jells magnificently, in spite of how Cole is experimenting once again with the instrumentation, now bringing in Lee Young on brushes instead of Costanzo on bongos. And here's the rub: Capitol was so overloaded with incredible music by Nat King Cole in 1950—and as his career was starting to go in a different direction in any case—that Capitol never even issued "Who's Who" until an English LP in 1987.[130] Yet this one marvelous track encapsulates just about everything we love about the King Cole Trio.

In art, as in history or politics, we tend to associate the end of something with a decline, whether it's the Roman Empire or the Three Stooges. With the Trio, however, the last two years or so were among the greatest of its fifteen-year existence. The Trio, with or without percussion, continued to play brilliantly even as Cole himself was being pulled six ways till Sunday. The March 9 date was the last that Cole would do for Capitol Transcriptions and included a full nine songs, all of which were issued at the time on ETs. The first two songs are a bluesy novelty by Timmie Rodgers titled "If I Were You Baby, I'd Love Me," which is immediately contrasted with a rather dour, patriarchal lament about single ladies titled "Third Finger, Left Hand," and then a lively new song in the old-fashioned, Dixieland two-beat style "Calico Sal," by Irving Gordon. (Remember that name.) We also get two of Cole's inspired updates of worthy songs from the Roaring '20s—the ballad "After My Laughter Came Tears" and the jazz standard "'Deed I Do"—and two very nouveau style bop numbers, "Peaches" and "All Aboard." Then there's "Ooh Kickeroonie,"[131] a 1947 Cole original that Costanzo helps transform from mere nonsense into a true Trio classic. As with the best of the Trio's novelties and nonsense songs, this is the sort of joyful inanity that you just can't help humming, and a song that gave birth to another, in that there's a counter melody, heard in the ensemble tutti that later became a tune on its own, titled "Rough Ridin'."

As these sessions indicate, by 1950, Cole was essentially playing every conceivable kind of music that was available to him in 1950: pop, jazz, bebop, swing, blues, R&B, ballads, comedy songs, children's music, Afro-Cuban, easy listening, dance music, a few country and western songs, even classical and concert music. No one else could claim anything like that kind of diversity, not even Louis Jordan or Sinatra, who were both, in distinct contrast to Cole, about to see their careers go into a sharp nosedive. As one journalist observed at the time, "Unlike many high-riding artists, Nat still wanted something original, and when other groups started copying his original style, [he] looked for a fresh angle."[132]

The March 9 session was also notable as the last "pure" session by the Trio, either the three-man or the four-man edition, and also the last of the Capitol Transcriptions. Yet doors were opening faster than they were closing, and Cole's horizons were expanding rather than contracting. As it happened, the final line-up of the Trio with Costanzo, as well as the "Rugolo era" in general, was particularly well documented on film and TV. Apart from the first Sullivan shows and the Universal theatrical shorts, Cole was a star player in a unique experiment that lasted two years and resulted in some priceless footage.

IT WAS THE LEGENDARY TROMBONIST (and occasional singer and bandleader) Jack Teagarden who came up with the idea for what became "Snader Telescriptions." Essentially, they were "Soundies for television," musical films, roughly the length of single records, containing one song per short.[133] At a party in early 1950, Teagarden met California businessman Louis D. Snader and gifted him with this idea; as Teagarden had hoped, Snader ran with it. Where Soundies had been shown in bars and restaurants, Telescriptions were meant to be sold as a library of programming to local television stations. The medium of TV was in its infancy, and there was virtually nothing happening in the daytime. One major deterrent that prohibited big name musical acts from appearing on live local stations was the American Federation of Musicians, whose highly aggressive leader, James Caesar Petrillo, was holding out for the best possible deal. Snader immediately made two brilliant moves: first, he worked out a deal with Petrillo, and second, he hired Louis Goldstone, known to one and all as "Duke."

Duke Goldstone had previously been a director of the George Pal Puppetoons, a brilliant, whimsical series of theatrical animated films that combined an innovative process (movement in three dimensions) with music by jazz headliners like Duke Ellington, Charlie Barnet, and Woody Herman; thus, Goldstone already was a connoisseur of jazz and African American talent. The director-producer was given a budget of $900 per title[134] and started working out the particulars: they would film for one day a week, at which time they would shoot a total of ten titles, five each by two different artists. The first date, announced on that day in *Billboard*, on July 22, 1950, resulted in five titles by Lionel Hampton and His Orchestra and an additional five by the lively duo known as "Martha Davis and Spouse" (the singer-pianist and her bassist-husband, Calvin Ponder).

The appreciable difference between the Soundies and the Snaders was that the earlier jukebox films were pre-recorded (the recording date was usually a few days prior to the "sidelining" date) much the same way Hollywood theatrical movies were produced. Conversely, Goldstone wanted the Snader shorts to be filmed "live," in other words, not pre-recorded and then lip-synched. This gives them an automatic advantage over the Soundies, in which the lip-synching process is very much apparent. Thanks to Goldstone, there are no fewer than fifteen excellent short films of classic numbers by the 1950–51 edition of King Cole and His Trio. The Snaders include almost all of the Trio's hits prior to 1951 (the major exceptions are "The Christmas Song" and "It's Only a Paper Moon") as well as their most notable contemporary hits ("Too Young," "Mona Lisa") and in general are very watchable—the backgrounds are nondescript and non-distracting.

Ten months into the firm's history, in spring 1951, Snader was going great guns—or so they wanted you to think. Lou Snader was successfully raising investment money and Duke Goldstone was continuing to put it to good use. At that point, they announced that they had produced some 400 short films in those first ten months. What's more, they also proclaimed that for their second "season," 1951–52, all their titles were going to be in full color.[135] This was remarkably far-sighted: there wouldn't be any regular color programming on TV until the end of the decade. Still, they filmed three numbers by King Cole for a second time, now in the color process.

Alas, what seems to have happened is that, to put it in the terminology of a 21st-century "start-up," they ran out of runway before they found market share and the path to profitability. In other words, the money was gone before it started coming back in at a sufficient rate to keep the company afloat. The investors lost their shirts, but they couldn't complain that the funds had been mis-used, since Goldstone had hundreds of finished films to show for it. There were also rumors of a sex scandal involving a company official (not Goldstone) and eventually, there was bound to be further trouble with the AFM. Snader was, evidently, also trying to position his company to represent all their musical artists in all their television appearances; obviously, General Artists Corp., Carlos Gastel, and the other talent representatives were not going to support that idea. The company folded after less than two years, but the fifteen short films that Cole made for Snader are a major part of his visual legacy.

IF TELEVISION WAS THE MAJOR NEW MEDIUM Cole was exploring, his next new direction was to Europe, and his experiences there would have a major impact on his music. Cole and Gastel had been fielding offers from abroad almost as soon as the war had ended. "We had a recent offer to go to England, but I'd like to wait a while," he said in January 1948. "Conditions are too shaky right now—particularly where your money is concerned. Living must not be so bad, because Lena Horne and some of the others said they got along all right. But I'd rather wait awhile."[136]

Cole toured overseas for the first time in September and October 1950, and it was an unqualified success, although some parts more so than others. He played through the United Kingdom (Birmingham, Liverpool, Manchester, Glasgow, and several venues in London, including the Palladium), and then Stockholm, Copenhagen, and Zurich. The surviving highlight is a brilliant concert from the latter. Just like the American jazz fans who crowded the concert halls to hear the Trio-Herd combination, the Swiss audience reacts enthusiastically to the group's many instrumental features: Ashby is spotlighted on his own original, "Nothin' to Fret About," while "Go Bongo" is built around the playing of Costanzo. "Tea for Two" was most often a piano tour de force for the leader, but here it's a showcase for Joe Comfort, and, in fact, it amounts to Comfort's shining hour with the Trio. Like Art Tatum, Ella Fitzgerald, and Cole himself, Comfort utilizes well-timed "quotations," thrown in at what seem like random moments, to keep the crowd interested: "Holiday for Strings," appropriately for a bass fiddle solo, the bebop standard "Ornithology" (based on "How High the Moon") and last, the classical warhorse, Debussy's "Reverie."

There's no shortage of Cole's piano on the Zurich show, especially on a beautifully extended reading of his piano signature "Body and Soul," and one of his own classically styled features, "In the Cool of the Evening." There's a unique Gershwin collage, built mostly around "Summertime," a standard he never played on any other occasion (with a wonderfully subtle Ashby guitar), which leads briefly into "It Ain't Necessarily So" (also from *Porgy and Bess*) and then into an abbreviated run through "Embraceable You," in which he sings Ira Gershwin's lyric much more convincingly than was possible in 1943 when he first recorded it.

If the crowd noise is any indication, fans loved the all-jazz program in Zurich just as much as they did on the two surviving 1949 concerts from New York and Los Angeles. But reports from London suggested that not every number went over equally well. *Down Beat*'s local correspondent observed that the crowds loved the big vocal hits, like "Nature Boy," but they weren't so crazy about the bass and bongo solos, nor about the instrumentals in general; during these numbers, "many of the elderly folk in the theater were seen leaving."[137] Roy Holmes, Cole's number one fan and collector in the British Isles, was present at the Palladium that night and told me that fans there had no interest in jazz; it was Cole the pop star that they wanted to hear. It's sometimes reported that it was during the British trip that Cole made the fateful decision to feature his own vocals more and more, to present himself more like a standup pop star. This may have been, in fact, the turning point: the Trio had brought him as far as Europe, but now to go even further, he had to strike out on his own.

There was one song that the London audiences wanted to hear more than any other—his latest #1 hit. He doesn't seem to have even bothered with it for the more jazz-centric crowds in Stockholm and Zurich, but the more pop-oriented Brits refused to let him off the stage until he sang it. This song, recorded at the same March 11 date that had produced "Who's Who," was the number that would, in the long run, do more than any other to make Nat King Cole a truly international star. It was called "Mona Lisa."

ACT TWO

Nat King Cole

6

Nat and Nelson

"MONA LISA" TO *TWO IN LOVE*, 1950–1954

I was trying to be as successful a vocalist with Nelson as Nat was. I never did find out if we made it or not.

—FRANK SINATRA

FOR NAT KING COLE, the start of the 1950s was marked by two blessings and a disaster, or as his many Jewish friends would have said, two *mitzvahs* and a *shanda*. On the positive side, his second child (and first "birth child"), Natalie, was born in February, and, a few weeks later, his next blockbuster hit was also "born" so to speak. What's more, the latter brought with it a new collaborator who would, in many ways, be his all-time most significant, the musical partner who did more than any other to help Cole achieve his greatest heights.

At the same time, these triumphs were counterbalanced by an epic struggle with the Internal Revenue Service (IRS), which had begun to heat up later in 1950 and even more so over the following few years, that very nearly cost him his home and threatened to undermine everything that he had achieved thus far.

WITH THE ARRIVAL OF NATALIE, known as "Sweetie," on February 6, 1950, his family was complete for most of the rest of his life. It was the strength and support of that family that empowered Cole to weather the worst storm since the travails of moving into Hancock Park in the summer of 1948. Between 1946 and 1950, with the start of his succession of game-changing hits, Cole's income had expanded too fast and he spent too freely. The wedding had cost him as much as $25,000, almost the most expensive in the entire history of Harlem, and the new home set him back $85,000 in 1948 dollars. He fell behind in his tax payments, and the IRS claimed he owed $150,000. The Coles were not aware of it, but they were also being monitored by another acronymic government agency at the same time. FBI overlord J. Edgar Hoover seems to have regarded every prominent African American as a potential Communist and subversive (particularly after Paul Robeson's infamous speech at the Paris Peace Conference in 1949), even one as openly apolitical as Nat Cole. The FBI file on Cole is full of unconfirmed hearsay, indicating that the artist may or may not (mostly likely the latter) have been a member of such-and-such a group that may or may not have had a possible connection to Communist front organizations. On April 20, 1951, one unnamed agent filed a report full of such rather meaningless speculation, which concluded, "no particular Communist activity on [Cole's] part has been reported.[1] By 1951, the tax situation had threatened to overwhelm and engulf him. Thankfully, he enlisted the aid of ace tax attorney Phil Braunstein, who went to work negotiating with the Federal Government. Thanks to a loan from Maria's Aunt "Lottie" (Charlotte Hawkins Brown), and a sizable advance from Capitol Records, he was able to give them $50,000.

Carlos Gastel told the press at the time that they "recently offered [the IRS] another $20,000, which they refused."[2] In March 1951, while Nat and Maria were on the road, the tax men raided their Hancock Park house and carted off anything that looked valuable, including her minks and his new Cadillac—and this was, apparently without having first tried to attach his salary (which normally precedes the seizure of property). The black community smelled a rat. No one denied that the debt was legitimate, but, as *Down Beat* suggested, it was suspected the white pressure groups who had tried to extricate the Coles from Hancock Park two years earlier had connections that enabled them to use the tax situation as a means of forcing them out. The implication was that if it had a been a white man who had the debt, or a black man who had the common sense to stay where he belonged, then the measures taken by the IRS would not have been quite so draconian.

In one of his most extreme examples of turning the other cheek, Cole somehow managed to extract some showbiz mileage out of the tax dilemma. He appeared at the Apollo Theater in March 1952, at which point the difficulties were still far from resolved. For this run, he was sharing the bill with longtime friend, comic-songwriter Timmie Rogers. "An added treat is that . . . during the run King Cole and Timmie will make one of the oddest switches in show business. King Cole will sing 'It's Crazy,' written by Timmie, and Timmie will do a comedy routine on taxes written by Nat King Cole."[3]

AT THE SAME TIME COLE WAS TAPING his final Trio classics, he was also introducing into his music the remarkable Nelson Riddle, who would help him create more classic songs and hit records than any other collaborator. The brilliant orchestrator came into Cole's career through the back door and immediately began to bring about profound changes in his music. Cole "discovered" Riddle in the same way all the best things happened in his career, through his unending search for something new and his unceasing willingness to experiment.

However, the "something new" that Cole was betting on at the start of 1950 was not the something new that would eventually work for him. He sang his first Riddle arrangement, "Mona Lisa," at the Capitol session of March 11 (before they got to "Who's Who"), but the primary focus of the date, the song that he and everyone else was putting their money on to be the next big hit, was something completely different. The number everyone thought was going to be the money song was a rather outrageous faux-gospel number titled "The Greatest Inventor of Them All." As the 1940s became the 1950s, the charts seemed to be dominated by such pop-spiritual numbers as "The Old Master Painter" and Frankie Laine's "That Lucky Old Sun." "The Greatest Inventor of Them All," by Dok Stanford, author of the minor Trio classic "I Can't See for Lookin',"[4] seems directly cast from the same general mold as "The Old Master Painter." In that widely recorded song of the previous year (Sinatra on Columbia, Peggy Lee and Mel Tormé on Capitol), the old master painter is a colloquial description of The Creator Himself, The One who gave us all the beauty and colors of nature.[5] Thus, where God was a painter in 1949, now, in 1950 He is the Great Inventor who created everything: "He took a lot of nothing / Made it into something / He's the greatest inventor of them all." The track opens with a dramatic, out-of-tempo verse, but from then on, the King and his men—Ashby, Comfort, and especially Costanzo—keep it light and moving. The finished record is more fun than it is pious, and you can see why everybody thought it would be a hit.

The "Greatest Inventor" needed a choir, so to direct the date, producer Lou Busch hired Les Baxter. Then best known as a group singer (with Mel Tormé's Mel-Tones, among others), he was quickly establishing himself as a creator of choral-centric pop music. Baxter was assigned to conduct on all four of the orchestra numbers, but Nat needed someone else to write the actual charts, particularly for the remaining three numbers, which were all grandly European and semi-classical in tone and texture: "Always You," "The Magic Tree," and "Mona Lisa." Busch recruited two then-anonymous young men: Gus Levene, to arrange the first two, and Nelson Riddle, to handle the third. "Always You" boasted a Tchaikovsky-derived melody, and "The Magic Tree" was another philosophical tone poem in the same general stylistic universe as "Nature Boy" with enchanted vegetation that makes wishes come true.

"Always You" wasn't bad, but clearly not a hit; however, "Magic Tree" was a total misfire, just about the doggiest "dog tune" that Cole had yet recorded.

Even long after the session, everyone was still betting on "The Greatest Inventor of Them All." Two months later, when Cole made his second appearance on Ed Sullivan's *Toast of the Town* on May 7, he still was plugging "The Greatest Inventor of Them All." However, by June, it was clear that "Mona Lisa" was the next big song in Cole's life—bigger than anything since "Nature Boy" two years earlier.

"MONA LISA" HAD ITS ROOTS in *No Surrender*, a 1942 novel by Martha Albrand, a German writer who had immigrated to the United States shortly before the outbreak of the war. In 1949, Paramount Pictures adapted *No Surrender* into *Captain Carey, U.S.A.*, a tale of American spies and German troops fighting for the soul of occupied Italy. In this context, you might assume that the song "Mona Lisa" would be a romantic signifier between the hero, Alan Ladd, and leading lady, Wanda Hendrix, but no. Director Mitchell Leisen uses the melody to advance a plot point, and as the story develops, the biggest clues to the larger mystery are a painting and a song.

Those words and music had been written for Paramount by two of their contracted writers, Jay Livingston and Ray Evans, who had already won the Academy Award for best song in 1948, with "Buttons and Bows" from *The Paleface* (a #1 hit single for Dinah Shore). The *Captain Carey* song "wasn't an important assignment," Livingston told me.[6] "In the story, the Italian Partisans were on their way to warn Alan Ladd and the Americans that the Nazi patrol was coming, so they said, 'Why doesn't somebody sing a little song,' you know? So, they figured a street musician, playing accordion or guitar, would play and sing this song, to warn Alan Ladd to get the hell out of there and hide the shortwave radio. We were actually busy writing the score for the first Martin & Lewis picture *My Friend Irma* (1949), and they said, 'If you don't have time, we'll use a public domain song.' "

The team's first idea for an Italianate song title was "Prima Donna." It was Evan's wife, a connoisseur of fine art and paintings, who gifted them with the title of "Mona Lisa."[7] Now, the song was more or less in its final form, but both the title of the song and the title of the film would be changed several times. At first, the movie title was going to be *O.S.S.* (for the Office of Strategic Services, which later became the CIA), then at one point, both the number and the film were going to be called "After Midnight." (Jay sang that lyric for me: "I'm so lonely though it's only after midnight. / Did we leave the candlelight and wine too soon?") But when the movie title was set as *Captain*

Carey U.S.A., the composers persuaded Paramount to let them go back to their original conception title and lyric, "Mona Lisa."

And that was almost as far as it went.[8] Alan Livingston, then a fledgling producer at Capitol Records (and the younger brother of songwriter Ray Livingston), remembered, "It was not an important song in the picture, it was only incidental music, and it wasn't even a musical to start with."[9] The movie *Captain Carey* came and went in February 1950 without any attention being paid to the "Mona Lisa" theme. The songwriters seemed to be the only ones who thought "Mona Lisa" had potential beyond its brief exposure in the movie. "But you know a lot of people wrote [to Paramount Pictures], they got a lot of letters, saying, 'What's that song he's singing?' It must have had something that grabbed people." Livingston recalled in 1977, "After it was written, we both got the idea, wouldn't this be great for Nat Cole?"[10] However, when I talked to Livingston twenty years after that, he insisted that their first idea was to make the rounds of all the Italian American crooners crowding the airwaves at that particular moment, Sinatra, Como, Vic Damone, Dean Martin, Frankie Laine (Tony Bennett, Al Martino, Julius LaRosa, Jerry Vale and still others were on the horizon)—but they all turned it down.

Larry Shayne, who ran Famous Music, the music publishing wing of Paramount Pictures, had the idea of bringing the song to Nat King Cole. Shayne reached Cole via Louis Lipstone, the head of Paramount's music department, who happened to be friendly with Carlos Gastel. As Alan Livingston remembered, "Louis Lipstone called up Carlos, and he said, 'I have never done this in my life before, but I'm putting it on a personal basis. I want Nat to record this song.' Carlos was a good-hearted guy, and he went to Nat and he says, 'Nat, we've got to do this for him.' "

Jay picks up the story from here: "Well, Nat didn't like to listen to [demo records of] songs, he wanted to have a copy of the music and work on it himself. He was such a gentle soul; he didn't want to say no to people." He continued, "We got over to Nat's house and I sang it for him. And there was a little girl went around ... giving me a lot of trouble, making a lot of noise, that was Natalie.[11] I didn't know she was going to be a star! And he said, 'Yeah, fine." He took the music and he kept it. And he didn't know whether to record it or not from what I heard." Livingston later heard that Cole didn't want to sing it at first because, "Who wants to sing a song about a girl with no arms?" "He was thinking of the Venus De Milo." Likewise, Livingston also later heard that Bing Crosby (who recorded it much later on) initially "turned it down because he considered it sacrilegious—he was thinking of the Madonna" (the Virgin Mary). Supposedly, Cole only agreed to do the song on the insistence of Carlos, who was doing a favor for Lipstone—and if Maria's memory is accurate, they both felt they owed it to Paramount Pictures; in this account, Nat said, "I recorded that song to get that Shayne fellow out of my hair."[12] Either way, they all agree, Cole only begrudgingly agreed to record it.

That's the part of the account that I believe Jay and Ray—and I knew them both—embellished to make for a better story, the kind of tale that songwriters love to tell. Knowing that Cole had already picked "The Christmas Song" and "Nature Boy" as hits, how could he fail to recognize that "Mona Lisa" was a quality song, and one that was perfect for him? He also did the song a favor by putting it on the back of "The Greatest Inventor of Them All," which they felt was the song likely to hit the charts.

As we have seen, throughout Cole's long relationship with the label, he generally recorded more masters than the label actually issued—they released only those titles that they thought had definite sales potential. When it came time to decide the fate of "Mona Lisa," there was no consensus. Lou Busch, who produced the recording, gave it the thumbs up,[13] but his boss, Jim Conkling, then the president of the label, was completely opposed to it. Jay remembered that, fortunately, the moment of decision occurred while Conkling happened to be out of town on business. Conkling later told Livingston that if he'd been around at the time, he wouldn't have let them release it at all. "They took a full-page ad in *Billboard*, for 'The Greatest Inventor' and never even mentioned 'Mona Lisa.' 'Mona Lisa' was nothing. Jim didn't think it was commercial at all. But then we went on a junket for Paramount for two weeks, going to all these theatres and doing our little act. And we took the record with us; these were 78s, and in every town we got to, we went to the disc jockeys. I think we did it, I really do; by the time we got back they were playing it everywhere."

The song hit number one in June; by the summer and fall, it was all that audiences (especially in England) wanted to hear. There were several factors in the song's success—and the fact that it had been briefly heard in a spy movie was hardly one of them (even though it did win an Oscar that year for best original song from a motion picture). There's Cole's voice and his interpretation, which perfectly captured the combination of strangeness and familiarity that the songwriters were going for. Cole and Riddle made vivid what Livingston and Evans had implied, in effect, a proper love song for a *film noir*, wherein you're never completely sure exactly what's going on; is the song about the painting itself, or about an actual woman with a smile like the woman painted by da Vinci? For that reason, Cole didn't include the verse (although his brother Freddy and Bing Crosby later did) which resolves that question in the first line: "In a villa in a little old Italian town / Lives a girl whose beauty shames the rose."

But the most salient factor is the orchestration of Nelson Riddle. It was as different from "Nature Boy" as "Nature Boy" had been different from what came before it. Riddle made prominent use of the guitar of Irving Ashby; in fact, he plays more here than on virtually every other Cole record, but it hardly sounds anything like the King Cole Trio. In writing a faux-Italian song, Livingston and Evans kept the whole thing more folkloric than operatic, and Riddle did what he would do countless times in the decades to come in writing a profoundly complex arrangement of a gloriously simple song. It also was grandly European; even Ashby, one of the great jazz guitarists, was directed to play in a way that suggested the columbine and Pierrot of old Venice. It was the kind of melody and provocative lyric that having heard once, you couldn't forget, and Cole and Riddle both brought that out, focusing on the fundamental melancholia of the music and words. Riddle's string writing was profoundly harmonically ambiguous; like the Mona Lisa's actual smile, you could never tell if it was happy or sad. Back in the days of phonographs, whenever I listened to "Mona Lisa" on the *Unforgettable* album, I somehow always assumed my turntable was running at the wrong speed—I kept trying to adjust the pitch, but I could never get it to conform to any conventional definition of "correct."

It was pretty heady stuff for a precocious twenty-eight-year-old arranger whose biggest credit up to that moment was having played trombone and arranged for Tommy Dorsey. Born in 1921, Nelson Riddle had come up with various big bands, including Tommy Reynolds and Charlie Spivak, and he had also served with both the Merchant Marines and the "regular Army" during World War II. He studied arranging for big band with the sagacious Bill Finegan (of Glenn Miller fame) and for strings with the innovative violinist Alan Shulman. By 1950, Riddle had already written successful arrangements for such stars as Bing Crosby and Doris Day, albeit anonymously. "Mona Lisa" was Riddle's first assignment for Capitol Records—and it would be the beginning of a beautiful, career-making relationship with both the label and the artist. "Les Baxter was doing some recordings for Nat Cole and he asked me if I would write one of the arrangements, so I did and it was 'Mona Lisa.' Nat liked it very much and that was my wedge," as Riddle recalled many years later,[14] meaning that was the avenue by which he eventually ascended to personally conducting for Cole—with his name on the label—rather than merely ghostwriting.

In this "creation myth," it's easy to paint Les Baxter as a bad guy because Riddle didn't receive any credit for the chart, but that's the way it was usually done then; the record label states "Nat King Cole with orchestra conducted by Les Baxter," all perfectly true. "He was credited because he was the bandleader," said Riddle. "They would presume or assume that the bandleader or conductor wrote the arrangements; he didn't even have to lie, he just had to say nothing, and it was okay. Les had authorized me to put in a bill for $6 a page. The A&R man at that time [Lou Busch] said 'I can't okay this, I'm only authorized to pay you scale, which in this case is $3.99 a page, he says, we'll round it off, let's make it $4.00.' So, four times thirteen is $52. In my estimation, Nat Cole used that arrangement so many times that he ended up using it for less than a penny a time." It was actually even less than that: the paperwork for the date shows that Riddle was paid $51.87.[15]

It was actually Pete Rugolo who let everyone know the name of the man who actually wrote the arrangement for "Mona Lisa." "I told Carlos that Nelson should be given a chance, because he was so good." Cole himself was very generous to the man who became his closest musical associate for the next ten years: "This date really showed everybody what Nelson Riddle could do. Later on, he was discovered by a lot of singers. It's easy to discover a gold mine when you can see it shining."[16]

THE BULK OF COLE'S SESSIONS for 1950 were conducted by Rugolo; Nat and Nelson next crossed paths in February 1951, when Les Baxter was recruited once more, this time to do another number with a big pseudo-Gospel choir. "The Lighthouse in the Sky" finds God switching careers again, from master painter to great inventor, and now we find Him becoming a lighthouse keeper—in the sky, yet. The concept, by the young Hal David (then known as Mack David's kid brother and later as Burt Bacharach's principal lyricist), was pretty obvious from the title: when you lose your way in the ocean of life, the big Lighthouse Keeper in the Sky will show you the path. Again, it was suited to Baxter's choral style, but this time, despite recording it on two different sessions, the label decided not to issue it at all. Baxter conducted on all four numbers; the other three were arranged by Riddle: the patriotic "Early American" (more Burke and Van Heusen, and a lovely if lesser-known song), "Because of Rain" (by the Coles' old friend, Ruth Poll, and also memorable enough to be a minor hit), and "Too Young" by Sid Lippman, which was instantly a #1 hit, Cole's biggest number since "Mona Lisa."

For the second time, Cole, by now at last known primarily as a popular singer, and Nelson Riddle, still unknown and uncredited, had landed a huge hit. Yet they were just a few steps ahead of Peggy Lee, who, it turned out, also had her eyes on Lippman's song. "I remember once that I wanted to find some new material, and someone said, 'Well, go in that room there. There's a whole stack.' There were stacks and stacks. Hundreds and hundreds of songs. And I went through them and I found just one song that I thought that I would really like to do. And I came out and I said, 'This is it. This is the one.' And they told me that Nat just picked that one out. It was 'Too Young.'"[17]

Again, everyone agreed that Riddle's chart was a key factor in the song's success. "By this time I had ingratiated myself, first with Carlos Gastel, who in turn introduced me to Nat Cole, and by August 1951, I was doing my own dates with Nat," said Riddle. "The first date I did had 'Unforgettable' on it." As Riddle relates, this was a session of three tunes, all by writers Cole had worked with previously: Marvin Fisher's "My First and My Last Love," Redd Evans's "Lovelight," and Irving Gordon's "Unforgettable." That last song came to Cole through his old friend Claire Phillips, who was then Mrs. Irving Gordon. Gordon (1915–1996) had landed several hits (like "Me, Myself and I (Are All in Love with You)" and "Christmas Dreaming"), and even one standard ("Prelude to a Kiss," with music by Duke Ellington). The song that became "Unforgettable" began life as a "white elephant," as Mrs. Gordon described it— an "ugly duckling" of a song, one that was nearly aborted at every step of the way, in the composition, in the publishing, and even in the title.

When Gordon originally wrote down the melody, he used several modulations as a means of getting in and out of the bridge. [18] That was the only way he could think of to make the melody work, but he wasn't happy with it: the key changes were awkward; there had to be a better solution. Gordon was already a veteran songwriter, but he couldn't think of anything, so he sought the counsel of two highly experienced musical friends, the arranger-bandleader Benny Carter and the songwriter Walter Kent. Yes, they agreed that the way Gordon had cast the melody was rather ungainly. But no, they couldn't come up with anything that would actually improve it.

Reluctantly, Gordon brought the song to a publisher as it was. He wasn't under a strict contract to any single firm; instead, it was his practice, when he had written a dozen or so saleable songs, to make a business trip to Manhattan every few weeks or so and hit the rounds of various publishers at the Brill Building at 1619 Broadway and across the street at 1650 Broadway. A few days later, Gordon called his wife with good news; he had found homes for all of his new songs—except for "Unforgettable." None of the publishers wanted it. Mrs. Gordon then gave him the bright idea of trying the Bourne Company, which, in the past, had been more responsive than other "pubberies" in terms of doing something with offbeat and unusual songs. She was right; the Bourne people took it. But they had a change that they wanted to make.

According to one account, Gordon's original title for this song was "Uncomparable."[19] However, the publisher people thought that this was a weak title. The word "uncomparable" wasn't exactly overwhelming praise; it merely indicated two things that can't be compared, as in "pigeons are uncomparable with tractors." What Gordon was aiming for was to talk about someone who was so wonderful that she couldn't be compared with anyone else, and that word was "incomparable." However, "incomparable" was also a subpar title; the word just doesn't sing—try humming either "uncomparable" or "incomparable" to Gordon's now-famous melody and you'll agree. However, the publisher instead suggested "Unforgettable," and Gordon wisely went with that. William Gordon, Irving and Claire's son, remembered that the original penultimate line was: "It's regrettable that someone so unforgettable, / Would not think that I'm unforgettable too." This, admittedly, was very awkward. The publisher wisely changed it to the line we all know, "That's why, darling, it's incredible, / That someone so unforgettable / Thinks that I am unforgettable too."[20]

Yet even after all these changes had been made, to the melody, harmony, and lyrics (at the very least), the Bourne Company still couldn't interest any artist, record label, or A&R man in the song. But Claire had one more idea: "I'll call Nat Cole and ask him if he'll listen to it," she remembered. "This nice man hadn't become too big and famous to remember his old friends." They didn't even have to play it for him; he took the music and, the inevitable cigarette dangling from his lips, proceeded to play it himself. Within a few minutes, he was not only trying out different keys for himself, he was, effectively re-harmonizing it. "Irv and I listened to him and sure enough, the song sounded better with Nat's chords. He had also improved on the little run which returned the song to the original key."

In fact, what Cole seems to have done was figure out a way that the melody and the lyrics could work without any modulation whatever. "Unforgettable," as we now know it, is published in G major, with no key changes. Also, it's in a highly unusual format that might be called AA': there are two 16-bar halves (each of which might also be designated AB), the first of which ends on the V chord (D), the second of which ends on the IV chord (C major). In its published form, the song doesn't have anything like a traditional bridge.

The next man who helped make "Unforgettable" into something truly memorable was Nelson Riddle. He realized that this would be the first Nat King Cole record in which Riddle would get his name on the label, and he made the most of the opportunity. As would become his trademark (in a manner inspired by the King Cole Trio), he devised a strikingly original introduction that, once heard, would be no less unforgettable than the rest of the song. The record opens with an absolutely sparkling few bars of keyboard harmony, a combination of celesta and piano playing together, on a five-note phrase that corresponds to the five notes of the song title ("un-for-get-a-ble") in block chords. The overall sound of the intro is directly reminiscent of the George Shearing Quintet, and it also underscores the specific use of block chords that Shearing learned from the King Cole Trio.[21] The five notes of the intro recur throughout the chart, and in the instrumental break, Riddle embellishes the keyboard part with no less distinctive pizzicato strings.[22]

"It was a bonanza for all of us," Claire Gordon concluded. In hindsight, it seems hard to believe that "Unforgettable" only reached #12 on the pop charts—and that was in America; it doesn't appear to have charted in England at all. Irving Gordon's song gradually became much more important to Cole's legacy over the decades, starting in 1952, when Capitol used the song as the title of Cole's first primarily vocal album (which collected most of his major hits from the 1949–1951 period, including "Mona Lisa" and "Too Young"). In 1959, the song's iconic status was cemented by a new hit single by Dinah Washington, and two years later, Cole re-recorded it for *The Nat King Cole Story*. Throughout his lifetime, when people heard Cole singing the song, they knew it was a man singing about a woman, but Natalie was wise enough to realize that since her father's death, the term "unforgettable" had become increasingly attached to Nat King Cole himself.

For Riddle in 1951, "Unforgettable" marked the cap of a rather unforgettable parlay: by summer 1951, he had worked with Cole exactly three times—although the third session was the only one when Riddle himself conducted—and each of those three dates yielded a signature hit: "Mona Lisa," "Too Young," and now "Unforgettable." Clearly it was fate that Cole and Riddle had to keep on working together—as they would for roughly ten years and approximately 250 tracks. Occasionally, Cole would bring in other arrangers for different orchestral colors, like Billy May and then Gordon Jenkins, even while Riddle worked with a wide range of other artists (most famously, beginning in 1953, Sinatra), but during this period, Nelson was Nat's main man.

Cole's ongoing success was particularly predicated on his remarkable knack for encouraging the right songwriters and continually finding the right songs. Cole sang "Your Voice" by Sid Lippman well before "Too Young," and "Calico Sal" by Irving Gordon prior to "Unforgettable." No other artist could find so many superior songs to begin with, then work so much magic on them, both as a kind of musical dramaturg (as he had done with "Unforgettable") and then as a singer, presenting them better than anyone else possibly could. Now, armed with the inestimable help of Riddle, Cole was regularly achieving the impossible: to take an underdog of a song that the composer's own wife had written off as an ugly duckling, a white elephant, and other unflattering zoological metaphors, and transform it into something truly "Unforgettable."

IN 1951, COLE NOT ONLY BEGAN WORKING with his most important long-term musical director, but he also gained a permanent producer. At the same time that Nelson Smock Riddle, whom Cole, Sinatra, and many others addressed as "Nels," was finding his place in Cole's music, so too was Capitol Records executive Leland James Gillette, known to all as "Lee." Earlier, Cole's first dates at the label had been supervised by Johnny Mercer himself, and others were done by Jim Conkling, soon to become the label's president. Occasionally Capitol also brought in working musicians, such as pianist Lou Busch and guitarist Carl Kress, the latter on New York dates. Gillette first worked with Cole in 1946 as part of his role as head of Capitol's Transcription service, and he supervised most of the Trio's transcription sessions from the late 1940s, and then he became Cole's full-time producer in 1951. If Carlos Gastel deserves props for helping to shape the overall arch of Cole's career, and if Riddle provided the specific musical colors for the songs he sang, most of the credit for Cole's recordings (after the artist himself) goes to Gillette, who also became Cole's most direct conduit to the upper management at Capitol Records.

Gillette had been born in Indianapolis on October 30, 1912, and grew up in Peoria and then Chicago.[23] An experienced musician (guitar, drums, arrangements), he was also, as Dave Dexter described him, a "disc jockey, yacht captain, world traveler, and connoisseur of food and spirits." (In the latter category, he was highly compatible with Gastel.) In the late jazz age and early Depression years, Gillette sang with two Chicago dance bands, Harry Sosnick and Buddy Rogers. In 1944, Gillette became the first formal "producer" to be hired by Capitol, and his initial assignment was to run their hillbilly music division (not yet re-christened "country and western"). Clearly, he was doing something right: in 1947, he produced "Smoke, Smoke, Smoke (That Cigarette)," by Tex Williams and his Western Caravan, the record that is cited as Capitol's first million-seller.[24]

Gillette had been best known for his work in the country field, yet he encouraged Cole's love for the traditional American songbook, past and future. As we've seen, Cole recorded virtually no new Broadway or Hollywood songs in all of the Trio period for Capitol, but once Gillette entered the picture, many more contemporary film and show tunes start to appear in his sessions. One of the first to benefit was Cole's old friend, Johnny Mercer, still a part owner of Capitol though no longer actively involved with the company. On September 14, 1951, Cole cut two especially lovely new Mercer ballads with orchestra, "O.K. for T.V.," a love song with Mercer's own music, from the burlesque comedy *Top Banana*, and "Here's to My Lady," with a melody by Rube Bloom.[25] In this season, Cole also sang "I Still See Elisa," the loveliest ballad from Alan Jay Lerner and Frederick Loewe's 1951 Broadway success, *Paint Your Wagon*—in some ways that single anticipates Cole's later, very productive relationship with Lerner and Loewe's score to *My Fair Lady*. In 1953, Cole sang "I Am in Love" from Cole Porter's *Can Can*, which resulted in a striking display of multi-harmonic pyrotechnics from Riddle, while "Alone Too Long" (1954, by Arthur Schwartz and Dorothy Fields) was a worthy ballad from a less successful Broadway show, *By the Beautiful Sea*.

The combination of classic standards and new songs that had the potential to be hits served Cole well as he continued to make inroads into television. His best friend in the new medium, for many years to come, continued to be Ed Sullivan, who played host to the artist roughly twice a year for most of the decade. Frequently Cole would start his Sullivan show segments with a hits medley, which served as a summing up of his best-known songs to that point, along with one or two other numbers that he was hoping to promote into hit status. On May 16, 1954, for instance, along with the medley, Cole performed one new swing number, an up-tempo treatment of "Lover, Come Back to Me," and a big ballad, "Answer Me, My Love." In certain ways, these performances are even better than the Capitol versions: "Answer Me" features the Riddle arrangement but without the big choir (what producer Michael Cuscuna refers to as "the Cecil B. DeMille chorus") and the more intimate sound makes the number resonate more meaningfully.

"Lover, Come Back to Me" likewise starts with the Billy May arrangement (recorded by Cole in January 1953), but in a way that makes better use of Cole's touring rhythm section, including solos from Cole himself as well as guitarist John Collins, and prominent participation by Cole's old friend and new-old drummer, Lee Young. "Every time you hear a drummer on a King Cole record, it's me,"[26] Young once told me, and it's only a slight exaggeration. Young elaborated, "In '53, I joined Nat again, and I went on the road with him as his drummer and [eventually] conductor, and I was with him for nine and a half years." In discussing Cole's performance style, Young explained, "He would just get up from the piano but rarely move more than 10 or 15 feet away from it." Young said that in the beginning, Nat was "very pigeon toed, and looked like he was going to fall down actually, all the time."

But by 1954, Cole was able to comfortably move around on stage, with or without the crutch of a Steinway or Baldwin. His developing onstage skills are particularly well documented in the 1954 Sullivan show performance of "Lover, Come Back to Me," in which he starts at the piano, stands up, walks away, comes back and hits a few notes, and then does it all over again, all the while looking perfectly comfortable, smooth, and very casual. It became a signature that was at once visual and musical; as he stands up, he hits the high A at the top of the keyboard even as he turns and smiles at the audience. Young concluded, "You know, the guy was just a great performer and a very gifted musician."[27]

The Sullivan shows contain no shortage of surprises: the October 23, 1955, show includes a duet with Maria (and their chemistry together counts for a lot more on video than on the audio-only medium of recordings) on "I Can't Believe that You're in Love with Me," and "Little Girl." The latter is a long-time Cole favorite, but here he introduces a very exciting big-band arrangement, clearly based on his familiar Trio version, with a brass elaboration on the artist's familiar piano runs. Cole is especially animated and moved by the spirit of the moment—and the energy from the studio audience—on this live TV performance.

By the early '50s, Cole was appearing on other TV shows well beyond *Toast of the Town*. Nat and Maria are both guests on an early CBS series called *Star of the Family*, in which they interact with another married couple, Mary Healey and Peter Lind Hayes (well before they co-starred in the cult classic *The Five Thousand Fingers of Dr. T*), and Nat introduces "Walkin' My Baby Back Home" as a song picked for him by his wife.[28] On ABC's *Showtime USA* (1951) he's introduced by the veteran producer Vinton Freedley playing and singing his latest record, "Jet."[29]

Cole was also a hugely popular guest with hosting superstar comedians, including two he could see eye to eye with, Sid Caesar (on *Your Show of Shows*) and Red Skelton, the latter on February 8, 1953. He joined Milton Berle on the *Texaco Star Theater*, on December 11, 1951. Cole starts with a hits medley at the piano, then rises to sing a stand-up version of his latest big chart-topper, "Too Young." He also participates in a musical sketch depicting a boisterous, noisy street scene—which he launches by singing Rodgers and Hart's "Manhattan" off-camera and then plays a loud-mouthed newspaper peddler opposite Berle as a garbageman with a Hitler mustache. The number is an elaborate comedy medley with comically mundane lyrics set to iconic classical themes, like "Libiamo ne' lieti calici" from *La traviata* (Giuseppe Verdi), "The Blue Danube (waltz)" by Johann Strauss II, and the familiar

Mexican waltz "Sobre las Olas" (Over the Waves) by Juventino Rosas. Silly though it may be, Cole's work in these kinds of productions would be good training for his own later variety series.

It's worth noting that on all of these television appearances, Cole is afforded the same dignity (or lack of same) as any white headliner. On September 12, 1953, Cole was the guest host of the season premiere of *Your Show of Shows*, on which he sings two relatively recent Capitol recordings, "A Fool Was I" and Cole Porter's "I Am in Love." The non-musical comedy highlight of the episode, not featuring Cole, is an extended and very funny parody of the big hit movie of the year, "From Here to Obscurity," with Sid Caesar as Montgomery Clift's embattled bugler and diminutive Howard Morris in the Sinatra role—which also serves as a useful reminder of precisely where Cole's colleague was at this particular point in his own career.

NOW WITH GILLETTE ENSCONCED as his permanent producer and Riddle on the team as his most-frequent arranger and conductor, the time had come at long last to officially "retire" the King Cole Trio. In September 1951—fourteen years to the month after the formation of the original group—it was formally announced that, going forward, the billing would no longer be "The King Cole Trio" or even "King Cole and His Trio," but "Nat King Cole." Gastel informed the press, "Effective as of this date, Nat King Cole will be presented as a solo attraction."[30] The final Capitol single to bill the Trio on the label was "Get to Gettin'," released in October 1950.

At this time, Irving Ashby and Joe Comfort were replaced by a guitarist and bassist who expected much less in terms of both their paycheck and a share of the spotlight, namely, John Collins and Charlie Harris, who remained with Cole for the rest of his career. Collins told me that he was, in fact, disappointed, at first, in how little they actually got to play; he was hoping to fill the shoes of his hero, Oscar Moore, and be a true collaborator of Cole's; instead, he was just playing mostly fills and backing up a solo star.[31] (However, there would be many remarkable exceptions, as we shall see.) Costanzo, who would later rejoin Cole for many projects (including the classic 1956 album *After Midnight*), was essentially replaced by traps drummer Lee Young, though Jack would also rejoin Cole's group on many occasions.

In a sense, the King Cole Trio had been doomed from the moment that Oscar Moore had turned in his notice back in 1947. Cole had spent ten years perfecting his sound with Moore, and five with Miller, until he reached the point that it was truly perfect. In fact, perhaps that was an unlikely sort of frustration as well, that it was literally impossible for the Trio, with Moore and Miller, to get any better; to keep growing artistically, he had to find new mountains to climb.

Then, the Trio of 1948–1951, with Ashby, Comfort, and Costanzo, was a brilliant follow-up act. But by 1951, Cole realized that there would be no point in following that, in turn, with still another Trio; the time had come at last to move onto something entirely new. But for all the influence of Maria and Carlos, and now Lee and Nelson, my personal theory is that had Oscar never left the King Cole Trio, Nat would have kept it going forever. He loved the Trio that much; it was that special to him.

And the Trio never completely went away, not permanently. Cole continued to tour with a core rhythm section of guitar (Collins), bass (Harris), and eventually drums (Young), with the latter also occasionally credited as "conductor." He never brought along another pianist for live shows. He still played on several numbers of every performance, and if they needed another keyboardist, it would be some semi-anonymous member of the musicians' local.

His relationship with jazz was changing as well: as we've seen, in 1946, he promised more of it for his fans, and in 1949 he was singing the praises of modern jazz and expanding the Trio's scope with bebop and bongos, resulting in stories with headlines like "Nat Nominates Himself Advance Man for Bop."[32] But in 1951, Cole says in numerous interviews that he feels disappointed with modern jazz—not the music itself, but the public's lukewarm reaction to it. Clearly, bebop was going in one direction and the mass market taste in another, and Cole felt forced to have to choose between the two. But he was far from bitter about it.

"No matter what anyone says, I think I'm a very lucky guy," he said around this time. "When I look back on my work so far, I realize I could play both sides of the fence, musically. When I wanted to play jazz I could do it. Now that I'm not playing so much jazz, I can still please a lot of people and—this is important—I enjoy what I'm doing. In fact, I may be doing jazz a lot more good than some of those really hip, cool people who put everybody down. I could play and sing for a lot of folks you could label square. But they trust me—you know what I mean. They have confidence in what we're doing, so we can sneak in some jazz, and they like it because it isn't being forced down their throats."[33]

AND YET, AS SOON AS THE TRIO had been officially put away, again, like some kind of a childish thing—Cole's very next full-length project was a new piano instrumental album, cut in 1952, at the point in which three of the top ten records of the year were by Cole, "Somewhere Along the Way," "Unforgettable," and "Walkin' My Baby Back Home," all following on the heels of "Mona Lisa" in 1950 and "Too Young" in 1951. And yet he still loved to play—probably more than anything.

Was he conflicted? After having worked so hard to transform himself into a popular vocalist, he was now starting to worry that audiences would forget that he had ever played the piano. "Everybody seems to have forgotten about my piano; just as they forget that Billy Eckstine was a pretty fair musician and bandleader, people think I've always been a vocalist. The young kids more than anyone else, they're even surprised that I play a piano at all. I mean the kids who started buying records a few years ago when 'Mona Lisa' was popular. All they've ever heard me do is sing with big bands and strings in the background."[34]

That was "the real reason," he told *Down Beat*, that he "cut his piano-only album"; to show the multitudes who were buying his pop singles that he could still play. Still there was more to it than that: he wanted to keep the piano as part of his music, but lately there was less and less opportunity for him to play it in his contemporary hits. And he also wanted to keep experimenting, if not to find a new sound, then at least to see if something new and different could be done with the piano.

The finished album, titled *Penthouse Serenade*, sounds light and effortless, but, according to Lee Gillette, getting it recorded was a major effort. "We really had some problems, first of all, to try to talk him into making a piano album. Now here is a man who was considered one of the great jazz pianists of our time and he's been singing so long that he's afraid to go in and record a piano album. Well, we first of all set it up and went over to his house with a tape machine and had him just sit there and play with no accompaniment, just to play some piano things. Well that didn't work out though. He froze, froze up on that occasion.

"I finally got him into the studio, and we started to record this album and Nat froze up again. He, first of all, he didn't want anybody in the studio. He didn't want anybody in the control room, but me and [the engineer], nobody else. Well, it took us . . . quite a time to get that album made. And then what happened? [Capitol accidentally] erased some of it after we had made it. So, we had to go in and . . . do a few of the sides over again. Well, that really made him a little upset, that he [had] finally gotten through it. Now he had to come back and do some more of it."[35] The session sheets confirm that Cole went into the studio to work on this project several times in March and April of

1952, trying to work out his ideas, and then returned to the project in July to re-do the tracks that had accidentally been erased.

As with his piano instrumental sessions of 1944 and 1947, he cut the complete original album as issued—all eight tracks—in a single date, July 18, 1952. The session took place while Cole was appearing at the Tiffany Room and utilized his then working rhythm section (Collins, Harris, Young, plus, on several tracks, Costanzo). Like the previous piano albums, this package is Cole's piano all the way, with no true solos by anyone else. There's also little of what could be called out-and-out improvisation. Rather, this is a vivid display of Cole's highly melodic style working its magic on a set of mostly familiar standard melodies. It's also another example of how Cole's piano and his singing came from the same place. Both here and on the 1955 *Piano Style of Nat King Cole*, Cole is essentially singing through the keyboard, delivering the melody (and, implicitly, the words) with absolute crystalline quality. He feels no need to muddy it up with a lot of abstraction or unnecessary notes. It speaks to Cole's mastery of the art of melody that he can completely personalize a tune without substantially altering it.

The 1952 album also represents the most extreme example of Cole's ability to make the piano sound like two different instruments being played by two different musicians. This he achieves primarily by accentuating the contrast between two different approaches to melody: one is a fully chordal kind of playing, which gives his playing an orchestral sound, and the other is expressing the melody more in single notes, like a horn or, even more so, a vocalist. It becomes obvious that Fatha Hines's concept of "trumpet-style piano" would have been a key inspiration here, and throughout *Penthouse Serenade*, Cole continually alternates between chordal/orchestral playing and horn/voice-like single-note playing.

Cole's 1943 "It's Only a Paper Moon" uses note-doubling between the piano and guitar in a way that anticipates the Shearing Quintet, although Shearing never directly imitated Cole. But unlike Shearing, Cole never reused the idea in the same way; where Shearing did a lot of subsequent numbers that were essentially variations on his breakthrough hit, "September in the Rain," Cole never brought the "Paper Moon" approach to any other song.

Cole never seems to have objected to the term "cocktail piano," yet this is hardly ambient background music. The pianist keeps everything swinging, lightly perhaps, but still irresistibly; this is still far from the "businessman's bounce" tempo of sweet bands like Guy Lombardo. The title track, "Penthouse Serenade," has a tinkly texture but a thoroughly thoughtful melodic variation, proving that Erroll Garner was his only conceivable competition in this area. "Rose Room" alternates between block chords on the "head" or first chorus and the melody phrased in individual notes in the second chorus, which is closer to an improvisation here. Cole frames the inherent rusticity of "Down by the Old Mill Stream" with cosmopolitan cool, the combination of modern musical elements with a laid-back style making this piece a kind of example of "bop-tail" piano. The more romantic "Laura" opens with a slow, rubato intro and first chorus, Cole playing one of the longer unaccompanied piano passages of his career, with the bass and drums abstaining until the bridge.

Cole opens "Polka Dots and Moonbeams" with a rubato chorus, block chords again rather than single notes this time, but that changes when he shifts into tempo and is joined by the rhythm accompaniment on the bridge. The lustier "Somebody Loves Me" again contrasts locked hands chords on the first chorus, single notes again in the second, effectively suggesting a flow from ensemble to solo playing.

Things slow down again with "Once in a Blue Moon," which is the first known recording of a song by the young composer Burt Bacharach, who had based the melody on Anton Rubinstein's famous "Melody in F" (op. 3). "That was a song that I wrote with my dad when I was in college," Bacharach later remembered, "and Nat King Cole recorded it. Actually it's Rubinstein's 'Melody in F,' so it was a real cop or a hat's off."[36] Further, as if the combination of Bacharach and Rubinstein wasn't enough, Cole also references a 1923 song of the same title by Jerome Kern. The album ends with "If I Should Lose You," a slow and romantic reading of a standard most famously recorded by Charlie Parker.

Penthouse Serenade was originally released in early 1953 as a ten-inch LP but it sold so well that Capitol wanted to reissue it in the new twelve-inch format. Thus, three years almost to the day after the original session, Cole and company returned to the studio. Perhaps now he felt more comfortable with the format, or knowing that the album was already a success, he was thus empowered to play around with it more. In any case, listening to the two sessions in chronological order reveals that Cole's playing is considerably looser and even more interesting here than on the earlier 1952 tracks. In fact, some of the 1955 playing is so futuristic it could almost pass for early Bill Evans.

First, Cole spins beautifully complex and intricate webs around "Don't Blame Me" (his third treatment of the McHugh-Fields perennial) and then he romps through Burke and Van Heusen's jazz standard "It Could

Happen to You." "I Surrender Dear" finds him fragmenting the melody in arpeggiated runs that harken back to Art Tatum (in whose combo Collins played before joining Cole); an alternate take shows Cole's overall approach is even more adventurous. "Little Girl" is the least cocktail-styled track on the album and the most like straight-ahead swing piano. Both the artist and the label had every reason to be pleased with the results, especially on the twelve-inch edition. "People who know me know that I'll never leave jazz," said Cole at the time. "My roots are in jazz and that's the music I love."[37]

THE TRANSITION FROM "The King Cole Trio" to "Nat King Cole" was made more seamless by Cole's participation in a series of tours from 1951 to about 1955 titled "The Big Show" or "The Biggest Show." These were concert "package" shows that enabled artists to consolidate their collective drawing power in order to play the big theaters and concert halls. The tours, which continued long into the rock 'n' roll era, usually combined several star singers and small groups with a big band, and often comedians and dance acts as well. (They were a direct outgrowth of the movie theater stage shows of the 1930s and '40s, except that they didn't accompany a film program.)

The 1951 and '52 Big Show tours featured Nat King Cole as the top headliner, supported by Sarah Vaughan and with Duke Ellington's Orchestra, as well as comic-singer (and occasional songwriter) Timmie Rogers and the remarkable one-legged tap dancer, Peg Leg Bates. It's a credit to Cole's skills as a businessman, and his ability to pick the right people to work with, that by 1956, he and Gastel were producing the tours themselves—and reaping the profits.

The 1951 Big Show tour was remembered very vividly by Billy Strayhorn, traveling as part of the Ellington entourage. He was asked if he and Duke Ellington would ever consider making an album with Cole. "Nat King Cole? Well, that'd be lovely. Of course, we've played with him, too, we did. Oh, we had fun, with the 'Big Show of '51.' " The composer continued, "Oh, he played the piano then—we got him to play the piano. We toured for about 12 weeks with Nat and Sarah Vaughan and Timmie Rogers, and Peg-Leg Bates. Every now and then, every third or fourth evening, why, Nat would get carried away—he'd play 'Route 66.' He'd sing it first; of course, it would goose him, and he'd play a half a dozen choruses. Of course, everybody is egging him on, you know."[38]

In 1953, the "Biggest" show, as it was called, was fully integrated, and Cole shared the bill (if not necessarily the stage), with, at different times, Betty

Hutton, Stan Kenton, and Billy May. One song exists from one of the 1951 shows,[39] and it's a triple rarity in that it features Cole duetting with Sarah Vaughan, accompanied by the Ellington orchestra on the Duke's "Love You Madly," his only extant performance with either Sassy or Duke—and there's a spoken interjection from the Maestro himself.

In between big tours and big clubs, Cole had found an ideal spot to play in closer to home, the Tiffany Room where, in early 1952, he was caught by critic, songwriter, and friend Leonard Feather, who noted that the place was "intimate . . . barely big enough to hold the members of Stan Kenton's concert orchestra [about forty people] without their instruments."[40] The Los Angeles club was one of the few venues Cole now played where all he needed was Collins, Harris, and occasionally Costanzo; he told Feather he had a new piano album coming ("to our delight") and Feather enthused that Cole should work with this combination in Tiffany-like rooms in New York and everywhere else.

THAT WAS THE IMAGE that Cole was promoting in the early 1950s, not necessarily a jazz artist but an entertainer who appeared in only the most high-class establishments. And with the coming of Maria, the zoot suits and hipster outfits of the Trio years are replaced by formal business attire and tuxedos. (There are hardly any photos of Nat from the pre-Maria period that show him in a tux.) He's depicted this way in all of his films from the period, starting with the next two Universal International two-reelers, both, like the 1950 *Nat King Cole and His Trio*, set in posh nightclubs. Unlike the earlier film, however, Cole is now the only black entertainer in both of these musical revues. *Nat 'King' Cole and Joe Adams Orchestra* (1952), has him singing a stand-up "Destination Moon" (along with "Too Young" and "That's My Girl")[41] and sharing the spotlight with a band led by the promoter Joe Adams, an infamous music business character who later took over as personal manager of Ray Charles.

Nat 'King' Cole and Russ Morgan and His Orchestra (1953) co-stars Cole with the veteran bandleader and occasional songwriter.[42] That 1953 featurette was less notable for its co-stars than its technological breakthroughs: it was filmed in the relatively short-lived medium of 3-D, and shown alongside the 3-D science fiction feature *It Came from Outer Space*. Cole doesn't engage in any three-dimensional antics here, although he does share the film with a dance troupe that mimes a bullfight in 3D. Cole is literally segregated from the rest of the proceedings—two chorus girls open a special set of doors revealing the artist in a special room within the nightclub set, where, seated at the piano, he plays and sings two of his best numbers of the period, Timmie Rogers's "It's Crazy" and the hit "Pretend."

Similarly, Cole is shown singing from the piano, also in conspicuously luxurious surroundings, in most of his subsequent feature films, especially the next two, *Small Town Girl* and *Blue Gardenia*, both from 1953. He not only plays that same role in both pictures but in both scenes, and his functions in them are suspiciously similar, if not to say identical, even though one is a frothy technicolor musical and the other a gritty monochrome *film noir*. In both, he is a virtual cupid, compelling couples to fall in love—whether they want to or not. In *Small Town Girl*, Jane Powell is the title character, who wants nothing less than to be stuck with the smug, spoiled rich boy played by Farley Granger; in *Blue Gardenia* (somewhat inspired by the infamous "black dahlia" case), Ann Baxter as "Norah Larkin" finds herself being drawn, against her better judgment, to the slyly seductive "Harry Prebble." (The character is played by Raymond Burr, which is a tip-off for the audience if not for Baxter.) In the first, it leads to romance; in the second, to something more sinister (no spoiler alert here). But none of this is Cole's concern—his only function is to lure these unlikely couples into each other's arms; what they do after that is strictly their own business.

Both of Cole's songs in these movies employ metaphors from the natural world to illustrate both the inevitability of love and its no less inescapable ending. "My Flaming Heart" (Leo Robin and Nicholas Brodszky) is in the same mold as the 1949 movie theme song "My Foolish Heart" in that the protagonist directly addresses his own heart as if it were a sentient entity unto itself. Instead of saying "Beware, my foolish heart," he's telling it, "Burn low, my flaming heart,"[43] advancing the idea that love, like a fire, is a chemical reaction, one in which neither the beginning nor the ending is controllable. In the second, the title theme "Blue Gardenia" (Bob Russell and Lester Lee) tells us that "love bloomed like a flower" and lasted "till the petals fell." (Here, Cole is backed on screen by his usual touring trio plus violinist John Creach, not yet a famous blues player.)[44]

Both pictures were directed by European emigrés, the second by the highly renowned Fritz Lang from Germany, the first by the practically unknown László Kardos from Hungary, a reliable craftsman who happened to be the brother-in-law of producer Joe Pasternak. In both movies, Cole and his song are there for contrast: in *Blue Gardenia* he provides a note of optimism in an otherwise dark narrative, and in *Small Town Girl*, his is virtually the only serious moment in a colorful musical where the other musical numbers are by the girlish soprano Jane Powell, the pneumatic Ann Miller, and the energetic Bobby Van. The songs contribute significantly to the plot points of each film; in fact, were it not for Cole the troubadour stoking the fires of romance, there would be no story.

The image of Cole in these films was consistent with the way Capitol Records depicted the artist on his album covers of the period: the front jackets of *Unforgettable* (1952), *Ballads of the Day* (1956), both of which were collections of successful singles, and *To Whom It May Concern* (1959) contain progressively sunnier paintings of Cole gazing approvingly, from a distance, at a couple in a clinch in a public park. The cover of *Nat King Cole Sings for Two in Love* (1953) shows said couple sans Cole, hands slyly meeting beneath the serviette with cocktails for two in a restaurant, Cole presumably being just beyond the frame of the painting, sitting at the piano. It's inevitably a white couple, but perhaps it was too much to expect Capitol to be any more "progressive," as they said at the time, than that in the Eisenhower era. Likewise, Sinatra is depicted in a similar fashion on the covers of his own classic Capitol albums of songs for young and/or swingin' lovers. Troubadours such as Cole and Sinatra were invariably instigators of love rather than participants in it.[45]

But singing on-screen was only the smallest part of Cole's involvement with the movies. Gradually, he was singing ever more movie themes for Capitol, such as "Lost April" and "A Portrait of Jennie." But it was "Mona Lisa" that established Cole's ability to make a hit out of a song that was barely even heard in the movie that introduced it. A few months after "Mona Lisa," Lou Busch brought Cole back to sing "Song of Delilah." This was the latest movie title theme with a lyric by the "Mona Lisa" team, Jay Livingston and Ray Evans, although this one (from Cecil B. DeMille's biblical epic, *Samson and Delilah*) boasted a melody by veteran Hollywood tunesmith Victor Young.

On "Delilah," Young's music evokes a classical theme, and the orchestration, by Heine Beau (an arranger and reed player who pops up all over the canons of Cole and Sinatra, usually anonymously), dips its toe into the waters of exotica first explored by Cole with Pete Rugolo (as in "Land of Love"). Everything about "Delilah" is intended to depict an exotic, forbidden love, from Costanzo's sensual percussion and the use of the lower registers of the strings as well as the deep bass clef of Cole's piano, which are effectively contrasted by high notes from Ashby's guitar—all of which paint a vivid picture of a belly dancer moving the lower half of her body. "Delilah" wasn't a chart hit for Cole, but no shortage of younger, black modern jazz musicians learned it from him, among them Clifford Brown, Blue Mitchell, and Bobby Hutcherson.

And that was only the beginning: about a year after "Delilah," Livingston and Evans returned to Cole with yet a third Paramount Pictures film theme, "The Ruby and the Pearl," from *Thunder in the East* (1952). This latest exotic adventure again starred Alan Ladd, this time in newly independent India, with the famous French actor Charles Boyer as the Hindu prime minister, proving that, in Hollywood, non-American nationalities are somewhat fluid. This time, the chart was conducted and perhaps actually arranged by Baxter, who aids Cole considerably in capturing the mood of Eastern mysticism.

Jay Livingston remembered that Paramount Pictures was at least trying, somewhat, to keep the overall mood authentic. "We went to play [the theme] for the director and the producer, and as I'm playing, I look up and there is an Indian standing in the doorway. I mean, from India, a big tall guy about six feet, wearing a white turban, standing with his arms folded, just staring at me. I realized he was a technical advisor, as they called them; he was the guy they would ask if they had any questions about India. So, they asked him about our song, 'What do you think of this?' He said, 'No, not for India. We would never compare our love to the ruby and the pearl.' And I was kind of upset. I said, 'Why not?' He said, 'Because it's too mundane, too worldly.' I asked, 'Well, what would you compare your love to?' And he said, 'The white orchids and the cockatoo.' "

Rubies, pearls, orchids, or cockatoos—just as "Nature Boy" sounds like it could be by Rumi, Jay and Ray wrote "Ruby and the Pearl" to sound like a leftover from *The Rubaiyat of Omar Khayyam*: "Can love be as warm as the Ruby? / Can love be as pure as the Pearl?" Cole again somehow transforms the whole enterprise, inauthentic though it may be, into something remarkably credible, which is why his version, though it only reached #25, scored considerably higher than Perry Como's RCA single. Como just isn't believable with this sort of text. As with "Delilah," Cole inspired multiple generations of modern jazzmen to take up the tune, most notably tenor saxophonists such as Wayne Shorter, Tina Brooks, and Branford Marsalis.

The Cole exotica film theme series climaxes in two epics, "Return to Paradise" (1953) and "Hajji Baba (Persian Lament)" (1954), both with melodies by the Ukrainian-born Hollywood composer Dimitri Tiomkin, lyrics by Ned Washington, and exquisite orchestrations by Nelson Riddle. "Return to Paradise" was a #15 hit for Cole, his closest competition being Percy Faith's orchestral version on Columbia (#19), and in comparing the two, it's hard to believe Faith came even that close. Faith's version (particularly the nearly seven-minute track on his album *Music from Hollywood*) is a big deep-sea snooze. Riddle, conversely, keeps everything popping, with unusual percussion, pan-American bongos, Middle Eastern cymbals, and highly arresting polytonal string writing.

Cole had competition on "The Ruby and the Pearl" and "Return to Paradise" (Shirley Horn, much later, on the second) but no one wanted to challenge him on "Hajji Baba (Persian Lament)." His vocal over the main titles is the only exceptional moment of the film, a 1954 "tits-and-sand" *Arabian Nights*-style epic, boasting, apart from Tiomkin and producer Walter Wanger, an otherwise all B-list crew and cast, starting with stars John Derek and Elaine Stewart. Both Cole and Riddle sound like they're trying to create the wildest and most outrageous Middle Eastern extravaganza yet, not only with classical woodwinds and a full contingent of percussion but also a mixed choir and a solo "air voice" (probably Loulie Jean Norman) singing behind Cole. Washington came up with the idea of chanting the words "Hajji Baba" over and over, like a mantra, until Cole sounds like a whirling dervish on a Persian rug in a Persian market flying somewhere over Istanbul (not Constantinople). The lyrics are yet another Hollywood approximation of Islamic poetry:

> *Deep in each soul, carefully hidden,*
> *There's a desire to be indiscreet.*
> *Hajji has said, "When love is forbidden,*
> *Love is so sweet; love is so sweet."*

And if all this weren't exciting enough, Riddle increases the stakes with a series of suspenseful modulations. Usually key changes are supposed to be subtle and imperceptible, barely noticeable, but the modulations in "Persian Lament" are so overt that they have the feeling of jump cuts in a Jean-Luc Goddard movie or even Doctor Who time-traveling. Surely, no other combination of talents, other than Tiomkin, Washington, Cole, and Riddle, could have pulled this off. As it stands, "Hajji Baba (Persian Lament)" may be way over the top and far from politically correct, by millennial standards, but you'll never get away with describing anything this well-crafted as "kitsch." The only thing to call it is quintessential pop music.

BUT IT WAS "MONA LISA" that literally opened up a whole world for Cole, and not because it was a movie song. Granted, it wasn't really Italian, but this song's overwhelming success launched Cole on an international campaign, which would be one of the distinguishing characteristics of the second half of his career. The 1950s and 1960s would be the international years of pop, and the two leaders of this movement would be a pair of African American entertainers who doubled as singer-instrumentalists and crossed over from jazz, Nat Cole and Louis Armstrong.

Virtually all of Armstrong's hits of the 1950s ("La Vie en Rose," "I Get Ideas," "Kiss of Fire," "The Faithful Hussar," "Mack the Knife," "Skokiaan," "The Dummy Song") originated outside the United States. Cole's foreign and/or exotic numbers, particularly in the years 1951 to 1954, tended to fall into two categories, genuine and ersatz, but these were by no means indicators of the quality of the material. Other foreign songs were somewhat less exotic—but hardly pedestrian—like the German "Answer Me, My Love" and the quasi-French "Darling, Je Vous Aime Beaucoup." Both were recorded in 1953 and feature Cole with a large mixed chorus and very dramatic but highly musical orchestrations of the kind we've come to expect from Nelson Riddle.

"Answer Me" was brought to Cole by Gillette. It had been written by Gerhard Winkler and Fred Rauch, and published in Hamburg, Federal Republic of Germany, 1952, under the title "Mutterlein"; the main phrase is often translated as "Answer Me, My Lord." The original English lyric, by Carl Sigman, began with the line, "Answer Me, Lord Above," and this version had been a big hit in the UK.[46] "There was a big record on it," Gillette remembered in 1977. "So I got with the publisher in New York and we went over the song and I said, 'You know, I'd love to record this with Nat Cole, but we just aren't going in that [religious] direction. Why don't you change the title of it, and rewrite a couple of lyrics? Instead of 'Answer me, oh Lord above,' make it 'Answer me, oh my love.' And he did. And we recorded it. And that was a million seller."[47]

The lyric change was slight but significant; it refocuses the text from the spiritual to the romantic by making it "Answer Me, My Love." This is another Cecil B. DeMille–like epic that Cole and Riddle made palatable, not only for themselves but for a subsequent generation of R&B stars, such as Etta James, Ray Peterson, and Clyde McPhatter (whose version is closely patterned after Cole's). Cole himself came back to the song in 1961, for the *Story* album, and again in the original German, as "Mutterlein," in 1964.

"Darling, Je Vous Aime Beaucoup" derives from the Wisconsin-born international supper club star, Hildegarde. The song had been written for her by Anna Sosenko, who served as manager, life partner, and, in this case, personal songwriter to the iconic entertainer. The singer and pianist first recorded it with a British band for the French market in 1935, and it was popular enough in France to be performed by local stars like gallic crooner Jean Sablon and guitar legend Django Reinhardt. "Darling" was a perfect song for Americans during World War II, thanks to Bing Crosby and Hildegarde herself, even as the Allies were gearing up to liberate Paris, but it didn't become a major hit until Cole and Riddle took it on in August 1953. The original 1935 Hildegarde version opens with a spoken intro by the pianist and singer, "This song is about an English boy who falls in love with a French girl. Of course, not knowing the language, he expresses himself like this." The lyrics are written in a combination of French and English; little by little the English boy gets his point across. The 1953 Cole-Riddle version doesn't use the verse at all—it doesn't need it—but there is a large chorus to help him drive the message home. Cole's version reached #7 in America (though surprisingly, not in the UK) and became a permanent part of his songbook—he uses it as the climactic number of his 1955 biopic, *The Nat King Cole Musical Story in Technicolor*.

Another huge hit, "Pretend" (#2 Pop, #10 R&B, #2 UK, 1953), was also featured prominently in the biopic, and as with "Answer Me," this time Cole himself had to negotiate for a specific set of lyrics to be written. The song was first popularized by the Italian-born trumpeter and bandleader Ralph Matererie, a key hitmaker in this international era, and Cole discovered it when he heard Matererie's disc on local radio. He immediately contacted the publisher in search of a set of lyrics but was told that Marterie had an exclusive on the song and no one else was allowed to record it. Lured by the prospect of bigger sales and convinced that a vocal version wouldn't compete with the instrumental record, the publisher finally relented and gave Cole both a set of lyrics and a green light.[48]

These were unusually rich and rewarding years for the team of Cole and Riddle. Though they would later create a string of memorable and classic albums together (*Nat King Cole Sings for Two in Love*, *The Piano Style of Nat King Cole*, *St. Louis Blues*, *To Whom It May Concern*, and *Wild Is Love*), the partnership would be best remembered for their hit singles; it seemed that for most of the 1950s, they were hardly ever off the charts. As Pete Rugolo pointed out, Riddle wasn't only a brilliant orchestrator from a purely artistic standpoint, but he had an innate commercial sense; between his work with Cole, Sinatra, and other singers, Nelson Riddle probably sold more singles and albums than any other musical director.

Yet the Cole-Riddle canon also included art songs. Cole never lost his passion for unearthing unusual offbeat numbers that didn't fit the ordinary profile of a hit or conform to any formula. There was always the likelihood that he might discover another "Nature Boy" or "Mona Lisa," but it was okay if he didn't; he basically sang these songs because he liked them, such as "Strange" and "Sweet William," both from 1952. The first was the result of an ongoing relationship with the songwriter Marvin Fisher, whose songs included some of the most "commercial" in Cole's canon, as well as some material obviously commissioned directly by the artist, such as the duets Fisher wrote with Roy Alfred for Cole to sing with Maria in 1950 and Dean Martin in 1954. Yet Fisher would also pen some of the most exquisite, artistically oriented numbers Cole ever sang: "For Once in Your Life," "It's the Sentimental Thing to Do," "When Sunny Gets Blue," and Cole's majestic, late-career torch song, "I Keep Going Back to Joe's." "Strange" benefited from a brilliant lyric by John LaTouche (librettist for *Cabin in the Sky* and *The Golden Apple*), a sumptuous arrangement by Riddle, and a typically high-class vocal by Cole. Indeed, Freddy Cole has consistently named "Strange" as his single favorite song by his older brother - which is hardly strange. "Sweet William," another highly unconventional art song (this one about love between anthropomorphic flowers), was the first song he would sing by composer Joe Sherman, who, both with and without his brother Noel, would write any number of significant songs for Cole in his last decade.

No fewer than four of Cole's most celebrated songs from this period originated in Mother England: "Red Sails in the Sunset" and "That's My Girl" (both 1951) and then "A Blossom Fell" and "Smile" (both 1954). "Smile" (#10 US, #2 UK) immediately became a key part of Cole's signature songbook. To this day, "Smile" is sung by artists who give all the credit to Charles Chaplin, the legendary comic-filmmaker-cultural icon and occasional composer. However, it's sometimes bruited about that the melody was inspired by a strain from Puccini's *Tosca*, and it's also quite possible that film composer David Raksin (best known for "Laura") deserves at least some of the credit for the original tune. That key part of the melody is first heard on the soundtrack of Chaplin's 1936 classic *Modern Times*, on which the young Raksin served as an orchestrator.[49]

But much of the credit for the final song should go to a pair of British songwriters, James John Turner Phillips (credited as "John Turner") and Geoffrey Parsons. The team specialized in English language adaptations of foreign numbers, and a month after "Smile," Cole recorded "United," a Turner-Parsons treatment of an Italian song. With "Smile," the two did more than put words to a 1936 film theme; when you listen to the ending of *Modern Times*, you'll hear that perhaps ten bars, at most, of the score (whether it was by Chaplin or Raksin) turned up in the song "Smile." The bulk of the tune and all of the lyrics were added fifteen years later by Turner and Parsons, who had the good sense to use Chaplin's line "What's the use of crying?" from the film (actually "trying" in *Modern Times*).

After Cole's death, "Smile" was revived most successfully by Tony Bennett in tribute to both Chaplin and Cole, and later still by dozens of singers and pop stars including Michael Jackson. Despite the contributions of others (real or speculated), we all like to think of "Smile" as Charlie Chaplin's song. Ironically, that's because Turner and Parsons did such a great job of capturing Chaplin's spirit in the lyrics, and Cole and Riddle further distilled and consolidated that spirit. We're all drawn to the idea of a great clown as a master tragedian, and one of the reasons we think of Chaplin as a greater artist than, say, Buster Keaton is because pathos is a no less important element of Chaplin's work. "Smile" ingeniously plays into that aesthetic, and it derives its power from the way the words deliberately work against, rather than with, the tune: the words are telling us to smile, but the music is maneuvering us to do precisely the opposite. It's a wonderfully complex kettle of emotions to instill into a basic 32-bar ABAB form.[50] Here's a very melancholy song about the act of smiling.

"Smile" was one of the songs that revealed Cole's increasing maturity and emotional range, with its combination of bittersweet, major-minor melody, and optimistic lyrics—it's the kind of song that Cole couldn't have sung ten years earlier, and indeed, it's hard to think of another popular singer who could have made such a success out of it in 1954. Yet, like "Unforgettable," "Smile" was to become even more permanently attached to him in later generations. In hearing either the 1954 original or the 1961 stereo remake today, it's hard not to think about how Cole, in spite of struggles with institutionalized racism that left other men cold and bitter, was still able to light up our collective face with gladness, and how he continues to do so, even after his tragically early death. In that sense, both Cole and Chaplin have become imbued with that exquisite happy-sad quality that is so much a part of what has become a classic song.

WHERE RUGOLO MOST SUCCESSFULLY captured Cole's modernistic side and Riddle his exotic (and overtly commercial) side, his work with Billy May brought out other aspects of his musical personality: bluesy, sexy, funny. At the time of their first session together they had already known each other for twelve years and written a song together, the cheeky novelty "Ooh, Kickeroonie." In 1951, May was not regarded as an accompanist, like Riddle, but a co-star, like Stan Kenton. After Carlos Gastel had parted company with Kenton, he began talking to May, a longtime personal friend, about taking a band of his own out on the road. "Oh, Carlos was a promoter," as May described the canny Honduran;[51] "you know, he was always looking out to make a buck." May said this admiringly and not as any kind of a criticism—nothing wrong with making a buck. He and Carlos were drinking buddies and once even swapped wives—permanently.[52]

It was Gastel's idea to team Cole with May, and the song that they started with was selected by Maria—she later said it was the only time she ever suggested a song to her husband. "Walkin' My Baby Back Home" was an early Depression number from 1930 (written by Fred Turk and Roy Ahlert, composers of "Mean to Me" and Bing Crosby's theme, the waltz "Where the Blue of the Night (Meets the Gold of the Day)"), and twenty-one years later, Maria happened to stumble across it on her aunt's player piano. But Cole was undoubtedly familiar with Louis Armstrong's 1931 recording, and the song had been widely recorded by other leading entertainers and dance bands in that year. Small wonder: during the Depression, nightclubs, ballrooms, and even movies were too expensive for young couples, and suddenly walking became the primary dating option—a few months later Harry Warren followed suit with "Would You Like to Take a Walk?"

Unlike many of the subsequent songs recorded by Cole with May, there's no blues content in "Walkin' My Baby" except for the sound of the band itself, replete with the arranger's sonic signature, the "slurping saxophones" as they were called—wherein the whole of the reed section would play a distinctive glissando à la Johnny Hodges or Willie Smith, going from one note to another while hitting all the microtones and blue notes in between. Here, the lead alto part is played by one of May's favorites (along with Smith), Arthur "Skeets" Herfurt.

"Walkin' My Baby" was 1951's answer to the previous year's "Orange Colored Sky," combining Cole with a famous Capitol Records bandleader, and it was nearly as successful, reaching #8 on the mainstream pop chart. Cole phrases swingingly on the beat, surrounded by May's bright brass and moaning reeds, those idiosyncratic touches that listeners had already begun to recognize from May's instrumental dance records. Cole took a forgotten song and made it into a new standard; soon the histrionic R&B shouter Johnny Ray would also land a hit with it and Universal would make a movie with that title (starring the power trio of Donald O'Connor, Janet Leigh, and Buddy Hackett) in 1953.

Cole sounds at once cheerful and innocent—if he's intent on any boudoir action, he doesn't let on—having first encountered his baby in the *flash, bam, alakazam* of an orange-colored sky, now all he wants to do is walk her back home. In retrospect, the song—and the Cole-May performance in particular—seems a perfect symbol of the sexually repressed '50s (more so than the pre-code early '30s): Cole's expressive vocal is a model of cool machismo, while May's libidinous saxes and orgasmic brass better convey what's transpiring below the surface. By their very partnership, Cole and May have presented a perfect picture of *naïveté* laced with licentiousness.

The other three tunes on the date were all new novelties and likely hits. "What Does It Take" was another charmer by Burke and Van Heusen with a Lester Young–inspired tenor solo by Ted Nash. Another ambulatory number, "Walkin'," was really the blues, in traditional 12-bar form, written by Mary Lou Williams, featuring a prominent piano part played by Jimmy Rowles and bluesy guitar from Barney Kessel. "I'm Hurtin'" feels like a country and western song, blues'ed up and polished by Cole and May.

In 1953 and '54, Cole and May re-teamed for five more tracks (as well as the two duets with Dean Martin, which were actually arranged by Riddle): "Angel Eyes," "Lover Come Back to Me," "Can't I?" "Papa Loves Mambo," and "Teach Me Tonight"; all rank as exemplary examples of pop music at its zenith. "Angel Eyes," from the 1953 film *Jennifer*, amounts to the most significant love theme from a *film noir* since "Laura": Cole's singing is oblique and full of mystery; May's chart is at once brash and steamy. It's of a piece with other noir-ish film songs like "Blue Gardenia" and "My Flaming Heart." When Matt Dennis wrote "Angel Eyes," the first singer he gave it to was Ella Fitzgerald, and later Sinatra made it his own, but Cole's record is clearly the one that put the song on the map.

"Can't I?" and "Teach Me Tonight" bring our two protagonists back into the realm of the sultry and seductive. "Can't I?" had been written by the R&B-oriented pianist-bandleader-songwriter Leroy Lovett, and Cole had originally attempted it in a session directed by Dave Cavanaugh, Capitol's jack-of-all-trades. Several months later, Cole decided that the tune really needed Billy May's by-now-patented reed section sound, so he commissioned May to write his own arrangement of "Can't I?" Those stylishly-slurping saxes, led by Willie Smith, are all over the place here, playing a distinctive countermelody that's at least as memorable as the central tune. Cole and Dinah Washington made "Teach Me Tonight" into an R&B standard in October and November 1954, and Cole's voice captures perfectly the sensual, soulful mood.[53] Anchoring the whole thing with Chuck Gentry's booming baritone sax, May divides up the bridge in the instrumental interlude between piercing brass and slurping saxes, as if to insinuate that the two sections are slow-dancing together.

Formerly a rather dignified lady, the operetta ballad "Lover, Come Back to Me" (from *The New Moon*, 1928) is transformed into a real swinging chick in the hands of Cole and May. The two outfit her with bongo drums, Willie Smith's hot alto saxophone, and the expert thumping of Ralph Pena, May's personal favorite bassist. Even the vocal chorus—entering on the word "no!" near the end—swings heavily. May's ensemble plays boppish variations that could have had their origins as a great improvised solo. Billy later told me a story that's almost too good to be true—that the singers, known as the Encores, were in the studio for another (non-Cole) project and he and Nat decided spontaneously to work them into the arrangement. However they happened to be there, they contribute much to the swinging presence.

Finally, for Cole and May in this period, "Papa Loves Mambo" is a gonzo masterpiece, fully on a par with such extreme mock-exotica as "Hajji Baba (Persian Lament)." Every time there was a new dance or musical trend, from the waltz and mazurka to the twist (even to "My Baby Likes to Bebop"), Tin Pan Alley was ready to take advantage of it, and Al Hoffman and Dick Manning were just the guys to do it—these were the songwriters responsible for "Takes Two to Tango," "Hawaii Swings," "Honolulu Rock & Roll," "Pa-Pa Ma-Ma Cha-Cha," and many others of that ilk. A hit for Perry Como and also recorded by Xavier Cugat and Johnny Ray, "Papa Loves Mambo," which takes its title from the 1923 "Mama Loves Papa," would have been just a simple harmless, one-joke gag number.

But, as with so many songs throughout his career, Cole and his collaborator elevate this simple novelty into something transcendently brilliant, by dint of Cole's rhythmic acumen and sheer class, and May's imaginative arrangement. Neither Cole nor May is the least daunted at the challenge of working in this entirely new musical idiom. (A few years earlier, in the dawning of the mambo craze, Capitol released a series of hot Latin dance discs by a group identified only as the "Rico Mambo Orchestra"; ultimately, Mr. "Rico Mambo" himself turned out to be Billy May.)

"Papa Loves Mambo" isn't at all authentic, but that doesn't matter in the least—it's ballsy and full of chutzpah, and impossible to resist. This is what American pop does best; anyone who bought the record would have found himself playing it over and over, at least ten times in a row.

"WHEN THERE ARE CLOUDS in the sky," as Cole sang in "Smile," "you'll get by." Those clouds were increasingly gathering around the Coles in the early 1950s, as Nat and Maria gradually settled into a hostile new neighborhood, now with two little girls who were potentially at risk from neighbors firing shots into their windows. These were also the years of Cole's widely publicized troubles with the Internal Revenue Service.

Perhaps even more painfully, just as he was emerging from the skirmish with the IRS, as we shall soon see, Cole was temporarily put out of commission by bleeding ulcers, which prevented him from working for much of that spring.[54]

Yet these were years of incredible achievements: quite possibly more Cole signature songs come from this period than any other. In the first half of the 1950s, Cole recorded a total of approximately 150 different commercial masters for Capitol (that number includes many songs like "Who's Who" which were first issued after his death), and thirty-three of these became genuine hits, or more than one in five, whether on the *Billboard* American pop chart, the R&B listing, the UK chart, or, most often, some combination of all three.

On December 17, 1953, Capitol Records decided to honor their top-selling artist with a gala party celebrating his tenth anniversary on the label; according to the company's own information, he had sold a total of fifteen million singles (as well as five million albums). That came out to $2.5 million dollars' worth of business per year, of which the artist himself took home roughly 10 percent, or $250,000.[55] "One of the mainstays of the Capitol label, Cole's record of achievement is one that few artists attain." *Billboard* wrote, "Since 1944, when his first records were released, Cole has managed to come up with at least one big hit in each of his 10 years on Capitol." The label took out an ad with Cole's picture, listing at least one blockbuster hit for each year. Of the ten biggest-selling records in the relatively short history of Capitol, four were by Cole. "He is our most consistent solo artist, among perhaps twenty we have under contract," said Glenn Wallichs. "All the publishers offer us a tune for him first, because they know if Cole sings it, they have an eighty to twenty chance of having a hit."[56]

There's every reason to believe that Sinatra was present at that party, raising a glass of Jack Daniels to toast his friend's success. By the time Wallichs issued that statement, that list of "perhaps 20" artists under contract to Capitol Records now included Sinatra, who had done his first sessions for the label in April 1953. Sinatra would never catch up with Cole in terms of sheer sales volume, especially with regard to singles—such was probably not even his ambition. Sinatra was a fiercely competitive man, but he was smart enough to realize that trying to consistently out-sell Cole would have been a fool's errand.

With the success of Sinatra on Capitol Records, aided equally by his Oscar-winning performance in *From Here to Eternity* as well as his own partnership with Nelson Riddle, Capitol realized that they had both of the industry leaders in the pop music field on their roster. It was inevitable that they would try to put the two icons together on a session. Naturally, Riddle was chosen to write the charts, and he was commissioned to write duet arrangements of four songs for Cole and Sinatra: two old-timers "Ain't She Sweet" and "Long, Long Ago," and two new songs: "What to Do," and "Open Up the Doghouse."[57]

The date was planned for Wednesday, February 3, 1954. But it didn't happen. Cole arranged for the session to start at 4:00 p.m. so that his daughters could come after school—this was probably also part of birthday festivities for Sweetie, who was just about to turn four. Then, at some point, it was decided that Cole would sing two sides with the little girls on this date, and that he and Sinatra would try again in the fall. The February sides, "Ain't She Sweet" and "What to Do," are two of the most charming recordings of Cole's entire career: the two girls are just plain adorable and his love for them is more than palpable.[58]

Then, in September, Cole would record "Long, Long Ago" (an Eisenhower-era update of a traditional English song, circa 1833) and "Open Up the Doghouse" (both credited to Roy Alfred and Marvin Fisher) as duets with Dean Martin rather than Sinatra. These are fun and goofy numbers with lots of one-liners and are just as much of a hoot as his earlier teamings with Johnny Mercer, Nellie Lutcher, and Woody Herman. If it was decided that these tracks wouldn't work with Sinatra, they were probably correct—try as I may, I can't imagine Sinatra's voice in place of Martin's on these.

Cole and Sinatra had sung "Exactly Like You" together convincingly on Sinatra's radio show in 1946, but for Nat and Frank to get together in the studio, they would have to wait for the perfect opportunity to come up with something extra special—that's the way Sinatra did a few years later with another of his peers, Bing Crosby, on Cole Porter's "Well, Did You Evah?"[59] A Sinatra-Cole duet was nothing to knock off casually, unlike the Dino duos. It would have taken forethought and preparation—or else why do it? And these years were just too busy for either man to take the time to do it right. (There also was something of a contretemps between Cole's right-hand man, Dick LaPalm, and Hank Sanicola, who ran Sinatra's publishing interests and apparently demanded a piece of the publishing action for himself.)

To what extent were Sinatra and Cole competitive? They each made a point of telling everyone what dopes they were to miss out on each other's hits. On his 1969 *Man and His Music* TV special, Sinatra loudly declaims that when the composer of "Nature Boy" presented the song to him, his response was, "I told that guy with the toga and the whiskers to get out!"

Music publisher Tommy Valando[60] told me a similar saga of how Cole missed the boat on "Young at Heart." Yet there's no way "Nature Boy" would have been a hit for Sinatra, and while I have a hard time believing Cole would have failed to recognize what a great song "Young at Heart" was, no other artist could have done for it what Sinatra did—it was the perfect vehicle to launch the greatest comeback in all of American popular culture. Still, after Sinatra's single hit the charts, the next time Cole encountered Valando, he turned around, bent over, and instructed him thusly: "Go ahead! Kick me in the ass!"

IN JANUARY 1953, while "The Voice" was still wandering in the wilderness—his own "Last Temptation of St. Francis" period—Nat and Nelson entered the studio together and strolled into Sinatra's eminent domain. In 1945, Sinatra had created the first modern pop concept album, titled *The Voice*, and while Cole had released seven original albums by 1952 (starting with *The King Cole Trio* in 1944), he had yet to do one that reflected his new identity as a popular vocalist. So, on January 27 and 28, 1953, working with Riddle, Cole taped his first album of vocal standards with orchestra, and though Sinatra was an obvious precedent, even he had not yet done quite so ambitious a project, with such a large orchestra.

This album was originally set to be titled *Love Is Here to Stay,*[61] although it would be released a few months later in 1953 as *Nat King Cole Sings for Two in Love*. With it, Cole would underscore what Sinatra had first brought forth in 1945: the artistic and commercial viability of a collection of familiar standard songs, rendered by a single vocalist and orchestrator, set in a similar mood and tempo, moving seamlessly from track to track, and imbuing the proceedings with a sense of narrative—not necessarily a linear story with a beginning, middle, and end, but a vague sense that all the songs could be describing the same relationship, the same boy in love with the same girl. The eight songs paint a fascinating and gloriously idealized picture of the perfect love affair, featuring Riddle's most mature arrangements yet and some of the most compelling singing of Cole's career.

We open with the original title song for the album, the Gershwin Brothers standard "Love Is Here to Stay," a note that might seem a better note to end on—the same way the song concluded George Gershwin's career. Yet Cole starts with this note of permanence, establishing the basic theme, and then setting off into different variations on that idea.

"A Handful of Stars" had originated as a warm-up phase that Ted Shapiro, best known as Sophie Tucker's musical director (and composer of "If I Had

You"), would use to start rehearsals. Songwriter Jack Lawrence wrote the lyrics, but thus far, Glenn Miller had been the only notable artist to take up its cause. Both Shapiro's celestial melody and Lawrence's lyrics inspired Riddle to create a shimmering sonic starscape, a beautiful backdrop for Cole's otherworldly baritone. Rodgers and Hart's "This Can't Be Love" (from *The Boys from Syracuse*) is the first of several upbeat numbers, a testament to Cole's perfect timing as well as his skills as a lyric interpreter: note those compelling pauses, especially in the first chorus, that allow him to bring out the greater meaning of the text just by stopping and starting. "There Goes My Heart" and "A Little Street Where Old Friends Meet," from 1934 and 1932, respectively, further testify to Cole's knowledge of the Great American Songbook and his skills as a tune detective with the ability to find the absolutely most perfect song for his voice.[62]

The B side of the original 10" album opens with the only two downer notes in the set, "There Goes My Heart" ("There goes my happiness, it couldn't be / There goes somebody else in place of me") and "Dinner for One, Please James," a rare song with a melody that begins on a sharp tonic note. The latter is a rather British, stiff-upper-lip tale of love, loss, and what to tell the servants, from 1935, in the same vein (if not quite as melodramatic) as Cole Porter's "Miss Otis Regrets." Cole learned it through a singer whom he had loved in his youth. On a 1954 radio program, he introduces "Dinner for One" as follows: "Nelson Riddle is the conductor of the orchestra and the song is one that goes back a good many years, way back to the days when Ray Noble and His Orchestra were first attracting attention in the United States. He had a wonderful singer in his orchestra at that time, a talented young South African lad named Al Bowlly. I've never forgotten him, and how he sang the song that I'm about to attempt now. Alright, Nels, in memory of the late Al Bowlly."[63]

We end on a more positive note with another up-tempo, "Almost Like Being in Love" and then especially with "Tenderly." The first is essentially Cole's arrangement, which he had been doing with the Trio since 1948, when the song was still being heard in *Brigadoon* on Broadway. Riddle used the Trio version (which has been issued on CD courtesy of a 1950 radio transcription) as a foundation on which he built a sturdy structure of brass and reeds. "Tenderly," the one standard of note by studio pianist Walter Gross, boasts another lyric by Jack Lawrence. "Tenderly" is notable as the first Cole classic to originate on an album rather than a single. It captures perfectly the intended mood of the album, two in a permanent state of love, not the beginning of love, not the end of it (except for those two tracks), but ongoing, romantic love, both a Sunday kind of love and a forever one. Cole and Riddle treat "Tenderly" like another one of his tone poems, with the feeling more of an art song or *lied* and a somewhat Chopinesque piano passage—rather than just another 32-bar pop song.

Remember that Capitol Records reported that by the end of 1953, Cole had sold half a million albums altogether. He had only made seven albums, and sales of 70,000 per album would not be impressive numbers say, by the standards of the 1960s, but remember that this is the age when long-playing technology was brand new and very pricey, and hardly anybody had it. It was at this point, as Mitch Miller of Columbia Records told me, that he was loath to let Tony Bennett or Rosemary Clooney make albums because practically no one could play them. These sales figures indicate that just about everybody who owned an LP turntable owned a copy of at least one of Cole's albums.

When the 12" technology was perfected and popularized two years later, Capitol re-released *Nat King Cole Sings for Two in Love* and expanded it to 12" length by adding four more songs. "Let's Fall in Love" and "There Will Never Be Another You" are especially suitable (in that the latter features Cole himself on piano), although it was a mistake to put anything after "Tenderly," which was a perfect closer. To my ears at least, the very famous French chanson, "Autumn Leaves" never quite fit; it's much too sad, especially in Riddle's very beautiful arrangement, which makes the whole enterprise sound rather like a Bach fugue. Beautiful indeed, but too much of a downer for this particular album and better suited to the concert hall rather than the boudoir. However, Pete Rugolo's 1952 arrangement of "You Stepped Out of a Dream" is absolutely marvelous, and like all Riddle's best work, it's modish and harmonically ingenious without distracting from the narrative or the star singer. It captures the mood perfectly and compliments the rest of the album.

Some of the 1955 additives are worthwhile, but they're all ultimately unnecessary—the eight-song, 1953 edition was perfect unto itself, and a major step forward for Nat King Cole, the singer of love songs and ballads. *Nat King Cole Sings for Two in Love* was, in fact, on a par with the best of Sinatra, and quite possibly the greatest pop vocal album that had yet been made.[64]

JUST ABOUT THE TIME that *Two in Love* was being recorded, Cole set forth on his major tour of the year, the 1953 "Big Show" package, sometimes billed as "The Biggest Show." The 1951 and the 1952 tours had been highly successful and helped to ease the transition from Trio to solo, but his participation in the 1953 edition would be curtailed by a near-fatal illness.

Not that the tours always ran smoothly. The 1953 tour started in Oakland, California, and was a truly integrated package, combining Stan Kenton and

His Orchestra with explosive singer-comedienne Betty Hutton, plus Nat King Cole, billed as a single, and Louis Jordan's Tympany Five.[65] As Kenton's lead trumpeter, Buddy Childers, later told John Pizzarelli, it was Cole's tradition to travel in a car, ahead of the band, who were on the band bus. They were playing through Texas when it was arranged for the rest of the tour to meet Nat and his group at a certain diner. When the bus pulled in, the band, were surprised to see Nat and company in the parking lot, eating a meal off the hood of their car. Stan went inside to complain about this treatment, where he noticed the restaurant had a jukebox, and virtually every record therein was by the King Cole Trio. He pointed this out to Nat, who answered, "That's the only reason that they even allowed us to order take-out." In other words, an "ordinary" Negro wouldn't have even been allowed to buy food and leave. Childers remembered distinctly that it was mostly the white Kentonites who were incensed; Cole acted like he was accustomed to it—it was just business as usual.

By April, Kenton had left the tour to be replaced by Billy May's Orchestra, and it was on the fifth of that month, Easter Sunday, which was also Nat's fifth wedding anniversary, when the trouble started. Cole was scheduled to do two shows at Carnegie Hall with Sarah Vaughan and Billy May, but his ulcers suddenly started bleeding. Somehow, he got through the first show, but just as he was preparing to go out for the second, he had to be rushed to the hospital instead.

In their review, *Down Beat*[66] noted that Vaughan filled in by singing an extra set. "Her pianist having already left"—this was, as noted, the second show, and the hour was getting late—"she sat at the piano and accompanied herself and went off to a great hand." Trombonist Dick Nash, who was then part of May's brass section, remembered that date vividly. According to Nash, "Sarah did her own thing just before that intermission, and then of course, Nat was the headliner, but he had an attack of ulcers. Then Sarah said, 'I'll do Nat's act!' Sarah sat down at the piano, sideways the way he did, and did his whole act, exactly note for note!"[67] Cole would be laid up for most of the spring; his next known appearance was at the Tiffany Club—his favorite, low-key regular joint close to home in Los Angeles—on June 7. He didn't return to the recording studio until August.

After the illness, Cole was back up to speed for most of the summer and fall of 1953, but as 1954 dawned, he wanted to do something special, possibly to make up for lost time: his first international touring since 1950. He spent much of spring 1954, from mid-March to mid-May, in Europe. The international tours of 1954 were nothing short of a triumph, even more so than his first trip overseas four years earlier.

This second European trip was so overwhelmingly successful that he started 1955, the second half of the decade, in Australia and New Zealand, and then played Honolulu on the way back. Cole was especially flabbergasted by his reception in Whenuapai: fully five thousand "well-wishers" and "welcomers" had mobbed the airport even before he landed. This was the kind of crowd that Sinatra had drawn at the Paramount theater a decade earlier, or that Elvis Presley would attract in his first golden period of fame. It was all the more special to Cole, because, unlike Sinatra or Presley, he was receiving this kind of mass adulation not at the beginning of his career, as if he were merely some exciting but possibly short-lived novelty phenomenon, but in the middle. This audience was the result of his paying his dues and making the right moves over a professional career that was already twenty years old by 1954–55. And yet it was only the beginning, a mere warm-up for what was to follow. At thirty-five, Nat King Cole was just getting started.

7

Assault on a King

1955–1956

I can't stand to see white people applauding a Negro. This is the time to fight. I'm plenty mad. There's going to be another day.
—WILLIE RICHARD VINSON (of Anniston, *Alabama). One of the four men convicted of attacking Nat King Cole on the stage of the Birmingham Municipal Auditorium on Tuesday, April 10, 1956*

ONE DAY IN THE MID-1950S, Nelson Riddle and his youngest son, Christopher (born in 1950 and thus the same age as Sweetie), were visiting Nat and Maria and family at their home on South Muirfield when they heard a crashing noise coming from outside. It appears that someone—possibly, but not necessarily, a neighbor—had done a hit-and-run job on one of the Coles' cars, driving right into it and inflicting as much damage as they could in a few seconds, then beating it before they could be seen. The Riddles were furious, but Nat acted like this was an everyday occurrence; clearly, he had long been desensitized to these petty, dehumanizing acts of anonymous violence. Nelson and Chris wanted to call the police, but Nat and Maria told them not to bother. In this world, you have to pick your battles, and this wasn't much compared to being shot at in 1948 or, as we shall see, being attacked on stage in 1956. This was just routine, everyday vandalism, and thus hardly worth bothering about. There was a lot more at stake than a car here, or even a house.[1]

BY 1955, NAT KING COLE was by far the most famous African American in the world, and, simultaneously, the single dominant figure in popular music, with more hits on the charts than anyone, outpacing even Sinatra (who was boosted by his film career) and Perry Como (ditto his long-running TV series).[2] He was also the most visible family man in American popular (or at least musical) culture. Partly thanks to Maria's vision of reinventing her husband from Central Avenue hipster to upper middle-class dad, they were constantly profiled far beyond the reaches of the music trade publications or the black press. The mainstream media was flooded with images of the Coles as a perfect family, a handsome star and his beautiful wife with their two adorable girls, living in a mansion in a respectable neighborhood. Not for nothing did Natalie describe her family as "the black Kennedys."

An April 1954 profile in the *New York Sunday News* was typical. Nat is quoted as saying, "'Cookie is taking dancing and ice-skating lessons. Little Natalie is a real ham, wants to do everything Cookie does, so she's taking dancing lessons too. Cookie goes to the neighborhood public school, and lately the older kids have been asking her for pictures of me. She knows I'm in show business, but she can't quite figure out why they want my picture. Love those kids,' Nat grins."[3] Three months later, there was an even more visible profile in an extensive article in the *Saturday Evening Post*, which described Cole as a "$12,000-a-Week Preacher's Boy."[4] These were just a few of the many stories depicting the four Coles as a supremely happy family in a hundred-thousand dollar home, who just happened to be a black family in a white neighborhood.

The most impressive of these was broadcast on November 1, 1957, when Nat became one of the very few black entertainers to be interviewed, in his Hancock Park home, by Edward R. Murrow on CBS TV's widely popular *Person to Person*. They start in the living room, where the Coles are listening to a "late release," Nat's recent album *Love Is the Thing*, and gradually travel throught the house. Throughout, Murrow addresses Maria as "Mrs. Cole," treating her no less respectfully than the wife of any white celebrity. It seems hard to believe that this was barely a generation after it was still considered acceptable for white movie stars to appear in blackface and less than a decade since Hancock Park residents did everything but burn a cross on the Coles' front lawn.

None of these points, as you'd expect, is discussed with Murrow. Instead, Maria describes their furnishings in copious detail for the benefit of the monochrome broadcast, from the pink-and-lavender living room, to the pink-and-white color scheme of the bedroom, and the TV sets they had installed in former fireplaces. Nat, for his part, talks about his ongoing NBC TV series and his forthcoming film, *St. Louis Blues*. The interview and tour winds up in Natalie's room, and, as if the two girls, Cookie, thirteen, and Sweetie, seven, aren't adorable enough, the four Coles are shown doting on a litter of month-old boxer puppies.

As we've seen, Nat and Maria had already appeared together on other TV shows, like *Star of the Family* (1951) and Ed Sullivan's *Toast of the Town* (1955).

This was all part of Maria's vision, to reinvent her husband and reposition him into the absolute epicenter of middle-class American culture in the age of the nuclear family. Cole's appeal transcended and encompassed all races (white, black, and, soon enough, the entire Spanish-speaking world). He was the successor to Bing Crosby, in terms of what Crosby had represented during the Depression and war—much more than Sinatra, who at this time exemplified a very different societal role, that of the swinging bachelor, or Elvis, who was perceived, incorrectly it turned out, to be rebelling against those very bourgeoisie values that Cole had come to represent.

This was why it was so vital that they buy the house in Hancock Park and why they had to hold onto it, despite the harassment from the neighbors and then the IRS. The Hancock Park home was worth many times what they paid for it in terms of what it did for Nat's image. In the *Person to Person* interview, Murrow informs us that there's something of a cultural generation gap in the Cole household, which was simultaneously occurring in millions of households across the forty-eight states. When Cookie tells Mr. Murrow that kids her age would rather listen to rock 'n' roll than anything else, millions of parents nodded their heads and said to themselves, "Oh, that's just like my kids." By the end of the twelve-minute interview, Nat and Maria were no longer black people. They were just people.

This was another reason Nat insisted over and over (he does so again to Murrow) that all his success was pure good luck: there was nothing special about him. Rather, he was the most ordinary guy in the world. You can read between the lines in all of these interviews with Nat and Maria: "Look at us," they are saying. "We are not exotic. We are not *other*. We are *you*."

It was a powerful message that was profoundly underappreciated in its day, at a time when the younger factions of the civil rights movement began to criticize Cole for not taking a more militant stance with regard to civil rights, and especially for continuing to appear before segregated audiences. Yet Nat King Cole did indeed pose a serious threat to the established order of segregation; but this, ironically, was most keenly appreciated and understood by the other side, the most extreme segregationists and white supremacists themselves. His success was bound to be resented by some of the less-intelligent, less-educated sectors of the country, most unfortunately by a terrorist organization, based, again ironically, in Nat's own home state. Their attitude was, "How dare he live the American dream better than we do?" He had already faced the wrath of his Hancock Park neighbors and survived an assassination attempt by one of them, as well as what many believed was racially motivated persecution from a major federal agency. Yet the most frightening challenge was about to come.

AS WITH THE REST OF COLE'S CAREER, the mid-1950s are another period of constant evolution, experimentation, and transition. These years were the high point of his decade-long relationship with Nelson Riddle and also the first period of his great albums, in which he crafted long-playing masterpieces with such brilliant collaborators as Billy May and Gordon Jenkins (not to mention Dave Cavanaugh, and the orchestras of Armando Romeu Jr. and Count Basie), in addition to Riddle, then his "main man." These are the years of his total ascendancy to the pinnacle of pop music as well as producing, at the same time, four transcendent jazz albums: *The Piano Style of Nat King Cole* (1955), *After Midnight* (1956), *Just One of Those Things* (1957), and *St. Louis Blues* (1958). He was still turning out successful singles and regularly averaging about ten chart hits per year, but most of his signature songs from the second half of the 1950s were introduced on albums rather than singles, such as "Stardust," "When I Fall in Love," and "For All We Know." This was also the period when he went up against—and ultimately made his peace with—the new, youth-directed form of popular music known then known as rock 'n' roll .

The musical marriage between Nat and Nelson was a committed one, though hardly exclusively monogamous. In many ways, the absolute pinnacle was the 1953 (and 1955) album *Nat King Cole Sings for Two in Love*; out of Cole's determination not to repeat himself, the team would never again make a "straight down the middle" album of vocal standards, although there was their highly swinging set of piano instrumentals with orchestra (*Piano Style*, 1955), a very specialized and brilliant set of blues classics (*St. Louis Blues*, 1958), an album of mostly brand-new songs by a wide range of composers (*To Whom It May Concern*, 1958), and last, their remarkable all-original song-cycle/suite/concept album, *Wild Is Love* (1960). And there were also dozens if not hundreds of singles. At the same time, Cole was also doing albums with May, Jenkins, and Cavanaugh, even while Riddle was also working not only with Sinatra but also on occasional projects with Judy Garland, Keely Smith, Ella Fitzgerald, and others.

In a radio interview not long after Cole's passing, Riddle was asked about the differences between working with Cole and Sinatra. "I think the personalities of the people involved were key. I know that as Sinatra's albums came out, a couple of the boys in Nat Cole's group [specifically drummer Lee Young] came to me and said, 'How come you don't write for Nat the way you write for

Frank? I think he'd love it.' I said, 'I don't think he would. I think he's a simpler, less complicated person, and I feel that what I'm writing for Nat is right for Nat, and what I'm doing for Frank is right for him. I just became aware of the person and tried to match what I felt was their characteristic. That's all."[5]

It's a fascinating opinion from the single greatest orchestrator of popular music. Granted, Sinatra was a hugely complex personality, but Cole too had more levels than he let on; his musical character not only incorporated his personal journey, from jazz pianist to pop crooner, but also his intricate, storied relationship with his times. If the background noise of Sinatra's career is the marriages, the mob, the Kennedys, and the tumultuous personal life, the leitmotifs of Cole's music are the civil rights movement and the often precarious balance of artistic excellence and mass popularity. But the best of what Riddle wrote for Cole, in particular Cole Porter's "I Am in Love" and all of the *Two in Love* and *St. Louis Blues* albums (to name just a few examples), could hardly be described as "simpler" or "less complicated."

COLE BEGAN 1955 ON THE ROAD in the South Pacific, where, as we have seen, he toured Australia and then played through Hawaii on the way back. He wasn't home for long when he headed for Las Vegas in early February, to play his first of many high-profile engagements at the Sands Hotel; along with the Chez Paree in Chicago and the Copacabana in New York, this was one of his three most prominent homes-away-from-home (he mentions all three to Murrow in 1957). Sinatra was already a part owner at the Sands, but Cole would be, over the next ten years, the highest-paid entertainer yet to appear at this "Place in the Sun."

That was the good news. The bad news was that Nat had to cut the Sands engagement a few days short, in order to rush to Chicago to be at the bedside of his mother, who was dying of cancer. She passed a few weeks before Nat's thirty-sixth birthday on February 23, 1955.

Back home in Los Angeles, Nat and Nelson did several important concerts together at the Shrine Auditorium and the UCLA campus. But, surprisingly, his first big project of the year was not an album or a singles session but a movie. This was Cole's fourth featurette for Universal International, *The Nat King Cole Musical Story*, released in 1955. The previous three UI films had all been revue-style musicals set on a nightclub stage, and the most recent, the 1953 short with Russ Morgan's orchestra, was produced in 3D. The 1955 release was much more ambitious, a seventeen-minute biopic released in Cinemascope and Technicolor.

Over the years, Universal had seemed determined to keep the big-band era alive, not only with its ongoing two-reelers but also with highly successful features like *The Glenn Miller Story* (1954) and *The Benny Goodman Story* (1955). Unlike Goodman or the late Miller, Cole was still at the height of his career, and the main point was to include as much footage as possible of Cole singing his best-known signature songs and hits—from "Sweet Lorraine" and "Straighten Up and Fly Right" to "Pretend" and "Darling, Je Vous Aime Beaucoup." So director Will Cowan took a tip from the 1950 biopic of another African American cultural hero, *The Jackie Robinson Story*, and had Cole portray himself in scenes from his own life.

The two-reeler begins in a rowdy nightclub, with Nat playing the very familiar piano intro to "Sweet Lorraine." "Sure, you recognize that style," narrator Jeff Chandler tells us; "it belongs to one of the greatest jazz pianists of all time." No lie there. From this point forward, all the myths and half-truths that Cole himself and the Capitol Records PR department had promulgated for years are exhumed, dramatized, and immortalized, such as Cole singing for the first time at the insistence of a persistent drunk and being spontaneously dubbed "King Cole." "So, he sang, and the two men listened to his rhythmic wares. What would be the destiny of this new sound?"

In addition to Chandler as narrator, Ray Walker played "Carlos Gastel," the only figure from Cole's actual life who is directly named. The main falsehood that the story perpetrates is the idea that Cole was an overnight hit; as we know, it took at least six years of very hard work after the formation of the Trio for Cole to reach any foothold of success. The script builds to Cole's life-threatening illness and the canceled concert at Carnegie Hall in April 1953. Although the doctor tells Cole, "You're a very sick boy," the presentation of an African American entertainer is, overall, admirable, and not as condescending as it might have been. The film is most impressive visually and musically rather than in terms of the accuracy of the script or Cole's own acting ability, and the Technicolor and Cinemascope are fairly spectacular. (Alas, as with Cole's previous three UI featurettes, there's never been a proper Blu-ray restoration.)

The Nat King Cole Musical Story was a one-off, but it was a fall 1954 release, *The Adventures of Hajji Baba*, that would have greater long-lasting ramifications for Cole's film career. He had been recording movie title themes for Capitol since "Lost April" in 1947; but starting with *Hajji Baba*, he was now singing them over the actual main titles of the movies themselves. Over the next ten years, he would fulfill that function in no fewer than ten feature films: *Hajji Baba* was followed by *Kiss Me Deadly*[6] (which he apparently taped around the same time he was working on the *Musical Story*), in which he is heard singing "I'd Rather Have the Blues," an effective, minor key noir torch song composed by "Nature Boy" arranger Frank De Vol. Then there were *Autumn Leaves*, *Raintree County*, *In the Cool of the Day*, *Felicia*,[7] and four more in which he was also featured on-screen: *China Gate, St. Louis Blues, Night of the Quarter Moon*, and *Cat Ballou*.[8] Surely that's a record: no other popular vocalist sang over so many movie main titles. (And still, he continued to record even more movie themes for Capitol, like "Marnie," from the 1964 Alfred Hitchcock thriller of the same title, a rare song with a melody by Hitch's longtime musical collaborator, Bernard Hermann.)

COLE MADE A COUPLE OF PERSONAL APPEARANCES here and there in early spring, but only one major trip: this was his second visit to Kingston, Jamaica. He had played the Carib Theater and Colony Club two years earlier, in March 1953, and returned to the Carib in March 1955. Kingston native Montgomery Bernard Alexander was then a ten-year-old aspiring jazz piano player. Today, he describes the Carib as having been "our answer to Radio City or the Paramount, it featured all of the best movies that came out."[9] He vividly remembers the two life-changing shows he saw around that time: Louis Armstrong and His All-Stars (in May 1957) and Nat King Cole and his group (in March 1955). All of Cole's shows were sold out, but Monty and his mother were somehow able to get tickets for the matinee set, which meant that he had to miss much of the show because of school. When he reached the theater, Cole was almost finished, and his mother "was sitting there with a big smile on her face, because she just loved Nat King Cole. That voice!" He remembered all the King's men were present, guitarist John Collins, bassist Charlie Harris, and drummer Lee Young,[10] not least because he worked with many of them years later. "He had a kind of an *After Midnight*-style band. He walked in with this shiny 'Mr. Sharkskin suit,' and he walked with the pigeon toes. Then he sat at the piano and really whipped it up. So that was my one time to see Nat Cole." (Later on, Alexander would perform live with both Natalie and Freddy Cole in helping to keep Nat's music and memory alive.)

In April, Cole and company played through the Midwest as part of a package tour put together by the Moe Gale Agency; at different points he was joined by various doo-wop, R&B, and big band acts: LaVern Baker, the Drifters, and Erskine Hawkins at the Mosque in Pittsburgh; June Christy at the Riverside Theater in Milwaukee. Then in May, he settled in for a five-week run at the Chez Paree in Chicago. There, to his surprise, his shows were attended by the last person in the world he expected to see at the Chez Paree: his father, the Reverend Edward Coles, Sr.. "He didn't come to see me work, particularly in nightclubs, until about two years ago, when my mother passed. She used to come visit with me a lot and come watch the different shows. But he, being a minister, didn't think that he should be in these type places. But when she did pass, he told me, 'Well, Son, I guess I'll have to take up where your mother left off.' And he came to visit me the last time I was in the Chez Paree in Chicago, and he's been coming quite frequently ever since."[11]

Toward the end of the run, Cole made a series of sessions for Capitol Records using Bill Putnam's Universal Recording studio on 111 East Ontario. Gillette and Nelson Riddle flew over from Los Angeles, and Cole's rhythm section (guitarist John Collins, bassist Charlie Harris, and drummer Lee Young) teamed up with an orchestra of as many as thirty-six members of the Chicago Musician's Local. Over five days, Cole and company made five dates (including what was officially listed as two separate sessions on June 7) for various projects, including a few singles and his ambitious instrumental album, *The Piano Style of Nat King Cole*.

THIS WAS A PARTICULARLY PIANO-CENTRIC SEASON. Everyone had been happy with *Penthouse Serenade*, so Nat decided not only to record four more tracks for the expanded 12" edition but to do an all-new piano album as well. The key point regarding Cole's four piano albums—*King Cole at the Piano* (1947), *Penthouse Serenade* (1952), *The Piano Style of Nat King Cole* (1955), and *After Midnight* (1956)—is that they're all sui generis; each was a success, artistically and commercially, but none of them repeats any ideas from the previous ones. Cole was continually on the lookout for new contexts in which he could showcase his instrumental prowess. The idea here in 1955 was to use Nelson Riddle's orchestra to back Cole the pianist in the same style as Cole the popular vocalist; to give Cole the player the same advantage he had enjoyed as a singer. Within a few years, Oscar Peterson, Joe Bushkin, and especially George Shearing would be frequently recording in this format, pushing instrumental jazz over the line into Jackie Gleason-style "mood" music, but it was a new idea at the dawn of the 12" LP era in 1955.

Cole was inevitably somewhat defensive about his piano playing when speaking with the jazz press. At the time of *Piano Style*, he told *Down Beat*, "I've been doing some thinking about this piano thing and you know something? At the start, when I was playing piano a lot, no one thought that I was so much. But now that I sing more, why, everyone says, 'Gee, that Nat Cole used to play great piano.' "[12] Cole seems to have been so excited about the piano solos-with-orchestra concept that he ambitiously selected no fewer than sixteen songs, making this his longest "concept" album ever. He described the selections "as all standards, but nothing that's been played too much." Nat and Nelson would start the album in Chicago in June and finish it in Los Angeles in August.

Piano Style is a spectacularly colorful album, and for sheer excitement, it ranks side-by-side with its much better known successor, the 1956 *After Midnight*.[13] On the up-tempo numbers, especially "My Heart Stood Still" and "Tea for Two," the royal digits flash across the keyboard with more joyful abandon than in anything Cole had recorded since some of his jam session numbers ten years earlier. In effect, *Piano Style* is a double whammy—some of his best keyboard work and in a completely unique setting. The pianist is obviously inspired by the new format and responds with his most animated and inspired playing.

As Cole said at the time, "This is the first real serious piano work I've done in a long time."[14] Cole worked out two different approaches to the material, as he put it, "eight sides with rhythm and eight sides with strings." Half the material consisted of swinging up-tempos rendered in something more like a familiar big-band style, and the other half were romantic ballads played in the semi-classical setting of a large string orchestra. Both approaches were distinguished by Cole's regal and remarkable capacity for melody, a factor that defined his music whether singing or playing. As a pianist, Cole was very vocally oriented: you could always hear the tune in everything he played; even his improvisations have a beautiful singing quality to them, here more than ever in the context of Riddle's exceptional orchestrations.

The major tactic that he does not choose to employ here is block chords. He phrases melodies in octaves and thirds but does not create an orchestral sound with the keyboard, simply because such a sound would be redundant with an actual orchestra working behind him. On the eight ballads especially, he phrases instrumentally almost exactly the same way he phrases vocally, "singing" the love songs with the piano. Yet as straightforward as they are, the romantic numbers have some surprising elements that would not have been available to Cole if he were singing instead of playing. In "Love Walked In" and "Stella by Starlight," Cole and Riddle flip-flop the foreground and background. Cole moves from being accompanied by the orchestra to accompanying it himself, improvising piano obligato underneath the strings as they play the tune.

"Love Walked In" opens with Cole stating the tune in octaves—two fingers hitting the same notes several octaves apart—while "Imagination" boasts both a very tender ad-lib sequence and a glissando inspired by foremother Mary Lou Williams. Both "Imagination" and "Stella by Starlight" in particular benefit from beautifully voiced altered harmonies, "Stella" especially revealing Cole's knowledge of diminished scales. All the ballads could serve as models of playing with a relaxed feeling—especially in what must have been a high-pressure situation—as well as the nearly lost art of stating a familiar melody simply and beautifully.

"I See Your Face before Me" is a standout for several reasons; this was the first song that Riddle had ever attempted to orchestrate (as a seventeen-year-old in 1938) and only a few months earlier he had scored it for Sinatra's *In the Wee Small Hours*. Arthur Schwartz's melody inspires the pianist's most restrained performance here, with Cole's comparative coolness contrasted with a valve trombone solo and a prominent alto sax obligato by two musicians, Juan Tizol and Willie Smith, who would both play an even more important role on the *After Midnight* album.

The faster numbers reveal that Cole's skills as a jazz pianist had continued to grow even though this was no longer his primary focus. The medium-fast "My Heart Stood Still" has Cole using repeated notes in patterns that parallel what Erroll Garner was doing at the time. "What Can I Say after I Say I'm Sorry" has Cole stylizing the tune by lagging behind the beat, and his use of quarter-note and eighth-note triplets points to Wynton Kelly and other later pianists. "What Can I Say after I Say I'm Sorry" finds him using bebop phrasing on top of a swing band backing. Some of the swingers are set up like vocal numbers; others, like "Just One of Those Things" and "I Hear Music," have Cole playing, for the most part, with just the rhythm section. The big band plays more around him than with him, commenting from the sidelines, like a swinging Greek chorus.

"I Never Knew" is a particularly brilliant collaboration between soloist and orchestra; you can't miss how, at the end of his solo, Cole signals for the orchestra to come back in by hitting a G octave. Virtually all these charts have thoughtful, elaborate climaxes in which Riddle referees over call-and-response interplay between the piano and the rest of the ensemble. "Tea for Two" (one of Cole's longtime keyboard perennials) has not only a stunning coda but also a grandiose, Kenton-esque intro by the band. This quotes from composer Vincent Youmans's actual verse, but then Cole's piano intro utilizes the melody rubato, as if it were a verse.

"I Didn't Know What Time It Was" and "If I Could Be with You" startle the listeners by exploiting still another aspect of Cole's talents, his propensity for the blues. Cole thoroughly personalizes these melodies, reshaping them with blues harmony and feeling, taking them light years away from Richard Rodgers's and even James P. Johnson's original conception. On the second especially, he modernizes the rhythmic concept in a way that James P. would find amazing. "I Hear Music" has Cole excavating churchy harmonies like one of Horace Silver's soul sisters. "I Didn't Know What Time It Was" shows Cole at his most tender and romantic; there's no way such warmth could ever have been notated into a printed score.

"Takin' a Chance on Love" is arranged in more of a Broadway style—perhaps Gillette's idea—emphasized in a quote from "Puttin' on the Ritz." (The Berlin melody also makes a brief appearance in "Just One of Those Things.") Conversely, on "I Get a Kick Out of You," the bouncing, Basie-like "terp tempo" and swaggering trombones (offering an original countermelody that's all Riddle and not Cole Porter) make this pure Riddle at his finest. Cole plays it cool in the best sense of the word, smoothing out rhythmic lines as if he were ironing wrinkles in a pair of pants.

As Cole said in a radio interview in September, "In fact, while we were at the Chez Paree, not so long ago, we started [recording the album] there, and made about eight [tracks] in Chicago and I just finished the other eight just last week in Hollywood. So, I'm quite proud of it now. But it was quite a tough job. I didn't realize what I was getting into!"[15]

It all added up to a terrific album. Cole promoted it diligently, playing many of the arrangements on his TV series in 1956 and '57, including "Just One of Those Things" (which he also played on *The Ed Sullivan Show*), "Stella by Starlight," and "Tea for Two." Alas, the album was hardly a top-seller. It more or less disappeared until being reissued on CD in 1993[16] with the addition of a substantially longer alternate take of "My Heart Stood Still."[17] Cole himself would never make anything like *Piano Style* again, although Riddle would go on to make an orchestral album with Cole disciple Oscar Peterson in 1963. In the 1955 *Down Beat* interview, Cole deprecates his playing in comparison to the performances of other master keyboardists who had emerged in the early '50s, specifically Shearing, Peterson, and Billy Taylor: "I'm just glad I don't have to compete with them on piano." Yet his four piano-centric albums of 1947–1956 proved that he could more than compete with those three savants—or anyone else. Although *Piano Style* is not the instant classic that *After Midnight* was, in many ways it's an even more satisfying achievement.

Piano Style is completely unique; it is the one project that presents Cole the pianist as superstar and monarch with no claims to jazz's democracy.

AT THE HEIGHT OF HIS SUCCESS in the mid-1950s, Nat King Cole was hardly a prophet without honor in his own country—at least not as far as Chicago was concerned. (Alabama, as we shall see, was another story.) While working on the *Piano Style* album (and singing at nights at the Chez Paree), Cole also did two sessions of pop singles vocals on June 10 and 11. Chicagoans continued to regard him as a local boy who had, as they say, made good—so much so that two local publications covered the session. One was the *Chicago Tribune* and the other was *Playboy* magazine. The second was a national publication not yet two years old (this was years before the clubs or even the original Chicago mansion), and throughout its first years it had a rather Illinois-centric point of view; its writers were much more likely to cover Cole at Universal Studios (at 111 East Ontario) than at the Capitol Tower in Hollywood. Hugh Hefner sent over one Bernard Asbell,[18] who, though not a music specialist, was a close friend of the folk singer Pete Seeger. It's not known how many of these June sessions Asbell attended, but his article concentrates on the date of June 10.

Cole was never filmed in the studio (neither was Sinatra, at least not until considerably later in his career), and no complete session recordings have ever been circulated.[19] Thus, Mr. Asbell's article, which ran some sixteen months later in the November 1956 issue of *Playboy*, is perhaps the most complete document (of any kind) of a Cole recording session. Unlike most commentators in a general interest publication, which even at this point were referring to Cole as "a Negro entertainer" or a "dusky vocalist,"[20] Asbell, commendably, never dwells on any kind of racial issue. He does describe him, on seeing Nat at such close range for the first time: "He was trim and mobile like an athlete, taller and darker than his pictures suggest."

The other details are telling: Gillette and Cole are ostensibly running the session together, although since Gillette has the advantage of objectivity, he is generally given the final word. One recurring thread is that Cole, like a lot of artists, expresses a persistent need to go for additional takes, and Gillette is most often the one who tells him it's not necessary. After they get what Gillette feels is a satisfactory take of the first number, Cole asks, "Why don't we make one more in a hurry?" and Gillette answers, "We have what we want now and we still have three more tunes to cut. You want to sing for your own excitement at these prices?"[21] Gillette's meaning could not be clearer: every time Cole insists on an additional take, one way or another, it's going to come out of his own pocket. This means that all the expenses of every session are indirectly charged against the artist; the more expensive the session, the more records he has to sell, and the longer he has to wait to receive any royalties.[22] You can tell that Cole trusts Gillette explicitly, that the producer was able to maintain a strict balance between the two ends: he wouldn't let Capitol release any performance by Cole that was less than his best, but, at the same time, he wouldn't run up an enormous bill by making take after unnecessary take.

Five or so years into their relationship, Cole had come to rely on Gillette to a remarkable degree.[23] Gillette would arrange for the studio to be set up so that he and Cole would have continual eye contact[24]—and also so that Cole wouldn't have such contact with anyone else in the control room (that is, the engineers). Cole would never stop in the middle of a song unless there was a big, obvious mistake; otherwise he would totally depend on Gillette's judgment.

Asbell only describes what he actually witnesses. He doesn't discuss anything that happened before the session, such as where the songs came from. (In fact, he doesn't even tell us what the song titles are—more about that later.) As we know, songs came to Cole from a bewildering range of sources: Capitol Records, publishers, film studios and Broadway producers, songwriters themselves, and Gillette. Like Sinatra, and unlike most artists of the period, Cole had both first choice and final approval on what he sang and what he didn't.

It's also somewhat deceptive how little Nelson Riddle has to say at the actual session. That's because the great majority of his creative input has transpired beforehand, that is, in actually writing his orchestrations. We know that Cole gave Riddle largely a free hand in his arrangements and that Riddle's only major collaborator who gave him very specific guidelines to follow was Sinatra. On his classic "concept" albums especially, Sinatra made a point to tell Riddle specifically what he wanted on a measure-for-measure level—strings here, a trumpet solo there, a key change in the middle, and so on. Cole apparently didn't provide Riddle with more than a key and a tempo, which is fitting, since the majority of what they worked on together were brand-new songs intended for singles. There was less leeway or room for interpretation in a new song like "A Blossom Fell," which was Cole's first big hit single of the second half of the decade (#2 US, #3 UK), unlike something like "I've Got You under My Skin," originally composed by Cole Porter as a slow, romantic bolero and reinvented by Riddle and Sinatra as a high-octane swinger.

Riddle is heard from only a few times on the Chicago date, and he is highly flexible: at one point, Gillette tells Riddle that a particular flourish of the clarinets is getting in the way, and, without hesitation, Riddle tells the woodwinds to cut it out entirely. At least once, Gillette asks Riddle if he feels the tempo is okay. Riddle quickly offers his thoughts when asked, but he virtually never pipes up and volunteers an opinion. The idea is that he's done his part, and now it's up to Cole and the musicians to make something of what Riddle has already done, with Gillette overseeing. Riddle was flown out to the session mainly to make these spontaneous last-minute changes, not necessarily because of his conducting skills—which, as many of his musicians have told me, was not nearly at the same level as his writing.

Gillette functions not as judge and/or jury, but as a traffic cop, keeping everything running smoothly, and not "making an arrest," that is, requesting an additional take, unless absolutely necessary. The most notable example of that is a take which is otherwise superior but wherein Cole accidentally "pops" a "P" sound. Gillette and engineer Putnam make a plan to edit together a composite master from various takes, working around the popped P.

Also present are two Chicago disc jockeys, Jay Trompeter and Bill O'Connor, and Asbell deploys them as spokesmen for his own incredulity concerning the state of recording in 1955. In this modern age of recording tape and multi-tracking, it is now, for the first time, possible to combine various takes and also to record various components separately and then later mix them all together. When they start the second number, Trompeter seems to have no idea what's going on, and Gillette explains that they're recording one number over multiple sessions: on this session there are more violins, so the more elaborate string intro will be taped today, but the next session will be much more brassy, so they'll record those parts tomorrow. "But where's the song?" the deejay asks, and the producer responds, "That comes tomorrow."

Fate, it seems, has a sense of humor. This is virtually the only time a journalist attended a King Cole recording session and provided us a detailed account of the creation of a single track. But alas, we can't compare the results to his description because the four songs taped that day seem to have immediately and utterly vanished from the Capitol vault—somehow they never made it from Chicago back to Los Angeles. The only way that we know precisely what session they came from is because Asbell gave us two master numbers, #13990 and #13991, which correspond to "Wishing Well" and "I've Learned." Cole and Riddle then went on to a third song, which, like the previous two was also a new (and otherwise completely unknown) one, "Half a Mind" (the full title may have been "I've Got Half a Mind to Kiss You, But the Other Half Says No").[25] But it was the fourth—also, unfortunately, completely missing—title that we would most like to hear: "But Not for Me."[26] Alas, fate determined that this Gershwin classic was not for him.

AT LEAST TWICE IN THE MID-1950S, Cole and Riddle came close to making a follow-up to the classic *Two in Love* (1953 and 1955)—in other words, another straight-down-the-middle album of vocals with orchestra. They started work on two projects that seem to have been slated to be that: the first of these, a set of new songs, eventually saw the light of day as the CD *Night Lights*. The second, which resulted in several sessions of swinging standards, has still never been issued in anything like the form that Nat and Nelson had intended. Not surprisingly, the standards project is, overall, a more exciting undertaking, but the *Night Lights* collection also contains some absolutely classic material.

Most of the *Night Lights* project was recorded over the end of 1955 into the start of 1956. Following the Chicago sojourn and the *Piano Style* sessions, Cole played through the Midwest again (including a two-week run at the Chicago Theater), and then did his second stints at the Hollywood Bowl (August), the Copacabana (October into November), then the Sands (November into December).

However, the big commotion that moment at 401 South Muirfield Road was not about Nat but rather over Maria's proposed return to show business. She played Ciro's in October, and then, that same month, sang a brief duet with her husband ("I Can't Believe That You're in Love with Me") on *The Ed Sullivan Show* on Sunday, October 23. In December 1955 and April 1956, she recorded two solo sessions for Capitol, and a few months later, Nat was still telling the press, "My Maria is still under contract to Capitol Records and she will definitely embark upon a career in the movie and television field." Nat also announced, "My daughter Sweetie will have a children's [song] on the Christmas market.' "[27] Maria's attempt at a renewed career would peter out by the end of 1956, however, this statement indicates that Natalie Cole was already planning a musical career for herself. Two years after her 1954 session with her father and older sister, Sweetie taped her first solo track, "Good Will," on September 19, 1956 (on the same date that her father recorded "Ballerina").

Night Lights is a fascinating album, even though it wasn't perceived as such for many years; it was the theory of Cole discographer and researcher Roy Holmes that these sessions were intended to be an album. Eventually, Cole would, in fact, do an album of brand-new songs that he liked: *To Whom It May Concern*, released in May 1959. It's hard to know precisely how the late Holmes arrived at this conclusion; there's no written evidence, no period documentation to support it, but *Night Lights* was a very welcome CD release just the same. The package contains several signature songs and hits, and in epic productions like "The Shadows" and "To the Ends of the Earth,"

Cole and Riddle are once again stretching the boundaries of what pop music is—and going for something entirely new.

The twenty tracks, whatever they were originally intended for, span six sessions from late December 1955 into January 1956. Of these, only five songs were actually issued as singles at the time, but remarkably, four of the five were bona fide chart hits: "My Personal Possession," "That's All There Is to That," "To the Ends of the Earth," and "Never Let Me Go." The only one of the five that didn't chart, "I Just Found Out about Love," became even more of an instant Cole classic. The same could be said about "To the Ends of the Earth" and "Never Let Me Go," and all three of these latter-mentioned titles were widely heard on *This Is Nat King Cole,* one of the singer's best-loved long-playing anthologies.

On *Two in Love,* Cole and Riddle had the job of making time-honored standards like "Love Is Here to Stay" sound fresh and exciting; here, they faced the no-less-daunting challenge of taking new and completely unknown songs and making the world love them. You could say that the Cole-Riddle combination is so strong that the quality of the song itself is almost a secondary issue and the fact remains that the three best songs were, in fact, actually released at the time. Still, many of the unissued items here are more than worthy.

Jimmy McHugh (1894–1969) was, like Johnny Burke, a veteran songwriter who was part of Cole's inner circle (and more than most tunesmiths, a prominent figure on the Hollywood social scene); Freddy Cole remembers hanging out with his big brother and the composer.[28] Best known for his jazz standards like "I Can't Give You Anything but Love" and "On the Sunny Side of the Street,"[29] McHugh had less success with his Broadway book shows, although his first, the 1948 *As the Girls Go*, ran well over a year. *Strip for Action,* which, like the 1948 show, had lyrics by Harold Adamson, was virtually his last. As the title suggested, the plot, such as it was, concerned the backstage life of a burlesque company and was mostly a framework and an excuse to show more female flesh than had ever been attempted before in "legit" musical comedy. The production barely (in both senses of the word) made it out of Philadelphia, and then in Boston, it was completely killed by both the critics and the censors.[30] "Jimmy McHugh in tears over fate of *Strip for Action*," Walter Winchell reported.[31]

Well before the company took to the road for the out-of-town tryouts, Cole recorded four of its songs: "I Just Found Out about Love," "Dame Crazy," "Love Me as Though There Were No Tomorrow," and "Too Young to Go Steady." As a photo shows, McHugh paid a visit to Nat in the studio on the December 29, 1955, session. Even though *Strip for Action* disappeared without a trace, "Too Young to Go Steady" became a substantial hit for Cole and "I Just Found Out about Love," became a Cole classic. (In fact, thanks to Cole, those two songs made more money for McHugh and Adamson than many a number from an actual hit show.)

Though "Too Young to Go Steady" was the hit (peaking at #21 in the US and #8 UK), the real winner in the long run was "I Just Found Out about Love," an absolutely irresistible swinger. Boasting clever words and a catchy tune (not to mention a Riddle orchestration cast from the same mold as "I've Got You under My Skin," featuring Willie Smith in the intro), it's absolutely everything that a great pop song should be. Cole has a way of swinging on a fast number that's quite remarkable, at once easy and relaxed and yet exciting and intense. His rhythmic placement here is masterful, especially on the line "I can tell by the way that I feel" at the end of the bridge (the form is roughly AABAC, the C section being a special tag), which is somehow staccato (with dramatic rests between notes) and legato at the same time.

The other songs are a mixed bag, though Cole and Riddle are never less than consistently excellent: Roy Alfred's "Mr. Jukebox," with its very white-sounding pseudo-doo-wop choir, is very much in the same vein as Sinatra's "Hey Jealous Lover" and was obviously right for the juke medium. The choir returns on another up-tempo, "I Got Love," whose spelling sequence anticipates Cole's later "L-O-V-E." (It's credited to Dennis Farnon, part of the Canadian-English-American musical dynasty of Farnons, including also Robert and Brian Farnon.) "Stay" is a bouncy round of "delay-the-lady" à la "Baby, It's Cold Outside." Another light swinger, "Believe" by Moose Charlap (best known for the 1954 Broadway *Peter Pan* and for being the father of top jazz pianist Bill Charlap), sounds like a rather cutesy leftover from one of his lesser shows, like *Kelly* or *Whoop-Up*.

The bulk of the new ballads were recorded in January 1956. "I Promise You" is a professionally constructed if uninspiring tune by two old pros, Sammy Lerner and Ben Oakland. "The Way I Love You" is a French tune with an American lyric by Jack Lawrence, boasting archetypical Riddle flutes.[32] "Once Before," by Ray Evans without Jay Livingston, has an artful lyric, personifying love anthropomorphically, and overall, it has the general aroma of a movie theme. The choir sticks around for "I'm Willing to Share This with You," which boasts lots more flutes, celesta, and characteristic Cole tenderness. "Make Me," by Larry Spier, composer and publisher and one-time partner of Tommy Dorsey, may not be deep and profound, but it's simple and effective.

At fifteen, Cole organized his first dance band, "Nat Cole and His Royal Dukes." This was an invaluable experience: by writing all the band's material himself, he learned first hand what went into the writing of a good song and the creation of good arrangement.

The young Nat Cole at the piano, probably Los Angeles, ca. 1940. Just as he knew what to do with a microphone, Cole always had a loving relationship with the camera; there's never a shot in which he looks awkward or uncomfortable; rather, he's often gazing out into the faces of those watching with warm, knowing eyes.

To Johnnie Merce
a great artist

Johnny Mercer, already a successful Hollywood songwriter and former bandsinger, had first come to hear the King Cole Trio at Jim Otto's Steakhouse in fall 1938. (In fact, that September, the first song they ever recorded was Mercer's "Mutiny in the Nursery.") Five years later, Mercer would sign the Trio to his "start-up" label, Capitol Records. Three photos from the early years at Capitol, when Mercer was still personally producing many of the sessions himself: The first shows a bespectacled Nat and is autographed directly "to Johnnie [*sic*] Mercer, a great artist, sincerely, Nat King Cole." The next was taken during the session of August 20, 1947, when Cole and Mercer recorded Cole's biggest hit of the year "Save the Bones for Henry Jones." (Special Collection and Archives, Georgia State University Library) Last, Cole and Mercer with road manager Mort Ruby and Capitol producer Walter Rivers. (Property of the University Archives and West Florida History Center at the University of West Florida)

The original King Cole Trio, with guitarist Oscar Moore and bassist Wesley Prince, plays at the opening of Music City, the retail outlet owned and operated by Glenn and Oscar Wallichs, July 1940. Nat had known both Wallichs and Johnny Mercer for several years before they founded Capitol Records in the Spring of 1942. (Courtesy of Capitol Records, LLC under license from Universal Music Enterprise).

Nat stirs up "The Frim Fram Sauce," the Trio's biggest hit of 1945. This was one of dozens of songs that Cole recorded by Redd Evans, who himself was one of many songwriters whom Cole recorded, supported, patronized, and, eventually, published. Guitarist Oscar Moore and bassist Johnny Miller take care of the "chefafa on the side."

Eden Ahbez (one of the songwriter and guru's many names) and "Nature Boy" had more to do with changing the course of Cole's career—from jazz pianist to popular singer—than any other factor. In a portrait of the songwriter that he autographed to Cole, ahbez proudly inscribed, "To Nat, every king has his fool—I'm yours, Eden ahbez."

In 1949, Cole added Jack Costanzo to the Trio (with Irving Ashby and Joe Comfort), explaining that the fourth man gave the group more "scope." The percussionist also helped Cole keep up with two new musical trends of the late 1940s: bebop and Afro-Latin jazz. With Perry Como on the *Chesterfield Supper Club*.

A mini gallery of King Cole's arrangers and musical directors. On opposite page: Of all Cole's collaborators, Nelson Riddle (1921–1985) was the one who most helped the artist realize his full commercial potential and completed his transition from jazz pianist to popular vocalist. For his work with Cole and Sinatra alone, Riddle ranks as probably the single most valuable orchestrator in all of American music.

Billy May (1916–2004) did only two albums with Nat, but they're both standouts: *Just One of Those Things* (1957) and *Let's Face the Music* (1961). The two men are pictured here during the recording of that second one. (Courtesy of Capitol Records, LLC under license from Universal Music Enterprises)

Contrastingly, the main contribution of Gordon Jenkins (1910–1984) to Cole's catalog was sheer beauty. In albums like the best-selling *Love Is the Thing* (1956) and *The Very Thought of You* (1958), the two men invented a whole new subspecies of romantic song. (© 1962 Capitol Records, LLC / Courtesy of Capitol Records, LLC under license from Universal Music Enterprises)

Above: Ralph Carmichael (born 1927) was the last major collaborator of Cole's career, responsible for most of the artist's greatest work in his final years, most impressively with *The Touch of Your Lips* (1960), *Nat King Cole Sings/George Shearing Plays* (1961), and his final project, *L-O-V-E* (1964). [Courtesy of Capitol Records, LLC under license from Universal Music Enterprises]

In early 1954, Capitol announced that its two star male vocalists, Nat Cole and Frank Sinatra, would be recording a duet single. That session didn't happen, but, luckily, another close friend, Dean Martin, stepped in to join Nat on two vaudeville-type novelty songs. Pictured with Nat and Dean are conductor Billy May and lyricist Sammy Cahn. [Courtesy of Capitol Records, LLC under license from Universal Music Enterprises]

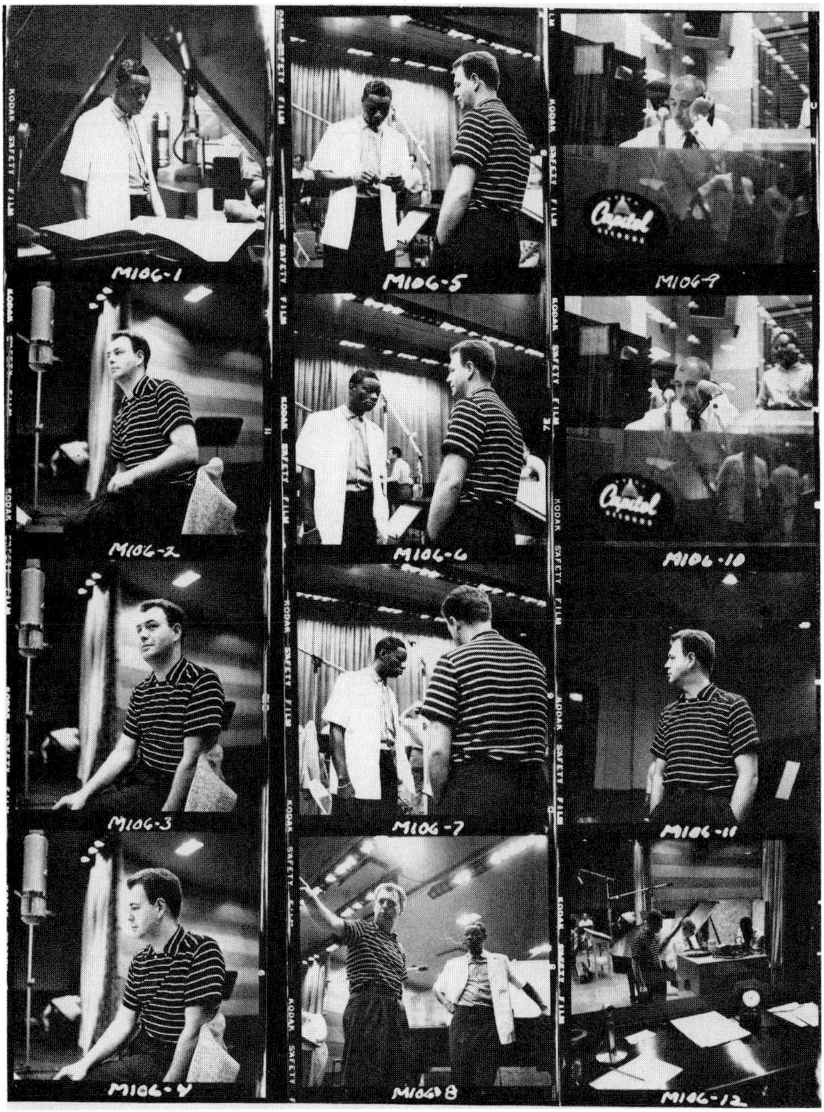

A contact sheet of rare images taken by photographer Kurt Reichert, featuring Nat, Nelson, and producer Lee Gillette in the new Capitol Tower studio, on August 23, 1955—during the recording of their classic instrumental album, *The Piano Style of Nat King Cole*.

Recorded in 1956, *After Midnight* was Cole's most celebrated post-Trio jazz project, as well as the only one of his four piano-centric albums in which he also sang. Nat and his touring rhythm section, with Charlie Harris, bass, Lee Young, drums, and John Collins, guitar (© 1956 Capitol Records, LLC / Courtesy of Capitol Records, LLC under license from Universal Music Enterprises) and with legendary hot violinist Stuff Smith, one of four remarkable guest soloists.

Songwriter Jimmy Van Heusen (1913–1990) was a major figure in the lives of all three of the most important singers of the mid-20th century (Bing Crosby, Frank Sinatra, and Nat King Cole). On March 17, 1957, the songwriter threw an elaborate party for Nat on his thirty-eighth birthday, at his rather expansive manse in Palm Springs, California. Nearly everyone then playing a major role in Nat's life was present, and most are captured in these photos by Van Heusen himself. Outside, with director Samuel Fuller, former Capitol executive James Conkling and an unknown. Inside, Nat tries out a song with pianist Joey Bushkin as accountant Harold Plant listens. (Courtesy Van Heusen Music Photo Archives)

In 1957, Cole became one of the first African American members of the storied Friars Club. The Los Angeles "monastery" of the Friars threw a gala dinner in Nat's honor on October 21, 1957, in Beverly Hills. Here's Nat with fellow Friars Frank Sinatra and Dean Martin.

Cookie (Carole, left), Maria, and Sweetie (Natalie) see Nat off at the Los Angeles airport for his 1960 engagement at the El Senioral. As the sombrero indicates, by 1960, Latin American music and Spanish-speaking audiences were an important part of Cole's musical makeup.

The 1961 album *Nat King Cole Sings/George Shearing Plays* is more than a duo project; it's actually a three-way collaboration among three major musical minds, the sublime Nat Cole; the brilliant British pianist George Shearing, one of Cole's greatest disciples; and the exceptional orchestrator Ralph Carmichael. It added up to one of Cole's finest later projects.

On August 5, 1962, Cole celebrated his twenty-fifth anniversary in show business with a gala dinner at the Ambassador Hotel, Los Angeles. One side benefit of the occasion is that this is the only time he was ever photographed with his original piano hero, Earl "Fatha" Hines. Also pictured: Maria and Eddie Cole and two unknown ladies. (© 1962 Capitol Records, LLC / Courtesy of Capitol Records, LLC under license from Universal Music Enterprises]

San Francisco, December 2, 1964: A rare shot of Nat not looking particularly happy, and, for once, not caring who knew, as he and Ralph Carmichael struggle to finish what Nat knew would be his triumphant final album, *L-O-V-E,* before his cancer incapacitated him.

"The Story's Old" is distinguished by more flutes and great Riddle harmonies. It's hard to find anything distinguishing about "Sometimes I Wonder" and "I Need a Plan," other than what Cole and Riddle bring to them.

While "Too Young to Go Steady" was Cole's biggest hit at the time, "To the Ends of the Earth" and "Never Let Me Go" became highly significant additions to the Cole canon. And, in many ways, "The Shadows," a kind of counterpart to "To the Ends of the Earth," may be the most remarkable of all. It derives from the long history of Nat King Cole and the Sherman brothers (not to be confused with Robert and Richard Sherman, famous for their work on Disney films), Joe, who mainly wrote music, and lyricist Noel. They had been in Cole's inner circle since the early '50s, and he would record more than a dozen of their songs, separately and as a team, over the span of that many years.[33]

After Noel's discharge from the army, the first notable song that the brothers did together was "To the Ends of the Earth" in 1955. Joe recorded a demo disc and put together a lead sheet—"I laid out the chords and tried to put down the feeling that I thought it should have," he said—and then sent both to his publisher, the former bandleader George Paxton. Eventually the Shermans and Paxton had a meeting at Capitol with Gillette. "He told us, 'I want this song for Nat.' "[34]

Two minutes and sixteen seconds of sheer bliss, "Ends of the Earth" was only a minor hit at the time but is much beloved among those who know Cole's music well, such as his brother Freddy and pianist Monty Alexander, both of whom recorded it more recently. Apart from Cole's glorious singing, two aspects of Riddle's orchestration distinguish the chart: its innovative, samba-like rhythm and low-pitched male chorus. The typical thing to do with a choir is to have them come in like angels, singing high up above the central voice, which Cole and Riddle did earlier with "Hajji Baba" and also here with "Once Before," both of which employ the ethereal "vapor" voice of Loulie Jean Norman.

However, on "Ends of the Earth" and "The Shadows," Riddle surprises us by recruiting an all-male choir of mainly deep baritones and bassos—the choral equivalent of his beloved bass trombones—and pitches them below Cole's smoother, higher baritone. Riddle also mixes in low-range woodwinds, such as bassoons and oboes, and integrates them within the choir. The combination of the sonic textures and the unusual rhythm, not to mention the King's sensational crooning, makes "Ends of the Earth" one of the great experiences in pop music. (Incidentally, Joe Sherman made no claims for these innovations—they were strictly Riddle's ideas.)

The unreleased "Shadows" is the tune recorded right before "Ends of the Earth" and makes a fascinating forerunner to it. The male voices are employed in the same way, although there's a slightly different Latinate rhythm going on underneath. There's also some of the exotic percussion and cymbalism à la the 1954 Nat-Nelson "Hajji Baba," plus a string countermelody that anticipates the faux-Asian motifs used later in James Bond and other 1960s movie themes. The orchestral voicings utilize another one of Riddle's signature sounds, what pianist Bill Miller described as the arranger's "polytonal" approach, familiar to listeners from Cole's "I Am in Love," Sinatra's "Not as a Stranger," and Billy Eckstine's "Sea Breeze." In all, "Shadows" has a highly unusual text, by Fred Ebb, who went on to one of the most imposing careers in the history of musical theater (alas, this is the only song of his that Cole would record), and a melody by a completely unknown composer named Pierre Dupriez, which Cole and Riddle bring to life quite evocatively. Perhaps even more than "Ends of the Earth," "The Shadows" is a polytonal Nelson Riddle spectacular—an epic orchestration, utilizing such dazzling harmonic fireworks that it's hard to believe this was once considered pop music. As an ingenious, classically influenced arranger of jazz and popular music, Riddle is easily in a class with Billy Strayhorn. This is one of the most complex, intricate examples of orchestration ever arranged by anyone and completely puts the lie to Riddle's own assertion that his writing for Cole was inherently simpler than what he did for Sinatra.

But we're not done with classics yet: "Night Lights" is essential Cole, not least for Riddle's contribution. The Chester Conn-Sammy Gallop song is catchy enough by itself, and yet the orchestral writing by Riddle is virtually the whole show. There's also a yummy piano solo in the center. On the Capitol recording, it's played by Sinatra's piano partner, Bill Miller, who told me that whenever he played for Cole, "I always tried to imagine, 'How would Nat play this?' "[35] When Cole performed the "Night Lights" on his NBC TV series (as he did at least twice), he played the piano part himself. The most salient feature of "Night Lights" is the brilliant vamp Riddle has running throughout, played by bass trombonist George Roberts over a background of flutes and celesta. It's heard first as an intro and then as a countermelody. Two years later, Messrs. Conn, Gallop, and Riddle (and probably Cole) got together again and reworked the chord progression and this vamp into a new song with new lyrics, entitled "That's You." Cole recorded it, as if you had any doubt; but although the new song, "That's You," didn't attain the hit status of the original "Night Lights," it's still a Cole classic.

Yet one more masterpiece remains: "Never Let Me Go," by Livingston and Evans, was introduced by Cole on-screen in the 1956 Paramount crime drama *The Scarlet Hour*, one of the final works of the legendary Michael Curtiz; Nat had already recorded and shot his number a few months earlier in summer 1955. Yet, though Curtiz had already directed several classic musicals, the director completely wastes both the song and Cole's performance; the artist is seen only briefly, singing a single chorus lasting roughly a minute. It did nothing for Cole's acting career, but it did provide him with yet another hit single. Riddle telegraphs the main motif of the melody in the intro with bird-like flutes, and what a melody it is, roughly 36 bars laid out like this: A (8) B (4) A (8) C (8) B (4) A' (4). Many orchestrations use rubato to stir up emotion—slowing down and abandoning the tempo is a sure-fire, almost stereotypical way to get the tears flowing—but Riddle here keeps the tempo flowing very nicely, even while Cole turns in one of his most effectively dramatic vocals. When he gets to what could be described as the C section, with the words "you wouldn't hurt me, would you?," Cole offers up some of the most emotionally vulnerable singing of his entire career. Although the tune wasn't a blockbuster on the level of the team's "Mona Lisa," both of those composers have named "Never Let Me Go" as their favorite of their own songs—this as opposed to any of their three Academy Award winners and many more nominations. (The song quickly caught on among jazz musicians, particularly pianists, like Red Garland, Bill Evans, McCoy Tyner, and Tommy Flanagan.)

THUS, COLE STARTED THE NEW YEAR of 1956 at his home base of Los Angeles, working with Riddle on this string of *Night Lights*–associated dates, and, in mid-January, he was also working nights at Ciro's. In February, Cole played Sydney, Australia (as he would every winter for three years in a row, starting in 1955), and in March, he did a week at the Tropicana in Havana, the first of his three annual appearances in Cuba. Later that month, he filmed another appearance in a Hollywood feature film. Cole announced a few months later, "You will soon be able to see the new Errol Flynn movie *Istanbul*, in which for the first time, I sing and act, portraying the role of 'Danny Rice' instead of Nat Cole."[36] Cole looks marvelous in Technicolor and Cinemascope in his final film for Universal—a feature at last. The 1957 *Istanbul* was a remake of *Singapore* (1947) and a general retread of *Casablanca,* with Errol Flynn as a rather charmless British Bogie. Director Joseph Pevney cast Cole as a six-foot Dooley Wilson (called "Danny" rather than "Sam") singing "When I Fall in Love" and forty seconds of "I Was a Little Too Lonely (and You Were a Little

Too Late)"[37]—the title of that song being longer than Cole's whole scene. "Danny Rice" gets barely a few moments on screen and just a little dialogue here and there; even so, this was Cole's most important "acting" role so far.

Even as he filmed his sequences for the movie, Nat and Carlos were at work on a special venture—a touring package of their own, set to play through the South in the spring. They called it the "Record Star Parade of 1956," and the additional acts, whether by coincidence or design, were all white: singer June Christy and the vocal-instrumental group the Four Freshmen, who were both associated with Cole's longtime friend Stan Kenton. This was also, coincidentally, a rather historical moment in the trade relations between the musicians' unions of the United Kingdom and the United States: for the first time, the Kenton Orchestra was allowed to tour Great Britain while Ted Heath and His Music, the most popular jazz orchestra in England, came over to join Cole in this tour of the southern United States. (Shortly after the tour was finished, the Heath Orchestra recorded its premiere concert at Carnegie Hall.) Two additional acts were on the bill: dancer Patty Thomas[38] and the young comedian Gary Morton, later best known as the second husband and partner of comedy icon Lucille Ball (and who would open for Cole again at the Copacabana in New York and the Sands in Las Vegas in 1962).

Cole had toured with "mixed" packages before, particularly in terms of co-starring bandleaders: he never discriminated against white bands and had already gone on the road with Stan Kenton, Woody Herman, and Billy May. This particular roster, a black headliner with an otherwise all-white line-up, was hardly out of the ordinary even in 1956. Still, that was possibly the straw that broke the back of a certain staunch segregationist who was then planning attacks around Alabama. Looking backward a few weeks later, Cole said, "I was aware that there was a lot of racial tension in the South right now, but I felt that people would forget it when it comes to entertainment. They usually do. If they didn't want to be entertained, they just wouldn't come."[39] Obviously, such an attitude seems naïve in the aftermath of what happened.

"A lot of racial tension" is putting it mildly: this was at the height of the first big salvo of the civil rights movement, the city-wide boycott of buses by African American passengers in Cole's hometown, Montgomery, being led by the Reverend Dr. Martin Luther King Jr. The "anti-King" spiritual leader of the pro-segregation, anti-civil rights movement was "Ace" Carter. Born Asa Earl Carter and later known as Forrest Carter, he had already organized the North Alabama Citizens Council, a more up-to-date, contemporary offshoot of the Ku Klux Klan. Carter and his white supremacist thugs felt no need to hide behind sheets; their white faces and their real names were plainly visible for all to see. They took considerable pride in espousing their anti-integration, anti-Negro and anti-Semitic rhetoric and unspeakable acts of terrorism in full view of the whole world.

The most famous words ever to come from the mouth of Nat King Cole were "The greatest thing you'll ever learn / Is just to love and be loved in return." The most famous words to come from Asa Carter, which he put into the mouth of George Wallace, in his inaugural speech as governor of Alabama, were, "Segregation now! Segregation tomorrow! Segregation forever!"

Carter (1925–1979) was a terrorist mastermind who was consistently able to manipulate others—an intensely loyal network of ignorant redneck stooges—to do his dirty work, and he never had to serve any jail time himself for his violent, sociopathic conspiracies. Carter was so extreme that he was even cautioned by other white supremacists. More than a slippery character, Carter was a Jedi master—an imperial wizard even—at distorting truth and promulgating lies, starting with his own identity, in order to advance his agenda. He was born Asa Earl Carter, but went by "Ace" apparently because he realized that "Asa" sounded Jewish. (It was, in fact, Al Jolson's actual first name.).

Carter had spent his early career as a vehement propagandist, preaching racial and religious intolerance in print journalism and, more successfully, on southern radio stations. Later in life, he became "Forrest Carter," the beloved author of Western novels, including *The Outlaw Josey Wales* (famously filmed by Clint Eastwood), and *The Education of Little Tree*, an alleged memoir (eventually revealed to be largely fictitious) which is actually sympathetic to a minority group (Native Americans), their way of life and spirituality. Yet no one could imagine Asa Carter, as opposed to Forrest, expressing anything like empathy for any non-white race. Carter hadn't changed his views, only his spots.

Carter was particularly keen on targeting popular culture and music as a progressive social force that, in his eyes, had to be stopped: he frequently organized his followers to picket and disrupt concerts with signs proclaiming, "Jungle Music Promotes Integration" and "Bebop Promotes Communism."[40]

On Tuesday, April 10, 1956, four Citizens Council hoodlums attacked Cole on stage at the Municipal Auditorium in Montgomery; typically, Carter wasn't among them, but he had been the force behind the attack. It was, both morally and logistically, a highly imperfect crime: the two gang leaders, Kenneth Adams, identified as the "leader of the white citizens council in Anniston [Alabama]"[41] and Willis Vinson, were eventually charged with intent to murder, but their stated intention was to kidnap Cole. What was supposed to happen next? It seems, in anticipation of Charles Manson a generation later, that Carter expected an apocalyptic race war to spontaneously break out, in which the whites would emerge victorious.

It's doubtful that Adams and Vinson even realized precisely why they were tasked to carry out this assault. Nat King Cole was hardly the only African American singer or musician to be appearing in Alabama—black headliners frequently toured Alabama, Mississippi, and other states in the Deep South, usually trepidatiously, because that's where their audiences were. Carter had repeatedly expressed his opposition to both rock and bebop, but even he knew well that Cole wasn't playing any of that. He was also on the warpath against any kind of inter-racial marriage or relationship, but Cole couldn't be accused of that either.

Ace Carter targeted Nat King Cole for one very specific reason, and, in his twisted logic and demented brain, he was entirely correct to perceive of Cole as a threat. With Nat and Maria, Cookie, and Sweetie projecting such a positive image of African American family life, the segregationist policies that Carter would have fought to the death to defend (or so he said) seemed increasingly ridiculous. To have regarded the Coles as children of a lesser God, as people who somehow deserved to be held back by discrimination or relegated to second-class citizenship, was as meaningless as killing a mockingbird. By constantly smiling in the rotogravures and even on television, with his handsome face, his beautiful family, and perfect house, Cole was showing the Ace Carters and Ken Adamses of the world that he was better than they were—and they knew it. He was proof that a poor black boy from Montgomery—their own state no less—could rise to the absolute top of the social and economic ladder. Cole embodied the very entity that the Ace Carters of the world feared most: a role model for both black and white people alike. His very existence was testimony to the validity of integration and equal rights. Nat King Cole didn't have to play "jungle music" or chase white women to incur their wrath. All he had to do was exist.

The big tour got under way on April Fool's Day, possibly not a good omen, with six dates in six different cities in Texas, then three days in Louisiana, starting with three shows over two days in New Orleans, and then, in one day, Monday April 9, they were set to hit two different cities in Louisiana, an afternoon performance in Grambling followed by an evening concert in Rustin. Tuesday, April 10, was the only date scheduled for Cole's home state, at the Municipal Auditorium, Birmingham. Beforehand, Cole didn't think his presence as the sole black artist on the bill would provoke anyone, although he admitted later that this was probably a factor in the attack.

Although it hurt him bitterly, Nat had agreed to play to segregated houses: an early show for a white audience and a later show for "colored patrons." It was during the first show that the trouble occurred—obviously, since the "white citizens" wouldn't have been admitted to the later show. "I guess it was a case of a few rabble-rousers trying to start trouble," said Cole; "I had just finished singing 'Autumn Leaves' and was going into 'Little Girl.' The attack itself occurred so fast it was over before I realized what had happened."[42] (Leave it to Cole to remember vividly exactly what song he was singing at the moment of the assault.) As drummer Lee Young remembered, "Nat started singing and we heard some women scream. One woman was screaming, 'They're gonna get him!' Guys came down the aisle, and one guy reached up. But [the police] knew about it, because they must have had fifteen or twenty detectives backstage. And one guy reached up and grabbed Nat by the ankle and pulled him down. And another guy jumped up on stage and hit him. But by that time, the detectives had them, and they were taking these guys away."[43]

The arresting officer, Patrolman H. E. Schotts testified, "I hit Vinson once with the night stick," while another officer grabbed Adams, and then, Schotts continued, "I hit Adams, knocking him off the stage."[44] John Collins later remembered, "I never heard so many people yelling *[N]-bomb, [N]-bomb*, and that was the police!"

Immediately afterward in his dressing room, Cole somehow made light of the attack and was quoted as saying, "Man, I love show business, but I don't want to die for it!"[45] It may seem amazing that he somehow found the fortitude to go through with the late show, the one for an all-black audience, but the man who taught the world to "pretend you're happy when you're blue" and to "smile, though your heart is aching" could hardly do otherwise.

In the aftermath, whenever Cole spoke about the occurrences of April 10, he always stressed the events that transpired immediately after the assault—the reaction rather than the crime itself. This enabled him to put a positive spin on the entire affair. As soon as the police had led the terrorists off and the incident was over, all 4,000 white people in the audience immediately rose to their feet and gave the artist a standing ovation which lasted, some say, for fifteen minutes. "Some of the best people in Birmingham, including the mayor, were out there," Cole said; "I know that they were trying to show me that they didn't sanction what had happened. So, I went out and spoke to them for a few minutes. I thanked them for coming to the show and told them I knew they didn't hold with what just occurred. I noticed that some people were even crying. Even the Mayor sent a representative backstage with an apology." (Sixty years later it seems heinous in the extreme that the mayor, who was actually in the auditorium, didn't come backstage himself and personally apologize.)

Maria Cole learned about the incident, from, of all unlikely people, Sinatra. Not yet known as the "Chairman of the Board," he already had deep connections in politics, government, law enforcement, and, it has been alleged, still other reaches of society. Somehow Sinatra knew about the attack on her husband even before Maria did. Sinatra also arranged for a plane, Maria said, to transport Cole and his entourage from Birmingham to Chicago the next morning.[46] Lee Young remembered that flight for another reason. "In defense of Birmingham, I have to say, that was only a certain portion of the people [who condoned the assault] because, ironically enough, we had a flight leaving the next morning at 8:00, and we were fogged in. I would venture to say that close to 100 people came to the airport and walked over to the group and were apologizing. 'We want you to know that all of us here don't feel that way.' And I thought that was very commendable. And that's about the only thing that I can think that was distasteful that really ever happened to us."[47]

Remarkably, Cole only canceled the rest of the week; his wounds were treated in Chicago, and then the tour resumed on Saturday, April 14, in Norfolk, Virginia.[48] For the next few weeks, he was occasionally joined by Maria, who left Cookie and Sweetie in care of family and servants back in Hancock Park. In interviews given that spring, Cole went so far as to say that the attack was, counterintuitively, an "aid to integration" and to the cause of racial equality. As he viewed it, this was intended to be a divisive act, yet everyone who spoke about it afterward, from the Deep South to all over the rest of the world, came out on Cole's side—not one prominent individual interpreted the events of April 10 as showing that racial mixing was a dangerous thing and that the races should stay segregated. Twenty years earlier, the old southern Dixiecrats would have said that the incident proved precisely that. In 1919, the year Cole was born, if a group of white men had helped to put an "uppity" Negro (and that would not have been the word that they would have used) in his proper place, then they would have probably been given a medal by President Woodrow Wilson.

Hard to believe as it seems sixty years after the fact, Cole received more flak from black militants than he did from any Caucasians. It was around this time that he sent a $500 check to the National Association for the Advancement of Colored People (NAACP), an organization he had already frequently supported by giving benefit performances, for a lifetime membership. He was accused of not being sufficiently radicalized, of not taking a strong enough stand against segregation. When Cole was growing up, it was considered a major achievement for a black artist to perform in front of white audiences under any circumstances; even to work in segregated houses was considered a step forward; in the phrase of Duke Ellington, Cole was trying "to build a church of his own." Now he was "being taken to task" for performing in such circumstances. Dr. George Cannon, the African American former president of the Manhattan Medical Society, wrote, "Wake up, Mr. Cole, you're not that hungry. What do you want, more and more money even if it is any kind of money?" The criticisms stung.

Louis Armstrong, one of Cole's first and greatest heroes (or, as the man himself would say, one of Cole's "inspirators"), sprang to his defense. Armstrong demanded to know, in a radio interview with the Voice of America, "why those boys in Harlem took King Cole's records off the [jukebox] just because they think they should?" Armstrong went on, castigating the northern black press for their failure to support Cole. At a time like this, he argued, "They should stand by this man. We only have a few in our race that's on top in this music game. And I think that if we get together and stick by each other, we could have a few more."[49] Another African American icon, Jesse Owens, the hero of the 1936 Olympics, also came to Cole's defense: "If we are going to convince [white] people of the job we can do, we certainly can't do it by staying away from them."[50]

Some of the fallout from the attack took a bizarre turn: the police chief of Charlotte, North Carolina, one Frank N. Littlejohn, sent word to Nat, "Come to Charlotte. We here are heartily ashamed of the indignity to which you were subjected."[51] But in the same city, a local deejay was fired for commenting on the incident and for broadcasting pre-recorded comments by various city residents who, like him, denounced the attack.[52] Overall, rather than inspiring the Aryan people to take arms against the mongrel races, the attack served to "take the piss out of" the segregationist groups; the Birmingham White Citizen's Council reported that membership and meeting attendance numbers started to fall off almost immediately after the assault. The chairman of that organization, Carl Richardson, officially announced, "I'd like to make it clear that we had nothing to do with what happened at the auditorium. I would not go along with anything like that. I'd rather just call it quits and get out."[53] In other words, it was actions like these that were giving white supremacists a bad name.

Despite the criticisms from the black press, Cole resumed the tour and even, in a few instances, played for additional segregated houses. The overall tour was an overwhelming financial success. The papers reported that they took in a remarkable $83,412 in the first week alone; the three shows in New Orleans grossed $37,000 by themselves. Carlos Gastel announced, "We had 'em standing in the Levees!"[54] On April 28, they played the Municipal

Auditorium in Charleston, West Virginia, to a crowd of 7,000. "All seats were reserved and sold out two days ahead of the show."[55]

For his part, Cole was never shy about discussing the Birmingham attack, when and if anyone ever asked him directly about it, but it's doubtful that he ever brought it up himself in an interview. However, he offered his response to the incident at his next recording date, which took place roughly five weeks after Birmingham. The tour wound up in Washington, DC, where they played a few nights at the National Armory and were interviewed by the Voice of America.

Cole was next booked for a return engagement at the Chez Paree in Chicago, and he already may have been aware of a major event about to occur in Detroit from June 30 to July 4. "The Panorama of Progress," as it was titled, would be the brainchild of two prominent Michigan politicians, Congressmen Charles C. Diggs Jr. and his father, Charles C. Diggs Sr. The Panorama of Progress had a theme song, "We Are Americans Too," by Eubie Blake and Andy Razaf, who had both known Cole early, at least indirectly through his brother's association with Noble Sissle. The song had been published by W. C. Handy, who, in June 1956, donated 100 copies to Dr. King, then in the middle of the Montgomery bus boycott. King accepted the donation and wrote back to Handy, praising him for having "made such a rich contribution to the musical field in America."[56]

"We Are Americans Too" had actually been written in 1940 for an all-black revue entitled *Tan Manhattan*. Razaf had come up with a kind of song that was a rarity in the prewar period: an anthem of Afro-American pride, that would celebrate the accomplishments of the "race" in a "God Bless America"–like fashion. However, the final version of the song, which Cole was the first to record, was very different from the first lyric that Razaf originally submitted. Blake remembered, "He really gave the white people hell."[57] There was even a spoken "recitative," Blake said. "This thing went right from the lynching of Negroes to *everything!*" Neither the composer nor the producer, the pioneering black impresario Irvin C. Miller, could change Razaf's mind. The latter thundered, "How in the hell am I gonna charge [white audiences] money for you to tell them how lousy they are!" It was finally Razaf's wife, Jean, who persuaded the songwriter that these lyrics would turn "the whole black world against you, the intelligent ones. . . . This isn't the way to do it. You can't sell it back to the people."

So Razaf changed the song, putting it into the form that Cole recorded in 1956. But back in 1940, it was all for naught: although *Tan Manhattan* ran successfully in its out-of-town tryout at the Howard Theater in

Washington, DC, the closest it came to Broadway was a brief run at the Apollo Theater in February 1941. But during World War II, "Americans," which was now a celebration of Negro achievement rather than a vehement excoriation of the white race, was heard occasionally as a pro-American, patriotic song.

Cole was in the middle of his run at the Chez Paree when he decided to record "We Are Americans Too," on May 17. He used the club orchestra as well as its house music director, Brian Farnon (brother of the more famous Robert and Dennis Farnon), to arrange and conduct. Cole herein embodies the famous phrase of Teddy Roosevelt, singing mostly softly but carrying a big stick; there's an undercurrent of both pride and defiance in his voice. Farnon writes with a snare-heavy military band style while providing just a hint of that martial swing. It's a stirring record, which more than makes its point without preaching or accusing.

By now, the spoken intro, which had evolved from Razaf's more incendiary prose, started with, "I feel that the Panorama of Progress telling the story of the Negro's contributions to the progress of America is a noteworthy and patriotic service to all freedom-loving people, whose hopes and aspirations find expression in our Democratic way of life." And it concluded, "So, it is with humble respect for those who helped make this history, but with great pride, that I dedicate the recording of 'We Are Americans Too' to the youth of America, who are the inheritors of a great tradition."

In terms of the lyrics and the story it tells, "Americans" is very significant both for what it says and for what it chooses to leave out. Unlike similar songs written earlier, such as "Lift Ev'ry Voice and Sing," or later, "A Change Is Gonna Come" or "I Wish I Knew How It Would Feel to Be Free," there's no reference to any history of suffering, enslavement, or persecution of the Negro in America. "Americans Too" is exclusively flag-waving sentiment about the loyalty and steadfastness of Americans of Color, and entirely positive. There's not the slightest hint that the Negro has ever had to overcome any kind of hardship or that this has ever been anything other than mutually beneficial.

The spoken introduction spells it out even more clearly: "From Crispus Attucks to Ralph Bunche, the Negro people have played a significant part in the building of this great country of ours. America has meant much to the Negro and the Negro has contributed much to America. It is a glorious history, that of the Negro in America." Cole actually performed the song at the Chez Paree, which clearly indicated that he was certain everyone in the house was familiar with the Birmingham attack. The *Chicago Defender* wrote that by recording and performing "Americans," Cole was "getting back in the

[good] graces of most Negroes," which suggested that he had offended some African Americans by not offering a more militant response to the assault.[58]

"We Are Americans Too," Capitol Promotional Single PRO-267, was never released commercially, but forty copies were pressed by Capitol and distributed to Michigan radio stations to promote the Panorama of Progress.[59] Diggs Jr. and Sr. were both overjoyed at Cole's contribution to their event, and wrote, "It is indeed timely and fitting that an artist of Mr. Cole's immense stature and a great business, respected for its democratic principles, should join us in paying tribute to the achievements of our fellow Americans."[60] "We Are Americans Too" wasn't heard from again until it was at last issued commercially fifty years later in 2006.[61]

There was another, completely unexpected repercussion of the attack: it made Cole a serious political figure, whether he wanted to be one or not. For the first time, the larger forces of that world beyond show business began to pay attention to him. First, he was asked to appear at the annual White House Correspondents Dinner for the president, around May 25. "I was more nervous there than when I broke into the business," Cole said immediately after the event; "I had these butterflies 'way down there. I couldn't have been more nervous if I had been going out to fight tigers."[62] Dwight D. Eisenhower would be the first of three presidents whom Cole would meet. It's known that he sang "Too Young to Go Steady" and one would like to think that he also did "We Are Americans Too."[63]

And that was hardly the end of it: a few months later, on August 23, he participated in the National Republican Convention, held at the Cow Palace in San Francisco. All of this attention would have truly made Ace Carter and his teeth-gnashing henchmen toss their grits; they had done more to help the career of Nat King Cole and to hurt the truly lost cause of segregation than they could possibly realize. It was the conservative Republicans, the Eisenhower administration, that were essentially extending a formal apology for what happened and offering an olive branch.

The invitation to sing at the White House had come at the last minute, and Cole needed to miss a few days' worth of his run at the Chez Paree to accept it. Fortunately, he had a substitute in mind to fill in for him in Chicago. Tony Bennett was then a twenty-nine-year-old pop-and-jazz singer from Astoria, Queens, who had already had a few notable hits; he had worshipped Nat ever since discovering the Trio's music while serving as a private first class a decade earlier. "When we first met, Nat was tickled by the idea that I was still taking the city bus to local gigs, even though I had all these hit records," Bennett said. He would forever be grateful to Cole, he said, because up through 1956, his fame and success were confined to the New York area, and the Chez Paree gig afforded him his first chance to work in a major venue in the Midwest.[64]

Even though Bennett had already encountered racism at several points in his young life—directed at himself, as an Italian American, and his many black friends—he found the attack on Cole particularly disturbing. As Harry Belafonte, a mutual friend of both artists, put it, "How would anyone attack Nat? He was the sweetest, nicest guy in the world." In the immediate aftermath of Cole's death in 1965, Bennett became perhaps the most prominent white celebrity to join Sammy Davis Jr. in the legendary march for civil rights in Selma, Alabama, led by Dr. King.

In 1962, Cole was honored at a special dinner, celebrating his twenty-five years in show business, at the Ambassador Hotel in Los Angeles. Nat's old friend Steve Allen was the emcee, and he remembered a casual comment that, although Cole tossed it off without any particular significance, was tremendously poignant. "Nat and I happened to walk in side by side, as we entered the ballroom in the hotel; it was one of the large ones in LA, and we had to walk through the kitchen, just so we could enter behind the dais, rather than walk through the audience. And I remember Nat made a little joke, 'You know, this is the way I've always had to come in to these hotels.' He was not a complainer, but just that once, in that one little moment, he revealed the suffering that that sort of cruelty inflicts."[65] In the last few months of his career, the Civil Rights Act of 1964 was finally passed, thus outlawing "discrimination based on race, color, religion, sex or national origin." It's one of the great tragedies of the short life of Nat King Cole that he did not live to see an age in which most of the country believed, after a struggle of hundreds of years, that black people were Americans too.

AFTER FINISHING THE HIGHLY PROFITABLE spring tour and the interrupted Chez Paree engagement, Cole returned to the Sands from the end of June to the end of July. He then began August at the Hollywood Bowl (his third annual appearance there) and ended that month at the Fairmont in San Francisco in August, at which time he also put in his appearance at the 1956 Republican Convention (on August 23).[66]

A year earlier, Cole had gone on record as saying that the *Piano Style* album was "one I'm happy about," but that didn't mean he didn't keep searching, and especially for ways to bring his piano playing into this new phase of his career as a popular entertainer. Less than a month after the Birmingham incident, Cole was interviewed by the Voice of America, and while almost anyone else would have wanted to dwell on the attack, the number one thing on Cole's mind was an idea he had for a new keyboard project. "In fact, we're doing a piano album pretty soon, this summer when we get back to the coast, which will be quite a treat for me. There won't be any holds barred on this one. So many people have been requesting for me to play a little, so I finally got enough nerve to try it again. It's going to be mostly standards, I'm going to revive a few of the things I did a long time ago, like 'Sweet Lorraine' and 'Embraceable You.' Some of the things I did in the early Trio days."[67]

As always, he was looking for ways to bring the piano with him into this new phase of his music and career. With *After Midnight*, released in 1957 (and taped almost exactly one year after *Piano Style*), Cole seems to have satisfied that urge. As he put it, *After Midnight* "may have bridged the commercial gap."[68] Of the four piano albums, *After Midnight* is the only one that's purely a small group jazz project, and the inspiration is less the late, lamented King Cole Trio than the jam sessions that Cole played on for Norman Granz from 1942 to 1946. By a coincidence, Granz was in the Capitol Studios at the same time *After Midnight* was being recorded, along with two of Nat's friends and personal heroes, Ella Fitzgerald and Louis Armstrong. Ella and Pops visited Nat in the studio, and a photo was taken capturing the three giants, along with Carlos, Lee, and, thanks to the kindness of fate, Nat's six-year-old daughter, Sweetie.

Cole told his brother, Freddy, another story about how *After Midnight* came to be. Nat and his old friend Harry "Sweets" Edison were at a baseball game in August of 1956, and they were so overjoyed when their team won that they spontaneously went into the studio and started playing—after rallying the rest of Cole's touring group (John Collins, Charlie Harris, and Lee Young). Both stories are partly true; Cole was already planning to do a jazz album when, on one joyful summer night following a particularly inspirational ball game, he and Sweets decided to just go for the gusto.

When Cole and Gillette then listened to the tapes, they liked what they heard so much that they booked three more sessions in roughly the same format: Cole's rhythm section plus one special guest soloist. To keep the flame burning, they called alto saxophonist Willie Smith, valve trombonist Juan Tizol, who, like Edison, had already both been a part of Cole's music, and Stuff Smith, dean of hot violinists. The finished album was titled *After Midnight* to convey that loose, relaxed mood.

Perhaps ironically, it's also the way Cole sings on *After Midnight*, as well the fact of it, that makes this the best-remembered of all of his piano projects; his singing is more in the fully developed, open-throated, completely realized style of the second half of his career rather than the more cautious, singing-around-corners approach he used in the mid-1940s. Like such later milestones as *John Coltrane and Johnny Hartman, The Tony Bennett / Bill Evans Album,* and the *Sinatra-Jobim* team-ups, *After Midnight* is a de facto collaboration as well: this is the only one of his original albums on which Cole both sang and played all the way through, the most significant meeting of Cole the vocalist with Cole the pianist. Stuff Smith opined, shortly after Cole's death, "Nat didn't really want to sing. He wanted to have a group. Nat wanted to play piano, I think. I might be wrong! Commercially speaking, it was a good thing he sang. You know, to make some loot. Well, loot's great."[69] Despite Smith's take on the subject, Cole certainly sounds like he's enjoying himself both playing and singing, and that's a key factor in what makes *After Midnight* one of the most remarkable works in his canon.

The first session on August 15, 1956, was the purest in that it genuinely seems to have been completely spontaneous, with Cole playing and singing only songs that were already in his repertoire—he wanted to capture the feeling of the moment. That's what a jam session is: extemporaneous improvisations on songs everybody knows rather than a time to learn something new. Three of the songs were long-standing signatures of the King Cole Trio: "Sweet Lorraine" and "It's Only a Paper Moon," which were both standards that Cole obviously had been playing for many years even prior to the Trio, and "(Get Your Kicks On) Route 66." Edison sounds like an afterthought here, and, to a degree so does Young, when Cole, Collins, and Harris are so perfect in and of themselves. While these versions may lack the sense of purpose of the originals, it's hard to argue with such outstanding playing.

Cole began the date with two songs that were not generally regarded as part of the Trio's history, even though he had recorded them both before, and these are both among the album's highlights. "You Can Depend on Me" is a standard by Cole's original inspiration, Fatha Hines; Cole had played with the Capitol International Jazzmen in 1945, but now he sings it as well. Slow and relaxed, even with a few hints of guitar intermingling with Cole's piano intro (a Trio trademark), it shows that Cole was a whole other artist making a whole other kind of record than he had in the 1940s.

"Candy" is equally tasty. The song was one of the big hits of the World War II era, as recorded by Johnny Mercer and the Pied Pipers, one of the more durable songs by Alex Kramer and Joan Whitney, whose tunes were on the charts consistently in the war years. Cole had sung "Candy" in 1945 on a V-Disc (distributed by the U.S. Army to servicemen only), and this is a major instance where the 1956 version is unquestionably superior. Cole's vocal is much more intense and full of details (as when he bites down on "*I* wish that there were four of her . . ."), the piano solo is fuller and more luxurious, and overall the vibe is much sweeter in a "Candy" sort of a way.

When they resumed recording, a month later on September 14, the next guest was William McLeish Smith. Professionally billed as Willie, Smith was a swing era alto colossus second only to Johnny Hodges. He had been the blues and ballad soloist supreme with the great Jimmie Lunceford band, then enjoyed a renaissance in a long-term association with Harry James and His Orchestra, and for a time replaced Hodges with Duke Ellington. He had previously played with Cole as one of the Keynoters, on a "Just Jazz" concert, and in the saxophone sections of both Riddle and May.

Cole attempted most of the newest material on this date, starting with "Don't Let It Go to Your Head," co-credited to Hollywood studio pianist Charlie LaVere (who plays on Cole's *Love Is the Thing* album); it's a slightly awkward lyric that Cole makes sound better, perhaps, than it actually is. The other two new songs are "You're Lookin' at Me," and "I Was a Little Too Lonely (And You Were a Little Too Late)." Of the three, only the last, the one fast novelty number in the batch, truly amounts to a King Cole classic. Bobby Troup's "You're Lookin' at Me" is not in the same class as his "Baby All the Time," "Route 66," or "Come to the Party," but it's a solid enough effort and worthy of Cole's attention. It achieved some cachet when Carmen McRae made it, rather surprisingly, the title of her 1983 tribute album to Cole.

"I Was a Little Too Lonely (And You Were a Little Too Late)" is by far the most satisfying of what we might call the "new new" [*sic*] songs on *After Midnight*. It was written by a pair of old pros, Ray Evans and Jay Livingston (authors of Cole's breakthrough hit "Mona Lisa" and his classic "Never Let Me Go") for the Cole film *Istanbul*. At first, there were big plans for this song: Cole was to sing it in the movie, and Capitol hedged their bets by having him make what appear to be two very different versions of it. One was here, at the second *After Midnight* date, and the other was in the middle of a session for the album *Love Is the Thing* with Gordon Jenkins (although it's impossible to imagine how this rhythmic tune might have been done by Jenkins with his massed army of fiddles). It was a terrific song for Cole, absolutely in the tradition of such swinging and funny classics as "The Trouble with Me Is You," "Now He Tells Me," and "The Best Man"; no wonder Cole had high hopes for it. Alas, it was barely heard in the movie (only about forty seconds) and then neither recording was issued; finally, it turned up on the expanded edition of *After Midnight*, some thirty years after the fact.

There was only one standard on the Willie Smith date, but he and Cole make the most of it—the 1929 "Just You, Just Me," which the Cole Trio had recorded as an instrumental for a 1946 Capitol transcription. Cole makes the most of the words here, but delivers them with the sensitivity and attention to detail that characterizes his mature work—like his colleague Sinatra, he can now be romantic, even at swingin' tempos. Cole had been an early advocate of pan-American rhythms, including calypso as well as rhumbas and congas, and for the third session (September 21) he brings in two guest stars to help create an exotic, Latino kind of mood: the Puerto Rican trombonist Juan Tizol and the Cuban percussionist Jack Costanzo.

Juan Tizol also worked extensively with Harry James, following his long tenure with Duke Ellington. Unlike Cole's other guest stars, he was not primarily an improvising soloist but was best known as a composer of exotic jazz standards (of which "Caravan" is the most famous) and an atmosphere specialist. The main order of business here is "Caravan," which Cole had first transcribed in 1938, and which, by 1956, had become a rare tune from the big-band era that had become even more popular in subsequent decades among modern jazzmen. "The Lonely One" was composed by saxophonist Lenny Hambro, who for much of his career was associated with the Cuban composer and bandleader Chico O'Farrill. The playing of the Cole-Tizol-Costanzo composition makes it a perfect companion piece to "Caravan": equal parts Latin and Middle Eastern, this is background music for a Havanese belly dancer. Lyrically, "The Lonely One" sounds like "Nature Boy" 's kid brother.

Then Costanzo sits out, and Cole and Tizol deliver the best two slow ballads of the album. "Blame It on My Youth" and "What Is There to Say" were composed by members of George Gershwin's inner circle, respectively, Oscar Levant and Vernon Duke. Both are slow, but "What Is There to Say" is vaguely optimistic rather than melancholy. Duke and E. Y. Harburg wrote it for the posthumous 1934 edition of the *Ziegfeld Follies,* but it quickly became a jazz perennial rather than a pop hit, embraced by the swing bands and then modernists like Gerry Mulligan. These two ballads show that the small group format isn't only suited to a Jazz at the Philharmonic (JATP)-style jam session, but that the intimate format also uniquely supports Cole as a crooner of love songs; both are exquisitely bittersweet.

Cole was saving the best "Stuff" for last: Hezekiah Leroy Gordon Smith (1909–1967), or Stuff, had been one of the major stars of New York's Swing Street in the mid-1930s and was generally regarded as the greatest of all jazz violinists; as the Danish virtuoso Svend Asmussen told me, "I thought that Joe Venuti was the greatest, but then when I heard Stuff for the first time,

I forgot about Joe!" Smith's celebrity had faded after the war, but ten years later he was enjoying something of a renaissance: Granz was recording him extensively as a leader and also with Dizzy Gillespie and Ella Fitzgerald, and he also turns up on a Capitol Session with Nelson Riddle.

Smith was a brilliant choice for the project. Like the violinist, Cole too had also been nurtured on Fifty-second Street. "Ah, there was a session!" As Smith later said of Cole, "There's a boy, man. He can play all the piano you want to hear." He continued, "Nat King Cole was one of the finest piano players in the country, I mean for swinging, man." Smith continued, "Yeah, he played beautiful, I mean to me, some guys just kind of fit you, and other guys don't. But he fitted me." The violinist was right: he and Cole "fitted" each other beautifully, and their four tracks are easily the album's highlight. Even apart from the rest of the album, the four Cole-Smith tracks represent a sainted collaboration, two masters at their absolute pinnacle, bringing out the best of each other.

This fourth and final date (September 24) starts out with a subtle ice-breaker, "Sometimes I'm Happy," in which both the principals are laid back in a blissfully bittersweet fashion. Clearly, both Cole and Smith are inspired heavily by Cole's earlier collaborator, Lester Young, and his 1943 interpretation of the Vincent Youmans classic, both iconic and laconic. (Too bad they didn't call Pres himself for one of these sessions as his brother was already present.) The 1927 melody is set in an ABAB structure: the violinist and pianist alternate on each 8-bar section, with Cole taking the two bridges. "I Know That You Know," also by Youmans (another Gershwin buddy), was already a Cole perennial. It's also perhaps the fastest tune on *After Midnight*, delivered like a jam session standard at horse race tempo—again, very much in the Jazz at the Philharmonic spirit of a bunch of soloists trying to outplay and even outrun each other. Smith plays gloriously here, full of warmth and swing, showing that the jazz violin, in the right hands, can easily compete with the saxophone or trumpet for sheer soul. The piano-violin exchanges constitute the finest "trading session" on the album, and while Lee Young is rarely included on anyone's list of great jazz drummers, his playing here is perfect.

Considering that "When I Grow Too Old to Dream" was written by Oscar Hammerstein and Sigmund Romberg for a Hollywood opera (*The Night Is Young*, 1935), the song has a surprising pedigree in the African American musical community: Putney Dandridge, the Cats and the Fiddle, Helen Humes, Dizzy Gillespie (with the Tempo Jazzmen), Rose Murphy, Sheila Jordan, and many others. Most jazz versions are breathtakingly fast, but Cole gives the song space enough to breathe. The singer pauses luxuriously between the first few words: "When . . . I grow too old to dream . . ." Smith responds with that same phrasing in his solo, emphasizing the first note and then pausing before continuing with the phrase. Guitarist John Collins also takes his best solo on the album, and, collectively, they show that one doesn't have to play at a breakneck tempo to truly swing.

"Two Loves Have I" represents the nexus of two major African American icons, Josephine Baker and Nat King Cole. The great transcontinental diva's theme song was titled "J'Ai Deux Amours" in French and later briefly became "Give Me a Tune" in England before becoming a postwar hit in the United States. Cole's treatment is relaxed, with a prominent bass vamp by Charlie Harris; the track isn't an exciting highlight, but it's a valuable low-key contrast to the other Stuff Smith numbers. It's also more Paris, Texas, than Paris, France, and Smith gives it something of a hillbilly feel.

In January 1957, presumably just as the album was coming out, Smith appeared on Cole's TV show and backed him on "I Know That You Know." Later in the spring, Cole promoted the album by spotlighting Tizol, then a regular member of Nelson Riddle's studio orchestra, and reprising their treatment of "Caravan." In October of that year, Cole's somewhat estranged old friend Norman Granz brought an entire Jazz at the Philharmonic troupe onto the Cole show, which gave the pianist a chance to reunite with such colleagues as Stan Getz and Coleman Hawkins.

With the sessions for *After Midnight* completed, Cole knew that he found what he was looking for; he had made the perfect piano-vocal-jazz album. In a way, that wasn't entirely a good thing, because he stopped looking and never made another piano-centric album again. This is the way he would incorporate both jazz and the piano into his act in the final years of his short career; surviving concert recordings from the 1960s, on both video and audio, often feature an *After Midnight* segment, in which Cole performs "Sweet Lorraine," "It's Only a Paper Moon," and a few others, not in the original Trio arrangements but in the looser versions he worked out for the 1956 sessions.

Afterward, he stayed in contact with Stuff Smith, and, according to the violinist, expressed an interest in recording an original song that Smith had written, titled "Miracles." Cole asked the violinist to demonstrate the tune for him, and Smith said, "He is a nice guy, but he wants everything perfected. Which is great. I will drop by his house when he gets to town and show him how 'Miracles' should be played."[70]

After Midnight's great strength is its spontaneity, which also insured that the circumstances that produced it would have been difficult to repeat, making it virtually impossible to replicate the album and even more so to surpass it. "And, you know," as Stuff Smith said of Nat King Cole, "he had so much music in his heart, man!"

FOLLOWING THE *AFTER MIDNIGHT* SESSIONS, Cole came East to play several weeks at the Latin Casino in Philadelphia, a month at the Copa (comedian Shecky Green was the opening act), and a week at the Three Rivers in Syracuse; believe it or not, for Cole this amounted to a comparatively light season. In fall 1956, Cole, for the first time since his career had started to really pick up in spring 1944 (other than when he took off a few weeks after the ulcer attack in spring 1953), began to slow down on his usual routine of constant touring, one-nighters, and record dates: he was concentrating all of his energies on a new and remarkable project, *The Nat King Cole Show*, which premiered on NBC TV on November 5, and about which more shortly. He was so busy with the program that it shouldn't be surprising that he never quite finished the one album project he was working on around this time.

We still don't know whether the tracks that eventually went into the *Night Life* package, from December 1955 and January 1956, were actually intended to comprise an album. However, there is indisputable evidence, in the form of a handwritten list by Cole himself, that the fall 1956 tracks were, at one point, supposed to be part of a new album of standards with Riddle. A few of these "orphan" standards had already started to pop up at various sessions. In Chicago, around the time of *Piano Style* in 1955, Nat and Nelson had cut a subtly swinging version of the 1926 Richard Whiting song, "Breezin' Along with the Breeze." (At the same date, they also laid down a stunning treatment of a new song by Marvin Fisher and Jack Segal, "Nothing Ever Changes My Love for You," which became an instant Cole classic.) Then, a month later in Hollywood, Cole and Riddle concocted a raucously jazzy reinterpretation of Governor Jimmy Davis's "hillbilly" standard, "You Are My Sunshine."

But the project, to which Cole gave the rather rudimentary working title of "Swing Album," gathered the most steam with seven tracks done over two sessions in September and October 1956, around the time of *After Midnight*. Six out of these seven songs were originally written for movie musicals, between the dawn of talking pictures and the start of World War II; the proposed album might have been eventually titled something like *Nat and Nelson Swing Hollywood!* The arrangements jump with a remarkable warmth and familiarity, not least because so many old buddies are present. Sweets Edison, Willie Smith, and Juan Tizol, who had all just played on *After Midnight*, are all audible throughout, as are Cole's two favorite royal deputies on piano, Jimmy

Rowles and Bill Miller. Likewise, in the song selections, Cole favored close personal friends like Johnny Mercer ("How Little We Know," "Tangerine"), Jimmy McHugh ("I'm Shooting High"), and Burke and Van Heusen ("Like Someone in Love").

Nearly four minutes long, "How Little We Know" (from the Hoagy-Bogie classic *To Have and Have Not*) was clearly planned as an album track rather than a single. Cole's vocal is wise and knowing, especially in the way he extends it with an original tag ("Well now maybe you're meant to be mine / And to have you would really be fine"), as is Smith's alto sax solo. Most of the arrangements are short and punchy, none more so than "Should I," an early talkie hit (from the 1929 *Lord Byron of Broadway*, reprised in *Singin' in the Rain*) that both Cole and Sinatra were fond of for its rhythmic possibilities. Cole dances around stinging brass in staccato jabs, almost as if they were throwing punches back and forth—Cole literally spars with the ensemble, and the piece gets steadily higher and more exciting.

Richard Whiting's "True Blue Lou" derives from another 1929 all-talking, all-singing, all-dancing epic, *The Dance of Life*, in which it was very movingly talk-sung by the quickly forgotten Hal Skelly. The lyrics, by Sam Coslow and Leo Robin, simultaneously suggest both a classic saloon song and a parody thereof. Cole takes it medium slow and highly melodically (Tony Bennett's later version is more talk-singing), with saloon-y piano by Miller under the vocal. Cole is a master storyteller here; this is a classic example of what he meant when he said, "I like to lean on the lyrics."

Even though the tracks were never assembled into an album, the arrangements would prove valuable for Cole; these bright, bouncy treatments of familiar songs were ideal both for high-class niteries like the Copa and for TV appearances. At a minute-and-a-half, "I'm Shooting High" served as a perfect opener for Cole's 1958 appearance at the Copa[71] as well as no less than four episodes of his NBC TV series. Cole shoots high and hits a bullseye, building to a quick climax with blaring brass, modulating upward and stretching out his final note in what could be a vocal approximation of a trumpet glissando. "Like Someone in Love" (introduced by Dinah Shore in *Belle of the Yukon*, 1944) was already a much-recorded standard thanks to modern jazzmen attracted to Van Heusen's memorable melody, unusual structure (ABAB'), and major-to-minor harmonies. Riddle opens with Edison and Tizol in a distinctly minor mode, before Cole enters stealthily, dancing, around a two-beat break. "Tangerine" (the Jimmy Dorsey hit from *The Fleet's In*) contrasts Smith's sweet-toned alto against Riddle's swinging brass. Cole's vocal is at once as sweet and tart and tangy as the citrus fruit that gives the titular senorita her name. Riddle's chart uses a lot of effective hi-fi contrast but remains true to the spirit of one of his key inspirations, Sy Oliver.

The most durable of these seven swinging standards was "Ballerina," by two songwriters who were both more usually lyricists, Carl Sigman and Bob Russell. Originally a #1 hit for the board-stiff Vaughan Monroe, "Ballerina" told a melodramatic tale of a dancer forced to choose between love and a career, and thus encapsulated the regrettable postwar moment when women were chased out of the workforce and back into the kitchen. That was in 1947; a decade later, Cole introduced it on his TV show as "a somewhat different arrangement of an old favorite."[72] The Cole-Riddle treatment is saturated with a Sinatra-like swagger and irreverence, as if he doesn't take the rather chauvinistic lyrics at all seriously (and kudos for him) but would rather swing it like crazy. The Cole-Riddle "Ballerina" had a life of its own on TV and concerts, most famously on *Nat King Cole Live at the Sands* (1960), but the studio version has been heard less often. This standout performance shows that Sinatra wasn't the only one re-imagining classic standard songs for swinging lovers.

BY FALL 1956, Cole had become a very familiar face and voice on television, and, what's more, he had enjoyed a fruitful relationship with the National Broadcasting Company for nearly twenty years. With the staggering popularity of his recordings, NBC finally decided to give him a real shot on his own weekly program; thankfully, a time slot became available, thanks to another, very different piano player. From August to October 1956, the society bandleader Frankie Carle had starred in his own fifteen-minute variety series on Monday evenings, titled *The Golden Touch of Frankie Carle*. When the Carle show went off the air, Cole's agents at General Artists Corp., Carlos Gastel and Tommy Rockwell, jumped at the opportunity.[73] They reached out to Harold "Hal" Kemp, a veteran NBC executive and producer, who was able to get the show greenlighted on a sustaining (non-sponsored) basis.

From the beginning, it was a gamble; a few black singers and entertainers, like Hazel Scott and Billy Daniels, had tentatively tried smaller-scale shows, but *The Nat King Cole Show* was the major leagues. In 1954, Cole was taking in at least $12,000 per week on the road, and the stakes in Las Vegas, where he brought in $50,000 on most weeks, were much higher. NBC couldn't pay him anything close to that, at least not at first, but the idea was to start small, and as the show grew in popularity, then a major sponsor would climb on board, and the budget and Cole's salary would expand along with it.

NBC broke the news in early October; "The smooth-voiced singer will become the first Negro performer to star in his own weekly coast-to-coast show," the *Philadelphia Inquirer* announced.[74] The black press was understandably ecstatic, calling it "one of the most unprecedented and momentous moves in the hectic history of television," and added, "Nat King Cole now becomes a full-fledged star of five mediums of entertainment: records, radio, stage, screen, and television."[75] The *Nat King Cole Show* premiered on Monday, November 5, 1956, at 7:30 p.m. EST, broadcasting out of New York, with Gordon Jenkins as the first conductor. (Veteran keyboardist Dick Hyman was on piano.)

NBC promoted the new show by having Cole make guest appearances on other shows hosted by Perry Como and Walter Winchell. On December 11, Como welcomed two towering (literal) giants of showbiz, Nat Cole and Carol Channing; Cole and Como converse about Nat's ongoing appearances at the Sands (he sings the same arrangement of "Thou Swell" that he would record live there in 1960) and, more locally, at the Three Rivers club in Syracuse. He also sings, for the first time, a number from *My Fair Lady*, "I've Grown Accustomed to Her Face." And he mentions that he now has his own show on the same network, NBC. They sing together on "I'll See You in C - U - B - A," a vintage Irving Berlin song from the dawn of Prohibition in 1919.

The *Courier* pointed out, "The Nat King Cole show will be different in other ways. It will not depend on guest artists to carry it" (as distinct from, say, Ed Sullivan, who was entirely dependent on guest artists). Instead, "it will rely on the sheer magic of the Cole personality," and then noted that Cole had already sold forty-nine million records' worth of such magic. They also added, "At this writing, the show is not sponsored but NBC believes it has a good shot at obtaining one." That, at least, was the plan.

Stay tuned.

NINETEEN FIFTY-SIX WOULD CONCLUDE with Cole recording his most successful album of the late 1950s. *Love Is the Thing*, which could be considered the greatest album of optimistic love ballads of all time (in sharp contrast to Sinatra's darker and more suicidal saloon songs), could have also been a tenth anniversary present to Maria.

Maria Hawkins Ellington and Nathaniel Adams Coles fell in love with each other and the music of Gordon Jenkins at the same time. It was on one of their first cautious dates in spring 1946; Nat was still married, although somewhat estranged from his first wife, and he and Maria were working on the same bill at the Zanzibar on West 49th Street. Now, it was about 5:00 a.m. , and they were afraid to be seen together, so they sat in Nat's car, listening to the radio. Just as the sun started to come up, "suddenly, Gordon

Jenkins's beautiful *Manhattan Tower* came over the radio."[76] How could they not fall in love? *Manhattan Tower* is a singularly amazing work, equal parts romantic and ambitious, one that fully captures the unique, short-lived spirit of postwar optimism: Jenkins's music portrays a world where anything is possible, where a bright-eyed youngster from Webster Groves, Missouri, can grow up to become a famous maestro and compose a classic work, and also where a poor boy from Alabama can grow up to be the king of show business, and claim as his queen a beautiful princess from the right side of the tracks.[77]

In 1956, Jenkins ended his long-term affiliation with Decca Records and switched allegiances to Capitol. Almost immediately, both Cole and Sinatra made plans to work with him, and Cole got there first. He announced the album in October, although it wouldn't be recorded for another two months, "We just closed a sensational record-breaking stint at the Coconut Grove [he would also play Philadelphia and Salt Lake City that same month], and, after busily rehearsing, I am going to record for Capitol Records with the big studio orchestra under the direction of Nelson Riddle. I feel that Nelson Riddle is one of the top men in the music realm, and we have been on many hit records together. However, I am [also] going to do a string recording date next month with another ace conductor, Gordon Jenkins. We have a tentative title for the album, *Love Is the Thing*."[78]

The presence of Gordon Jenkins ensured that this album project would have a unique sound, immediately different from the singles with Riddle and his other, more recent, piano-centric albums. What's more, this would be his first project in stereo.[79] Lee Gillette had another idea about how the new album might further distinguish itself from both Cole's and Jenkins's earlier work. "I wanted Gordon to do a background that was all strings, I didn't want him to include any French horns, or reeds, or brass of any kind.[80] Well I had quite a time talking Gordon into that, he said, 'How can I write anything with just violins and cellos and violas? How can I do this?' I said, 'Gordon, you're a master at this, at getting a beautiful sound out of strings. Just don't clutter it up.' He finally agreed."[81] This is also one of the few albums where Cole didn't bring in his regular rhythm section; those roles are filled by the conductor's preferred guys, guitarist Allan Reuss, bassist Jack Ryan, pianist Charlie LaVere, who joins Cole's drummer, Lee Young.

A major inspiration for both collaborators was the music of songwriter and film composer Victor Young, who had been Jenkins's mentor and who had died about a month before the sessions. On November 26, Cole devoted most of that week's episode of *The Nat King Cole Show* on NBC to Young's music. *Love Is the Thing* includes four tunes by Young, including the opener,

"When I Fall In Love," "Where Can I Go without You," "Love Letters," and the title track and closer, "Love Is the Thing." Just as rhythm songs like "Route 66" on *After Midnight* would be internalized by multiple generations of jazz singers, "When I Fall in Love" would become a staple not for only crooners and balladeers but R&B and soul singers. Pop stars of the of the 1960s, '70s, and '80s were singing it (as well as "For All We Know," from the follow-up album, *The Very Thought of You*) over and over long before Natalie Cole re-hipped everyone to the rest of her father's catalog.

Love Is the Thing, like *Two in Love* before it, also provides us with a clear-cut distinction between Cole and Sinatra. A Sinatra love song is either the heights of rapture or the depths of despair, but when Cole sings about love, he often goes straight down the middle. In these two albums especially, love is a state of being that enables us all. Being in love is more important than being rich or poor, beggar or king—whether that love is requited or not. Later on, Sinatra's 1960 album *Nice 'n' Easy* became his answer to Nat Cole's style of optimistic love songs and Cole's 1962 *Where Did Everyone Go* is his version of the classic Sinatra-ian suicidal saloon songs.

Gordon Jenkins (1910–1984) was the perfect partner for *Love Is the Thing*. Where younger arranger-conductors, like Riddle (and most of Stan Kenton's staff), were enamored of the more recent European classical masters, from the French impressionists to Stravinsky, Jenkins was more solidly in the camp of Brahms and Tchaikovsky. In twenty-five years of arranging for big bands and pop singers, Jenkins had perfected a sound and a style that was uniquely his own. It was grandiose, unabashedly pretentious—at times excessively so, and other times delightfully so—but always sincerely so. Jenkins was as direct and honest an orchestrator as Cole was a singer and they suited each other perfectly.

Jenkins first became aware of Cole in the late '30s when the King Cole Trio was doing odd work in bars and as well as various studios around Los Angeles and he was a young arranger on staff at NBC. "Oh, yeah, I always dug Nat, I love the way he sang," Jenkins remembered on a radio interview in 1974. "He sang on a radio show at NBC, he was working across the street in the Bowling Alley bar with his Trio, and, I think, they gave him fifteen or sixteen dollars to do a thing, the first time I'd ever seen him. And I was quite taken with him as a jazz piano player, which he was, of course, expert at. But he's such a good musician."[82] Jenkins is talking about the Radio Room, where the Trio played in 1940 (and which housed a bowling alley in the back). The Trio also shared at least several weeks of a radio series with Jenkins "and his swing band" on NBC in May 1939. [83]

When asked about working with Cole, Jenkins replied,

> He was such a gentleman, a nice person to work with. He had great manners. And he didn't ever try to impress you with how good he was, and you knew [that whatever you wrote] he was going to sing it good. You could write in any kind of a trick chord and it didn't have to be easy for him to come in. Some people don't have good ears, you have to get down to a child's level, a rock-n-roll level, whatever, where they can hear what you're doing, so they don't have any trouble hearing, getting in. But with Nat I just wrote anything I wanted. You try to color the arrangements to fit the personality, and the way that he's going to sing it. He's going to approach a song completely different from Frank or Judy. I keep going back to those three, because they were the ones I worked with the most.[84]

What was Jenkins's approach to working with Cole? "Well, you sit down at the piano, and he'd sing it through, if he had an idea, he might want to start with a verse or he might want to do this, but he never said how he wanted the backgrounds written. He'd heard things that I did that he liked, so he figured I would know." Jenkins also noted that Cole was such a professional that often one take was all they needed; however, if Jenkins thought they needed another take, no matter how many they'd done, Cole would always go along with what he wanted. (He also added that to get this out of Garland, contrastingly, he had to "lock the door of the studio and *make* her do it again!")[85]

No one ever seems to have asked Jenkins if he had a hand in selecting the songs on the two albums, but, as it happens, a lot of them do derive from the maestro's own experience, at least indirectly. Jenkins came of musical age during the height of the radio era of the '30s, when there was a phenomenon that has long since been forgotten known as the pop-music maestro. These were larger than life characters who were to radio what auteurs like Alfred Hitchcock and John Ford were to the movies, such as Isham Jones and Victor Young, two of Jenkins's key mentors. Others, Johnny Green, Andre Kostelanetz, and British Ray Noble, were all composers, songwriters, conductors, orchestrators, and marquee-name bandleaders, a genre that largely vanished after the war.

Young, who, as we've seen, had died just a few weeks earlier at the age of fifty-six, exerted a particularly pertinent influence on Jenkins. A Jewish composer who studied classical music at the Warsaw Imperial Conservatory, Young wrote songs that were much favored by black musicians (more than the songs of most of his contemporaries), and a disproportionate number of them became all-time jazz standards. "Love Is the Thing" had already been recorded by two of Cole's favorites, Ethel Waters and Billy Eckstine (as well as the Mills

Blue Rhythm Band and Andy Kirk); black female jazz pianists were also fond of it, among them Hazel Scott, Beryl Booker, and Cleo Brown.

Conversely, the album's iconic opener, "When I Fall in Love," had virtually no history at that point, but had most likely come to Cole by way of a young pianist-singer who had cut her teeth on the King Cole Trio. Young and Heyman had written it for a quickly forgotten film called *One Minute to Zero* and doubtless it would have fallen off the face of the earth had it not been for Jeri Southern, who recorded it with her own piano and orchestra conducted by the composer in 1952. Cole would then inspire dozens if not hundreds of jazz musicians (most notably Bill Evans) as well as soul singers to pick up the song's mantle. Young's "Where Can I Go without You?," which boasts a stellar lyric by Peggy Lee (a consistent songwriter), and "Love Letters" are both songs of separation; Jenkins had helped Dick Haymes make the latter a hit to begin with in 1945.

Along with the four Victor Young songs, much of the rest of *Love Is the Thing* comprises songs that Jenkins had worked on at some point earlier in his career, such as Mack Gordon's "Stay as Sweet as You Are" (sung by tenor Lanny Ross in *College Rhythm*), Fats Waller's ur-jazz standard "Ain't Misbehavin'" (here in a rare incarnation as a slow ballad), and Harry Warren and Gordon's movie theme for Glenn Miller, "At Last." (This is most likely the recording that inspired Etta James's soul classic in 1960.) "Maybe It's Because I Love You Too Much" is a relatively obscure number from the Irving Berlin songbook. The legendary songwriter was always gracious when he heard a recording that he liked of one of his songs (and he wasn't always easy to please), but he was especially effusive when he wrote to Cole, "Your record has given me one of the greatest thrills I've had in my career."[86]

The most obscure song on the set is "I Thought about Marie," with both words and music by Jenkins, who had written and published it in 1951.[87] In a studio outtake from the *Love Is the Thing* sessions, Cole mentioned that the song's publisher, Sam Weiss (who was also present at the December 1956 sessions), had presented him with the song about four years previously. Obviously Cole was inspired by the coincidence that the song has his wife's name in it, even if it describes a couple who are getting back together after a fight and a separation. (He also sang it on the August 6, 1957, episode of the NBC series in front of a large photo of Mrs. Cole.)

Apart from the standards and the existing songs that Cole was transforming into standards, *Love Is the Thing* did introduce one new song, and it's an absolute classic. "When Sunny Gets Blue," perhaps the single greatest composition by Marvin Fisher, the ever-reliable composer who had been steadily supplying

Cole with excellent material since 1945. (A few months later, Cole would record another of Fisher's topical novelties, "When Rock and Roll Come to Trinidad.") Sometimes Cole is at his best with a simple song, like the closer, "Love Is the Thing," and sometimes we just yearn for him to sink his teeth into a more harmonically complex piece of music, a more cryptic lyric, and a melody that rarely goes in the direction we expect it to. "When Sunny Gets Blue" is a prime example of the latter, it takes half a heartbeat for us as listeners to realize that "Sunny" is a girl, and Jack Segal's expert text plays up the contrast between the states of sunniness and being blue, and the irony of a girl with a Sunny name being in a blue mood. He sings it with tenderness, compassion, and empathy that's remarkable even for him. The Fisher-Segal song immediately became a jazz-pop perennial, lovingly sung by many who learned it from Cole, such as his most prominent rock-era disciple, Johnny Mathis.

If the most memorable new song is "Sunny," then the greatest old-new song is "It's All in the Game." Composed in 1912 as "Melodie in A" by the soldier, statesman, and composer, General Charles Gates Dawes, who later served as vice president under Calvin Coolidge, it was originally conceived as a semi-classical showpiece, especially for virtuoso instrumentalists such as saxophonist Rudy Wiedoeft and trombonist Tommy Dorsey. Around 1950 or 1951 (not long after Dawes's death), lyrics were added by the veteran tunesmith Carl Sigman, and it became a hit for Tommy Edwards, an African American balladeer who can safely be described as a Nat King Cole disciple. The team of Louis Armstrong and Gordon Jenkins recorded it at the end of 1951, and this was clearly the blueprint for Cole and Jenkins five years later. But then the 1956 Cole-Jenkins recording, unquestionably the definitive reading of the song, inspired Edwards to do it again, this time with a rock-pop beat (16th note triplets and a doo-wop-ish vocal group), and this 1958 remake became Edwards's signature hit.

When *Love Is the Thing* was released, it immediately became not only Cole's most successful album yet—his first to hit #1 on the *Billboard* pop album chart—but one of the biggest sellers thus far in the brief history of the long-playing record. It seemed apparent to everyone, even in the heat of the moment, that Cole and Jenkins were making pop history. At least three of the major mainstream columnists sang the praises of the album: Dorothy Kilgallen announced the project a whole month even before recording began;[88] Earl Wilson, who selected it as the number one record of the week,[89] and even the most iconic syndicated columnist of them all, the infamous Walter Winchell, told readers in papers across the country, "Album a Sell-Out: Nat King Cole's latest album, *Love Is the Thing*, sold out in its first three days."[90] (Flash!) This was a remarkable trifecta of positive media attention from the three most widely read columnists in America, none of whom would have paid so much attention to Cole ten years earlier.

There are many reasons that *Love Is the Thing* was such an instant classic, starting with the opening "When I Fall in Love" and the closing title song, not to mention "When Sunny Gets Blue," "It's All in the Game," and "Love Letters." But the number one reason for the album's success was undoubtedly "Stardust." It was Gillette's idea to include the thirty-year-old standard, which, almost from the beginning, had been regarded as an archetype of the American songbook. Jenkins had remembered the moment when Victor Young wrote the arrangement that transformed Hoagy Carmichael's melody from a jazz instrumental to a romantic ballad, and Cole had been doing the song at least since 1954. "I hate to sing 'Stardust,' " he said at the time; "it wears me out."[91]

That being the case, Gillette had to put his foot down. "We got to choosing the material and we came to 'Stardust,' and Nat looked at me and he said, 'You gotta be out of your mind! Me, do "Stardust"?! It's got a thousand recordings!' I said, 'Yeah, but we don't have one by Nat Cole.' So, when we finally got that settled, and got the key set, I said 'Now Nat, there's one other thing . . .' and he said 'Oh no, I'm not doing the verse!' I said, 'You've got to do the verse.' Well we argued an hour or so on that. I finally convinced him to do the verse."[92]

Although the tentative title for the album from the beginning was *Love Is the Thing*,[93] at one point they considered calling the album *Stardust*, and that's what it says on Capitol's recording sheets. But apparently Cole was still unconvinced, even after they made the first take, and it seemed to be apparent to everyone but the singer, especially Gillette, that this was a "Stardust" for the ages. Jenkins cited this song as the only one he and Cole had a disagreement about concerning an additional take. "But Nat would hear it himself and he'd do it over if it needed it—except 'Stardust.' He didn't want to do it [again]; he said, 'That's all. Next.' And it turned out to be great, it's a great record."[94] Gillette concluded, "Well, after it was all done and released and it got tremendous airplay, Nat admitted, 'It was a good move, I'm glad we did it. But I had no eyes for doing "Stardust" at the beginning.' And he didn't; he fought 'Stardust,' then he fought the verse of 'Stardust,' but it's one of the best recordings of 'Stardust' that I know of."[95]

Cole's "Stardust" is especially well used over the main titles of the classic comedy *My Favorite Year* (1982), in which it serves as a means to transport viewers back to the hopes and dreams and bittersweet optimism of the 1950s. After Cole's voice, the first thing we hear is the main character, "Benji Stone," played by Mark Linn-Baker, who is, as soon revealed, narrating the story from the vantage point of many years later, even as Mitchell Parish's sagacious lyrics likewise depict a man "narrating" a nostalgically remembered incident from his youth—the two are perfect parallels for each other. The three-minute track opens with the arranger's trademark—throbbing moaning strings, which suggest waves breaking on a tropical shore in the middle of the night as well as twinkling, dusty stars. Cole's crystalline voice is perfectly balanced by Jenkins's celestial strings.

Of all the classic songs in what gradually came to be known as the Great American Songbook, the two most notorious examples of songs that were never quite sung by Sinatra are "Lush Life" and "Stardust," although he attempted both, unsuccessfully. Clearly, after he heard Cole, the Chairman realized that there wasn't much left to be done with either song.

The final notable aspect of *Love Is the Thing* is the cover, bearing a remarkable painting of Cole by Capitol's house artist, Jim Jonson.[96] Cole is more than handsome here. The artist somehow makes him look "pretty"; the face is distinctly feminized, and his eyes and mouth are both half-closed. He's not looking straight out, at the "camera" or the viewer, but slightly to his right, as if he's noticing something—we don't know what, since we can't see it. All of this seems contrived not only to make him look as attractive as possible but also as non-threatening. This was deemed an acceptable way to present an African American singing love songs on an album that, Heaven forbid, white women might actually listen to.

It was safe, at least, for a black man to project his hopes and dreams into the stars, but back home on Planet Earth, there was still a long way to go. Small wonder then, that he put his faith in the stardust and the night lights; he had no choice, at a time when everyone else was afraid of the dark.

8

Years of Stardust, Night Lights, and Fear of the Dark

1957–1959

Thirty-nine and still a maid.
I thought for sure by now I'd be
Better off than this
Thirty-nine-year-old,
I should be somewhere being kissed
by Nat King Cole.
—from *Caroline, or Change (2003), book and lyrics by Tony Kushner*

IN THE FIRST TEN WEEKS of 1957, Nat King Cole played three major extended runs: the Paramount Theater in New York (with Ella Fitzgerald, Count Basie, and Joe Williams), the Tropicana in Havana, and the Eden Roc in Miami. All these engagements (which ran a week or two each) were fulfilled in and around some eleven episodes of his Monday evening NBC TV series.

Then, on Sunday, March 17, Nat celebrated his thirty-eighth birthday with a lavish party, hosted by one of his closest personal and professional friends, Jimmy Van Heusen, at the songwriter's opulent home in Palm Springs. All of Nat and Maria's close music industry buddies were there: Carlos, Lee, Nelson, as well as his traveling rhythm section guys, John, Charlie, and Lee, plus other assorted pals. Van Heusen, who among his various pursuits (composer, test pilot, swinging bachelor) was also a talented photographer, documented the occasion with several dozen photos. Many of these show Hollywood's musical elite wearing Robin Hood-style beanies; the event was apparently also a fund-raiser for a Palm Springs charity that was going with a Sherwood Forest–style theme. Van Heusen's former partner, lyricist Johnny Burke, and composer-pianist Joey Bushkin introduced several new songs, which Cole recorded a year and a half later. The iconic Hollywood auteur Sam Fuller offered up a birthday toast to his newest star, Nat Cole himself, who had just wrapped up his best-ever acting role in Fuller's latest production, the forthcoming *China Gate*.

Cole received the best birthday present he could hope for: his new album, *Love Is the Thing*, was released to widespread acclaim and sales. Even Walter Winchell himself was announcing to "Mr. and Mrs. America and all the ships at sea" that it was selling out in record stores everywhere. Likewise, his winning streak on the singles charts showed no sign of slowing down: he was still outselling both Sinatra and Como, his two major competitors.

Yet, as we shall see, he would spend much less time in 1957 working on albums or singles and instead devote most of his energy to television and movies; this was the year in which he would star in both of his most substantial film-acting roles. And everyone still had high hopes for the TV series; surely, with a program this well received, a sponsor was certain to step up to the plate sooner than later. Two days after the birthday celebration, he was back in Hollywood, recording the Capitol version of the title song from his latest film, *China Gate*. It was in this period, from 1957 to 1959, that Cole enjoyed his most productive years as a film actor, with four genuine acting roles: *Istanbul* (1957), *China Gate* (1957), *St. Louis Blues* (1958), and *Night of the Quarter Moon* (1959).

Of all his film-related performances, *St. Louis Blues* was, at long last, his first (and final) full-scale starring role in a major motion picture. But his best acting job, however, and his only really satisfying performance other than from a strictly musical standpoint, is in Sam Fuller's *China Gate*, playing "Goldie"; produced in late 1956 and early 1957, it was released in spring 1957. For the only time in his career, Cole was cast in the production because of on-screen image rather than his voice and his success as a cashbox champ. "I'd given Goldie a soldiering background very much like my own," Fuller later wrote. Darryl F. Zanuck, head of Twentieth Century Fox, "asked me about who I had in mind to play the part. I said I wanted a man's man, but a guy with a warm, tender-looking face. I picked up an album on top of a pile next to Darryl's record player. If my soldier was black, he'd look just like the guy on the album cover, Nat King Cole." Zanuck responded with incredulous laughter, "Sammy, Cole's a big star. We paid him seventy-five grand just to sing a title song. He's the most popular singer in the country. Do you have any idea how much he'd ask for appearing in your picture? He probably makes in a couple of weeks the entire budget for your film.' " But Fuller was determined; "I was infatuated with that face on the album cover, so I persisted," he said. "A dinner was arranged so that I could meet Nat and his exquisite wife, Maria. They were both moved by my story for *China Gate*. I told Nat point-blank that I didn't write the part for a 'black actor.' I needed Goldie to be diametrically opposite to Brock, the bigot who rejects his own child because of the little boy's slanted eyes. Nat agreed to do the picture right away and asked only for a minimum fee."[1]

For the only time, *China Gate* gave Cole a real director to work with; Fuller, whose specialty was well-crafted, intelligent action films—westerns (*I Shot Jesse James*), crime stories (*Underworld USA*), naval adventure (*Hell and High Water*), and war movies (*The Steel Helmet*). *China Gate* is also noteworthy as practically the only Hollywood movie of the 1950s to address the ongoing and worsening conflict between communist and free-world forces in Vietnam. The director's own script has Cole and Gene Barry as American soldiers of fortune, trying to help the locals fight off the invading forces of Ho Chi Minh, armed with weapons from Soviet Russia and Red China.

China Gate also boasted a distinguished main title song, announced on screen as the final work of Victor Young, with a poignant text, inspired by Asian haiku poetry, by Harold Adamson. This was precisely the kind of intelligent cinematic exotica (in the realm of "Hajji Baba") that was grist for the mill of Cole and Riddle. They recorded the soundtrack vocal on January 8 and the Capitol single on March 19 on an ethnically diverse session, right after cutting Marvin Fisher's lively Calypso, "When Rock and Roll Come to Trinidad." That first number featured the bongos of Jack Costanzo, who then left immediately for a gig in Vegas. *Down Beat*'s John Tynan, who was there observing, described "China Gate" as "a wistful, dreamy melody loaded with rather overt Oriental orchestral effects"; he called attention to the "two-string Chinese violin, a long stick about as high as a cello with a barrel stuck in the middle."[2] This was played with a cello bow by one Irving Lipschulz—clearly, not an Asian musician. As the engineers struggled to get a balance on the instrument, Cole stood in the doorway and observed, "Pretty weird!"

Cole is third-billed in *China Gate*, after Gene Barry and Angie Dickinson, then not yet the sweetheart of the Rat Pack. Unlike his co-stars, Cole gets a vocal on screen: in the opening sequence, we are shown a South Vietnamese citizen of the kind the Americans are trying to protect, a small boy, who in turn is trying to protect a puppy—and keep it from being eaten. He and Cole (as "Goldie")[3] encounter each other in the bombed-out ruins of a building. Goldie doesn't speak the boy's language, so Cole, in a charmingly paternal moment, calms him and reassures him by whispering—not even crooning—a soothing lullaby. He sings almost under his breath, very low-key indeed, as he guides the child to safety. Cole is perfectly winning throughout; lanky and lean—he's one actor who never had to lose weight for a role—and physically convincing as well. His film career would have been much more substantial and memorable with just a few more roles like this one and a few more directors like Fuller.

AS THE TV SERIES CONTINUED, Cole stayed comparatively close to Los Angeles for most of the year: Tucson, the Sands in Vegas, after shooting for *China Gate* wound up, and then, in May, the premiere of the picture at the Fox Theatre in San Francisco. That same month (May 1957), he played through Seattle and left us a remarkable document, a thirty-minute concert recording that is one of the best-sounding live performances of his career.[4]

Over the summer, Nat hit the Chez Paree again and the 500 Club in Atlantic City. He was back in Los Angeles to do his weekly TV broadcast, and then, in June, to work on his next film project. *China Gate* had proven that you didn't need a big budget to make a decent movie (even Angie Dickinson, in *Madame Butterfly* drag, came off well), just a director who knew what he was doing. Cole's next film, conversely, was a big budget flop that proved all the money, technicolor, and A-list talent in Hollywood often isn't enough to guarantee a success. With *Raintree County*, Cole was probably glad that he didn't have an onscreen acting role; the main title song, sung by Nat, is the only aspect of the enterprise that's remotely palatable.

MGM's *Raintree County* was a kind of belated follow-up to the studio's 1939 sensation, *Gone with the Wind*, a new civil war epic based on a highly respected novel by Ross Lockridge Jr. The theme was composed by Johnny Green, who had long been MGM's number one music director. Earlier in his career, Green had been a successful songwriter, but after he moved to Hollywood, he made a lateral move into composing instrumental film scores and ultimately running the studio's music department. "The Ballad of Raintree County" started as a strictly instrumental theme, but it was a singularly beautiful one that Green regarded as something special. Studio head Dore Schary and "I decided to lyricize and make a song out of that instrumental theme, to make it something more than a movie theme," said the composer. "But even before Paul Webster wrote the lyric, there was only one voice, in my brain's inner ear, that was right for that. It was Nat. I got Nat on the phone, I never had to deal with any manager or anything like that, because we were good friends, and I had Nat's private number and he indeed had mine."[5]

Nat took the call. Some songwriters had a hard time reaching him, but not Johnny Green. After all, here was the composer of "Body and Soul," a jazz standard that was virtually a sacred text and a signature showpiece for Cole the pianist. "And I got him on the phone, and I told him that we had this song. By that time, Paul had written the lyric. and I told him also what the pressures were on me and I said, 'I know you're in the midst of rehearsing, is there some way I can come down there and play it for you?' And he was so concerned. He said, 'Well, do you mind if there are other people around?' What a considerate thing for him to say! 'Because the only thing I can think of is we'll knock off a few minutes for you in the rehearsal hall.' And he also said, 'Be sure and bring an extra copy so you can leave one with me. . . . So if you can be here at quarter of three, If you don't mind sitting around a little bit, we'll do it.' So I went down there at the time, and I sat for maybe ten minutes [while] they knocked off rehearsing, and Nat came over and sat down at the piano with me. And he instantly loved the song."

Nat had other reasons to love the song, 17,500 of them—that was the amount MGM paid him to sing it over the main titles. (What didn't go to the taxman probably went to pay for a lot of college for Cookie and Sweetie.) Even though the rest of the production was a disaster, the main title music is stunning, especially in the way that Nelson Riddle incorporates the distinctive timbre of a harmonica, giving it a 19th-century Americana sound, alongside modern string textures that suggest Aaron Copland. In later years, Green said more than once that "Raintree County" was his favorite of the songs he'd written. This was probably because it came years after the rest of his most famous songs and proved to Green that he could still do it. But even so, considering that this was the man who wrote "Body and Soul," "Out of Nowhere," and "I Cover the Waterfront," that was really saying something.

THE FIRST SEVEN MONTHS OR SO of *The Nat King Cole Show*, in a fifteen-minute slot on Monday nights, had served as a sort of trial balloon, which Cole and his team passed with flying colors. Originally NBC had assigned a writer-director named Jim Jordan to the series, but Jordan had a drinking problem, and a few months later he was replaced by Robert Henry, a young and "hungry" director who remained in charge for the duration of the series.[6] On July 2, the show expanded to a much more ambitious half-hour slot on Tuesday nights and now featured guest stars, starting with Frankie Laine. In a sense, Nat's ten years on television from 1948 to 1957, and indeed, the radio years before that, had been a warm-up allowing him to become acclimated to the technology and the rhythms of live broadcasting. By this point, after half a year on the air, he was totally relaxed and ebullient in front of the camera. It helped to have an old friend with him as he expanded into the new format. Cole had known Laine, he tells the audience, since 1943, when the young singer and occasional songwriter brought him what Laine tells us is his "first tune," "It Only Happens Once."[7]

In expanding to a half hour, Henry and Cole were doing more than just adding songs; now, by featuring a guest star, there was also going to be considerable interplay between the host and the visitors: chatter, jokes, and duets, both comic and serious. The first expanded show makes this clear: Cole and Laine do a familiar guest-host routine, the kind we have since seen on a million variety shows, where the host and the guest exchange extravagant praise, compliments, bromides, and pleasantries, until they both step out from behind the fourth wall, laugh and point out how silly the whole thing is—the old vaudeville and variety show tradition of letting the audience in on the joke.

The centerpiece of the episode is an elaborate comedy medley wherein the two entertainers parody the idea that popular singers have now become a fixture on television; we learn that all kinds of programming are becoming more and more musical in nature—not just variety shows—but Cole and Laine demonstrate musical westerns, musical detective shows, musical quiz shows, musical news programs, musical sports commentary, and even musical commercials (such as "Try our pizza" to the tune of "Mona Lisa"). Both Laine and Cole are completely game and deliver the gags and puns with energy and zest. It was many times more ambitious than having Nat just come out and sing three or four songs; someone, usually Bob Wells, had to write all that "special material." This tradition of comedy medleys would eventually culminate in Cole's most famous piece of special material, "Mr. Cole Won't Rock and Roll," written for him by Joe and Noel Sherman.

Within a few weeks, Cole and Henry had found their footing. NBC must have realized that in launching Cole in his own series, they now had all three top singer-hosted variety shows, adding to *The Dinah Shore Chevy Show* on Sunday nights, launched in October 1956, and *The Perry Como Show*, which ran on Saturday nights from 1955 to 1959 before it morphed into the new *Kraft Music Hall*. The network's top "general" variety show (somewhat more comedy-centric) was hosted by Cole's longtime friend Steve Allen, and this was the one NBC scheduled directly opposite their number one rival, *The Ed Sullivan Show*, long a Sunday night institution on CBS.

Como, Shore, and Allen were all given a full sixty-minute slot, but Nat's show was never longer than thirty minutes. This was primarily because a half hour was expensive to produce without a sponsor, but Cole and Henry turned it into an advantage. It's worth noting that a few months later, in fall 1957, Sinatra himself took the plunge and accepted an offer from the upstart

American Broadcasting Company to do his own weekly series, and, like Cole, his was also a thirty-minute show.

Each Cole show was framed by the theme song, Harry Warren and Al Dubin's "The Shadow Waltz,"[8] for which Cole concentrated on a few slightly rewritten lines, "In the evenings may I come and sing to you? / All the songs that I would like to bring to you." Cole would start with a bright and brassy opening number: "Breezin' along with the Breeze," "Takin' a Chance on Love," "Almost Like Being in Love," or "Lulu's Back in Town"—which he usually does in front of a mixed singing/dancing chorus of six. Cole would often then announce the guest, and then sing either a ballad or a recent hit (frequently they were one and the same thing) before bringing out the guest. Usually the guest would do at least one solo number before joining the host in a duet, whether straightforward or something of a comedy-parody nature.

At the start, the show didn't have an ending theme, until the young songwriter Alan Bergman presented Cole with one. One of Bergman's mentors had been Leo Robin, who had written, by accident or design, theme songs for no less than three major entertainers: Jack Benny's "Love in Bloom," Bob Hope's "Thanks for the Memory," and Eddie Cantor's "One Hour with You." Robin encouraged Bergman to try to do the same, and he and his partners, composer Lew Spence and co-lyricist Marilyn Keith, came up with a closing theme for *The Nat King Cole Show* titled "It's Just About That Time Again." "Nat was just the nicest guy," as Bergman said many times when we spoke in 2019; "he was just so thrilled that we had written a song for him." Bergman was well aware that dozens of songwriters were writing songs for Cole all the time, but Nat still acted excited and flattered that the Bergmans (Alan and Marilyn were soon married) and Spence had gone to the trouble.

Nat was often joined on stage (especially in the first year) by his rhythm section, all of whom were black, but he also was backed up by a six-member singing-and-dancing backup group, sometimes billed as "The Cheerleaders," all of whom were white. The guests were fairly evenly distributed; after the first half-hour Tuesday night show, the guests on the next show (July 9) were two jazz-oriented singers, June Christy and Mel Tormé. Then for the next three weeks in a row, the headlining guests were all African American: Pearl Bailey and her (white) husband, drummer Louis Bellson (July 16), Sammy Davis Jr. (July 30), and Harry Belafonte (August 6). Later episodes would feature Ella Fitzgerald (September 10 and November 19), Eartha Kitt (October 8), Cab Calloway (October 22), Mahalia Jackson (November 12), the Mills Brothers (December 10), and Billy Eckstine (December 17).

The half hour format gave Cole and Henry leeway to create something special that would have been more difficult to sustain for a full sixty minutes. One particularly charming episode was on August 27, when the guests were singer Margaret Whiting, who had been close with Nat since their shared early days on Capitol Records, and the long-lasting popular vocal quartet the Merry Macs. The conceit this time is that they're all performing at a summer stock theater and everything is dressed up to look like a quasi-makeshift stage in a barn somewhere. They stick to the theme of vaguely seasonal songs: Whiting sings her signature song, "It Might as Well Be Spring," while Nat's final number is a lovely ballad arrangement of the turn-of-the-century vaudeville air, "Shine on Harvest Moon" (which he never sang on any other occasion). The big finale number is "Chopsticks," a revival and a revision of an arrangement he performed with the Trio twenty years earlier; he and Whiting start off on twin upright pianos, with Cole showing a lot of technique and Whiting, by contrast, making a gag out of playing as little as possible. Next, the Merry Macs enter with the rather dopey lyrics to "Chopsticks," and last, the three components, Cole, Whiting, and the vocal group, interact for a grand finale.

Another delightful thirty minutes is the show of August 13, which, we are told is set in Paris (no, they weren't actually trying to fool anyone) and is a tribute to the City of Light. The primary guest is Lisa Kirk, best known to history as the original "Bianca-Lois" in Cole Porter's *Kiss Me, Kate*. She was the only Broadway headliner to appear on the Cole show, and that was likely due to her husband, songwriter Bob Wells. Her performance on the show is a reminder that Hollywood missed a good bet when it passed over Kirk; even Ann Miller, who took essayed Kirk's role(s) in the MGM *Kiss Me, Kate* doesn't have her vivaciousness. Kirk was a major figure on live television, in multiple senses of the term. Here, she sings a fetchingly *franglais* piece of special material, including "Hi-Lili, Hi-Lo" (possibly inspiring Cole to sing it a few years later) and is completely winning all the way.

Cole and Kirk are joined by virtually the only comedian to appear on the series, James (billed as "Jimmy") Komack, then best known as a supporting player in Broadway's *Damn Yankees* but who went on to a substantial career on television. Here he's masquerading, not convincingly but appealingly, as a master of ceremonies in a Pigalle nightclub. At one point, Cole is beset by four little boys—two of whom are black—with whom he sings "Alouette" and then distracts them by pointing them in the direction of Elvis Presley. For the finale, they join forces on the most popular French song in America at that point (associated with African American entertainers like Louis Armstrong and Eartha Kitt), "C'est Si Bon." Cole sings it fast and jazzy, followed by Kirk, slow and sultry, and then Komack, loud and funny in fractured French. Taking their tip from the 1953 Kitt record, they then indulge in an extended coda in which each of the three recites an extended list of material goods that might be on their Christmas list; for Nat, it's "une magnum de French champagne—manischewitz" and "cherche du hit record, un grand million seller, comme si 'Son of Nature Boy.'" Television was still a very young art at the time, but still, it never got any better than this.

The climactic "duets" of both the August 13 and 27 shows take somewhat elaborate precautions. Rather than present something that might be construed as a love song between a black man and a white woman, they added a third element: Komack in "C'est Si Bon" and the Merry Macs in "Chopsticks." Neither was a love song to begin with, both were more frantic than romantic, but you couldn't be too careful. On the December 3 show, Cole teams up with the dynamic, not to say explosive, Betty Hutton, and again the producers came up with an ingenious idea for them to sing together: the set-up is that Hutton is making a new album, so she calls Nat for ideas for songs, and the two talk back-and-forth via split screen. Every song she suggests for herself is one of his hits, and every song he recommends is one of her signatures (like "Doctor, Lawyer, Indian Chief" and "His Rocking Horse Ran Away"), finally, they get together on a song identified with both of them—"Orange Colored Sky"—which they sing together, but still in split screen, until the last eight bars.

The show had zero budget but no shortage of imagination from Henry and Cole. The basic ideas and setups were remarkably simple, as with two guys named Tony, both of whom were co-stars on shows done live from the stage of the Sands Hotel. On October 1, the guest is one of Cole's biggest fans and admirers, the young Tony Bennett. (His hit record that summer, which he performs on the episode, was "In the Middle of an Island," a novelty song that the singer didn't care for then or now.) Here the gag is that the guests, Tony plus the singing group the Beachcombers with Natalie (what would have then been called a "mixed race" quartet, with three white guys and an Asian female lead singer), are going to let Nat take a break by taking over all the announcing and hosting duties. That idea may be more contrived than most, but it works better in the actual show than here on paper, and Cole sings outstanding live versions of "Little Girl," "I'm Gonna Sit Right Down and Write Myself a Letter," "Raintree County," and "Stardust."

The September 17 show with Tony Martin is even more straightforward and sprightly; here the conceit is that this Tony is curious about how TV variety shows are done, so Nat lets him stand on stage and on camera next to him, so for the whole show they're continually interacting. It's ridiculously simple, but charming. At one point, Nat hands him what he calls a "Morris chair" to sit in, and Martin confesses that his original name was "Morris" (indeed it was). At another, Nat joins him on "Manhattan," which leads to "Sunny Side of the Street" (there are sunny streets in Manhattan, after all), for which Cole unleashes his keyboard skills (both he and the piano are standing upright) and Martin, who started as a reed player, takes out his clarinet and plays—not badly. Considering that all the major variety stars—Sullivan, Hope, Como, Shore, Allen, and the various hosts of the Colgate Comedy Hour were, as usual, taking the summer off, *The Nat King Cole Show* was virtually the only show worth watching during July and August. With a program this good, surely a sponsor would come forward summarily. There could be no doubt.

IN BETWEEN HIS TWO BIG ACTING ROLES in *China Gate* and *St. Louis Blues*, and roughly fifty episodes of his TV series, Cole made only one album in all of 1957, but it was an all-time classic. This was *Just One of Those Things*, Cole's first of only two full-length collaborations with the legendary Billy May. They taped it in July and August 1957, at which point Nat was not only continuing to do the NBC series (without, as we have seen, taking a break for the summer) but also doing his fourth annual "Cole at the Bowl" concert at the Hollywood Bowl and a summer run at the Coconut Grove.

As we have also seen, Cole preferred to leave the more extreme ends of the emotional spectrum to Sinatra: *Love Is the Thing* was happy but not euphoric, unlike *Songs for Swingin' Lovers*, and *Just One of Those Things* was melancholy but not despondent. In Frank Sinatra Jr.'s memorable phrase, one should listen to Sinatra Sr.'s saloon-and-suicide albums "by prescription only." However, on *Just One of Those Things*, Cole may be down but he's not out, even though he plays the role of a loser in love, there's no shortage of wry humor in the proceedings, in his own singing as well as Billy May's darkly comic orchestral contexts.

May (1916–2004) had first become aware of Cole in fall 1939, probably at the Swanee Inn;[9] he had first landed in Los Angeles as a trumpeter and arranger for Charlie Barnet's band. They had come to play the Palomar Ballroom that October, but, as often happened in those days when seemingly everybody (especially Cole himself) walked around with a lit cigarette all the time, the venue had burned to the ground just before the band arrived. That left Barnet and his men without a gig, and with unexpected time on their hands, they thoroughly checked out the local Angelino music scene and were immediately drawn to the King Cole Trio, by far the hottest combo in town.

Billy and Nat got to know each other two years later, when May returned to Hollywood as a member of Glenn Miller's orchestra to film the first of that band's two cinematic epics, *Sun Valley Serenade*. May was immediately impressed with Cole's prodigious skill as a pianist and also enjoyed the group's jive-style unison vocalizing. They became friendlier still after May settled in California and both men entered long-term relationships with Capitol Records. At some point the two even wrote a song together, the exuberant novelty "Ooh, Kickarooney," which the King Cole Trio actually performed in two different film appearances (the 1948 all-black feature *Killer Diller* and the 1950 Universal short, *Nat King Cole and His Trio*). The story has long circulated that Cole and May composed "Kickarooney" between shows during a movie theater gig. However, when the song's publisher, Cole's friend Ivan Mogul, presented May with a royalty check forty years later, May claimed that he had absolutely no recollection of ever having been involved with this Slim Gaillard–style nonsense number.

The eventual collaboration of Cole and May was preordained not only because they were both under contract to Capitol Records but also because both were closely connected to Carlos Gastel—he was not only the manager of both artists; he was their best friend. By 1951, Cole and May were each enjoying bonuses from God in terms of careers they had never expected—Cole as a chart-topping pop singer, and May, who had been a completely anonymous sideman and uncredited orchestrator for so many years, as a recording star in his own right. They worked together successfully, as we have seen, between 1951 and 1954, on three sessions of singles (including the all-time hit "Walkin' My Baby Back Home") as well as the spring 1953 tour. In May 1957, May presided over the R&B-centric recording session that produced the hit "Send for Me" (about which more shortly) and then in July they cut *Just One of Those Things*.

Cole and Gillette began putting together the song list, and when they had a few tunes selected, Gillette called May and asked him to start work. "They'd just give me three or four to start, and they'd still be picking them," May recalled. "It took me maybe two or three days to write them. Then, I'd do a date with Nat and we'd record them, and then at the end of the week I'd go back to doing a television show or something. Then I'd have to do something else the next week, and then maybe some more songs would come in from Nat, and so on. So, I never sat down and figured out the whole thing for the package. All I did was take down the tunes, the keys, and figure out the tempos—and away we went."

As distinct from the pure string backgrounds of *Love Is the Thing*, it was decided to make *Just One of Those Things* using essentially the standard big-band format. May remembered that this was, at least partially, a budgetary consideration (which is surprising, considering the high profits Cole's recordings inevitably generated). In being asked to do sad songs sans strings, May hit upon the idea of making the set at once a ballad album as well as a dance album. At some level, he and Cole may have both been inspired by *In the Wee Small Hours*, the 1955 masterpiece by Sinatra and Riddle, which was at once a ballad album, a set of sad songs about the end of love, and a jazz album, perhaps the loosest and jazziest that either one of them would ever make.

May started with the standard big band setup of brass, reeds, and rhythm, but his first move was to beef up the format with several additional instruments for coloration. On various tracks, he adds Helen Hutchinson on harp, and she flourishes fancifully on, among other tracks, the after-coda to the set's "bonus" item, "You'll Never Know." As was also mandatory for May sessions, an additional percussionist, here Frank Flynn, was brought in, primarily for vibes but also carting a plethora of percussive implements, such as the kettle drums that get the last word on "A Cottage for Sale."

Most important, Red Callender, who had worked briefly with Cole in 1942, supports the entire ensemble and gives it more bottom via his tuba. As the conductor said, simply, "Red played wonderful tuba." Callender holds up the whole works like Atlas with the globe on his shoulders and is particularly effective on the countermelody on the opener, "When Your Lover Has Gone." He also contributes mightily to "I Understand," while on "Who's Sorry Now," Callender provides contrast to Willie Smith's super-high alto squeaks, signifying May's most outrageous juxtaposition of sounds from the rooftop and the basement. The contrast also vividly illustrates the new sonic possibilities of the hi-fi recording medium; little of May or Riddle's best work would have been audible in the pre-tape era of recording, just a decade earlier.

In fact, the chief weapon in May's arsenal is contrast; it's the element that keeps everything interesting—the conflict between high and low, loud and soft, fast and slow, sweet and hot. "These Foolish Things" starts quite romantically, with just Cole and John Collins's guitar in rubato. The tempo gradually picks up in the chorus, with Cole piling several choruses on top of each other as if they were modular-style blues units, with Cole's regular drummer Lee Young swingingly accenting the afterbeats with brushes in a manner reminiscent of May's favorite drummer, Alvin Stoller. (On hearing the album for the first time in decades, May thought that Young *was* Stoller, which is as great a compliment as he could pay any drummer.)

No player ever had a greater sense of color than Harry Sweets Edison, favorite mute man of both Cole and May (not to mention Basie, Sinatra, and Riddle). May left an open space in "Just for the Fun of It" for Edison to improvise his own solo, and Sweets makes the most of it by offering a rich juicy chorus; it's one of his most satisfying on a vocal date and considerably more involved than the usual *beep-beep-beeps* that he gets to play in most of his dates with singers. May even has the entire section of trumpets beep à la Edison on "Cottage for Sale," and throughout, the arranger uses the vibes as an extension of the trumpets to accentuate high-note *beeps* in the brass section.

The instrumental sections of "Once in a While" and "Don't Get around Much Anymore" contain homages to two of Cole's and May's favorite musical auteurs. "Once in a While" pits a very large sound—the whole horn section—against a very minimal triangle *ping*, in the manner of Sy Oliver's whimsical arrangements for the Jimmy Lunceford band. "Don't Get Around ..." has May re-interpreting not only one of Duke Ellington's best-known songs but referencing the Ellington orchestral style on the whole, with Rowles as a suitably ducal deputy on piano, and May spinning his own take on Ellington's signature harmonic dissonances; the entire ensemble surges through glissandi in a chromatic love affair like a collective Johnny Hodges. When asked if Ellington had influenced him, May responded emphatically, "Damn right! He wrote the book."

Yet there's no better instrument for catching the upbeat yet melancholy mood of the tracks than the King himself. In a microcosm for his own entire career, it's Cole's strengths as a rhythmic master that make him so effective on an emotional level. For instance, the title track, "Just One of Those Things," far from being the usual trip to the moon on gossamer wings, becomes a ferocious swinger. He quite cleverly unwinds "The Song Is Ended" from an archaic waltz into a surprisingly potent rumination on lost love. Cole packs an extra emotional wallop on the final "the moon de-scend-ed," carefully syllabicating the word so that the rhyme works but also conveys exactly the right emotional color (he does the same with the two utterings of "the mel-o-dy lingers on"—repeated for emphasis—in the coda).

Likewise, the bridge on "I Should Care" contains a section where the speaker falls off his train of thought to declaim an observation that just occurs to him then and there ("funny how sheep ..."), all of which Cole captures perfectly. He gets the same despondent disposition going in "The Party's Over," the only contemporary tune in the collection (from *Bells Are Ringing*, then still running on Broadway, and which he had sung in two very different arrangements on the NBC TV series). May throws one mountainous crescendo at him after another, and yet far from worrying that these outsize episodes will break the mood, Cole is instead so coolly confident that he even engages in a call-and-response meeting with the ensemble.

Just One of Those Things was taped precisely in between the two more famous Jenkins albums, *Love Is the Thing* and *The Very Thought of You*, and like them, mixed moods very brilliantly, balancing sad songs of dysfunctional affairs with a mood that's far from melancholy—instead of telling broken-hearted lovers to cry there in the gloom, Cole and May are motivating them to face the music and dance. For four years, *Just One of Those Things* would be a solitary event in the Cole catalog, until Cole and May reunited in 1961 with a new album that got the message across even better.

IN FALL 1957, while continuing to star in the NBC series on Tuesday evenings, Cole filmed *St. Louis Blues*, his most ambitious feature film project ever, which had been in the making for several years at that point. *St. Louis Blues* was part of the continuum of Hollywood's ongoing tradition of musical biopics and was also an indirect response to the "school integration crisis in the south."[10] The original idea of a biopic of songwriter, bandleader, and entrepreneur W. C. Handy was conceived by a music buff and record producer named George Garabedian, who might have been partly inspired by a classic album, *Louis Armstrong Plays W. C. Handy* from 1954. Handy, who was eighty when that album was recorded, had long been a central figure in American vernacular music—and also, as Garabedian knew from Handy's autobiography, *Father of the Blues* (1941), his life story was a colorful and dramatic one.

Cole had actually crossed paths with Handy several times previously. "The first time I met Mr. Handy was when we played a benefit together" around 1942, Cole later said; "I remember bringing up [the idea of] a movie about his life, but he thought a story about a Negro wouldn't be accepted by everybody." He continued, "Nothing whatever came of the proposal way back then in 1942, and certainly I wouldn't have been so presumptuous as to suggest myself for the Handy role, but here I am finally doing it."[11] The two met again in 1947, when the Father of the Blues appeared on NBC's *King Cole Trio Time* and presented Cole with his Esquire award.[12]

Garabedian approached Handy with the idea of doing a movie based on his life and his book, but he wasn't the only one; in addition to other Hollywood producers, Edward R. Murrow wanted to produce a documentary about

Handy (as he had recently done for Louis Armstrong) and, Garabedian said, Oscar Hammerstein, who already had one successful all-black musical to his credit (*Carmen Jones*) was rumored to be interested in a Broadway show built around Handy's life and music. "Previously, he had always felt that the time wasn't quite propitious. But at the moment I approached him, the question of the school integration crisis in the south was becoming sharper and getting more and more publicity. This encouraged him and led to my success where others had failed."

In 1955, Garabedian decided on his leading man. "To be quite frank," he admitted, "at first I had a little doubt as to Cole's acting abilities. At the time, he had never made a picture, I'd never seen him act." But it was the 1955 "autobiographical" featurette, *The Nat King Cole Musical Story*, that convinced Garabedian that Cole "could carry off the part with conviction." Garabedian then brought the idea to Cole via Carlos Gastel, and they were both enthusiastic. There were a few snags when an attorney allegedly representing Handy tried to call the deal off, for which Garabedian blamed Gastel for "offering Handy an unacceptable deal," but soon enough they straightened the matter out and "from then on, it was clear sailing."

Garabedian then contacted all the major studies and agencies in Hollywood, but, as he found, "Nobody was interested, no studio in town would touch an all-black picture. It was generally understood that [the film versions of] both *Carmen Jones* and *Cabin in the Sky* had lost money.[13] But in recent years, Negro actors had begun to make a place for themselves in Hollywood. A case in point is the short Nat made for U-I." Although Universal International had already produced the Miller and Goodman biopics and also enjoyed a long relationship with Cole, the project wound up at Paramount Pictures—not least because, at the time the proposal was being pitched in January 1957, Cole was in the middle of a run at the New York Paramount Theater[14] and the home office couldn't miss the point of the smash business he was doing.

That was the end of Garabedian's involvement to the project; hopefully he got to put a little something in his pocket for his efforts.[15] From that point on, the picture, now titled *St. Louis Blues*, was being steered by Robert Smith, who produced the picture and co-wrote it with Ted Sherdeman. The good news was that Smith filled out the cast with an all-star roster of African Americans, starting with Ruby Dee (who had already played the leading lady in *The Jackie Robinson Story*) as Handy's sweetheart "Elizabeth," the vivacious Eartha Kitt as "Gogo," a singer-dancer-entertainer who becomes the other woman in Handy's life, the eleven-year-old Billy Preston as the young Will

Handy, and Cab Calloway as "Blade," an unscrupulous club owner who takes advantage of the composer. (Calloway had also been represented by Irving Mills, so he had a role model there.) Trumpeter Teddy Buckner, clarinetist Barney Bigard, Red Callender, and Lee Young all play musicians in Handy's bands, and there are musical cameos by Ella Fitzgerald and Mahalia Jackson. (Virtually all of these artists also appeared on *The Nat King Cole Show* during the fall of 1957.) Shooting took place mostly in September and October, and Cole recorded most of his vocals for the film in early October. On November 1, he announced that filming had been completed.[16]

Cole had certain things in common with Handy; he too had a valuable copyright taken from him, much the same way Handy did with "Memphis Blues," and he also experienced an internal conflict between the music he originally set out to play and the music he wound up making for the latter part of his career. But Nat was severely handicapped in many other aspects: Crosby, Sinatra, and Day were all singers who made the transition into acting, but they were given considerably more of a ramp-up than he. They had started in fun and frivolous musicals, like *Anything Goes, Anchors Aweigh*, and *Romance on the High Seas*, before they were asked to appear in heavier dramas like *Going My Way, From Here to Eternity*, and *Love Me or Leave Me*. For his first starring role, Cole was given a relatively heavy drama; there was music, yes, but it was hardly light and "frivolous."

Besides which, Bing, Frank, and Doris all benefited from the expertise of name-above-the-title directors like Leo McCarey, Fred Zinnemann, and Michael Curtiz; these were practiced hands who knew how to coax Oscar-level performances even from relatively inexperienced actors. But the director assigned to *St. Louis Blues* was Allen Reisner. This was his only theatrical feature; he spent the rest of his career directing television episodes—and though he was later praised for his work on *The Twilight Zone, The Green Hornet*, and *Mannix*, it's not surprising he never did another movie. Reisner isn't much help here to Cole, who seems to spend the whole movie brooding and sulking—a far cry from the jubilant and charismatic entertainer we see on *The Nat King Cole Show*.

Harry Belafonte, Sidney Poitier, or even Sammy Davis Jr., who all had real acting chops, could have played the role much more convincingly. With all these cards stacked against him, Cole would have been wiser, in retrospect, to turn the project down. But, let's face it, how many leading man parts were coming his way?

OR, FOR THAT MATTER, how many TV series? By fall 1957, the hard work of Cole and Bob Henry was starting to pay off. Now there were three factors in play here: first, there was everything Cole had worked for in the twenty years since he arrived in Los Angeles, his excellence as a performer, his status as a number-one hitmaker, and the goodwill he had long been generating all over the world. Then, there was the general excellence of the show itself, thanks not only to Henry but also to Cole's increasing skills as a host and star. Last, there was the unwavering support of the National Broadcasting Company. It all added up: "By summer's end, *The Nat King Cole Show* was the number one variety show in New York City. In Los Angeles it had landed in the top ten and pulled within three Trendex rating points of CBS-TV's *$64,000 Dollar Question*, a show that ranked fourth among all programs of the 1956–57 season."[17]

Surely the sponsors would be lining up, all over Madison Avenue, to have their products featured on such a well-received, top-rated program. But no. In 1946, the Wildroot company had no qualms about hiring Nat King Cole to sell their hair cream to a general audience, but ten years later, manufacturers of hair care products and cosmetics could not be convinced that black people ever used such goods and, for that matter, neither did those millions of white people who enjoyed the music of a hugely popular black artist. Cole was told that when NBC approached "a cosmetics manufacturer," they informed the network that "Negroes can't sell cosmetics"; he, in turn, responded, "What do they think we use? Chalk? Congo paint? And what about corporations like the telephone company? A man sees a Negro on a television show. What's he going to do—call up the phone company and tell them to take out his telephone?"[18]

Rheingold Beer, to their everlasting credit, stepped up to the plate, but on a limited basis, and their support was not enough to keep the show from losing money. What's especially frustrating is that Cole and Henry had taken enough precautions to please everybody. A woman in Raleigh, North Carolina, who described herself as a longtime "Southern Segregationist," wrote NBC directly to explain, "Were I owner of an industry, I'd be happy to sponsor him," and concluded, "It isn't fair to whites nor Negroes in any section of the country to deprive them of the enjoyment Nat brings through TV."[19]

That was the opinion of someone who, by the standards of the day, might be considered a "reasonable Segregationist": she didn't approve of fraternization between the races, but even she still loved the great Negro entertainers. Yet others were far more vehement. The owner of one local southern station was quoted as saying, "I like Nat Cole, but they told me if he came back on, they would bomb my house and my station."[20] He didn't even have to get any more specific as to who "they" were.

When "General" David Sarnoff, the autocratic chairman of NBC, who ran the network like a military operation, watched the episode co-starring Harry Belafonte—an African American entertainer far more outspoken than Cole (and who had married a white woman), he redoubled his determination to keep the show on the air. He placed a call directly to the network's head of advertising and thundered, "I want that show to be sponsored or heads will roll."[21] General Sarnoff took it as his personal mission to do whatever he could to keep *The Nat King Cole Show* on the air. Scholar Bob Pondillo believes that Sarnoff, a Russian-born Jew and staunch anti-communist, saw more than commercial possibilities in the television medium; to Sarnoff, it was a legitimate platform to counter Soviet propaganda. Where radicals like Paul Robeson had for decades openly criticized the United States for its deeply entrenched racist policies and politics, *The Nat King Cole Show* could be taken as proof that America was truly the land of the free. Its value was more than commercial or even musical; it was also highly political. Sarnoff was, in effect, saying, "Take that, Nikita Khrushchev!"

Alas, even with that impetus behind it, NBC could not afford to keep Cole on the air, and Cole couldn't afford to keep working for practically nothing. Indeed, as his accountants kept reminding him, compared to the fees he was now commanding on the road, he was literally losing money by scheduling his whole week around rehearsing and preparing for the show. In November, they all bit the bullet. NBC offered to keep the show on the air, but in a much less attractive time slot and less ambitious format, similar to the original series of November 1956 to June 1957. After Cole and Henry discussed the proposal, they decided to turn it down.

Cole skipped a week, using the gap to pick up some much-needed real money by spending that time in Sydney, Australia, and then returned to Los Angeles to do the final three episodes. On the last show, December 17, Nat and another old smoothie, the legendary Billy Eckstine, crossed a cadenza, as Bing Crosby would have said, on "Life Is Just a Bowl of Cherries," which Eckstine had recorded with Woody Herman in 1951. (As he had with Herman, Eckstine chides, "You know, Nat, that's cool philosophy, you gotta live it and love it, 'cause when you leave it, you're a long time gone.") This leads to "Rosetta," dedicated to Nat's first hero and Eckstine's first boss, Earl Hines, for which they both sing the lyrics. Next, they trade back and forth, Nat improvising on the piano, Eckstine scatting then soloing on trumpet (also not badly) and then surprising us by soloing on the normaphone, a truly bizarre instrument that looks like the love child of a trumpet and a saxophone.

If the idea had been to prove a political point—that a black man can star in his own series and have it become an undisputed success, a great show with top ratings and top reviews, then the point had undeniably been made. *The Nat King Cole Show* had a been a labor of love, a labor of racial inclusion, and a labor of artistic excellence, but due to factors beyond the control of the star, the director, and even the network and its imperious commander-in-chief, it was never to be a labor of profit. Cole said in the *New York Times*, "There won't be [television] shows starring Negroes for a while."[22] (An accurate prediction: the next was Sammy Davis Jr. in 1965.) This was because, as Nat had said a few months earlier, in what is quite likely—and, alas, unfortunately—the most quoted phrase he ever uttered, "Madison Avenue is afraid of the dark."[23]

THE STORY GOES THAT in the weeks following the final episode of *The Nat King Cole Show* on NBC TV at the end of 1957, Nat, Carlos, and Lee were pow-wow-ing, and debating the strengths and weaknesses of Cole as a record-seller in comparison with other top pop singers. Perry Como and Dinah Shore had TV shows. Sinatra and Doris Day had the movies. And lately, all of these veteran hitmakers now also had to contend with a younger generation of pop stars, like Elvis Presley and Johnny Mathis (both only twenty-two in 1957) who had more direct access to the ever-expanding youth market.

What advantages, exactly, did Cole have that the others did not? He could sing the title theme for films, but rarely appeared on screen in a substantial role. He could be a top-paid guest star on variety shows, but because Madison Avenue had prioritized prejudice over profits, he could not host his own series. He was the highest-paid entertainer in Las Vegas up to that point, but for most of his life, he couldn't stay in the very hotels where he headlined. Yet from the beginning, Cole's key strength was his unique understanding of his listeners, what appealed to them and what didn't; in the final phase of his career, his superpower turned out to be his ability to attract entirely new audiences with music such as no other pop stars were capable of making. This would be music from Mississippi, Havana (as well as Rio and Mexico City), Nashville, and other faraway places with strange-sounding names.

How far was Nat King Cole willing to go to find new audiences? To the ends of the earth.

ALL WAS NOT BAD NEWS at the start of 1958. Cole retreated from a losing proposition and headed back toward a place where he could make some "serious coin," as *Variety* would have said, when he opened the year with a lucrative month-long run at the Copa. Even better, while in New York, he recorded still another classic album, *Nat King Cole Sings Songs from St. Louis Blues*.

Most of Cole's albums up through 1956 had served to remind listeners that he had started as a jazz pianist, but this album was one of two in 1958 that brought him back even closer to his roots in blues and gospel music, *St. Louis Blues*, followed by *Every Time I Feel the Spirit*. When the film *St. Louis Blues* was released in April 1958, it was both a critical and a commercial disappointment—which is how he remembered it three years later. That "picture that should have had everything—with that cast—and [instead it] had nothing."[24] But he was wrong in at least one regard: *St. Louis Blues* inspired one of the most remarkable albums—not strictly a soundtrack—of any movie in the classic years of Hollywood.

As we've seen, whether playing piano, singing, or doing both, Cole performed essentially two kinds of blues. When they were slow, and usually sad, he brought to the form all the tenderness and sincerity of a great love song. And conversely, when he sang a fast blues, it was with unbridled exhilaration and swing. The approach to the blues perfected by Cole and his major collaborator, arranger Nelson Riddle, is so exciting (even when Cole sings a quiet or contemplative song, it can be described as exciting) that *St. Louis Blues* qualifies as one of the artist's all-time strongest statements as a stand-up vocalist.

Producer and co-writer Robert Smith constructed his script out of two different sets of movie clichés: the bandleader biopics produced by Universal around this time and the *Jazz Singer* variations that went back to the dawn of talking pictures (but were still around, notably in the tepid 1953 remake of *The Jazz Singer*). But one thing that the script did not draw on were the actual facts of the life of the composer, W. C. Handy, that the movie was supposed to be about. On the positive side, as in the case of songwriter biopics like *Words and Music* and *Till the Clouds Roll By*, there's an all-star cast of singing actresses doing the composer's songs; these included Pearl Bailey and Eartha Kitt, portraying the women in Handy's life, while Mahalia Jackson and Ella Fitzgerald made cameo appearances in all-singing, non-speaking roles. (Cab Calloway gets a few lines of dialogue, but, alas, wasn't given the chance to sing.)

The sole redeeming aspect of the movie was the music and the way that, as with the Miller and Goodman stories, *St. Louis Blues* kindled new interest in the music of its subject. But unlike the bandleader biopics, the *St. Louis Blues* album wasn't merely celebrating the past; rather, Nat and Nelson were truly creating something new—something that possibly surpasses even *Two in Love, Piano Style*, and *Wild Is Love* as their greatest collaboration—and in the process, it re-established the ongoing artistic validity of a quintessential American composer. It also counts as a career landmark for Sweets Edison, who puts his distinctive stamp on almost every track, and in this case, the pianist standing in for the King himself is the extraordinary, New York studio keyboard virtuoso Hank Jones.

Working primarily in the second and third decades of the twentieth century, W. C. Handy (1873–1958) would devote his life to the cause of moving vernacular black music into the mainstream of American popular culture. Known as the "Father of the Blues" (also the title of his autobiography), the widely successful Handy proved himself a role model for successive generations of African Americans both from a musical and an entrepreneurial standpoint. The Cole album illustrated how well those ideals had been carried out since the period covered in the film, the years when Handy debuted his classic blues. The album was a testament to black and white solidarity, between a black star and a white musical director, a black composer and a thoroughly "mixed" ensemble of section players and soloists. Handy died at the age of seventy-four in March 1958, which means that he might have lived to hear the Cole album; if that was the case, I can't imagine he ever heard his music sound better.

The first track is an opening title-style overture-medley. *St. Louis Blues*, the album, opens with the famous opening strain of Handy's 1912 classic, treated in a semi-classical fashion, not pompous like the old "symphonic jazz" of the 1920s but with overtones of Aaron Copland. From there, the familiar opening blues theme transitions into an instrumental passage identified as "Love Theme" (not by Handy but by Riddle), the transition suggesting a Broadway overture but rendered with more sensitivity than most pit bands could play it. The opening track then introduces Cole the vocalist with something listed as "Hesitating Blues." There are several early jazz standards with that name, but this song. which begins with "Procrastination is the thief of time . . .," seems to be unique to this project. It could be that the piece Cole sings is an obscure section of Handy's song (many of his compositions have all kinds of unexpected strains, some of which are rarely performed) or more likely a new concoction by either Riddle (à la "Love Theme") or Mack David (à la "Morning Star," as we shall see). Whatever the provenance of Cole's "Hesitating Blues," it's a stunning example of the artist's unique way of blending the idioms of blues and love songs. Cole's concept of "crooning the blues," not just on this album but going back at least as far as his 1943 "Gee Baby, Ain't I Good to You," is one of the major innovations of his career and a substantial influence on a whole school of followers that included Charles Brown and Ray Charles.

Cole's first full vocal is heard on "Harlem Blues," circa 1926, one of Handy's relatively later and lesser-heard works. Cole and Riddle do a swinging version of what Handy conceived of as a moody piece in which, as originally written, the lyrics comically protest the transition in Negro life from the rural South to the urban North. It's a twist on eighty zillion Tin Pan Alley tunes by post–Stephen Foster composers singing the praises of a southern paradise, but this one rails against Harlem life without quite celebrating home sweet home in a little shack back in Alabammy or wherever. Cole and Riddle swing it into good health.

Considering that Handy's world-famous blues classics describing the towns of Memphis and St. Louis helped make those cities famous—especially outside the United States—it's a surprise that Handy wrote so little about New Orleans, the birthplace of jazz. "Chantez Les Bas" was inspired by a Louisiana Creole tune, with lyrics in both English and Creole-French patois—it means "Sing 'em low." It's another later Handy work, originally published in 1931 but not widely heard until Artie Shaw recorded a classic big-band treatment of it in 1940. The Cole-Riddle treatment is a laid-back, bluesy folk song, with the singer every bit as relaxed as an old man puffing on his pipe and rocking back and forth on his porch in the middle of the Louisiana swamp.

"Friendless Blues" was listed on the cover of the second issue of this album as "Friendliness Blues"; no, that's not exactly the same thing. Whatever the title, it's a regulation 12-bar blues; Riddle deploys a vaguely Basie-like brass obbligato off and on throughout. "Stay" (which is not to be confused with an entirely different song that Cole recorded in 1955) is one of the few songs associated with Handy that doesn't even allude to blues form, sounding more like a standard pop song of the Harlem Renaissance era; it could be by Eubie Blake, Don Redman, or Fats Waller, who recorded it in 1936 in a duet with the composer's daughter, Elizabeth. (The bridge melody is especially tasty.) The Cole track opens with very solid Sweets Edison, beeping away as brilliantly as ever, backed by a descending reed line. Cole interprets the song as a sort of a predecessor to "Baby It's Cold Outside." The instrumental break is notably unbluesy, with eight bars of prominent celesta.

"Joe Turner's Blues" (most famously recorded by the blues giant Big Joe Turner in 1940 but also beloved of early country and hillbilly musicians) is the big butt-kicking swinger here. If the arrangement sounds different from the rest of the album, it's because it's the work of producer-orchestrator-Capitol employee Dave Cavanaugh. It lacks the sophisticated Debussy-ian harmonies of Riddle's "St. Louis Blues" and the self-aware, wise-guy sense of humor of "Beale Street Blues," but it compensates with a raw and groovy directness. Apparently, Cole wanted at least one comparatively simple chart that he could use on the road, and Cavanaugh's "Joe Turner," which doesn't require any string section (or the same level of skill as Riddle's polytonal Coplandisms), was eminently more transportable.

Cole swings "Joe Turner" with glorious aggression that takes us right to the very heart and soul of the blues. Handy explained that this song was about black families in the post–Civil War era being torn apart when their men were carried off involuntarily and forced to live and labor far from their loved ones. In the best tradition of the blues—and African American music in general—that tragedy has herewith been turned around: the looming threat of the breadwinner being forced away from the family has been transmuted into the message, "you better appreciate me now, woman, because soon enough I shall be gone"—the same idea that can be found in many songs of the "classic blues" era. Cole defuses a potentially tragic situation and responds by vigorously swinging it—true to the blues ideal of smiling in the face of trouble and making light of catastrophe. Cole would swing it with even more excitement almost exactly two years later, when he re-recorded the chart on his *Live at the Sands* album.

"Beale Street Blues" offers Riddle's comment on the way the blues were traditionally rendered by big bands, with lots of blaring brass and dramatic stop-time breaks—after "If Beale Street could talk," the horns come in with a great big "WHAMP!"—rendered in what almost seems like a caricature of Basie-style exaggerated dynamics. When Cole finishes his choruses, Edison just keeps going in what amounts to an extension of Cole's vocal, expressed on a highly vocalized trumpet solo, on top of the same backdrop. This 1916 classic was kept alive for many years by trombonist and singer Jack Teagarden, who made it almost as important a part of his act as "Basin Street Blues." (The song also inspired James Baldwin's classic novel, *If Beale Street Could Talk*, and the acclaimed 2018 movie adaptation.)

"Careless Love," from 1921, offers more old-codger-style mock ranting—in this case, inspired by a soap box orator Handy heard railing against mass-produced products and foodstuffs. Handy himself transposed that sentiment into a comic protest against the liberated sexuality of the 1920s, which he characterizes as "loveless." He argues that since the government has levied a "pure food law" to protect us from unhealthy additives in groceries, why shouldn't the legislation also protect innocent folks against the often equally unsavory ways of thoughtless lovers? Along with "Yellow Dog Blues" and

"St. Louis Blues," "Careless Love" was one of the three major Handy classics immortalized early on by the great Bessie Smith. Again, Cole's crooning and Riddle's Ellington-influenced mixtures of brass and reeds emphasize the love song aspects of the text. Cole sings of "Loveless Love" as if he were doing a 12-bar torch song, with an "Angel Eyes"–like diminuendo at the end.

"Morning Star" is a new song by Mack David, written for the film, borrowing only the title of an older, more spiritually oriented Handy piece. While I do regret that Cole didn't sing the actual Handy composition (which Pearl Bailey sang quite wonderfully on her own *St. Louis Blues* album), the new Mack David tune is also excellent, very much in the vein of Judy Garland's "Friendly Star." Where the movie itself was largely about strained parent-child relations, this new piece is a clear-cut anthem of maternal love. This is Riddle's most ambitious string section orchestration here.

One of the few things the film does get partially right is the origin of "Memphis Blues," Handy's first notable composition and the second most famous work of his career. As the picture shows, "Memphis Blues" was originally written as a political campaign jingle; but in the interest of not igniting inter-racial hostility, Paramount Pictures does not show us how the song was swindled away from Handy by a pair of conniving white publishers. Had the movie been made in 1968 rather than 1958, this plot point would surely have been depicted differently. This is the only lyric to one of Handy's major compositions that's not by the composer himself, being the work of George Norton (also the lyricist on "Melancholy Baby"). Handy got cheated out of his royalties, but, almost as if to make it up to him, Norton used the text as a kind of promo for the bandleader-composer, in lyrics that sing the praises of the remarkable Memphis maestro. Cole's treatment is both traditional and literal, as when he sings of "the trombone's croon." The unknown trombonist (sounding something like Bill Harris) also plays in the break, trading fours for a 12-bar chorus with an open-bell trumpeter and he winds up with a Teagarden-esque coda.

The 1914 "Yellow Dog Blues" is, like "Joe Turner," based closely on traditional folk-blues sources. "Yellow Dog" also makes light of a sad situation—men packing up and heading north, joining the Great Migration to Chicago, Detroit, and Harlem (as indeed the Coles family did in 1923), but leaving their women behind. "Where the southern cross(es) the dog" refers to the meeting of the train line and the Yellow Dog River in the Mississippi Delta—"Every cross-tie bayou, burg and bog." In 1925, Bessie Smith established "Yellow Dog" as one of the archetypical women's blues, which laments how the menfolk are free to jump on the rails and ride, but the unliberated women of the day are forced to remain at home—tied down by their own apron strings. The train itself becomes a kind of mechanical rival, the instrument of desertion.

The three most famous vocal performances of "Yellow Dog" are by Smith, Armstrong, and Cole, and the first two treated the material as cautionary tales of love and loss; contrastingly, Cole and Riddle swing the "Yellow Dog" with a vengeance. Cole expresses the rapture of the man who may be leaving his woman, but more important, is hoping to leave the oppressive Jim Crow ways of the Old South for the freedom and dignity he hopes to find up north.[25]

"St. Louis Blues," one of the most famous compositions of all time, climaxes the album and elaborates on the semi-symphonic snippet that began the opening overture, this time expanded into a full-length treatment with a Cole vocal. "St. Louis Blues" is essentially a woman's song—she sings of how the man she loves was seduced away from her by a St. Louis hussy with a powdered face and store-bought hair. Cole and Riddle seem to be distracting from the issue by playing up the concerto grosso aspects of the arrangement and by making it relatively short—just one chorus of all four famous strains. It's dramatic and it's great, and like many tracks on the album, one wishes there were more.

The film *St. Louis Blues* tanked, but the album was a success and, eventually, a classic. The original 1958 *Nat King Cole Sings Songs from St. Louis Blues* (Capitol SW 993) stayed in print long after the movie had been forgotten and was reissued in 1963, with a new cover, as *Nat King Cole Sings the Blues* (SW 1929).

In an odd way, what works best on the *St. Louis Blues* album is the same element that destroys the movie: the film was absolutely inauthentic and took virtually nothing from Handy's actual life. But what's great about the record is the way Cole and Riddle take chances with the Handy canon and both modernize and personalize it, adding overtones as they saw fit from sources as varied as Maurice Ravel and Count Basie. The Cole-Riddle partnership was never more inspired, particularly in the climax of the remarkable "Yellow Dog Blues."

The repeat of the last line in the coda provides an appropriately mythic ending to this tale of the legendary "Joe Turner," while Cole himself imbues the vocal with autobiographical relevance. You can't sing about Joe Turner this convincingly unless you've been him. He was here with me last night, that rascal, but by the time the rooster crowed, he had left, gone where the southern cross' the dog.

With this project, Cole and Riddle proved Albert Murray's dictum that "the blues is not the creation of a crushed-spirit people. It is the product of a forward-looking, upward-striving people."

IN THE MONTHS LEADING UP TO the release of the film, when Cole still had high hopes for it, he had another piece of good news to share with the music industry. He and his new partner, Jack Gale, had re-structured his publishing interests into three firms, "Comet," "Sweco," and "Tri-Park." From this point going forward, Cole owned the publishing of many of his singles and at least one song on all of his albums (with the exception of *My Fair Lady*). Even though the *St. Louis Blues* album consisted almost entirely of vintage material by the storied composer and publisher, W. C. Handy, Cole procured the publishing rights to one of the few new songs in the project, Mack David's "Morning Star."[26] In general, he was pursuing his publishing business somewhat more aggressively than Sinatra, as a point of comparison, but considerably less so than Elvis Presley and Colonel Parker.

AS *ST. LOUIS BLUES* CONFIRMED, the blues medium was yet another of Cole's superpowers: here was a classic album that none of his rivals—Sinatra and Como in one area and Ella Fitzgerald in another—could compete with; only Joe Williams and Dinah Washington (both, like Cole, born in the Deep South and raised in Chicago) ever made a comparable album of swinging, sophisticated blues. At the same time, Cole's biggest-selling singles of the era were also the blues, but blues of a very different sort.

Cole played and sang the blues consistently through the Trio years. He even did a few boogie-woogie numbers, even though he seems to have generally agreed with Fats Waller's assertion that the form was a rather shallow, crowd-pleasing stunt ("two handfuls of nothing," as Fats put it). In the early 1950s, he entered his most "European" phase and delved into the blues only rarely. Still, even then there were a few notable exceptions, like Mary Lou Williams's "Walkin'," which he cut with Billy May in 1951. And then, at the very end of 1954, he began singing a new kind of blues that was starting to take the music industry by storm.

"Rock 'n' Roll," as it came to be called, was essentially a dumbed-down but highly exuberant form of the blues that innovators like Cole and Louis Jordan had pioneered ten years earlier. By 1955, it was embraced by teenagers, who thanks to the postwar baby boom, were now becoming the culturally dominant generation and making this new-old music into the top-selling musical style. As Nat's own thirteen-year-old daughter, Cookie, tells Edward

R. Murrow, "I explained to Daddy that us teenagers like rock 'n' roll better than any other kind of music. I finally got him to make 'Send for Me' and it made a big hit." At which point, Nat adds, "I'm glad I did, in fact, I'm coming to her for all my information from now on."[27] At this point in the *Person to Person* interview, the adults, Nat, Maria, and Ed Murrow, all chuckle—the notion of teenagers dictating trends in popular music still seemed hysterical even as late as 1957.

As if knowing that 1955 would be the year when everything would start to shift from the Sinatra kind of thing to the Elvis kind of thing, Cole had made his first quasi-rock/doo-wop record at the very end of '54. "If I May" was taped on December 20, the same date as some of Cole's most classically styled music, with the Debussy-influenced orchestrations of Nelson Riddle. He recorded three significant hits on the same date, the other two being the British song, "A Blossom Fell," and the almost operatic "The Sand and the Sea," which boasts a big, Cecil B. DeMille–like choir. "A Blossom Fell" was the biggest hit of the session (#2 US, #3 UK) but "If I May" (#8 US) did even better than "The Sand and the Sea" (which was still noteworthy, topping at #23).

"If I May" was essentially a doo-wop record, Cole being backed by a tight male vocal quartet called the Four Knights, who, like the Delta Rhythm Boys, had started (in 1943) as a gospel-centric group. There are also some exaggerated guitar "stings" by John Collins, but it's the constant wah-wah-wah-ing by the Four Knights (and, after all, a King must have his knights) that make this an embryonic, at least, doo-wop enterprise. (It's also the first of half a dozen rock era songs Cole would record by the R&B-centric lyricist Charles Singleton).[28] This is very early in the development of the music, made only less than three months after "Earth Angel" by the Penguins, one of the breakthrough doo-wop hits.

Cole followed it up a year later at the end of December 1955, with two more numbers in a similar vein, "My Personal Possession" and "That's All There Is to That." Again, both were recorded at the tail end of sessions of more "conventional" Cole material with Nelson Riddle. The majority of the orchestra would head home, and Cole would stick around with his rhythm section, joined again by the Four Knights. Most of Cole's rock 'n' roll and doo-wop records seemed to have been composed and arranged according to a strict formula, using a bouncy beat, a male quartet background, and the inevitable sixteenth-note triplets. We are now in the realm of such iconic period groups as the Cadillacs, the Platters, the Coasters, the Marcels, and Frankie Lymon and the Teenagers.

There would be many follow-ups to "If I May," leading to his next big hit in the genre, the 1957 "Send for Me" (done with Billy May) and eventually a series of sessions in 1958 and '59, eleven tracks of which were later gathered into the *Looking Back* LP. Cole and Lee Gillette elected not to "cover" any established hits of the period; you would never hear Cole warning anyone not to step on his blue suede shoes (except as a gag reference in "When Rock and Roll Come to Trinidad"). Rather, the singer-producer team consistently attempted to create original hits of their own. They generally relied on a small pool of writers who were already experienced with the idiom, and thus the same few names recur on song after song, including Singleton, Herman McCoy (who also conducted the vocal group on a number of Cole dates, and often on the NBC TV show), and the team of singer-songwriter Brook Benton, producer Clyde Otis, and arranger Belford Hendricks (on "Nothing in the World," "Thank You, Pretty Baby," and "Looking Back.")

Ollie Jones, who had started with Cole[29] as one of the Four Knights, was responsible for the most successful song of the entire R'n'R series, "Send for Me," which had been brought to Cole's attention by song-plugger Marvin Cane. He recorded it in May 1957, on a date supervised by Billy May, along with "With You on My Mind," one of several songs Cole co-wrote with his wife's sister, Charlotte Hawkins. Nat test-marketed "Send for Me" by playing the demo for Cookie; when she spontaneously started dancing, he knew he had a potential hit.[30] "Send for Me" is much more of a genuine blues, albeit one with a bridge, and overall, it's the most compelling of Cole's rock-ish numbers. Herman McCoy supplied the backup singers and there's a driving tenor solo by Plas Johnson (formally known as Plas John Johnson Jr.), who, for a whole generation, was the preeminent rock-pop saxophonist on the West Coast. "With You on My Mind" was also successful; the single reached #30 and Cole sang it memorably on his NBC TV show (with the two-tenor team of Flip Philipps and Illinois Jacquet), but "Send for Me" was clearly the hit, becoming a permanent part of the Cole canon.

When Capitol issued "Send for Me," backed with "My Personal Possession" (recorded two years earlier), the single made it to #6 on the mainstream pop charts and #1 on the R&B listings; it was Cole's biggest hit since "A Blossom Fell," two years earlier. When Cole performed "Send for Me" in his nightclub act, he often added the comment, "If you can't beat 'em, join 'em!" A reviewer observed that at one swanky joint, the Eden Roc in Miami, "Send for Me" elicited "a stomping reception by mink clad and otherwise expensively clothed patrons."[31] In clubs, Cole probably performed the song in more of a traditional big-band arrangement.[32]

The rest of the date, which included a doo-woppy arrangement of Rodgers and Hart's "Blue Moon" (unlike Elvis, Cole included the bridge), contained nothing particularly memorable and the tracks were not issued until the CD era. This illustrates the way it went with this material; whereas nearly every track on all of the classic albums (or even the lesser ones, like *Tell Me All about Yourself*, 1958) is worth listening to, the rock-pop material, conversely, is entirely hit or miss. Some tracks, like "Send for Me" and "With You on My Mind" are quite enjoyable, but the bulk of them, like the other three songs on that 1957 Billy May date, were total duds.

In November 1957, Cole and Riddle bit off three more rock-ish numbers, "Angel Smile," "It's None of My Affair" (also unissued at the time), and "Nothing in the World"; of the three, the last is by far the loveliest, suggesting a halfway point between Cole's traditional style and the current doo-wop approach, but the first, "Angel Smile," is the one that charted. Despite the mild chart success (#33), one still wonders why Gillette is wasting Riddle's time with this stuff—what they want on these sessions is precisely the opposite of what Riddle's strengths are. That situation was soon rectified: this was the last of Cole's rock-style sessions to utilize either Riddle or May. Going forward, his musical director in this series would be Dave Cavanaugh, who had considerably more experience with this kind of material.

The next date in the R&B series would be Cavanaugh's first with Cole (at least since a one-off in 1952), and it occurred on February 4, 1958, shortly after Cole and Riddle had finished their album of considerably more sophisticated blues compositions by W. C. Handy. Taped in New York, the session utilized not only Cole's touring rhythm section (Collins, Harris, Young) but the team also recruited several local "ringers": a second guitarist, John Pizzarelli, known to everyone as "Bucky," and even closer to home, Nat's kid brother, Freddy, both of whom had more experience with pop-rock/R&B style than Cole's usual crew. Decades later, Freddy naturally remembered the session (his only professional collaboration with his superstar big brother) more than the music itself, since most of the songs weren't particularly memorable.

However, as was by now a kind of tradition, three of the songs, "Thank You, Pretty Baby" (which survives in a seventeen-minute slice of session material, including thirteen partial and complete takes), "Make It Last" (which didn't), and "Just as Much as Ever" went nowhere, but "Do I Like It?" was a minor hit (#62) and another, "Looking Back" made it to #5 pop and #1 R&B, and thus became Cole's biggest hit in three years, even more than "Send for Me." "Looking Back" was something new in R&B: a melancholy, reflective song that seems far outside the emotional experiences of the teenagers who were buying such records in 1958.

Listening to "Looking Back" sixty years later, one can't help but notice that in retrospect it sounds much more like a Brook Benton record than a Nat King Cole record. Songwriters Benton, Otis, and Hendricks then brought Cole a follow-up song, a similarly moody, grown-up number titled "Just a Matter of Time," and Cole immediately agreed to record it. But even as he was making plans to take the new song into the studio, Benton and Otis were making a professional transition from songwriters to singer and producer. Otis decided that "Just a Matter of Time" would be the perfect song for Benton to launch his own singing career with, and he turned out to be right. They then somehow summoned up the nerve to ask Nat *not* to record it, and he graciously agreed. "Nat really wanted those songs," Otis later told Colin Escott, "but I told him what had happened with Brook and how I had this new job, so he laid off them." [33] A few months earlier, Ed Murrow had asked Cole, "Have you ever turned down an eventual hit tune?" "Well yes," he answered; "I've made those blunders. I'm sure there are a lot of performers have turned down songs they didn't quite feel. But we always figure, if we've lost one, we can always find something else."[34] This, however, wasn't a "blunder" of any sort, but a kind of noblesse oblige, an established artist stepping aside so that an emerging talent could have his chance. As they predicted, "Just a Matter of Time" became the breakthrough hit for Benton.

Cole seemed to realize that with "Send for Me" and "Looking Back," he had gone has far as he could with the quasi-rock style. He and Cavanaugh made several more such sessions in summer and fall 1959, resulting in six vocal numbers, as well as two funky piano instrumentals, "Whatcha Gonna Do" and Duke Ellington's "In a Mellow Tone." Most of these ("I Must Be Dreaming," "Midnight Flyer," "Sweet Bird of Youth," "The World in My Arms," and "Time and the River") seem rather half-hearted and have little to recommend them (although "Midnight Flyer" is at least legitimate 12-bar blues). A few made it to the distant regions of the top 100 chart, but it was clear that this phase of Cole's artistic evolution was over.

There were roughly twenty-six songs in the Cole "rock" series, recorded between 1954 and 1959, eleven of which were included in the posthumous album, *Looking Back*; to take a sad song and make it worse, the producers of that 1965 LP overdubbed a contemporary-sounding rhythm section to make the tracks sound even more rock-ish. By and large, this is the ass-end of the Cole canon, the least interesting music that he ever recorded.

However, "Again," recorded in November 1958, was a major exception. This was a 1949 movie theme, written for Ida Lupino to sing in the film noir *Road House*, music by Hollywood royalty Alfred Newman and a lyric by the little-known Dorcas Cochran. Cavanaugh's arrangement splits the difference between the doo-wop style and Cole's traditional music, using a rock-ish rhythmic underpinning (more sixteenth-note triplets) but lush strings like Riddle or Jenkins. Rather than canceling each other out, the disparate elements work together to support Cole's voice and his especially tender crooning. Fittingly, the only really decent song gets the only really decent arrangement in the whole series. It didn't happen again.

IN ADDITION TO BEING COLE'S MOST PROLIFIC YEAR as a recording artist, 1958 was also his most amazingly diverse one. This was a lesson Cole learned from Bing Crosby, that variety was the spice of keeping record-buyers interested. *St. Louis Blues* sounded nothing like *The Very Thought of You* which in turn sounded nothing like *To Whom It May Concern, Every Time I Feel the Spirit,* or *Welcome to the Club*. The most different of all these projects, and certainly the one that was intended for the most far-flung audience, was *Cole Español.*

The mid-to-late 1950s were the high point of the relationship of Nat Cole and Carlos Gastel. Throughout these years, the canny Honduran still exerted a powerful force in Cole's life and music; there are copious shots of them together at nightclubs and at the Palm Springs birthday party in 1957. Gastel (who would officially part company with Cole in 1963)[35] gets credit for the concept of the *Cole Español* project, which seems logical as the San Pedro Sula-born manager was a native Spanish speaker. As early as October 1944, Carlos reported that the Trio was getting offers from Mexico City, and he "revealed that he is planning a post-war tour of Central and South American countries with a crack unit which will be headed by the Trio."[36] Gastel realized that Nat had an international appeal that other artists didn't; as we've seen, many of his 1950–1955 hits were songs that originated in other countries, and he was singing in languages besides English as far back as the 1953 "Darling, Je Vous Aime Beaucoup" (which, ironically, has a lyric about *not* being able to speak another language).

Other singers had recorded in languages other than English prior to this; Crosby was genuinely multi-lingual, and the highlight of Dean Martin's output was his string of Italian ballads and novelties, but Cole set a precedent by recording in a foreign language specifically for that market: listeners and record-buyers who actually lived in the Spanish-speaking world. Gringos were welcome to buy it too—at the time there was a major market for rhumbas, cha-cha-chas, and mambos (as celebrated in Cole's 1954 "Papa Loves Mambo") across the forty-eight states. But North America was strictly a secondary consideration; the target audiences were Central and South America, and *El Madro España* herself. Gastel and Cole even came up with a clever title, one that capitalized, so to speak, on the way that Cole's last name happened to rhyme with the Spanish word for "Spanish": *Cole Español.*

The team, Nat, Carlos, and Lee, decided to cut this album in February while Nat was working at the Tropicana nightclub in Cuba. "The first Spanish album we did with Nat was done in Havana," said Gillette. "We had a local conductor. The arrangements were for the most part done by Dave Cavanaugh. And so Dave came down, he wrote some of the arrangements after we got to Havana and did a remarkable job."[37] Cavanaugh is generally regarded as the overall music director, even though the team was using the house band from the Tropicana under the baton of Armando Romeu Jr.

Additional arrangements were written by Romeu and a few were also by Nelson Riddle—notably "Lisbon Antigua," a Portuguese song that had been a rare hit instrumental single for the arranger in 1955.

On February 17, 1958, the entourage convened in the Panart Studio in Havana. Cole seems to have actually recorded two English adaptations of Spanish language songs, "Lisbon Antigua" and "Come Closer to Me" (Acercate Mas) then and there; he did fine with the English texts but wasn't happy with his Spanish. He couldn't fudge this, especially because the primary audience for the album was to be native Spanish speakers. Thus, the decision was made to keep going with the session, but to record only the backing tracks in Cuba. Cole would later record the vocals back in Hollywood, after first having the Spanish lyrics written out phonetically.

Thus, over four dates from February 17 to 20, Romeu and his crew recorded nine orchestral backgrounds, including instrumentals and, in some cases, background vocals (by the Facundo Rivero Four). An additional two were recorded in the Capitol Tower on June 9, "Cachito" and the Mexican "Noche De Ronda" (Be Mine Tonight) with Dave Cavanaugh conducting an orchestra of mostly Hollywood Hispanics, including the veteran Cuban pianist and composer Rene Touzet.

The eleven songs on the final album were divided between lively, uptempo dance numbers ("Cachito") and slow, romantic boleros—*musica romantica*—("Acercate Mas" and "Quizas, Quizas, Quizas"), and every gradation of tempo in between (like the half-fast "El Bodeguero"). They were also chosen from all over the spectrum of Latin American music: "Las Mananitas" and "Adelita" are Mexican mariachis, with prominent brass and solo violin (on the album back cover, there's an indication, "with mariachis"); "Lisbon Antigua" originated in Portugal; "Acercate Mas" and 'Quizas, Quizas, Quizas" are both archetypical Havana rhumbas by Cuban composer Osvaldo Farres.

A few were well known in the Northern Hemisphere—namely, "Maria Elena" (dedicated to the former First Lady of Mexico) and "Te Quiero Dijiste (Mucho, Mucho) (Magic Is the Moonlight)," but this doesn't seem to have been a factor in the song selection. There's even one Italian song in there, the famous "Arrivederci Roma (Goodbye to Rome)," also sung in Spanish (it was hugely popular in Mexico) as well as a piano instrumental, "Tu Mi Delirio." Otherwise, the piano parts on the album (the Cuban sessions) are played by Bebo Valdés, one of the most famous Cuban musicians of all time, whose son, Chucho Valdés, went on to become a superstar of contemporary Cuban music.

The idea of singing to pre-recorded backgrounds—in order to concentrate on the Spanish lyrics—truly paid off; additionally, Cole was in terrific form, relaxed and confident, even though he was working in what was yet another whole new medium. He sings beautifully, and especially on some tracks, such as Riddle's wonderful arrangement of "El Bodeguero." Hispanics and Gringos alike could easily imagine Cole is cha-cha-cha-ing through the aisles of a local *bodega*, taking delight in the foodstuffs he finds, especially those *frijoles negros*.

Cole Español was a resounding success; "El Rey" Cole was accepted in the Spanish-speaking world like no North American star before or since. International sales figures are impossible to ascertain, but we know the album was a huge hit all over the world, especially in its target countries—and it also reached #12 in the United States. Cole went to the trouble of memorizing some of the more popular songs phonetically so that he could sing them live; among other domestic outlets, he plugged the album on the *Patti Page Show*, singing "Quizas, Quizas, Quizas." There's a 1961 "television concert" from Tokyo in which he sings, "Quizas," "Acerte Mas," and "Cachito," with considerable animation and empathy. Even better is an audio recording from the New Latin Quarter in Tokyo in 1963, where he invests "El Bodeguero" and other *Español* songs with *mucho fuego Cubano* (Cuban fire). From 1958 forward, Latin music would be one of the recurring themes of his life.

IN APRIL 1957, *Love Is the Thing* reached number one on the Billboard album charts, the first 12" Nat King Cole release to do so. Clearly a follow-up was in order, and for the first time, Cole decided to do a direct sequel to one of his albums. This was *The Very Thought of You*, recorded by Cole and Jenkins eighteen months later in May 1958, at which point Cole was in the middle of a month-long stint at the Coconut Grove and was getting ready for a major tour of the Pacific Northwest, from Portland and Seattle to Winnipeg and Saskatchewan. Overall, *The Very Thought of You* is so similar to *Love Is the Thing* that even I have a hard time remembering which tracks are on which album. Still, two albums hardly constitute a "formula" but rather more of the same greatness. (The major difference, all but inaudible, is that this time Cole's own guitarist and bassist, John Collins and Charlie Harris, joined Lee Young in the rhythm section.)

Where the composer of choice the first time around was the late Victor Young, this time the music man of the moment was the still very active Harry Warren, who had only one song on *Love* ("At Last") but fully three on *Thought*: "I Found a Million Dollar Baby (In a Five and Ten Cent Store)" comes from Warren's early Broadway/pre-Hollywood period (the 1931 revue *Billy Rose's Crazy Quilt*), and two from his 20th Century Fox Technicolor era with Mack Gordon, "My Heart Tells Me (Should I Believe My Heart)" (from *Sweet Rosie O'Grady*, 1943) and "The More I See You" (*Diamond Horseshoe*, 1945). Jenkins's chart on "Million Dollar Baby" is particularly ingenious in its use of pizzicato violins to depict the raindrops in a "lucky April shower."

Jimmy Van Heusen also has two: "But Beautiful" (*Road to Rio*, 1947) with lyrics by Cole's very close friend Johnny Burke, and the equally beautiful "Making Believe You're Here" with text by Sammy Cahn. The latter is one of Cahn's most poignant lyrics and in a class with "All My Tomorrows," which the team wrote for Sinatra that same season. It's reminiscent of the many World War II songs of separation, à la "Love Letters" (on *Love Is the Thing*). It's altogether likely that Sammy and Jimmy wrote it at Cole's request; he got the publishing for his own firm, Comet, which suggests that Nat might have given them the title.[38]

Three more songs come from film sources: "I Wish I Knew the Way to Your Heart [Notorious]," is not to be confused with Harry Warren's "I Wish I Knew" (which Cole recorded later in 1958) but is the work of another Italian songwriter, Carlo Alberto Rossi, and an English lyric by the prolific Al Stillman. "Magnificent Obsession" was a collaboration of Columbia pictures house composer Fred Karger and Cole's close friend Frankie Laine, although it has no connection with the classic 1954 Douglas Sirk film of the same title.[39]

"Paradise" is another of Jenkins's goofy, wonderful ideas, and a track that garnered considerable attention at the time. The song is in ABAB form and was originally written (for the 1932 *A Woman Commands*) in a way that requires the singer to hum as suggestively as possible at the end of each line in the A sections: "And then she holds my hand—la-de-da-dum . . . " This worked for Bing Crosby in 1932, but one can't imagine Cole semi-scatting in this lush orchestral context, and at this ballad tempo. Jenkins solved the problem by arranging for the string section to "hum" the phrase instead. It's an idea that could have come from no one but Jenkins. (However, Cole does verbalize a part of the song that was previously done only instrumentally.) Remarkably, according to Lee Young, this particular form of non-verbal communication was judged as too salacious. "When we did an album with Gordon Jenkins and did 'Paradise,' they took that song off the air. ... They took it out because the humming was 'too suggestive.' That was in the 1950s. We live in a changing world, don't we?"[40]

"Paradise" also had a profound effect on one of Cole's original Capitol Records rabbis, Dave Dexter Jr. "It's the only pop record I ever heard that, probably the first fifty times I heard it, I'd start crying, the way those strings go up, the way they jump an octave at the end," he told Bruce Jenkins. "And mind you I'm a jazz guy. That's my real bag. But it's so beautifully orchestrated, and Nat was at his very best. ... You think I'm exaggerating. I tell you, I cried. Time after time. It gets down to those last sixteen bars, those strings. And I don't feel [that] I'm an emotional guy."[41]

The young Johnny Mathis was taken backstage to meet Cole at a show not long after the album was released, and he spoke with him about this song. "I remember specifically the time that I met him in the dressing room, he had to sing either 'Stardust' or 'Paradise,' 'Stardust' is a very difficult song to sing, and he was complaining about the fact that it was so difficult, but he had to sing it, he had just had a hit recording with Gordon Jenkins. And 'Paradise' was also a difficult song, because of the open vowels, in 'Paradise,' and the phrasing of it." Reminiscing about the conversation twenty years later, Mathis marveled that he had had the chutzpah to share his wisdom with the most successful singer in the world. "I was young and brash of course, so I gave him the benefit—ha!—of all my studies and told him he should keep his vowels open a little longer and it would make it easier for him to sing the song."[42]

The Very Thought of You opens with the title song by British composer and bandleader Ray Noble, a key inspiration for both Cole[43] and Jenkins. There are two somewhat mysterious pseudo-French chansons here: "Cherchez La Femme" is by Bob Marcus, who also wrote three additional, lesser items in the Cole canon,[44] in collaboration with Lorenzo Pack, who began his career as a prizefighter before graduating, as it were, to the more dangerous bout known as the music business.[45] "Cherchez La Femme" is the best song that either wrote; in the spirit of "Darling, Je Vous Aime Beaucoup," it's in true *franglais*, it's both catchy and memorable, and a perfect choice for this album, even its faux-European pretensions. (Contrastingly, "Cherie, I Love You" credited to one Lillian Rosedale Goodman, unheard of before or since, is strictly faux Euro-trash.)

Along the way, we also hit "Impossible,"[46] written by Steve Allen for a 1956 TV show titled *The Bachelor* (his other song from the score, "This Could Be the Start of Something Big," became a standard) although Allen later used "Impossible" on his own series. "I used to use it as a closing theme on my Sunday show, and because of that, a lot of singers heard it and got used to it, and fortunately Nat was one of them."[47] Then there's also the Maestro's own "This Is All I Ask," later a success for Tony Bennett and then Sinatra, an especially poignant song about growing old for a thirty-nine-year-old singer who would never grow old.

"For All We Know," which Jenkins first encountered in his salad days with Isham Jones, and "Don't Blame Me," by buddy Jimmy McHugh, were both originally done by the King Cole Trio. "For All We Know" is probably the single best-remembered song on the album, and it's easy to see why Cole thought so highly of it, with its masterfully melancholy lyric and the idea that "we may never meet again, so let's make the most of this moment"—an idea that increasingly became a leitmotif of his short life. The melody, somewhat reminiscent of the opening notes of Mozart's "Jupiter" symphony, is, like, "Paradise," cast in an ABAB form.

"Don't Blame Me" and Isham Jones's "There Is No Greater Love" were not included on the original stereo LP but are on the CD editions. On the whole, if forced to compare the two, *Love Is the Thing* has at least a slight advantage over *The Very Thought of You*; the original is almost always better than the sequel, and this is no exception. Being the first, *Love* has a little more energy to it, which you might not think is the general quality that one is necessarily looking for in a ballad album, but there's a more tangible feeling of greater inspiration throughout. And overall, there are more standout tracks. But *Thought* is rich with stunning performances as well.

Perhaps the single most impressive is "But Beautiful": Cole's phrasing of a slow love song has never been more masterful. It grew ever more so as he kept singing it, and his 1963 live performance on BBC TV is greater still than this 1958 studio performance. His use of space and silence is at a level that exceeds any pure singer, even, possibly, Sinatra. The slow, even, deliberate way he delivers the melody, with a lot of room around each note, is reminiscent of some of the piano solos on Jenkins's own orchestral records, using a minimal approach to get as much out of the tune as possible. It's nothing but pure melody and pure emotion. Like *Love Is the Thing, The Very Thought of You* is a stunning testament to Cole's ability to tell a story and Jenkins's gift for helping a singer to do that.

At every step of his life, Cole was creating not only amazing new music but whole new forms that had never existed previously. It's easy to forget that the idea of a singer working this way with a string orchestra, in a hi-fi or stereo recording on a 12" long-playing 33⅓ RPM was radically new—as new in 1956–58 as the Trio was in its day. Until the day he died, Nat King Cole was constantly inventing new kinds of beauty.

To give Jenkins the final word, the maestro later confessed that whenever he listened to his own recordings he couldn't help but pick them apart and find flaws—things that he would have liked to re-do—except, as he made clear, his work with Cole. "He did everything good. I was just playing some tapes in a car; I can't find anything wrong with anything. He never made a mistake. I never heard him make one. He had a very high standard, a very high level of performance, much more than probably anybody."[48]

COLE TAPED *THE VERY THOUGHT OF YOU* in three sessions over the first week of May 1958 (it was released in November), in the middle of the *Cole Español* project, which he finished in June (and released in August); before June was finished, he had started work on two more albums, *To Whom It May Concern*, with Nelson Riddle, and *Welcome to the Club*, with Dave Cavanaugh. But the big event for Nat in summer 1958 wasn't a new album or even a tour, although after he and Nelson returned from the Northwest in early June, he then worked extensively across California in June and August. The news that occupied most of Nat and Maria's attention—along with the rest of Los Angeles—was the premiere season of the town's first Major League Baseball team, the Dodgers, recently imported from Brooklyn.

"He loves baseball as some men love women or drink," *Ebony* magazine observed in 1956. Said Nat, "If I ever get rich, I'm gonna buy me a plane and get a box in every ballpark in the country, then I'm gonna fly from city to city and do nothing but watch baseball games."[49] The arrival of the Dodgers in time for the 1958 season was a major moment for the Cole family and the city and served as a socializing force to make Los Angeles feel more like a community—which it never had been previously. The movie colony and non-showbiz folks alike gathered at the Los Angeles Memorial Coliseum stadium, and the Dodgers games quickly became a social ritual; Doris Day, among many others, had fond memories of sitting with the Coles at numerous games.[50] Vin

Scully, who announced the team's games for sixty-seven years, fondly remembered how Nat and Maria made "micro-wagers" with each other: 'I bet you a nickel this will be a ball that will be a strike!'" He continued, "Nat was at every possible game imaginable, you know? He came up to the booth one time and was one of the few celebrities that we have ever had on the air. We had Nat on to plug the celebrity game and chat with him."[51]

Scully also remembered that Nat's cigarettes, now ensconced in a three-inch holder, were ever present. Not a good sign.

DAVE CAVANAUGH, WHO WAS BORN a few days before Nat Cole on March 13, 1919 (and who died in 1981), was a shining example of what a record producer used to be: someone who was extremely competent musically, had great taste, and never made the mistake of thinking he was more important than the artists he produced—in other words, the polar opposite of Clive Davis and the other moguls who have dominated the pop music biz for the last fifty years. He started as a saxophonist, most famously with Capitol Recording artist Bobby Sherwood's orchestra, but he soon developed into a talented orchestrator, conductor, and composer. He was not singularly great at any one thing—as an arranger, for instance, no one would have put him in the top class (alongside Riddle, May, or Jenkins)—but he could get the job done, and his combined skills in all these areas made him a very capable A&R man. Along with Lee Gillette, Voyle Gilmore, and Bill Miller (not the pianist), Cavanaugh was an important part of the all-star production staff that presided over Capitol Records in the great years. He will probably be best remembered for his long-term relationships with Peggy Lee, George Shearing, and Nancy Wilson, but he also worked with virtually everyone at Capitol at one time or another, including Frank Sinatra and Nat King Cole. Everyone seemed to want to have "Big Dave" (as he was billed on some of his own releases) with him or her in the studio.

Freddy Cole remembered that Nat and Maria were especially close to Cavanaugh and his wife Mildred, and so was he. "Dave was the only one (of Nat's arrangers or producers) whom I knew really well. He was a very nice guy with a very nice family. I wish I could have known him better. Musically, Dave was very together." In 1952, Cavanaugh had arranged and conducted one singles session for Cole. Then, from 1958 to 1960, they were reunited for a series of projects that included some R&B-styled singles (some of which were on the *Looking Back* album), the first two Spanish albums *Cole Español* (1958) and *A Mis Amigos* (1959), Cole's first officially released live album, *At the Sands* (1960), and two studio albums of standards, *Welcome to the Club* and *Tell Me All about Yourself,* both recorded in 1958.

Cavanaugh had also already proven his mettle in terms of the blues. Capitol had released several albums of his studio band playing R&B instrumentals for dancing teens, and what's more, he had written an exceptional arrangement of W. C. Handy's "Joe Turner Blues," in addition to those dates of rock-ish material for Cole. It was probably on the strength of Cavanaugh's blues chops that they agreed he was the arranger best equipped to oversee *Welcome to the Club* (later reissued on CD as *Big Band Cole*), Cole's one in-studio meeting with the legendary orchestra of Count Basie.

"Nat and Basie were very dear friends," said Freddy Cole. "I know he enjoyed doing the album, and that was one of the swingin'est ones that Nat ever did." Most of Nat's friends shared his love for baseball, but when Nat and Maria got together with Bill and Catherine Basie, they indulged him in his favorite sport: horse racing. How better for jazz royalty, a King and a Count, to distract themselves than with the sport of kings?

Because Basie was then under contract to Roulette Records through much of the early LP era, when singers wanted to team up with him, the precedent was to not directly mention the presence of the band on the record, and also to include the band but not the Count himself, as Sarah Vaughan had done a few months earlier on the aptly titled *No Count Sarah* (recorded in January 1958). In the case of Nat's album, the record itself doesn't mention the Basie name, but the back cover verbiage does make reference to "a band you can count on." (No one would have failed to catch the hint.)

Prior to this album, Cole's most memorable teaming with the Basie aggregation occurred, as we have seen, at the New York Paramount theater in January 1957.[52] The billing described the line-up as "the incomparable" Nat King Cole (headliner), with "the Swingin'" Count Basie and His Orchestra featuring Joe Williams, and "the inimitable" Ella Fitzgerald. The whole aggregate was scheduled also to guest on Cole's NBC TV series,[53] but as it worked out, Basie and Ella appeared on the show without each other, Basie on January 28, joining Cole on the jam session warhorse, "Oh, Lady Be Good."

A year and a half later, the West Coast–based jazz piano virtuoso Gerald Wiggins was hired to play on *Welcome to the Club*, in effect substituting for two of the greatest keyboardists in all of jazz. Wiggins sounds especially Basie-ish on "Avalon," the 1920 Al Jolson song turned into a jazz standard by Benny Goodman; Wiggins offers glorious soft/loud dynamics in a call-and-response exchange between piano and horns, fully in the Basie tradition of soft shoe dancing on the keys. Drummer Sonny Payne plays a particularly spectacular solo here, just about the most exciting to ever be heard on a Cole record—the time feel is totally different from that usually supplied for Cole by Lee Young.

On one hand, this jazz setting would have been a perfect opportunity for Cole himself to play some jazz piano, but in the long run we can be grateful that he chose to focus on singing here. As is evident from the first notes of the opener, "She's Funny That Way," onward—Cole is playing an even more beautiful instrument here than the piano. Tender on the torch tunes and bitingly abrasive on the swingers, Cole is even more all over his "horn" than he was in the days when he made his living with his mouth shut; his gift for bringing a lyric to life has never been sharper. His overall interpretation—of the melodies as well as lyrics—renders crystal clear any story that he elects to tell. He's doing all the work with his voice and hardly needs any help from the keyboard.

Cavanaugh also completely catches the spirit of the "New Testament" Basie orchestra, although largely without the benefit of extended solos; the one prominent horn feature here is a brief tenor statement by Billy Mitchell on "The Late, Late Show" that seems to have caught both the engineers and the saxophonist (as if sight reading the chart for the first time) by surprise. "Avalon" and "Late, Late Show," for instance, begin most eloquently with "Whirly Bird"-style drum thunder by Sonny Payne, the percussionist who did the most to establish the new band's rhythmic feel. Throughout, Cavanaugh uses the current Basie band's trademark dramatic brass surges for punctuation, periodically contrasting them with feather-light tinkling from the piano bench. Basie-style exaggerated dynamics, those extreme loud-louds and soft-softs, are employed throughout.

"The Late, Late Show" is a romper with lyrics by old friend Roy Alfred to a tune by Cavanaugh himself, who frequently employed pseudonyms when he placed songs with artists he was producing; here, he's "Murray Berlin," while elsewhere, most famously with Peggy Lee on "I Love Being Here with You," he's "Bill Schluger."[54] "Late Show" was first heard instrumentally played by jazz organist Milt Buckner on the Capitol album *Rockin' Organ*, and was introduced lyrically by Dakota Staton on another Cavanaugh production. Even before Cole got to it in 1958, the song already had a history with the Basie organization.

So too did "I Want a Little Girl" and "Baby Won't You Please Come Home," both famously done by Basie with his original band vocalist, Jimmy Rushing. "Baby . . ." had been reprised more recently by Basie and Joe Williams and is one of the more notable popular songs to incorporate elements of the blues. That is, in fact, the same spirit that songwriter Vic Abrams intended in his blues song, "The Blues Don't Care,"[55] which had been recorded three months earlier by trumpeter Jonah Jones and the Five Keys (both on Capitol). These are songs with authentic ties to the blues, but "Wee Baby Blues," by two legendary Kansas City musicians, pianist Pete Johnson and singer Joe Turner, is the real thing, an authentic 12-bar blues.

Likewise, "Avalon" and Duke Ellington's "Mood Indigo" (lyrics by an uncredited Mitchell Parrish, another victim of Irving Mills's machinations),[56] were well established jazz and big band standards. The less familiar songs are generally worthy of being heard in such fine company: "Look Out for Love," by Broadway actor Danny Meehan, is a cautionary tale in the tradition of Sinatra's "The Tender Trap" and Louis Jordan's "Beware."[57] "Anytime, Any Day, Anywhere" is a superior song by Victor Young, co-written and associated with the great jazz singer Lee Wiley.

Over the course of these dates (June 30, July 1, and July 2), Cavanaugh and Cole recorded a total of twelve tunes with the Basie band, including "Madrid," a swinging pop-song adaptation of the famous "Habanera" from the 1873 opera *Carmen*. This was possibly to be part of the *Club* album, even though it was an odd fit. It didn't quite match the Basie style that they were going for, and it was arranged by Billy May rather than Cavanaugh. "Madrid" was released as a single in the United States and the United Kingdom several weeks prior to the *Club* album, but it was quickly banned by the BBC, who frowned on the concept of swinging the classics (much as they had barred Sinatra and May's treatment of "Mandalay" on *Come Fly with Me*). It was omitted from the album but restored to the CD, and even charted as a single. "Madrid" is swinging and exciting, especially when Cole also performed an exuberant version with a full dance troupe on the Perry Como *Kraft Music Hall* in 1959.

Welcome to the Club enjoyed a particularly meaningful afterlife; at the height of the "Unforgettable" era in 1991, it was reissued on CD as *Big Band Cole*. Under the new title, it gained a whole new status in the 1990s, when, all of a sudden, songs like "Avalon" and "The Late, Late Show" were being included in Cole tributes (the latter was particularly well done by John Pizzarelli Jr. in collaboration with George Shearing). In the overall context of Cole's career, *Welcome to the Club,/ Big Band Cole*, is doubly notable as the closest he would come to an official collaboration with Count Basie as well as the first of two jazzy albums of standards with his great friend, Dave Cavanaugh. If Cole had lived a little bit longer, into the late '60s, when record companies began to loosen their contractual restrictions and both Basie and Duke Ellington were pretty much free agents, I have no doubt that Cole would have worked more extensively with both of those legendary bandleaders. As it stands, it's still notable as the meeting of a Count and a King.

Welcome to the Club didn't make the charts in 1958, but Cole was happy enough with Cavanaugh's work to reunite with him a mere three months later (for three sessions in New York in late October and early November) for *Tell Me All about Yourself*, released in 1960. As with *Welcome to the Club, Tell Me All about Yourself* was a mixture of standards and suitable new songs (which gave the albums their titles), both with Cavanaugh at the podium and with many of the new songs being published by Cole's own firms. Both are highly swing-oriented and, in this case, budget-conscious—that is, there was no need here to go the expense of a string section.

The linchpin for the second of the two is the title number, "Tell Me All about Yourself," written by Hollywood arranger Hub Atwood, best known for the Sinatra standard "I Could Have Told You." The song is a sprightly rhythmic romper that sets the tone for the album; as always, Cole himself is an irrepressible swinger, and he matches the swinging intensity of the band beat for beat. He's especially compelling when he emphasizes a low note on the downbeat, "*Tell* me all about yourself!" and in the last chorus when he lets the band play the first four bars of each A section instrumentally (". . . things you like to say and do . . . bring me up to date on you"), reminiscent of the way Cole would trade phrases with the guitarist and bassist back in the Trio days.

As with *Welcome*, the primary focus is standards from the big-band era: "Until the Real Thing Comes Along," a song that originated in Kansas City, then was revised by Sammy Cahn and Saul Chaplin to become a hit for Cole's colleague, Andy Kirk; Cole's treatment is refreshingly reharmonized. "I Would Do Anything for You" is the best-known composition of two well-known Harlem-based composer-pianists, Alex Hill and bandleader Claude Hopkins. Both songs were associated with high-falsetto tenors: Pha Terrell on the first and Orlando Roberson on the second, and as such, they both suit Cole's high baritone very well—and he is considerably more accomplished than either of his predecessors in terms of both rhythm and emotional content. "For You," by Joe Burke and Al Dubin, originally recorded as a waltz in 1930, and "Dedicated to You" (also Cahn and Chaplin) were both widely recorded in the swing era, and then both enjoyed a long history with African American and jazz artists.

Three further songs derive from the early postwar period, which could be considered the late swing era: Irving Berlin's "The Best Thing for You" (from *Call Me Madame*); the Billie Holiday standard "Crazy She Calls Me," by Carl Sigman and Bob Russell, two extremely prolific hitmakers who would individually and together write a number of significant songs in the Cole canon);[58] and Warren and Gordon's "This Is Always," from the Fox musical *Three Little Girls in Blue* (which also yielded "You Make Me Feel So Young"). And even though the last was a minor hit for the team of bop savant Charlie Parker and Eckstine-styled crooner Earl Coleman, it has been done by surprisingly few major singers.

There are four newish songs besides the title track, nearly all by authors with a long-standing connection to Cole, starting with the singer-pianist himself. "My Life" is co-credited to Cole and Roger Simon; Nat's treatment of the bridge is especially warm and compelling. Apart from the songs published by Cole, "You Are My Love" is another example of double-dipping. Cavanaugh wrote it under a pseudonym (as "Stanley Bass") and it was originally heard as an instrumental on a Hank Jones album Cavanaugh had produced earlier that year;[59] Noel Sherman added the lyric for Cole.

Cole's very dear friend Johnny Burke, now working with pianist Joe Bushkin, supplied "When You Walked By" and "You've Got the Indian Sign on Me." A few years earlier, Burke had told Bushkin, "There's one song I always wanted to do with Jimmy but he never liked the idea." He then started pounding on the table in the kind of a mock-tom-tom rhythm used to portray Native Americans in Hollywood westerns; not long after, they introduced the song at Cole's thirty-eighth birthday party at Van Heusen's Palm Springs mansion.[60] For me, this is the highlight of the album, although it's hard to imagine it ever being heard again (much like Berlin's "I'm an Indian Too" and Comden and Green's "Pass That Peace Pipe") in the politically correct 21st century.

Where *Welcome to the Club/Big Band Cole* became much more important in the CD era, *Tell Me All about Yourself* is almost completely forgotten. There's no denying it would have been more memorable had it been done under the baton of Riddle, May, or Jenkins. Cavanaugh's arrangements are serviceable, in the mid-1940s big-band tradition, with an occasional nod to Basie, but somewhat generic. *Tell Me All about Yourself* is roughly like Sinatra's *Nice 'n' Easy* or Ella Fitzgerald's *Like Someone in Love*: hardly a masterpiece but rewarding listening just the same.

BY THE SUMMER, there could be no doubt that for Cole, 1958 was a marathon year for albums, possibly to make up for lost time, having devoted so much of the previous year to the TV series. You would think that in preparing and recording so many long-playing projects, he wouldn't have had time to do anything else, but no, he continued to actively turn out singles and toured constantly, mostly in the western states.

Where *Tell Me All about Yourself* was an album of first-rate songs but a second-tier arranger-conductor, *To Whom It May Concern*, was a set of lesser-known songs but an absolute superstar musical director. This penultimate album by Cole and Nelson Riddle was taped over five sessions at the Capitol Tower and then back in New York, which resulted in a total of thirty tracks. Twelve of these became the album *To Whom It May Concern*, while the others enjoyed the usual fate of Cole's miscellaneous tracks: most were released as 45 RPM singles, some turned up on compilation LPs, both domestic and international, and some were never released until many years later.

To Whom It May Concern was predicated on the same concept that drove the 1955–56 *Night Lights*, as the artist himself explains the theme in the original album notes:

> I'm the kind of singer who likes nearly every type of tune. But the ones I enjoy most are the ones we call "standards"—I don't mean only the big favorites that are heard all the time; I'm including songs that have the unforgettable "something" in their sound that nearly always marks them for a spot in the standard shelf. . . . So, while I've recorded quite a few albums of proven standards, and always enjoyed doing them, this time I decided to try and find a set of great new tunes that have this wonderful "something" . . . tunes that really sound like they'll make it over the long pull. Personally, I hear the magic in all these selections. It will be interesting to see whether I'm right.
>
> With warmest regards,
> Nat

Cole was wrong and he was right—few of the twelve songs on this album (Capitol SW 1190) were ever recorded by other artists, and, unlike many of Cole's albums, *To Whom It May Concern* did not remain in print for very long. Yet he was correct that the twelve sections do have a kind of "magic," even though, in most cases, said magic derives more from the singer and the arranger than the actual songs themselves. *To Whom It May Concern* was the third Cole album cover, after *Unforgettable* and *Ballads of the Day* (both compilations of hits and other singles), to feature an artist's rendering of the singer in a city park, playing Cupid and making couples fall in love via the romantic sound of his voice.

The title song, "To Whom It May Concern," uses the conceit of a business letter—working rather than relaxing in the park—to tell its tale. Much of the drama of the narrative comes from the tension between the formality of an inter-office communique with a more openly passionate love song, becoming ever more so as it progresses across 32 bars. Capitol's art director extended the metaphor that the song presents in that the track listing and Cole's own album notes were also laid out like formal correspondence using a courier/typewriter typeface. In this office-like context, the song "In the Heart of Jane Doe" leads us to assume that the titular Ms. Doe is a secretary; the whole thing reads like a romance story from a woman's magazine of the period ("She took love for granted / and that wasn't smart").[61]

Most of these new songs are excellent, and nearly all derive from sources close to home: his new publishing houses, his old friends (Johnny Burke, Marvin Fisher, Jack Segal, Bob Haymes, Cahn, and Van Heusen), and even his family. The title track was co-credited to Cole and his wife's sister, Charlotte Hawkins Sullivan;[62] this, along with "You're Bringing Out the Dreamer in Me," with words and music by Johnny Burke, and "Lovesville," co-written by Ralph Freed, were all published by Comet. Many of the others were owned by Ivan Mogull, Cole's closest friend in the music publishing business. "Unfair," which Cole had attempted in both 1955 and '56, was also co-written by Mogull under the pseudonym of "Phil Belmonte."

The absolute gems of the *To Whom* sessions are three songs by the great Marvin Fisher (two with words by Jack Segal), two of which made it onto the actual album. "Love-Wise," a collaboration with Kenward Elnslie, an aspiring Broadway librettist otherwise best known for the Barbara Cook flop *The Grass Harp*, makes use of the 1950s lingo tradition of sticking the suffix "-wise" after unlikely words (parodied in the movie musical *It's Always Fair Weather*). It's an admirably simple, well-crafted set of words and music that perhaps had the greatest shelf-life of the *To Whom* songs, with notable later recordings by Mabel Mercer, Marilyn Maye, and Nancy Wilson, among others.

"Can't Help It" is sultry and bluesy, centering on an elegant, descending phrase. Cole and Riddle are never better than when they're being literal, as when he snaps his fingers "like so" and the whole ensemble goes into a fermata. Riddle keeps the orchestra suitably *piano* behind the vocal but then breaks out with an arresting *forte* in the instrumental break, using a Basie-like dynamic contrast. Cole's re-entrance ("I'd give my soul" . . .) right on the beat, when even the beat itself is behind the beat, is the quintessence of cool. "Something Happens to Me" is absolutely top drawer, one of Cole's best songs of the era—it's a total mystery why this song didn't make the album. Capitol stuck this on an EP, but largely ignored it ever since; it was up to Freddy Cole, who has used it to open many a set, to snatch it from the jjaws of oblivion. It's a beautifully constructed song (in ABAB form), with finely tuned self-contained melodic and lyrical logic, and Riddle's arrangement, with chromatically rising strings behind Cole in the last eight bars and effective use of stop-and-start rhythm in the finale bridge, sets it off brilliantly.

Two of the cheerier tunes that made it onto the album were from the first session, in June. "Too Much," by Sinatra pally Dok Stanford, has a warm, slow-dancing tempo, and Riddle effectively emphasizes the main two-note title phrase by having the various sections repeat it after Cole. Likewise, "Lovesville" is also danceable and hummable; on both, the strings are way in the background, and the reeds, for the most part, assume the typical string role. Johnny Burke wrote both music and words for "You're Bringing Out the Dreamer in Me"; it's a very Van Heusen-esque melody and overall, it's easy to imagine Crosby singing this in a Road movie.

"My Heart's Treasure" introduced Cole to the young songwriters Dotty Wayne and Ray Rasch and thus set in motion the *Wild Is Love* project (album and TV special), one of the major triumphs of his later career. The package ends with an exceptional song, "This Morning It Was Summer," by Bob Haymes, best known for his standard "That's All" (recorded definitively by Cole and Riddle in 1953) and for being the occasionally singing younger brother of Dick Haymes. "This Morning It Was Summer" closed the *To Whom* album, and to make it more like a musical theater piece, the track and the album conclude with Cole and a choir doing a brief reprise of the title song, "To Whom It May Concern."

To Whom It May Concern could have easily been a double album: there were at least twenty-four first-rate songs in the sessions that Cole and Riddle recorded over summer and fall 1958. Some of the best that didn't make it onto the album were "When You Belong to Me" with a rather unusual bridge (music by Mahlon Merrick) and a memorable lyric by Dorcas Cochran (of "Again" fame). "Laughable" is a rare example of Cole aping a familiar Sinatra format, with celesta and Pied Pipers-like background voices in the manner of "Don't Change Your Mind about Me." "Bend a Little My Way," by Noel Sherman and Dick Wolf (the "Welcome to the Club" team), gives Cole the chance to do what he does best, as when the lyric repeatedly reiterates the title phrase but takes the last word, "way" up a half-tone on the final occurrence—thus he's literally bending it his way.

The very best of these, however, was a direct sequel to "Night Lights." As mentioned earlier, "That's You" grew out of the intro and countermelody Riddle had written for "Night Lights," and he wound up sharing the credit for it with Sammy Cahn and Chester Gallop. "That's You" is possibly even snappier. Another superior song that didn't make it onto the album was "As Far as I'm Concerned," and one can only speculate that Cole left it off because he didn't want to appear to be overly concerned with "concern."[63]

The *To Whom It May Concern* album was also connected to Cole's current film project, a B-level melodrama titled *Night of the Quarter Moon*, released by MGM in 1959. Following *Istanbul*, *China Gate*, and *St. Louis Blues*, this was Cole's last on-screen "acting" role in which he had an actual character and dialogue. This was the only one of his films to address, albeit in rather lurid fashion, the contemporary issue of race in America, in a tale of a light-skinned "mulatto" woman who marries the scion of an old-money San Francisco WASP (white Anglo-Saxon Protestant) family. The leads are both curios: singer Julie London, who was soon to actually wed Cole's old friend, songwriter-singer Bobby Troup, and John Drew Barrymore, much better known as the son of one famous star (John Barrymore) and the father of another (Drew Barrymore).

Still, the only real energy in the picture comes from the redoubtable Agnes Moorehead. Best known as the feisty mother-in-law on TV's *Bewitched*, here she's unforgettable, even terrifying, as Barrymore's unabashedly racist mother, a maternal ogre who repeatedly insists that respectable young men from respectable families simply do not marry those kinds of women. The tag line of the poster loudly proclaimed, "I don't care what she is, she's mine!," depicting London with the back of her dress ripped off, like a plantation slave about to be whipped.

Cole doesn't get much to do on screen—he plays a respectable representative of the African American middle class whose sole purpose is to show Barrymore and the audience that, contrary to what his mother may believe, not all "colored" people are libertine savages. He does get to sing the main title song, and it's a good one, written by the reigning kings of movie title songs, Jimmy Van Heusen and Sammy Cahn. As Cole mentioned in the notes to the *To Whom* album, the song "To Whom It May Concern," is also heard in the film, albeit briefly. Regrettably, the "Night of the Quarter Moon Song" did not make the album, but "If You Said No," by Cahn and arranger Paul Weston, did.

It's almost as if Nat realized, as early as 1958, that his storied collaboration with Riddle was winding down and that he wanted to get as much done with the great arranger as possible before they parted company. The fall of this year would be an extremely busy one for the two of them, well beyond *St. Louis Blues* and *To Whom It May Concern*, taped in winter and summer, respectively. Once again, Cole was experimenting, trying out all sorts of songs, from venerated standards to new foreign songs. It's also notable how few of these tracks were issued at the time—or even since.

The most familiar tune in this stack originated out of a group of European imports, of which one, the Italian "A Thousand Thoughts of You," by Ulpio Minucci, with an English lyric by Sammy "Night Lights" Gallop, made it on to the *To Whom* album. Intriguingly, "A Thousand Thoughts of You" (credited to one Robert Moseley, also responsible for the blues "Midnight Flyer") doesn't sound particularly Italian, but "Give Me Your Love" is positively dripping with marinara sauce and sounded even more so when he sang it on the Perry Como *Kraft Music Hall* in January 1959 (along with "Madrid").

There's also one German song here, the very catchy "For the Want of a Kiss," with an original *Deutschlander* melody by Gerhard Winkler, composer of Cole's very successful "Answer Me, My Love,"[64] and an American text by Cole's old friend Redd Evans (of "No Moon at All" and a dozen or so other Cole recordings). "Lorelei" is not the Gershwin Brothers standard but a pseudo-Asian opus by one Jack Delgado. Here, Riddle seized the opportunity to do some of his oriental-style string writing—not to mention exotic bongos—and brings us back to the China Gate if not quite a return to Paradise. The traditional Mexican song, "Coo Coo Roo Coo Coo Paloma" herewith becomes a first cousin to "Skylark" and "Flamingo," in which the protagonist-lover instructs a pretty little dove to find his sweetheart and tell her that he loves her only. (Apparently this is what single folk resorted to in the age before Tinder.)

But *voila*! True to Cole's usual batting average, at least one song in this batch of imports became both a hit and a classic: "Non Dimenticar" is easily Cole's most enduring song of the entire era. Originally written by Michele Galdieri and P. G. Redi for a 1952 Italian film called *Anna*, the original Italian title was "T'ho Voluto Bene" (which translates as "I Wanted You Well"). The familiar lyric (the only work of note by one Shelley Dobbins) rather astutely gave the song another Italian title—"Non Dimenticar (Do Not Forget)." The song was gifted to Cole by Pearl Bailey on his NBC TV show of July 16, 1957; she sang it between bites of a slice of pizza, as Cole strolled by playing a mandolin, for extra Neapolitan effect. Whereas some American adaptations of European songs hide their "otherness," "Dimenticar" celebrates it in a manner of "Darling, Je Vous Aime Beacoup," and as with that 1955 hit, "Dimenticar" brilliantly translates the romance, in multiple senses of those words, of being an American abroad into the palpable form of words and music.

There's a photo of Nat in his parents' living room in Chicago in 1954, in which, we can see, above photos of brothers Eddie and Freddy on the mantel, a painting of a Venetian canal scene with gondola. Here, as with that painting, authenticity isn't the objective; imagination is. Cole isn't trying to beat the many Italo-American crooners, like Dean Martin (who sang Italian songs better than almost anyone), at their own game. Instead, he's singing foreign songs from an unpretentiously American perspective. During his European tour of May 1960, Cole performed the song on an Italian TV show (*Il Musichiere*) and that live version, rendered mainly with John Collins on guitar, is even better than the studio-recorded single.

The delights of the 1958 Cole-Riddle sessions hardly end there—Cole made a point to record yet more great songs with Riddle if only for no other reason that the brilliant arranger-conductor was available, even though he may not have had a definite project in mind. As we've seen, the two cut six swinging songs from the World War II era in 1956, then in August 1957, they recorded three lovely waltzes: Victor Young's "Around the World" (only a year old at that point); the 1938 "There's a Goldmine in the Sky," a western-concoction by columnist and songwriter Nick Kenny and his brother Charles; and "Fascination," written in 1904 by Fermo Dante Marchetti and Maurice de Féraudy.

In 1958, Nat and Nelson recorded six more standard ballads, a septet of tracks that are as stunningly beautiful as they are obscure: "You're My Thrill," "Sweethearts on Parade," "I Had the Craziest Dream," "I Wish I Knew," "You Made Me Love You (I Didn't Want to Do It)," and "Be Still My Heart." The singing here is some of Cole's most intimate; these are six of his prettiest ballads ever. Famously sung by Billie Holiday and Peggy Lee, "You're My Thrill" has an air of obsession, but Cole does it as more of a romantic love song. He also finds in "I Had the Craziest Dream" more of a feeling of melancholy than most interpreters, emphasizing not the rapture of the dream but the hard crash to earth when one wakes up to reality. In the instrumental break, Riddle effectively single notes the melody on a celesta contrasted with somber strings. Harry Warren's "I Wish I Knew," contrastingly, is more optimistic than usual; Cole's interpretation is more about knowing, rather than just a-wishin'.

Two old timers, the 1914 "You Made Me Love You," by Joseph McCarthy Sr.,[65] and the 1929 "Sweethearts on Parade" (which he clearly learned from

Louis Armstrong) are spellbinding examples of Cole at his most hypnotic. Symbolizing the "parade," Riddle lines up a long procession of trombones marching way off in the distance—prefiguring an effect that Gil Evans used on Miles Davis's *Sketches of Spain*. Along with "Sweethearts on Parade," the 1934 "Be Still My Heart" is the prize of this subset. It's a British song (composed by the relatively unknown John C. Egan and Allan Flynn, recorded in London by the formidable African American singer Alberta Hunter) that was also popular in the United States. Cole probably learned it from Hunter or Al Bowlly, or possibly one of his own disciples, the blues and ballad singer Charles Brown, former pianist-singer with Johnny Moore's Three Blazers. The lyrics, inspired by the Shakespeare line "Be still my beating heart," are based on the conceit of someone directly addressing his own heart; they are terribly stoic ("though we'll miss her so / We'll never let her know") and get curiously militant in the bridge ("she hears the rumbling of a drum") and I would imagine Cole found a certain satisfaction in making the words seem incredibly down to earth and credible.

In 1960, Cole and Gillette made plans to release these six standard ballads as part of a projected album to be titled *Sweethearts on Parade*, ultimately never issued. There are roughly twenty of these mystery/orphan standards by Nat and Nelson from 1955 to 1958, which represent some of the best work ever by this legendary collaboration. Taken together, they would make a spectacular CD; this is some of the greatest, yet least-known music of the Cole-Riddle collaboration. There's a gold mine here indeed.

"I NEVER HEARD NAT MAKE A RECORDING that I thought he should have done over," Gordon Jenkins once said.[66] If *Sweethearts on Parade* was the album that Cole should have released, the one he shouldn't have bothered with was *Every Time I Feel the Spirit*. Taped five months after their second of three masterpiece collaborations, *The Very Thought of You*, *Spirit* was never mentioned by Jenkins in any of his interviews, nor by his son, Bruce, in his extremely thorough biography of his father. Even Cole himself, promoting the release of his 1963 album with Jenkins, *Where Did Everyone Go*, conveniently forgets that *Spirit* ever existed.

Perhaps Nat was motivated by the death of his mother, three years earlier, and the increased presence of his father in his life; if the Reverend Edward Sr. could now come into nightclubs, could the prodigal also come back into the church? Jenkins was recruited as conductor, apparently because he had much experience with choirs. Yet Cole and Gillette do not seem to have commissioned Jenkins to write any orchestrations for the project. The idea, apparently, was that Cole would do the traditional spirituals in a completely traditional way, singing as soloist with the fourteen-voice First Church of Deliverance choir and the standard church rhythm section of Hammond organ and drums. Yet with no disrespect to Jenkins, it's a mystery why Cole didn't go out and find a genuine African American church choirmaster, like Jester Hairston for, example, who might have been able to infuse the proceedings with a bit more animation. What was the point, one wonders, of hiring Jenkins, but then not letting him be Jenkins?

The original LP liner makes a great deal about the technical aspects of the sessions—this was apparently one of Capitol's first recordings of an authentic church choir in "full dimensional stereo." "Stereo Note: Stereo clearly separates Nat as the soloist in this recording, bringing his voice well forward from the choir. Nat doesn't stay in one place for every song but, rather, picks the spot where his solos will best blend with the accompaniments. The 14 voices of the choir are spread all the way across, with soloists singing from their regular positions. The organ, drums and other occasional instruments remain clearly to the left."

Perhaps they should have spent more time worrying about the musical content and less about the tech, and perhaps Cole was too, you should forgive the expression, reverential. He never really digs into the material—the same way he did so gloriously, say, with "Joe Turner's Blues." He and Jenkins and the choir just seem to have rushed through the sessions—twelve songs in two consecutive days—and Cole never really sounds invested. He never takes chances with them or puts his heart and soul into them. It's also one of Cole's shortest albums: only twenty-five minutes long, total. Overall, *Every Time I Feel the Spirit* is nowhere near in the same category as Louis Armstrong or Jack Teagarden's albums of spirituals, not to mention the glorious gospel recordings of Elvis Presley.

The other motivation for the album was hardly ecumenical: Cole and Jenkins copyrighted these "arrangements" in their name and therefore kept the entire publishing collection plate. But the album does have a few benedictions: it is a very well recorded document of traditional spirituals by an authentic inner-city church choir, not a Hollywood or Broadway recreation, and Cole is in very good voice. There are times when he seems close to actually feeling the spirit, as when he sings "it's not the butcher, but it's me, oh Lord!" ("Standing in the Need of Prayer") and plays with the time, delaying the beat. Yet it's ironic that sometimes even the tritest pop ephemera (like "I Feel So Smoochie") apparently elicited a more committed engagement from Cole than an all-time classic air like "Nobody Knows the Trouble I've Seen."

In fact, he sings with considerably more spirit on such Tin Pan Alley ersatz spirituals as "The Lighthouse in the Sky" (1951) and "The Greatest Inventor of Them All" (1950).[67]

Every Time I Feel the Spirit was slated for release on August 31, 1959.[68] The album tanked, but not for lack of promotion: Capitol Records hosted a pre-release event at a prominent Hollywood restaurant—what today would be called a "listening party." Then, on August 21, 1959, Cole gave his sixth annual "Cole at the Bowl" concert at the Hollywood Bowl. He devoted the entire second half to what seems to be a performance of all twelve songs from *Spirit*, accompanied by the 100-voice choir of St. Paul's of Los Angeles Baptist Church, conducted by the Reverend John L. Branham.[69] In October, *Jet* magazine published a photo of Cole rehearsing with Branham. Undoubtedly, he delivered the material live in concert with more passion and zest than on the studio album, wherein everything seems to have been ground out as quickly as possible.

In the early 1960s, Cole renewed his interest in Gospel music, not least as a way of keeping pace with the ongoing folk music boom and the emerging soul scene. Gospel songs proved to be a surefire crowd pleaser in live performances and on television appearances. He had already sung "Steal Away" in a duet with Mahalia Jackson on his NBC TV show in 1957 and would do a much more rousing version of "Every Time I Feel the Spirit" live with Dinah Shore.[70] In these years he regularly worked with Ralph Carmichael, a conductor who was much more invested in the world of Christian music, and the vocal group, the Merry Young Souls, who served as a de facto Gospel choir when necessary. As it stood, perhaps the most salient feature of *Feel the Spirit* was Jim Jonson's marvelous color painting of the artist, clasping his hands in prayer with his eyes slightly skyward.[71]

In 1959, Cole was asked why traditional spirituals were increasingly heard in nightclubs and saloons, and his answer was memorable: "Because that's where the sinners are."[72]

AT THE END OF 1958, Cole finally made it back east, to the Chez Paree and a generous, three-week run at Blinstrub's in Boston. Even on the road, he was constantly in the studios: two dates in Chicago (the *Feel the Spirit* album) and at least seven in New York. In New York alone, he taped the entirety of *Tell Me All about Yourself*, miscellaneous tracks for *To Whom It May Concern*, and the unfinished *Sweethearts on Parade* project and singles (both of the rock-ish and the more traditional variety), not to mention several TV appearances, including a considerable amount of screen time on Patti Page's show, *The Big Record*.

Where 1957 had been a year for film (both of his two biggest acting roles) and TV, 1958, as we have seen, was a marathon year for recording albums: in a twelve month span, Cole recorded the *St. Louis Blues* album, the first *Cole Español* album, *The Very Thought of You*, *To Whom It May Concern*, *Welcome to the Club (Big Band Cole)*, *Every Time I Feel the Spirit*, *Tell Me All about Yourself*, and numerous singles (including much of *Looking Back*). That's seven full albums in one year, all of which were released over the next three years (up through 1960), and lots of leftovers.

Conversely, 1959 would be a year of non-stop touring: he would reap the benefits of the remarkable success of *Cole Español* by playing for two whole months in Central and South America. As Capitol worked through the backlog of the previous year, Cole taped only one new album in 1959, and, not surprisingly, this was *A Mis Amigos (To My Friends)*, the second in the *Español* series.

The pan-American tour was set to begin in Havana on February 13, roughly a year after the sessions there that had led to the original *Español* album. Coincidentally, a year earlier, on February 8, 1958, the NBC (and former CBS) executive Manie Sacks had died of leukemia at age fifty-four and NBC was now mounting an all-star tribute on the first anniversary of his death. Cole was asked to participate, along with Sinatra, Como, Shore, and many others; it was set for a live broadcast on February 22, but because Cole was scheduled to be in Havana at that time, he videotaped his segment around the first of the month. As it happened, the special early taping date wasn't necessary; the communist revolution had started in earnest by the middle of the month; the Tropicana was essentially out of business and the engagement was canceled. Yet the early taping was a good thing: for some random reason, the segments filmed around this time (also including Kay Starr, Sinatra, and Shore) survive in color, whereas the rest of the program, the live portion, apparently does not.[73]

But 1959 was also a year for family. As Nat put it, "We had two daughters and it was only natural that we should want a son to complete the family circle. We could have had another child"—Nat and Maria were only thirty-nine and thirty-six at that moment—"but they tell me the only way a couple can be sure their next child is a boy is to adopt one. We adopted one." [74] They considered adopting a "Korean brown baby" but in the end went to the Children's Home Society of California. At the same time that the Coles were submitting their application, the boy that they would officially adopt five months later was being born.

Cole flew out of Los Angeles on March 26, then opened in Puerto Rico two nights later, and from there he moved on to two different cities in Venezuela. But it was the trip to Brazil that was truly staggering—and amounted to the biggest reception that a North American entertainer had yet received in South America. A huge mob greeted him at the airport in Congonhas on April 21, and the occasion was deemed so auspicious that Cole gave a formal press conference and was received by the president of Brazil. He formally opened the new opera house[75] in Rio and went on to play a week at the Night and Day Club in that same city. On April 17 and 19, he played multiple shows at the Ginásio do Maracanãzinho, a sports arena in the North Zone of Rio; the capacity was 20,000, and since he did at least four shows, we can estimate that he performed for roughly 80,000 paying customers over those two nights; in between, on April 18, he played a tennis stadium to a capacity crowd of 11,000 people.

During that week in Rio (April 13 to 16), he recorded the second of his *Español* albums, this one titled *A Mis Amigos (To My Friends).* As with the first album, the discographical details on this one are far from clear: we don't know what songs were recorded exactly on which days, but we do know that more numbers were actually done "live" (in tandem) with the orchestra rather than sung to pre-recorded tracks—but not exactly which. "Nat was very good at foreign languages," Gillette remembered, "originally, we would write them all out phonetically [but] It finally got so that it wasn't very rough for him to take a Spanish lyric and he could sing it off without [having to] write it out phonetically."[76]

For this second *Español* album, nearly all of the charts were by Cavanaugh, who also conducted. The focus was primarily on songs from Brazil, but there also were numbers from Mexico ("Ay, Cosita Linda"), Cuba ("Aquellos Ojos Verdes" [Green Eyes]), Puerto Rico ("Capullito"), Venezuela ("Ansiedad" [Anxiety]), and Argentina ("El Choclo"). The last was one of the most internationally famous of all tangos—a new rhythm for Cole—having been a hit for Tony Martin as "Kiss of Fire."[77] Among these were two very popular Latin ballads that had crossed over during World War II, the Brazilian "Perfidia" and the Cuban "Aquellos Ojos Verdes." "El Choclo" also boasts strings (as well as a Rene Touzet-like piano solo), as does "Suas Maos."

On "Nadie Me Ama" Cole receives the additional support of Sylvia Telles, already becoming one of the most famous singers in South America (a career that tragically ended when she was killed in a car crash at age thirty-two in 1966) and here serving as a background "vapor voice" singer. Cole recorded the Brazilian song in two different languages: the Spanish take ("Nadie Me

Ama") is on most editions of the original *Amigos* album; the Portuguese version ("Ninguem Ma Ama") was included on the Brazilian pressing (titled *Aos Meus Amigos*).

There's also one North American song, written in the pan-American style, "Fantastico," by Noel Sherman and Jack Keller, here outfitted with a Spanish text (Peggy Lee later sang it in English)—an export rather than an import. This and "Capullito De Aleli" are done with a red-hot Cuban-style rhumba band, also heard on "Nao Tenho Lagrimas."[78] On "Fanastico" especially, Cavanaugh's arranging style is very sure-footed and confident—much less tentative than on the previous album, and up to his very best work with Cole.

Cole was now well aware that projects like these—away from the all-controlling arms of the North American music publishers—were a perfect opportunity to pick up a little extra change via the publishing. For some traditional songs, it was possible to collect mechanical royalties for the adaptation, and for these Cole and Cavanaugh split the credit and the proceeds.[79] "Ansiedad" and "Yo Vendo Unos Ojos Negros" are both credited to Cole and Schluger. "Caboclo Do Rio" and "Ay Cosita Linda" introduce a backup group singing behind Cole, the Irakitan Trio, in addition to the brass and rhythm (there's not much in the way of reeds here). "Ansiedad" and "Yo Vendo Unos Ojos Negros" both feature much more intimate ensembles, stressing Latin guitar and shakers; the vocal trio is here but they are pretty much just background singers, guitar, and rhythm. "Ojos Negros" shows that we have transitioned from eyes of green to eyes of black.

A Mis Amigos boasts many highlights: the classic bolero, "Perfidia," is particularly lovely and a highlight of the album. There's also a lively, jumping, Brazilian carnival song, "Não Tenho Lágrimas"; in the 1958 sessions, Cole had sung it in an unissued English language take courtesy of Ervin Drake ("Come to the Mardi Gras"); he revisited it in Rio, this time in the original Portuguese, and that version was issued on the second album. There's also a bonus track, "Brazilian Love Song," recorded in English, one of the artist's many buried delights.

Cole's extensive singing of Brazilian songs, for an album actually recorded in Rio, puts him way ahead of the curve; other American pop stars, like Sinatra and Tony Bennett, wouldn't explore this music for a few more years. (Peggy Lee's response was her *Latin a la Lee* series.) *A Mis Amigos (To My Friends)* didn't chart in the United States but it was another huge seller all over the world.

THE COLES WERE BACK IN TIME to play his usual North American venues: the Sands and then the Coconut Grove for roughly a month each starting in mid-May, and then, on August 21, the Hollywood Bowl. In between, from mid-July to mid-August, he took a month off for family time. They got the call in July, while Cole was working at the Grove, that there was a healthy, five-month old African American baby boy that they should take a look at. "Now, I have been a parent by adoption and by the natural method. People say there is a difference. Well, when I stood in that room and looked at him for the first time, I felt the same way I felt when I looked at Sweetie in the hospital," he said at the time. "It was love at first sight."[80] It was apparently Maria's idea to name him Nat Kelly Cole, which was also Cole's way of paying homage to his St. Patrick's Day birthday, his long-standing faith in the luck o' the Irish, and the shamrock in his pocket.

As always, for Nat, family was closely connected to baseball, and that year, both of the cities that he called home were competing against each other in the World Series: the Chicago White Sox and the Los Angeles Dodgers. He managed to book himself into clubs in both areas to be able to attend the games, and in Chicago, at the second game, on October 2, it was arranged for baseball's biggest fan to sing the National Anthem. But it was hardly the triumph he envisioned. Unfortunately, Nat's close friend and promo man, Dick LaPalm, seems to have jinxed him about remembering the words. "Of course I know the words," he said, "But I take out my pen anyway, and I'm writing it out for him just in case."[81] Vin Scully picked up the story of what happened next: "That was the day the wind blew the words out of his hands, and he had to fake it and as only he could do. He could fake it and it was still a bolt of silk, a beautiful performance."

Others didn't receive the performance quite so kindly. Where the last two lines are written as, "Oh, say, does that star-spangled banner yet wave / O'er the land of the free and the home of the brave?", Cole fumbled and sang, "Over land and over sea, and the home of the brave?," thus omitting the mention of "the land of the free" and changing the nature about the concluding question; it was supposed to ask if the flag was still waving, not whether or not America was actually the land of the free. The mainstream press, represented by the *Chicago Daily Tribune*, wrote "The National Anthem took a beating from Nat King Cole, who is accustomed to working much smaller rooms."[82] (The sportswriters were obviously ignorant of how Cole had just played for well over 100,000 people in Brazil alone.)

The Negro press, however, gave Nat the benefit of a doubt, and viewed the lyric change as an expression of the ongoing struggle for civil rights. "Instead of attributing this to a slip of the tongue or a lapse of memory, we are more inclined to believe that when Nat got to the words 'land of the free,' they simply stuck in his throat. Even his patriotism cannot be placed in question because when an artistic expression was nullified by a political fact, like George Washington, Nat just could not tell a lie."

His last TV appearance of the decade, was also, surprisingly, focused on his home life. On December 17, Cole took his daughters to the NBC studio, ostensibly to rehearse a song for a benefit program supporting the National Kidney Disease Foundation (he was honorary chairman for the entertainment industry). But he was caught completely by surprise when the familiar host Ralph Edwards walked in and announced, "Nat King Cole—this is your life!" Over the next half hour, Nat found himself trapped on an episode of NBC's long-running *This Is Your Life*, and trying hard to be a good sport about it. Nat was greeted by his family, starting with Maria, and, surprisingly, his father, his sister Evelyn, and his big brother Eddie and his wife, Betty. NBC had also flown in four members of Nat's Chicago big band of the mid-1930s (Andrew Gardner, Charles Gray, Russell Shores, and Henry Fort) and the three men who changed his life when they helped him launch the trio in 1937: Oscar Moore, Wesley Prince, and Swanee Inn owner Bob Lewis. (The latter took credit for dubbing him "King Cole.") "When I look at the tape today," Natalie later remembered, "I can see that my father is wishing he could be somewhere else—anywhere else. But we definitely surprised him—on national television."[83]

For Nat, the arrival of his son and the big upset at the World Series were closely inter-related, and perhaps it was a bad omen. Nat seems to have never spoken publicly about wanting to pass along his gift for music to his children, but the main reason he wanted a son was to share his love of the national pastime. "Although it was premature"—to say the least—"I could see the little fellow playing his first game of softball. I could hear the crack of the bat as he walloped a long, long, drive."[84] One of Cole's most tender later ballads, especially aimed at young children, is a 1961 single titled "Goodnight, Little Leaguer." Ironically, even though Kelly was only six when his father died, it was already clear by then that the little fellow would never be much of a sports guy.

But Nat still could share the sport with other members of his family—Freddy, for instance. His three brothers were not seen very often—if ever—in Hancock Park. However, Nat was exceptionally close to Maria's sister, Charlotte Hawkins: they wrote songs together and generally enjoyed each other's company; the relationship roughly parallels that of Alexander Hamilton and his sister-in-law, Angelica. The children adored her too and called her "Aunt Baba." But that seems to be as far as it went regarding the mixing of the Coles and the Hawkins family. "With the exception of Baba, my mother's family generally disapproved of Nat," Natalie observed. "The mutual distaste between the two sides of the family created a lot of tension in my parents' marriage and made life awkward for us kids as well. Mom made it clear that she didn't have much in common with Dad's relatives." The younger daughters, Casey and Timolin, have expressed the view that Nat's family dismissed Maria just as quickly, instantly pigeonholing her as a "Miss High-and-Mighty" type without giving her a real chance. However it worked out, none of his children had memories of ever seeing any of their father's family at 401 South Muirfield Road.

Talking about his brothers in 1954, Nat told the *Saturday Evening Post* that Isaac (or "Ike") was working in an auto plant,[85] though he also worked as a musician from time to time, while big brother Eddy and his wife were living and working in Hawaii.[86] Nat reserved his most effusive praise for "Freddy," describing him as the "most talented" of his siblings. Nat was already out of the house when Freddy, who was born in 1931, was growing up. He would see his big brother sporadically over the years; for instance, he remembers well the first time he saw his brother work: a *King Cole Trio Time* radio show that the Trio did live from Chicago, in 1946 or '47. Although the *Post* article dismissed Freddy, then all of twenty-two, rather unfairly as "a singer who imitates the style of his more famous brother," anyone who has had the pleasure of experiencing Freddy Cole in performance knows well that isn't true. On the contrary, over the years, Freddy has often played and sung songs associated with his legendary brother (specializing in the lesser-known ones), but he never imitated Nat or coasted on his coattails; Freddy Cole would have had a remarkable career no matter who his brother was.

For much of the 1950s and '60s, Freddy lived in New York. In February 1958, he became the only one of Nat's brothers to participate in one of his recordings (at least since Eddie in 1936), when he played piano on the "Looking Back" session. But Freddy's favorite memories of Nat are of sharing ballgames with him. He remembers one occasion—the details are long lost to memory—when they were in the same town, when Nat had a recording date in the morning, before the two of them took in a ballgame in the afternoon, and Nat then did a second record session in the evening. Another date that stands out occurred around October 1, 1959, when Nat was in town to appear on *The Pat Boone Chevy Showroom* on ABC TV. (He and the host sang a rather bizarre medley of "Nature Boy," done doo-wop style, and the Coasters' hit, "Poison Ivy." A few weeks later, he returned to New York to guest with

Rosemary Clooney and Perry Como for his fourth appearance on the latter's NBC series, which climaxed in a lengthy medley of cowboy songs.)

One night, instead of a game, the two brothers went to Birdland, where the jazz icon Miles Davis was headlining. "We came in there and Miles was glad to see Nat, we talked, they were good friends, Nat and Miles. Nat was a big jazz fan, and he asked Miles to do that song, 'It Never Entered My Mind.' I know that was one of Nat's favorite songs. I'm surprised that Nat never did it. I suggested to Nat that he should make a record of that song, since he was so fond of it. He said, 'I'll have to look into that.'"

IT WOULD HAVE BEEN another great standard song for Nat King Cole to sing. Nat had turned forty the previous spring, and it must have seemed like there was still time enough for him to play or sing every wonderful song that had ever been written. A whole new decade was about to dawn, and it would be, in many ways, his most successful period yet. Much of his greatest work—including his only official live recording and his most ambitious concept album, as well as a brilliant series of projects with a brand-new collaborator—was still ahead of him. No one could have guessed that Cole was about to attain an even higher level of achievement, both as an artist and as a human being, that he would have even bigger hits, explore even more kinds of new music, create yet more classic albums (at least eight in his final five years), consort with presidents and monarchs, and bring his artistry to the world entire.

But the flip side of this disc is that, likewise, no one knew that the next half decade would be his last. That he would be gone well before his son was even of age to join the Little League.

It simply had never entered his mind.

9

The Ends of the Earth

1960–1961

It was just great fun to work with Nat, because if you got a nod of approval from him, it was like the sun was shining.

—RALPH CARMICHAEL

EVERY CHAPTER IN THE SHORT LIFE of Nat King Cole was distinguished by musical and artistic triumphs. But beyond the music and the work itself, the second half of the 1950s was marred by tragedy and disappointment: the assault in Alabama (which he managed to spin into a victory of sorts) and the equally shameful failure of Madison Avenue to support his television series. Yet the 1960s would begin with a very different vibe, one that was precisely the opposite. In fact, the five years between 1956 and 1961 seem more like a half century than half a decade in terms of the progress that had been made, at least from Nat's perspective.

The watershed year would be 1961. It began with the Inaugural Gala for President John F. Kennedy on January 19, produced by Sinatra. Remember that Cole had been born during the presidency of Woodrow Wilson, who had insisted that segregation was the best possible policy regarding African Americans: "For their own good," as he put it. Now, in 1961, a Democratic president was inviting no fewer than four outstanding African American artists (Mahalia Jackson, Ella Fitzgerald, Harry Belafonte, and Cole) to perform in his honor.

Then, ten months later, something even more remarkable occurred. The evening of November 18 began with Cole performing at a fundraising concert for the Democratic party, held at the Hollywood Palladium, at which he again sang for President Kennedy. This in itself would have been unimaginable just a few years earlier, but then JFK stunned the world when, a few hours later that same evening, the president spontaneously appeared at the debutante ball of Cole's oldest child, Cookie, at the Links Cotillion being held at the Beverly Hills Hilton. He made no secret of his presence, either; he graciously posed for pictures and he stood up and spoke. "Nat was at our dinner tonight, so I thought I would reciprocate. I congratulate you girls and your families, and I am grateful that you let an itinerant President come to your party."[1]

A president of these United States very publicly paying his respects to an African American family by gracing them with his presence? Woodrow Wilson would have rather set himself on fire than allow such a thing to happen. For his own good, of course.

YOU CAN TELL THAT THIS HAPPENED a long time ago—so long ago that the nine-year-old daughter of one of the most famous men in the world was allowed to play outside her home without any bodyguards or security, or indeed, any adult supervision whatever—something that seems unfathomable today. One day in late summer 1959, a white woman approached the Cole home in Hancock Park. She handed a package to Sweetie and asked her to give it to her Daddy, adding that he was expecting it. When Nat opened it a few hours later, he knew what it was going to contain, but he may have been surprised that it had arrived so quickly. It was the basic twelve songs that would form what would become his one of most successful albums ever, *Wild Is Love*.

In the final five or so years of his career, Cole would be more determined than ever to conceive and explore new ways to reach his audiences that weren't dependent on traditional show-business models: new kinds of shows; new kinds of albums (among them his only official live album); new kinds of movie roles; new ways to tell stories, to present and frame narratives, and to sing songs. The most successful of these were *Wild Is Love, Sights and Sounds,* and *Cat Ballou*.

The Nat King Cole Show went out live for the last time on December 17, 1957, with guest Billy Eckstine; the credit roll for the final episode includes a full list of all the guests who had appeared on the series since the beginning. But NBC, to their credit, seemed determined to make it up to him: in the last years of the 1950s and the start of the 1960s, he was repeatedly seen on *Perry Como's Kraft Music Hall, The Dinah Shore Chevy Show*, and the *Steve Allen Show* for Pontiac. He was by now commanding record high fees for guest appearances (and he had been getting $2,000 a pop as early as 1953). You can tell from the way that hosts such as Como, Shore, Allen, and Patti Page introduce Cole that they considered it a coup to land him on their programs.

But for his most significant TV appearance in fall 1959, he asked only a token fee. This was the premiere episode of *Playboy's Penthouse*, which Cole taped during his October run at the Chez Paree. Host Hugh Hefner and his co-producer, Victor Lownes, were trying to advance the cause of integration by having Cole intermingle with the otherwise white guests and converse with them as an equal—something that had not yet been done on either talk or variety shows. Alas, it was decided that he wouldn't perform (which today seems like a wasted opportunity but was significant at the time), but he did discuss a very interesting impending album.

BUT BEFORE HE COULD GET AROUND TO that project, he had another first on his calendar. Cole had begun the decade rather auspiciously at the Sands Hotel in Las Vegas. Since 1955, he had worked regularly at the Sands, appearing there at least twice a year, once during the winter months and again during late spring or early summer. But this run, which began on December 30, 1959,[2] was going to be special. For the only time in his career, he was officially making a live album for Capitol Records and therefore this was set to be an unique performance.

Nat Cole and Las Vegas had pretty much come up together: he first started working in the city long before he became an international, "cross-over" super-star, which was also long before the city in Nevada grew into one of the showbiz Meccas of the world. In his earliest days in Vegas, the singer-pianist, who was still leading the King Cole Trio, worked at the El Rancho. However, in 1955, Gastel negotiated a switch to the Sands, with the help of Jack Entratter, who ran the place, and the encouragement of Sinatra, who was a part owner.

Apart from the increase in his fee, there was another, equally important reason that Cole was delighted to make the switch. Up to that time, Las Vegas might as well have been Mississippi: black musicians, performers, and even headliners were subject to legally enforced segregation and prohibited from mixing with white customers or eating in the regular restaurants. In the early days, Cole and his Trio weren't allowed to stay in any of the hotels they were headlining in but had to sleep in a special trailer out back. Under the auspices of Sinatra, however, the Sands launched a policy of integration; African American entertainers like Cole, Sammy Davis, Harry Belafonte, and, soon enough, Johnny Mathis, were invited to stay at the Sands even when they were appearing elsewhere in Vegas.[3] The FBI was paying attention: on October 8, 1957, agent Mark Felt (later infamous as "Deep Throat" during the Watergate incident) reported that "top flight colored entertainers [such as Nat Cole and Pearl Bailey] have been allowed to stay at the hotel where they were performing." Felt elaborates, "the problem is . . . complaints have been received concerning Cole's actions. One citizen insists that the Sands Hotel be closed for permitting such activity."[4]

Thus, it was no surprise that when Cole decided to make a live album, he would do it at the Sands. He was actually late to this particular party: Ella Fitzgerald, Mel Tormé, and Louis Prima and Keely Smith had been making such albums for years; in 1955, Noel Coward made the first really famous live album "at" Las Vegas; and in 1960, Billy Eckstine, Tony Martin, and Lena Horne all recorded live in the city. Cole's was no ordinary show, as the artist's publicist and close friend, Dick LaPalm, who had been pushing for Nat to make a live album for many years, explained. The decision was made to record at 2:30 in the morning so that everybody from all the other spots in town could attend; among those present were Louis and Keely, singer-pianist Frances Faye (a Cole favorite), and comedians Jackie Gleason, Jack Carter, and Joe E. Lewis.

Because this performance was planned for recording, Cole did not sing his usual nightclub set. Normally, he included at least a few of his big hits, but, as LaPalm observed, he had only previously recorded three of the numbers from the January 14, 2:30 a.m. show: "Funny (Not Much)," "Ballerina," and "Joe Turner's Blues." The bulk of the songs were arranged for the occasion by Dave Cavanaugh, credited as co-producer and musical director, although the orchestra was directed by the house conductor, Antonio Morelli.

The band was also essentially Sands regulars, whose names are lost to history, plus Cole's regular rhythm section (John Collins, guitar; Charlie Harris, bass; and Lee Young, drums) and his touring lead trumpeter, Irving Bush. Importantly, the ensemble also includes a few key men imported from Los Angeles. Among these are the famous trombonist Milt Bernhart, who later related that it was Sinatra who instigated this tradition of beefing up a local Vegas band with Hollywood studio players.

"In the beginning, in Las Vegas, they didn't have enough musicians to go around," Bernhart remembered. "It was still a small town. It was 1952 or '53 or '54, and believe me, the standards were high. There would be a call out in Hollywood, Los Angeles, for players that he would want to come to Las Vegas in a hurry. And money was paid; you know, [they] paid very handsomely. It was almost a regular event. If [Sinatra] was going to open in Vegas, I almost expected it. And a couple of trumpet players, a trombone, and several fiddle players—and maybe a saxophone."[5]

It was obvious why Cole and Sinatra, who were used to working with the greatest musicians in the world, would regard most of the union members working elsewhere as being not quite up to the level of the New York and Hollywood studio men. However, even with Bernhart and a few top-drawer "ringers" interspersed, the orchestra on the Sands album sounds rather bush-league, at least compared to the orchestras on Cole's studio sessions. Yet, in a way, that's part of the album's considerable charm; the band with all its imperfections (especially contrasted with Cole, who essentially has none) helps to transport us back to a very specific moment in American cultural history.

The album *Nat King Cole at the Sands* was originally released with eleven songs including bow music (the vamps played under the applause as the headliner bows) on the first track ("Ballerina") and the last ("Joe Turner Blues"), in 1966, a year or so after Cole's death. The 2002 CD edition added one song, the eight-minute "Mr. Cole Won't Rock and Roll." Still later, in 2013, a much-expanded edition of the music, titled *Live at the Sands: The Complete Lost Concert*, was released on a semi-private label from Europe.[6]

The expanded edition opens with the voice of comedian Marty Allen, introducing himself as "Kelly Cole—Nat's kid."[7] The crowd titters, knowing that Nat and Maria's newly adopted son, Kelly, was less than a year old in January 1960. Then, getting serious, Allen tells the crowd that this is their "last time to see Nat Cole before he leaves for the Orient" (actually Cole would tour Europe a few months later in the spring but didn't get to Asia until a year after that). He introduces Cole as "truly one of the nicest guys you ever want to meet, a great artist, and our pride and joy."

Cole then takes the stage; he lets the audience know that a recording is being made (although they doubtless already know), introduces the two producers from Capitol standing in the back, Gillette and Cavanaugh, waves at his fourteen-year-old daughter ("Carole, what are you doing?"), and explains why he feels the need to have lyric sheets in front of him (even on "songs I've been singing for years"). He also tells the crowd to react as loudly as they wish with their approval, for the benefit of the microphones. It's a wonderful opening speech, one that shows how relaxed and assured Cole was in front of a crowd, and it perfectly sets up what we are about to hear. (During a brief pause, we hear the unmistakable voice of Joe E. Lewis, somewhere in the house, uttering his famous opening catchphrase, "It is now post time.")

The orchestral introduction on the expanded edition is at least a minute longer. We get a full chunk of "Too Young" before the familiar "Unforgettable" (Cole's mantra if not his theme song) and spoken announcement by Bob Bailey ("Ladies and gentlemen, the Sands Hotel takes pleasure in presenting . . . Mr. Nat King Cole!")—that begins the intro. The intro leads directly into Cole's opener, his 1956 hit "Ballerina." The *Sands* album treatment is slightly faster and considerably less subtle than the Riddle-conducted studio single; the treatment of Riddle's opening riff is notably less nuanced. If anything, however, that makes it an even more exciting opener and puts us in the mood for the high-octane show that is to follow. (Cole would continue to use "Ballerina" in many of his live appearances, including several that were recorded.)

The second song, "Funny (Not Much)," is the closest thing on the album to an established hit that Cole reprises for the live album. The single was a #26 hit for Cole in 1952, in the original Pete Rugolo arrangement (which he uses here in 1960). He obviously loved the song: he sings it twice here (the second version is in the expanded *Complete Lost Concert* edition; the "new" take has a tentative opening wherein Cole seems to be chuckling over the first word) to get it precisely right, and then he sang it all over again at the end of 1960 on *The Touch of Your Lips*. We'll probably never know the precise provenance of the song, originally credited to Marcia Neil, Philip F. Broughton, and Hughie Prince, except that Bob Merrill's name is attached to it on most references from after 1970.

We get to the new charts by Cavanaugh in the third number, "The Continental" (the first Academy Award–winning song, which Cole had sung on the *Kraft Music Hall* the previous October); Cole, in his best royal fashion, swings it hard, landing right on the beat. The main melody or A section is more rigidly rhythmic, whereas the bridge is more legato and romantic—that's where the strings come in.[8] Cole stays in a continental mood with Charles Trenet's "I Wish You Love," with an English lyric by Lee Wilson (published under the pseudonym "Albert A. Beach"). This had already become a signature on Capitol for Keely Smith, in an arrangement by Nelson Riddle (who also arranged Cole's chart here) and would later become one for Gloria Lynn; Cole's is the tenderest of all recordings of this song of parting, so much so that Sinatra obviously didn't want to compete with him, and thus when he recorded it with Count Basie in 1964, he turned it into a finger-snapping swinger.

"Thank you! You're a cutie," Cole says to the audience, "in fact, you're so nice . . . as he leads into "You Leave Me Breathless," a 1937 movie song (introduced by Fred MacMurray in *Coconut Grove*) that Cole probably learned from Billy Eckstine. Cole swings it luxuriously, with complete relaxation and strong staccato emphasis on each note: "you—leave—me—breathless," but letting it flow more conversationally in the bridge. In contrast to the lyric, Cole sings it like he has breath to spare.

"Thou Swell," arranged by Riddle, is another of the treasures of the *Sands*. It opens with a Nelsonian vamp; Cole doesn't dwell on Larry Hart's mock-Shakespearian text but again swings the melody with a vengeance. The chart takes on Basie overtones, even more so than the ones that Cavanaugh wrote for the King and the Count in the 1958 *Welcome to the Club* album. Cole had sung a shorter version of this chart on his 1956–57 TV show, and here it goes over so well that he takes an extra bow at the end. This was the end of the first side of the original LP. (Riddle probably wrote the chart at the same time as the "Ballerina" chart for the aborted "swinging standards" project of 1956.)

Following "Thou Swell" on the *Complete* edition, we hear what is probably the voice of Lee Gillette, way off "in the back," saying what sounds like "Side Two!" and then "Side Two, get ready." Clearly, he and Cole had planned the album so carefully in advance that they knew where the break in the two sides would occur; Cole then introduces his rhythm section (Young, Harris, and Collins) and conductor Tony Morelli. The second side of the album originally began with a "very lovely wonderful oldie," "My Kind of Love," by the esteemed composer Louis Alter and the equally esteemed Afro-American lyricist Jo Trent from 1929, first put on the map by Jack Teagarden and Bing Crosby. Cole's version is tender but with a beat and a blues-style stop-time beat at the end of the second bridge: "when you meet it . . . steal it, beg or borrow," in which he interrupts the general rubato feeling with a large "whomp" from the brass.

We next hear from Richard Rodgers; Cole would record roughly a dozen songs by Rodgers in his career, and three of them are on the *Sands* album. "Surrey with the Fringe on Top" was a 2/4 bouncer in scene one of "Oklahoma!" The song had been already adopted by jazz musicians, but no one had revved it up into swing time as Cole does here. Normally a lot of lyrics and "patter" can slow down the momentum of a swing number, but Cole uses Oscar Hammerstein's additional choruses to increase the excitement. With the same ultra-precise articulation he originally brought to his piano playing, he rolls out the tricky lyrics with machine gun intensity, not only Hammerstein's but an original patter chorus of unknown origin ("when we ride in the surrey / we'll just hide every worry . . ."), delivered over a boppish background (a melody vaguely similar to "Anthropology"). He would keep this treatment of "Surrey" in his book for a few years—in fact, he would sing it almost exactly a year later at the JFK inaugural on January 19, 1961—growing more comfortable the more he did it.

The expanded edition only includes one song that's not on the original LP, titled "It's Not What You Say," credited to Clint Ballard Jr. and Hank Hunter but arranged by Nelson Riddle; I can't blame Gillette for leaving this one off. It sounds like a single, and not a particularly good one, although Nelson's arrangement makes productive use of the house string section. There's then some verbal exchange with Gillette, who advises Nat to set up the intro for "Where or When," which gets under way as Nat shouts, "And now a little piano!" Normally, Cole would accompany himself on one or two vocals, but here, in this special recording set, he chooses not to sing and play on the same track. "Where or When" is in the mold of Cole's 1955 album *The Piano Style*, being a piano solo with orchestral accompaniment; in fact, he and the orchestra play *around* each other more than *with* each other. Parts of it are certainly improvised, but it builds to a pre-arranged climax much the same way his vocals do, and, as with *Piano Style*, one feels like it's a vocal orchestration in which Cole happens to play rather than sing.

Of the major writers of the Great American Songbook, Cole Porter (whom Nat introduces by name) was by far the least represented in the Cole canon; he recorded fewer than a half dozen of Porter's classic songs. "Miss Otis Regrets" is a major addition to the very small dual legacy of Cole and Cole. Nat's vocal is very straightforward and sincere, but Riddle's arrangement is deliberately over-the-top in the drama department; on the whole it's somewhat reminiscent of Pete Rugolo's "tone poem" treatment of "Lush Life," not to mention the kind of dissonant background scores that Elmer Bernstein and Bernard Herrmann were currently writing for crime movies. The subtlety of the singer is heightened by the contrast with brashly Kentonian brass interludes. The juxtaposition between singer and background could be perceived as an extension between the formal nature of Porter's text (which uses the conceit of a servant addressing an employer) and the violent nature of the narrative that the text is describing. At four and a half minutes, this piece, which should be considered a "concert arrangement" (like those on *The Concert Sinatra*), is certainly one of Cole's more ambitious dramatic performances—for him to have recorded this in a live album was doubly impressive.

Even more so, however, is the original album's closer, "Joe Turner's Blues," which is here twice as long and even more exciting than the 1958 studio version; in fact, it's one of the most exciting things Cole ever sang. The Vegas band, even with the ringers thrown in, can't compete in the precision department with the Capitol Records studio ensembles. But throughout this live recording, it's the jazz numbers, like "Ballerina" and "Where or When" where the musicians really come alive—never mind that they sound comparatively tepid and even sloppy on some of the slower ballads. On "Joe Turner" in particular, the Sandsmen, to use the vernacular, really kick ass. Here, they might be compared to the great territory bands of the '20s and '30s, making up in energy and togetherness what they lack in intricate nuances. The tempo is faster and Cole himself much more supercharged; he really tears into it—noticeably influenced by the rabble-rousing Joe Williams-Basie blues spectaculars like "Ev'ry Day I Have the Blues." The band plays the counter-riff a few times instrumentally before Cole comes back and sings an encore chorus. You not only feel the energy of the singer, the rhythm section, and the band, but the crowd, stomping their feet and going nearly hysterical as Cole bows and the band repeats the riff a few more times instrumentally. It's an incredible moment, and one can hardly blame Gillette for ending the original LP there, even though at thirty-seven minutes it would be a fairly short one.

On both major CD editions (but not the original LP), Cole then returns and treats us to a rather remarkable piece of special material; this was "Mr. Cole Won't Rock and Roll," custom-written for Cole as an encore by the reliable Joe and Noel Sherman. "That was the time that Presley was coming in and rock was starting," said Joe Sherman. "Mr. Cole Won't Rock and Roll" was originally written around 1957 or '58, at the height of the first wave of rock 'n' roll, and the point where this new, youth-oriented genre of pop music was starting to usurp the more traditional. Sherman continued, " 'Mr. Cole' started at a dinner table; we had taken Nat out to dinner and sitting there, we were talking about trends in music. And Nat said, 'This thing called rock 'n' roll—I just don't dig it.' We discussed it, pro and con, and my brother, who was the lyricist of the family, always had an ear for what people were saying.[9]

"On the way home, Noel said, 'You know, remember we were talking about rock and roll? I have an idea, I'd like to write a song called "Mr. Cole Won't Rock and Roll." It's about how he doesn't like it—he won't do it! Maybe Nat will do it in his act!' We wrote it on the spur of the moment. When Noel was inspired, we would just keep going night and day until it was done. We just thought it would be fun to show it to Nat. He had not done special material until then, just his hits, or new songs, or play the piano. He had never done a piece of special material of the kind that my dear friend Sammy Cahn would write for Sinatra."

The brothers played it for Cole where he was staying at the Waldorf-Astoria. "He said, 'Well, I've never done anything like that, with such a long lyric, let me have the lead sheet.' That was the last the two brothers heard of it, until about two years later, in 1959, when Cole was about to open at the Chez Paree in Chicago. "Dick [LaPalm] called and said 'Listen, you guys wrote "Mr. Cole?" Nat found it in his trunk, and he pulled it out and he's gonna try it out in Chicago.' Word was it was a big hit in Chicago, he had an arrangement done and it went over. He worked on it more, polished it, and then included it when he played the Copacabana in New York—he always played there in September. The song went over so well he had to do it three times—in the same show! I swear to you, three times! He did it once, they applauded, they stood on their feet, he did it again and he had to do it a third time.'"

"Mr. Cole," which Cole sang again on the *Dinah Shore Chevy Show* of October 9, 1960, was a natural for the invited audience at the Sands, which consisted of a lot of showbiz insiders who felt the same way about rock 'n' roll that Cole did; even so, one can hardly blame Capitol for not including it in the LP when they finally released it in the very different atmosphere of 1966, at which time it would have seemed dated and reactionary. One thing that the Sherman brothers concoction does make clear is that although rock 'n' roll was only a few years old in 1960, it took the music remarkably little time to accumulate a stockpile of verbal, melodic, and orchestral clichés, nearly all of which have been worked into this performance piece. Much of the humor comes from the juxtaposition of the contemporary and the traditional, or, as the lyric tells us, the romantic versus the frantic.

The number is divided into two parts, an all-original chorus by the Shermans (in roughly AABA form) and an additional section in which Cole parodies his own signature hits by interjecting references to rock 'n' roll, doo-wop, rockabilly, and other youth-directed hits: "Why Do Fools Fall in Love?" (by Frankie Lymon and the Teenagers), "Kookie, Kookie, Lend Me Your Comb" (Edd "Kookie" Byrnes), "Oh Oh, Get Out the Car" (by the Treniers) which segués into Cole's hit "Pretend," then "Answer Me, My Love," combined with "Ko-Ko-Mo" (actually a chart hit for Perry Como), "Too Young" merged with "Rag Mop" and "I Want You to Be My Baby," and "Too Young to Go Steady" with "Eddie, My Love" by, respectively, the Chordettes and the Teen Queens. Then we get more "Ko-Ko-Mo" into "Mona Lisa," climaxing with "Nature Boy," rewritten to describe Elvis Presley, the original rock 'n' roll superstar (then currently serving in the US Army, and stationed in Germany), with a mention of "Heartbreak Hotel." The climactic line, parodied from "Nature Boy," is "The greatest thing you'll ever learn / Is just to rock and be rolled in return." But the most telling statement comes as the band plays its final vamp, and Cole announces to the crowd "Mr. Cole Won't Rock and Roll—but I could if I wanted to!" True, that.[10]

As mentioned, Capitol sat on *The Sands* LP until 1966, allegedly because too many live albums by too many other artists were coming out all at once (the blockbuster *Mack the Knife: Ella in Berlin* among them), and certainly in 1960 Capitol was still catching up with Cole's marathon year of recording in 1958.

Cole recorded another live show at the Sands two years later, twenty-five minutes of which have been issued on another semi-private collector's label. This particular show would be well worth a wider release, particularly if more material can be excavated.[11] The eight full songs on this CD are all singularly excellent. There's only one "iconic" Cole signature song, "Unforgettable," and the rest are more offbeat: such as "Aren't You Glad You're You" and "I've Got a Lot of Living to Do" (from *Bye Bye Birdie*). The most valuable item is Cole's slow and sultry interpretation of the old blues hit, "Why Don't You Do Right" (originally known as "The Weed-Smoker's Dream"), which, unlike the famous Peggy Lee and Lil Green versions, is heard in an ingenious new lyric meant to be delivered by a male singer. ("The bees give the honey to the honeycomb / To me, there's no honey, 'cause you're never home . . ." He follows and contrasts this with the loud and up-tempo "Wild Is Love," and eventually simmers back down to the waltz ballad, "In Other Words" ("Fly Me to the Moon"). The 1962 tape also includes a long segment in which Cole introduces Mrs. and Mr. Jerry Lewis in the audience; following this, the comedian stands up and joins Cole in a demonstration of the twist.

Cole returned to the Sands twice more in 1962, at the end of September and again at the end of November, at which point he was riding high on his massive hit, "Ramblin' Rose." No recording survives from either engagement, but the occasion was well remembered by Tony Bennett, who happened to drop in to one of the rehearsals with Cole, the orchestra, and Sands majordomo Jack Entratter. Tony remembered that Nat had the idea of walking off the stage during one number and strolling through the house while singing with a handheld microphone—then a relatively new technology. [12] "Nat was very gregarious, he was going to go walk from table to table and make everybody comfortable." Entratter, however, was of the old school and maintained that there should be a respectful distance between the performer and the audience and wouldn't agree to the idea. By this point, Tony had entered the showroom, but Cole and Entratter didn't notice him, as the argument was growing increasingly heated and voices were being raised. After listening for a few minutes, Bennett himself got engaged in their row and all of a sudden, he yelled out, "Don't worry, Nat, you have the number one song in the country, do whatever you want! You tell him!" Since no one had any idea that Tony

Bennett was in the room, they were so surprised by this unexpected outburst that the tension was broken, and both men started laughing hysterically.

Tony remembered another occasion. "Jack and everybody at the Sands treated Nat very well. Once they gave Nat and his family a special dinner, his daughters were there. It was in one of the big ballrooms upstairs just themselves, about fifteen people, with his relatives and everything, and he invited me. It was just one of those things where you could tell the respect that they had for Nat. He was treated like a king at that dinner." As great as Cole was on recordings, he was even more dynamic and intimate in person. You just had to be there, and the great thing about *Nat King Cole at the Sands* is that you feel like you actually were.

It may or may not be a coincidence that the very month Capitol released *Nat King Cole at the Sands*, Sinatra went into that same venue and recorded his own, no-less-classic album *Live at the Sands* with Count Basie. Sinatra must have personally loved Cole's album even as he simultaneously relished and resented the competition; even in death, Nat Cole was kicking his ass.

AFTER THE SANDS, in January 1960, Cole was gearing up for a big European tour, his first in six years. He went east briefly in January (the Eden Roc and the Copa) and did a few concerts in the larger halls of California (Long Beach, Pasadena, Santa Monica) even as he prepared to record what, in many ways, would be his most ambitious album ever—the one that he had talked up to Hugh Hefner a few months earlier. On that premiere telecast of *Playboy's Penthouse*, Hef and Lenny Bruce had been discussing the new popularity of stand-up comedy and spoken-word albums, and Cole mentions that he has a new album in the works where he will, for the first time, speak as well as sing. "I'm getting ready to do an album pretty soon, not a 'talk' album, but one where I do recitations prior to the song that I'm going to sing. This is a story, and all the songs join in to make one big story. And prior to each track I say something, leading in to each song. Say, about half a minute—no poems, but talking. Each song takes this guy through a whirlwind of mad love, and he ends up at the end, still way out."[13] This was *Wild Is Love*, an entirely original work that took the form of a Capitol album as well as a full-length TV special, produced by Cole himself on the Canadian Broadcasting Corporation and later shown on American TV as well. It stands as one of the signature achievements of Cole's career and, in particular, the culmination of roughly two decades of work in the visual mediums, film and television.

Bing Crosby famously described Cole as a modern-day troubadour and a strolling player. (He was being diplomatic in not using the term "minstrel" in reference to an African American artist.) As we've seen, Cole's album covers tended to depict him as an enabler of romantic relationships rather than a participant in one; with *Wild Is Love*, he found a brilliant way to turn that role to his advantage. It was a perfect fit, especially because of the two other factors that were at the top of his mind: first, as he acknowledged, he had little skills as a dramatic actor, and second, even if he had possessed the acting ability of a Poitier (or, for that matter, an Olivier), there was relatively little call for a romantic leading man who happened to be black.

In *Wild Is Love*, he circumnavigated all these issues, avoided his weaknesses and consolidated his strengths: *Wild Is Love* centers on Nat as the musical narrator, who tells the story in both speech and song; he is the sage, he is the dispenser of wisdom—he is the embodiment of Nature Boy himself. For Cole, this is what he'd been looking for. The only comparable role in Sinatra's career is his portrayal of the narrator, known as "the stage manager," in the one-shot TV musical production of Thornton Wilder's *Our Town*. (That would have been a great role for Cole as well. In fact, he described *Wild Is Love* as "a kind of *Our Town* in reverse.")[14]

Wild Is Love also checked another important box for Cole: it was almost completely unique and unprecedented. One of the defining characteristics of Cole's career, as we've seen many times, is a consistent desire to find something new to do, something other artists, other piano players, bandleaders, and singers, were not doing. As we'll continue to see, in the last part of Cole's career, he was even more determined to explore new avenues and ideas that would set him apart from everybody else:the *Español*albums, the country-and-western records, as well as such diverse projects as *Those Lazy-Hazy-Crazy Days of Summer* and *L-O-V-E*. No other artist could have done them. Cole would spend much of 1960 and 1961 working on two such uncategorizable ventures, *Wild Is Love* and *I'm with You*, both of which were ideas that took him well beyond the usual kind of album and beyond a traditional supper club or concert hall program. "You gotta keep moving, trying," Cole said in 1961. "Even with records. That Capitol album we made, *Wild Is Love*, that was trying. You can't stand still."[15]

Both *Wild Is Love* and *I'm with You* were all-original works by the hitherto-unknown team of Ray Rasch (music) and Dotty Wayne (lyrics), and had their beginnings in 1958, when Cole met the two aspiring songwriters, thanks to his old friend, Eddie Beal. Beal had been a popular pianist around

Los Angeles's Central Avenue in the '40s, and had also led the back-up singers on a few episodes of Cole's NBC show. One night, around May 1958, when the singer was working at Hollywood's Coconut Grove, Beal brought the two kids over to meet him. Cole liked one of their songs, "My Heart's Treasure," well enough to include it on his next album *To Whom It May Concern*, taped a few months later.

Wayne then pitched Cole on the idea that became *Wild Is Love*. Cole was intrigued but noncommittal—naturally, he'd have to get some idea of the music first. Fair enough. The two of them then spent the next two weeks rushing to write the twelve songs for the *Wild Is Love* project, figuring that they had better strike fast while the iron was still hot—in other words, while Cole was still potentially interested. [16] Generally, it took a lot longer, even for well-oiled professionals, to write twelve songs for a show, but, according to Wayne, they somehow did it quickly enough to get the finished work to Cole while he was still open to the idea.

Then came the day, probably in mid-1959, when Dotty Wayne dropped off the music to *Wild Is Love* with Natalie Cole in front of the family's home in Hancock Park. Wayne later told me, with some irony, "I didn't really need to know the exact address. When I got to South Muirfield, there was only one house with a little black girl playing in front of it." One of the songs in the work was titled "He Who Hesitates" and that was one thing Nat Cole did not do; he called Wayne later that same day and told her he liked what they had done. He was going to record it. Nat was almost predisposed to like the idea of *Wild Is Love*; remember that he and Maria originally fell in love with each other while listening to Gordon Jenkins's pioneering *Manhattan Tower*. That 1945 album had already inspired a very short list of subsequent works, which combined the elements of song cycle, concept album, musical comedy, and jazz, such as Mel Tormé's *California Suite* (1950) and Jo Stafford's *Ballad of the Blues* (1959).

Wild Is Love would be the last Cole project to be arranged and conducted by Nelson Riddle; ten years after "Mona Lisa," their collaboration was winding up with a bang. Cole and Riddle had come up together, but even though they remained friendly, Cole needed a musical director who could make Cole his first priority. "Nelson had pledged his allegiance to Frank," as Ralph Carmichael put it, and, in fact, on March 1 and 2, 1960, the same nights that Riddle was conducting on the *Wild* sessions for Cole, he was also recording two out of the three sessions that became Sinatra's *Nice 'n' Easy*. He had long since become better known as Sinatra's chief co-pilot, and his own career as a recording artist and as a composer for film and television was also leaving less and less time for Nat. Riddle would arrange and conduct all the songs for *Wild Is Love*, but the narration tracks would be recorded at a session conducted by his successor, Carmichael. However, everyone remembered that the sessions went very smoothly—that there was no tension whatever between Nat and Nelson, even though they were about to dissolve their professional partnership.

As we have seen, *Wild Is Love* was written incredibly quickly by two unknowns, who composed little else of note.[17] Rasch had done occasional work writing and arranging for films and television but mainly supported himself by playing piano in bars and clubs around Los Angeles.[18] But despite the two creators' general lack of experience, most of *Wild Is Love* is surprisingly satisfying, not least because the work of Rasch and Wayne is considerably enhanced by the combined talents of Cole and Riddle.

From the beginning, it was clear that *Wild Is Love* was (unlike, say, *Tell Me All about Yourself*) going to be something more than just another album. Capitol gave Cole their total support from the git-go: not only did Nat and Nelson record it with a forty-piece orchestra—plus a full mixed chorus—but Capitol also agreed to package the finished LP with a deluxe twelve-page full-color photo booklet. The models were fully clothed, but other than that, the whole section looked like it could have been a "pictorial" from *Playboy* magazine. When all was said and done, the total cost of the recording, the packaging, and the promotion, came to a total of $100,000, an unheard-of budget for a pop album (or any recording) at that point.[19] The figure was regarded as so astronomical that Capitol decided to use it as part of the marketing, and market the project in press releases as "The $100,000 Album."

By early spring, *Wild Is Love* was in the can and being readied for release. As Cole prepared for his European tour, he told interviewers that he was planning to develop the work into a Broadway musical. "I've been wanting to do a Broadway show for four years," he said, "but I've been waiting for the right vehicle. So, when these two kids came along with their songs, and we recorded them, I knew we had the theme for the show. When you hear this music, you begin to see pictures, and develop a book." He announced rather boldly that the *Wild Is Love* Broadway musical would be produced by Paul Gregory (better known as a film producer) and open in Times Square after Labor Day.[20] By May, he was announcing that the release of the album was being timed to coincide with the show in September. "It isn't going to be either an assortment of just standard songs identified with me or a regular musical comedy," he explained; "I think I'm old enough now to try a new audience. ... They'd probably stone me if I tried something like this in a nightclub, but Broadway, on the legitimate stage, is where you can take your liberties. It's not a case of trying to show Broadway my versatility, but just showing Broadway a new kind of musical show."[21]

MARCH 1960 WAS A BUSY MONTH. In addition to the *Wild Is Love* album, there were the last of Cole's quasi-R&B singles, "Magic Night" and "Is It Better to Have Loved and Lost?," arranged and conducted by Cavanaugh. Then he made a reunion session with Stan Kenton; this time their brief collaboration was instigated by Gillette rather than Gastel. Alas, the team was not able to make that "Orange Colored Sky" magic happen again, although the 1960 titles are highly entertaining. Both are pop-oriented: "Steady" uses swinging Cuban polyrhythms, featuring percussionist Mike Pacheco. Both songs incorporate Kenton's signature contrast of screamingly high trumpets with earthy, low baritone sax and bass trombone. Ollie Jones's "My Love" is a big-band blues in an AABA pattern, and is roughly in the spirit of his earlier "Send for Me." In addition to the dissonant, Kenton-esque brass, we also get Plas Johnson on honking tenor and a doo-woppy female choir, all rendered over a heavy shuffle beat. It's the kind of thing that would have doubtless been a big hit five or six years earlier.

Cole seems to have recorded all four of these vocals, the Cavanaugh titles and the Kenton titles, on March 9, 1960, and then he came back only two days later for his first date with Ralph Carmichael. (He was about to head back to Nevada, Lake Tahoe, and then the Sands in Vegas again, and then off to the continent.) On March 11, Cole finished up the *Wild Is Love* album and started a new project, which seems to have been a *To Whom It May Concern*–type collection of excellent new songs, mostly by top-tier, highly respected songwriters. "Someone to Tell It To" by Cahn and Van Heusen with Dolores Fuller was so good that he decided to save it for a big album in 1962, and "When It's Summer" was a lovely ballad co-credited to Johnny Burke and Cole himself. The other two, "Baby Blue" and "You Are Mine,"[22] were also worthy, but most important, they proved to Cole that his new man could deliver with unfamiliar—but worthy—songs. Soon, Ralph Carmichael would get the chance to prove his mettle with the classics.

COLE FLEW OUT OF LOS ANGELES on April 14, accompanied not only by his touring group (Collins, Harris, Young, and lead trumpeter Irv Bush) but also by Maria, Cookie, and Sweetie. The first stop was the Kurzaal in Ostend, Belgium, and the last was the Palladium in London; in between they played through Paris, Vienna, Berlin, Hamburg, Stockholm, Copenhagen, Oslo, Zurich, Munich, Frankfurt, Rome, Milan. When he'd played the London

Palladium in 1954, he had been billed on the legendary theater's huge marquee as "America's Sensational Coloured Recording Star." Now, only six years later, King Cole was playing the Royal Variety Show and officially being presented to Her Majesty herself.

While in London, Cole videotaped his first TV special, produced by future Lord Lew Grade for his ITV (Independent TV) Network. ITV's plan was to show it all over the world, and in some countries it was titled *A King Called Cole*. The program showed Cole visiting England, Rome, and Paris (all recreated on a London soundstage), where he interacted with local comedians, entertainers, and musicians. It opens with "C'est Magnifique," a *franglais* show tune by Cole Porter, and climaxes in a slow, stately rendition of the majestic Gordon Jenkins arrangement of "The Very Thought of You" (by British songwriter Ray Noble), as interpreted by a full-scale dance company.

But it was the continental part of the tour that yielded the most interesting music. Here, Cole interfaced with an old friend, Norman Granz, who booked the European engagements, as well as a new one, the young arranger-conductor Quincy Jones. Jones would, well before he was thirty, work with such old-school headliners as Sinatra, Lionel Hampton, Count Basie, Peggy Lee, Ray Charles, and Cole. At the time, he was twenty-seven and had been working and studying in Europe for most of the late 1950s. "Q" had put together a remarkable jazz big band, composed of both black and white, American and European musicians, as a pit orchestra for a touring, all-black show called *Free and Easy*. This was essentially an update of the 1946 Broadway musical *St. Louis Woman*, by Harold Arlen and Johnny Mercer. However, even as it had fourteen years earlier, the production once again closed unexpectedly, and the orchestra was now "at liberty." Granz got wind of this and arranged for this high-powered jazz ensemble to serve as Cole's backing group for the spring 1960 tour.

Relatively few live recordings of Cole in concert survive, and two are from this run, Paris (April 19) and Zurich (May 1). They show that with the encouragement of Granz and the inspiration of Jones's all-star jazz orchestra, Cole was inclined to play much more piano—and more jazz—than he was otherwise doing in his later years. The Paris concert (the CD issue of which contains music from two different sets on the same night) is much jazzier than the January Sands concert, but the Zurich show is even more so; in fact, there's comparatively little material here that seems to have been aimed at general "pop" audiences. The Zurich recording is divided into two "acts" that each begin with a few Quincy Jones big band instrumentals. Cole starts with a signature, "Unforgettable" and then "Madrid," before he completely surprises us with no less than three extended piano instrumentals: "Tea for Two," an outgrowth of the *Piano Style* version as well his earlier piano concerto style treatments (including a paraphrase of the *Rhapsody in Blue*); "Laura," a piano feature from the latter part of his career that was never officially recorded; and "On the Sunny Side of the Street," a unique interpretation very different from the much earlier King Cole Trio arrangement.

"It was a real interesting tour," as Jones later remembered the concert. "He was one of my favorite musicians, a real influential musician. We played a couple of places like Switzerland, and the people didn't want to hear him sing commercial songs, they wanted to hear him play piano. Nat, in a way, was kind of cornered, but it didn't matter, because he had the ambidexterity to go both ways. And so, he came out, we finished our first hour and the people were really happy, they were screaming and everything. And we started to announce Nat, but they kept screaming for the band to play more, and he kept saying, 'Go back out there and play!' But I said, 'No, you come out and play piano.' And from then on, we put [Nat's] piano with the band, and it was beautiful."[23]

The second "act," if, indeed, that's what it is, has two more instrumentals by the big band, followed by only one "pop" hit, "Darling Je Vous Aime Beaucoup." Then Cole goes into his *After Midnight* segment, with three Trio classics that had been remade in the 1956 sessions, but, more surprisingly, they're all heard here in newer, even more modern arrangements: "It's Only a Paper Moon," is missing the famous block chord intro, and likewise "Route 66" goes without the familiar introductory vamp, but with a highly stylized second vocal chorus wherein he clips off the last words of key lines, as "get your (pause) on (pause)." But in between there's a truly remarkable extended piano improvisation on "Sweet Lorraine," followed by an Oscar Moore–inspired solo by guitarist John Collins that's among the best he ever played in his long career with Cole. Obviously inspired by this, Cole returns to play a second piano solo, this one almost entirely improvised, full of block chords and quotes, more like the way he traditionally played "Body and Soul." He climaxes the concert with a driving rendition of "Joe Turner's Blues," played considerably better by the Jones all-stars than the Sands house musicians.

It's both part of the triumph of Cole's career as well as its tragedy that he didn't live long enough for his music to ever become predictable.

WHENEVER RALPH CARMICHAEL, who was born in 1927 and, as of this writing, is still a spry ninety-two, is asked about his five-year-collaboration with Nat King Cole, he always starts his answer the same way, by pointing out that they had a lot in common, starting with their parentage: both were the sons of preachers. This is much more prevalent in African American music: W. C. Handy, Sam Cooke, Lou Rawls, Jon Hendricks, Fats Waller, Aretha Franklin, and many other black music icons literally grew up in church—it's considerably less common among Caucasians. It isn't surprising that Carmichael prefers to emphasize his spiritual connections to Cole, since he has spent the great part of of his long career creating music for worship. After Nelson Riddle, Carmichael would be the most prolific and significant of Cole's collaborators, and his often-brilliant arrangements are among the major virtues of this final chapter of the Nat King Cole story.

Born in Quincy, Illinois, Carmichael grew up in North Dakota and then his family settled in California. He was immersed in the church and its music from infancy, and studied piano, trumpet, violin, and voice even before he was ten. Pastor Carmichael saw no inherent sin in popular music, and unlike many fundamentalists, did not discourage his son from listening to the radio. Ralph played in the San Jose Civic Orchestra as a teenager but was never formally schooled in orchestration and composition. However, he did attend Southern California Bible College (currently known as Vanguard University) and it was there he first began to think about modernizing traditional Christian music. "I was captivated by the chordal explosions I heard on the radio," Ralph said. "I felt a sadness that we didn't have that in our church. Our church orchestra sounded weak and terrible by comparison. It was embarrassing. Why? Why did we have to settle? Why couldn't we use those gorgeous rhythms, sweeping strings, the brass, the stirring chords? That [idea] started to control everything I did." Just as, ten years earlier, black innovators like Thomas A. Dorsey brought the energy and rhythm of the blues to traditional Afro-American spirituals and created Gospel, Carmichael began looking for ways to rejuvenate church music with the panache of pop. The phrase that is most often attached to Carmichael is "The Father of Contemporary Christian Music."

In college, Carmichael formed an orchestra and choir that utilized elements of contemporary jazz and pop ideas, which was not welcome in many more conservative church venues because it was deemed "too worldly." Still, Carmichael persisted and around 1950, he was asked to audition for a local television station, and then was given the opportunity to do a weekly series called *The Campus Christian Hour*; writing so much music every week gave him his first taste of deadlines. The show was at first not welcomed by the local Christian community, but they gradually warmed up to it in a big way when area parents realized that their teenage kids were now listening to Christian music and actually liking it—which had been Ralph's idea all along. After eighteen months or so, the show was eventually shut down, not by the church but by the musicians' local for using student and other non-union players.

However, Carmichael's career was beginning to flourish, and he was asked to score a series of films produced by the evangelist Dr. Billy Graham (which would later include the famous *The Cross and the Switchblade*) and, to his surprise, also found himself fielding offers from the world of secular entertainment. He started near the top, serving as a writer of "incidental music" for *I Love Lucy* and soon was also composing for such western shows as *Bonanza* and *The Roy Rogers and Dale Evans Show*. He first began working with major mainstream pop singers thanks to his friend, the widely employed keyboardist Buddy Cole. Through Buddy Cole's advocacy, Carmichael was hired to direct the choir on Bing Crosby's annual TV Christmas special as well as *Hymns from the Heart,* a 1959 album by Rosemary Clooney.

It was as a choral singer that Carmichael first met the other Cole. "The first time I saw Nat in the flesh, he was doing a show at NBC. It was in downtown Hollywood and Nelson [Riddle] had the band and occasionally they would call Randy Van Horne to direct the chorus, which was six or eight voices. I got a call, because I was doing some studio singing to learn how to write for voices. And I went and did it and we were in the same studio with Nat King Cole. And so, afterward we all left the studio and several of us followed Nat and he was with Nelson, his manager, and an engineer."[24] (Carmichael is visible on camera in several episodes of Cole's 1956–57 NBC TV series.) Carmichael was, at that time especially, a young man of many parts. In addition to working in both the sacred and the secular music fields, he was also employed as both a studio singer (as he said, to learn more about scoring for choirs) and as an arranger and conductor.

"Now in the meantime," he continued, "I had been doing a lot of big orchestra stuff for a label called Sacred Records, and it was all Christian music. And we were using Studio A in the Capitol Tower. So, we were in there recording and my engineer was a guy by the name of Val Valentin. He rolled off something on quarter-inch tape and gave it to Lee Gillette who was Nat's producer at Capitol. They played some of the string stuff that I'd been writing, and that's how it all started. That's how I got the Christmas album."

THE OVERALL ARCH OF THE CAREER of Nat King Cole can be described as a journey, from the fringes of society, in which he began by playing a very specific music for a very special segment of the American public, and then, over the course of roughly three decades, steadily made his way to the very epicenter of American culture. Christmas music helped Cole make this journey into the heart of whiteness, and after "The Christmas Song" he recorded roughly a dozen seasonal songs, nearly all of which had two things in common: they were all new, contemporary numbers (not traditional carols), and for the most part they were aimed at kids: "Frosty the Snowman," "Mrs. Santa Claus," "The Little Boy That Santa Claus Forgot," the Italian "Buon Natale (Means Merry Christmas to You)" and two songs involving anthropomorphic trees, "The Little Christmas Tree" and "The Happiest Christmas Tree."

The Magic of Christmas was Cole's answer to *A Jolly Christmas from Frank Sinatra* (1957) and *Ella Fitzgerald Wishes You a Swinging Christmas* (also 1960). Having just returned from a tour of England, Cole was inspired to bypass the American pop songbook and concentrate on traditional Christmas songs, mostly from 19th-century England—the era of Charles Dickens, from whence most of the familiar images of a traditional English/American holiday celebration come. At this particular point in musical history, dozens of white pop stars were "appropriating" black music; *The Magic of Christmas* is a unique example of an African American artist going straight for the heart and soul of white Anglo-Saxon identity. As with many a Christmas album, *Magic* was taped in July, after Cole had followed his European sojourn with a three-week run at the Coconut Grove.

It was an interesting notion that served several key purposes. By singing the likes of "I Saw Three Ships" and "God Rest Ye Merry Gentlemen" and other Dickensian fare (as opposed to, say, "I'll Be Home for Christmas"), Cole automatically distinguished this project both from his earlier Christmas singles and from the albums of his colleagues. But perhaps the larger part of Cole's motivation was economic: as they had on some of the *Español* albums, by using public domain material, Cole and Gillette could copyright the adaptations and collect mechanical royalties on them—thus making an album of traditional Christmas songs more potentially lucrative than an album of hit Christmas songs written by Irving Berlin and Sammy Cahn. Carmichael, whose entire background was in sacred music, was a perfect choice to arrange and conduct.

The profit potential was high but then Cole and Gillette were also very generous with their audiences, giving them a full fourteen rather than the usual twelve tracks. Twelve of the fourteen were copyrighted by Cole and Gillette (who used his wife's maiden name, Edith "E." Bergdahl). Although most of the actual authors are anonymous, even the few who are known are not credited—most famously George Frederick Handel and Felix Mendelssohn, whose music was utilized in, respectively, "Joy to the World," and, "Hark the Herald Angels Sing." Most of these carols were published and codified in their familiar form in the Victorian era, many in the book *Christmas Carols Ancient and Modern* (1833) compiled by William B. Sandys.

The Magic of Christmas (1960) does not repeat the mistake of *Every Time I Feel the Spirit* (1958), which suffered because neither singer nor arranger seemed fully invested in the material. Carmichael's arrangements, which stress the choir as much as the orchestra (which is mostly brass) are faithful to the traditional meaning of this music, but at the same time they make the music sound current and exciting, with something of the feeling of contemporary movie underscoring. None of the tunes ever quite breaks into swing time, but they don't have to, Cole and the singer and musicians dig into the music with much energy and *gusto con brio*.

As Carmichael remembered, "That was done at Capitol Studio A with a full orchestra and a choir. And of course, in those days there was no tracking, you know, everything was 'simul'—even Nat's voice. Those were the early days and it was a real challenge for the mixer because you couldn't let the brass spill too much into the strings, and you had to separate the voices. As I recall, at Capitol, they had these big glass and plasterboard panels that went twelve or fourteen feet in the air, and they put the choir behind those. So, there we were! We had a studio full of people, I'll tell you."

The two most magical tracks on the Christmas album are the two new songs. "Caroling, Caroling" (credited to A. Burt and W. Hutson) is a lively ride on a one-horse open sleigh; the jaunty tempo really gives it a feeling of fast travel and the use of three-quarter time suggests the clippity-clop of hoofbeats. "A Cradle in Bethlehem" is by Larry Stock[25] and Alfred Bryant (1871–1958), who wrote the children's song "I Wanna Be a Friend of Yours" (on *Cole for Kids*) but is best remembered for the perennial "Peg O' My Heart" (which Cole recorded with Lester Young). "Cradle," is unquestionably the album's high point. The text combines the feel of a traditional holiday song with a slightly more 20th-century sensibility, and as Cole sings it, he unfurls the fullest extent of both his tenderness and his conviction. He makes

"Cradle in Bethlehem" into a modern Christmas classic through the power of his performance.

The album was very successful, and was frequently reissued, sometimes with "The Christmas Song" added and often with different titles and covers; as far as I know, it has never been re-released with the original cover, with two Hummel-like children gazing in awe at a well-appointed Christmas tree. *The Magic of Christmas* was also, as Carmichael noted, a gift that kept on giving. "About a year or so later, Lee called and said, 'I'm buying a new boat thanks to the Christmas album. I want you to come down and we're gonna have a big party and christen it.' He was celebrating the Christmas album 'cause it got a lot of airplay and it was very popular. And in those days, I think 200,000 units would've been a smash hit, you know."

How could it not have been a smash, with both Cole and Carmichael working on material that inspired them to operate at peak levels of artistry? The new partnership was off to a great start, with tidings of comfort and joy.

FOR COLE, *THE MAGIC OF CHRISTMAS* was something old and something new at the same time. In the spring, he had promised a new musical production for the live stage; at one point it was going to be based on his still unreleased concept album, *Wild Is Love*, but it turned out to be a brand-new work by the same authors, designed from the ground up for theatrical performance, titled *I'm with You*. As he indicated in the spring interviews, Cole was trying to create something wholly original, along the lines of a Broadway revue, and he invested a huge amount of resources, both his own, and Capitol's. Dick LaPalm[26] remembered that the label invested $150,000 in *I'm with You*, which was a loss—except in the sense that it further strengthened the bond between the artist and the label. So strong was the bond that when other labels would come along with offers (LaPalm maintained that RCA Victor was a persistent "suitor"), many of whom were dangling a higher royalty rate or more incentives than what he was getting from Capitol, Cole refused to even take the call.

We don't know much about *I'm with You*, other than that it also had a score by Rasch and Wayne and that it co-starred a young black singer from Chicago named Barbara McNair (who had been "discovered" for the production by Maria Cole); this was a full two-act production that Cole hoped to bring to Broadway. Many in Cole's immediate camp thought this was overly ambitious and told him so. Nat and Maria's longtime attorney, Leo Branton, was one of these: "I said 'This play is gonna flop. It's not good enough. The people you have are really not doing a good job.' And he said, 'Oh, Leo, you're a lawyer. Don't try to be an artist.' I said, 'Nat, you forget two things, my background was in arts. And I'm also an ex-actor. And I also am a consumer. And if I don't like it, your public's not gonna like it. There's two things wrong. This play is not ready and you should not open in San Francisco. San Francisco is a very sophisticated theater town.' "[27]

Branton, who would soon turn out to be very wrong indeed about a number of things (as we shall see), was, unfortunately, correct about *I'm with You*. McNair herself admitted that while she thought the music was fine, the narrative, such as it was, and connecting material, were the crux of the problem.[28] *I'm with You* opened at the Geary Theater in San Francisco on October 31, 1960, where it was set to run for two weeks before moving to Minnesota and then Detroit. Branton continued, "So we opened in San Francisco and got panned, got really panned by all of the critics. Every newspaper panned us." Although McNair agreed that some of the criticisms were valid, she also felt that many reviewers were prejudiced against *I'm with You* because of the free and easy integration of black and white performers, even though Cole was smart enough not to include any inter-racial romance. (That wouldn't come to Broadway until *No Strings* in 1962.) Bob Wells, who had started his career with "The Christmas Song" and gone on to considerable success as a lyricist, TV producer, and writer of "special material for headliners," was brought in as a consultant, but to no avail. After San Francisco, *I'm with You* ran four nights at the St. Paul Theater in Minnesota and then about five at the Riviera Theater in Detroit, and that was the end of it.

Branton concluded, "And they finally folded because it was obvious that it wasn't gonna make it. So, Nat's life's dream of going to Broadway died. He always wanted to do that. And I always wondered, why do singers wanna be actors, actors wanna be dancers, dancers wanna be something else? Why don't they play on their strengths?" Branton has a point, but if Cole had only played "to his strengths" for his whole career, that is to say, played it safe and never took a chance on anything new or different, he would have never been anything more than an anonymous, non-singing piano player in Chicago; every accomplishment of his life had meant going out on a limb and taking a risk. "I suppose every singer wants to be a comic like every comic wants to play Hamlet," Cole himself admitted. "You know, I never was much of a talking man on the stage, even in night clubs. But I'm going to do a little talking, inject a little humor. I want to try this."[29]

Obviously, not every such risk would pay off, and in retrospect, Nat's major mistake in 1960 was coming out with two such major ventures in such a short time, both *Wild Is Love* and *I'm with You* reached the public at almost exactly the same moment. (The precise reasons why still seem unclear almost sixty years later.) Even his most ardent fans were bound to be somewhat confused, but it was obvious that the market couldn't support both.

But while *I'm with You* was a disappointment, *Wild Is Love* was a resounding hit—exceeding all expectations of both the artist and the label. Capitol promoted it like crazy and encouraged radio stations not just to offer highlights but to let their listeners hear the whole thing. They "told broadcasters they would give them a full-week's advance release of the album to those stations who would air it in its entirety. To spare jockeys the temptation of playing only selected tracks, Capitol is furnishing them with continuous groove copies."[30] They announced that the album would sell for a hefty price tag of $7.98 (mono) and $8.98 (stereo) but that there would be a special "introductory price" of $2 less in each format between the release of the album, on September 19, 1960, and the end of the year, thus making it a major imperative as a holiday present. This was underscored by the images, which could have been taken for extremely hip Valentine's Day cards. Here was now a deluxe gift package that a guy could present to his sweetheart on anniversaries or other romantic occasions—a picture book with an album attached. *Wild Is Love* may be the world's first and only coffee table LP.

But ultimately what sold the album were the stunning performances of Cole and Riddle; the partnership was at an all-time pinnacle just as it was officially dissolving. And the songs of Wayne and Rasch, combined with the rather spectacular photo insert, worked together to perfectly capture the zeitgeist of the era. It turned out to be prescient that Cole had first told the world about *Wild Is Love* on the *Playboy* TV show, right at the moment when we were about to elect the supreme playboy himself of all as our 35th president (and Cole would sing at his inaugural). The 1950s were turning the corner into the 1960s, and the pheromones of the sexual revolution, women's lib, and racial integration were already in the air.

Wild Is Love made it all the way to number four on the pop album charts, the most successful Cole LP between *Love Is the Thing* and *Ramblin' Rose.* This was no small accomplishment, since, like *Manhattan Tower* before it, it was an album of wholly original songs, no hit singles or standards. It also was nominated for a Grammy Award (best engineering, and also "album of the year"), and because Cole's ASCAP publishing company, Comet, owned the songs, the album was a double windfall for him. Thus, once *I'm with You* had played itself out (although elements of the production would be re-used in other Cole ventures, like *Sights and Sounds*), Cole turned his attention back to *Wild Is Love*.

In the interim, he had also developed a production titled *The Merry World of Nat King Cole*, which he presented at the Greek Theater in Los Angeles in August 1961. He explained at the time that most of his big concerts in the area, including seven annual "Cole at the Bowl" shows at the Hollywood Bowl, were more like elaborate nightclub sets. "I'm fortunate, man. I could get out on stage, sing 15 or 20 songs, and get the hell off. People could take me for what I am and pay me—and it would be all right, everybody would be happy. That's pretty much what I've been doing each year at the Hollywood Bowl. During the years I've been playing the Bowl, the Greek has been dogging me to do a show for them. But then I kept saying to myself, 'What can I bring to the Greek? Can I contribute something? It was certain that I couldn't do the straight one-man concertized show. That would be too much like things I've done at the Bowl. So, I just got together with Ike Jones, my producer, and [writer] Les Pine, and we dreamed this up."[31]

The *Merry World* was presented like a "musical travelogue" featuring Cole and, among other performers, a small chorus of dancers, performing songs from all over the globe, with Cole singing in multiple languages. Once again, as with *I'm with You*, he expressed the ambition that it would take him into other arenas, both literally and metaphorically, "We dreamed this up just for the Greek. though we're going to break it in in San Diego. Later? Who knows? Maybe we'll tour it. Maybe play on Broadway. But this year I'm too bottled up to do this show [again] after the Greek."[32]

He was, as he said, "bottled up" with the process of turning *Wild Is Love* into a TV special, but even before Cole could get that project into production, a French ballet company staged their own version on "the French national TV network," in January 1961. As the Negro press reported, "Since its release in France two months ago, *Wild Is Love* has been a runaway best seller."[33] The special, in which the company danced to the entire album, ended with a ten-minute transcontinental interview with Cole, in which he "revealed plans for a forthcoming album to be sung in French." In 1961, *Wild Is Love* would become a TV special closer to home as well.

COLE WAS DISAPPOINTED by the failure of *I'm with You* but, at the same time, thoroughly energized by the smash success of *Wild Is Love*, so he decided to take his lawyer's suggestion and do what he did best, and what he did better than anybody: an album of standard ballads and classic songs. Ralph Carmichael had a good reason for remembering that album, *The Touch of Your*

Lips, so fondly. "Around that time, all the big artists were coping with what was happening in the marketplace, with the rock and roll stuff and all that. So, they were all trying to make time with the kids, the younger set. Nat was no exception. Oh, they tried some country and western with him, and they eventually tried some kind of rockish, R&B type stuff. The arrangers, of course, had to go along with that."

But *The Touch of Your Lips* was the album that Cole and Carmichael chose to make for their own mutual satisfaction. They would prove their cashbox credibility as a team with *The Magic of Christmas, Those Lazy-Hazy-Crazy Days of Summer*, as well as the various Latin and country projects. "But, with *The Touch of Your Lips* we just went our own direction. Nat said, 'I'm gonna pick a bunch of ballads and we don't have to worry about the marketplace. We'll just go in and do it.' And that's why *Touch of Your Lips* is my favorite album with Nat, because there were no market constraints, you know? We didn't have to try and get airplay. We just did what was fun and Nat had a ball recording it—he just enjoyed that liberty in not having to worry about getting a hit record."

He continued, "I think that Nat and Lee picked the tunes. Every now and then, when Nat was playing Tahoe or Las Vegas, they'd bring me up there for a production meeting. And when I would come in, Lee would have his lists and have lead sheets and so I could tell that they had done some homework before I got involved."

Like all the great pop-jazz vocal albums by the masters, *The Touch of Your Lips* has a mood and a feeling all its own. Cole seems to have instructed Carmichael to pay close attention to the writing of Jenkins; on one of the arrangements for the title song, "The Touch of Your Lips,"[34] Carmichael writes down a note for himself, "Listen to 'Love is the Thing'—simple but not simple chords." The very brief (one-sentence) album notes also play up the similarity to the Jenkins albums, "In the romantic mood of *The Very Thought of You* and *Love Is the Thing*, Nat King Cole brings his wonderfully appealing warmth to this program of rich ballads."

Throughout all these albums, there's a deeply romantic and subtly optimistic feeling. *Touch of Your Lips* doesn't have the euphoric, urgent rush of *falling* in love (as Cole exemplified on the title tune of *Wild Is Love*) but rather the luxuriously secure feeling of *being* in love: love as a constant and dependable state. Cole is singing of how much he enjoys being in this state, and that he has no fear that things are going to change—love is not in the past or future tense, but here with us now, in the present. He sings "You're Mine, You," not "You Were Mine Once" or "You Will Be Mine Someday." Here, his interpretation of the Johnny Green-Edward Heyman classic is so miraculously tender that he defuses what could easily sound like an alpha-male song of possession and domination.

The sources were also somewhat unique: of the twelve songs, nine were established standards and three were new songs, mostly by writers whom Cole had favored in the past. Around the same time in 1960, Cole and Carmichael recorded five other songs with arrangements that suggest they might have been considered for *The Touch of Your Lips* at one point or another.

The album begins with the title track, *The Touch of Your Lips,* which, like "Paradise," helps set the tone of love in the present tense, a vivid description of a romantic encounter even as it is transpiring. Yet the album's most famous track is "I Remember You," which accomplishes that same task even more adroitly: lyricist Johnny Mercer exploits the contrast between past and present; the act of remembering leads us to think the protagonist is reflecting on the past, but then he quickly establishes (both in the verse and the refrain) that he is "remembering" something that happened just "a few kisses ago." At points (especially the verse) there seems to be more reverb on the voice than usual, suggesting the blurry effect used in movie flashbacks, as if the singer himself were trapped in someone else's memory.

In many of these lyrics, the message is "I will always love you, even as I do right now." Even when the protagonist projects ahead to the future ("when my life is through"), he then looks backward from that vantage point, that is, to the present. As the titles indicate, the two songs here by Johnny Burke (both written for Bing Crosby) are also written with the idea that love is always, forever, and ongoing: "Sunday, Monday or Always" (with Jimmy Van Heusen) and "Only Forever" (with Jimmy Monaco). Appropriately for a song about the beginning of the week (and the beginning of a life together for a couple), the arrangement of "Sunday" is especially notable for the opening and closing. Cole and Carmichael begin by calling the bridge ("No need to tell me now . . .") into service as a verse; the ending has Cole modulating upward and then repeating the last line in the new key for a dramatic resolution. "Only Forever" opens with the contrast between low dark basses and high violins as if to illustrate the conflicting ideas in Burke's title—"only" makes it sound like it's going to be light and trivial, where "forever" is just the opposite.

"A Nightingale Sang in Berkeley Square," the most famous of all British love songs from the war years, describes a relationship in terms of "the night we met," but Cole makes it clear that this romance is current and ongoing. At nearly five minutes, this is one of the longest vocal tracks Cole ever recorded—and he doesn't even sing the verse ("when true lovers meet in Mayfair . . ."), he just luxuriates in the chorus. Not that it's necessarily slow, but, rather like the lovers walking home on air that night in Mayfair, it's just not in any particular hurry. The chart is two choruses, and the first 16 bars of the second are given over to a sumptuous Carmichael instrumental.

"Lights Out," comes from Billy Hill, an American composer of the '30s who combined a New York and a cowboy sensibility, especially evident in his hits "The Last Round Up" and "The Glory of Love." This is the shortest tune on the package, but "Poinciana," is another longish epic from a far-flung locale, masterfully sung by Cole. It seems jointly inspired by the pop version by Bing Crosby, which also included the verse (like Cole's, set to a bolero-like beat) and the jazz piano instrumental hit by Ahmad Jamal. This is no minor foreign melody with a second-rate English text tacked on, but Cole and Carmichael make it clear that the Buddy Bernier words are truly those of a superior pop song. (One wishes Cole had also recorded Bernier's other major song, "The Night Has a Thousand Eyes.")

The first American hit version of "Poinciana," however, was not by Crosby or Jamal, but by the arranger and conductor David Rose, whom Carmichael has mentioned as one of his key influences. *The Touch of Your Lips* was the thirty-three-year-old orchestrator's first chance to show what he could do with a great singer, great songs, and a canvas that was fully as expansive as he wished. Almost fifty years after the date, Carmichael still remembered the instrumentation: customarily, for most projects, it was twelve violins, four violas, and four cellos, and here the stakes were 50 percent higher: eighteen violins, six violas, six cellos, plus three flutes, and Cole's customary rhythm section. "So, we could just have fun," he added.

Carmichael described his string writing as being influenced by the famous Glenn Miller reed section, and even more so by the writing of David Rose (as on "Holiday for Strings") but incorporating horns as well. "So that's when I first began to experiment with strings, like the Dave Rose sound. But then, when I began to write for brass, we got four trumpets and we got four trombones—so now we got eight sounds. So, somewhere along the way I thought why don't I do that with the strings—have four violin parts, two viola parts, and two cello parts. And that's what I was beginning to do with *The Touch of Your Lips*." Carmichael was experimenting with this sound throughout his early recordings with Cole, and it's clearly heard on "If I Knew" (from Meredith Willson's upcoming *The Unsinkable Molly Brown*), recorded three months before *The Touch of Your Lips* sessions.

"Now, it wasn't always pleasing to the string players. Felix Slatkin was a wonderful concertmaster. Both Felix and his wife Eleanor played on all those sessions. He called me one time and he said 'Ralph, I wanna talk to you about your string writing.' " The veteran violinist (and father of the celebrated conductor, Leonard Slatkin) "castigated" Ralph for his use of minor seconds, "when you've got two notes that are right together. That happens a lot on your 13ths and your flat fives, the hot chords. And you've got where they're buzzing, they'll be just a half step apart." But Carmichael realized that effect was what made his writing stand out and gave it such a unique sound. "I kept doing it anyway. By and by, Felix and Eleanor were very proud of it. They listened to the end result—and it sounded pretty hot to them—so they liked it."

Of the three new-ish tunes, two were by Alfred Frisch,[35] "My Need for You" (with Allan Roberts) starts with an intriguing couplet that justifies Cole's faith in the song: "If I were the moon / You'd be the night / If I were the sun / You'd be the light." It's a worthy effort in an ABAB pattern, although if it's not as memorable as it might be, it's because the title phrase isn't heard until the last line—perhaps the title should have been "If I Were the Moon." "Not So Long Ago" (with Harry Tobias) is also a highlight (and when Nat lingers on the phrase "heart to heart," it sounds like a reprise of "You're Mine You"), and extends the theme of talking about love in terms of the very recent past and the present. "Illusion" has both a title and a waltz-time signature that makes it reminiscent of Cole's recording of "Fascination." "Illusion" throws in a somewhat different light on the album, since it's a song of romantic entreaty—of wanting something rather than having it.

"Funny (Not Much)," however, is a more serious departure from the mold—it's the only song of the twelve about having lost something. It's also neither a new tune nor not exactly a standard but a song out of Cole's own past. This is Cole's third official recording, but by far the most impressive: Cole's voice has achieved a new maturity, a richness and a warmth that makes even his best recordings of the '50s pale by comparison, and his interpretative skills have grown even more. By now he's truly invested in the idea of a melancholy, bittersweet song in which the key word is "funny"—a songwriter's idea of irony that becomes something deep and profound in Cole's singing.

As mentioned, Cole concludes with the shortest tune here, "Lights Out," in which both the words and music sound like a variation on "Goodnight, Sweetheart," the Ray Noble tune that closed a million proms. In fact, the last sound you hear on the album is Cole intoning that very phrase. Fortunately, it wasn't "good night" but only the beginning for the team of Cole and Carmichael.

Here's one last memory from Ralph of the original sessions, this one concerning a playback of a take rather than a specific recording of one: "On one of the tunes, they dimmed the lights and played back the tracks. It was so beautiful that a couple of ladies in the string section were crying."

COLE TAPED *THE TOUCH OF YOUR LIPS* over two dates (December 22 and 23), right before Christmas 1960. Following the holiday, his second with his son Kelly (now almost two), he headed for Vegas for his customary winter run at the Sands, and then January would be marked by an all-time career pinnacle followed by an equally major career *kerfuffle*. On January 19, 1961, Nat made one of the most auspicious appearances of his life, introduced by Janet Leigh and Tony Curtis and accompanied by Nelson Riddle, at the John F. Kennedy Presidential Inaugural Gala, singing two popular song classics that could be considered quintessential slices of Americana, Dave Cavanaugh's hard-swinging *Sands* arrangement of "Surrey with the Fringe on Top" and Gordon Jenkins's now-classic chart of "Stardust." After the Inaugural, he traveled to Boston for a week at Blinstrub's (opening on Saturday, January 21), and then to New York, probably on January 28, where he was set to make his first appearance on *The Ed Sullivan Show* since 1958.

The plan for the January 29 show was, as usual, for Cole to sing several all-time hits plus "Illusion"; this was a new song (by Sol Parker, who had earlier written "This Love of Mine" for and with Sinatra) which Cole and Carmichael had recorded a month earlier for *The Touch of Your Lips* and which the artist liked so much that he decided to make it his next single. Capitol Records was all good to go, having rushed advances to "reviewers, disk jockeys, distributors, and salesmen" who were all informed that the song was to be featured on the *Sullivan* show.[36] But then, to everyone's surprise, Sullivan himself pulled the rug out from under them; he too had been at the Gala, and was so impressed by Nat's performance that he decided that he wanted him to sing "Stardust" instead of "Illusion."

Cole was informed by producer Bob Precht (also Sullivan's son-in-law) that they were vetoing the new song in favor of something "better-known." The usually affable host was then going through a hissy-fit, one of his periodic temper tantrums—around this time he was also ranting against NBC TV hosts Steve Allen and Jack Paar. Precht informed Cole that "the Sullivan show is not used for exploitation" and Cole responded, logically enough, that virtually every moment of the Sullivan show was pure exploitation and promotion. "I said, 'What are those excerpts from movies and Broadway plays but exploitation? Or those rock 'n' roll kids who make one hit record?" They came to a standstill, and then it was Cole's turn to totally surprise everyone by telling Precht and Sullivan that unless he could do the song that they had already agreed upon, he wasn't going to go on at all. Thus, he sat in his hotel room as nine o'clock, Sunday evening, came and went. (He was due to open at the Twin Coaches, Uniontown, Pennsylvania, on the far western side of the state, closer to Ohio, on the next day.)

In March, Cole gave an extended interview in which he laughed and said, "Oh Ed's all right. We've been pretty good friends for years. I don't know what to attribute the misunderstanding to. But when he wanted me, as an artist to sing what he selected, this was an affront to my integrity. I don't have to get on TV to identify myself." He would get the chance to promote the song in question, "Illusion," twice in April, once on Sullivan's own network, on *The Garry Moore Show* (April 4) and then a week later on Jack Paar's relatively new NBC late-night talk and low-key variety show (April 14), both occasions would have rankled Sullivan. Elsewhere, Nat said, "Ed's too nostalgic. He wants me to sing the same old songs. How many times can I sing 'Nature Boy' or 'Mona Lisa?' "[37]

COLE LINGERED AROUND the East Coast that February (Pennsylvania, Washington, DC, Miami) before getting in one more Sands run over the first two weeks of March. It was at the end of March that business brought him to Manhattan: the New York Disc Jockey convention, a full month at the Copa, and then an epic recording project that required no fewer than ten full sessions. This was Cole's major undertaking of 1961, a new stereo album package containing thirty-six of his biggest hits thus far, from the beginning of the Capitol era (1943) onward.

Capitol Records had already pioneered the idea of the deluxe gift-package album, like *The Kenton Era*, a four-LP boxed set from 1955; Jackie Gleason's *Lover's Portfolio*, a two LP set packaged in a cardboard briefcase; and Cole's ambitious *Wild Is Love* with its greeting card/candy box—like a gatefold cover. *The Nat King Cole Story* took them all a big step further: here was a deluxe, three-LP package that came with a twenty-eight-page booklet, with tons of photos and text by three of America's best-known jazz critics, enclosed in a box that made it look like a coffee table booklet for people who didn't drink coffee.

The *Story* project had originated out of the artist's desire to consolidate the gains he had made since 1943. In later years, the major record labels would become more inclined to simply reissue the vintage recordings of a legacy artist, but Capitol had also set a precedent for hi-fi and stereo recreations by major bandleaders such as Benny Goodman, Harry James, and Kenton; Cole's friend June Christy had already made two albums of stereo remakes of classic mono works. For the label, it gave them a deeper catalog; for the artist, it gave them the chance to market tracks that were already hits at a noticeably higher royalty rate. Cole and his current business partners, Ike Jones and Leo Branton, had set up an organization called "Associated Arts" that would hold Capitol's royalty payments in what was essentially a trust, and the first project to be covered by Associated was *The Nat King Cole Story* album.

Ralph Carmichael flew to New York. Between the Copa and the album sessions, Cole was in town for one of his longer stays. Nat used the occasion to visit with his brother, Freddy, then living with his wife, Margaret, in Brooklyn; Ralph and Freddy, who were closer to the same age, also became friendly at this time. While Nat was singing—and presumably, eating—at the Copa nearly every night, Ralph often found himself taking the subway out to Freddy's place for a home-cooked meal, even on nights when Nat couldn't join them.

Carmichael wasn't expected to write any new arrangements for Cole to sing on the *Story*; his main job, as musical director, was to conduct the orchestra behind Cole as he revisited his classic hits. On many of Cole's bigger songs, like "Mona Lisa," which he still sang occasionally on in-person appearances, there were no problems. "Most of those charts, to Lee's credit and Capitol's credit, were archived and we just pulled them out," said Carmichael. However, there were some songs that Cole hadn't sung in a while, and he and Gillette had lost track of the original music; those would have to be "taken down," or transcribed from the recordings. Carmichael did the bulk of this work himself, and several New York arrangers were also recruited, including the veteran Russ Case (on "Somewhere along the Way") and one newcomer from Germany, Claus Ogerman. Most of the "take-downs" were no problem, but others proved so difficult and time-consuming to recreate that Ralph found himself wishing that he could have been allowed to just start from scratch. Two of these, coincidentally, were both the work of Pete Rugolo; "Orange Colored Sky" was transcribed for this project by Kenton arranger (and Clint Eastwood collaborator) Lennie Niehaus.

And the other was "Lush Life"; this was by far the most difficult number in the entire project. Cole hadn't sung Rugolo's chart of Strayhorn's song in years, and no one could find the chart, including Pete himself. Carmichael started trying to take it down even before he left for New York. He explained, "The first night I went to work on it, I fell asleep. Then I woke up and tried it again. And I quit about 3:00 or 4:00 p.m. in the morning. I mean it's the toughest chart. I couldn't get past the intro. [Pete used] the 'atonal clusters' approach; it was just unbelievable. I put it aside and I told Lee 'we'll do it later.' So, I took it with me back to New York and thought 'well, you know, late [after one of the sessions] at night I'll finish it up.' "

Cole opened on March 16, and on March 22 and 23, he and the rhythm section went into the Capitol studio to cut what he deemed were his four biggest hits with the Trio: "Route 66," "Straighten Up and Fly Right," "For Sentimental Reasons," and "Embraceable You." (One applauds the decision to include the Gershwin song, complete with the all-important pianistic allusion to "Le Secret," even though "You Call It Madness," as a ballad, was a much bigger hit for Capitol.) The orchestral sessions started the next day, but meanwhile, Carmichael hadn't gotten any further with "Lush Life"; try as he might, he still couldn't retrace Rugolo's steps.

As it happened, there was a visitor at that first orchestral session, the young orchestrator Richard Wess, who had already made a name for himself with one of the most successful albums of 1959, Bobby Darin's *That's All* (a breakthrough LP which contained two huge hit singles in "Mack the Knife" and "Beyond the Sea," all arranged by Wess). Carmichael remembered, "He's got a real sharp looking raincoat on and he's very dapper, a personality kid." Like Carmichael himself, Wess was young and hungry, and was hanging around Cole and Gillette, trying to ingratiate himself—arranging for Nat King Cole would have been a definite feather in his cap. "So, he struck up a friendship with Nat and on the breaks he and Nat would hang out and laugh and joke and everything."

Soon enough, Wess's networking skills (as they would say in the 21st century) would pay off. "So sometime during the date, I saw Nat go in and talk to Lee Gillette. And Lee called me in then and he said 'I know you've still got some work to do; do you have something that you could give to Dick Wess? Because Nat would like for Dick to do something.' And I said, 'Aah, boy! Do I have something for Dick Wess!' "

A highly religious man, Ralph didn't have an uncharitable bone in his body, but here was an opportunity not only to get a difficult job done but of dealing with a potential rival who was, very obviously, as we would say today, trying to eat Ralph's lunch. However, it was Ralph who came to regret it when the idea backfired on him: Wess took the record home, and a few days later, made an excuse for not having done it. "I went back to the hotel and there was a package there and a little note in the package. He had returned the album and the little note says, 'I've been too busy to do 'Lush Life.' I'm so sorry, I hope I haven't let you down.' " Wess made it look like he was too busy to do it, but Carmichael knew that it was just too difficult for him, or *anybody*, to take down. So, it still wasn't done.

Recording proceeded: after a set of orchestra and string dates with Carmichael, Cole remade his three biggest R&B-styled hits with a small group featuring the New York soul saxophone star, King Curtis (Curtis Ousley) on April 3: "Send for Me," "If I May," and "Looking Back."

Then Cole put the whole project aside, first for a singles session, then for his long-awaited tour of Japan and the Far East. In Tokyo, he gave a singularly excellent "studio concert" for the benefit of Japanese TV, which is highlighted by a superb reading of "Stardust" and a culturally stunning "Autumn Leaves," which he sings in both Japanese and English (you haven't really appreciated "Les Feuilles Mortes" until you've heard it in Japanese). The Tokyo concert also gives us a four-song segment of *Cole Español* numbers: "Acercate Mas," "Cachito," "Quizas! Quizas! Quizas!," and "El Bodeguero."[38] This is virtually the only footage that has surfaced of Cole singing in Spanish and it's very special indeed.

Cole then played Harrah's in Lake Tahoe for most of June and was ready to get back to work on *The Nat King Cole Story* project again in July, starting with "Orange Colored Sky," once again with the full Kenton Orchestra.[39]

There would be two more sessions for the album, and Ralph put off dealing with "Lush Life" until the very last one, on July 20. As he vividly remembered, "When I got home, I checked with my call service, and there was a message from Pete Rugolo and it was one of the greatest messages I ever got in my life: 'Ralph, I found my worksheets on "Lush Life." Call me if you still want them.' It was the score, not the individual parts, but the overall score. So I called him and said 'I'm on my way.' I went over and picked them up, took them to the copyist, he copied it off, and we recorded it. And that's what you hear, the 'Lush Life. And if you listen to that, you'll see what I'm talking about. It's an arranger's nightmare. But we lived through it—because Pete Rugolo came through!" Everyone was so overjoyed that they invited Rugolo to come the last date and conduct his 1949 orchestration himself.

The final package consisted of thirty-six tracks, of which thirty were newly recorded ("Embraceable You," was recorded but not used at the time), and six were taken from albums that were originally recorded in stereo. Of the thirty-one recordings made for the album, twenty-one were done in New York over seven sessions, between March 22 and April 3, and the remaining ten were taped in July at the Capitol Tower back home in Los Angeles. The set was released in time for gift-giving, Christmas 1961.

Recreating his career chronologically, Cole began the project by going back to the beginning in two sessions that contained all of his early hits with the King Cole Trio. The two most recent songs among the recreations are "Looking Back" and "Non Dimenticar," both from 1958. Of the six songs where the original recordings were used—"St. Louis Blues," "Stardust," "Paradise," "Oh Mary Don't You Weep," "Ay, Cosita Linda," and "Wild Is Love"—not one was a hit single of any kind, but rather, these were very well remembered album tracks—"deep cuts" as they say today—that Cole was especially proud of.

In the notes to the package, Cole himself pointed out, "It was a great trick redoing some of these tunes. The way I think I feel now, I'm a little amazed that I picked some of them originally, but I'm glad some of my choices turned out so well. You know, we didn't have to change a single key when we remade them. As a matter of fact, I find that I'm singing out more than I used to. I can belt when I want to and give a song more impetus."

The long-term success of the 1961 performances is both a matter of Cole's vocal quality—the increasing maturity of his voice and his approach—and the question of whether or not the songs themselves would actually benefit from a deeper approach. The recreated Trio numbers come off very well, with the possible exception of "Straighten Up and Fly Right," in which, in the trio unison vocals in particular, Cole sounds like he's trying to put on the same suit he wore in 1943 and that it no longer fits. (Apparently he found it difficult to go home again, and this particular song required nine takes to get it right.)

Yet the other four trio tunes sound considerably better, especially the three slow ballads, "Sweet Lorraine," "For Sentimental Reasons," and "Embraceable You"—this 1961 performance is, in fact, Cole's definitive treatment of the Gershwin classic. Here, John Collins's guitar solo doesn't strictly re-create the solo Oscar Moore played eighteen years earlier, but Cole's much-briefer piano part is pretty much exactly the same, beginning with the same series of treble triplets from the original 78.

To me, the least successful remakes here are the songs from the early '50s: big epic songs like "The Sand and the Sea" and "Answer Me My Love" seem so specific to the era that created them that they come off as naïve ten years after, despite the best efforts of Cole, the quality of his voice and the excellence of Riddle's work. Yet "I Am in Love" is a triumph, a great song that one suspects he included in the story package to show that yes, he could get on the charts with Cole Porter—that Sinatra didn't have a monopoly on the upper echelon Broadway composers. The 1961 "To the Ends of the Earth," however, doesn't work as well as the original—the combination of the song, Cole's voice and Riddle's brilliant use of the deep male choir was something that couldn't be replicated.

And it's not only the more complicated ideas and productions. The two simplest, most innocent songs Cole ever sang, "Nature Boy" and "The Christmas Song" (his first two "crossover" hits with strings) are very much improved in the new treatments. So too is "Orange Colored Sky," which, of the dozens of novelty and comedy songs Cole recorded throughout his career, is the only one that made it to this autobiographical collection. In other cases, the success or failure of the new versions has nothing to do with vocal quality in and of itself: Cole's voice is actually younger and prettier on the original "Somewhere along The Way" (composed by friend Jimmy Van Heusen under a pseudonym), but in 1952, Cole can't even begin to fathom the subtleties and nuances he would bring to the song nine years later. The same goes for "Smile" and especially for the infamous "Lush Life." Even though Cole repeats his original lyric fluff ("siren of song" instead of "siren song"—a risible mistake), the new treatment is thirty seconds longer and a dozen years deeper.

When *The Nat King Cole Story* was released in mid-September, it proved to be a major success—and not just because of the copies it sold on both LP and, thirty years later, on CD. It made economic sense for Cole to have new state-of-the-art recordings of his signature songs; in most cases, these were the tracks that would be issued and reissued most over the subsequent decades. When, in 1991, Natalie Cole recorded her studio-created "duet" with her father on "Unforgettable," she went to the 1961 recreation rather than the 1951 original; not only was Nat singing better, but the *Unforgettable* project would have been nearly impossible without the multi-track stereo master.

For Ralph Carmichael, it was a fun project because of classic charts like Billy May's "Walkin' My Baby Back Home" (which according to the AFM sheets, was conducted by May himself). Said Ralph, "That's such a nice, loose, swinging arrangement—just a classic. And I really enjoyed the project, getting to conduct all of those arrangements, like Frank De Vol's 'Nature Boy,' Nelson's 'Mona Lisa,' and all the Billy May things. All these guys were my heroes. It was amazing to be walking through the forest of giants."

IN LATE SUMMER AND EARLY FALL 1961, Cole worked in San Diego at the Greek Theater, this time with his *I'm with You* co-star, Barbara McNair. But in addition to the biggest album project of his career, he was about to give birth to his biggest visual project, his most successful television venture, as well as to the latest and final wing of his family.

In June 1960, Cole had announced the formation of his own production company, Kell-Cole Productions, named after his year-old son. His partners were Leo Branton, who had long worked for Nat and Maria as an attorney but was increasingly assuming a greater role in his general management, and Ike Jones, the first Negro graduate of the UCLA School of Dramatic Arts.[40] Astute readers will note the absence of Carlos Gastel from this list of partners; Cole's longtime manager and one-time best friend was gradually ceding more and more of Nat's management job description to Branton.

The good news was that Maria had been pregnant since January 1961, and she was due in September. At the exact same time, Cole, Branton, and Jones were making the rounds of the networks, trying to shop *Wild Is Love* as a TV special, but not even General Sarnoff and his faithful friends at NBC seemed interested.

The only network that was receptive to the idea of a special featuring a black star was the Canadian Broadcasting Company. "Television has not yet 'grown up' to the extent that it would allow such a show to be produced in this country," as Branton wrote in 1964.[41] No less important, the CBC was willing to cut a highly advantageous deal with Kell-Cole. The arrangement was made that Nat and company would split the proceeds fifty-fifty with the CBC. Ike Jones would produce, working with Stan Harris, a thirty-year-old Toronto-born director who was placed in charge of the project (he would later go on to do specials with Jack Benny and George Burns). Cole's company "furnished certain ingredients, namely the story idea, the original music, the musical director [Nelson Riddle's orchestrations], [and] the star."

Harris started putting it together, with choreographer Alan Lund and musical director Bert Niossi assigned to conduct Riddle's charts, in what turned out to be a neck-and-neck race with the stork. Nat had been working for most of September at the Latin Casino in Philadelphia, but he flew back home on September 20, in time for the new arrivals. It turned out to be twins and the delivery was difficult. Geri Branton, Leo's wife, told the nurse, "I know the rules of a Catholic hospital such as this. If there is a decision to be made, you always save the child. Well, Mrs. Cole is not Catholic." Hearing this, Nat piped up, "I don't know anything about those babies. Just save my wife!"[42]

It worked out fine, thankfully. Two healthy baby girls were delivered on September 26; in accordance with his tradition, he gave them both Irish names, albeit unusual ones. "Casey" was named after Casey Stengel (it was hardly surprising that he named his daughter for a ballplayer, but it was that he so honored one of the New York Yankees) and "Timolin" was inspired by Johnny Burke, this being the name he had given his own third daughter in 1954.[43] As soon as it was confirmed that mother and children were all doing fine, Cole flew to Toronto.

When the Cole party arrived, they saw that the production was in good order: everything was cast and choreographed, the sets were all built and the two locations were set, and everything was good to go. But then, they noticed something: the entire cast of dancers and performers was completely and utterly Caucasian. This simply would not do; a show with a black star had to have some other non-white faces in it. Harris and the CBC crew were stymied; they somehow hadn't thought of that. Alas, they responded, there wasn't much that they could do, because "(1) the cast had already been selected and contracted." In other words, legally binding contracts had been signed with the local guilds and unions. And,(2) there were "understandable limitations on the availability of Negro talent in Toronto."[44] With just a day or so left before filming had to begin, Jones and Harris located "one Negro girl and one Chinese girl for a scene in the production." The fifty-three-minute special was then shot in the first few days of October 1961.

While the album is excellent, the TV production is better still. Although the LP has been reissued several times in the digital era, the TV special has never been available on any form of home video. A poor-condition copy at one point found its way onto youtube.com, but apart from that, the program has hardly been seen over the last sixty years.

Wild Is Love begins with a highly dramatic orchestral fanfare, with fast-moving fiddles racing upward and a nearly ecstatic choir chanting the phrase "Wild Is Love" as if it were a mantra; Cole then enters, atop a somewhat calmer, pizzicato violin passage, like a calm eye in the center of a musical hurricane, reciting an old, anonymous poem that could practically be a biblical proverb:

As a rule, man's a fool,
When it's hot, he wants it cool;
When it's cool, he wants it hot,
Always wanting what is not.

The opening "movement"—the eponymous "Wild Is Love"—is easily the most outstanding song in the work; this otherwise unknown pair of writers, Wayne and Rasch, had at least this one truly great song in them. [45] It's an absolutely awesome, rhythmically irresistible track—and a true Cole classic. Between the cacophony of the fanfare and the cool Confucian logic of the "proverb," Cole and Riddle find a swinging middle ground. After Riddle's distinctive, brassy introduction (the strings and the choir are not heard on this track), Cole leaps into the fray, keeping his balance amid all this excitement with the steadiness of a drunk in an earthquake.

On the album, the track is only two minutes and two choruses long, but Riddle makes the most of every second. The song is in an ABAB format, and, for the second chorus, Cole sings the B sections while the A's are given to instrumental solos—coincidentally, to two of the first black musicians to work regularly in the Hollywood studios. The first is by tenor saxophonist Plas Johnson; the second is by Cole's longtime friend Red Callender on tuba (as he had done on the 1957 *Just One of Those Things*). Where Billy May himself played tuba and used it frequently, "Wild Is Love" marks Riddle's most notable use of the instrument—like the harmonica on "Raintree County" and the Asian violin on "China Gate."

The program opens with Cole on a soundstage, standing in front of a veritable jumble of letters spelling out the word "love," in neon, in cutouts, in standees just as tall as he is. The message is clear: love is all things to all people, and larger than life. In the album, Cole delivers the spoken prelude just before the title song, but on the show, it comes after the opening number. Nat is wearing his houndstooth hat, and later in the show he combines it with a trench coat that makes him look even more like Henry Higgins in the opening scene of *My Fair Lady*, which is obviously intentional: Cole is the Higgins of romantic relationships, a kind of super-spiritual uber-lifecoach. (Cole later wore this same combination on the cover of his own *My Fair Lady* album.)

"You know there's not a person in this whole world whom love hasn't touched," he tells us "There's hardly anybody." This is a cue for his co-star, Larry Kert to appear: strolling over from stage left, he introduces himself to Cole as "hardly anybody." In 1961, the handsome and talented Kert was known for two things: for creating the leading role in the 1957hit original Broadway production of *West Side Story* and for being unfortunately overlooked for the same role in the lackluster Hollywood version of that classic show. Casting him opposite Cole was a masterstroke: throughout the show, Kert looks exactly like the anonymous male half of the Caucasian couple on the *Two in Love* album. More important, Kert and Cole are highly copasetic costars; he's young enough, innocent enough, tall enough (just about an inch or so shorter than the host), and with just enough left of the juvenile leading man about him. When Kert claims to not know anything about love, Cole says (to the audience) "talk about Adam and *naïve*!"

Their brief exchange leads to the second number, which begins with more spoken narration (also heard on the album): "When did you first discover love? That wonderful moment when the world takes on a new and beautiful glow?" The spoken portions sound somewhat kitsch-y on the album, but they're perfectly appropriate on the show. "Hundreds of Thousands of Girls" could be a main title theme for a 1960 romantic comedy, exactly the kind that Cahn and Van Heusen would write for Dean Martin—it has a very ratpacky feel, similar to "You Can't Love 'Em All." Cole sings it accompanied by a male chorus, and in the show the song is illustrated with both still pictures and live shots of dozens of attractive twenty-something actresses and models (including the two non-Caucasians); "They're so hard to resist / Every one of them ought to be kissed!"

If the title track is the album's best swinger, the best ballad overall is "It's a Beautiful Evening." The song is pure simplicity, Cole intoning the title phrase twice, followed by a gentle breeze of a string passage. The singer and arranger don't just perform the notes and the text; they make the images come alive in your brain. "It's a Beautiful Evening" is the only other song from the project to have a life beyond it.[46] The sequence was filmed in the lagoon of the Toronto Islands, shot "in the afternoon but camera-filtered for dead-of-night closeups."[47] Cole sings while boating down a river through the middle of the park (a rather literal manifestation of all those album covers), mostly courtesy of a blue screen effect. We also see Kert, an accomplished dancer, in white dinner jacket and a romantic pas-de-deux with a stunning blonde named Maureen Hill. Joined by six more couples, the two literally dance until the sun comes up, and the beautiful evening gives way to a beautiful morning. It's a beautiful number indeed, which ends with Kert and partner dancing up to Cole on a park bench, where he finishes the song.

Act Two begins with Cole and Kert discussing the events of the night before in what we gradually realize is Kert's bachelor pad. Importantly, Cole addresses Kert as "Larry" but Kert calls him "Mr. Cole." We hear Kert's singing voice for the first time, "Last night I kissed her / I kissed my baby" and eventually they sing together. "Tell Her in the Morning" is another of the better songs in the cycle, earning an exciting bluesy chart by Riddle and steadily modulating upward toward a high-note climax. It's a solo by Cole on the album, but the duo by the two men on the show is even more exciting.

The next scene opens the following morning in a diner, with Larry and his girl at one table and Cole in an adjoining booth. Following Mr. Cole's advice, Larry tells his girl that he loves her, they talk and she in turn tells him that she loves "books, good paintings, and jazz . . . and unfortunately, somebody else." Overhearing this news, Cole strolls over to Kert's table, and, once again playing the role of the voice in the young man's head, sings "Are You

Disenchanted?" This is the most melancholy number in the package, and the chart is classic Riddle, making use of his signature windchime flutes.

The next act (following a commercial break) has Cole advising that the cure for the blues is to "make the scene—get in that car—let the top down, brother—get on that boulevard and cruise." Which leads to two songs filmed al fresco on Yonge Street in the middle of the night on October 2. Yonge is "Toronto's main thoroughfare—which was roped off by police from midnight to five AM and specially watered for reflection."[48] As Cole sings "The Pick Up" ("Hey, baby can I give you a ride?"), the lyrics are enacted visually in a late night street scene (the streets of Toronto standing in for Anytown, USA) wherein Kert in his convertible trails after a hot but distant blonde (Marilyn Rollo) in slacks. In the final shot, a chauffeured limousine pulls up and whisks her away.

Pan to Cole, still in full Henry Higgins drag, now commenting musically on how Kert has failed to pick up the blonde he was after, by singing of loneliness and rejection in "Beggar for the Blues," which alludes to blues harmony and imagery. The album track features prominent Callender tuba obbligatos throughout, plus growling trumpet and wailing alto—the most prominent moments by the great Pete Candoli and the even greater Benny Carter. "World of No Return" is the cycle's answer to Rodgers and Hammerstein's "dream ballets" from *Oklahoma!* or *Carousel*. Kert is shown dancing around a set of white, flowing curtains with a dozen different female dancers, one at a time; the song is introduced by Cole but sung by the full mixed choir—sounding very angelic. The whole sequence is, indeed, rather wet-dreamy.

"As months go by . . . soon Autumn turns to winter . . . you find yourself falling in love too easily," Cole tells us, which leads not to a number but a comedy sketch, which has no counterpart in the album, but was expressly written for the CBC production by Paul Wayne. This is a sitcom-type scene that we've seen in lots of period romcoms, of which the archetype was the 1955 Sinatra movie, *The Tender Trap*. Kert is presented as the ultimate make-out man, trying to make love to three different girls at once (Pam Hyatt, Carol Starkman, and June Sampson) while hiding them from each other in different rooms of his swinging bachelor pad.

The comedy is then counterbalanced by a more somber song with a somewhat generic title, "In Love Again," sung by Cole in the hallway outside "Larry's apartment." It warns against the danger of falling in love too easily ("Fool, you tumble much too fast, / Fool, you know that it won't last") with somber, polytonal chords from Riddle and a prominent female "vapor voice" trailing Cole.

"But you can't stop now! Who you kidding? So, you might as well laugh it up, live it up, because you know you can't give it up." Cole re-enters the apartment, to find himself in the middle of a swinging cocktail party, a scene that mimics the Playboy party he participated in two years earlier in Chicago, with men in suits and ties, women in furs, gowns, and opera gloves. Cole wanders around the room, inspiring romance among all manner of Canadian Caucasian couples as he sings the rhythmic, "Stay with It." The songwriters once again channel the spirit of the Rat Pack poets Cahn and Van Heusen, utilizing a triple-rhyming scheme, and it's another delightful combination of scene-and-song made perfect by Cole and Riddle as well as the staging by Stan Harris. Even better: Cole then sits at the piano and treats us to an entire chorus of the song, even throwing in one of his familiar quotes (the vintage march, "American Patrol").[49] He ends with the concluding line, "Just move your heart right in / And stay with love!" giving the piano the last word, as he ends with a resounding plink of a high A, which is a device we've heard him use a thousand times but provides the perfect note, right here and right now. (The album version features Callender again, along with vibraphonist Emil Richards and pianist Lou Levy.)

How could it get any better than this? Well, it does, for "Larry," at last: "Just when you're ready to pitch it all, you're through looking, you're through caring, then one day out of left field . . . there she is! You've found her, at last." The scene reveals Kert seeing "her" across crowded room, and somehow, he knows, he knows even then. So, he sings "Wouldn't You Know?" Cole croons it beautifully on the album, but having Kert sing it here has much more dramatic impact; the opening line is "Wouldn't you know / Her name is Mary?" and he sings it to Joan Roberts, the dancer who personified the "shy" girl earlier (in "Hundreds and Thousands of Girls") and they do a sweet and simple dance together. It's a lovely, intimate moment.

We then cut to the exterior of a church, in time to watch the newly married couple—Larry and "Mary"—get showered with rice by their wedding party; Cole follows, and sings, this time really for us rather than for Larry, "He Who Hesitates" ("He who hesitates when it comes to love / He will never know all the wonders of a kiss, a sigh . . ."); as he sings, the churchyard set comes apart and we're returned to the opening soundstage with Cole singing in front of about a dozen signs beaming the word "love." In the final moment before the end credits roll, he sings a brief reprise of the title song in front of those same letters, this time enhanced by the entire female company of dancers and models. "And while wild is the wind, and wild is the roaring sea / Nothing could ever be, as wild as love!"

Wild Is Love was broadcast over forty-six stations by the CBC in November 1961. *Variety* gave the production a rave review, "A tribute to Cole and his cast, this was easily the most elaborate show in the CBC's variety classification and kudos should go to Stan Harris." The show was well received across Canada, without any problems, given "one of the highest ratings ever received by a television show in that country."[50]

As he had with the album a year earlier, Cole must have felt vindicated by the wonderful reception that the CBC version was given in Canada. But even then, alas, little progress was made in terms of bringing the show to America. Kelly Cole, who though still a toddler at this time, was later told about a fateful telegram that sealed the fate of the show in the United States. The deal-breaker was the final shot: "Larry Kert ... sang a duet with Dad and at the end of it, Dad puts his arm around him, and they walk offstage. Well, they got a telegram saying the only way the sponsor would take the show was if that segment—the approximately three-and-a-half seconds when two men—a white and a black—had physical contact, was cut." Kelly concluded, "They [Cole and Harris] declined to cut the segment."[51]

Wild Is Love was finally shown on American TV in January 1964, via syndicated distribution. The whole process had simply taken too long; by that point, the show's moment of impact was over. The tragedy of November 1963 had proved to be a cultural turning point, marking the end of an era, of Camelot, of the Kennedys, of the Rat Pack, and of the original *Playboy* mindset. It all ended with the gunshots in Dallas. By the mid-1960s, the party was over, and now it was time to get serious, with the Great Society and the Civil Rights Bill on the immediate horizon. No one wanted to see *Wild Is Love* in the mid-1960s; by then, everyone's idea of a good time was to get stoned and then go out and protest something, not to put on a tux and pick up girls at cocktail parties.

Alas, *Wild Is Love* got noticed for all the wrong reasons in 1964. In 1961, Cole couldn't get the show on American TV because of too much fraternization between the races; in 1964, he was criticized for just the opposite reason. After describing the program as "one of the rare and delightful moments of this year's season on the big tube," *Los Angeles Sentinel* columnist Stanley G. Robertson felt obliged to "take Mr. Cole to task for not using a greater percentage of Negroes in the cast. Only for a fleeting instance was there a Negro girl even shown on camera, a fact which is pretty disgusting in these days and times, particularly in a show starring and produced by a Negro!"[52] Several months later, the debate continued, when Leo Branton explained that the whole production had been put together by the time the Kell-Cole team arrived in Toronto.[53]

The larger point was that the moment for *Wild Is Love* had already come and gone. Today, however, it's possible to appreciate *Wild Is Love* for the truly exciting hour of music, dance, comedy, and, yes, even wisdom that it is; no less than the classic works of the Trio, his best albums, the highlights of the NBC TV series, and his best dramatic role (in *China Gate*), *Wild Is Love* ranks as one of Cole's pinnacle achievements.[54]

BACK IN HANCOCK PARK, after taping *Wild Is Love* in October 1961, Nat tried to take time off to be with his family, which now numbered five children; there was a testimonial dinner at the Beverly Hilton for the legendary moviemaker Mervyn LeRoy, then his fall run at the Copa, and, finally, the much-anticipated evening of November 18, which began with Cole singing at a Democratic Party fundraiser and ended with JFK himself making a surprise appearance at Cookie's coming out party. Nat was obviously in ebullient spirits in November 1961, and thus it was a perfect time for him to make a new and classic album with Billy May.

Cole's appetite was obviously whetted when, on July 20, he and May recorded a new stereo version of their 1951 hit, "Walkin' My Baby Back Home" for *The Nat King Cole Story*. Where their previous album, *Just One of Those Things* (1957), employed some notably radical instrumental juxtapositions, the 1961 collaboration was a straight-ahead set of what trade papers at the time referred to as 4/4 "terp tempos," using the standard swing-band-plus-strings format that Cole and Sinatra had helped perfect in the early '50s. Naturally, May brought along his sense of humor, expressed in the use of such offbeat instruments as those found in the arsenal of percussionist Emil Richards, a legendary collection among Hollywood studio musicians.

The new album, *Let's Face the Music*, also featured a very special guest artist on electric organ. In Cole's nightclub act of the early '60s, Cole had played a device described as a "two-octaved clavietta" but had never recorded on it, and he also occasionally played celesta, most famously the *King Cole for Kids* album in 1947. Still, the five Hammond organ solos on *Face the Music* constitute Cole's only substantial solos on a keyboard other than a traditional acoustic piano. As we've seen, in the second act of his career, most of his professional associates, especially Gastel and Gillette, were continually encouraging him to play more; according to May, it was Lee's idea that Nat should play electric organ on *Let's Face the Music*. May also felt that there was likely a commercial motivation; "He was always pushing to sell records," said Billy, "There was probably a hot organ record out at that time."

On "When My Sugar Walks Down the Street" (one of the earliest standards by close friend Jimmy McHugh, which Cole and May probably remembered from the 1938 Ellington-Ivie Anderson version), Cole shows he can match the entire massed ensemble for both volume and momentum on the Hammond, and "Tweet! Tweet! Tweet!" By contrast, "Too Little, Too Late," accurately described in the original jacket copy as "a slow rocker," has Cole whining cowboy-style on the keys, suggesting Ray Charles. On the titular "Let's Face the Music and Dance," the arranger sets up an ingenious background and foreground pattern by positioning the organ's electrified tones against the strings. ("I've written about a hundred and forty fuckin' arrangements of that tune," May pointed out to me, the most famous being on Sinatra's 1979 *Trilogy*.) Cole's organ playing here is a whole other animal, much more aggressive and horn-like than most of his piano work.

This isn't to say that the seven tracks where Cole simply sings—without playing—aren't just as good. The original opener, "Day In, Day Out" amounts to one of the most powerful swingers in the entire Cole catalog (he would reprise it on one of his final TV appearances, on *The Jack Benny Program* in 1964), with both principals embodying the full force of "the ocean's roar, a thousand drums." May had previously scored this, also at a roller-coaster clip, for Sinatra's 1958 *Come Dance with Me* set, and he does even better by the Johnny Mercer-Rube Bloom standard here.

May and Cole also use tempos as a crucial element of cross-genre pollination. The Gershwin show tune "Bidin' My Time" (from *Girl Crazy*), for instance, lopes along at a square-dance tempo—an example of Times Square sophisticates poking fun at the hicks from the sticks—whereas "Cold, Cold Heart," by hillbilly hitmaker Hank Williams (and arranged by Bill Loose) only starts out that way. It gently picks up juice, especially during his solo, wherein Cole shows that the Hammond can truly cook more than just jambalaya. Where previous mainstream pop renditions (Tony Bennett, Dinah Washington, Louis Armstrong) had treated the tune as a ballad, Cole reanimates the 1951 country classic as a bluesy stomp.

"Moon Love" (arrangement by Heinie Beau) and "Ebony Rhapsody" take us from the far West to the middle of Europe, both being swing era adaptations of classical warhorses. Perversely, the first piece, inspired by Tchaikovsky (the second movement of the fifth symphony), who was hardly known for his jazziness, turns out to be one of the most audaciously swinging selections in the set, in which horns aggressively punctuate the organ solo. "Ebony Rhapsody" represents many levels of interpretation: Nat Cole singing an orchestration by Billy May inspired by a record by Duke Ellington of a song by Sam Coslow based on the Hungarian Rhapsody No. 2 by Franz Liszt. This was May's favorite tune on the set, the late conductor told me, and also that he simply copied the chart off Ellington's 1934 record. He didn't. May brilliantly added his own distinctive touches even while maintaining an inherently ducal feel. For his part, Cole doesn't replicate the vibrato of Ellington vocalist Ivie Anderson but instead deconstructs Liszt into a series of riffs, underscored by Emil Richards's tinkly little percussion instruments.

Yet no matter what the source or the speed, Cole continues to excel at the sensual singing that he had become known for. "Something Makes Me Want to Dance with You" amounts to a swinging seduction in foxtrot time. The strings move like crazy here, and Richards enhances the undulation with light touches of marimba. Cy Coleman and Carolyn Leigh's "Rules of the Road" finds Cole combining compassion with slight filigrees of irony and sarcasm.

"I'm Gonna Sit Right Down and Write Myself a Letter," one of only a select few songs in Cole's canon that were associated with Fats Waller, went from this album into Cole's nightly act (he included it in his show at San Francisco's Fairmont in 1962 and in Australia in 1963). "Warm and Willing," a unique collaboration of multiple generations of songwriters close to Cole, Jimmy McHugh with Jay Livingston and Ray Evans, is an extraordinary song (later revived in the Broadway revue *Sugar Babies*) that inspires one of Cole's sexiest vocals ever; as he skims the upper ceiling of his voice and then travels downward for some tasty low notes, he truly makes "every golden moment thrilling."

One of the triumphs as well as the tragedies of this album is its showing that Cole could have easily incorporated his keyboard playing into more of his vocal albums; even though his instrumental work was no longer the focus, his playing contributes mightily to our enjoyment of *Let's Face the Music*. Cole was continuing to play on his live appearances, even if 1961 saw his last recorded keyboard performances. (He had worked out a special instrumental arrangement of "Laura" that he played extensively throughout the early '60s that he never recorded.)

Billy May (who later arranged several Nat Cole signatures for Natalie) was never one of your more maudlin chaps. It was hard to imagine him getting all choked up even when he talked about people who meant a great deal to him. He was an extreme professional, who expected no less from the artists he worked with; the worst insult he could pay someone was to say that the person acted unprofessionally, that he or she gave him a hard time and caused a lot of trouble in the studio; his highly colorful *sobriquet* for such individuals was that they were "a pain in the ass."

His memories of Nat King Cole were precisely the opposite—in fact, they were about as sentimental as I ever heard Billy get. He regarded most singers as prima donnas, but Nat, he said, "never gave anybody any trouble." Billy told me, "He was just a wonderful guy. He was also a talented and a very capable musician. He had a very open mind about music . . . and everything. He was a wonderful man."

JUST HOW BUSY WAS NAT at the end of 1961? There's a photo of him taken during the middle of *Face the Music* sessions: we see him in the now-familiar houndstooth hat, perched at the Hammond organ, in the vocal isolation booth. Through the window, there's no mistaking the rotund, friendly form of Billy May. Cole has the sheet music for one of the *Face the Music* songs on the organ, where it ought to be, but near the vocal mic, there's a music stand, and it contains an entirely different song: it's "Magic Moment," which he would record five days later. In other words, Nat was so busy that even while he was in the middle of one album—one of the best of his career—he needed to find time to study a new song from his next session.

This was already close to the end of 1961, and Nat was looking forward to spending his first Christmas with his newly expanded family. But before the dawn of 1962, he still had time for yet one more major extended engagement (his eighth annual run at the Coconut Grove) and, amazingly, yet one more classic album.

Throughout 1961, in addition to the album sessions, Cole had found time to turn out singles; usually these were done in the afternoon, when he was working at night (at the Copa in New York in May and the Coconut Grove in Hollywood in November) and all these sessions but one were conducted by Carmichael. The outlier was a Manhattan date directed by Richard Wess, who had been given a shot with Nat before dropping the ball on "Lush Life." Most of the 1961 singles are a mixed bag; there are a few more R&B/rock 'n' roll-style numbers, with nervous-sounding string parts and repetitive sixteenth-note triplets, and there are also many foreign-import songs. Wess's major contribution was an Italianate up-tempo titled "Cappuccina" very much in the vein of his chart on "Beyond the Sea" for Bobby Darin.

This marked the beginning of yet another whole new sound for Cole: the "Euro-swinger." That same year, he also cut "Step Right Up (Sucu Sucu)," perhaps the single most worldly song in his entire canon. The Bolivian musician Tarateño Rojas wrote it in 1959 as a celebration of solidarity between Bolivia and Argentina. It soon was being heard in every country in the pan-Americas, and then in Europe, not to mention Scandinavia, the Middle East, and even Asia. Smelling opportunity, Ivan Mogull purchased the rights to an English language adaption, and the song charted for Cole, but only at #106.

Two of Cole's best singles with Carmichael allowed him to incorporate his major avocational obsession and also to serve as a ramp-up to a performance he would give in July at the Baseball Writers Dinner in San Francisco. "Goodnight, Little Leaguer," with a lyric by Dorcas Cochran,[55] mixes in another ingredient that clearly appealed to Cole: the idea of singing to a child—now that Kelly had recently turned two and the twins were on the way. "The First Baseball Game," conversely, combines athletics with spirituality and copious humor. Written by the highly successful team of Don Raye and Gene De Paul,[56] the song derives from one of the more famous poems in sports literature, "Brother Noah Gave Out Checks for Rain," first published anonymously in 1906 and believed to be the work of one Arthur Longbrake. The piece was recited on an Edison wax cylinder (under the original title) in 1907. Cole and Carmichael show that preachers' sons do have a sense of humor when it comes to religion. The text wittily uses baseball jargon to re-enact episodes from the Old Testament in a way that makes it, in the words of baseball historian Warner Fusselle, a "sermon on the mound." (A sample: "Goliath was struck out by David, / A base hit was made on Abel by Cain, and the Prodigal Son made a great home-run.") Play ball!

The baseball songs aside, two other singles from these sessions are absolute stunners—and near the very top of the list of classic achievements by the Cole-Carmichael team—and both are from contemporary Broadway musicals by veteran composers. "Magic Moment" comes from Arthur Schwartz and Howard Dietz's reunion project, the ambitious but unsuccessful *The Gay Life*. Carmichael's use of a prominent guitar gives the arrangement a distinctly European feel, and the string figures seem to genuflect in the general direction of Nelson Riddle. The song is written so that the last phrase—"Magic moments all our own" is spoken, *parlando*-style, though Cole doesn't take this as far as Barbara Cook did in the actual show itself.

The other is "Look No Further" which is, likewise, the highlight of the score to *No Strings*; this is the apex of Richard Rodgers's career after the death of Oscar Hammerstein, and the only show for which he wrote lyrics as well as music. Rodgers deploys a very specific rhyming scheme that only a composer could think of, with lines like, "Don't move an inch away—stay," "This is the journey's end—friend," and "Making my life complete—sweet": these are some of the most purely musical lyrics ever written—the kind of thing that Nat King Cole can really sink his teeth into.

I ONCE INTERVIEWED GEORGE SHEARING regarding a completely different subject, but when he started thinking about his absolute favorite albums, he immediately began talking about Nat King Cole and "the album that we did together."[57] He was very specific—he didn't just refer to it as "Nat King Cole and George Shearing" or something like that; he quoted the title exactly right in a way most musicians rarely would, as *Nat King Cole Sings / George Shearing Plays.* If he could have managed some Victor Borge-style phonetic punctuation, he would have pronounced the slash as well.

Shearing gave credit for the basic idea—for putting the two of them together—to Ralph, something that Carmichael never claimed for himself. "Ralph Carmichael had the idea. And it might have been either Dave Cavanaugh [Shearing's producer at the time] or Lee Gillette who started talking about it. And it didn't take very long to sell me on Nat Cole. Not only was he a marvelous singer, but he was also one of the most underrated jazz pianists I've ever met in my life. I mean, unfortunately or fortunately, probably his singing became such a big hit that not too many people around today know about the King Cole Trio and what great piano there was on that."

The finished album would be co-credited to Gillette and Tom Morgan as producers, although Cavanaugh also helped pick some of the tunes. And while Shearing gave a lot of credit to Carmichael, many of the charts were worked up from quintet arrangements by Shearing himself. Carmichael's major credit was located on both the front and the back, as an extension of the album title: "Nat King Cole Sings / George Shearing Plays . . . with String Choir Directed by Ralph Carmichael."

"We had some meetings, of course," said Shearing, "about what we were going to do." Carmichael remembered the pre-production meetings on that project very vividly. "It was in the Tower. And I had my score paper there and I was taking notes and, oh it was terrible! Because, we'd get everything set and then Nat would say 'Wait a minute, I think George should take the first instrumental break when we finish the first chorus.' So, I'd erase everything and put the new directions in, but then George would say 'Let's see, what key were we going to do it in? No, I don't want to do that in D flat—I think E flat is a better key for me.' So, I would have to erase and start again. Well, we spent about two hours up there, and when we finished, I don't think we had routined more than two or three tunes. It was just a waste of time."

Rather than talk it through, they decided they would set the routines—the basic outline of the arrangements—together in the studio, with Shearing at the piano. Carmichael found it was easier for the two to play and sing their way through the songs rather than plan them in the abstract. "And that way we could record all of those changes and all I'd have to do would be to go through about 30 or 40 minutes of talk, fast forward to the last two or three minutes, cause the final decision would be right there at the end, you see. So that worked out real good—we got all the keys and the routines. Wouldn't it be something to hear those tapes now? I don't know where they were, but it was a hoot 'cause I did listen to them after the fact, you know. I kept them around for quite a while. I don't know what ever happened to them, but I should be kicked in the britches for letting them get away."

This was the rare Cole project that didn't use any of the King's men, his regulars in his touring rhythm section. Rather, the whole point was to use Shearing's idiom, his sound, his approach, his guys—vibraphonist Emil Richards, guitarist Al Hendrickson, bassist Al McKibbon, plus a ringer on drums, Shelly Manne, the storied percussionist, already a bandleader to be reckoned with, who would make several guest appearances with the Shearing Quintet.

Cole and Shearing were predestined to make beautiful music together. The two men were born just a few months apart (Cole in March 1919, Shearing in August) and both were among the preeminent jazz piano players of all time. Extending the parallel, both first came to the attention of the jazz public via the remarkable small combos that they led, the King Cole Trio and the George Shearing Quintet. In 1950, Cole said of Shearing, "He's a fine player, and he's done more than anyone else in America to interest the ordinary people in modern jazz. Of course, he didn't think up the locked-hand style of playing; I guess Milt Buckner did that. But he did the music business a lot of good, especially in New York."[58] (However, Shearing had probably learned the "locked-hand" style from Cole rather than Buckner.) Both Cole and Shearing achieved even greater fame and rewards by adding a pop dimension to their music, which they brought about by annexing orchestras and strings to their sound.

It was probably Cole's idea that the set should primarily consist of ballads. Both these men were originally known as jazz musicians, but at this point in their lives, they had love songs on their mind. The mood throughout is similar to *The Touch of Your Lips*, but despite an approximately equal number of strings and the addition of Shearing's piano and his quintet, the sound is even lighter and, as musicians like to say, "transparent." The orchestral textures are completely open, beautiful but not syrupy, and enticing without being dissonant. In fact, even without the element of Cole's marvelous voice, these are some of the most attractive backgrounds ever written for Shearing's piano (quite a compliment, in that Shearing worked with Billy May and many other giants of pop-jazz orchestration, in addition to being a distinguished arranger himself). Carmichael would also write settings for the piano playing of Stan Kenton, Earl "Fatha" Hines, and pop star Roger Williams, but nothing would surpass his work here.

Cole / Shearing is a remarkable piece of work from start to finish: not one of the songs here is obvious or overdone, nor is the way they are sung, played and arranged. Just looking at the list of songs selected tells you that here were two major musical mavens looking for the best and most interesting material they could possibly come up with. There would be plenty of time to make hits, as Cole's catalog from this period attests, but the idea here was simply to produce the most exquisite music that it was possible for two great artists, working in collaboration, to make.

The album was taped over four dates, from December 19 to 22, 1961, about a week after Cole returned home from his winter run at the Sands. On the first date, Carmichael remembered, "What George doesn't know is that Nat always comes about 20 to 30 minutes late. Not because he doesn't care, but as a favor to me—he knows that gives me a chance to run a couple of the tunes and get the clams out. And so, he can walk in and we can go right to work without having him stand around while I'm making corrections, you see. So, George arrived on time, and as a matter of fact it was during that wait that he complimented me on the arrangements, how much he liked them, before that first date. Now on the second date, Nat is coming 30 minutes late, but George comes 45 minutes late! Now on the third date, we got to laughing, because we thought neither one of them would ever show up, because they were always trying to outdo each other. We finally got the album done, but it was fun to see the one-up-manship, how each one would want come a little later than the other one."

The project seems to have been put together in that same spirit of friendly give-and-take; what you might call "coop-etition." For instance, George says, "How about 'Let There Be Love?'" He would know that one, since it was a British song from the early war period when he was one of the stars of the London jazz scene. Then Nat says, "How about 'There's a Lull in My Life?'" and I'll bet anything he remembered it from Duke Ellington and Ivy Anderson. The same thing goes for "I Got It Bad (And That Ain't Good").[59] And so on. Each collaborator also took the opportunity to include several songs from his own past. Apart from the parallels between the careers of the twin protagonists, the relationship between the two men and their material was equally organic. For Cole, there were two remakes, Otis Rene's "I'm Lost" (1943) and the *Bishop's Wife* theme, "Lost April" (1948). (One suspects that he was thinking about these older songs.)

It was Cole, Shearing recalled, who insisted on including Jerome Kern's "Pick Yourself Up," which had been a signature song for the Shearing Quintet since they recorded it in 1950. "When Nat said, 'Let's do 'Pick Yourself Up,' well, I'll tell you, years after my original conception of 'Pick Yourself Up,' I was no longer that enamored of it." The pianist said, "I mean I still love the tune and the lyric; I was just tired of my 1950 conception of it. I did it at that fast tempo because I wanted to get that little fugue-thing in at the beginning. But I couldn't really see Nat doing it like that. But Nat said he had a new idea for it, and he hummed it for me. And that was the kind of inspiration that happened all the way through that album on those meetings, because if he initially had an idea that hadn't occurred to me, it took him precisely two seconds to sell it to me."

"Let There Be Love" makes use of a gospel-style choir of strings, and the countermelody they play is very similar to Bobby Timmons's hard bop classic "Moanin'." "Let There Be Love" became, over the years, the "hit" from the album, and the track one most often hears on the radio, an arrangement used as a template by other, later groups. As a representation of this particular Anglo-American alliance, several of the selections have international leanings: "Let There Be Love" is British, "Azure Te" is jazz organist Wild Bill Davison's depiction of Paris, and "Serenata" by Leroy Anderson and Mitchell Parrish is treated in a lightly Latin fashion that suggests that the three principals were already familiar with the bossa nova. Ellington's "I Got It Bad" was already a jazz standard and Bart Howard's waltz "Fly Me to the Moon" was about to become one. "I Got It Bad" was normally done either bluesy and torchy, but Cole and Shearing take it more romantically, and that ain't bad at all—in fact, it's good. This is three years before the iconic Sinatra-Basie version of "Fly Me to the Moon"—and here, on the original album front cover, the song is listed under the original title "In Other Words," but on the back, it's given as "Fly Me to the Moon."

Cole / Shearing is also the album that made "A Beautiful Friendship" into a hip favorite; if the album had a title other than the names of its two co-stars, this should have been it. This was an outstanding song by the team of Kahn and Styne—not Sammy Cahn and Jule Styne—but Donald Kahn (the son of the famous Chicago-based lyricist Gus Kahn) and Stanley Styne (son of Jule). It's a beautiful song for Cole, and it's in the tradition of his great Trio numbers, winding up with what Scott Fitzgerald once called "a *Saturday Evening Post* ending," and it's a worthy successor to "The Best Man" and "I've Got a Way with Women."

The closest thing to a misstep on the original album is "Don't Go," a pleasant-enough song by two old pros Al Stillman and Guy Wood (another Brit), but not up to the other eleven on the LP. It's regrettable that the two principals chose "Don't Go" instead of Wood's authentic masterpiece of a song, "My One and Only Love." (We'll have to content ourselves with Sinatra and Johnny Hartman on that one.) Two absolutely stunning standards, "Everything Happens to Me" and "Guess I'll Go Home This Summer" had to wait another twenty-five years to be released. (The third "bonus" song is "The Game of Love," a tricky Latin tune by Shearing percussionist Armando Peraza that they were wise to leave off.)

Ralph Carmichael recalled one more incident that illustrated the camaraderie between himself, Nat, and George. (Incidentally, for those who may not know, this is a good place to mention that the late Shearing was blind.) "We were in the studio—it was the first date. And here again, Capitol had given me a few extra strings, because I asked for them. This was in the first twenty minutes or so, so Nat was not yet here. But George was sitting over at his piano. And George knows the layout of the studio—he knows where the mikes are, and how not to bump into things, and music stands, and all that. So we do this run through and the strings have a lot of stuff going on, and George is sitting a little bit behind me and to my right—probably a distance of twelve or fifteen feet. And we finish, and it's quiet in the studio. And I'm looking over at him and he's pushing his piano bench back, and he gets up and he shuffles over to me, puts his hand out, finds my shoulder, puts his face right up to my ear and he says, 'You're a son of a bitch!' That was his way of telling me he liked the chart! And then he turns around and shuffles back. That's the greatest compliment I ever had in my life!"

Nat King Cole Sings / George Shearing Plays was a milestone project in the careers of both stars. Shearing told me on several occasions that the one album he always wanted to make, but was never able to, was a collaboration with Sinatra. But of all the albums he actually did make, including team-ups with Peggy Lee, Nancy Wilson, Dakota Staton, Carmen McRae, Mel Tormé, and John Pizzarelli (*The Rare Delight of You*, 2002, which recreated the famous cover shot of the 1961 album), his favorite was *Cole / Shearing*.

"A Beautiful Friendship?" *Nat King Cole Sings / George Shearing Plays* was all that and much more.

THE LAST TWO MONTHS OF 1961 yielded two of Cole's all-time greatest albums, *Let's Face the Music* and *Cole / Shearing*. In the last five years of his career, his output was, more than ever, at a remarkably high level: there would be at least six undisputed masterpieces (*Live at the Sands, Wild Is Love, The Touch of Your Lips, Let's Face the Music, Cole / Shearing,* and *Where Did Everyone Go?*), as well as four near-classics (*Magic of Christmas, My Fair Lady, L-O-V-E,* and the uncategorizable *Nat King Cole Story*), and five more commercial releases that paid a lot of bills (*Ramblin' Rose* and the other two country albums, *Those Lazy-Hazy-Crazy Days of Summer*, and the final Spanish album, *Mas Cole Español*).

If the best news of 1961 had been the arrival of Timolin and Casey, his one regret was probably the falling out with Ed Sullivan. This wasn't necessarily for professional reasons; he would achieve his final three blockbuster hits, "Ramblin' Rose," "Those Lazy-Hazy-Crazy Days of Summer," and "L-O-V-E" without any help from Ed, and, in fact, with precious little support from television at all (although Sullivan surely would have been supportive in helping to promote *Wild Is Love* when it was finally broadcast on American TV). As Cole said in March, "Personally I can't knock Ed. He's a great guy. But professionally, I can, because he's not ... a real entertainer. Why, on his program once, he forgot Carmen McRae's name."[60] For a guy he was supposed to be feuding with, Nat had little to say about Sullivan that wasn't overwhelmingly positive, and he gave him credit for putting his taste where his money and his mouth were—the implication between the lines being that Sullivan was the first major TV impresario to regularly feature black entertainers and present them with the same respect and dignity as his white guests.

Sadly, Nat never did return to the famous CBS Studio 50, which would be renamed "The Ed Sullivan Theater" at the time of the twentieth anniversary of the show in 1967. However, less than a year after his death, on January 23, 1966, Maria Cole appeared on *Sullivan*, backed by her one-time employer Duke Ellington, and proceeded to give the performance of a lifetime on "'There Will Never Be Another You." This was truly the best she ever sounded. At forty-three, Maria looked fantastic and delivered the lyrics with amazing conviction and energy—something sadly lacking from her other extant performances. This was obviously because at this moment, those particular words rang so very true to her.

And she was right. There wouldn't be.

10

Requiem for a King

1962–1964

Some performers—like myself—have to be loud and rambunctious. But Nat was just Nat.
—SAMMY DAVIS JR.

IN NOVEMBER 1962, Nat King Cole starred in a live radio concert and conversation on WNEW Radio. By that time, radio had been relegated almost exclusively to the deejay format, and Cole hadn't sung on the radio in years. But the station's idea was to present something unique on the radio "lest it become a total waxworks."[1] The broadcast consisted of eight songs by Cole, with a full twenty-three-piece studio orchestra, and some highly convivial conversation between Cole and host (and New York broadcasting legend) William B. Williams. At one point, Williams asks Cole if he would consider singing one of the station's jingles; Cole consents, but, he says, half-kiddingly, only if Williams will also sing one. Williams, being a game guy, says he'll go along with it. We then hear the famous deejay and announcer squeaking out the words and the notes, more or less, to the jingle. As he finishes, the following dialogue transpires:

COLE: "You've got that husky sound, like I have. Keep working on it!"
WILLIAMS: "How do you mean that, keep working at it?"
COLE: "Keep smoking!"
WILLIAMS: "I got no place to go but up."
COLE: "Funny thing, if I ever cleared up my voice, I'd go out of business. That's why I keep smoking."

We hear this today and we cringe because we know that two and a half-years later, Cole would be dead, precisely from smoking too much. From the age of about thirteen or fourteen onward, Cole was almost never seen without a cigarette. Cruel as it seems to put it this way, Nat Cole earned his cancer; it did not just randomly strike the wrong guy. It seems especially unkind that he willfully entered into his addiction to cigarettes without being fully aware of the dangers it brought, and even more cruel that it struck him down at such a young age. Sammy Davis Jr., Cole's close friend, was such an unrepentant chain-smoker that even Sinatra, hardly one in a position to begrudge other people their unsavory habits, nicknamed him "Smokey the Bear." And yet fate let Sammy live another twenty years of his life expectancy, well beyond Nat.

As we've seen, during spring 1953, Cole was hit by an ulcer attack, which forced him to cancel a concert at Carnegie Hall on Easter Sunday and kept him out of work for most of the season. After he recovered, some friends, particularly Carlos Gastel, persuaded him that it might be better for his health if he started using a cigarette holder, and he went along with the idea. "One of his most familiar trademarks in recent years was a long ivory cigarette holder which dangled from his lips during performances in nightclubs and theaters."[2] Some stories claim that "he gradually tapered off and had quit smoking completely at the time he was stricken."[3] This seems unlikely, and there are later photos of him (including one with the young Bobby Darin) where he is shown smoking a pipe.

In early 1964, he told friend Ivan Mogull that he had given up cigarettes (Mogull credited this change to a certain new friend in Nat's life) and showed him his pipe to prove it.[4] It's not known whether using a cigarette holder or switching to a pipe helped, or even slowed the cancer at all. Longtime valet Sparky Tavares said that the holder would keep the cigarette constantly burning even when he wasn't actually smoking, causing him to go through many more cigarettes than he actually smoked. "He didn't smoke as much as people thought he did." But even if so, all those decades of constant use of tobacco products had long since taken their toll on a body that was already much weakened by ulcers.

IN THE EARLY MONTHS OF 1962, Cole wrapped up one series of albums and launched another. But first, he started the year, as usual, at the Sands, then went up to San Francisco and southeast to the Eden Roc in Miami. In March, he taped the third and last of the Spanish albums, *More Cole Español.* This time, the location was Mexico City, and the musical director was Ralph Carmichael, who refers to the album more properly as *Cole Español Mas.* He remembered that it was done in the afternoons while Cole was appearing at nights at the *El Senioral* nightclub. They had traveled down with "Jonesy" [Reunald Jones] on lead trumpet.[5] John Collins, Charlie Harris, and Lee Young were also there, but this trip was the final stop on the tour for Lee

Young. Never much of a diplomat, Young got into an argument with his boss during this trip and the two never spoke again. Cole replaced him with Leon Petties, a California modernist who had most recently been working with tenor saxophonist Harold Land (his good friend, the legendary Shelly Manne, who had played on *Cole / Shearing* encouraged him to take the gig with Nat).

In Rio, Cole had sung sambas and then the trip to Havana yielded mambos, thus the Mexico City sojourn found him making music in a mariachi manner—the album opens with a blast of mariachi trumpets and brass before Cole enters singing "La Feria De Las Flores," another of the seemingly endless parade of pan-American songs that concern themselves with flowers and/or birds—"La Golondrina" (The Swallow) follows soon.[6]

Nat's progress with languages other than English was proceeding apace. In a promotional interview distributed by Capitol, he said, "Whenever I appear anywhere, like recently when I was in Mexico City to make this last album, ninety percent of my act was all in Spanish, which they really got a great kick out of."[7] He then adds that he learned to speak the language "by singing it. When I first made the first album, I was singing it phonetically. You know, it's not an easy language to sing, particularly with so many vowels in their words, that you have to get all in one note! But after I got into the feel of it, and as I got more used to the pronunciation, I began to learn it and also to learn more about what I was singing about."

The faster numbers here are in traditional Mexican dancing tempos, such as the rousing "Guadalajara" (familiar to North Americans via Xavier Cugat and Desi Arnaz) and "Las Chiapanecas" (known in English as "While There's Music, There's Romance"), which customarily accompanies the famous Mexican Hat Dance. Yet Cole is even more of a lover than he is a dancer, and the most memorable numbers are the ballads, "Tres Palabras" (Without You) and Augustine Lara's "Solamente Una Vez" (You Belong to My Heart), both of which became popular in the States in the years of President Roosevelt's good-neighbor policy. "Vaya Con Dios" (May God Be with You) had been a hit ten years after that, in a multi-tracked novelty single by Les Paul and Mary Ford.

On the whole, the pickings are slimmer here than on the Havana and Rio journeys—Mexico had less of an impact on North American pop and, probably because of publishing reasons, several of the more famous south-of-the-border songs are not included. Cole does not do "Besame Mucho," which he had sung with the Trio on a MacGregor transcription in 1944 but never in a commercial recording, or "Granada," by Augustine Lara, the author of "You Belong to My

Heart." Also, one of the most appealing tunes got in here under somewhat false pretenses: Bobby Capo's "Piel Canela" (Cinnamon Skin) had been used as the title theme for a Mexican movie in 1953 (and also famously recorded by Eydie Gormé), but is strictly Cuban salsa, not at all Mexican mariachi.

Cole sings very well throughout, particularly on the slower pieces like the gently undulating "No Me Platiques" which he and "Edith Bergdahl" (Gillette) were able to copyright. This is one of two numbers in which Cole is backed up by a small Mexican choir, or perhaps a quartet. But in terms of Carmichael's arrangements, the results are not on the level of several earlier charts that Carmichael wrote for Cole when he was really trying: the classic Brazilian song "Poinciana" on *The Touch of Your Lips* (1961) and Leroy Anderson's pan-American-styled "Serenata" on *Nat King Cole Sings / George Shearing Plays* (1962). These are both unbelievably lush and stupefyingly beautiful; if everything—or, indeed, anything—on *More Cole Español* had been this good, the album would be a masterpiece.

For Cole's next side trip, he would travel (at least metaphorically) to a locale possibly even more remote to him than Havana, Rio, or Ciudad de México: Nashville, Tennessee.

THERE WERE SEVERAL CHANGES on his spring tours: Cuba was now no longer a stop on the road, to say the least, but, following Mexico City, he played the El San Juan Hotel in Puerto Rico and then the Cat and the Fiddle in Nassau. The Chez Paree had closed in 1960, and Cole did his first gig in Chicago since 1959 when he played the Palmer House from March to April 1962; along the way, he opened the season at Comiskey Park on April 10. He then sang the National Anthem again two weeks later at the opening of the Cassius Clay–Sonny Liston fight; apparently with no lyric malfunctions. (He also sang in church at an Easter Sunday service that same month, so perhaps God was being kind.)

While he managed to conquer "The Star-Spangled Banner," he still couldn't get beyond the bigotry that dogged him and his family even as he extended his royal reign as one of the most popular entertainers on the planet. In 1958 and then again in 1960, Gastel had booked him into the Masonic Lodge in San Francisco; on both occasions, the management at first agreed, but then changed their mind and canceled. There was only one obvious reason they decided that they didn't want Cole, but when it happened in 1960, he did better by booking the San Francisco Civic Auditorium instead; it was twice as big and considerably less expensive.[8] Around 1961 or '62, the Coles were staying in New York, at a posh luxury hotel, when Johnny Burke brought his kids Rory and Kevin to visit; the Burkes were surprised to learn that Nat had been forced to rent not just a single suite but the entire floor. The assumption was that no white guest wanted to stay next door to a black couple, even a beloved celebrity.[9]

It was because of both the inconvenience and the expense of such incidents that the Coles decided to acquire a condo in Lincoln Towers, a new luxury complex in Midtown west, so named because it was around the corner from where the New York's forthcoming performing arts compound, Lincoln Center, was then being constructed. By a coincidence, his friend, the composer Joe Sherman, also had an apartment in the same building, undoubtedly subsidized by all the hit songs he had already written for Cole. The area would soon become ground zero for the high arts: opera, ballet, the symphony, and "legitimate" theater. It was thus an unlikely neighborhood to give birth to one of the biggest country-and-western (C&W) hit songs of the era.

One day, Joe's most frequent collaborator, his brother Noel, came over with the idea for a new song. "So, he came up and we wrote it," said Joe, "If I tell you it took 18 minutes, it was a long time! If you note the song, there are just three stanzas to it—no bridge. The next evening, we were at Noel's place writing, and Nat called us. 'Hey, I'm going to California tomorrow and there's one side open.' In those days, we used to do four sides on a session." The two brothers then argued about whether or not to show him their new work; Noel was for, Joe was against. "I couldn't see it at first. 'Ramblin' Rose' isn't for Nat Cole for Christ sakes! Nat's not gonna do that. Nat has strings with Nelson Riddle, it's 'Nature Boy,' 'Mona Lisa.' You're not gonna show that to him. We don't really have anything." Noel said, "I'd like to just throw it at him."[10]

They played the song for Cole, but he seemed only mildly interested. They had no lead sheet that he could take with him, so Joe quickly wrote out something while Nat waited. "He said, 'Listen, if I have fifteen minutes left over at the end of the session, maybe I'll do it as a simple thing, and I can just try it for you. Let me fool with it.'" Cole himself told a slightly different story of how the song reached him. "Sometimes the more you want a hit, the harder it is to get one. Jackie Gale, who runs my publishing firms, brought 'Ramblin' Rose' to the coast, I'll admit I wasn't too excited about it. I could have blown it. But we cut it and you know the rest. Joe and Noel Sherman wrote a good song and a good song always has a chance."[11]

After Cole tried it out at that session, he and Gillette began to get a sense of the potential commercial appeal of "Ramblin' Rose." He seems to have recorded some sort of test arrangement with Ralph Carmichael, but by then they had decided to shoot for the moon, which meant bringing in the single most "commercial" arranger they could think of—and that was Belford Hendricks. Even his name was imposing.

Ten years older than Cole, Hendricks was already one of the leading musical directors of R&B as it transitioned into Soul music and true mainstream popularity in the 1960s. Among his bigger successes were revitalizing the commercial potential of the great Dinah Washington and pretty much the entire career of his frequent writing partner, soul crooner Brook Benton. He and Cole had circled each other a lot around 1957, but Hendricks had not yet actually worked as musical director on a Cole session.

They now knew well what they had and were working toward a whole album with a new sound that would combine elements of country, pop music, and R&B. (Unlike Ray Charles's roughly concurrent experiments, there was relatively little of what might be considered jazz.) The first session with Hendricks occurred on June 19 and began with "Dear Lonely Hearts," which would become the title of the second Cole "country" album. Then, after "Rose" they tackled another song in the same vein, "Nothing Goes Up (Without Coming Down)," also released as a single (but, strangely, not included in any of either of the two country and western albums by Cole and Hendricks). Then, there were two distinctly youth-pop numbers, "The Good Times" and "Who's Next in Line?" Interestingly, the quasi-country songs represent just about the best work Hendricks ever did, whereas the two R&B-style tunes, particularly, are probably the worst. "The Good Times" is a likely candidate for the title of the all-time worst song recorded by Cole—this is Brill Building tripe at its most excruciatingly annoying. Yet, according to Sherman, "The Good Times" was originally the A side of the 45 single before "Ramblin' Rose" "broke out" in Philadelphia.

This idea of a rose that rambles is one of the more persistent icons in popular music; there are at least three previous songs that have those two words in the title, including a 1948 Perry Como hit by Joseph McCarthy and Joe Burke. But the Sherman Brothers' song is the only one that has entered the cultural bloodstream—and it's easy to see why. Lyricist Noel Sherman conceived of a song with folkish simplicity, an AAA structure with three 8-bar choruses. As Joe points out, there's no bridge; however, while the first and last A sections both begin with the title "hook" phrase, the second A does not. Cole also sings it somewhat more quietly than the first and last (another arranger might have put the second A in a different key, but Hendricks does not) so the overall effect is to make the second A into a more passive section that feels vaguely like a bridge.

When Cole finishes the first chorus, that's when the song really kicks into high gear. Up to now, he's been singing with a big choir close behind him, but in the last minute, Cole calls out the instruction "One more time, everybody now!" And all of a sudden, the appeal of the song becomes clear. Cole is tapping into the early '60s mania for singalong records, the legacy of Mitch Miller and his long-running *Singalong with Mitch* franchise, which manifested itself in best-selling albums as well as a long-running TV series. The Singalong album era lasted nearly a decade and coincided with the folkie boom of the early '60s, when Pete Seeger led the world in singing old-time traditional favorites—in fact, no one was supposed to actually *listen* to folk music; they were supposed to sing along with it. The ease of performing this music was one of its most salable features. (It was a long way from "Lush Life.")

Other artists took advantage of the singalong trend, notably Bing Crosby (and even Mickey Katz). But no other individual artist parlayed it into blockbuster success on the level of Cole and "Ramblin' Rose"—and then possibly even more so with "Lazy-Hazy-Crazy Days of Summer." After it caught on, Cole made "Rose" into even more of a singalong in his live concert appearances; he doesn't just wait for the out chorus to get the crowd singing with him, he energetically encourages the audience to join him from the first note, and he even feeds them the lyrics one line at a time in a method that Gospel singers call "outlining." At a show in Fresno, 1963, the crowd enjoyed singing the song so much that Cole had to reprise it twice.

Cole and crew put all these ideas together on the same plate: the big choir, the singalong feel, the "country-politan" sound, a few favorite C&W songs (including the Jim Reeves hit "He'll Have to Go" and the 1948 "One Has My Name"), and several 1920s pop songs, which had been around so long that they practically felt like traditional folk airs—especially "When You're Smiling."[12]

One night about midnight, a month or so after the Sherman brothers had last seen Cole, Joe got a phone call from the West Coast: it was Nat, playing his new track on the song for him. "And I said, 'Oh my God!' And I'm listening to this thing and Nat gets on and he says, 'What do you think?' I said, 'Nat, my God, it's different.' He said 'I know. Everybody loves it here. Maybe we'll see what happens.'" At this point, it became a familiar tale in pop music annals; what had been intended as the B-side of a single was embraced by disc jockeys and became the song that everyone wanted to hear.[13]

Sherman reports that he was driving near Philadelphia a short while later, when he happened to turn on local radio station WDAS. "And all of a sudden, I hear the voice of Georgie Woods, the biggest black deejay in Philly. And

Georgie says 'Now I'd like to play Nat Cole's next song. It's his new release. It's a fantastic song, but I'm not going to play this song for you first. I'm going to recite the lyric, and then I'm going to play it for you.' I wondered, 'What the hell?' He says 'Ramblin' Rose, Ramblin' Rose, why you wander, no one knows.' I thought I was gonna go off the highway! He recites the lyric, and then he plays the song. The next thing, he breaks it wide open in Philadelphia. And I got a call from an old song-plugger friend of mine [Pete Bennett][14] who called me about a week later and he said, 'Joe, you got a number one hit. The big station in Detroit that beams from Detroit right through down to Mississippi, all the way down South, it's popping up all over different playlists, going into country music.'" Cole himself pointed out that the song was a bonanza for him as a publisher as much as a performer. "With 'Ramblin' Rose,' we were sure enough of the tune to send out 75,000 unreturnable copies of the sheet music."[15]

By this point, Cole and Gillette were well on their way to building an album around the song. Surprisingly, it included only two sides from the June date (including, alas, "The Good Times") and ten tracks recorded over what was officially registered with the AFM as two sessions on August 11, 11:00 a.m. to 2:30 p.m., and then from 3:00 to 6:30 p.m.. The repertoire was deliberately diverse: Cole did classic country songs like Hank Williams's "Your Cheatin' Heart" (done in a manner completely different from his swinging treatment of "Cold, Cold Heart" on *Let's Face the Music*) as well as the fundamental folk song "Goodnight Irene" (credited to Leadbelly, popularized by Pete Seeger and the Weavers). The ancient nursery rhyme "Skip to My Lou" is slowed down into a somewhat melancholy square dance. The rather bloodthirsty "Wolverton Mountain" had recently been adapted from a folk source into a chart hit by C&W star Claude King. "Twilight on the Trail" is a Billy Hill–like Tin Pan Alley concoction retrofitted to sound like a traditional cowboy song, which Cole croons very sweetly.

Cole reserved two spots for brand-new songs, and he handed them out to old friends as a kind of Christmas in August. The Brothers Sherman were given another spot on the album that was already destined to make them zillionaires, and they gave him "I Don't Want It That Way." "It had a country feel," remembered Joe. "We thought maybe Nat would be interested. It wasn't an important song, but I think it's a nice song."

The other was just about the best song in the entire NKC / C&W series: Johnny Burke's "Sing Another Song (And We'll All Go Home)." There are good moments on these albums, and more than a share of bad ones; in fact, the first album concludes with the two most extreme tracks, the thoroughly mediocre "Good Times" followed by the beautiful "Sing Another Song," which allows the set to end with a genuinely profound moment. The titular opener, "Ramblin' Rose," paints mental images of Cole entertaining his friends and leading a singalong at a party, but the closer "Sing Another Song" completes the narrative. Cole is still at that party or bar, possibly playing piano, but it's getting to be time for the last call. "You're such a swell bunch of friends," he tells them. As the party begins to wind down, it becomes clear that the reason our hero is so extroverted and gregarious is because he's trying to hide a broken heart—there's a faint touch of "One for My Baby" amid all this merry-making. This takes us deep into the territory of country heartbreak, on a par with the best of Merle Haggard or Willie Nelson. It's also very nearly the last song Cole would sing by his dear friend and favorite Irish poet; Burke would die roughly a year before Cole, in February 1964. "Sing Another Song" doesn't quite conclude the relationship, but it winds up the album on a suitably bittersweet note.

The single would reach number two on the general pop chart, making it Cole's biggest hit of his final years, even more than "Lazy-Hazy-Crazy Days of Summer" in 1963 or "L-O-V-E" in 1965.[16] The album would make it to #3. By then, Cole and Gillette were already thinking about a second album. The song "Dear Lonely Hearts" was recorded at the same date as "Ramblin' Rose," immediately before the Sherman Brothers' opus. Cole and Gillette could have easily included it on the *Ramblin' Rose* LP, but apparently they realized that the song had "juice" enough to support an LP of its own. They taped the rest of the *Dear Lonely Hearts* package in two dates in November—another ten songs plus a couple of bonus items.

Surprisingly, none of the ten songs from November (on the *Dear Lonely Hearts* album) are country classics or even country- or folk-oriented; rather, virtually all were written by Tin Pan Alley professionals of the 1920s. Yet nearly none of them quite qualify as well-known standards; apparently, they were just vintage numbers that Cole liked, possibly remembered from his childhood, which he decided might work in terms of this quasi-country treatment. He also was repeating a lot of the same songwriters: there are three tunes by Benny Davis ("Oh How I Miss You Tonight," "Lonesome and Sorry" and "Yearning"), another three by either Harry or Charlie Tobias ("Miss You," "All Over the World," and "It's a Lonesome Old Town"), and two by Joe Burke ("Oh How I Miss You Tonight" and "Yearning"). (All of this indicates that Gillette had made some sort of a deal with the publishers.)

"Oh, How I Miss You Tonight" had been done by Sinatra that same year (on his *All Alone* album) with an even stronger waltz feeling, and Sinatra had also established "It's a Lonesome Old Town" as an all-time standard on *Only the Lonely*. "Why Should I Cry over You?" had also been revived by Sinatra as a swinging single with Riddle. But apart from these, the only tune that was revived with any regularity was Irving Berlin's "All by Myself. The least C&W-oriented is "My First and Only Lover," a hideous track with pizzicato electric guitars making chicken noises; this is the second album's answer to "The Good Times" on the first—another nadir.

There are more songs in 3/4 time here than on any other Cole album, even though the country settings make it clear that this is not the waltz time of Johann Strauss, or Richard Rodgers, or even Ray Charles. "All over the World," a new song by Charlie Tobias and Al Frisch, is a fairly clever piece of pop, with Cole and the choir singing contrapuntal choruses around each other (sort of like Berlin's "You're Just in Love") and it is the "least" lonely tune in the package. Cole and singers conjure up images of picnickers around a campfire, and it's a sort of prequel to Tobias's impending mega-hit with Cole, the lazy hazy crazy one. "Near You" is also comparatively cheerful, this being a country-ish tune that originated with a cocktail-style pianist in Nashville and later went on to serve as the theme song for Milton Berle.

The best song is probably the title, "Dear Lonely Hearts" (which was published with the subtitle "I'm Writing to You"), because here at least the quasi-country treatment fits the material. Yet the *Dear Lonely Hearts* album somehow seems like old news after "Ramblin' Rose"; even though the songs are frequently better here, the album seems like an afterthought—there's nothing on it as engaging as "Sing Another Song." Cole sang "Lonely Hearts" much more convincingly on an Australian TV appearance from 1963, in which he delivers it from the piano, accompanying himself in what seems like a mixture of his familiar jazz technique and the Nashville-oriented "slipnote" style keyboard. (This is one of many instances when a surviving live performance of a song is considerably more compelling than the studio version.)

Two bonus items also exist from the *Lonely Hearts* sessions, one of which was eventually issued, and the other not—with good reason. This is a bizarre German language overdub to "All over the World," with an unidentified female singer (probably Evangeline "Vangie" Carmichael, Ralph's wife) instead of Cole. Capitol apparently wanted Cole to sing it in German but waited too long. Cole sang a thirteenth song at the November dates, "Misery Loves Company," still another sad waltz, by the Georgia-born Jerry Reed, who would later write the Elvis Presley signature "Guitar Man." It was arranged for

Cole by his regular road conductor, Joe Zito, and included on the last date. Cole and Gillette elected not to include it on the *Dear Lonely Hearts* album (it remained unissued until 2006); perhaps they felt it was just *too* country.

THUS, COLE MORE OR LESS RECORDED the first two country albums, *Ramblin' Rose* and *Dear Lonely Hearts*, in rapid succession and, in some cases, at the same sessions. But this was hardly all that was happening in his life and career. He chose September to celebrate his twenty-fifth anniversary in show business (using the formation of the King Cole Trio in 1937 as a point of demarcation); there was a gala dinner at the Ambassador in August as well as celebratory articles in *Billboard* and elsewhere. But perhaps the most important move Cole made at this time was to record his final undisputed masterpiece, *Where Did Everyone Go?*

Arranged and conducted by Gordon Jenkins, *Where Did Everyone Go?* begins with the title song, which is perfectly logical, and it ends, rather literally, with another lesser-known song, "That's All There Is," by Jenkins himself. But it's also informative to listen to the album in the sequence in which it was originally recorded (which is much easier to do in the digital age). Cole ended, rather than began, the sessions with "Where Did Everyone Go?" It was the key song on the album, and perhaps he elected to save it for last because he wanted to wait until he was good and ready to sing it. Cole was biting off a lot on those two sessions—a total of fourteen songs, which was almost twice the union rule, and further, he was doing both in August, at the same moment when he was in the middle of a ten-night run at the Greek Theater. Ordinarily, he might have been afraid he would sound tired on the last tune of the date, but on the song "Where Did Everyone Go?" a certain amount of weariness (world-weariness and otherwise) was perfectly appropriate to the material.

The song he chose to begin the album date with is equally interesting: after warming up with a couple of singles, he launched into "When the World Was Young." He had already given the world the most famous recording of "Autumn Leaves," and now, here was Johnny Mercer's other great English adaptation of a classic French song.

What does this tell us—that he begins with "When the World Was Young" and ends with "Where Did Everyone Go?" Both of these songs, as well as many others on this amazing album, employ the dramatic conceit of time shifting, having a protagonist in the present looking back at the past and evoking a comparison. Such things are part of the very nature of torch songs: she used to be here with me, but now she's gone.

More specifically, the narratives behind these two songs reflect on each other like distorted images in a funhouse mirror, making it not surprising that Cole would bookend the sessions with them. "When the World Was Young" is about the loss of innocence, and "Where Did Everyone Go?" is about the loss of, well, practically everything—wealth, fame, emotional stability, and, not incidentally, love.

Because "When the World Was Young" was based on a French original, it doesn't use the familiar Tin Pan Alley AABA structure but rather a verse-chorus setup of ABABAB. In Mercer's lyric, the A's and the B's have a very distinct meaning: the A's tell the story of our hero and the *distingue*, sophisticated life he lives right now in the present tense, and how his nights consist of endless rounds of smoking, drinking, and carousing. The melody for these A sections are very tense and staccato—very minor. Contrastingly, the B sections are much more major, in which the jaded boulevardier reminisces about his bucolic childhood, his salad days of innocence in the French countryside, and the melody here is much more legato and flowing. It's as if Mercer and the original French authors (Angela Vannier and M. Phillipe-Gerard) have created a single great song by taking two other tunes, not exactly forging them together, but alternating between the two, to heighten the contrast between the then and the now.

The title song "Where Did Everyone Go?" is a milestone in the careers of both Nat King Cole and composer Jimmy Van Heusen, one of the very few he wrote with Tin Pan Alley veteran Mack David. Presumably, David (whose younger brother was the even more successful lyricist Hal David) came up with the idea of this Sinatra-style saloon song and decided that Van Heusen was the perfect guy to write the music. If so, he was right. Introduced by Cole on *The Dinah Shore Show* on December 29, 1961, in an orchestration considerably less grandiose than the one he would record for the album (eight months later), it was a suitably melancholy song for New Year's Eve.[17] "Where Did Everyone Go?" derives solidly from the tradition of the great Sinatra saloon soliloquies as well as the classic blues, such as Bessie Smith's "Nobody Knows You When You're Down and Out"; Cole's 1947 "That's a Natural Fact" also draws on both traditions. The speaker begins by informing us, "It wasn't my intention to eavesdrop"; with the best of such songs, the listener always has to feel that he's hearing something so extremely personal he wasn't supposed to hear it at all.

After we are introduced to the character sitting two stools away, he tells us, in essence, that it's a natural fact that nobody knows him now that he's down and out. But he used to be on top, you see; he had friends and flunkies following him around; he was the center of all attention, treating everyone to champagne and caviar, and tipping the hat-check girl with fifty-dollar bills. David's lyric almost seems inspired by Sammy Davis Jr.'s famous description of Sinatra during his "big nosedive" period in the early '50s, walking around Times Square by himself. The structure is essentially AABA, but the last A has a special tag, so it could be given as AABA'. Although "Where Did Everyone Go?" does not have two intertwined tunes, like "When the World Was Young," the tone constantly modulates emotionally: the verse is deliberately neutral, but this is contrasted by the first two A sections, which are almost comic in their over-the-top descriptions of our hero talking about his money and how he used to spend it.

This mood shifts once again in the bridge, where he starts reminiscing about "the beautiful girl" he once had: here the song starts to assume the melancholy character of a torch song. In the final A, and especially the tag, the speaker is fighting back tears, and the song is no longer serio-comic or even torchy, just overwhelmingly sad. He doesn't want to know what happened to his money or even his girl; he just wonders aloud, "Where did everyone go?"—emphasis on the "everyone." It's not any one person or any one thing; it's everyone and everything that has deserted him and broken his heart. Like the protagonist's life, the song has gone from way over the top to stark and simple. No wonder Cole wanted to start the album with this song; he wanted to catch us by surprise with its devastatingly defeatist ending, and placing any one of the other sad songs before it might have lessened its impact.

Thus, like "When the World Was Young," "Where Did Everyone Go?" is also about the contrast between earlier, happier times (whether they were more innocent or more licentious), and the harsh realities of the present. In that sense, both were perfect songs for 1962. The world was changing, and Cole was well-nigh changing with it. Although no one did jazz and Broadway-based standards better than he, the King was in step with changing times and had hits that were solidly in the increasingly profitable "and" genres of pop music: rhythm-*and*-blues, country-*and*-western, rock-*and*-roll. But he would keep making "art" records, like *Where Did Everyone Go?*, which was recorded, essentially, between the first two country albums and shortly before *Those Lazy-Hazy-Crazy Days of Summer*.

Where Did Everyone Go? was the last and, in many ways, the best of Cole's series of romantic albums with Gordon Jenkins, who created another pinnacle achievement that same year, Sinatra's *All Alone*. The Maestro's high style is most impressive on Rodgers and Hart's ironic and melancholy "Spring Is Here," the second tune recorded and the second-to-last tune on the finished

LP. Here's a masterful example of the Jenkins sound at its most epically *Grand Guignol*, with some twenty-five string players from the Los Angeles local sawing away in his dramatically over-the-top patterns of major-into-minor and back again.

Alas, *Where Did Everyone Go?* is by far the least known of the three main Jenkins-Cole projects.[18] This 1962 album didn't have any "breakout" song, like "For All We Know," "When I Fall in Love," or "Stardust"—a track which, while not exactly becoming a chart hit, had a life well beyond the album itself. In fact, it's probably because the album works so well as a coherent whole that it's hard to imagine listening to just one track from it—you have to hear the whole thing in toto, start to finish. For this and other reasons, *Where Did Everyone Go?* is overall the best of the three. Not that it's necessarily "better" to be dark and serious all the time, but where the first two packages are lighter and more optimistic—about the nature of falling in love and being in love—the 1962 album is about the aftermath, and therefore, cuts much deeper. The protagonist of virtually every song on *Where Did Everyone Go?* is fixed in a state of shock and denial.

In 1969, the psychologist Elizabeth Kubler-Ross published her widely accepted theory of the five stages of grief, but Irving Berlin and other songwriters had already crystallized some of those exact same sentiments into tangible musical form many years earlier. Berlin's "Say It Isn't So" (previously, that phrase had been most closely associated with the World Series scandal of 1919) offers a virtual textbook illustration of the Kubler-Ross state of "denial": please tell me this isn't really happening. Likewise, the bridge to Johnny Burke's "If Love Ain't There" is an archetypical example of what Kubler-Ross described as "bargaining": "And you can look / With a longing in your look, / And try every method in the book / And worship the smile / that kind of took you unaware." Then, fittingly, the final A section illustrates the stage of "anger," "depression" and "acceptance": "And you can weep and sigh, / You can say, 'Unfair.' / You can almost die of despair. / But if love ain't there, It ain't there."

"No, I Don't Want Her" is by Joe Bailey, a little-known singer-songwriter-pianist briefly championed by Cole in this period.[19](Cole also recorded his "How I'd Love to Love You" on the *L-O-V-E* album two years later.) Bailey's song takes its cue from another Berlin ballad, the more ironically comic "You Can Have Him, I Don't Want Him" (from *Miss Liberty*) in exploring what Kubler-Ross might call "the stage of sour grapes"—in other words, pretending you don't want something you know you can't have.

"Am I Blue?" is a classic song in the African American experience, written for Ethel Waters in the early talkie musical *On with the Show* (1929). It's a torch song imbued with elements of the blues, and Jenkins's ornate strings give it a distinct symphonic component as well. "The End of a Love Affair" is the sole song of note by one Edward C. Redding, an acquaintance of the cabaret chanteuse Mabel Mercer who penned this one outstanding song, already immortalized by Sinatra. "Laughing on the Outside," is, contrastingly, *not* a classic song. It was a 1946 hit for Dinah Shore by a second- or third-tier songwriter named Bernie Wayne, whom few would place in the Berlin-Rodgers-Van Heusen class. "Laughing" is a brilliant example of Cole and Jenkins, taking a grade-B song and upgrading it into a grade-A piece of artistry.

Yet "Someone to Tell It To" marks an even greater illustration of how interpretation and context can completely change the meaning of a song. This was a three-way collaboration between Van Heusen, Cahn, and an even more surprising third collaborator, one-time B-movie queen Dolores Fuller who by then was best known as a composer of special material for Elvis movies (the most successful being "Rock-a-Hula Baby").[20] Cole had recorded "Someone to Tell It To," in 1960, but the Jenkins arrangement is half a minute longer and many shades darker. In Ralph Carmichael's more cheerful arrangement, Cole makes you feel like the rainbows, plans and dreams, castles in air are all wonderful and beautiful because you have someone to tell it to; in the Jenkins chart, you feel like the whole works are useless, empty and bare, the moonlight is merely moonlight, there's no magic in "I love you," because you're all alone and have no one to share them with. It's the same song, the same singer, the same lyrics, even the same medium slow tempo, but it now seems like the saddest thing in the world. The 1962 treatment could be re-titled "No One to Tell It To." Jenkins himself chimed in with the very worthy "That's All There Is," a song of farewell and futility in the same vein as his more famous "Goodbye." "That's All There Is" had been introduced by Judy Garland as part of one of Jenkins's lesser works, *The Letter* (1959), and it serves as a fitting closer here.

Fisher and Segal contributed what is probably the best song on the album (at least neck and neck with the title track), the devastatingly beautiful "I Keep Going Back to Joe's." Where both "When the World Was Young" and "Where Did Everyone Go?" are comparatively complex narratives, "Joe's" is fairly straightforward; Segal's text (and Cole's interpretation) are as subtle and understated as Jenkins's orchestration is elaborate. The idea of a waiter setting a place for someone who isn't there is both morbid and pathetic—and just the opposite of what the protagonist of "Dinner for One, Please, James" asks of his servant (even though at the end of that song, he confesses that he can't bear to move the "favorite flowers" of his absent beloved). As with "Angel Eyes" and "One for My Baby" it's what the lyricist leaves out that tells the story: why did she leave him? Where did she go? We are never told. We only see that he's trapped in a set routine, like some kind of Freudian obsessive, "sippin' wine and starin' at the door," knowing full well that she'll "never show" (Segal's use of such colloquiums is singularly effective)—he seems to be in the "denial" and the "acceptance" stages at the same time. The simpler the song gets, the more profound it seems.

George Shearing told me that this was his all-time favorite song of Nat's. "I've loved 'I Keep Going Back to Joe's' for so many years, ever since I heard Nat do it," he told me. "Now, I do that song myself on my shows. *I* sing that baby!"

(At the start of the first session, Cole recorded two sad songs, "Farewell to Arms" by Allie Wrubel and Abner Silver, and Jenkins's own "Happy New Year." They're in a similar mood but don't belong on the *Where Did Everyone Go* project; the orchestrations are slightly different, and both make use of a background chorus, but the two songs aren't nearly up to the other twelve cuts that were used.)

Even more than *Face the Music, Where Did Everyone Go?* alas became one of Cole's most woefully underappreciated projects. Perhaps the cover has always been part of the problem: it would have been obvious and logical to have a cover shot of Cole nursing a drink in a bar, much like Sinatra on *No One Cares* or Nat's own *Just One of Those Things*. Instead, the cover showed Cole standing by himself in an underground parking garage—certainly all alone, perhaps wondering where everyone went, but hardly seeming like he was completely deserted. The song is about someone abandoned by friends, lovers, family; the photo makes him look like a guy looking for his Uber.

Where Did Everyone Go? is a towering achievement, one of the all-time great pop vocal albums. It was a milestone for a man who never set out to be a singer, who started his singing career with no more ambition than to tell us we should hit that jive, jack and / or straighten up and fly right. The album still serves as an antidote to those who think the final part of Cole's career was devoted exclusively to roses that rambled and the charms of pretzels and beer in the sweaty summertime.

AFTER THE FIRST TWO COUNTRY ALBUMS, Nat's big hit of 1963 would be a different kind of "Americana," one that had actually originated in Germany. He would spend the winter and spring of the new year far away from home, for his most far-flung, longest overseas tour yet. After playing the Hacienda in

Fresno (a recording survives) and then Harrah's in Lake Tahoe, he took off to spend the whole of February in Australia and the Far East.

The first stop was the Chevron Hilton in Sydney, and on February 15, he starred on the *The Mobil Limb Show*, on which he does comedy bits and patter with hosts Bobby Limb and Dawn Lake but also gets plenty of time on his own—more than on any American variety show. His opening ballad is "When I Fall in Love," followed by the spectacularly swinging Billy May chart of "I'm Gonna Sit Right Down and Write Myself a Letter" (from the yet unreleased *Face the Music* album) and a surprisingly satisfying trio version of Burke and Van Heusen's "Imagination" with Lake singing and Limb on tenor saxophone.

There's also excellent footage of Cole doing his "To the Ends of the Earth" travel medley, heard on several later concerts (including "Darling, Je Vous Aime Beaucoup," "Non Dimenticar," and "Acercate Mas"). The highlight is a "piano segment," wherein he plays "Where or When" (even better here than at the Sands) and "Dear Lonely Hearts," the latter in a Nashville-esque piano style à la Floyd Cramer. This live TV version is a major improvement on the studio recording and is easily Cole's most satisfying performance in the country idiom. And in Australia, no less.

A few days later, he arrived in Tokyo, where he played a concert venue (Sankei Hall) and a nightclub. This was the Latin Quarter (inspired by the earlier, so-named establishments in Paris and New York), which gave us the most valuable audio document of his tours at this time.[21] From the acoustics of the tape, this was not an intimate club, but a biggish Copa or Vegas-sized venue, with a full big band. Taped live on February 22, 1963, the recording features mostly the same mixture that we know from his American concerts like *The Sands*. There are hits ("Unforgettable," "Too Young," "Ramblin' Rose") and standards ("The Way You Look Tonight," "And the Angels Sing," two swing era classics he was singing in these years that he never recorded, both arranged by a young orchestrator new to his fold, Charlie Albertine), and signatures ("Stardust"). More than the *Sands* album of three years earlier, there's a generous sampling of world music: the classic French chanson, "Les Feuilles mortes" done in English ("Autumn Leaves") as well as Japanese ("Kareha"). Among the gems of both Japanese performances (as with his 1961 Tokyo TV concert) are four Spanish numbers. He's literally on fire in "Cachito," and makes his earlier studio versions (on *Cole Español*) sound tepid and tentative by comparison. "Quizás, Quizás, Quizás," now even boasts a new piano interlude by Cole. The Latin Quarter performance also features a wonderful piano/Trio segment, highlighted by a special arrangement of "It's Only a

Paper Moon" that combines the original Trio arrangement with big-band accompaniment. The performance ends with "Love Is a Many-Splendored Thing," done in English and Japanese.

In Korea, he sang the local folk ballad "Arirang" in that country's language, which is a fitting counterpart to the Filipino love song "Dahil Sa Yo" in Tagalog (which survives from a May 1961 appearance at the Araneta Coliseum, Manila). On the way back home, he stopped off in Honolulu and then did two weeks at the San Juan Hotel in Puerto Rico, at which point he and Maria celebrated their fifteenth anniversary; it was several months early, but by now there were chasms in the relationship, and this was among the last occasions we know of when Nat and Maria spent any meaningful time together. He then spent April and May first at the Sands and then the Coconut Grove, and, in the daytime, returned to the Capitol Tower to cut some singles and a new album.

WHETHER HEARD ON A 45 OR AN LP, "Those Lazy-Hazy-Crazy Days of Summer" is, perhaps (even more than "Ramblin' Rose") the Cole single that most of his professional associates took the greatest pains to distance themselves from. Alan Livingston, who was, at the time, president of Capitol Records, wanted to make it clear to me that these songs were in no way something that the label forced on their top-selling artist (meaning in the way that Mitch Miller pressured Sinatra to sing "Mama Will Bark"). In fact, Livingston distinctly mentioned that "Those Lazy-Hazy-Crazy Days of Summer" was the kind of song "that ordinarily we [meaning the Capitol A&R staff] would not have picked." Dick LaPalm also reported, "I told Nat I didn't want to work on 'Ramblin' Rose' and 'Lazy-Hazy-Crazy' and he laughed, he said it was okay; it didn't affect our friendship."

So, you have to admire Ralph Carmichael, the man who arranged the song for Cole: he admitted that it wasn't his "favorite kind of song" but at the same time refused to disavow his own work. He even tells a tale about how the song has, even from the beginning, succeeded in pleasing a large segment of the population while, at the same time, grating on the ears of everyone else. One afternoon, Ralph and trombonist Kenny Shroyer were hanging out at the Spotlight, a local bar frequented by musicians, but at this particular moment, about 3:00 p.m., the place was empty except for the two of them plus one patron who kept playing "Lazy-Hazy-Crazy Days of Summer" over and over, dropping in one dime after another. The two of them are trying to talk over the record, and, as Ralph remembered, "Now I can tell that Kenny's a little irritated." After a few more plays, "Kenny hits the bar and says, 'If I could find the son-of-a-bitch that wrote that chart, I'd kill him!' So, I put my hand out and said 'Kenny, you're meeting him right now.' "

As it happens, I personally think both "Ramblin' Rose" and "Those Lazy, Hazy-Crazy-Days of Summer" get something of a bum rap—I would rather listen to those songs and albums than the worst of the 1958–59 *Looking Back* material. Something about these two late career projects tends to stick in people's craw; perhaps it was because Cole had now gotten as far away from his roots as a jazz pianist as possible. What could be more Anglo than country and western music? What could be less Afro than the cover of *Lazy-Hazy-Crazy*, which shows a jolly party of Caucasians, consisting of four youngish couples, frolicking on the beach? (The only hint of cultural diversity here is a Chinese kite.)

Lazy-Hazy-Crazy, the album, depicts a mythic good old summertime that was more or less invented by Hollywood and popular culture. Few if any suburban, bourgeois white people, who had grown up in the Depression and the war, had actually experienced anything like it—but this is what the popular culture of the period wanted us to believe. *Lazy-Hazy-Crazy* successfully does for the summertime what television and Tin Pan Alley had already done for winter and Christmas.

"Those Lazy-Hazy-Crazy Days of Summer" originated in Germany, a country even whiter than Anglo-America. The song was published in Berlin in 1962, under the title of "Du Spielst 'ne Tolle Rolle" (roughly translated as "You Played a Great Role") with words and music by Hans Carste and Hans Bradtke; it was originally recorded early in 1963 by the Deutschland pop singer Heidi Armio. In the original lyric, a man is telling a woman, "You play a great role in my memoirs, which I will write one day"; that's the "hook," that became the title line of "Lazy-Hazy-Crazy." In the two main verses, he says he only needs a paper and pen and will write great stories of "you." He then states that he has seen her walking through Milan in a bikini and boxing with a friend. For the coda, he tells her that "compared to you, Brigitte Bardot is a small fish."[22]

Like many a prospective European import, "Rolle" eventually wound up in the hands of a Jewish publisher and songwriter in New York. "A music publishing partner of mine found the song and we heard a German record of it, in German, of course" said Cole. "We had a writer by the name of Charlie Tobias, who everyone knows over here as one of our great ASCAP writers. He put a new lyric to it and called it 'Those Lazy-Hazy-Crazy Days of Summer.' "[23]

Cole had a distinct fondness for musical families. He had come from one himself and been very supportive over the years to both the Fisher family (which included the father, Fred Fisher, and three songwriting siblings, Dan, Doris, and Marvin) and the Sherman brothers (Noel and Joe). And he also was very generous to Charlie Tobias and the Tobias brothers. Charles Tobias (1898–1970) was the most prodigious of a brood that also included Harry (1895–1994), both of whom were inducted into the ASCAP Hall of Fame, and Henry (1905–1997).[24] Their best-known song today may be Harry's "It's a Lonesome Old Town," the theme song of popular bandleader Ben Bernie and recorded by Sinatra on *Only the Lonely* and by Cole on *Dear Lonely Hearts*. Working with the brothers in his publishing companies, Cole recorded nearly a dozen songs by them in this period. Just as "Ramblin' Rose" was the culmination of Cole's long relationship with the Shermans, "Lazy-Hazy" was the highly profitable result of Cole's ongoing association with the Tobiases.

"Du Spielst 'ne Tolle Rolle" was purely a polka, and while the finished "Lazy-Crazy-Hazy" has some aspects of that Eastern European dance form about it (not the least of which is a reference to "pretzels and beer"), it's more of a showtune-y two-four. Tobias's text is a craftily conceived collection of rather harmless but vivid images, one-liner type gags and rhymes such as might make for a second-tier Broadway musical or "special material" for a TV variety show or a Las Vegas act: "girls in their bikinis" (rhymes with "weenies") "who never get 'em wet" or kids making out at drive-in movies. Here was a song that asked the musical question, "Are we having fun yet?" Only the most churlish of knaves would complain that he isn't.

"Those Lazy-Hazy-Crazy Days of Summer" was an instant party grafted to one side of a vinyl 7" disc spinning at 45 revolutions per minute. It was the polar opposite of *Where Did Everyone Go?*—as soon as the needle hits the grooves, you immediately feel like you are surrounded by friends. Even more than any of the country projects, this was an extreme sing-along number; the hook was so catchy and the simple lyrics were repeated so often that it literally defied you not to sing along with it. It was also impossible not to feel uplifted by this incessantly cheerful song. Arranger-conductor Ralph Carmichael was much more of a choirmaster than any of Cole's other key collaborators, and he came up with a choral sound that was full of pep and energy—more convincing and sincere, and much less grating or annoying, than any other arranger could have done. Cole and Carmichael recorded it in April 1963 amid a session of other foreign imports and rock-pop-style tunes (more about which later).

"That song wasn't my favorite kind of music," Ralph said, "and it certainly wasn't Nat's favorite kind of music. But at some level there is always a reward. If you ring the bell and it's what the marketplace accepts, then there's a certain fulfillment—because you've done your job. And when that hit, Nat loved to see people accepting what he's offering them. And it was definitely a hit!" "Those Lazy-Hazy-Crazy Days of Summer" belonged to the genre of summer songs, a key subset of youth-directed jukebox singles that had pretty much only existed since the start of the rock era—tunes like "Dancing in the Street" by Martha and the Vandellas and "School Is Out" by Gary U. S. Bonds.

Promoted by Pete Bennett, the song quickly reached number six in the singles charts, but at that point, team Cole was just getting started. When it became clear that this was the next mega-hit, they regrouped a month later in the Capitol Tower to quickly fill out an album. Where "Lazy-Hazy-Crazy" was the only song on the April session to use the big jingly choir, all the additional numbers from the May date use the combination of a large chorus and a relatively small band, although some of the ballads employ an eight-piece string section.

Extending the ideas of the "Lazy-Hazy-Crazy" lyric, the other eleven songs explore the idea of summer fun and frivolity—there's nothing as serious as "Summertime" or as wistful as "The Things We Did Last Summer," or Sinatra's later song of love and loss, "Summer Wind" (also German). Cole was careful to avoid anything that smacked of a deeper meaning or any sort of a subtext. These songs depicted chipper young lads strolling up and down the boardwalk in Atlantic City circa 1900, not minding the hot sun in their brightly striped suits and straw hats, dudes with handlebar mustaches in full-body bathing costumes, an era of banjos and tubas, riverboats and train whistles and calliopes and merry-go-rounds and newly invented ice cream cones. Not to mention baseball and mom and apple pie. It's a very Disneyland kind of an album.

Cole's choice of songs, such as "On the Sidewalks of New York," "After the Ball Is Over" (the classic waltz), "There Is a Tavern in the Town," (the classic drinking song), "On a Bicycle Built for Two" "In the Good Old Summertime," and "You Tell Me Your Dream," all of which depicted an American nation that was young and innocent, before World War I, Prohibition, and the Depression. Several of these selections were old enough to be in the public domain and thus Cole and "Edith Bergdahl" were again able to profit from their adaptations.

Cole spread the wealth around in other ways, too. He saved two spots for Joe Sherman ("That Sunday, That Summer," and "Don't Forget") and an additional two for Charlie Tobias, whose English words to a German polka had made the whole windfall possible. Tobias polka'ed all the way to the bank with three spots on the album: the title track plus the 1928 "Get Out and

Get Under the Moon" (recorded by Nat and Maria in 1950) and another new number, "That's What They Meant."

The *Lazy-Hazy-Crazy* album has sometimes been described as "nostalgia," but in reality, it is anything but; rather, it's an ecstatically cheerful reminiscence of a fictional, idealized past. Nostalgia, which literally means "homesickness," implies a bittersweet look back; even if the past is idealized or put on a pedestal, then there's a melancholy quality implied in the act of thinking about it. Yes, things were better then—don't you wish you could go back to those carefree, innocent times? Contrastingly, the songs on *Lazy-Hazy-Crazy* seem to have been carefully stripped of all such emotional resonance.

This rule also applies—for the most part—to the new songs. The Sherman-Weiss "Don't Forget" has something of a twist at the end—after telling the object of his affection not to forget the Ferris wheel and the penny arcade, he switches to the potentially poignant "don't forget *me!*" Likewise, on "That's What They Meant" ("That's What They Meant by the Good Old Summertime"), the narrator-singer is apparently standing in the present and looking back, and there is an implied distance between the today and yesterday ("When a nickel took you far / On an open trolley car"). In both cases, the songs could have been orchestrated and sung with a considerable amount of poignancy. But where, on most other albums, the singer and orchestrator would relish the opportunity to dig a little deeper, here Cole and company resist all temptation to make any kind of ironic or poignant juxtaposition of past and present. (Cole's 1954 duet with Dean Martin, "Long, Long Ago" has considerably more sarcasm.) "That's What They Meant" is rendered as a half-time vaudeville-style soft-shoe; "Don't Forget" has the repetitious rhythm of a calliope on a carousel; the percussion sounds like some mechanical drumming device.

Cole, however, permitted himself one exception to the album's rule—and that exception made for one of the most moving performances of his career. Composer Joe Sherman recalled, "He was riding very high in 1963 with 'Those-Lazy-Hazy-Crazy Days of Summer.' That was a huge hit and he wanted to do an album. You know, in those days, you have a single and they want you to do an album right after. So, he called me at home, and he said 'I need a song. Something about summer. Do you have anything like that? Because I'm just calling a few writers to see what they can come up with.'"

Sherman was then working with the veteran lyricist George David Weiss. "It was the one occasion when Nat specifically called us to write a specific song. We were very inspired and turned on by the fact that Nat called us, and we were writing together night and day. And I was at the piano and I started tinkling around with certain chord progressions, unconsciously, not thinking about what I was doing. And George was on the phone and he put down the phone and he said, "What's that you just played?" And then he came up with the first line. We wrote the whole thing in one afternoon." Sherman also noted, "The middle part [the bridge: 'Newborn whippoorwills . . .'] was the part that really grabbed me. And the part has always stayed in my mind—I guess one of the most exciting moments of my life of writing songs—when we came up with 'go on and kiss her' and the harmonies change."[25]

"That Sunday, That Summer" is one of the most stunning performances of Cole's entire prolific career. Yet it plays by all the rules of the rest of the album: there is prominent tuba and banjo, oomphing and clanging away behind Cole, and the choir is omnipresent; here is where the eight strings are most obvious. Lyrically, the song is reflecting on the past, yet it's not melancholy or bittersweet; there's nothing to imply that this is a romance that went wrong.

It's the unstated, implicit meaning of the song that makes it so touching: even when love doesn't go bad, even when you can find someone and be with them for fifty, sixty years, the most special moment, at least according to the song's own mythology, is that split-second instant of romantic discovery. It seems so cosmically special that even the forces of nature, the whippoorwills and the flowers, are in sync with you. It is a Zen-like moment in which you are not only perfectly in tune with each other, but one with everything.

Cole's vocal perfectly conveys the mixture of extreme excitement and total serenity that you feel—this is the happiest moment of your life. It doesn't get any better than this. Carmichael's arrangement is also letter-perfect; he has developed into a total master of bringing the various forces together and moving subtly in and out of tempo when it's appropriate. He begins and ends with the choir slightly rubato, gradually picking up speed as Cole comes in, and then chugging along like a walk in the woods as reinforced by the banjo, which keeps things moving below while the soaring strings represent the dreamy thoughts occurring in our hero's head. And Sherman is correct about the modulation at the end of the bridge being a heart-stopping moment. When the combined force of the singers and the orchestra changes key and repeats the phrase "go on and kiss her," it feels like the exact instance of romantic rapture has been pinpointed and extended, dwelt in and shared with the entire world. Hearing Cole singing this, one can't help but feel blessed.

Carmichael's ending, which seems so perfectly planned, was almost a complete accident, and it's also ironic that a song about such a sweet and endearing moment should underscore how Carmichael's career and his health were starting to go off the rails. Ralph was so overworked at this point, especially in trying to get this album done quickly enough, that he made it to the studio with this chart only about half done. "I think it was just an oversight—I didn't get an ending written for 'That Sunday, That Summer.' And we ran it down and it just stops. Boom! And there's nothing. So, I didn't know what to do because it's obvious it's an incomplete ending." So, Carmichael whispered this instruction beforehand, that when they reached the ending, even though there was nothing written, just to repeat the a capella choral intro from the beginning. "So anyway, we make the first take and we get to the written end and then there's just a brief moment of silence and then we reiterate the intro. And we look at each other and wink and all of a sudden, I see Lee Gillette coming out and he says 'Ralph, that's genius!' So, I got off the hook that time." He had inadvertently turned the song and the chart into a metaphor; as soon as you're finished replaying that one special moment in your mind, what do you do? You start to think about it all over again.

"That Sunday, That Summer" and "L-O-V-E" were the only two songs from the later part of Cole's career that Natalie included in her *Unforgettable* album. As Carmichael points out. "That was one of Natalie's favorite songs. She liked to think that her daddy was singing that to her. And that has a lovely melody, it's kind of a feel-good song, and I liked it too." If we had to choose just one song, out of the hundreds that Cole sang in the final five years of his career, it would surely be "That Sunday, That Summer." Cole not only crystallizes a moment of romantic rapture into tangible form; he literally makes time stand still.

WHILE NAT WAS BUSY MAKING MUSIC (and money), others were increasingly involved in a game of thrones–like power grab for control of his career—and money. We have no way of knowing: was Nat simply looking the other way, too immersed in his work, to notice that Leo Branton and Ike Jones were gradually phasing out Carlos Gastel? Branton "was known in Hollywood as the 'black Perry Mason,'" as Cookie described him, "but he was under Maria's thumb."[26] However, Timolin and Casey feel that Maria was not responsible for ousting Gastel; whenever their mother spoke of Carlos in later years, she had nothing but good things to say about the hearty Honduran—and she was not one to be unnecessarily diplomatic regarding people she didn't care for. Noting that Nat and Carlos had been working together for exactly twenty years, *Variety* made the announcement in June, "One of the longest performer-manager ties in showbiz will be severed Dec. 31 when Nat King Cole and Carlos Gastel will call it quits."[27]

Cole was brilliant at show business; there was no one better at maximizing profits from a concert or a tour or an album. From the mid-1950s onward, Cole was working less and less in movie theaters and more in top-of-the-line nightclubs and concert halls, or Vegas-style rooms that blurred the boundaries between the two. In the last ten years of his career, Cole and his team, first Carlos and then the Kell-Cole partners (Branton and Jones), would organize the show, rent the venue, pay all the expenses (including the musicians and other performers), but then would be able to keep the lion's share of the proceeds. Perhaps Irving Mills had done him a favor after all, following the "Straighten Up and Fly Right" debacle of 1943; he would never again, unlike so many other black performers, be a victim.

But even Nat, alas, was completely taken in when Branton got the Coles involved with a lowlife wheeler-dealer named Harry Margolis. Ostensibly a tax lawyer, Margolis seems to have been entirely focused on nothing else but fleecing Nat and Maria out of every last cent. Margolis set up a sham trust fund, and quickly managed to drain their bank accounts to the tune of several hundred thousand dollars—essentially Nat's life savings.[28] Everyone was fooled, including Nat, Maria, and longtime accountant Harold Plant, who had delivered them from the wrath of the IRS ten years earlier and saved their house. Was Branton in on the take? Was he corrupt or merely incompetent? Or perhaps he was just an attorney who, like Nat, was out of his depth in a rather complicated financial maneuver that he never should have gotten his clients involved in. We'll never know, but either way, the scam happened on his watch.

A decade earlier, weathering a major setback like this together would have strengthened the bond between Nat and Maria, as, indeed, the IRS disaster of the early 1950s seems to have done. Instead, this time, it exacerbated the mounting tension in the marriage. By 1963 there seems to have been a genuine rift between them.

When Cookie and Sweetie were young—and so was Maria—she seems to have had no qualms about putting the two girls in the care of nannies and her sister, "Aunt Baba," while she traveled the world in high style with her husband. And, to a certain extent, both Carole and Natalie grew up highly critical of their mother. In the late fifties, Mrs. Cole seems to have been looking forward to an empty nest and having her husband all to herself, since both daughters were leaving home for school on the East Coast; in 1962 (sometime after her coming out party with Preisdent Kennedy in November 1961), Carole began attending Cazenovia College, the alma matter (more or less) of her father's buddy, Jimmy Van Heusen, and in 1963, Natalie entered boarding school in Northfield, Massachusetts.

But as of 1961, Maria was suddenly now responsible for the welfare of three new babies; unlike Cookie and Sweetie, they were very young all at once, and she became more of a stay-at-home mom. As a result, among other things, to this day the two younger girls, Casey and Timolin are much more vociferous in their praise of their mother. In a certain sense, what happened to Maria was unfair, and she had never kept it a secret, from Cookie in particular, "that it was Dad who wanted to adopt me, not her. It was his idea, he insisted, he wanted me."[29] She told her this not out of anger, but blunt honesty. It was Nat who really wanted all those children, but he was like any other father of his day, in expecting his wife to care for them while he was out bread-winning. In fact, rather than spending more time with his five children when he was in his early forties, Nat was now so in demand that he was on the road more than ever. There's only one extended interval in all of 1963 when he spent any quality time in Los Angeles, and even then, he was playing the Grove in the evening and recording the *Lazy-Hazy-Crazy* album in the daytime.

Cole had been off the road for about three months when he headed east again, for what would be his final trek across Great Britain. For the second half of July, he played the Astoria Theater in London, as well as Glasgow, Leeds, Lewisham, Hammersmith, Cardiff, Birmingham, Manchester, Leeds, and Liverpool.[30] It had been arranged that the BBC would videotape one of the shows, and, making it all the more special, Cole is accompanied not only by his traveling group (Reunald Jones, Collins, Harris, and Petties) but one of the greatest jazz orchestras in the world, Ted Heath, and His Music. This time, their collaboration went down considerably more smoothly than in 1956, when Heath accompanied Cole on the infamous southern tour.

The BBC show captures Cole at his all-time swingin'est as a stand-up vocalist, particularly on Jerome Kern and Dorothy Fields's "The Way You Look Tonight," featuring a solo by the artist on clavietta, the 1936 Oscar winner. Cole's treatment of this (no less than "The Continental" on *At The Sands*) were likely inspirations for Sinatra on his more famous *Academy Award Winners* album of two years later. There's also an *After Midnight*–inspired small group segment, which includes "It's Only a Paper Moon" and "Sweet Lorraine". Counterbalancing all the jazz, there's a chorale segment, in which Cole is joined by a small mixed choir (the Cliff Adams Singers) for "Ramblin' Rose," in which he invites everyone to sing along (it's the only time we see the audience). Then we get three numbers from his latest smash hit album, "Those Lazy-Hazy-Crazy Days of Summer," "In the Good Old Summertime," and what would turn out to be his last great ballad,

"That Sunday, That Summer." When the program was shown in the States (in October 1963, a few weeks after the UK airing),[31] older African Americans who watched it were surely rubbing their eyes in disbelief: a black entertainer accompanied by a white orchestra and chorus, all deferring to him, like the King he surely was. He might as well have been walking on the moon.

The concert's most transcendent moments are a pair of classic ballads by Johnny Burke and Jimmy Van Heusen, "Here's That Rainy Day" and "But Beautiful," sung back to back. His singing here is a miraculous balance of sound and space, miraculous timing—what Sinatra would call "phrasing"—and heartfelt emotion. One can only imagine that Cole was thinking about relationships after all; Johnny and Jimmy were among his oldest and closest friends, and he remained close to both even after their professional "divorce." For Burke, "Rainy Day" had been particularly poignant; it was the song he wrote to commemorate the conclusion of the two most significant relationships he would ever have: his wife Bessie, the love of his life, and at the same time, the end of his partnership with his best friend, Van Heusen. Nat sings as if he's very much aware of all that, but he's also thinking about Maria. Fifteen years earlier, he left his existing marriage for her, put himself in debt and even risked his life to give her the home he thought she deserved, and she in turn gave up her career and incurred the wrath of her family to hitch her wagon to his star. But now, it was all starting to seem like a cold, rainy day.

The "Rainy Day" arrangement is one of the best written for Cole by Charlie Albertine, a young orchestrator who wrote many noteworthy charts for the artist in his last few years ("The Way You Look Tonight," also unrecorded but heard here and several times in live appearances throughout 1962–63, is probably his best swing number for Cole) and it ends rather chillingly with the dissonant clash of a cymbal. And it's all captured on videotape; this 1963 BBC concert is, overall, perhaps the single greatest visual document of Cole at his absolute pinnacle.[32]

COLE HAD BIG PLANS for the fall and well beyond; he announced that he was setting up a tour of Europe and the Middle East for 1964, including some places he hadn't been in a while, if ever: Paris, Madrid, Israel, Ghana.[33] No less ambitiously, he had decided to put together another touring show along the lines of *The Merry World of Nat King Cole*, in which he would be accompanied by, and interact with, a twelve-voice choir, not only mixed gender but mixed race as well, to be called "The Merry Young Souls."

Gunilla Hutton, who had been born in Gothenburg, Sweden, in 1944, is generally described as a "Scandinavian beauty." But she is much more Texas than Sweden; from the age of six, she grew up in Fort Worth rather than

Stockholm and would spend most of her professional career singing country music and acting in hillbilly comedy shows like *Petticoat Junction* and *Hee Haw*. After the family arrived in the United States, around 1950, she remembered, "We took a train from New York and I was later told by my brother that I got up and I walked up and down the aisles, singing an American song that I had memorized phonetically, and everybody was talking about me."[34] She wanted nothing more from life than to sing and make music, because it "just was a natural place for me to go."

By 1963, her family had moved to Los Angeles, where she was attending UCLA. She heard about a chance to sing professionally, an audition being held by "an older woman on campus," and gave it a shot, not quite knowing what it was for. "She had me come into her living room and I sang a few *bars a capella.* And then she said, 'Let me see your legs, and pull up your skirt just a little bit.' So, I did. She said, 'Yeah, you're going to get work.' And she called me the next week and told me about the audition for the Merry Young Souls. And I went and auditioned, and I really wasn't very good because I was so nervous, but they all were smiling. And then I got called back again, but I decided to get pretty strong with them. I said, 'You know, I have other offers.' I'm sure they saw right through it. But they said, 'Don't worry, you're hired.' And the next thing I knew I was off on tour. A bunch of friendly, nice people."

Hutton was right that it took hardly any time at all; the auditions were apparently held even before Cole had left for England. Then, within a week or so of his return to the states, the American tour had begun. The show was titled *Sights and Sounds* and it seems to have premiered at the Shrine Auditorium on August 8, a benefit concert for several civil rights organizations, including the NAACP, the Congress for Racial Equality, and Dr. Martin Luther King's Southern Christian Leadership Conference.

This particular US tour, which ran from late summer and fall 1963 and then deep into 1964, was one of Cole's busiest periods. The star and his company were continually on the road, and there's no point in his itinerary when he has more than a few days off between gigs. He almost seemed to be deliberately avoiding coming home to Hancock Park, especially now that Cookie and Sweetie were both away at school.

Cole had put together the Merry Young Souls to help him make a crucial transition: as a solo entertainer, or even leader of the Trio, he was essentially a nightclub act; but the addition of the featured chorale group turned his show into a full-blown concert attraction. He could now concentrate on the bigger, better-paying venues. But there was a trade-off: he got paid less in the clubs, but at least the upside was that he could stay in the same city for a week or more.

When you played the Shrine Auditorium, you were lucky to be able to fill it even for a single night. Therefore, while playing concert halls and theaters brought in much needed revenue, it meant a constant strain of one-nighters, which were exacerbating health problems that he apparently didn't yet realize he had.

"He told me that he was doing this tour—and it was a backbreaking tour—to pay off an IRS debt," said Hutton. We don't know if this was the same old IRS debt that first emerged in 1951–52, or, more likely, new financial problems that had arisen from the Harry Margolis debacle. She added, "He told me about that. Not untypical of entertainers and people in our field, his business manager [Branton] had really mucked things up. And so, Nat had this big debt, which was a tremendous surprise to him. And that's why he was doing this tour. And I don't think he planned to do another tour like that. I mean, he was such a, popular, best-selling artist, he was one of the biggest stars in the world." Nat loved working and generally enjoyed the road, but this was ridiculous: after the Shrine, in August and September, he played Denver; Washington, DC; Pittsburgh; Toronto; and finally a three-week run at the Latin Casino in Cherry Hill, New Jersey, whose patrons were mostly from Philadelphia. But even though he could stay put in Philadelphia, it hardly meant that he was able to relax in the daytime; now he was also recording a new album, *Nat King Cole Sings My Fair Lady*.

MY FAIR LADY, WITH MUSIC BY FREDERICK LOEWE and libretto by Alan Jay Lerner, opened on BROADWAY to overwhelming acclaim in 1956. It was not only immediately recognized as an all-time classic of the musical theater, but it established the Broadway cast album as a commercial force to be reckoned with in the music industry. The original *My Fair Lady* cast album (released by Columbia Records, which had invested in the show up front) was an enormous seller, and so were numerous spin-off albums, most notably the jazz interpretation of the score by Shelly Manne and André Previn. The original Broadway production ran until September 1962, making *My Fair Lady* one of the longest-running shows in history; a few months later, in 1963, filming began on the Warner Bros. movie version. When the film was released in 1964, there would be a new spate of recordings of the score that hoped to get in on the coat-tails of the movie: the jazz arranger Johnny Richards did one, and, coincidentally, so did both Shelly Manne and André Previn, now working separately, on their own new versions.

The film was released on October 22, 1964, but thirteen months earlier, the Cole-Carmichael team was working on the album that would be released with a full title of *Nat King Cole Sings Selections from Lerner & Loewe's My Fair Lady*. Although the high quality of the finished product would lead one to think otherwise, everything about this album was a case of a last-minute rush and "hurry up and wait!" Capitol Records seems to have been under the impression that the movie was coming sooner, and that it made sense to get their album in the stores as quickly as possible. Gillette staked out various studios in the city and decided to do the actual recording in a ballroom in the Philadelphia Athletic Club (formerly the Broadwood hotel) that had been outfitted with recording equipment. "We did that album in Philadelphia last fall," Cole said in a promotional interview from June 1964, when the album was about to come out. "We got quite a kick out of doing it. We used quite a big [portion] of the Philadelphia Symphony Orchestra to record this with us, and we recorded this in a very large ballroom, which gave us that big sound."[35]

Even while Nat was pushing himself to the limit, exhaustion was catching up with his thirty-six-year-old musical director, Ralph Carmichael, who was handling the bulk of Cole's orchestrations, especially for recording, and working for other clients as well. He had been working in the pop music business for less than five years by this time but was already trapped in the vicious cycle of destructive workaholism that killed or ruined the lives of many of the most successful pop music and movie-TV orchestrators (the same pressures that drove Billy May to A.A. and put Oliver Nelson in an early grave). Carmichael was simply working too much, neglecting his family, his health, and, equally unhealthily for Carmichael, his faith. By now, his first marriage was over and he was developing a problem with stimulants. (Eventually he would leave the world of secular music entirely and re-dedicate himself to the church.)

But in September 1963, Carmichael was still trapped in a downward spiral, trying to chase down deadline after deadline—and occasionally, to his great regret, even letting his old friends down. This was the only time Carmichael had unpleasant memories of a project with Cole. "It was horrible! I had my own copyist fly in from Los Angeles—but there was a big orchestra and there were so many notes! Lee sub-contracted the whole job to a bunch of local guys and they were up there in our hotel room, and they're copying and copying away!" By this point an orchestra full of union musicians and Nat King Cole are being paid to stand around waiting for the music. What made it worse was that they had to end the date so Cole could make it to a gala reception (described in the album notes) for local Capitol staffers, salesmen, and distributors at which "tea and crumpets were flown in from London."[36] "It was going to be a real social event," said Carmichael. So, Gillette didn't have the option of extending the session, which would have been expensive enough; he had to call a whole new session, which was even more so.

After the reception, Carmichael and Gillette were headed back to the hotel. "And we get about halfway up the stairs and Lee stops and he grabs me by the coat, and he swears at me and says 'Nat thinks it's the copyists, the orchestra thinks it's the copyists, but I know it's YOU!' He just vented his spleen on me. And I had to take it, because he was right. I was always just barely making the deadlines. That was the only time that I really missed a deadline for Nat."

Cole had previously sung several songs by Lerner and Loewe, notably "Almost Like Being in Love" from *Brigadoon* and "I Still See Elisa" from *Paint Your Wagon*. In 1956 and '57, when *My Fair Lady* was the hot ticket on Broadway, Cole sang "I've Grown Accustomed to Her Face" several times on his NBC TV series in an arrangement by Nelson Riddle, and he also sang "Hymn to Him" in several live concerts, which shows he had a real taste for the show. "I've always admired this score, and Ralph has always wanted to do it; for a change, I wanted to do something different. In fact, I do quite a bit of everything they do in the show, [including some numbers that most jazz and pop] singers don't attempt to do, most of the special material things," as he said in 1964, "like 'Hymn to Him.'" [37]

For the 1963 album, they devised an approach roughly somewhere between a pop single-style adaptation of a show tune and a more authentic Broadway-style orchestration. Stanley Holloway's "With a Little Bit of Luck," for instance, is a sprightly jig, but Cole's is a solid four swinger. It starts with a colorful English-march-style flourish, but by the second chorus, the groove is more like Count Basie than your average hometown British brass band. Likewise, "Get Me to the Church on Time" is a swinging flagwaver, particularly in the second chorus, wherein the orchestra plays the first three lines of the A sections instrumentally and Cole just comes in on the fourth (title) line. "The Rain in Spain" (arranged by Frank Hunter) is a tango, as in the show; only a nattering nabob of negativity would have pointed out to Frederick Loewe that the tango is from Argentina and that if he wanted a dance form more accurately representative of that soggy plain in Spain, he should have composed a *paso doble* or a *flamenco*. The episodes in "Rain in Spain" where Cole is interacting with the choir sound ("now altogether!") have much in common with the singalong-stye construction of "Ramblin' Rose."

As Carmichael remembered, "As far as my job, in terms of the arranging, is concerned, it could be just any twelve songs. Because you give them the treatment the lyric calls for, and we wanted it to be a combination of swing and Broadway. It was a fun project." In some cases, both Cole and Carmichael seem to have studied the 1956 Columbia cast album very carefully, and while they might have modernized the proceedings slightly, there's not a lot of difference. On "You Did It," when Cole (as leading man, Henry Higgins) describes being dogged by a "hairy hound from Budapest," Carmichael re-employs a witty device from the show's original orchestrator Robert Russell Bennett in liberally quoting from Franz Liszt's famous second Hungarian Rhapsody No. 2 in C-sharp minor of 1853 (the same piece that Cole had sung as "Ebony Rhapsody" in 1961).

Carmichael was especially pleased with the combined ensemble of singers and musicians that he was able to work with in Philadelphia: the Merry Young Souls, supplemented by four additional voices, were the choir; lead trumpeter Clyde Reasinger came down from New York, while Carmichael brought in his own lead alto saxophone, to head the reeds; the string players were mostly members of the Philadelphia Symphony. "So, I had a wonderful orchestra. The french horns . . . impeccable! It was just terrific. And the 'legit' woodwinds also were great. So, the timing just worked out great."

At least two-thirds of *Nat King Cole Sings My Fair Lady* is an uncompromised delight: some of the tracks, particularly the show's great love song, "I've Grown Accustomed to Her Face," have become Nat Cole classics. As interpreted by Cole, "Accustomed" can be viewed as part of the same stratum of lyric as "That Sunday, That Summer" in that it crystallizes the exact instant when the speaker realizes he has fallen in love. Even more so, in this case, like "Angelo" in *Measure for Measure*, professor Henry Higgins is pinpointing the specific moment when he realizes that he actually has a heart. Where "That Sunday" made a point of avoiding irony—indeed, it was a first-class piece of songwriting that took the long way around in not requiring it—"Accustomed" finds delicious irony in the idea that even as the hero is realizing his romantic condition he is cursing himself because of it. If Cole's interpretation leaves out the song's famous spoken introduction in the show—"Damn! Damn! Damn!"—it's because, as Cole sings it, the song is more about his feelings for someone else than talking about how love is affecting him personally. It could be said that in the show, Henry Higgins (Rex Harrison) sings "*I've* Grown Accustomed to Her Face," but Cole sings it as "I've Grown Accustomed to *Her* Face."

On Broadway, "With a Little Bit of Luck" and "Get Me to the Church on Time" were major dance production numbers that Cole herewith turns into big band swingers. Contrastingly, "I Could Have Danced All Night" is sung with much more maturity and sensitivity than by the young Miss Andrews; Cole's interpretation is more about the discovery and the realization of love than it is about dancing all night. "Show Me" may be the most radical reinterpretation: Liza Doolittle (Andrews) sings "Show Me" as a bravura, over-the-top showstopper to express how frustrated she is, but Cole's treatment is pure tenderness without a hint of that impatience or vehemence. To use a British expression, Cole "takes the piss out of" the lyric.

Yet at the same time, the idea of Cole singing a complete musical comedy score has its limitations—as Cole revealed in that selfsame "Show Me." At one point, Liza sings "Haven't your lips hungered for *mine* / Please don't *explain*, show me!" The point of that rhyme is that Liza wants to stick it to Higgins by backsliding into the cockney pronunciation of "explain" as "ex-pline." However, if you had heard Cole without having seen the show, you might wonder what the line was supposed to mean or what the rhyme actually was. Likewise, quite possibly as much as a third of the *My Fair Lady* album sounds like a waste of Cole's time. For instance, the best that Cole can do is rehash what Rex Harrison had sung on two of Henry Higgins's monologs, "I'm an Ordinary Man" (in spite of a lovely clarinet obligato behind the singer in some of the song's more melodic moments) and "Hymn to Him" (both of which were also the work of Carmichael deputy Frank Hunter), whereas "You Did It," is musical dialog more than an actual song in the usual sense. (Although it's tempting to imagine Cole playing Higgins an actual staged production.) In retrospect, knowing Cole's time was limited, one wishes he and Carmichael had spread the wealth around a little bit and done an album called *Nat King Cole Sings Lerner and Loewe,* which would have included such incredibly right songs for him, such as "If Ever I Would Leave You" (from *Camelot*), "Gigi" (from *Gigi*), "I Talk to the Trees" (from *Paint Your Wagon*), and "Come to Me, Bend to Me" (from *Brigadoon*). Then, too, I listen to Cole singing "Show Me," an out-of-the box choice if ever there was one, but a brilliant one, and realize anew that, whatever its missteps, no one needs to "ex-pline" that the *My Fair Lady* album is at the very least, a lesser Cole classic.

When it came time to reinterpret a classic Broadway score, Cole avoided any trace of a show associated with the Afro-American heritage. He could have made *Nat King Cole Sings Cabin in the Sky* or *Nat King Cole Sings Mr. Wonderful,* or any of the many black-oriented shows written by Harold Arlen (*St. Louis Woman, House of Flowers, Jamaica*). As with *The Magic of Christmas* and *Those Lazy-Hazy-Crazy Days of Summer*, Cole seemed to be deliberately looking for the most Anglo-Saxon project he could find. *My Fair Lady* illustrates that Cole had by now completely reinvented himself as the great American songster, part jazz, part big bands, part country, part pan-American and world citizen—and now part Broadway, part everything. In 1963, at least, there was still enough of him left to go around.

AFTER THE EXTENDED RUN at the Latin Casino and the *My Fair Lady* sessions—and apparently still without heading back to Hancock Park—Cole and company, including the Merry Young Souls, resumed touring – and how. First, they head north and east: Pennsylvania, Westchester, Boston, Syracuse, Scranton, Ottawa, Hartford, Baltimore. Then it was west: Columbus, Kokomo, St. Louis, Bloomington, Louisville, Nashville, Winnipeg, Minneapolis, Duluth, Sioux City, Chicago, Appleton (Wisconsin), Champaign (Illinois), West Lafayette (Indiana), Cedar Rapids, Aberdeen. It all added up to unending months of "backbreaking" one-nighters.

By fall 1963, Cole and Hutton were involved in an intimate relationship. Maria first acknowledged this not in her own 1971 book but in the Epstein biography, published in 1999.[38] For her part, Hutton has never spoken publicly about it, never confirmed or denied it. In looking over the state of Nat's personal life at this point, it does seem like the marriage was already on the rocks long before he met Hutton, and there's no real evidence of Nat having any extra-marital activity before this point. The burlesque star Tempest Storm later claimed that she had a fling with Cole in Vegas in 1956, and Eartha Kitt told a story about Nat filling her dressing room with roses when she appeared on his NBC series. (Maria then made sure that her husband never paid her any further attention, although this entire episode was likely nothing more than an amusing anecdote that Kitt imparted in her shows.) But the Hutton affair was real, as Maria admitted again in one of her final interviews: "A couple of years before he died, he did have a major . . . that's the only time, really, I can say he had an affair."[39]

Gunilla Hutton only agreed to speak with me on the condition that she would not be asked to speak about the affair itself. But she did want to speak about the man she knew: "He had an almost childlike wonder about things. That's one of the things that made him so fun. You know, because he could have been jaded, and here he was this glamorous figure, and he lived such a glamorous life, but he didn't look at it that way."

She also vividly remembered how devastated Nat was by the tragedy of Friday, November 22, 1963. The troupe had just played at the Aberdeen Civic Arena on Thursday, November 21, and were set to perform in Omaha, but nobody felt like singing that weekend. "When JFK was assassinated, Nat took that so hard. He just fell apart. He adored him." Finally, Nat made it back home to Hancock Park, to celebrate Thanksgiving, and when the subject came up—as it inevitably had to—he just started to cry. It was the only time Natalie would ever see her father in such a state.[40]

At long last Nat was back in California, but not for long, and he was still working. He played a week at the Melodyland Theatre in Anaheim, and videotaped memorable guest shots on both *The Jack Benny Show* and *The Danny Kaye Show*, the latter broadcast on Christmas Day. There were more fights with Maria, especially when she found out about the affair. Now, at the start of 1964, it really seemed that the Coles, after sixteen years, were about to split up. "Later on, when people would ask my mother, 'Do you think Nat would have stayed with you?'" said Timolin, "she would answer, 'The question is, would I have stayed with him?'"[41]

THE HOME SITUATION WAS BLEAK, and so was his health, although he didn't yet realize it, except possibly on an unconscious level, or even a spiritual one. Otherwise, he was more visible than ever: on January 9, Nat paid a call on the new president, Lyndon B. Johnson, at the White House, in conjunction with "a Senate Office Building luncheon sponsored by the Hollywood Museum."[42] A few weeks later, he was part of the Joseph P. Kennedy Jr. Foundation Awards Ceremony, held at the Americana Hotel in New York, in honor of the late president's father. In San Diego, in April, he would be presented with the National Brotherhood Award by the National Conference of Christians and Jews.

Cole was now routinely accepted into the upper brackets of politics and government as well as in showbiz. In late 1963, he had been honored to be asked to produce a gala opening night concert for the Dorothy Chandler Pavilion, part of the Los Angeles Music Center, which was scheduled to open at the end of the year. For Nat, this was the same kind of cultural validation that Sinatra had felt when President Kennedy had asked him to produce the Inaugural Gala in 1961—perhaps even more so, because he was carrying the torch not only for his profession, as musician and entertainer, but for his people.

"People think of a performer as a minstrel, they don't expect him to have the time or the civic pride to get into things like this. They expect the doctors, the lawyers, the businessmen to be there. But a performer, he's there but he's not really there," Nat was quoted as saying. "They consider us a diversion. Wind us up and we'll dance. Right there when you need entertainment. But when you're looking for a citizen to work with other people, whoever thinks about calling us in?" He added, "I walk on the world, but I'm not usually in it, a non-entity once off-stage. That's why I'm delighted to work with The Music Center. To take time. Take pride. Prove that entertainers would like to be involved citizens and maybe—most of all—advance the appreciation of all music."[43]

Cole put out feelers to three other headliners whom he wanted to be involved, starting with Tony Bennett. "He kept saying to me, 'I've got a big item for you. There's a theater that's opening up in Los Angeles, and I want you, Ella Fitzgerald, Count Basie and myself. Now, put it on your calendar; it's a year from now.' I didn't even know what it was. It was the Dorothy Chandler Pavilion. He had great friends who owned it, and they wanted him to open it." As Tony recalled, the plan was for Count Basie "to open the show, I would close the first half, and then Ella Fitzgerald and Nat Cole, and we would all have a jam session at the end." Tony remembered how proud Nat was, and how he made sure to keep reminding everyone to hold the date. "About every two months he'd call me up and ask me 'Are you blocking that off?' "[44]

Cole was, likewise, receiving proper respect on television. In his early years on TV, the hosts tended to treat him, usually without any racial condescension, as a welcome but flashy newcomer with a few hot hits. Now show biz legends like Danny Kaye and Jack Benny were rolling out the red carpet and treating him like fellow royalty. His appearance on the Benny show is another of his finest visual moments: after the host introduces Nat as "The best friend a song ever had," he bursts out of his dressing room and, strolling among the hardware of film and television production—cranes, lights, miscellaneous paraphernalia—sings Billy May's fast-and-swinging arrangement of "Day In, Day Out." Then, following some patter with the host, he moves on to Gordon Jenkins's now-iconic string-laden ballad orchestration of "When I Fall in Love."

The chit-chat between Nat and Jack is scripted, but it's sincere and authentically based on their genuine affection for each other. They joke about Nat's record sales (Capitol Records just told him, he informs us, that he's currently selling about seven million records a year) and his songs (there's a very funny riff on "Mona Lisa"). This old-school showbiz acceptance continued on January 27 in New York, when, for the second time in his life, he was honored by the Friars Club, at a luncheon presided over by George Jessel. The supreme toastmaster "started off with a high level crack tracing Cole's beginnings as a choirboy on the East Side named Nathan Cohen."[45] Tony Bennett attended and Johnny Carson also spoke, directing his best zinger at Jessel, saying that the toastmaster's *bar mitzvah* pictures had been taken by Mathew Brady. But Nipsey Russell had the best line of the afternoon. In reference to the minister and congressman who had performed the wedding ceremony for Nat and Maria sixteen years earlier, Russell explained that the initials "N.A.A.C.P." stand for "Never Antagonize Adam Clayton Powell."

On January 14, Nat, Ralph, and Lee went into the Capitol Tower to spitball a bunch of ideas and songs, with the general idea of starting work on a new follow-up album to *Ramblin' Rose* and *Dear Lonely Hearts*. Where those 1962 albums were "pop country," this latest session was more like "pop folk" music, of the kind that Bobby Darin was making on albums like *Earthy* and *Golden Folk Hits*. They went through six folkish numbers on the date, "Silver Bird," "A Rag, a Bone, a Hank of Hair," Joe Sherman's Bob Dylan-esque "Let Me Tell You, Babe" and "My True Carrie Love," all of which brought him into the "tuxedo folk music" territory of the Kingston Trio and the Village Stompers.

"My True Carrie Love" didn't make it on to the album, but it's a winning single, an up-tempo "hootenanny" that he used to open his last appearance on a major, prime time variety show, *The Hollywood Palace* of March 21, 1964. The live performance gives a better indication of what Cole was going for; it's a hand-clapping, foot-stomping number with the Merry Young Souls—a big band swinger with an audience participation element added utilizing simple, nonsensical words of the sort that Mel Brooks would describe as "authentic frontier gibberish." ("Olem piccolo, Carrie / Olem piccolo doo."). The heavy use of audience participation also invokes the pop Gospel style of the period.

The most surprising track from this date is "People" from *Funny Girl*, set to open on Broadway in March. This was clearly not part of the country project; whereas everything else on the session uses mainly guitars and violins, "People" adds three trombones (Dick Nash, Lloyd Ulyate, and Kenny Shroyer playing the bass instrument), which can be clearly heard among the strings. It's an outstanding song, but one in which Cole and Carmichael seem somewhat constricted by a very pop-single-style arrangement and tempo—it's not quite up to "Magic Moment" or "Look No Further" or anything on the *My Fair Lady* album. Still, unlike Barbra Streisand, who would introduce the song on Broadway, Cole sings it like a person who actually needs people.

"I Don't Want to Be Hurt Anymore" had come in over the transom of the publisher Bregman, Vocco, and Conn about three years earlier. This was the first song of one Charlotte McCarthy, a secretary based in San Francisco. Already, a number of publishers had passed on it, but Jack Bregman decided to give it a chance. Then, when demonstrating a bunch of songs for Cole in 1963, all of which were by "established composers," Bregman slipped in Ms. McCarthy's effort, and Cole, as Bregman reported, "just went out of his mind about it."[46]

Cole and Gillette decided to make "I Don't Want to Be Hurt Anymore" the title track of what would be the last country-ish album, especially after it charted the highest of the batch of singles released in February. In the meantime, he was on the road again; in addition to the ceremonial and philanthropic appearances, there was still money to be made at the Copa in January and then the Sands in February; in between, his choral group, the Merry Young Souls, made their own recording debut. He was now off and running with *Sights and Sounds of 1964*, throughout the northwest (Vancouver, Oregon, Seattle), then another swing through California and Nevada.

In May, having gauged the results of the January session, he went ahead with the rest of *I Don't Want to Be Hurt Anymore* over two dates. The January and May sessions employed a fairly stellar studio orchestra, including not only jazz stars (among them his own ex-bassist, Joe Comfort) but two celebrity guitarists, James Burton and Glen Campbell. The most prominently featured musician is the pianist, Don Robertson (1922–2015), a major figure in the history of country music, both as keyboardist and composer. Robertson had been following King Cole since hearing "I Just Can't See for Lookin'" on the very first Trio Capitol release.[47] He later remembered hanging out with Nat and Carlos at Hancock Park, how one evening Cole treated everyone to an impromptu recital of "solo jazz piano," and how he continued to be blown away whenever he heard Cole play.

At one point in the 1950s, Robertson developed a new way to phrase certain notes and chords on the piano that gradually became the keyboard sound most associated with the golden age of country music. "I adapted certain figures from country guitar players and fiddle players and singers to the piano." Various Nashville players, especially Floyd Cramer, picked up on it, but they all acknowledged that Robertson was the creator of what had become known as "slip note"-style piano.

In 1964, Robertson was honored when Cole and Gillette invited him to play on *I Don't Want to Be Hurt Anymore*. "That would be like a cellist being called to play some solo cello passages on a Yo Yo Ma session," Robertson said. "Nat, in my opinion, was the ultimate jazz/pop pianist. He had been my idol and accompanied himself superbly. I really don't know how I worked up the nerve to do it, but somehow I got through it." Robertson is a consistent and welcome presence throughout the album, as on "Brush Those Tears from Your Eyes."

The tune stack for the third C&W album is another eclectic mix, including yet more offbeat tunes from the Depression, like "Was That the Human Thing to Do?" (associated with the Boswell Sisters and including a new line about Coles's stereo) and Harry Warren's "You're My Everything." The very-Nashville "Only Yesterday" is Carmichael's most notable tune as a composer for Cole and has an 8-bar acoustic guitar solo by Campbell. It's all very pleasantly done, and certainly Carmichael's charts lie easier on the ear than those of Hendricks. Nothing on the album is as bad as the worst of the tracks on *Rose* and *Hearts*, but again, as with *Hearts*, there are few tracks that stand out from the others. Still, the somewhat grating sound of Hendricks's charts was actually a plus in the world of pop singles. There's a reason Hendricks had so many hits—sometimes it pays to be irritating—even though Carmichael was a vastly superior musician.

One bonus track from the *I Don't Want to Be Hurt Anymore* album was another version of the title song, sung in Japanese for that market. It seems to be a whole new recording rather than Cole simply singing in a different language over the existing orchestral track: for one thing, the background choir is also singing in Japanese.[48]

Nat told Joe Sherman a story about singing "Ramblin' Rose" at some event where the master of ceremonies introduced him with "a whole soap opera" and a big "dramatic story" about the song. " 'This is a song that has the roots of America in it; it's so much a part of the heartlands, the soul of America.' He's going on and on, being very poetic about it. And at the end of it, Nat tells the guy, 'To be honest, this was written by two Jewish boys from Brooklyn.' " (This is, in fact, the way he would frequently introduce the song in clubs and concert halls.) For Nat, any notions of cultural authenticity were strictly secondary; rather, it was all about the diversity.

A COUNTRY-AND-WESTERN SONG in Japanese? It shows how truly international Nat King Cole had become in the final phase of his life. He had gradually transformed himself into the ultimate voice of multi-culturalism: he wasn't going for just Spanish-speaking listeners with the Latin albums nor just C&W fans with the "country" albums, but he was trying to get everybody on board with everything that he was doing.

Around the time that "Ramblin' Rose" was climbing the charts, Cole officially celebrated his twenty-fifth anniversary in show business and *Billboard* noted correctly that Cole had made his first records for Ammor.[49] That same season he was asked, in a promotional interview for *More Cole Español*, if there would be any further *Español* albums." He responded, "I hope so! In fact, I hope to branch off into some other languages such as French, Italian, German, and possibly a little Japanese. Now that's a ringer!"

Having finished the latest country album, he now briefly headed east in early June where, for virtually the only time in his life, he invaded the halls of higher education. On June 1, he received an honorary degree from one of the oldest "historically African American" universities in the country, Morgan State University in Baltimore.

Then, there was an event that was even more meaningful: on June 7, he attended Carole's graduation ceremony at Cazenovia College. This upstate New York institution, located near Syracuse, had apparently come up as a choice for Nat's oldest child because the family's great friend, Jimmy Van Heusen, had attended the university in about 1930. Unlike Van Heusen, who was famously expelled for his rather unscholarly antics, Carole was actually graduating—although at this point, she was carrying a secret (that's one way of putting it) that she wasn't yet sharing with her father or anyone else.

For the ceremony, Nat and Cookie were happy to be joined by the ever-lovable Van Heusen and his no-less-irrepressible partner, Sammy Cahn. When the composer, who wouldn't marry until he was almost sixty and had no children, talked about the event a few years later, it was clear that he loved Cookie and was as proud of her as if she were his own daughter. Nat was still in the doghouse with Maria; the trouble between them was far from being resolved, and to stay, as much as he could, on her good side, he had promised his wife that he would not sing or play at the ceremony. Do not, she warned him explicitly, pull focus from your daughter; this night was about Cookie, not about Nat.

But then Sammy and Jimmy performed a whole set of their biggest hits, some with new topical "special material" lyrics dishing the latest Cazenovia campus dirt, written an hour before. Poor Nat could only stand so much. "We were such a smash," said Van Heusen, "that Nat just had to get up. He sang 'Ramblin' Rose,' which was his big hit then, and about eight other songs. He caught hell from Maria, but he just couldn't help himself."[50] Nat was bursting with pride over Cookie, and delighted to share the moment with Sammy and Jimmy. It was one of the happiest occasions of his entire life, and one of the last magic moments he would share with his eldest child.

In between the two academic events, he had done yet another recording session in Los Angeles, perhaps the most important one of his final year. We have seen how, in this period, Cole stayed ahead of the competition with his now-established pattern of trying lots of different ideas; then, when something seemed to hit, he and his team, with Lee Gillette and Ralph Carmichael, would pounce on it and build an album around it. With the exception of *My Fair Lady*, all of his albums from 1962 onward—*Ramblin' Rose, Dear Lonely Hearts* (both 1962), *Those Lazy-Hazy-Crazy Days of Summer* (1963) and *I Don't Want To Be Hurt Anymore* (1964)—had all been constructed in this fashion. "We'd go in and record some singles and throw 'em at the wall," said Carmichael, "and if one of 'em stuck. they'd take that single and build a whole album around it. So, they'd parlay the hit single into a hit album."

He may not have realized it, but the country series was now complete, and so he turned all of his energies to an "international series"; this would be a direct extension of both the three pan-American albums and the many English and European songs he'd been doing regularly for at least a decade. In April 1963, he had not only taped the hit "Lazy-Hazy-Crazy Days of Summer" but also three other imports, "In the Cool of the Day" (Greek), "Felicia" (Italian), and "You'll See" (French) (and also, the lamentable "Wishing Well," which smacked of 1958 rather than 1963). All three were exceptionally lovely and fit with the international program: "Cool of the Day" was by Manos Hadjidakis, best known for "Never on Sunday"; he was the closest thing that Greece had to an international superstar maestro on the level of Bert Kaempfert (Germany), Michel Legrand (France), or Antonio Carlos Jobim (Brazil). Moving forward, Cole's singles output for 1964 consists almost entirely of internationally oriented material; the only exceptions are a trio of movie themes. At the June 1964 session, he cut the "money" song, "L-O-V-E," and it's a testament to his highly developed skills at knowing what would be a hit even though this German song was not much of a success when it was first released as a single in September.

The summer of 1964 was the last point in his life when he spent any meaningful time at home, mostly with the younger children; Carole was then acting in summer stock. Before and after three productive recording sessions in August, Nat played the Greek Theater and the Cow Palace in San Francisco. The music from these summer sessions is, quite literally, all over the map. There were some familiar Cole import hits, now sung by him in their native tongues, as well as other Cole hits translated into various languages. There are also a few brand-new songs he had never recorded previously and a mix of vintage arrangements (mostly by Riddle) and new charts by Carmichael.

Cole sang in these other languages, for the most part, phonetically. "I remember specifically a project that we did in a couple of different languages, German and French," said Carmichael. "And the reason I remember the French is because we were over in Las Vegas working on another project—or picking tunes and keys—and there was a gal that was headlining at the Lido de Paris, a very famous French actress—she was the star of the show—and it was arranged for Nat to have a session with her and she was going to teach him the phonetic pronunciation of some of those songs. But I remember there was a meeting and she was helping him with pronunciation of the French." Gunilla Hutton told a similar story, "He just adored singing in other languages, not just Spanish but German and French. And I remember my mother helped him with one German song that he was doing."

Among the re-done classic Cole imports are "Answer Me, My Love," now restored to its original German title and lyric, "Mutterlein." He actually sings the 1953 Riddle chart in German, then in English in the out chorus, overdubbing the orchestral track from the 1961 stereo remake. Then there are two foreign-language versions of "Autumn Leaves," which Cole and Riddle (on the 1955 edition of *Two in Love*) had helped make into perhaps the single most popular French song in the English-speaking world. On the original arrangement, Riddle had employed some suspiciously minor string sounds that Carmichael turns to his advantage: on the French language version ("Les Feuilles Mortes")[51] he brings in accordionist Carl Fontina; on the Japanese translation ("Kareha"), Asian musician Kazue Kudo plays koto.[52]

Cole recorded four additional European songs at this point, two of which he never sang in English: Andre Clavier's "Le Bonheur C'est Quand On S'aime," which also employs Senor Fortina's accordion, is a jaunty little strut down the Champs-Elysee. "You Are so Amiable," is the English transliteration of a very pretty Italian song somewhat reminiscent of "Sorrento," which Cole recorded in both Italian ("Tu Sei Cosi Amabile") and Spanish ("Tu Eres Tan Amable"). The first arrangement is slightly more Neapolitan, with accordion; the second more Iberian, with Spanish-style acoustic guitar.

There is also a pair of extremely tasty French dishes in this pan-European mixed grill menu: "Passing By" is one of the most famous songs by that most melodic of all Frenchmen, Charles Trenet. Cole had already sung his "I Wish You Love" at the Sands, and he had also done Jack Lawrence's English lyric to "Passing By" on his NBC TV show. This is quite the nicest of all of Cole's French items—making it all the more regrettable that he didn't also sing Trenet's "Boom" or "La Mer" (aka "Beyond the Sea"). Very nearly as nice is Gilbert Becaud's "Crois-Moi, ca Durera" which he recorded a year earlier as "You'll See." In both versions Cole has a perky choir and a tempo change from ballad to dance in the second chorus; either way, they are both *magnifique!*

The August 1964 singles are a fascinating pool of material, and at the time of his centennial in 2019, fourteen tracks were collected onto a CD titled *International Nat King Cole*. Still, they don't add up to an actual album. Fortunately, Cole had just enough time and energy left to complete one last project, which would represent the culmination of both his fascination with international music as well as his lifelong status, whether playing or singing, as a great jazz musician.

IN JANUARY, WHEN THE FRIARS TOASTED and roasted Cole, they presented him with a deluxe set of golf clubs for being such a good sport. It's not known if he ever used them. By fall, he was a very sick man. In September, he flew to New York to videotape an episode of *The Jack Paar Program* and then drove up with Sweetie to register for the new semester at the Northfield School for Girls. She recalled that he was, as usual, "smoking non-stop," and when they arrived, "his presence nearly caused a riot. No one had expected Nat King Cole to show up at this small prep school, and there was no security to prevent hundreds of girls from crushing in to shake his hand or to get a closer look. Dad was cool as always." She later would remember this as the last truly happy time she would ever spend with her father, even though she later realized that he was already suffering from crippling back pain, caused by the cancer.[53]

He was putting off visiting the doctor and getting a proper diagnosis; there was still too much to do, projects to finish, and his house to put in order. His bassist, Charlie Harris, had already grown tired of the road after more than a dozen years, so Nat helped him make a lateral transition into the world of furniture retail in Baltimore, and he never looked back.[54] Cole still had some contracted engagements to fulfill, including, unbelievably, two extended engagements in Nevada. Plus, he had an album to finish and, to his surprise, one last movie to make.

As with everyone in Tinseltown, there had been all kinds of film projects that were bruited about for Cole but never came to fruition, including two Hollywood films mentioned in 1961 and two foreign productions announced the following year. *Reprieve* was a prison drama written by Millard Lampell, in which Cole was to play a supporting role as Ben Gazzara's cellmate. "Straight acting, no singing,"[55] he promised. He was also interested in a "wonderful script" by Lester Pine, who had written the continuity for his 1961 Greek Theater show, *The Merry World of Nat King Cole*. "It's called *Adam*, and it's the story of a jazz musician. But an authentic jazz musician—and they've never done that in movies. It's a tragedy." The first was apparently never produced, but the second became the 1966 drama, *A Man Called Adam* starring Sammy Davis Jr.[56] Cole seems acutely aware of his limitations as a dramatic actor; he's not kidding himself or anyone else. The title role of "Adam," he said, "is not a part for me—it calls for a great actor like Sidney Poitier. I'd be in it, but not in the starring part."

In 1962, Cole was slated to appear in a feature that would be shot in Mexico City and had a working title of *The English Teacher*. It was to co-star Cole and the iconic Mexican actress and Hollywood star Dolores Del Río and would have been co-produced by Kell-Cole (and Ike Jones) and Mexican producer Miguel Zacharias. "The comedy [is] about a nightclub entertainer who wanders into a convent and winds up teaching English there."[57] The other was *The Loved and the Lost* "to be produced independently in England early next year."[58] Cole was supposedly to co-star with blonde bombshell Carroll Baker, but, in both cases, it's dubious that Cole would have played a romantic leading man against either of these white leading ladies, even if one was *Latina*. (Around 1953, there had been talk of a new production of Eugene O'Neill's *The Emperor Jones*; I think it's safe to say that it's a relief that this one never made it in front of the cameras. Alas, Cole doesn't seem to have ever been considered for any production of *Othello*, though Sinatra would have made a great Iago.)

Then finally, unexpectedly in 1964, came *Cat Ballou*. If *China Gate* was Cole's best dramatic film, then *Cat Ballou*, which he filmed in September 1964, would be his best comedy, his best musical, and his best and only western, all in one. The project began when producer Harold Hecht (who'd won an Oscar for *Marty* in 1956) read *The Ballad of Cat Ballou*, a 1956 novel by Roy Chanslor, a straight-ahead western action story albeit an unusual one with a very pro-active, empowered young female protagonist at its center.

Catherine Ballou begins the story as the innocent daughter of a prominent rancher, who then watches as her parents are killed by a corrupt local "corporation" (a fancy facade for a pack of crooks), who, in cahoots with the local law, are scheming to take over the family's ranch. Over the course of the novel, "Cat" Ballou gradually transitions from merely wanting to protect her ranch, to seeking revenge on her father's killers, to gradually becoming a full-fledged bank robber and outlaw queen. After Hecht brought in screenwriter Frank Pierson, the story morphed from a conventional western to something much more like a parody. It was Pierson's idea to bring in Elliot Silverstein to direct, even though all of his experience up to that time had been in television. Both were making their theatrical feature-film debuts.[59]

There had been tough women in movies before, even in westerns, like both Joan Crawford and Mercedes McCambridge in *Johnny Guitar* (1954), but Silverstein and Pierson wanted someone soft, feminine, and girl-ish, the last girl you'd expect to reinvent herself as a dangerous desperado: the very first shot of "Cat" shows her looking as demure as can be, sewing up the dress that she's apparently going to be wearing when, in a few hours, they hang her. The initial choice was Ann-Margret, but her agent rejected the offer, without even telling her. Still, the twenty-six-year-old Jane Fonda was perfect, one can't imagine anyone else doing it better; her then-husband, French director Roger Vadim, encouraged her to take the role, saying, "The woman is courageous, but tender, modern, and funny. It's just right for you at this stage in your career."

Likewise, the men in her "gang," are Michael Callan as the love interest, Dwayne Hickman, then and now most famous in the lovable, girl-crazy doofus title role in the classic, long-running sitcom *The Many Loves of Dobie Gillis* (1959–1963), and Tom Nardini as a Native American. They're fresh-faced, young, and cuddly, looking like they belonged in a beach party movie rather than a western. The only real manly man in the bunch is Lee Marvin (who, coincidentally, had a prominent supporting role in *Raintree County*), cast at Silverstein's insistence, as an atypical gunfighter with a drinking problem (to put it mildly) and even an alcoholic horse.[60] In fact, as if to maximize his masculinity, he played a dual role as both of the two manliest men in the picture, not only the dysfunctional hero, "Kid Shelleen," but also, the bad guy, "Tim Strawn."

As we've seen, Cole already had sung the main title themes for roughly a dozen movies, and thus, in a sense, he was a kind of narrator who sets up the story in song. And while he had never done a western, story-songs were very prominent in the genre. Pierson was also clearly inspired by *The Threepenny Opera*, which begins with "Moritat" (or "Murder Ballad" or "The Ballad of Mack the Knife") a tale of an extravagant criminal as performed by a "street singer." It was apparently Pierson's idea to open this drama with two "street singers" singing "The Ballad of Cat Ballou," which also details the exploits of a highly unusual anti-hero. Silverstein started to cast the two street singers, billed on screen as "shouters." "I wanted Stubby Kaye, whom I'd worked with in musical theater one summer," the director said, probably remembering how Kaye's numbers in both *Guys and Dolls* and *Li'l Abner* did much to set up the action in those two hit shows. "But I didn't know who the other one should be." It was Mitchell "Mike" Frankovich, then the vice president in charge of production at Columbia Pictures, who "came to the rescue. He said, 'How would you like Nat King Cole?' And I said 'Terrific, terrific!' That was not a period of time when black performers were so easily welcomed into feature films. And I remember thinking how really great that was, for Frankovich, the head of a major studio, to come out and do just that."[61]

For Cole, it was a reunion with Frank De Vol, who had served as arranger-conductor on the breakthrough hit, "Nature Boy," in 1947, although they had not worked together since.[62] Now famous as a musical director for film and television, he was billed simply as "De Vol." It's not quite known how they settled on the team of Mack David (the older brother of the more famous lyricist Hal David) and Jerry Livingston (no relation to the more famous Jay and Alan Livingston); they had several notable songs to their credit, including those from Disney's 1950 *Cinderella*, but no major hits or standards.[63] Still, this was the right choice. David and Livingston wrote two excellent new songs for the production, "The Ballad of Cat Ballou" and "They Can't Make Her Cry."

Cole and Kaye rehearsed and pre-recorded their vocal tracks around September 22. The company went on location for ten days in early October,[64] at which point Cole did two benefit concerts, at Marineland Sea Arena in Manhattan Beach and his final appearance (October 4) at the Hollywood Bowl. The latter was produced in opposition to Proposition 14 and against housing discrimination in California. In what is his last extant live performance, Cole who is introduced by a remarkably julibilant Milton Berle, sounds surprisingly good in his 20-minute segment.

Then the crew returned to shoot for ten days on the western town set on the Columbia Pictures backlot. This would have been difficult enough for Cole, but at the same time, he was also working at Harrah's. He would film his scenes all day, then take a plane for the 430-mile trip to Lake Tahoe, do several shows, and then fly back. This schedule would have been enough to crush a healthy man. Cole and Kaye shot their scenes on Columbia's outdoor backlot, beginning on Monday September 28. (For relaxation, at some point Cole took a few hours off here and there to go trout fishing with co-star Michael Callan.)

"When I first read the script, the two street singers were in it," Silverstein continued. "However, they were not 'presentational'; they were part of the life of the town. And so, I said, 'Oh my gosh, I'll take these two singers and I'll make them tell the story of the 'Ballad of Cat Ballou.' We'll [have them] directly address the audience and they'll be invisible to everybody else. They'll pop up and make odd appearances here and there. And that's just one of my favorite things in the film." The finished film, released in June 1965, is a classic western comedy, and though, admittedly, not everything in the film works as well as everything else, no one would argue with Silverstein that the use of music is the best thing about *Cat Ballou*.

The movie opens with a bang, literally, with the iconic Columbia Pictures logo, the so-called "torch lady" who morphs before our very eyes, courtesy of traditional "cel" animation, from a stately variation on the Statue of Liberty into a two-gunned, red-headed firebrand of a female outlaw. We hear two plinks of a banjo and there we are, staring right into the faces of Stubby Kaye and Nat King Cole, both in full western drag, playing banjos (and with guitars strapped to their backs) and singing in harmony. "Well now, friends just lend an ear / For you're now about to hear, the ballad of Cat Ballou." But before they proceed, first they have to introduce each other: Cole sings solo as he acknowledges Kaye, "It's a song that's newly made, and Professor Sam the Shade" and then Kaye in turn bows in deference to Cole, "and the Sunrise Kid are singing it for you."

This opening sequence is particularly convincing: after introducing each other, Cole and Kaye set up the story, telling us that we're in Wolf City,

Wyoming, 1894, and the town is just about to hang "the wildest gal in the West since Calamity Jane." They walk around the gallows, and then stroll down the Main Street of Wolf City, as Silverstein suggests, totally unnoticed by townspeople, singing and strumming all the way. They pause in front of the city jail, and we see armed guards in front; seated on a bench, a wizened, bearded old pioneer reads what looks like a vintage 1894 *Police Gazette*; the opening credits are then shown as pages in this magazine.

Following the credits, we see "Professor Sam the Shade" and "The Sunrise Kid" still singing, strumming, and strolling, now approaching a procession of rather tightly wound women who have formed an ad-hoc Salvation Army-style band and choir. They march up to the jailhouse, entreating the prisoner "Pray, Jezebel, pray / If ye would seek salvation." They look like a veritable orchestra of Linda Tripps, precisely the kinds of harpies who seek to punish any and all members of their own gender who step out of line and have anything resembling fun. The moods of the two interlocked melodies, the antic fun of "Cat Ballou" and the dismal piety of "Pray Jezebel" are acutely contrasted, as Cole and Kaye sing back and forth in counterpoint with the female choir. As the sequence continues, the camera pans into the window, and there we see Jane Fonda as "Cat Ballou," whom we have already heard quite a lot about; as mentioned, she looks especially demure, in very proper 19th-century undergarments, putting a finishing touch on a dress more appropriate for a wedding rather than a hanging. The music slows, as do the two street singers, and the shouts quiet to a whisper. Then, we pan past Cole, now singing solo, "Cat, your time has come. As you stand on the brink, / it's sure making you think, 'bout your life of sin. / How they're now gonna hang you, and how did you begin?"

The rest of the movie, going forward, is a flashback. (The idea was repeated in two Broadway classics, *Evita* and *Wicked*, which both open with the death of the main character.) We now see Jane Fonda, as she looked just a few months earlier, appearing even younger and more innocent; characters are introduced, inter-relationships are anticipated in a train sequence. After leaving the train, Cat is seen in a horse-drawn carriage carrying her out to her father's ranch, and she just happens to pass the two shouters, the Professor and the Kid, who are standing in the street, strumming and singing the first reprise of the "Cat Ballou" theme.

Cole and Kaye have perhaps their most memorable sequence at the exact halfway point: Cat has just witnessed the bad guys murdering her father in cold blood (spoiler alert) but she screws her courage to the sticking place and vows, as God is her witness, that "You'll never make me cry." Jump cut to the shouters standing stiff as boards on top of a hill, with the sun setting picturesquely in the background. Now the Professor and the Kid are playing guitars, rather than banjos, and Cole sings in solo, "There are teardrops in her heart / But they can't make her cry."

Much of the "Cat Ballou" song is intended as dramatic irony, a good clean fun kind of a song about this wicked woman, this western "Elphaba," whom, the shouters tell us repeatedly, is "mean and evil through and through." Still, everything else tells us something completely different, and the movie goes to great lengths to show us that rather than being "wicked," her transgressions are altogether justified. "They Can't Make Her Cry" is something else entirely, the song is completely straightforward, without a trace of irony, and Cole sings it in a manner that's remarkably tender, even for him. "She's lost all the kin that she's known / And the tears will turn into stone."

"The Kid" and "the Professor" turn around, and we then see Fonda and her three amigos (Callan, Hickman, and Nardio) riding along dejectedly at the bottom of the hill; some brief dialogue transpires while Cole continues to sing. The next scene is the dramatic turning point, where Cat decides to join the outlaw band and get revenge on Wolf City: "I'll make Sherman's march to the sea look like a bird walk!" (A scene that's effectively punctuated and contrasted by some drunken shenanigans from Lee Marvin.) Cut again to the shouters standing outside, resuming the "Ballad of Cat Ballou": "So that mournful day, became part of a legend." When reprising the "Ballad" this time, they "intercut" back into "They Can't Make Her Cry," and the two songs are again juxtaposed—although when heard this time, rather than being slow and tender and in minor, now they are louder, in a major key, and in a considerably more defiant, martial tempo. "Cat Ballou made her mind up," they tell us, "to make this country bleed!"

The other most memorable sequence comes as we build to the big climax: a major caper is foreshadowed in a house of ill-repute. This time, the Kid and the Professor are staying in one place and Lee Marvin and the other cast members walk past them. Like any great Cole venture, the producers thankfully found one opportunity for him to play the piano; we see him pounding away at the upright, singing with Kaye and accompanying an aging trollop (played to the fullest by Dorothy Claire). This is a vintage bar-room ballad, "Why Are You Weeping, Sister?" by one Herbert Kaufman, from 1911. (On the Columbia Pictures pre-record disc, the song is titled "Tarnished Virtue.") The piece is written as something of a call-and-response, with Cole, occasionally joined by Kaye, asking the questions:

"Why are you weeping, Sister?
Why are you sitting alone?"

and Claire responding,

"I'm bent and gray
And I've lost the way!
All my tomorrows were yesterday!
I traded them off for a wanton's pay."

They all join in on the last phrase ("and now you are wrinkled and old"), in a way that seems both poignant and mock-poignant at the same time. We follow Marvin up the stairs, and we hear the three singers and the piano recede into the distant background of the soundtrack. Having spoiled enough, I won't give away the ending, but I will tell you, that Professor Sam the Shade and the Sunrise Kid are a key part of it.

Writing about *Cat Ballou* in the Fall 1965 issue of *Film Quarterly*, Pauline Kael whined, "There are even two minstrels—wasn't Cole enough? Is it perhaps that Stubby Kaye makes it *cuter*? A black man and a fat man—so nobody can fail to realize that the ballad singing is 'for fun.'" With this observation, Kael seems as humorless as the harridans outside the window of Cat Ballou's prison cell. She doesn't seem to have any sense of comedy or of music here; what's more she makes all these things, to be black, to be fat, to be cute, and to have fun, all sound like dirty words. To directly answer her question, yes, Nat Cole by himself would have been great, but there are times in the theater and music when a duet is, in fact, more entertaining than a solo. Just because the director is underscoring the fun—much like *Blazing Saddles*, this is rather broad comedy, not Oscar Wilde or Sir Noel Coward—doesn't mean he's undercutting it. Elsewhere in the review, Kael does make some worthwhile points, including listing Cole's singing "They Can't Make Her Cry" as one of the high points of the picture (although she might have noticed that this was an occasion when Silverstein agreed that Cole by himself was "enough"), and some of her criticisms are on-target. Still, I can't imagine that anybody who's ever seen the picture would walk out of the theater not only humming the title song but thinking that Cole and Kaye are especially magical together.

Cat Ballou was worth the trouble and the pain that Cole went through; it turned out not only to be the best-remembered movie of his career, but it was one of the major hits of 1965, taking in $20 million at the box office when that was still a ton of money. It proved a formidable push for the career of Fonda, establishing her as a major Hollywood star, and even more so for Marvin—who won the Academy Award. Like *Wild Is Love* in 1960–61, 1965 was precisely the moment for *Cat Ballou*, a story about an empowered woman in a dominant role at the start of the women's movement, and which made fun of a venerable American institution, the western movie, at a time when people were just beginning to question more than a few other venerable American institutions.

On the *Jack Benny Show*, in January, the host and the guest had shared a quip about Cole's movie roles being eminently forgettable. Now that statement was no longer true. My personal feeling is that Cole would have been delighted with *Cat Ballou*, and especially his own part in it, if only he had lived long enough to see it.

But he didn't.

IN HIS TRADITIONAL VENUES, like the recording studio and the clubs of Nevada, Cole was able to act as though nothing was wrong—and no one was the wiser. But he was on a movie set in October, well outside of his comfort zone; as Harry Belafonte put it, "I don't think Nat King Cole was ever as uncomfortable anywhere in the world as he was in front of the camera being required to act."[65] Even though most of the cast and crew on *Cat Ballou* had never met him before, they all could tell something was wrong. Silverstein, Callan, and Hickman all said so. He was not acting like someone in good health. Said Silverstein, "I must say that one of the sad memories I had was that, nobody knew why, but Nat was coughing quite a bit, particularly when we got up into the thin mountain air. Later, it turned out, of course, he had lung cancer and it was shocking to know that while he was moving forward, there he was a sick man." He added, understatedly, "wonderful guy."

Nat finished both the movie shoot and the Harrah's engagement around the end of October, and even then, he wouldn't rest; he was completely booked for November. For the first three weeks, he would be working at the Sands, and then he would travel directly to San Carlos, California, and play the Circle Star Theater for a two-week run. Toward the end of that run, he would also finish the album he had been working on. It was now clear to almost everyone what was happening; Sparky Tavares, his valet, knew something was amiss when his boss kept repeatedly asking him to punch new holes in his belts, and his clothes were starting to droop from his thin frame.

For Gunilla Hutton, the tip-off was even more dramatic, and for her, unbelievable. "I knew something was wrong. He just coughed continuously. And he said that he was going to check with his doctor when he got back to Los Angeles. And then he did, apparently, get some x-rays taken, but he didn't tell me about it. I only found out later. He kind of kept that from everybody, not just me. But me, and some other people close to him, we were all nagging him. 'Please go to the doctor.'" Finally, she was presented with the smoking gun, an occurrence that left her with no doubt that Nat was deathly ill, and it wasn't holes in a belt. In surveying the vast legacy of performances, studio and live, that Cole left us, it's literally impossible to find an example of him singing flat or missing even a single note. But then, in Vegas, the unthinkable happened. "He never missed a note. He never slid off a note or cheated a high note. But one night in Vegas, he missed the high note [the high E flat in the last two words of] 'Mona Lisa'—"Mona *lee*-sa"—"and his voice just cracked on that note." Never before. "I knew then that he was very sick. But he just kept on keeping on until he collapsed in San Carlos."

He was now experiencing violent chest pains, so much so that the show had to be rewritten so that Cole did as little as possible and left as early as he could.[66] Thus, a doctor was summoned to his room at the Fairmont on December 1, and told him what he and everyone close to him already knew: it was a lung tumor. These days, the medical cliché regarding cancer is that "we could have cured it if we had caught it right away." But not in Nat's case: "It was, as post-mortem examinations showed, already in an advanced state that would have been impossible to arrest."[67]

THE CIRCLE STAR WAS A DREAM ENGAGEMENT: for years he'd been trying to establish himself as something more than an individual performer; he wanted to be at the center of an elaborate musical package that would enable him to play the big rooms, and, at 3,743 seats, the Circle Star was one of the biggest in California. In that sense, Cole was again anticipating the movement of rock and pop stars into sports arenas and other really big rooms, as Elvis and Sinatra would later do, at the end of the 1960s. No, it wasn't exactly Broadway, and *Sights and Sounds of 1964* was hardly *Fiddler on the Roof*, but the dream that Cole had been working toward had essentially come true.

So, who could blame him, when the doctor gave him the prognosis, for not instantly dropping everything to rush to the hospital? No, he would finish the *Sights and Sounds* engagement, and he would finish the album. He still had some "L-O-V-E" to share with the world.

IT'S VERY SATISFYING THAT NAT KING COLE'S final project should be *L-O-V-E,* recorded at the end of 1964 and released at the beginning of 1965. This was by far the jazziest of his albums ever since *Let's Face the Music!* in 1961. With this heavily swing-oriented set, Cole was getting back to his jazz roots—roots that he had never entirely abandoned. But at the same time, *L-O-V-E* was highly international in its appeal, and it illustrated how much of a "world citizen," to use Tony Bennett's phrase, Nat King Cole had become. With *L-O-V-E,* Cole was moving backward to the beginning of his career and forward into a future that he would never live to enjoy at the same time.

Like *Lazy-Hazy-Crazy, L-O-V-E,* began with a German song; "L-O-V-E" originated as an instrumental by Bert Kaempfert, the Hamburg-born composer, bandleader, and producer, who would write important songs for Elvis Presley ("Muss I Den" or "Wooden Heart") and Frank Sinatra ("Strangers in the Night"), and who was the first to record the Beatles. Already well known in Europe, Kaempfert had started to crack the US market thanks to the assistance of another producer-songwriter, Milt Gabler, who had produced some of Cole's sessions for Decca in 1941 (also known to history as the uncle of Billy Crystal). As a single, "L-O-V-E" wasn't anywhere near the hit that "Lazy-Hazy-Crazy" was, but Cole knew it had potential for an album, thanks not least to Carmichael, who provided a swinging, lean-and-mean arrangement that cut straight to the chase, and to trumpet soloist Bobby Bryant. At the same date in June, Cole taped "Wanderlust" and "More and More of Your Amor," two songs in a somewhat similar style that would also later become part of the *L-O-V-E* album (although not until the CD era); the date also included "Marnie," a movie theme, for Alfred Hitchcock no less, released as a single.

As Carmichael remembered, "We did 'L-O-V-E' as a single, at Capitol Studio A. As I recall, I used Nat's rhythm section, but there was a trumpet player named Bobby Bryant who was quite popular. He [was dating] Della Reese and I remember at the time that he had been playing lead for Della in Tahoe. Bobby was a real powerhouse trumpet player and of course he played that great trumpet solo."

During the August sessions, Cole and Carmichael re-recorded 'L-O-V-E' in five additional languages for release on foreign singles (later, the five takes were edited into a composite, multi-lingual master). Finally, Cole, as exhausted as he was, decided to cut the rest of the necessary tracks in San Francisco while he was working an hour or so away at the Circle Star. It was now clear to everyone that if he didn't finish the album soon, he might never have the chance.

The first man that Gillette called was Ralph Carmichael. "After 'L-OV-E' became a hit, it was decided that we'd put a whole bunch of tunes around that and call it the *L-O-V-E* album." The sound that Cole and Carmichael created for the album could be viewed as a more subtle and genuinely musical expansion of what Bobby Darin and Richard Wess had wrought on "Mack the Knife" and "Beyond the Sea," which itself used a template of Sinatra and Riddle's "I've Got You Under My Skin." "Skin," "Mack," and "L-O-V-E" all begin comparatively quietly, then they all gradually mount in intensity and excitement; "Mack," in particular keeps modulating upward, getting higher in pitch as well as volume.

The original idea had been to mimic the sound that Kaempfert had created for "Wonderland by Night": "There was a very commercial sound at that point. Bert Kaempfert had a hit record, and the 'Bert Kaempfert sound' was going around." Carmichael's memories of the session are borne out by the music itself; the issued tracks from December 1, "How I'd Like to Love You" and "Coquette," both sound more or less like Kaempfert instrumentals. But then, Carmichael continued, "Nat said he didn't want any more of that Bert Kaempfert stuff. He wanted some straight-ahead swing. So, he rebelled. He didn't want to chase the market. He wanted some nice, pretty, and swinging stuff." And then, the arranger said, "We stayed up all night after the first session, rewriting the charts. Good thing. We changed the rhythm. Jimmy Rowles came up the next day and we rewrote the things, because he wanted more of a punchy brass feel. And so, we were up all night and got a bunch of the charts done and copied, so then the next day, it felt a little better." Rowles was joined by saxophonists Bud Shank and Charlie Kennedy (the latter best known for his work in Louis Prima's '40s big band and, later, Terry Gibbs's Dream Band), and trumpeters "Jonesy" (Cole's longtime lead brass man, Reunald Jones) and Al Porcino.

The majority of the songs on the project were either European in origin or specifically concerned themselves with the theme of international travel and romance, or both. "More" was an Italian movie theme that had hit in the States for Steve Lawrence (a rare example of a Jewish singer scoring with a song by an Italian composer, rather than the other way around); "The Girl from Ipanema," the breakthrough hit by Brazilian composer Antonio Carlos Jobim; and "My Kind of Girl," a hit for London crooner Matt Monro written by Leslie Bricusse, which had anticipated the British invasion.

"Swiss Retreat," "Wanderlust," and "More and More of Your Amor" (from the June session and added to the CD edition) were all about wandering and lusting, and they fit directly into the "L-O-V-E" pattern: like "Mack," they continually modulate, which further fits the profile: they convey the idea of loving and moving on so effectively that even the key signature can't stay in one place. "Wanderlust"[68] is an especially breezy, witty lyric of loving and leaving; "Swiss Retreat" cleverly ends with a low "whoomp!" (probably played on bass trombone) as if to suggest an Alpine *oompah* band; while "More and More of Your Amor" opens with a jazz flute solo by Bud Shank, itself a rather exotic sound in 1964.

Characteristically, Cole saved room at the table for one of the Tobias brothers (Jerry, "Swiss Retreat") and a Sherman brother (Joe and George David Weiss, on "There's Love" and "More and More of Your Amor"). (Most of these new songs were published by Cole's firms, Comet and SWECO.) Two new songs from the December 2 session—"Your Love," co-credited to Carmichael, Gillette, and Wayne Dunstan,[69] and "There's Love," by Weiss and Sherman—seem like musical and lyrical variations on the original "L-O-V-E," based on the same chord changes; all three songs could be countermelodies to each other.

"There's Love," along with Joe Bailey's "How I'd Love to Love You" and Bob Marcus's "Thanks to You" are as close as the set comes to a ballad in the original eleven tracks; though quieter, they too follow the same trajectory, gradually rising in pitch and intensity. "Thanks to You" incorporates an introductory vamp and countermelody that uses doubled notes and block chords in the rhythm section that seem jointly inspired by the King Cole Trio and the Shearing Quintet. These comparatively quieter tracks are no less jazzy, being also similar in mood to Count Basie's classic slow dances, like "Li'l Darlin'." Two of the best new songs, "Wanderlust" and "More and More of Your Amor," were taped at the June date, and though they fit brilliantly along with the rest of the material, Cole left them off the original LP. ("Amor" was a Comet publication, which proves that Cole wasn't necessarily biased toward songs that he owned a piece of.)

Nat had showed up at the June date wearing a formal suit; this was a break from his normal attire at sessions, which, under Maria's influence, had become "elegant casual." Said Ralph, "We commented about that. Why would he dress up to come to a recording? He must have been valuing every day. Maybe he knew his time was short." He was more customarily casual at the December 2 date, and Ralph remembered that he was so focused on rewriting and getting the charts ready, and dealing with a lack of sleep, that at the first he didn't notice anything wrong—but soon enough he did. "Nat was irritable and less cheerful than I'd ever seen him. I could tell something was bothering him"—and it wasn't the charts.

Cole's voice is somewhat raw on the faster numbers; there's a slight bit of gruffness on "Wanderlust" that actually further enhances the narrative. There's no hint of the blues form or harmony in this number, but Cole incorporates some of the raspiness we heard, for instance, on his gag version of "Joe Turner's Blues" from the 1960 Sands soundcheck. Perhaps the message is similar to "Joe Turner," "Yellow Dog Blues," and Jimmy Rushing's famous "Goin' to Chicago." A man is telling his woman that he's moving on; only in this case, he's not going north but heading for the next world. But it's hardly a lachrymose self-eulogy. Cole is joyful about it, swinging, upbeat, even euphoric. He's not about to leave us on anything but a high note.

The final session, December 3, concluded with a track that had an international provenance but was almost certainly not intended for the *L-O-V-E* project. "No Other Heart" was a British song, with music by David Lee, a composer who worked frequently for the BBC, and lyrics by Herbert Kretzmer, the South African playwright and librettist who later got very rich by writing the English adaptation of *Les Miserables*.[70] It's a very touching ballad, which starts with, "No other heart will touch this heart / Nor find again it's secret place / Through all the Autumn years that lie ahead."

It's almost impossible not to think that Nat King Cole knew then these would be the last words that he would ever sing.

AFTER THE FINAL DATE, December 3, 1964, Lee Gillette got busy. Even as Cole was being treated in St. John's Hospital, Capitol Records rushed the album out—perhaps that's why there are only eleven tracks; clearly, everybody was in a hurry. It reached stores before the end of January 1965, and in that sense, it was the greatest gift that could be given to Cole as he prepared to leave the world behind. To everyone's satisfaction, the *L-O-V-E* album reached #4 on the pop album charts—this at a period when all of Cole's biggest-selling works were inevitably the so-called commercial projects, the country albums and the singalongs, the rambling roses and the lazy-hazy-crazies. He hadn't released a jazz record that sold like this since . . . well, practically forever. It undoubtedly gratified Cole, in his final weeks, to realize that his last will and testament would be a genuine jazz album. This was the way he would have wanted to make his exit: rejoicing, even in the face of the abyss.

This album, and "Girl from Ipanema" especially, suggests where Cole would have gone had he lived another few years: surely his next project would have been a fourth pan-American project, this one dedicated to the bossa nova and contemporary songs of Brazil. There are many post-1964 songs that seem so right for him that I can easily hear his voice singing them in my mind's ear: "The Windmills of Your Mind," "Like a Lover," "The Fool on the Hill" (a text that seems directly inspired by "Nature Boy"), all the work of international composers. As all of his associates agree, Nat King Cole still had so much music left in him at the time of his death.

Gunilla Hutton confirmed, "He was always a very curious, interesting man, who just had such a wonder about the world, and he was also very spiritual. He was like a wide-eyed boy, a fellow with so many plans. So much to learn. So much to do."

He was hardly used up, or spent; rather he was just getting started. There's no telling what he could have done, or where he would have gone, had not the butcher cut him down.

Postscript: The Afterlife

1965 AND BEYOND

For God's sake, let us sit upon the ground
And tell sad stories of the death of kings.
—*KING RICHARD II, Act 3, Scene 2*

CHRISTMAS 1964 WAS UNQUESTIONABLY the bleakest holiday in the history of the Cole family. By a bizarre quirk of fate, three key figures, each representing a different generation, and each in a different part of the country, were all in the hospital at the same time. Two of the three were leaving the world, even as the third was bringing a new life into it. At the St. Therese hospital in Waukegan, Illinois, the Reverend Edward J. Coles Sr., father of Eddie Jr., Evelyn, Nat, Ike, and Freddy, lay on his deathbed. At St. John's in Los Angeles, Nat King Cole was fighting a losing battle with lung cancer; he would hang on for another six weeks or so, but he was already so ill that the doctors wouldn't let him go home to Muirfield Road for Christmas Day. And Carole Cole was 3,000 miles away from her family, in Lenox Hill Hospital on East 77th Street in Manhattan. On Christmas Day, Cookie gave birth to a healthy baby girl, a blessed event that was then viewed with no less horror than the impending death of both her father and grandfather.

IN 1964, CAROLE COLE, then twenty, still attending Cazenovia College, had fallen in love with a young man named Stanley Goldberg, who was attending nearby Syracuse University. Cookie later described him as "tall and lean," which means that, in his body type at least, he must have reminded Cookie of her father—except that he was white. "With a killer smile, straight black hair, and long lashes to match. His fashion sense? 'Snappy but effortless.'"[1] By January, Cookie was smitten. By March, she was pregnant. By the summer, after she graduated and was performing in summer stock, she had told Maria.

To look at the situation from Mrs. Cole's point of view, if the daughter of any famous entertainer in 1964 had had a child out of wedlock, it would have caused a scandal. No one seems to have considered the idea of Cookie and Stanley getting married; for a prominent black girl to marry a white Jewish boy would have launched an even bigger tumult. This was only three years after Sammy Davis Jr. had been ingloriously disinvited from the 1961 Inaugural Gala because he had recently married a white woman. Cole's business partner, Ike Jones, was married at the time to the Swedish actress Inger Stevens, a fact they had to keep secret from the press. If liberal Democrats like the Kennedys hadn't the stomach to publicly support an inter-racial marriage, then imagine how all those evangelical conservatives in the red states, the ones who were buying those millions of copies of "Ramblin' Rose" and "Lazy-Hazy-Crazy Days of Summer" would have felt.

It would have given the Ace Carters and George Wallaces of the nation another excuse to rail against the very existence of Nat King Cole. You can imagine what they would have said: "This is what happens when you treat a Negro [not the world they would have used] as an equal and let him sing love songs to white women." It would have given them another torch to throw on the flaming cross. Maria doubtlessly imagined mobs of racists burning King Cole records in bonfires on the streets of Tuscaloosa, much like they did those of the Beatles when John Lennon made what was taken as an anti-Christian remark two years later.

But Maria hardly had to say anything; her voice and her logic were already resounding in Cookie's head. "How can you possibly think you can raise this child? People will talk. What will you say? The newspapers will have a field day. This could RUIN your father's career!"[2] By the time Carole's pregnancy started to show, everything had been arranged; she would register with the Spence-Chapin Adoption Agency under the name of Carroll Gale, and for the last few months, she would stay out of sight, ensconced in an institution rather uncharitably named "The Washington Square Home for Friendless Girls."

This was in Greenwich Village, near where the King Cole Trio had played in 1941. And this was where Nat returned, at some point in November 1964—probably when he had a two-night break from the Sands. Even in this brand-new age of jet travel, it couldn't have been easy for Cole to fly cross country, especially when he was dying as much from overwork and exhaustion as from cancer.

He closed at the Circle Star on December 6, and the next day he returned to Los Angeles and checked in to St. John's; he was leaving the world in the same place where his twin daughters had recently come into it. While Nat had been working in San Francisco, Maria had been traveling in Europe, and then stopped by the Lincoln Center condo on the way back. On December 7, she had been to see their friend Sammy Davis Jr. in his greatest triumph yet, the Broadway musical *Golden Boy*, when she got the message from her sister, Aunt Baba, to come back to Hancock Park at once. That first day at St. John's, as Maria later remembered, was the most painful for Nat—she had been driven there by Glenn Wallichs, who was still running Capitol Records. "It did not take long for Nat's condition to deteriorate," she said.

On Sunday, December 6, the same day he finally finished in San Carlos, the *Los Angeles Times* magazine published an extensive article on Cole, focusing on the gala concert that was scheduled for a few days later on Friday, December 11. As we've seen, he had been planning this event for more than a year and had secured the services of Tony Bennett and Count Basie many months earlier. This was to be his last interview, and he speaks with considerable pride and love for his adopted home town. "This city has to take pride in The Music Center. The people deserve it. The place is finally unified enough to build, appreciate, participate, in a home for music. Once it opens, the very fact of its being here is going to unify us some more. In another way, the Dodgers coming out here gave us a community excitement to root for. This is going to do the same thing, and only deeper as music is more important in the long run. The idea is to bring people into the Center. You give them what they want; you also give them the whole range of what music represents."[3]

The original line-up that he planned, as Tony Bennett remembered, was Cole, plus Ella Fitzgerald, Count Basie, and Tony. Fitzgerald hadn't been able to do it, and, apparently, already aware of how sick he was, Nat then reached out to his closest and most famous friend. By Sunday, December 6, it had been announced that Sinatra, who was then appearing with Basie at the Sands in Vegas, would co-star alongside Cole, on the evening before the Chairman's forty-ninth birthday. Cole had appeared at Sinatra's request at the JFK Gala in 1961, and now he was returning the favor; there was even a possibility that they might perform together, something that hadn't happened since two brief radio appearances twenty years earlier.

But it was not to be. All year long, Nat had been keeping in touch with Tony, reminding him about the date, but the calls had dropped off by late fall. Tony was wondering what was going on, so he contacted friends in Los Angeles, one in particular. "I knew Dean Martin real well. Nat and I both loved him," said Tony. As it happened, Dean had just seen Nat in his final Vegas run, at the Sands, after which he had followed him for a few nights before Sinatra and Basie came into the Sands. Tony continued, "So, I called Dean and said, 'How's Nat?' Try to imagine, if you can, Dean Martin getting serious, however briefly. 'He's got the cancer real bad,' Dean answered. 'He's not going to make it.' "

During the final few days before December 11, when it became apparent that Cole was too sick to go on, serious changes were made. Now, instead of concentrating on three or four select headliners, the event became more of an all-star variety show. A review from the next day mentions Sinatra, who began by giving props to Cole and reading a telegram from Cole expressing regret at being too sick to be there, along with Mexican pop singer Vicki Carr, country and folk artist Jimmie Rodgers, singer-actress Diahann Carroll, and Shelly Manne (the brilliant jazz drummer who played with Cole and George Shearing on their 1961 album together) and His Men.[4] (Tony also remembers that Peter Lawford and Joey Bishop were there, although they're not mentioned in the *Times* review.) Tony was disappointed on multiple levels; he was allowed to do only two songs, but that might have been a good thing, since he was so distraught over Nat's condition that it's hard to imagine he had the wherewithal to do a longer set. "And it angered me. So, when we came out, the Basie Band and me, we greased up the walls. It was unbelievable, with the two songs. . . . The people went insane. It was just the hottest thing I ever did!"

There was only one act that could follow the Bennett-Basie combination, and it did. As the *Times* observed, "For the last two weeks, Sinatra has been doing nightclub 'concerts' with Basie in Las Vegas and it was if the entire engagement was rehearsal for this moment." Sinatra sang only three songs, ending with the arrangement of "Hello, Dolly" that he and Basie had done on their 1964 studio album, *It Might as Well Be Swing*, which paid homage to Louis Armstrong. But like Bennett, Sinatra was thinking about another African American icon in that moment. He had finished, but the crowd "didn't want to let him go. The applause continued, on and on. Finally, he sighed and said he was sorry—he could do no more. And he left the stage." The *Times* concluded, "Jazz came to The Music Center. It was a night to remember."

AS THE HOLIDAYS DREW NEARER, Maria remembered, "I was standing in the hallway at the hospital one day when [Nat] said he would like to come home for Christmas. I went to the doctor, who was standing at the nurses' desk, and asked him if we could do it. 'I don't see why not,' he replied, and then added, 'It might be the last Christmas he'll ever spend at home.' "[5] Maria looked at the faces of the staff, who couldn't believe that the doctor was being so undiplomatic, so insensitive, and so blunt, but she at least personally appreciated that he was giving it to her straight.

One day early in the stay, Nat picked up the phone and said goodbye to Gunilla Hutton, said Maria, who, in her later years, described Nat's final six weeks as a period of reconciliation between the two of them.[6] Not long after, she wrote, "We were coming out of the Cobalt Therapy treatment place in the Santa Monica Hospital and the photographers were there. I looked at them and tried to stop them; he said, 'No, Skeez [his nickname for her], let 'em take the picture. And I did. And they cried."[7] The world needed to see, he said, what this disease did to people.

The holidays that year, said Maria, "seemed like a wake";[8] everybody had hoped Nat would be released from the hospital to spend Christmas at South Muirfield, but no such luck. Meanwhile, on that very day, December 25, 1964, Cookie gave birth to a beautiful "biracial" baby girl. The original plan was that Cookie would name her "Gretchen" and she would be adopted by her father's younger brother, her Uncle Freddy, and his wife, Margaret. But, as always, Maria had the last word, and Maria, Freddy said, "would have none of it."[9] Nat's first grandchild was, instead, adopted by Robert and Vera Clarke, both teachers in the New York City school system, and raised in one of the better neighborhoods of the Bronx. Coincidentally, they named her "Caroline" and wasn't until almost forty years later that anybody noticed the coincidence of the mother's and daughter's names.

Thankfully, Nat did come home to Hancock Park for two days around New Year's. "But Nat was so ill he could not help but be a bit irritable, and Casey and Timolin, our three-year-old twins, seemed to be a little frightened of him."[10] So observed Natalie, back home for the holiday break. "When I saw Dad, there was no mistaking that singular voice, but otherwise I might not have recognized him. He'd lost a lot of weight and looked ancient and skeletal. I was numb with fear when I realized that this person in front of me was but a shadow of my father."

The new year brought no good news from inside St. John's, but there were welcome tidings from Capitol Records. The new album, *L-O-V-E*, was a huge hit, one of the most successful albums of Cole's career. Cole had given birth to yet another new kind of music, one that he wouldn't live to explore, and he had also gained a granddaughter. But death was in the air: Cole's father, the Reverend Coles, died in Illinois on February 1 and he would never get to meet Cookie's child. At St. John's, Nat kept telling his doctor, Robert Kositchek, "Bob, get me well so I can get on television and tell people to stop smoking.

He said this again and again. All during this time, he wanted to live, to be able to tell people to quit smoking."[11]

On Valentine's Day, Maria was allowed to bring him in a wheelchair for an outing to see a beach house she was thinking of buying; after staring at a beautiful vista of the Santa Monica oceanfront for a few moments, he asked to be turned around. Then he said, "Go ahead and buy it, Skeez." He made it through the day, but a few hours later, he died in the wee small hours of the morning of February 15.

Perhaps ironically, his death was, to a degree, absorbed into the uproar of the civil rights movement and other kinds of tension in the Afro-American community. Even on February 16, when the *New York Daily News* ran the picture that Maria described, showing the two of them outside the cobalt therapy center, the main headline was about Malcolm X. On February 20, the *New York Amsterdam News*, along with dozens if not hundreds of newspapers and magazines across the country, ran a lengthy memorial feature on Cole. Then, the following day, Malcolm X was assassinated in the Audubon Ballroom in Harlem. On March 13, the *Amsterdam News* ran a eulogy for Malcolm, a moving and heartfelt tribute by none other than Martin Luther King. And directly under Dr. King's story, there was an equally moving and passionate letter by A. S. "Doc" Young, a veteran African American journalist based in Los Angeles. Young chided the paper for giving a disproportionate amount of coverage to Malcolm and giving him more attention than Cole. He described the late artist as "a tremendous gentle man, who did more good in the world than probably any combination of six Negroes who ever lived before him."[12]

WHEN I WAS ABOUT TWENTY, I worked full-time in the jazz department at Tower Records on East 4th Street in Manhattan—the original New York store—at the same time I was attending NYU a few blocks away. During that time, I had two experiences regarding the music—and the larger meaning—of Nat King Cole that, to quote old Nick Carraway one more time, I have been turning over in my mind ever since.

One of my best friends there was an African American kid about my age, who was also working in the jazz department. This was hardly remarkable in New York in the 1980s, but even at that point it might probably have been noteworthy in Alabama, the state where Nat King Cole was born and where I spent a great deal of my childhood.

I wish that I could remember my friend's name, but I do remember that like me, he was from Brooklyn and had roots in the Deep South. I was already a fan of all the major jazz-influenced popular singers, Bing Crosby, Frank

Sinatra, Louis Armstrong, Billy Eckstine, Joe Williams, Mel Tormé, and especially Nat King Cole, and what's more, thanks to my father, who was a major jazz buff, I grew up loving Cole just as much as a jazz pianist as a popular singer. But even though I was already a passionate Cole fan, my appreciation of Cole's music was comparatively intellectual: I couldn't relate to Cole on the same level as my friend.

I found this out one day when I put on a Nat Cole album. It wasn't anything special, probably just a basic collection of greatest hits. But as soon as the needle hit the groove (this was shortly before the advent of the compact disc), my friend started crying. It may not have even been a sad or a romantic song; it might have been "L-O-V-E" for all I remember. But the sound of that voice took him back to when he was a little kid, in his grandmother's kitchen, with the sounds of Cole coming over the radio or the phonograph. When he first started listening to music on his own, as a young teenager, he was originally attracted to Motown and other purveyors of 1960s soul and pop. Then, in his high school and college years, he became a jazz fan, like the rest of us, and listened mostly to hard bop and 1950s Blue Note LPs—that's why we were all in the jazz department at Tower.

But his connection with Nat King Cole was profound and visceral; it was like every emotion he had was hard-wired to the sound of that voice. It took him way back and instantly moved him to tears, something not often seen at the Tower outpost on Broadway and 4th (unless it was over the salary, all of $3.85 an hour). I asked him why, and he said, "It takes me back to good times, man, good times." It took him back to well before soul or jazz, the music he discovered on his own, back to the music of his family, the music that he was born into. In that sense, the music of Nat King Cole was his birthright.

IN 1965, THE FIRST "TRIBUTE RECORDING" made to honor the late Cole was made by his dear friend Tony Bennett in Nat's home town, Chicago, on March 11, with Joe Marsala, an old time Windy City clarinetist. It's a slow, stately, and passionate reading of "Sweet Lorraine," delivered by a trio of clarinet, voice, and Bobby Hackett, best known as a cornetist, but here playing guitar as he had done with Glenn Miller twenty-five years earlier. Clearly, Tony is thinking of Nat with every note, every word, and weighing the loss of this incredible force—both his own personal loss and that of the whole wide world.

In 1965 and early'66, following the bestseller *L-O-V-E,* Capitol released a slew of new albums and collections, among them *Songs from Cat Ballou*, which was a collection of songs associated with Cole's films (including *Raintree County, China Gate*, and *Blue Gardenia*); *Nature Boy*, a collection of classic Cole hits and signature songs from the orchestral period; *Looking Back*, which gathered all of his rhythm and blues and rock 'n' roll-type hits from the late 1950s; and, at long last, in 1966, *Nat King Cole at the Sands*, which had been originally taped in January 1960. There also was a new edition of the early hits collection, *Unforgettable* (with a new cover), and a new anthology of Trio material, *The Nat King Cole Trio* (subtitled "Original Vocal and Instrumental Recordings of the Easy Listenin' Favorites") with a very mod, Peter Matz-style cover. All were successful, but none was anywhere near as popular as *L-O-V-E*.

The funeral was held on February 18, at St. James Episcopal Church on Wilshire Boulevard. Four hundred invited mourners were inside, thousands more lined the streets. This was one of only two occasions when Sammy Davis closed his Broadway show, *Golden Boy*; the other would be a few weeks later, when he, Harry Belafonte, Tony Bennett, and hundreds of others joined Dr. King for the March on Selma.

With the death of Cole, then that of Malcolm X a few days later, and then the historic march, it was a rather tumultuous moment to be black in America. As Leonard Feather noted, "Nat went to his eternal rest in Glendale, the community where neo-Nazis recently planted roots and where Negroes have never been welcome alive—and not, until recent years, were they welcome dead."[13]

Rather than someone from the world of jazz or popular music, the eulogies were given by two representatives of old-school mainstream (Jewish) show business, Jack Benny and George Jessel. Benny was particularly appropriate, since he and Cole had become close friends in his final years, and he was the most persistent of all visitors to Cole's hospital room in St. John's. Eddie "Rochester" Anderson, from the *Jack Benny Show* cast, who had more or less introduced Nat and Maria to each other at the Zanzibar in 1946, was also there with his wife.

Among the other attendees were entertainers George Burns, Johnny Mathis, Billy Daniels, Ricardo Montalban, Danny Thomas, Bobby Darin, Jerry Lewis, Milton Berle, Jimmy Durante, Steve Allen, and Frankie Laine; Cole's own musical collaborators, Billy May, Gordon Jenkins, Nelson Riddle, Ralph Carmichael, Stan Kenton, John Collins, and Charlie Harris; songwriters Jimmy McHugh, Sammy Cahn, Jimmy Van Heusen, Marvin Fisher, and the publisher Ivan Mogull; Alan Livingston and Lee Gillette from Capitol Records and Jack Entratter from the Sands; Peter and Pat Kennedy Lawford, and California governor Edmund G. Brown; Dr. David Daniels and Dr. James Scott; Sy Devore, tailor to the stars, and Carlos Gastel, who had meant so much to Nat for so many years. And Frank Sinatra. (Surely Cole's death was a major motivation for Sinatra to contemplate his own mortality a few months later, when he turned fifty, with the *September of My Years* album, and other inward-directed projects.)

Jessel informed the mourners that "until Cole, Negroes had not been welcomed into the Friars"; Feather opined that this was a noteworthy achievement, even if Jessel was telling us this "the wrong way at the wrong time."[14] Benny's eulogy focused on Cole as a human being rather than an artist or a star. He repeatedly used the phrase, "a nice man," and for once the use of the word "nice" didn't seem passive or noncommittal. "A nice man [who] knew how to live and knew how to make others glad they were living." He continued, "In accepting the belief 'Thy will be done,' many times we are prompted to question the justice of events such as the one that brings us here today. Nat Cole was a man who gave so much and still had so much to give. He gave it in song, in friendship to his fellow man, devotion to his family. He was a star, a tremendous success as an entertainer, an institution. But he was an even greater success as a man, as a husband, as a father, as a friend."

Marvin Fisher, who had probably written more songs for Cole than anybody, and served as an active pallbearer, was overheard saying, "He's been carrying us all our lives. Now it's our turn to carry him."

Benny closed with a few sentences that were widely quoted in the subsequent obituaries, and since: "Time, as always, will work its healing ways. And I know that someday the dew drops will glisten on the 'Ramblin' Rose' again. The 'Ballerina' will dance again, and the 'Mona Lisa' will smile."

Notes

The following biographies and memoirs were referenced in more than one chapter:

ADAMS	Berle Adams, with Gordon Cohn, *A Sucker for Talent*, published by Berle Adams, 1995.
CAROLINE	Caroline Clarke, *Postcards from Cookie: A Memoir of Motherhood, Miracles, and a Whole Lot of Mail* (New York: Harper, 2015; Kindle Edition).
DME	Daniel Mark Epstein, *Nat King Cole* (New York: Farrar, Straus and Giroux, 1999).
GORDON	Claire Phillips Gordon, *My Unforgettable Jazz Friends* (Arroyo Grande, CA: Phase V Press, 2004).
GOURSE	Leslie Gourse, *Unforgettable, The Life and Mystique of Nat King Cole* (New York: St. Martin's Press, 1991).
HAMPTON	Lionel Hampton, with James Haskins, *Hamp: An Autobiography* (New York: Warner Brooks, 1989).
HASKINS	James Haskins, with Kathleen Benson, *Nat King Cole* (New York: Stein and Day, 1984).
KT	Klaus Teubig (compiler), *Straighten Up and Fly Right: A Chronology and Discography of Nat "King" Cole* (Westport, CT: Greenwood Press, 1994).
KW	Kat Wisker Productions, *Nat King Cole: Biography in Sound*, eight-part radio series (presented by Bill Moran), 1977.
MARIA	Maria Cole, with Louie Robinson, *Nat King Cole: An Intimate Biography* (New York: William Morrow, 1971).

NATALIE	Natalie Cole, with Digby Diehl, *Angel on My Shoulder: An Autobiography* (New York: Time Warner Brooks, 2000).
RGH SCRAPBOOK	Privately published by scholar and archivist Roy G. Holmes, Surrey, UK, circa 1995.

Book Epigraph: Iona Opie and Peter Opie, *The Oxford Dictionary of Nursery Rhymes*, 2nd ed. (Oxford: Oxford University Press, 1951, 1997), 134–55.

ACKNOWLEDGMENTS

1. "A Step in the Right Direction—Nat King Cole Discusses His Role in Television," *TV Guide*, September 7, 1957.

INTRODUCTION

Epigraph: Performed by the Roots words and music by Illmind (or !llmind), based on "Who Lives, Who Dies, Who Tells Your Story" from *Hamilton* by Lin-Manuel Miranda.

1. The only other fact I have been able to learn about them is that they also wrote one other song that Cole put on the charts, the 1955 "Dreams Can Tell a Lie"; this was not nearly as good a song nor as big a hit as "A Blossom Fell." Also, although "Blossom" was first published in the UK (John Fields Music Co., Ltd., 1954), I don't know of any recordings by any English artists—or anyone else—prior to Cole's.
2. There actually is a similar superstition in Romania: "If you bite your tongue while eating, it's because you recently told a lie." (https://travelaway.me/66-funny-romanian-superstitions/) However, I would not care to hear Nat King Cole sing about that.
3. KW, 1.
4. Ralph J. Gleason, "Nat Always Comes Through," *Down Beat*, July 13, 1951.
5. Thomas Thompson, "A King of Song Dies, and a Friend Remembers Him," *Life* magazine, February 2, 1965, 36.
6. Discussion with Ernie Harburg, December 2017. All details about the writing of "Paper Moon" here come from Mr. Harburg. Was it fair that Rose put his name on it, even though he didn't write any of the words or music or even the title? In his defense, he was responsible for the basic idea and the fact that it was written to begin with. In general, he did a lot more to earn his author's share than, say, Irving Mills ever did on all the songs his name is on.
7. Cole himself gives Buckner credit for the technique, in an interview with Steve Race. "We Had to Break the Monotony a Bit, so I Started Singing, Says Nat King Cole," *New Musical Express*, September 15, 1950.

8. Cecil Smith, "Nat Keeps Movin' in Musical Experiment," *Los Angeles Times*, August 27, 1961, N10.
9. Ren Gravatt, "25 Years in the Business, Nat Cole Finds There's No Rest for Talent," *Billboard*, November 16, 1962, 4, 49. As you'll see in the first chapter of this book, Nat Cole was a full-time professional musician at least as early as fall 1934, when he was fifteen, so he could have actually celebrated his twenty-fifth anniversary in "the biz" in 1959.
10. "A King of Song Dies, and a Friend Remembers Him," *Life* magazine, February 26, 1965.
11. Cecil Smith, "Nat Keeps Movin' in Musical Experiment," *Los Angeles Times*, August 27, 1961, N10.
12. Ren Gravatt, "25 Years in the Business, Nat Cole Finds There's No Rest for Talent," *Billboard*, November 16, 1962, 4, 49.
13. J. A. Rogers, "Noble Sissle and Orchestra Hold Prize Job of Continent," *Philadelphia Tribune*, July 17, 1930, 6.
14. For the record, the band is Arthur Briggs, Tommy Ladnier, trumpets; Billy Burns, James Revey, trombones; Rudy Jackson, "first" (probably alto) saxophone; Ralph (or "Rudy") Duquesne, clarinet; Frank Goudil, second alto saxophone; Ramon Usera, tenor saxophone, reeds; the rhythm section includes two pianists (Antonio Spaulding and Lloyd Pinckney), and two basses, one string (Sherman Edwards) and one brass (Coles), and Frank Ethridge, doubling banjo and violin.

Part Epigraph: Buster Sherwood, "Ole King Cole," *Orchestra World*, April 1945.

15. Gordon, 85. Both the 1920 and the 1930 United States Census also confirm 1919 as the birth year. At the time of his death in 1965, all the obituaries give his age as forty-five.
16. "King Cole Carries Shamrock in Pocket," *New York Amsterdam News*, March 22, 1947, 23
17. The 1930 census gives the Coles' family address as "South Parkway in Chicago," and a 1934 clipping gives his address as 4030 South Prairie Avenue. In 1930, Edward senior's occupation is listed as a "Baptist Minister" and his wife's (Nat's mother's) name is given as "Pelina" rather than "Perlina." It also states that three children were currently living with their parents, Nat, Evelyn, and Isaac, along with an older cousin, one William Robinson, who is described as working in a shoe-shine parlor.
18. Obituary page, "Rev. E. J. Coles Dies; Father of Nat King Cole," *Chicago Tribune*, February 2, 1965, B6
19. KW, 1.
20. Barry Ulanov, "Fly Right," *Metronome*, August 1944.
21. Sanford Josephson, *Jazz Notes: Interviews across the Generations* (Santa Barbara, CA: ABC Clio/Greenwood Press, 2009), 78.

22. A. S. "Doc" Young (editor), *The Incomparable Nat King Cole* (Fort Worth, TX: Sepia Publishing Company, 1965), 27.
23. Sharon A. Pease, *Swing Piano Styles* (column), "Nat Cole's Jazz Piano Wasn't Quite for Church," *Down Beat*, October 1, 1941.
24. Doyle J. Carr, "Have You Ever Heard of Nat King Cole's Brother?" *Pittsburgh Courier* magazine. Undated article (likely mid-1950s) found in the Claude A. Barnett Papers: The Associated Negro Press, 1918–1967, Part 3: Subject Files on Black Americans, 1918–1967, Series D: Entertainers, Artists, and Authors, 1928–1965.
25. "Eddie Cole's Band Goes on Road Tour," *California Eagle*, September 4, 1936. According to this source, Eddie had been in the Sissle band for six years when he left in 1935.
26. Ren Gravatt, "25 Years in the Business, Nat Cole Finds There's No Rest for Talent," *Billboard*, November 16, 1962, 4, 49.
27. Barry Ulanov, "Fly Right," *Metronome*, August 1944.
28. Cole viewed the stride style, whose greatest practitioner was Fats Waller, as something to be transcended. However, one curious point that he never acknowledged is that the most famous "quote" in all of Waller's music is the reference to Edvard Grieg's "In the Hall of the Mountain King" (from the *Peer Gynt Suite No. 1*, 1888); this is a key part of one of Waller's classic piano instrumentals, "The Viper's Drag" (1934). And, as apparently coincidentally, the single most famous quote in all of Cole's piano music is this same "Mountain King" phrase, heard in nearly every recorded version of his piano solo on "Body and Soul."
29. John Tynan, "First Part about a Pianist Who Turned Singer to Find a Kingdom," *Down Beat*, May 2, 1957 (two parts).
30. Stanley Dance, *The World of Earl Hines* (New York: Charles Scribner's Sons, 1977), 92
31. "Urge Billikens to Spread Christmas Cheer," *Chicago Defender*, December 6, 1930, 15.
32. KW, 1.
33. "Nathaniel Coles Wins Third Turkey," *Chicago Defender*, December 31, 1932, 16. Yes, here he gives his last name as "Coles," whereas two years earlier, the *Defender* listed him as "Nathaniel Cole."
34. Interview by Edward R. Murrow, Nat King Cole and family, *Person to Person*, CBS TV, November 1, 1957.
35. Max Jones and Mike Nevard, "Why I Made the Trio a Quartet," *Melody Maker*, September 23, 1950.
36. "Nat Cole's Prep Band Hits High in Chi," *Pittsburgh Courier*, March 16, 1935, A9.
37. In later years, Smith even claimed that he was the one who persuaded the Regal Theater to let Nat play there and thereby win those turkeys. In Smith's account, Cole was such a success that one year he actually won two turkeys; the two then went into a nearby cafe and gifted the owner with one turkey in exchange for having

his chef cook the other one for them. However, since we know Nat first appeared at the Regal at age eleven, this part of Smith's story seems highly unlikely.

38. Al Monroe, "Hot Jam Sessions Gave Us the King Cole Trio, Scribe Finds," *Pittsburgh Courier*, May 5, 1945, 17.
39. *Chicago Defender*, October 6, 1934, quoted in DME, 41.
40. Jack Ellis, *The Orchestras* (column), *Chicago Defender*, November 17, 1934, 8. The other musicians in this band are George Skinner, Leon C. Gray, Andrew Gardener, Robert Dade Jr., Charles Gray, Charles Murphy, John Dawkins, Russell M. Shores, "and Nat at the piano, featuring Arthur Hicks, vocalist."
41. Earl J. Morris, *Grand Town* (column), *Pittsburgh Courier*, December 1, 1934, A8. This report may not be entirely reliable: Nat is described, for the only time in his career, as being "small in stature"—which perhaps indicates that he didn't stand up from the piano bench for the whole set, since we know from other evidence that he was already at least six feet tall. Morris also reported, more accurately, that Cole "is usually immaculate in his costume."
42. Buster Sherwood, "Ole King Cole," *Orchestra World*, April 1945.
43. Throughout this period, the musicians who played in the Royal Dukes included trumpeter Charles Murphy; Robert Dade Jr. (probably a trombonist); reed players Leon Gray, George Skinner, Andrew Gardner, Charles Gray (or Nortes Gray), the latter listed as a clarinetist; and a rhythm section of John Dawkins on banjo, bassist Henry Fort, and drummer Russell M. Shores, plus Nat on piano. There's also a male vocalist, one Arthur Hicks.
44. Earl J. Morris, *A Grand Town Day & Night* (column), *Pittsburgh Courier*, December 1, 1934, A8.
45. "Band Leader," *Chicago Defender*, January 19, 1935, 8.
46. "Nat Cole's Band Is New Sensation," *Chicago Defender*, March 9, 1935, 8.
47. A. S. "Doc" Young, editor. *The Incomparable Nat King Cole* (Fort Worth, TX: Sepia Publishing Company, 1965), 36.
48. "Students Learn to Sing with Nat Cole," *Chicago Defender,* February 16, 1935, 24. "Young Cole in explaining his reason for the series of contests said, 'Among my student friends and acquaintances there is talent without an outlet. My object is to encourage those who have talent to become great just as I am being encouraged.' " The winner, for the record, was a Miss Pauline Wilson, singing Ellington's "latest number, '(In My) Solitude.' "
49. "Future Stars Given Much Applause for Their Acts," *Chicago Defender*, June 8, 1935, 15.
50. "Nat Cole's Prep Band Hits High in Chi," *Pittsburgh Courier*, March 16, 1935, A9.
51. Advertisement in unknown publication, found by Jordan Taylor, March 1935.
52. Advertisement, *Chicago Defender*, May 4, 1935.
53. "He's Marvelous," *Pittsburgh Courier*, May 4, 1935, A8.
54. Jack Ellis, *The Orchestras* (column), *Chicago Defender,* June 22, 1935, 7.
55. "Member of Cole's Band Is Drowned," *Chicago Defender*, August 10, 1935, 1. This is virtually the only early story on Nat where his correct age (sixteen) is given.

56. "Plan to Drain Quarry to Get Artist's Body," *Chicago Defender*, August 24, 1935, 3. In this story, Murphy is described as a "16-year old saxophone player," in the previous one, he's a seventeen-year-old trumpeter. (Trumpet is apparently correct.)
57. Dan Burley, *Back Door Stuff* (column), *Chicago Defender*, June 14, 1935, 5.
58. The first was probably John Kirby, who began leading his sextet on New York's Swing Street in 1937 and recorded starting in 1938. (Eddie might have also been familiar with the Kansas City territorial band, Walter Page and His Blue Devils, who recorded one session in 1929.)
59. Jack Ellis, *The Orchestras* (column), *Chicago Defender*, September 14, 1935.
60. Barry Ulanov, "Fly Right," *Metronome*, August 1944.
61. DME, 43.
62. In the meantime, Cole's ex-manager, Malcolm B. Smith, formed a new band of very young musicians and installed them in Cole's old spot on Sunday afternoons at the Warwick Ballroom. Cole was such a big deal in Chicago at this moment that Smith was still promoting himself as the "inventor" of the Cole band. In fact, when the *Defender* announced the news of the new band at the Warwick, the story mentioned Smith prominently but didn't even give the name of the band. Jack Ellis, *The Orchestras* (column), *Chicago Defender*, October 19, 1935, 9.
63. Two advertisements for the Savoy Ballroom in the *Chicago Defender*, September 21 and 28, 1935.
64. Jack Ellis, *The Orchestras* (column), *Chicago Defender*, October 19, 1935, 9. Also " 'Jelly' Coles and Brother Form a Band," *Chicago Defender*, October 26, 1935, 8.
65. Barry Ulanov, "Fly Right," *Metronome*, August 1944.
66. "'Jelly' Coles and Brother Form a Band," *Chicago Defender*, October 26, 1935, 8.
67. "Maurice Mitchell in Ben Skoller's Revue," *Chicago Defender*, July 25, 1936, 10.
68. "Eddie Cole's Theme Song Popular in Chi," *Pittsburgh Courier*, March 21, 1936, A6. Blanche Cole, whoever she was, was apparently no relation to Nat and Eddie.
69. Bob Hayes, "Cabaret," *Chicago Defender*, March 21, 1936. Quoted in DME, 54.
70. Earl J. Morris, "Eddie Cole's Band Rivals Earl Hines and Fletcher Henderson for Honors," *Pittsburgh Courier*, April 11, 1935, 18.
71. Biographical information on Nadine Robinson (also called Nadine Coles, Nadine Cole and, much later, Nadine Burnside), from Ancestry.com. California, African American Who's Who, 1948 [database on-line]. Provo, UT, USA: Ancestry.com Operations, Inc., 2011. This collection was indexed by Ancestry World Archives Project contributors. Retrieved by Jordan Taylor, August 20, 2018.
72. California State Library; *Negro Who's Who in California*; Page Number: 93; Call Number: E185.93.C2N43 1948.
73. "Maurice Mitchell in Ben Skoller's Revue," *Chicago Defender*, July 25, 1936, 10.
74. "Babe Matthews Is Headliner in Chicago," *Chicago Defender*, June 20, 1936, 10.
75. "Maurice Mitchell in Ben Skoller's Revue," *Chicago Defender*, July 25, 1936, 10.
76. One trumpeter named Kenneth was replaced by another trumpeter named Kenneth, one saxophonist named Tommy has been replaced by another saxophonist named

Tommy, all of which makes me think that perhaps the *Defender* got the last names of the musicians wrong when they listed the personnel in April.

77. Barry Ulanov, "Fly Right," *Metronome*, August 1944.
78. Natalie, 27
79. "Eddie Cole's Band Goes on Road Tour," *California Eagle*, September 4, 1936. (As reported in the *California Eagle*, the leading black press outlet of the West Coast; this was also the first time Nat or Eddie had been noticed by a media source outside of Chicago or Pittsburgh.)
80. Earl J. Morris, "Graham Artist Bureau 'Broke,'" *Pittsburgh Courier*, September 19, 1936, A7.
81. Obituary page, "Rev. E. J. Coles Dies; Father of Nat King Cole," *Chicago Tribune*, February 2, 1965, B6. Edward Sr. moved to the new position sometime in 1936.
82. That's the story he told to Barry Ulanov, in *Metronome*, August 1944, as well as to many other interviewers on many other occasions.
83. DME, 44.
84. Earl J. Morris, "Graham Artist Bureau 'Broke,'" *Pittsburgh Courier*, September 19, 1936, A7.
85. Jean Calloway had been working at least since 1932 as "Cab's little sister," except that she wasn't. Ms. Calloway, or whatever her name actually was, must have been grateful that *Wikipedia* didn't exist at the time; it would have been a simple matter to ascertain that Cab Calloway had one famous older sister, Blanche, and three other siblings (Bernice, Henry, and Elmer), but no younger sister. (There's no reason to believe, however, that Flournoy Miller knew about the deception or was a party to this low-class conspiracy.) More information at http://www.thehidehoblog.com/blog/2008/04/earres-prince-the-pianist-cab-never-appreciated, retrieved August 20, 2018.
86. "Unit Reviews," *Variety*, September 30, 1936, 51
87. Barry Ulanov, "Fly Right," *Metronome*, August 1944.
88. Jack Ellis, *The Orchestras* (column), *Chicago Defender*, December 5, 1936, 21.
89. Jack Ellis, "Kansas City Rockets to Open Chi's Cotton Club," *Chicago Defender*, December 19, 1936, 21. "Nat Cole's band and *Shuffle Along* layed [*sic*] over in Chicago in December 2 and kicked out on December 8. Swing!"
90. An ad exists from the *La Crosse Tribune and Leader Press*, December 11, 1936.
91. *Billboard*, week of December 19, 1936.
92. Advertisement, *Michigan Daily*, January 26, 1937. The movie was Edward Everett Horton in "the hilarious" *Let's Make a Million*.
93. Mrs. Floyd H. Skinner, *Chicago Defender*, February 6, 1937, 8.
94. "To Wed in Ypsilanti," *Chicago Defender*, February 6, 1937, 21.
95. Gordon, 75.
96. Jack Ellis, *The Orchestras* (column), *Chicago Defender*, February 27, 1937, 20. "The one and two week stands in RKO Houses" could actually be with the *Shuffle Along* company, although Ellis would have likely mentioned this if that were the case.

Ellis also gives us the personnel of the band at the time: Fostelle Reese, Kenneth Johnson, Russell Gilson, trumpets; John Thomas, N. Atkins, trombones; Bill Wright, George Skinner, "Sax" Mallard, Otis Hicks, reeds; Hurley Ramey, guitar; Henry Fort, bass; Jimmy Adams, drums. (Of these, the most famous was the Chicago guitarist Hurley Ramey, who had worked extensively with Earl Hines.)

97. The following engagements for *Shuffle Along*, for March, 1937, are listed in *Variety*, in the issues of March 3, 10, 17, and 24, 1937:
March 5–8, Garrick Theatre, Duluth, Minnesota
March 9, State Theater, Virginia, Minnesota
March 11–13, Palace Theater, Superior, Wisconsin
March 14, Paramount Theater, St. Loud, Minnesota
March 16 & 17, Egyptian Theater, Sioux Falls, South Dakota
March 19 & 20, Babcock Theater, Billings, Montana
March 21, Fox Theater, Butte, Montana
March 23, Wilma Theater, Missoula, Montana
March 24, Grand Theater, Wallace, Idaho
March 25–27, Empress Theater, Spokane, Washington
March 28, Capitol Theater, Yakima, Washington
March 30, Palomar Theater, Seattle, Washington
98. Jack Ellis, *The Orchestras* (column), *Chicago Defender*, February 27, 1937, 20.
99. "Shuffle Along Revue Reported 'Busted Up' in Long Beach, Calif.," *Chicago Defender*, May 29, 1937, 18.
100. "'Shuffle Along' Will Open Saturday at the Lincoln," *Los Angeles Sentinel*, May 6, 1937, 1. Note that this story is taken directly from the show's press release; the exact verbiage appears in a story in the Billings, Montana, local paper.
101. Harry Levette, "Thru Hollywood—Follow the Movie Stars and Players Weekly," *Chicago Defender*, May 15, 1937, 21.
102. Bernice Patton, "The Sepia Side of Hollywood," *Pittsburgh Courier*, May 22, 1937, 20.
103. Richard G. Hubler, "$12,000-a-Week Preacher's Boy," *Saturday Evening Post*, July 17, 1954, 30.
104. "Vaudeville Notes," *Billboard*, May 29, 1937, 15.
105. "Shuffle Along Revue Reported 'Busted Up' in Long Beach, Calif.," *Chicago Defender*, May 29, 1937, 18.
106. Richard G. Hubler, "$12,000-a-Week Preacher's Boy," *Saturday Evening Post*, July 17, 1954, 30.
107. "Shuffle Along Revue Reported 'Busted Up' in Long Beach, Calif.," *Chicago Defender*, May 29, 1937, 18.
108. Harry Levette, "Behind the Scenes . . . ," *California Eagle*, June 18, 1937, 4B.
109. "Birthday Party Honors Mattie V. Green," *California Eagle*, June 11, 1937. The Coles and the musicians were apparently only present as guests and not as paid performers. For the record, the seven listed were George Skinner, Henry Fort,

C. A. Mollard, William Bill Wright, Curtis Walker, and Nat Atkins, and the party took place at 3418 Denker Avenue.

110. Harry Levette, "Behind the Scenes . . . ," *California Eagle*, June 18, 1937, 4B.
111. "Hit on Coast," *Chicago Defender*, July 10, 1937, 10.
112. Jack Ellis, *The Orchestras* (column), *Chicago Defender*, July 24, 1937, 11. All of these proposed Chicago and Detroit gigs, none of which are believed to have actually happened, are listed in this column. Among the bands scheduled to appear at the big Chicago event were Roy Eldridge; Tiny Parham; Johnny Long, the white bandleader from North Carolina; Cole's pal Jimmie Noone; two pioneers of the jazz big band, the brothers Fletcher and Horace Henderson; and Cole's old sparring partner Tomy Fambro.
113. Donald Bogle, *Dorothy Dandridge: A Biography* (New York: Amistad Press, 1997). Meeting Nat and Marie Bryant, 43–44; proposed Dandridge-Cole TV series, 483.
114. KT, 25, has it the other way around; he states the Trouville became the Century; actually, the reverse appears to be true.

CHAPTER 1

Epigraph: Ralph J. Gleason, "Nat Always Comes through Bigger than Ever," *Down Beat*, July 13, 1951.

1. Buster Sherwood, "Ole King Cole," *Orchestra World*, April 1945.
2. "King Cole Carries Shamrock in Pocket," *New York Amsterdam News*, March 22, 1947, 23.
3. Buster Sherwood, "Ole King Cole," *Orchestra World*, April 1945.
4. Nat King Cole, "Get Your Kicks . . . A Gentle Discourse on California's Golden Jazz," *Esquire's 1947 Jazz Book*, 85.
5. Red Callender, *Unfinished Dream* (London: Quartet Books, 1985), 45.
6. Harry Levette, "Thru Hollywood—Follow the Movie Stars and Players Weekly," *Chicago Defender*, May 15, 1937, 21.
7. This is one of the most frequently cited quotes of the entire King Cole story. It seems to have originated in the *Saturday Evening Post* article, "$12,000-a-Week Preacher's Boy" (by Richard Hubler) July 17, 1954, 106. Within a short time, it was turning up in other places too, as when NBC TV issued their first press release for *The Nat King Cole Show* in 1956.
8. The name of the club is often given as "The Swannee Inn," with two n's, but in the majority of the ads placed by Lewis himself, he gives the name as "Swanee," so we'll stick with that.
9. Ralph J. Gleason, "Nat Always Comes through Bigger than Ever," *Down Beat*, July 13, 1951.
10. Ralph Eastman, "Pitchin' Up a Boogie: African-American Musicians, Nightlife, and Music Venues in Los Angeles, 1930–1945," in *California Soul: Music of African*

Americans in the West (Music of the African Diaspora), ed. Jacqueline Cogdell DjeDje and Eddie S. Meadows (Berkeley: University of California Press, 1998), 79.

11. Lionel Hampton with James Haskins, *Hamp: An Autobiography* (New York: Warner Books, 1989).
12. Hampton.
13. Hampton.
14. Barry Ulanov, "Fly Right," *Metronome*, August 1944.
15. In 1938, by which time the King Cole Trio was already working steadily, Moore also appeared with a vocal group called "The Original Sing Band" in an MGM short subject titled *Streamline Swing* (and possibly elsewhere as well). This was a group that could be described as the Mills Brothers doubled, a collective of eight or nine male voices accompanied by Moore on guitar. (Info from Mark Cantor, who also has a copy of the film.)
16. John Tynan, "First Part about a Pianist Who Turned Singer to Find a Kingdom," *Down Beat*, May 2, 1957 (two parts).
17. Hampton. In some accounts, Cole met Prince through Hampton and Prince introduced him to Moore, but in Hamp's own version, Cole and Moore were already together when Hampton met the two of them.
18. The earliest known account of the trio's formation, in "King Cole's Jesters New NBC Feature," *Chicago Defender,* November 5, 1938, 19, roughly corroborates this telling: Cole heard Prince "slapping a bass in a local night spot" and "Prince's rhythmic ability attracted Cole and he suggested they get together and form a trio with Oscar Moore, whose guitar is well known in the musical world."
19. John Tynan, "First Part about a Pianist Who Turned Singer to Find a Kingdom," *Down Beat*, May 2, 1957 (two parts).
20. KW 1.
21. Cole was willing to go only so far in terms of "branding." He later said that when they decided on this name for the group, Lewis insisted, "'If we are going to book you as King Cole, you will have to look the part,' and produced a gold leaf crown. 'I wore the crown for about three months,' says Nat, 'and then one night it mysteriously disappeared. It worked out as I hoped—he never did get around to getting another.'" Quote from Sharon A. Pease, *Swing Piano Styles* (column), "Nat Cole's Jazz Piano Wasn't Quite For Church," *Down Beat*, October 1, 1941.
22. Max Jones and Mike Nevard, "Why I Made the Trio a Quartet," *Melody Maker*, September 23, 1950.
23. Gordon, 71. Gordon (January 23, 1919–June 3, 2016) says it was fall 1939, and there's no reason to doubt her, but because she says it was such a big deal for them to come in and order a drink, and that they had to save their allowance money to pay for said drink, I can't help wondering if this was actually during the Trio's first and longer run at the Swanee in fall 1937, when she would have been eighteen. Gordon's obituary is at https://www.legacy.com/obituaries/latimes/obituary.aspx?n=claire-phillips-gordon&pid=180242171, retrieved September 7, 2018.

24. "Society," *Chicago Defender*, October 23, 1937, 14.
25. Advertisment, *Los Angeles Times*, December 24, 1937, 2.
26. "Thru Hollywood with Harry Levette, *Chicago Defender*, April 2, 1938, 18. They're also listed as appearing at the "Swanee-Inn" in the May 1938 issue of *Tempo* ("L. A. Band Briefs," 10) magazine.
27. Dave Hyltone, "Trombar's New Band Didn't Open Cold," *Down Beat*, May 1938
28. KT, 25.
29. Information regarding the Vogue debacle from *Pittsburgh Courier*, July 2, 1938, 21 and also *Down Beat*, August 1938 ("Paramount Music Head Says Sax Is Doomed," Dave Hyltone, 29). The Vogue theater was at 6675 Hollywood Boulevard, according to http://cinematreasures.org/theaters/496, retrieved December 26, 2017.
30. Earl J. Morris, "Grand Town," *Pittsburgh Courier*, July 2, 1938, 21, and *Pittsburgh Courier*, June 11, 1938, 21.
31. Earl J. Morris, "Grand Town," *Pittsburgh Courier*, June 11, 1938, 21. More details regarding the King Cole Trio on KECA radio in fall 1938 from researcher Dave Dawes, who has several listings that point to them being on the air starting around October 17. (Another listings clip is from the *Los Angeles Times*, December 5, 1938.)
32. "Electrical Transcription Producers," *Variety*, January 15, 1936.
33. *Metronome*, March 1940, quoted in KT, 41.
34. From a radio interview with Dick Strout, quoted in Maria, 41.
35. In 2019, Cole's various early recordings (including the radio-only transcriptions and the Decca sessions) were collected for the first time and issued in a comprehensive and authorized package titled *Nat King Cole: Hittin' the Ramp—The Early Years (1936–1943)* (Resonance Records HCD 2042). This contains virtually all of the artist's pre-Capitol recordings, including nearly everything discussed in this chapter..
36. Judy Garland later sang it, exuberantly but somewhat embarrassingly (in blackface), in the 1941 *Babes on Broadway*.
37. The two songs are the work of Al Jacobs, Jack Palmer, and Dave Oppenheim; their collective catalog includes several songs that Cole would later address, including "I've Found a New Baby," "'Taint Me," and "If I Give My Heart to You."
38. "King Cole's Jesters New NBC Feature," *Chicago Defender*, November 5, 1938, 19.
39. "King Cole and His Sepia Swingsters replaced Kay St. Germain & Co at Jim Otto's in L.A.," *Variety*, November 16, 1938.
40. Cleo Wilson, "Hollywood Chatterbox," *Chicago Defender*, November 26, 1938, 18. The Criterion Theater was at 642 Grand Avenue.
41. https://sites.google.com/site/downtownlosangelestheatres/criterion, retrieved December 26, 2017
42. Earl J. Morris, "Show Has Plenty of Stars, But . . .," *Pittsburgh Courier*, November 19, 1938.
43. *Chicago Defender*, November 26, 1938.
44. Earl J. Morris, "Show Has Plenty of Stars, But . . .," *Pittsburgh Courier*, November 19, 1938. The *Los Angeles Times* (November 11, 1938, 10) added: "F. E. Miller wrote

the book and lyrics and Sammy Scott and Nat Coles the music, and the staging and production are by Quintard Miller."

45. TED Talk, "Laws That Choke Creativity" by Larry Lessig, published on November 15, 2007, https://www.youtube.com/watch?v=7Q25-S7jzgs, retrieved December 27, 2017.
46. "New Radio Firm Offers Free Music," *Broadcasting*, June 1, 1938.
47. Earl J. Morris, "Grand Town," *Pittsburgh Courier*, November 19, 1938, 20.
48. Additional data re the Davis & Schwegler publishing operation from the research of scholar and pianist Alex Hassan, conducted primarily at the Library of Congress, in emails to the author.
49. Notes from NBC files, quoted in KT, 29. Also, Fitz Patrick (obviously a pseudonym), "Hollywood," *Swing: The Guide to Modern Music*, May 1939. There are also numerous listings and advertisements that confirm that *Swing Soiree* was being heard nationally: *New York Herald Tribune*, January 10, 1937; *Boston Daily Globe*, April 30, 1939.
50. Special thanks to musicologist and professor Edward Green for helping me clarify these observations.
51. "At Beverly Hills Nightery," *Chicago Defender*, June 24, 1939. The "Kelley's Night Club" gig is also referenced in ad in which Oscar endorses Epiphone guitars, in *Tempo*, June 1939.
52. *Down Beat*, September 1939, quoted in KT, 37. See also Dean Owen, "Hollywood and Los Angeles," *Billboard*, August 19, 1939, 8.
53. *Variety* cabaret bills, November 8, 1939. Listed for the "Swannee [*sic*] Inn" are "Arthur Tatum, Charlie Evans, King Cole 3."
54. All "personal" observations here are from Gordon, starting on 73. Incidentally, some of the details she offers suggest that she and her brother may have actually been hanging out with the Trio starting at their first run at the Swanee in fall 1937, rather than their return there two years later.
55. Gordon, 75.
56. DME, 85.
57. The late Gord Grieveson, sleuthing at the Los Angeles Musicians' Union Local (the information is in KT, 38), uncovered information that the Trio had recorded six titles with violinist William Bowers on September 28 for Cinematone (aka Penny Phono). "Trompin'" comes from another date, presumably around the same time. The Cinematone "Trompin'" (the Trio also recorded the tune for Standard) was both discovered and issued in 2019, in the boxed set, *Nat King Cole Hittin' the Ramp, The Early Years 1936-1943*. The Trio's connection to the Cinematone Corp. is also mentioned in "Many L. A. Bands Recording for Penny Phono," *Tempo*, March 4, 1940, 2.
58. *Down Beat*, January 1, 1940, 21. The normally reliable KT misinterpreted this to mean Kelly's Stable in Manhattan, rather than Shep Kelly's in Hollywood, but they didn't actually make it to New York until 1941. *Down Beat*, in this story, also reported that the Trio had "hooked up with William Morris," but that doesn't seem to have actually happened.

59. John Bustin, "Nat King Cole and His Trio Here Tuesday," *Austin American*, July 3, 1949, 14.
60. *Down Beat*, February 1, 1940, 19.
61. Barry Ulanov, "Fly Right," *Metronome*, August 1944.
62. Claire Gordon Phillips described the Trio as making their first session in 1939, but she's probably talking about the twelve Davis & Schwegler tracks (Hap Kaufman definitely had a hand in those) which were initially recorded for radio transcription use and only issued commercially after the fact (Gordon, 74). Some sources claim the Ammor date was on April 18; discographer Klaus Teubig says February.
63. http://www.vocalgroupharmony.com/4ROWNEW/AmmorLabel.htm, retrieved December 28, 2017
64. Other songs by the Rene Brothers include "That's My Home," also memorably recorded by Armstrong; "I Sold My Heart to the Junkman"; "Someone's Rocking My Dreamboat"; "Boogie Woogie Santa Claus"; "When the Swallows Come Back to Capistrano"; and three that would be subsequently recorded by the Trio: "I'm Lost," "Let's Spring One," and "Mexico Joe."
65. Quoted by Arnold Shaw in *Honkers and Shouters* (New York: Collier Books, 1978), 153.
66. Lee Young, interview with the author, circa 1990.
67. *Down Beat*, August 15, 1940. Quoted in KT, 40.
68. *Metronome*, September 1940, 19.
69. Again, thanks to Professor Edward Green for this observation.
70. Arthur Jackson, "Jazz King Cole," *The Gramophone Record Review*, May 1954, 351.
71. *Down Beat*, September 1939, quoted in KT, 37.
72. *Down Beat*, September 1939, quoted in KT, 37.
73. "Revue Slated for LACC Today," *California Eagle*, April 11, 1940.
74. "Hampton Breaks Up LACC Assembly," *California Eagle*, April 18, 1940.
75. Some sources credit "I'd Be Lost without You" to Hampton and Tommy Southern; others list "Donaldson, Wright, Forrest," presumably Walter Donaldson, Robert Wright, and George Forrest.
76. Gordon, 79.
77. Both "Jivin' with Jarvis" and "Jack the Bellboy" were dedicated to early disc jockeys: the first to Al Jarvis of KLAC, Los Angeles; the second to Ed McKenzie of WJBK of Detroit.
78. Hampton, 51–52.
79. *Down Beat*, October 1, 1940. Lunceford's chart on "Jivin' with Jarvis" was arranged by Bill Soderberg. Hampton and Cole at the Casa Manana from "Coast Spots Vie for Biz with Jam," *Down Beat*, September 1, 1940, 12.
80. Leonard Feather, "King Cole Trio Will Form Basis for New Hampton Ork," *Down Beat*, August 15, 1940.
81. Hampton, 71.
82. Arthur Jackson, "Jazz King Cole," *The Gramophone Record Review*, May 1954, 351.
83. Interview with Dave Dexter Jr. by Michel Montet, Hollywood, June 24, 1977.
84. "Hollywood Trio to Tour East," *Pittsburgh Courier*, January 25, 1941.

85. Unpublished manuscript, *The Conversational and Otherwise Art of Jimmy Rowles* by Rowles and Tad Hirschorn, courtesy Tad Hershorn.
86. This information from Mark Cantor, the highly respected scholar, archivist, and historian of jazz and African American–related cinema, who has copies of the films in his collection.
87. Earl J. Morris, "Famed Cole Trio Opens in Chicago," *Pittsburgh Courier*, February 15, 1941, 20.
88. Technically, "I Know That You Know," which Cole recorded most famously in his classic 1956 album *After Midnight*, was not originally written for the 1924 *No, No, Nanette*, but rather for a far-less successful 1926 show titled *Oh, Please*. However, the song was incorporated into some later productions of *Nanette*, including the 1950 Warner Bros. musical film *Tea for Two*, in which it was sung by Doris Day and the Page Cavanaugh Trio, in a manner very much inspired by the King Cole Trio.
89. I'm discussing *No, No, Nanette* in the main text because there is some specific period evidence (i.e., the 1941 *Pittsburgh Courier* profile) that Cole might have had some actual participation in that project. However, there are two more rumors of early appearances by Cole in major Hollywood films: *Too Hot to Handle* (1938) and *Citizen Kane* (1941). Austin Powell, guitarist and singer with the vocal-instrumental group the Cats and the Fiddle, told researcher Mark Cantor that both he and Cole were cast as jungle natives in the Clark Gable–Myrna Loy comedy. Orson Welles himself told Peter Bogdanovich that he hired the King Cole Trio for his all-time classic film, but possibly not to appear on screen or even the soundtrack, but to play off-camera for a party sequence. Neither claim has been substantiated, but I decided that they were both worth mentioning in this book as a footnote at least.
90. Actually, in the first recording, made for Standard in November, the opening lines are slightly different "When skinny *little* me went out with my honey / The boys *who saw us all* laughed . . ."
91. David A. Jasen and Gene Jones, *Spreadin' Rhythm Around: Black Popular Songwriters 1880–1930* (New York: Routledge, 2005), 333.
92. For many decades, no one even raised the possibility of a second guitarist on the first Trio Decca session, not until Gunther Schuller, writing in *The Swing Era: The Development of Jazz 1930–1945* (New York: Oxford University Press, 1989), 818, mentioned it. Even so, the second guitar is so faint that probably only a highly trained musician could even hear him. However, Nick Rossi, the guitarist, historian, and Oscar Moore specialist, supports Schuller's conclusion. It's believed that the second guitarist is most likely Oscar's older brother, Johnny Moore.
93. *Down Beat*, March 1, 1941, quoted in KT, 50.
94. "Hollywood Trio to Tour East," *Pittsburgh Courier*, January 25, 1941.
95. "Hollywood Trio to Tour East," *Pittsburgh Courier*, January 25, 1941.
96. "Famed Cole Trio Opens in Chicago," *Pittsburgh Courier*, February 15, 1941.
97. This evening is mentioned in Gary Giddins, *Swinging on a Star: The War Years 1949–1946* (New York: Little, Brown, 2018), 95, and also in Donald Bogle, *Dorothy*

Dandridge: A Biography (New York: Amistad Press, 1997), 85. Giddins describes the event as a party; Bogle describes it as a more formal benefit performance but doesn't list a theater or other venue.

98. Recorded in New York on December 19, 1940, "Gone with What Draft" was also known as "Gilly."
99. *Afro-American*, December 10, 1938, 9.
100. "Revue Slated for LACC Today," *California Eagle*, April 11, 1940.
101. Performance contract between "Fats Waller and His Victor Rhythm," his manager, W. T. "Ed" Kirkeby, and Murray Anderson of the Brent Inn, Burlington, Ontario, Canada, July 21, 1942, courtesy Stephen Hester.
102. Arnold Shaw, *The Street That Never Slept* (New York: Coward, McCann, & Geoghan, 1971), 214.
103. *Down Beat*, February 1, 1941, 21, and March 1, 1941, 5.
104. The Trio is believed to have recorded a total of twenty titles with Boyer, ten in February 1941 and another ten in July 1944. There are also sixteen or so additional titles by Boyer included on the four-CD set *The King Cole Trio: The MacGregor Years, 1941–1945* (engineered and produced by David Lennick, on the Canadian label Music & Arts as M&A 911). However, these additional sixteen are now believed to feature another pianist, guitarist, and bassist, and not Cole, Moore, and Prince.
105. "Famed Cole Trio Opens in Chicago," *Pittsburgh Courier*, February 15, 1941.
106. At one point it was announced (by the *Courier*, February 15) that they were set to open on Saturday, February 1, but various sources, including *Down Beat* and *Billboard*, indicate an opening date of Friday, March 7.
107. Adams, 49.
108. "Night Club Reviews," *Billboard*, September 9, 1941.
109. Jordan to Arnold Shaw, quoted in John Chilton, *Louis Jordan: Let the Good Times Roll*, 83.
110. Adams, 49. Adams distinctly remembers having the Tympany Five and the King Cole Trio on the same bill. However, no other source mentions this, and both groups were already prominent enough that the black press and the jazz press (especially *Down Beat*, which was based in Chicago) would have surely noticed. (*Billboard* did review the booking of Cole and Jordan when they shared a bill at the Capitol lounge in September 1941.)
111. *Variety*, April 9, 1941, 40, and April 16, 1941, 48. The "Romany Room is Jumpin'" was issued, in two takes, on the 2019 Resonance Records package.
112. Informal telephone and in-person conversations with William Gottlieb, 1990s. One of these images was used on the cover of the Vintage Jazz Classics four-CD package, *The Complete Early Transcriptions of the King Cole Trio: 1938–1941*.
113. DME, 85.
114. Confirmed in many listings in the *New York Herald Tribune*, June 11; *Billboard*, June 14; *New York Times*, June 19; and repeated listings in *Variety* cabaret bills, from mid-June through late August. Also Metronome, June 1941, 10.

115. Shaw, *The Street That Never Slept*, 214. The agent whom Watkins mentions, Frank Henshaw, worked for General Artists Corp.
116. "Night Club Reviews," *Billboard*, September 9, 1941; jazz violinist Eddie South and his band replaced.
117. Sharon A. Pease, *Swing Piano Styles* (column), "Nat Cole's Jazz Piano Wasn't Quite for Church," *Down Beat*, October 1, 1941.
118. Shaw, *The Street That Never Slept*, 214. The circumstances that Watkins describes and the pay rate that he mentions are more consistent with the Trio's status in 1939 than 1941. Watkins is definitely conflating multiple gigs in that he remembers the Trio working for him for nine months, which would indicate 1941–42.
119. Barry Ulanov, "Fly Right," *Metronome*, August 1944.
120. *Variety* cabaret bills, June 18, 1941.
121. *New York Times*, September 17, 1941, 17.
122. *New York Times*, October 29, 1941, 17.
123. Handwritten memoir by Norman Granz, incomplete and unpublished, courtesy of Tad Hershorn.
124. Alan Bergman, interview with the author, March 20, 2019.
125. Adams, 49.
126. Shaw, *The Street That Never Slept*, 214–15.
127. Don George, *Sweet Man: The Real Duke Ellington* (New York: G. P. Putnam's Sons, 1981), 77.
128. Shaw, *The Street That Never Slept* , 214.
129. Phoebe Jacobs (1918–2012), conversation with the author.
130. Gunther Schuller, *The Swing Era: The Development of Jazz 1930–1945* (New York: Oxford University Press, 1989), 818.
131. And, more recently, Diana Krall, John Pizzarelli, Billy Stritch, Christine Ebersole, and many others.
132. "Kicking at the Stable," *Afro-American,* November 8, 1941.
133. "King Cole Trio on Basin Street," *New York Amsterdam News*, January 10, 1942; "King Cole Trio Is Guest Starred in Radio Sketch," *Chicago Defender*, January 17, 1942; "King Cole Trio Guest Stars on Basin Street," *New Journal and Guide* (Norfolk, Virginia), January 24, 1942. For all of my criticism of the series, of course, we regret that no aircheck of Cole's performance actually survives, nor do we even know what songs they played.
134. Adams, 50.
135. "Cleve. Scandal Causes Cafe Mop Up," *Variety*, April 9, 1942.
136. *Cleveland Call and Post*, April 4, 1942. The full title of the story, and all the headlines and subheads, actually read: "Hold Nine on Vice Charges—Dailies Play Up Negroes in Vice Case Involving 4 White Girls Who Went 'Bad'—Teen-age White Girls 'Amaze' Police Officials with Revelations of Loose Living; Lay Early Vice Start to White Men."

137. "Vice Scandal Brings Firing of Negro Acts," *Variety*, April 16, 1942. Raynor's name is given as both "Ray" and "Roy" in different accounts.
138. "Hold Nine on Vice Charges," *Cleveland Call and Post*, April 4, 1942.
139. "Cleve. Scandal Causes Cafe Mop Up," *Variety*, April 9, 1942.
140. "Vice Scandal Brings Firing of Negro Acts," *Variety*, April 16, 1942.
141. "Vice Scandal Brings Firing of Negro Acts," *Variety*, April 16, 1942.
142. Adams, 50.
143. *Variety* cabaret bills, April 15, 1942. Around this time, the Trio may have also appeared at Nick's in the Village, for many years the home base of the traditional jazz guitarist and general "ringleader" Eddie Condon (Barry Ulanov, "Fly Right," *Metronome*, August 1944).
144. *Chicago Defender*, specifically the *Hollywood Through* column, written by Harry Levette, July 4, 1942.
145. Claudin's name later turns up in *Billboard*, April 14, 1945, as the California manager of Martin Block Music.
146. *Metronome*, October 1942, KT, 62.
147. *Metronome*, October 1942, KT, 62.
148. Jeffries was backed by a King Cole Trio–style combination of the popular Central Avenue pianist Eddie Beal (a close friend of Cole's who worked on the NBC TV series), guitarist Ulysses Livingston, and bassist Joe Comfort (remember that name).
149. *Pittsburgh Courier*, November 12, 1942. The two titles were listed as "All for You" and "Vom Wim Needle" [*sic*].
150. *Pittsburgh Courier*, November 21, 1942.
151. *California Eagle*, February 10, 1943, 2-B.
152. "King Cole Trio Score Over CBS," *Pittsburgh Courier*, March 6, 1943.
153. Sam Abbott, "Reviews," *Billboard*, March 6, 1943, 19.
154. Contrary to Adams's memories, the Beachcomber gig was not a frantic last minute occurrence; several papers reported it well in advance.
155. "Draft Gets Cole, Flat Feet et al.," *Afro-American*, March 13, 1943, 2.
156. *Down Beat*, May 1, 1943, quoted in KT, 66.
157. Maria, 62.
158. *Afro-American*, March 20, 1943, 10.
159. "King Cole Trio 'Solid' at Beachcombers Club," *Pittsburgh Courier*, April 10, 1943.
160. *New Journal and Guide* (Norfolk, Virginia), May 15, 1943.
161. "Bandleaders Weld a Little Close Harmony," *Pittsburgh Courier*, July 3, 1943; and "West Coast Lures Many Top Notchers to Tinsel City," *Pittsburgh Courier*, August 7, 1943. Also covered in *Down Beat*, July 15, 1943.
162. Researcher Mark Cantor has found a Universal contract, dated July 12, 1943, that substantiates that Cole, Moore, and Miller were paid, respectively, $45, $30, and $30 for three hours of recording on July 10th. *Top Man* was released on September

17, 1943, and thus pre-dates the Trio's first on-screen appearance in any film, which is *Here Comes Elmer*, recorded and filmed later in July and which was released by Republic Pictures on November 15, 1943 – and which is covered in chapter two.

163. "King Cole Trio Signed to Long Contract by Republic," *Chicago Defender*, July 24, 1943. On this program, they also were to appear with character actor Mischa Auer and director Wesley Ruggles.
164. John S. Kinloch, *Kinloch's Corner* (column), *California Eagle*, September 2, 1943, 1B. The Alpha Bowling Social Club was located at 29th and Western Avenue.
165. At least as listed by *Metronome* in October 1945: "Premier Radio Enterprises, 3033 Locust St, St. Louis."
166. John Tynan, "First Part about a Pianist Who Turned Singer to Find a Kingdom," *Down Beat*, May 2, 1957 (two parts).
167. Over the next fifty years, Scherman would sell and re-sell, license and re-license, the four Premier tracks many times; once, the early 1980s, he tried to talk the researcher and historian (and kindergarten teacher) Mark Cantor into taking the masters off his hands. (They weren't able to reach an agreement.) In 1945, the four tracks were reissued on a Los Angeles–based indie label called Atlas, including a pairing of "Got a Penny" and "Let's Pretend." At the time, *Metronome* commented, "a typical ballad, perhaps a little too typical, with the pattern that is now becoming over-familiar" (Barry Ulanov, "Fly Right," *Metronome*, August 1944). Even by 1945, the Trio was moving beyond what they had established less than two years earlier—all the more curious that Cole revived the song, now known as "Got a Penny, Benny" for his Soundies session of November, 1945.
168. In fact, the Trio had already been signed to Capitol (announced in October) when they did the Premier date in early November—they were probably merely seizing the opportunity to pick up a quick paycheck. (Plus, the Premier date had probably already been set up even earlier than that, say September.)
169. All ten of the 1943–43 tracks would be included, much later, in the 1991 boxed set *The Complete Capitol Recordings of the Nat King Cole Trio* released by Mosaic Records, which is exactly as it should be.
170. To Don Freeman, *Down Beat*, October 6, 1950; KT, 261–62; Adams, 50.

CHAPTER 2

WF: I was asked for a footnote for the opening epigrams to this chapter—the *Sullivan's Travels* quote should be self-explanatory. The other quote would be sourced as:

Marvin Fisher, phone conversation with the author circa 1990.

1. At least three of these photos were used in the booklet for the 1991 Mosaic Records King Cole Trio boxed set.

2. *Down Beat*, May 2, 1957, John Tynan, profile of Nat King Cole, "First Part of a Story about a Pianist Who Turned Singer to Find a Kingdom." Cole was never a stickler.
3. Norman Poirier and Lael Scott, "Nat King Cole 2. The Early Days," *New York Post*, February 18, 1965. In other accounts, Mercer was by himself the first time he heard the Trio and returned with Crosby.
4. Richard G. Hubler, "$12,000-a-Week Preacher's Boy," *Saturday Evening Post*, July 1954.
5. *Down Beat*, July 15, 1940, quoted in KT, 43.
6. From an unfinished and unpublished memoir by Johnny Mercer, the manuscript of which resides in the Mercer papers at Georgia State University, quoted in Philip Furia, *Skylark, The Life and Times of Johnny Mercer* (New York: St. Martin's Press, 2003), 136.
7. *Down Beat*, July 15, 1940, quoted in KT, 43.
8. Richard G. Hubler, "$12,000-a-Week Preacher's Boy," *Saturday Evening Post*, July 1954.
9. Interview with Dave Dexter Jr. by Michel Montet, Hollywood, June 24, 1977.
10. Richard G. Hubler, "$12,000-a-Week Preacher's Boy," *Saturday Evening Post*, July 1954.
11. The Liberty Music Shop was in business from the 1930s at least until the 1970s when I was first buying records; at one point they operated three retail outlets in the city. Throughout this time, they were regarded as something roughly akin to the cabaret and show music equivalent of the famed Commodore Music Shop a few blocks away on East 42nd St. Because Broadway, no less than jazz, was underserved by the regular commercial record industry at the time, Liberty launched what would today be called a "boutique label"of its own. The idea was, as veteran music buffs such as the late Roger Sturtevant told me, that you would see a show on Broadway or at a sophisticated club such as the Blue Angel in Times Square, and then pick up a record of a song you liked on your way home. The two most famous artists on the Liberty Music Shop label were Ethel Waters, who recorded her numbers from *At Home Abroad* and *Cabin in the Sky*, and Lee Wiley, who recorded her George Gershwin and Cole Porter songbooks for LMS.
12. Quoted in *Capitol Records 50th Anniversary, 1942–1992*, written by Paul Grein, a private limited edition volume published by Capitol Records in 1992.
13. Quoted in *Capitol Records 50th Anniversary, 1942–1992*.
14. *Capitol Records 50th Anniversary, 1942–1992*. Wallichs's chronology is slightly off: Mercer's disc of "G.I. Jive" was recorded at the very first session following the ban on October 15, 1943, and there also was a hugely successful hit version by Louis Jordan on Decca.
15. Interview with Dave Dexter Jr. by Michel Montet, Hollywood, June 24, 1977.
16. KW.
17. "Odd situation is that Oscar Wallichs will be one of the active directors of the new company [Excelsior Records]. Wallichs is the father of Glenn Wallichs who also

recently started a record company." *Metronome* magazine, October 1942 (quoted in 2). It might have seemed like the two new labels were not in competition; Excelsior was primarily a race label, run by the Rene Brothers, whereas Capitol in its first year didn't have any black artists. (They did record two titles by the legendary blues singer and guitarist T-Bone Walker in July 1942, but these weren't released as singles at the time.)

18. Interview with Dave Dexter Jr. by Michel Montet, Hollywood, June 24, 1977.
19. *Billboard*, October 23, 1943, 66.
20. This is from the episode of August 6, 1957. Cole sings only eight bars of "Straighten Up" here, but it's especially interesting in that, in this version, he sings it with a very swinging big-band arrangement by Nelson Riddle.
21. "The King Heeds His Father—Nat Cole Listens to Sermon and Sets It to Music," *Afro-American*, November 16, 1946, 8.
22. "Ole King Cole," Buster Sherwood, *The Orchestra World*, April 1945, 5.
23. KW.
24. *Pittsburgh Courier*, April 10, 1943, "King Cole Trio 'Solid' at Beachcombers Club." The Omaha gig may have been planned earlier and then pushed back after Cole received in his induction notice in early March. During this run, the Trio also played at least one local dance, at the Dreamland Ballroom, on March 28.
25. Adams, 50. In his memoir, Adams talks about three major gigs that he booked for the Trio: the Capitol Lounge in Chicago, the Sky Bar in Cleveland (and the infamous scandal connected with it), and the Beachcomber in Omaha. Adams described these as consecutive bookings, one right after the other; in reality, however, they were all at least a year apart.
26. The entire song is based on "Rhythm" changes, with the exception of the opening section, which might be called the intro or verse, which begins, "A buzzard took a monkey for a ride in the air . . ." The rest of the song is all "rhythm" changes.
27. This line is from a 1959 public service broadcast sent out to stations on behalf of the March of Dimes. In this semi-pre-recorded interview, a live deejay would ask questions from a script and Cole's answers were taped beforehand.
28. "Nat King Cole and Hal Singer at Auditorium Tonight," *Atlanta Daily World*, June 12, 1949, 12. Irving Mills was hardly "anonymous"; in fact, his name was on every copy of the song, every piece of sheet music, every recording.
29. The number, roughly fifteen songs by Duke Ellington that Irving Mills put his name on, comes from Mills's biographer, Donald McGlynn.
30. *Chicago Defender*, July 10, 1943, "Nat Cole's New Song Latest on Hit Parade"; *New York Amsterdam News*, "Cole Pens Tune Stunner." Note that all of the notices about the song, presumably written from the publisher's own press release, give full credit to Cole as the song's sole author; Mills doesn't seem to be trying to fool anyone into thinking he had anything to do with actually writing it.
31. *Chicago Defender*, July 24, 1943, "King Cole Trio signed to Long Contract by Republic." It was reported that they were "up for a three-picture-a-year contract"

by Republic, although they made only one other film for the studio, *Pistol Packin' Mama*, also released in 1943.

32. "King Cole Calls for Barristers," *Down Beat*, December 1, 1944. Note that in this account, Cole states that he never directly placed the song with Mills but that the publisher merely stepped up and claimed all rights to the song based on an earlier existing contract—which Cole states is "old" (and therefore, one assumes, invalid). At one point, about ten years later, Cole claimed that he had written "Straighten Up and Fly Right" much earlier, as when he told the *Saturday Evening Post* (July 17, 1954) that he had written the song in 1937 and then "sold it for fifty dollars' worth of room rent when he was broke." This may have been a deliberate dodge to convince everyone that he had written the song well before he ever met Mills and therefore Mills had no claim to it. By 1957, when he sang "Straighten Up" on his NBC TV series, he was back to admitting that he had written it in the "early forties."
33. In most publishing deals, the publishing rights revert to the author after twenty-seven years, but in this case Cole seems to have signed over all of his rights to Mills, past, present, and future.
34. Irving Mills was far from the sleaziest or most morally bankrupt publisher around. The reader is referred to *Black and Blue*, Barry Singer's excellent biography of Andy Razaf (the lyricist of "Gee, Baby Ain't I Good to You," among many other classic songs) for eye-opening anecdotage regarding Joe Davis, a music mogul who made Mills look like Mother Theresa.
35. Capitol cut seven masters on that date, by Jo Stafford, Johnny Mercer, the Pied Pipers (also singing "Pistol Packin'Mama"), all in various combinations.
36. *Good Morning Blues: The Autobiography of Count Basie*, as told to Albert Murray (New York: Random House, 1985), 275.
37. Although Capitol later launched an "Americana" series, featuring country and blues artists (their 40000 series), this was also hardly racially driven.
38. *Down Beat*, May 2, 1957, John Tynan, profile of Nat King Cole, "First Part of a Story about a Pianist Who Turned Singer to Find a Kingdom." The term A&R man refers to the label's "artists and repertoire man," who would, in later generations, be called a record producer.
39. June 3, 1957, broadcast live from Chicago.
40. Larry Kiner, *The Rudy Vallee Discography* (Westport, CT: Greenwood Press, 1985).
41. There's yet one other "Sweet Lorraine" pre-Capitol: in fall 1943 yet again, this time at a session starring the twenty-year-old saxophonist Dexter Gordon (and produced by Norman Granz), making his debut as a leader. Cole's great friend, trumpeter Harry Sweets Edison, plays the melody first, and Gordon does a beautiful melodic improvisation that sounds as though it could have been played by Lester Young, while the pianist, though just a sideman here, is unmistakably King Cole.
42. The two most famous, archetypical examples of a "quality problem" are 1. "What to do with all my money?" and 2. "What to do with all my hair?"

43. All of Bing Crosby's Decca albums up to this point were compilations of previously released material, with the exception of the 1942 *Holiday Inn* album (more fully titled, *Song Hits from the Paramount Picture Holiday Inn*). Gary Giddins, in *Bing Crosby: Swinging on a Star* (New York: Little, Brown, 2018), makes a case for this as a pioneering cast album, preceding the better known *Oklahoma!* album by about two years.
44. Barry Ulanov, "Fly Right," *Metronome*, August 1944.
45. "Embraceable You," "Sweet Lorraine," "Body and Soul," "The Man I Love," "Prelude in C Sharp Minor," "What Is This Thing Called Love," "Easy Listening Blues," and "It's Only a Paper Moon."
46. Quoted in "King Cole Shatters Apollo Theater Mark," *Pittsburgh Courier*, December 9, 1944, 13.
47. Some of this background information on the MacGregor company comes from Ivan Santiago's excellent, highly thorough discography of Peggy Lee. http://www.peggyleediscography.com/p/macgregor.php, retrieved March 2, 2018.
48. Michael Sparke and Peter Venudor, *Stan Kenton: The Studio Sessions* (Lake Geneva, WI: Balboa Books, 1998).
49. In 1995, a Canadian label called Music & Arts issued what is so far the definitive package of the Trio's work for the company, a four-CD package produced and restored by David Lennick, titled *The King Cole Trio: The MacGregor Years, 1941–1945*. Containing 120 tracks total, it features all fifty of the "prime" tracks by the Trio on its own, plus thirty-three with Anita Boyer, fifteen with Ida James, five with Anita O'Day, five with the Barrie Sisters, and an additional twelve tracks (discussed elsewhere) from 1944 that amount to Cole's first all-piano "album."
50. Gourse, 62.
51. The closest thing to an exception was "Is You Is or Is You Ain't My Baby?" which Cole performed on a MacGregor transcription and in a Soundies film with vocalist Ida James, but never on a commercial disc.
52. Cole did record two of Jordan's most successful songs, "Is You Is Or Is You Ain't (Ma Baby)" and "That'll Just about Knock Me Out," but only for MacGregor transcriptions, not Capitol proper.
53. Details on Carlos Gastel from his *Variety* obituary, November 18, 1970, as well as DME, 104–5.
54. "Member of Cole's Band Is Drowned," *Chicago Defender*, August 10, 1935, 1.
55. Gordon, 79–80.
56. *Down Beat*, January 1, 1940, 21.
57. Arnold Shaw, *The Street That Never Slept* (New York: Coward, McCann, & Geoghan, 1971), 214.
58. *Down Beat*, April 15, 1943, 6.
59. Adams, 50.

60. As Adams relates, the attorney who presided over the contracts was Lee Eastman, father of the future Mrs. Paul McCartney and already something of a music industry legal legend.
61. Adams remembered that this conversation occurred the Christmas before Cole died, but it was more likely the holiday season of 1963, since Cole was in the hospital in December 1964.
62. From the unpublished manuscript *The Conversational and Otherwise Art of Jimmy Rowles* by Jimmy Rowles and Tad Hershorn. Rowles's colorful account, which must be taken with at least a grain of salt, indicates that Herb Rose apparently also served briefly as the Trio's manager. Courtesy of Tad Hershorn.
63. Maria, 42–44.
64. Dixon Gayer, "Jazz in Small Packages," *Seventeen*, January 1947. Yes, some sources say the Trio earned $800 a week at the Orpheum and others say it was a full thousand.
65. "Los Angeles Band Briefs," *Down Beat*, April 1, 1944, 6. "Herb Rose shopping for an attraction to replace the King Cole Trio at the 331 Club."
66. Barry Ulanov, "Fly Right," *Metronome*, August 1944.
67. *Down Beat*, May 2, 1957, John Tynan, profile of Nat King Cole, "First Part of a Story about a Pianist Who Turned Singer to Find a Kingdom."
68. They also both had a propensity for publishing songs under the names of their wives, for contractual reasons, which is why you see "Nadine Robinson"and "Fleecie Moore" listed as authors on so many hits, by, respectively, the King Cole Trio and the Tympany Five.
69. A still incomplete count: "Hit That Jive, Jack" (1941), "Vim Vom Veedle" (1942), "I'm an Errand Boy for Rhythm" (1945), "Breezy and the Bass" (in the 1948 all-black feature film *Killer Diller*), "Cole Capers" (on *King Cole at the Piano*, 1947), "Lester Leaps In" (recorded live at the first Jazz at the Philharmonic concert in 1944, and again for Capitol Transcriptions in 1946), "Return Trip" (by Irving Ashby, 1947), "Airiness a la Nat" (with the Keynoters, 1946), not to mention "Straighten Up and Fly Right" (1943). Most of these were composed by Nat, and all of them use the "rhythm" changes to some extent, although, as we've seen, only in the bridge in some cases ("Veedle," "Jive," "Straighten"). Last, the Trio left us at least two versions of the actual "I Got Rhythm" melody itself, both cut for studio transcriptions, MacGregor in 1944 and Capitol Transcriptions 1946.
70. Marvin Fisher, phone conversation with the author circa 1990. The Trio version wasn't issued until 1991, but it was commercially recorded by Count Basie and also Cole's friend Timmie Rogers, who cut it for Cole's former label, Excelsior, with a KC3-style trio of piano, guitar, and drums.
71. In 1945, virtually everybody on the airwaves was cracking jokes regarding Sinatra's fine thin frame; someone surely noticed that the singer looks as if he could have used a hearty helping or two of *chefafa* on the side.

72. *New York Amsterdam News*, December 21, 1946. This particular fete was held at prizefighter Joe Louis's restaurant in Harlem.
73. Dixon Gayer, "Jazz in Small Packages," *Seventeen*, January 1947.
74. Quoted in *Minnie the Moocher and Many More* (1983 documentary and compilation of soundies and other early films of African American entertainers, hosted by Cab Calloway).
75. As footnoted elsewhere here, several were published under the name of his wife, probably for publishing contractual reasons, like Louis Jordan frequently did. "But All I've Got Is Me" is one of several songs he wrote with Don George. "I Can't See for Lookin'" was later recorded by several contemporary pianists in tribute to Cole, including Ahmad Jamal, Monty Alexander, and Loston Harris.
76. Haskins, 44.
77. Geoffrey C. Ward and Ken Burns, *Jazz: A History of America's Music* (New York: Alfred A. Knopf, 2000), 92.
78. Fischer was best known as the accompanist and collaborator of Frankie Laine, with whom he wrote the standard "We'll Be Together Again."
79. Leeds had an admirable pedigree of '40s novelties to his credit, among them, "Rip Van Winkle," "Joey's Got a Girl," and, in a more serious vein, the English language lyric to the Brazilian standard "Perfidia," later sung by Cole.
80. KW.
81. KW. We'll have to take Conkling's word that the guitar solo on the original 1944 recording was out of tune, because that master was destroyed and never issued.
82. Barry Ulanov, "Fly Right," *Metronome*, August 1944. If Cole ever actually wrote down any of the Trio's arrangements, this was likely not a long-term process, as literally none of these notations have survived.
83. "King Cole Trio Heading for Harlem Triumph Nov. 17," *Cleveland Call and Post*, November 18, 1944.
84. *The Nat King Cole Trio—Live at the Circle Room* (Capitol Jazz – 7243 5 21859 2 4).
85. *Down Beat*, April 15, 1944; Milton Benny, "Hollywood Periscope," *Metronome*, March 1944, 12. Benny added that Ernest Ashley was "not to be confused with [Irving] Ashby of Hampton guitar renown."
86. Carrie Miller, *Backstage* (column), *California Eagle*, May 4, 1944, 15.
87. Special thanks to the late Richard Lieberson for helping me with these observations regarding Oscar Moore.
88. Barry Ulanov, "Fly Right," *Metronome*, August 1944.
89. *Down Beat*, May 2, 1957, John Tynan, profile of Nat King Cole, "First Part of a Story about a Pianist Who Turned Singer to Find a Kingdom."
90. "King Cole Trio's Recipe for Success Is 'Like Your Work,'" *Cleveland Call Post*, March 29, 1947.
91. "King Cole Trio Heading for Harlem Triumph Nov 17, after Snub by New York in 1940," *Cleveland Call Post*, November 18, 1944, 9.

92. "King Cole Shatters Apollo Theater Mark," *Pittsburgh Courier*, December 9, 1944, 13.
93. Marvin Fisher, informal interview with the author, circa 1991.
94. "How Does It Feel," alas, was never issued until 1969, when Capitol overdubbed a disastrous strings and rhythm section over it on the notorious *There I've Said It Again* album; the *au natural* version wasn't heard until the 1991 Mosaic box.
95. Maria, 24.
96. *New York Amsterdam News*, December 12, 1944, "King Cole and Lorenzo Pack in Tune." There's a photo of Cole and Pack, with the story being a caption that describes Pack as a "former heavyweight contender" and mentions that Pack has written songs performed by Duke Ellington, Andy Kirk, and the Andrews Sisters ("Miss Sallie Sue"). Cole is referred to as "leader of the famous trio that recently smashed all records at Harlem's Apollo Theater."
97. "Confess" by Buddy Clark and Doris Day on Columbia was a bigger hit than the KC3 version on Capitol, while "A Boy from Texas, a Girl from Tennessee" was also waxed by crooner Johnnie Johnston and a few others, but these examples are relatively rare.
98. Interview with Lee Jeske, 1984, from the liner notes to the two-LP reissue, *Everything I Have Is Yours (The M-G-M Years)* (1985), quoted in Will Friedwald, *Jazz Singing: America's Great Voices from Bessie Smith to Bebop and Beyond* (New York: C. Scribner's Sons, 1990).
99. Dave Dexter, *Playback* (New York: Billboard Publications, 1976), 97.
100. James would appear in several features, both of them all-black poverty row pictures, *The Devil's Daughter* and *Hi-De-Ho* (starring Cab Calloway).
101. For not playing several of the last dates of the tour, the Trio's agency (and Carlos Gastel) were sued by Kirk's agency (who had put the tour together). Several months later, there was an article in the *Chicago Defender* which quoted Cole as saying, "We didn't decide to sue each other, it was our agencies' idea." September 21, 1946, "King Cole and Kirk Still Friends."
102. In the otherwise excellent documentary, *Nat King Cole: Afraid of the Dark* (2014), the claim is made that the central dancer in several of the 1945 Soundies is Nadine Robinson Cole, the artist's wife. This seems extremely unlikely; for one thing the dancer in question doesn't resemble any of the existing photos of Mrs. Cole, and we also know that he was generally traveling without her, especially in his increasingly long trips to New York, in this period.
103. *The Capitol*, April 1946, 7.

CHAPTER 3

Epigraph: John Collins, telephone conversation with the author, 1990.

1. The entire show is on youtube.com, at least as of September 14, 2018: https://www.youtube.com/watch?v=VkgWpZBqVnw.

2. "Jam Men," *New York Amsterdam News*, May 23, 1942. The photo also includes an individual identified as one "Jay Wishing," but it's not known who he was or what he played.
3. Dick Katz, "The Pianist," liner notes in the 1991 Mosaic box.
4. Red Callender, *Unfinished Dream* (London: Quartet Books, 1985), 49.
5. Handwritten memoir by Norman Granz, incomplete and unpublished, courtesy of Tad Hershorn.
6. Handwritten memoir by Norman Granz, incomplete and unpublished, courtesy of Tad Hershorn.
7. Interview with Granz by Tad Hershorn.
8. Interview with Norman Granz, by Patricia Willard, August 23, 1989. Courtesy Tad Herschorn.
9. General information from Tad Herschorn, *Norman Granz: The Man Who Used Jazz for Justice* (Berkeley: University of California Press, 2011), 40. Granz later said that Berg "opened" the club at this time; we know that Cole played there in 1937 when it was called the Café Century.
10. Interview with Norman Granz, by Patricia Willard, August 23, 1989. Courtesy Tad Herschorn.
11. Granz memoir.
12. Arthur Jackson, "Jazz King Cole," *The Gramophone Record Review*, May 1954, 351. Two additional points: first, Jackson quotes Cole as saying this happened in New York, but clearly he was misquoting, since this obviously was happening in Los Angeles. Second, Nat also describes this as "my only attempt at band leading,"—but as we know, it wasn't.
13. Callender, *Unfinished Dream*, 51.
14. Tad Herschorn, *Norman Granz: The Man Who Used Jazz for Justice* (Berkeley: University of California Press, 2011), 33.
15. "Jam Sessions begin in Hollywood," *Down Beat*, July 1, 1942, 7.
16. Freddy Doyle, "Swingtime," *California Eagle*, July 2, 1942, 2-B.
17. Callender, *Unfinished Dream,* 50.
18. *Down Beat*, August 15, 1942, quoted in KT, 61.
19. "And Still They Come," *Metronome*, October 1945,
20. *Down Beat*, August 15, 1942, quoted in KT, 61. Besides which, Nat was in Omaha with the Trio for at least six weeks in Spring 1943 in any case, as we have seen.
21. *Down Beat*, July 1, 1943, 6.
22. The sole reason Cole isn't in this classic film, undoubtedly, is because the Trio was then on tour, playing the East with Andy Kirk's orchestra at the time that it was recorded and filmed in September 1944.
23. *Down Beat*, July 1, 1944, 11.
24. *California Eagle,* February 3, 1944, 11. It's also worth noting that the *Eagle* ad mentions a "Membership Dues" fee of $1.00 rather than a conventional cover charge. The ad proclaims "ALL STARRED JAZZ CONCERT [*sic*]—featuring

NAT KING COLE, KIRK BRADFORD alto star of Jimmy [*sic*] Lunceford's Band, Oscar Moore and other stars of Cab Calloway's band, Illinois Jacquet, J. C. Heard and others."

25. A former clarinetist, Tony Martin would later co-star with Cole on the September 17, 1957, episode of *The Nat King Cole Show.*
26. "Jazz Concert at Music City," *California Eagle,* February 10, 1944, 12.
27. "Granz Inaugurates LA Sunday Swing Shows," *Down Beat*, March 1, 1944. The guitarist is properly credited here,
28. *Metronome*, March 1944, quoted in KT, 84; "Gastel Signs Up King Cole Trio," *Down Beat*, March 1, 1944.
29. Herschorn, *Norman Granz: The Man Who Used Jazz for Justice*, 56.
30. Leonard Feather, "Jazz Millionaire," *Esquire*, January 1957, quoted in Herschorn, *Norman Granz: The Man Who Used Jazz for Justice*, 99.
31. *Down Beat*, July 1, 1944, 11.
32. Gourse, 66. Paul is probably overdramatizing the reasons for Moore's absence; in general, Oscar seems to have deliberately avoided playing on Cole's non-Trio shows, but, apparently not wanting to hurt Nat's feelings, he usually never actually says "no"—rather, he just doesn't show up.
33. Arthur Jackson, "Jazz King Cole," *The Gramophone Record Review*, May 1954, 351.
34. This is the billing on the first ten-inch LPs issued from the July 2, 1944, concert, *Jazz at the Philharmonic, Volume Four* (MG V4). (The JATP recordings were not issued in the actual chronological order of the concerts themselves.) By the mid-1950s, Granz was perhaps glad that he had never incurred the wrath of Capitol Records since he would rent studio space for many Verve Records sessions in the famous Capitol Tower.
35. "D-Day" by Lew Spence, recorded for MacGregor transcriptions, however, rather than for Capitol Records, circa July 1944.
36. Hershorn, *Norman Granz: The Man Who Used Jazz for Justice*, 64.
37. Hershorn, *Norman Granz: The Man Who Used Jazz for Justice*, 63.
38. Gourse, 66.
39. "Lawsuit Almost Halts LA Jam," *Down Beat*, August 15, 1944.
40. Milton Benny, "A Jumping History: Dave Dexter's Project Augurs Well for Capitol and for Jazz," *Metronome*, August 1945, 11.
41. Benny, "A Jumping History," 11.
42. Benny, "A Jumping History," 11.
43. Benny, "A Jumping History," 11.
44. Dave Dexter, *Playback* (New York: Billboard Publications, 1976), 97.
45. Kay Starr, interview with author, 1990.
46. Morroe Berger, Edward Berger, and James Patrick, *Benny Carter: A Life in American Music*, vol. 2, 2nd ed. (Lanham, MD: Scarecrow Press, 2001), 174.
47. Dexter, *Playback*, 97.

48. Cole had accompanied Ida James singing "Stormy Weather" on a 1944 MacGregor transcription but that was it; he never sang it himself, certainly not for Capitol.
49. Kay Starr, interview with author, 1990.
50. Dexter, *Playback*, 98.
51. Referenced in *Chicago Defender*, July 7, 1945, 14, "When Will War End? Let Disc Stars 'Tell You When.'" The original story in *The Capitol*, July 1945, had a more dramatic headline, "When Will the Japs Surrender? Noted Musickers Submit Guesses," by Lou Schurrer.
52. "Patton and Doolittle Call 'Job Half Done,'" *The Sun*, June 10, 1945, 2.
53. Dexter, *Playback*, 97.
54. There's some disagreement as to Haymer's exact birthdate, and some believe that 1915 is more likely.
55. Buddy Rich quoted in *Jazz Professional*, July 1982, online at http://jazzpro.nationaljazzarchive.org.uk/Main/Rich%20interview.htm (retrieved December 4, 2019)
56. Alun Morgan, liner notes to two LPs, *Kicks* (Fontana FJL-132) and *Anatomy of a Jam Session* (Black Lion 28414), both British issues, released posthumously under Nat King Cole's name. (Capitol Records be darned.)
57. The last ten seconds or so of the alternate to "I'll Never Be the Same" are actually a first try at "Swingin' on Central."
58. "Round the Turntable: Jazz," edited by Denis Preston, *New Musical Express*, February 27, 1948.
59. Alun Morgan, liner notes to two LPs, *Kicks* (Fontana FJL-132), and *Anatomy of a Jam Session* (Black Lion 28414).
60. *Chicago Defender*, July 7, 1945, "May Be Off Rubber; FBI May Take Simmons' Car in Weed Case." Simmons was playing with Eddie Heywood's sextet at Billy Berg's when police searched his car and found "several sticks of weed." Although Heywood was also arrested, he "continues to deny any involvement in the crime."
61. Buddy Rich quoted in *Jazz Professional*, July 1982, online at http://jazzpro.nationaljazzarchive.org.uk/Main/Rich%20interview.htm (retrieved December 4, 2019). Also quoted in Pelle Berglund, *Buddy Rich: One of a Kind* (Hudson Music, 2019), 128
62. Dan Morgenstern, liner notes to *The Essential Keynote Collection 9, The Keynoters with Nat King Cole* (Mercury CD 830 967-2).
63. The matter of exactly who the pianist is on "Tailspin" and "Halfway to Dawn" will probably never be completely settled. Phil Schaap, who produced the 1994 CD reissue, feels that the documented evidence, scant though it is, firmly points to Strayhorn. However, historian and musician Kenny Washington has always insisted that the pianist is Cole, and his opinion is seconded by all the experts, pianists, and historians who listened to the tracks (at my request): Ehud Asherie, Loren Schoenberg, Eric Comstock, Edward Green, Dan Morgenstern, and David Hajdu. If, indeed, it is Cole, the most likely date that he recorded these tracks might

be August 13, 1947, the same date that he cut the entire *King Cole at the Piano* album at Radio Recorders.

64. *Norfolk New Jersey Journal and Guide*, October 26, 1946, 20.
65. *Variety*, October 23, 1946; KT, 153.
66. KW.
67. There are several very modern guitar solos here, on "Body" and "Moon," that I would like to believe are by Moore but in all likelihood are played by Barney Kessel.
68. Handwritten memoir by Norman Granz, incomplete and unpublished, courtesy of Tad Hershorn.
69. Arthur Jackson, "Jazz King Cole," *The Gramophone Record Review*, May 1954, 351.

CHAPTER 4

Epigraph: Richard Hubler, "$12,000-a-Week Preacher's Boy," *Saturday Evening Post*, July 17, 1954, 106.

1. Don George, *Sweet Man: The Real Duke Ellington* (New York: G. P. Putnam's Sons, 1981), 82–83. George's book is essentially a memoir of his experiences with Ellington. Notably, he goes on at great length about a particular moment when he helped Nat and Maria attend one of Ellington's performances in an exclusively white supper club, but he barely even mentions "Calypso Blues."
2. *Afro-American*, June 15, 1946, "King Cole Victor in Suit to Occupy Calif. Home."
3. *Afro-American*, June 15, 1946, "King Cole Victor in Suit to Occupy Calif. Home."
4. "Earl Griffin in Hollywood," *Cleveland Call and Post*, June 22, 1946, 7B.
5. Gordon, 81. This fact is reported by Claire Philips Gordon, a close friend of both the Cole and Ellington families, although it is notably, absent from Maria's own book and every other biography.
6. Natalie, 27.
7. Written for Dorothy Lamour in *Road to Utopia,* by Johnny Burke and Jimmy Van Heusen, although Maria later remembered, incorrectly, that the lyrics were by Johnny Mercer.
8. *Atlanta Daily World*, February 14, 1947, "'I've Never Been So Happy' Says King Cole Following Divorce Action."
9. Various sources (especially on the internet) will often give chart positions for recordings going back earlier than 1940, but these, in fact, are not taken from genuine *Billboard* listings. These were invented, for the most part, many years later by an author named Joel Whitburn for a book titled *Pop Memories, 1890–1954: The History of American Popular Music* (Menomonee Falls, WI, 1986).
10. A brief item in the *Chicago Defender* ("Music-Minded Champ," February 8, 1947) credits the song jointly to both Watson, then touring with a group called "Deek and His Brown Dots," and Best, who is identified as a guitarist. The story shows a picture of Deek Watson with heavyweight champion Joe Louis, and

it further mentions that Deek and His Brown Dots recently appeared at "Joe's Rhumboogie" and "are currently in their final week at Jordan Chambers's Riviera in St. Louis."

11. It even became a template for other songwriters: when Sammy Cahn talked about how he and Jules Styne wrote their own song, "The Christmas Waltz," it was pretty much taken verbatim from Mel's account.
12. Mel told the story many times, to me personally in interviews and informal conversations, and also for posterity in his 1988 memoir, *It Wasn't All Velvet*. Quotes and facts from Mel here are both from that book and my own conversations with him. I also spoke with Wells more than once and he never challenged Tormé's account. (Mel remembered it was July 1945, but he also remembered that they brought it to Cole at the Trocadero, an engagement that ended on June 20.)
13. Cole quotes from Leonard Feather's liner notes to *The Nat King Cole Story*, 1961. (Incidentally, the month was more likely May than June.)
14. The original Trio-only version was first issued, quite probably by accident, on a German LP circa 1979, and then eventually on the Mosaic box in 1991.
15. Earlier, in 1944 and '45, Cole had made several appearances on the Kraft show with Crosby himself, who was always a keen supporter of black talent. Bing was virtually the only man who addressed Louis Armstrong as "Lou" and Nat Cole as "King."
16. This information is from the author's 1990 interview with Charlie Grean, who went on to arrange and conduct one other major hit of the era, "Ghost Riders in the Sky" by Vaughn Monroe, in 1949. The label of the original record itself has no specific orchestra credit; it merely says "The King Cole Trio—with string choir—vocal by King Cole."
17. The session of August 19, 1946, not only included the string session but also a drummer, Jack Parker, who had worked extensively with such accomplished pianists as Mary Lou Williams and Pete Johnson. He's only faintly audible on "The Christmas Song" but unmistakable on "The Best Man," also recorded on this date.
18. "Billy Rowe's Note Book," *Pittsburgh Courier*, November 16, 1946, 16.
19. Bill Chase, *All Ears* (column), *Amsterdam News,* November 23, 1946.
20. Dixon Gayer, "Jazz in Small Packages," *Seventeen*, January 1947.
21. The 2014 CD *The Extraordinary Nat King Cole* also included a previously unreleased alternate take from the 1961 session.
22. "MacGregor, Capitol Disk Deal Off, But May be Resumed, *Billboard*, February 3, 1945, 20.
23. An opinion expressed at greater length by Capitol contract artist Margaret Whiting, in her memoir, *It Might as Well Be Spring* (New York: William Morrow, 1987).
24. Also from the online Peggy Lee discography by Ivan Santiago, http://www.peggyleediscography.com/p/captrans.php, retrieved March 2, 2018.
25. Fats Waller had previously recorded a brief reading of the "Wild Rose" theme as part of a medley; the midwestern pianist Herman Chittison recorded a treatment

the same month as Cole. (Chittison's starts slowly and then abruptly starts to rock in a Tatum-esque fashion.)

26. The story, by columnist Don De Leighbur, ran in at least three African American papers on January 12, 1946: the *Norfolk New Journal*, "Cole Promises New Wrinkle in Carnegie Hall Concert"; the *Cleveland Call and Post*, January 12, 1946, "King Cole to Carnegie Hall; and "King Cole Presents Novel Appearance in Carnegie Hall," *Pittsburgh Courier*, January 12, 1946.
27. Klaus Teubig (KT, 125) felt the Esquire concert took place at Carnegie, but most sources confirm that it was the Ritz Theater, used by ABC radio on some of their early broadcasts: *Afro-American*, January 26, 1946, "Backstage at Esky Rehearsal," and *Chicago Defender*, "Stars Shine on All-Star Bill: Orson Welles, King Cole, Woody Herman Kings"; both stories were apparently by syndicated columnist Dolores Calvin.

    The Duke Ellington itinerary also confirms that the 1946 Esquire concert took place at the Ritz Theater in New York, http://tdwaw.ellingtonweb.ca/TDWAW.html#Yr1946, retrieved January 31, 2018.
28. Some discographies, including Tom Lord's *The Jazz Discography*, report that Cole sat in with the Ellington Orchestra on the opener, "Take the A-Train." Alas, if that happened at all, it wasn't recorded. The version on the ABC broadcast and the issued LP (on Boris Rose's Session Disc label) clearly features Ellington himself, as usual, taking the piano solo. Also, since we have only an hour or so of the actual show, there's still a possibility that the Trio may have played some of their concert-style works on the portion of the show that wasn't broadcast.
29. *Norfolk New Journal*, February 2, 1946, "Chamber Music Champs Receive Esquire All American Awards."
30. *Down Beat*, March 25, 1946, "The King Cole Trio Plans Feature Serious Stuff."
31. *Down Beat*, July 1, 1946, 2, "Nat Cole Gets His Trio Set for Concerts," by William Gottlieb.
32. *Down Beat*, July 1, 1946, 2, "Nat Cole Gets His Trio Set for Concerts," by William Gottlieb.
33. *Down Beat*, March 25, 1946, "The King Cole Trio Plans Feature Serious Stuff."
34. *Down Beat*, November 5, 1947, 2.
35. Bill Gottlieb, "Nat Cole Gets His Trio Set for Concerts," *Down Beat*, July 1, 1946.
36. "'Our '47 Concerts Will Shock Listeners' . . . Nat," *Hollywood Note*, July 1947.
37. *Down Beat*, October 21, 1946, KT, 153. As we've seen, earlier editions of this series also co-star movie comic Edward Everett Horton.
38. *Pittsburgh Courier*, November 16, 1946, 16, "King Cole Trio Tops in Show, Radio Orbit."
39. *Pittsburgh Courier*, November 16, 1946, 16, *Billy Rowe's Note Book* (column).
40. "King Cole's Forgotten Love," *Tan*, September 1954.
41. Gertrude Gipson, "Gertrude Gipson's Candid Comments," *California Eagle*, January 30, 1947.

42. "Three More Weeks at the Bocage Starting August 6," *Variety*, July 23, 1947.
43. Thomas Thompson, "A King of Song Dies, and a Friend Remembers Him," *Life*, February 2, 1965, 36. Davis remembered that this was in 1941, and it does seem more likely that the audiences were less likely to be paying attention in 1941 than in 1947. However, the Trio's only known gig at the Million Dollar Theater was this run in July 1947, and the Trio played virtually no theater gigs before 1944.
44. Cole recorded both of these albums, *King Cole at the Piano* and *King Cole for Kids*, in August 1947. *Piano* was actually recorded several days prior to *Kids*, but *Kids* was released considerably earlier. (For the record, *King Cole for Kids* was released in late July/early August 1948, while *King Cole at the Piano* was released in mid-February 1949. These dates refer to the original 78 RPM albums; the LP editions and other formats came later.)
45. The most likely date for the MacGregor "piano" material is August 1944, as per KT, 97–98. (The date is given as November 21, 1944, in the booklet to *The Nat King Cole Trio: The MacGregor Years, 1941–1945* (Music & Arts CD911), which is probably incorrect, since the Trio was playing the Apollo at the time and none of the MacGregor sessions are believed to have been done in New York). The eight titles from the Capitol album were all cut on August 13, 1947.
46. *Billboard*. The tracks were listed on February 12, 1949, and the brief review comes from a week later on February 19.
47. *Down Beat*, March 25, 1949, 14.
48. Mercer and Cole had actually performed together once before, on NBC's *King Cole Trio Time* program of December 7, 1946; although the Trio would have certainly accompanied at least one number by Mercer, it's not known whether Mercer and Cole actually sang together on that show. Ten days after the Capitol date, on August 30, 1947, Mercer and Cole performed "Save the Bones for Henry Jones" live on the *Wildroot* show. They would do so again, ten years after that, on October 29, 1957, this time on the Cole TV show, also on NBC.
49. Minstrelsy was hardly part of the long-dead past in 1947. As late as World War II, Hollywood musicals still occasionally featured production numbers with white artists in blackface. The 1920 "Henry Jones" was recorded by J. Russell Robinson, a pianist, singer, and songwriter (best known as pianist with the Original Dixieland Jazz Band) who also wrote "Meet Me at No Special Place (And I'll Be There at No Particular Time)," which was a #3 hit on the Race chart by the King Cole Trio in 1947.
50. Bishop's other topical and funny songs were written for Louis Jordan ("Jack, You're Dead") and the team of Count Basie and Billie Holiday ("Swing, Brother, Swing") as well. Sinatra's most notable bebop number, "Bop! Goes My Heart." Bishop's son was the excellent modern jazz pianist, Walter Bishop Jr.
51. Alan Livingston, interview with the author, 1991.
52. Billy May, interview with the author, 1991.
53. Bing Crosby talks about the minstrel show number, "Keemo Kimo" in the first pages of his 1953 memoir, *Call Me Lucky* (New York: Simon and Schuster, 1953).

54. Richard C. Norton, *A Chronology of the American Musical Theater*, Vol. 2 (New York: Oxford University Press, 2002), 195.
55. Discography of Historical American Recording (online). "The Three Trees" was revived for the electrical age in 1928 by Frank Crumit, also for Victor, and later there were dance band arrangements, by Londoner Lew Stone (1933) and Horace Heidt and his Musical Knights (1940).
56. One other orchestral track from this session, an adaptation of the classic "Lullaby (Wiegenlied: Guten Abend, Gute Nacht)" by Johannes Brahms, went missing for decades. He sings it straightforwardly, but there are no Trio elements or piano. "Lullaby (Wiegenlied)" wasn't released until 1990 (on the CD, *Cole, Christmas and Kids*). It's the only 1943–1947 Capitol song by Cole to be deliberately left out of the 1991 Mosaic package. Not an inappropriate fate; this is more of a failed experiment than a lost treasure.
57. *Billboard*, August 14, 1948, 35.
58. *Down Beat,* November 5, 1947, 2, quoted in KT, 198.
59. *Down Beat,* October 8, 1947, 2, quoted in KT, 195. This concert was much more extensively covered by *Down Beat*, since that magazine's editorial offices were located in Chicago.
60. Maria, 45.
61. Lem Graves Jr., "5,400 Jam Arena to Hear King Cole Trio," *Norfolk Journal and Guide*, July 27, 1946. Two and a half bucks seemed like a lot of money for a concert ticket in 1946, but earlier in the same evening, Cole had already given another performance, this one completely for free, for African American servicemen at the Smith Street USO Center.
62. *The Norfolk Journal and Guide* story even includes a picture of Polk with Cole and Miller, but not the drummer.
63. *Down Beat*, August 26, 1946, KT, 148.
64. *Variety*, October 8, 1947, quoted in KT, 197.
65. "King Cole Plays Date as a Duet," *New York Amsterdam News*, October 25, 1947. The performance was also covered in *Variety*, October 8, 1947, quoted in KT, 197.
66. Maria, 55. Note that Mrs. Cole gets at least one key detail wrong; as she remembered it, Nat was playing solo for the entire evening, but according to both *Variety* and the *Amsterdam News*, Miller was present for at least part of the concert.
67. DME, 156.
68. Max Jones and Mike Nevard, "Why I Made the Trio a Quartet—by Nat King Cole," *Melody Maker*, September 23, 1950. Many of the biographical and career details regarding Irving Ashby, Joe Comfort, and Jack Costanzo also come from this source.
69. "Nat 'King' Cole and Hal Singer at Auditorium Tonight," *Atlanta Daily World*, June 12, 1949.
70. *Down Beat,* November 5, 1947, 2, quoted in KT, 198.
71. Leonard Feather, "The Blindfold Test—'My Heart Is Still with Jazz'—Nat," *Down Beat*, July 3, 1952, 12.
72. Steve Race, "Interview with Nat King Cole," *Musical Express*, September 19, 1950, 3.

73. The rest of the bill included "[singer] Connie Haines, Bob Evans, Bobby Lane & Claire, and Randy Brooks and His Orchestra." "King Cole 3 Close Top Paramount Run," *Pittsburgh Courier*, December 6, 1947, 16.
74. *New York Amsterdam News*, December 27, 1947, 17.
75. In 1947, Paramount Pictures announced that the King Cole Trio would appear in a forthcoming film to be titled *Catalina Island*, but the movie doesn't seem to have actually been produced. ("King Cole Headlines Million Dollar Show," *Pittsburgh Courier*, July 26, 1947, 17)
76. Production details re *Killer Diller* courtesy of Mark Cantor. The approximate date of shooting (about December 20, 1947) is from "King Cole 3 Close Top Paramount Run, *Pittsburgh Courier*, December 6, 1947, 16.
77. "King Cole's Mother Week-Ends in City," *Cleveland Call and Post*, October 18, 1947, 16-B.

CHAPTER 5

Epigraph: There are several sources for this quote (one is *Time* magazine, July 30, 1951), and also several variations on it.

1. The songwriter and philosopher, who was also known as "George Alexander Aberle" and "George McGrew," preferred to give his name in lower case letters, which is how we shall refer to him here. The name is also given in conventional uppercase letters and is sometimes spelled "Ahbe," without the "Z."
2. Carole Cole, telephone conversation with the author, 2005.
3. Unknown author and unknown (British) publication, included in RGH Scrapbook, 135.
4. To name just two papers in which this ad appeared: the *Chicago Daily Tribune*, May 14, 1948, and the *Buffalo Courier-Express*, May 23, 1948.
5. Most of our information on eden ahbez comes from a May 19, 1948 *Down Beat* profile, "'Boy' Author Ahbez [*sic*] Bearded Vegetarian" (no byline), supplemented by much additional data from an excellent website devoted entirely to Ahbez, his life and his music, titled "Eden's Island," and located at https://bcxists.wordpress.com (retrieved May 3, 2018).
8. The 1946 film *The Razor's Edge* introduced the song "Mam'selle," which Cole performed on the *King Cole Trio Time* radio show of April 26, 1947.
9. Another movement of the suite, "Nature's Symphony," was later recorded by veteran crooner Tony Martin for RCA but never released. Martin kept a copy of the unreleased single, which he later bequeathed to singer-scholar Michael Feinstein.
10. Frank De Vol, phone interview with the author, circa 1990.
11. Frank De Vol, phone interview with the author, circa 1990.
12. 1946 Goldenheart Press edition of "Nature Boy" courtesy Brian Chidester.
13. Information on the 1946 publication from Brian Chidester, "Eden's Island" website in note 5 above.

14. Maria, 29.
15. Dolores Calvin, "Nature Boy Brings Legal Misery to Its Exotic Composer"; this story was carried in several papers, including the *Pittsburgh Courier*, May 29, 1948, also *Afro-American*, May 29, 1948.
16. Mort Ruby told the story many times, but this version is from the Kat Wisker (KW) radio biography of Cole. As if to illustrate that no one story re "Nature Boy" is completely accurate, the Paramount Theater gig of which he speaks was five months earlier, and they had spent the entire year thus on the road in the east, but not in New York.
17. "Cole's 'Boy' Starts 'Mad Discery' Whirl," *Down Beat*, May 5, 1948. Pollard said that he approached several publishers, including Lou Levy of Leeds Music, and Nicky Campbell, and asked for $1,000 for the song, and also Eddy Howard, but was turned down by all of them.
18. Maria, 30.
19. E. B. Rea, "Echoes and Encores," *Afro-American*, March 22, 1947, 6. In addition to the guarantee of $3,000 per week, they were also to receive "one third of the take over $5,000."
20. Cole and Gastel had actually set up a firm called "King Music" a year earlier. "Two Leaders to Publish," *Down Beat*, October 7, 1946. The second of the "two leaders" was Stan Kenton, who also set up a publishing firm in partnership with Gastel at the same time, this one titled Leslie Music. Both firms had "Capitol's Mickey Goldsen in the production and selling-agent slot."
21. Leonard Feather, liner notes to *The Nat King Cole Story* (1961). According to Maria and other accounts, Cole recorded a straight trio version (no strings) of the song—if that indeed happened, no trace of that unissued master has ever surfaced. Discographer Michael Ruppli has also suggested that the orchestral parts on "Nature Boy" were recorded separately and then overdubbed, but this seems even less likely.
22. Frank DeVol, interview with author, circa 1990.
23. Don C. Haynes, *Down Beat*, October 8, 1947, quoted in KT, 194.
24. "King Cole's 'Nature Boy' Became Hit Over Night [*sic*]," *Chicago Defender*, May 22, 1948. Note that Maria uses this phrase and other details, obviously taken from this story, almost word-for-word, "At the end of 1947, a rumor had spread throughout the industry to the effect that Nat Cole had made a recording that would be one of the greatest in history, but no one had heard it." Maria, 34–35.
25. "King Cole's 'Nature Boy' Became Hit Over Night [*sic*]," *Chicago Defender*, May 22, 1948.
26. Wiki and other sources, including DME, 168, give a release date of March 29, but information from the March 20 and 27 issues of *Billboard* indicates that the first week of April is a more likely date.
27. Both *Billboard* write-ups are from the issue of April 3, 1948.
28. "Cole's 'Boy' Starts 'Mad Discery' Whirl," *Down Beat*, May 5, 1948.

29. "'To Wax or Not to Wax?—Nature Boy' Scramble But Bing No Cut," *Billboard,* April 17, 1948.
30. "Everybody Wants In on 'Nature Boy' Act," *Down Beat,* June 2, 1948, 9.
31. "Cole's 'Boy' Starts 'Mad Discery' Whirl," *Down Beat,* May 5, 1948, 3.
32. *Billboard,* April 17, 1948, " 'Nature Boy' Scramble But Bing No Cut." Pollard even denied having been fired at all; he said that he left for personal reasons, going to work for Johnny and Oscar Moore and the Three Blazers. Cole replaced him with Sparky Taveres, who remained his valet until the end.
33. The Calvin News Service (CNS) ran this story in several papers, with slightly different headlines, including "King Cole's ex-Valet Denies Being Fired Over Nature Boy," *Afro-American* June 19, 1948, and "King Cole's Ex-Valet Says He Knew 'Nature Boy' When . . ." *Philadelphia Tribune,* June 19, 1948.
34. Dolores Calvin, "Nature Boy Brings Legal Misery to Its Exotic Composer"; this story was carried in several papers, including the *Pittsburgh Courier,* May 29, 1948, and the *Afro-American,* May 29, 1948.
35. Richard G. Hubler, "$12,000-a-Week Preacher's Boy," *Saturday Evening Post,* July 1954.
36. " 'Boy' Author Ahbez Bearded Vegetarian," *Down Beat,* May 19, 1948, 2.
37. "Everybody Wants In on 'Nature Boy' Act," *Down Beat,* June 2, 1948, 9.
38. *Washington Post,* September 5, 1948, 8S.
39. This was also the story that Cole and ahbez gave out to the media, as reported, among other sources, by Don Tranter, "Radio Comment," *Buffalo Courier,* June 1.
40. Another special thanks to ahbez's biographer, Brian Chidester, for unearthing this kinescope in an archive maintained by the City of Chicago.
41. http://www.musicvf.com/Nat+King+Cole.art (this is the best reference for chart hits etc. overall)—also https://en.wikipedia.org/wiki/List_of_Billboard_number-one_singles_of_1948—note that wiki says (on the nature boy page) it reached #11, but elsewhere on wiki it says that it was #1 for seven weeks. Wiki frequently contradicts itself.
42. "The Nat King Cole Nobody Knows," *Ebony,* October 1956.
43. Maria, 111–12; she details several such incidents at the Bismarck Hotel in Chicago and the Mayfair Hotel in Pittsburgh.
44. Maria, 112.
45. Haskins, 84.
46. *Nat King Cole: Afraid of the Dark* (Documentary, 2014) includes a handwritten receipt from Bradford, acknowledging having received $5,000 "from Nat Coles" as "part payment on down payment on prop(erty) at 400 Murfield Road. Bal(ance) 29,000 - 33:40.
47. DME, 179.
48. *Nat King Cole: Afraid of the Dark* (Documentary, 2014), appx, 33:00 and 36:00.
49. *Nat King Cole: Afraid of the Dark* (Documentary, 2014), 36:30.
50. Haskins, 85.

51. KT, 226.
52. DME, 183.
53. "Householders Object to Negro Neighbor," *The Irish Times*, July 4, 1948.
54. *Nat King Cole: Afraid of the Dark* (Documentary, 2014).
55. Interview with Bobby Short by Whitney Balliett, *New Yorker*, February 21, 1977; the younger singer-pianist had first met his hero in Omaha in 1943.
56. Haskins, 96. It's worth mentioning that even though Maria has nothing but positive things to say about Gastel in her 1971 memoir, she didn't even start writing until after his death in 1970, almost as if she wanted to wait until he wasn't around before she told her version of the story.
57. "Obituaries," *Variety*, November 18, 1970, 87.
58. Author's informal interviews and conversations with Mel Tormé, 1980s and 1990s. Other examples include Paul Whiteman's Rhythm Boys with Bing Crosby, but an example in reverse would be the career of Connie (later Connee) Boswell, who was never as strong as a solo act as the Boswell Sisters had been as a trio.
59. Bob Kreider, "'Swing Will Never Die!' Says Nat King Cole," *Musical Express*, April 23, 1948.
60. "King Cole to Play Xmas Eve at Renaissance," *New York Amsterdam News*, December 18, 1948, 22 (also a display ad on 24).
61. John F. Goodman and Sy Johnson, *Mingus Speaks* (Berkeley: University of California Press,, 2013).
62. There is some debate as to the year and place of Joe Comfort's birth. Some sources, including Klaus Teubig (KT, 15) place it as 1919 in Los Angeles; others, including the majority of his obituaries from 1988, place it as 1917 in Alcorn, Mississippi. If Comfort wasn't actually born in Los Angeles, his family moved there when he was very young.
63. Cole sings the praises of both Noble himself and his band vocalist, Al Bowlly, in a 1954 broadcast produced by Dave Dexter for Radio Luxembourg, *The Capitol Show*, Nat Cole, guest; Show #94 (in the Dave Dexter collection at University of Missouri, Kansas City). Also, Cole titled two of his greatest albums after songs by Ray Noble, *The Very Thought of You* (1958) and *The Touch of Your Lips* (1961).
64. "Nat 'King' Cole and Hal Singer at Auditorium Tonight," *Atlanta Daily World*, June 12, 1949.
65. KT, 15.
66. "Cole Trio, Child Singer, in Picture," *Los Angeles Sentinel*, October 7, 1948. On September 30 and October 28, the Trio also guest-starred on *The Chesterfield Supper Club*, with star and hostess Peggy Lee; I've not been able to hear either of these shows.
67. Information on Nat King Cole and Bill Evans from two biographies of Evans, Peter Pettinger, *How My Heart Sings* (New Haven, CT: Yale University Press, 1999), 15, 21; Keith Shadwick, Everything Happens to Me (San Francisco: Backbeat Books, 2002), 52.

68. Sid Kuller, one of the credited co-authors of "Bang Bang Boogie," was best known as a writer of special material for entertainers in clubs and TV variety shows; he worked with Duke Ellington on the breakthrough revue *Jump for Joy* in 1941 and with Peggy Lee on her signature lyrics to the hit "Fever" in 1958.
69. A favorite line: "I'm an old maid—and no one knows more about love than an old maid."
70. The credited co-writer of the song is one Gordon Burdge. His trail apparently goes no further than this movie.
71. Incidentally, Wiki states that the title theme became a hit for Cole, but it doesn't appear on any chart. The song, however, was used on the 1952 album *Unforgettable*, and has been heard on every permutation and reissue of that extremely popular LP.
72. *Billboard*, March 5, 1949, 38: "Gene Gilham, WBZ Boston, thinks highly of a tune called 'How Lonely Can You Get.' Reason: Gene wrote it (his first), and it's been published by Mills Music."
73. Barbara Hodgkins, "Backstage with Nat," *Metronome*, August 1948.
74. Again, much of the biographical info regarding the "new" trio (Ashby, Comfort, Costanzo) comes from Max Jones and Mike Nevard, "Why I Made the Trio a Quartet—by Nat King Cole," *Melody Maker*, September 23, 1950. This source also lists three film titles that Costanzo allegedly appeared in as a dancer: *Mary Lou, Champagne for Two,* and *Thrill in Brazil.*
75. *Variety*, June 16, 1948, quoted in *Stan Kenton: This Is an Orchestra* by Michael Sparke (Denton: University of North Texas Press, 2010), 76, reported that Gastel "tried to induce Kenton to tinkle terp arrangements [in other words, play for dancers] to hold a larger following. Biz on several concerts in southwest has been blowzy [bad]. The pair couldn't see eye-to-eye on the reason, so they parted."
76. *Nat King Cole: Afraid of the Dark* (Documentary, 2014).
77. "King Cole Adds Banjo Player to Trio," *California Eagle*, February 17, 1949.
78. "King Cole Adds Banjo Player to Trio," *California Eagle*, February 17, 1949.
79. Max Jones and Mike Nevard, "Why I Made the Trio a Quartet—by Nat King Cole," *Melody Maker*, September 23, 1950.
80. John S. Wilson, "Nat Nominates Himself Advance Man for Bop," *Down Beat*, April 22, 1949, 1.
81. *Metronome*, May 1949, in DME, 189.
82. Interview from *Nat King Cole: Afraid of the Dark* (Documentary, 2014), but Mogull never does quite explain exactly who he means by "they."
83. "King Cole Unhappy Soul over Dixie Bias; White Bonga [*sic*] Drummer Barred from Dates," *Pittsburgh Courier*, July 9, 1949. Some sources state that Costanzo was apparently allowed to play in Little Rock, and some claim that he was barred.
84. *Down Beat*, August 26, 1949, quoted in KT, 240.
85. "King Cole Unhappy Soul over Dixie Bias; White Bonga [*sic*] Drummer Barred From Dates," *Pittsburgh Courier*, July 9, 1949.
86. "Cole and Cornbread Stuffing Dixie Coffers," *Pittsburgh Courier*, July 2, 1949, 18.

87. "Cole 3 to Hawaii," *Pittsburgh Courier*, August 20, 1949, 19.
88. Haskins, 97.
89. Haskins, 97.
90. *Down Beat*, August 12, 1949, 2.
91. Don George, *Sweet Man: The Real Duke Ellington* (New York: G. P. Putnam's Sons, 1981), 84.
92. *Down Beat*, August 12, 1949, 2.
93. Leonard Feather, liner notes to *The Nat King Cole Story*, 1961.
94. George, *Sweet Man*, 84. Of the two conflicting accounts, Feather is certainly the more reliable witness. George quotes Cole as saying, of Strayhorn, "Isn't he the little guy who works with our friend Duke?"—never mind that nobody in the world talks like that. George's strength was writing lyrics, not dialogue—or history. (We also know that Strayhorn attended Nat and Maria's wedding, as did Feather.)
95. *Down Beat*, August 12, 1949, 2.
96. Interview with Billy Strayhorn, March 1962 meeting at the Duke Ellington Jazz Society, New York, courtesy David Hajdu.
97. Interview with Billy Strayhorn, March 1962 meeting at the Duke Ellington Jazz Society, New York, courtesy David Hajdu.
98. *Down Beat*, August 12, 1949, 2.
99. Interview with Billy Strayhorn, March 1962 meeting at the Duke Ellington Jazz Society, New York, courtesy David Hajdu.
100. *Down Beat*, August 12, 1949, 2.
101. Pete Rugolo, multiple interviews with the author, circa 1991–1992. All quotes from Rugolo are from these interviews. In actuality, Cole shared a bill with Kenton in a long run at the New York Paramount in fall 1946, but they didn't extensively tour together until later, in the "Big Show" Tour of 1952–53.
102. David Hajdu, *Lush Life: A Biography of Billy Strayhorn* (New York: Macmillan, 1997), 110–11.
103. Although, according to the 1955 Universal featurette *The Nat King Cole Musical Story in Technicolor*, the Strayhorn song actually sold 50,000 copies. This isn't necessarily a reliable source or an accurate number, but it is at least an indication of the esteem in which Cole held the song, and that he considered it one of his signature achievements.
104. Don Freeman, "Critics to Blame for Confusion," *Down Beat*, October 5, 1951.
105. The interview ran in *The Capitol*, the label's house organ publication, April 1946, 7.
106. Flournoy Miller's *Sugar Hill*, which, like *Shuffle Along*, was a book musical rather than a revue, had originally played Broadway for one week at the end of 1931. Miller tried to bring *Sugar Hill* back to Broadway in a revived production in 1949, but although it played for three months in Los Angeles at the Las Palmas Theatre, it never made it to New York. Johnson wrote the score to both versions but composed new songs, including "You Can't Lose a Broken Heart" (also recorded as a duet by Billie Holiday and Louis Armstrong) with lyrics by Miller. This was Cole's

last connection to Flournoy Miller. *Variety*, December 29, 1931, and *Los Angeles Sentinel*, June 30, 1949.

107. "All I Want For Christmas (Is My Two Front Teeth)," "You Can't Lose a Broken Heart," and "Bang Bang Boogie" were all recorded at the session of August 2, 1949, for which the Trio was accompanied not by the Alyce King Vokettes but by another white vocal group named "The Starlighters," which included Pauline Byrns, Vince Degan, and Howard Hudson, who had recorded with Cole for Standard Transcriptions ten years earlier, then billed as "Pauline and Her Perils."
108. "The King and His Men Take Off," *Pittsburgh Courier*, September 3, 1949, 18 (also DME, 203). The song, "(Here Is My Heart) Nalani," is credited to Gerda M. Beilenson and Alvin Kaleolani Isaacs.
109. This movie number was inspired by another rowdy racetrack comedy song performed by a group of character actors, "The Horse with the Dreamy Eyes" from the 1937 *Saratoga*. *Riding High* itself is a Frank Capra–directed remake of his own 1934 film, *Broadway Bill*, and in the 1950 movie Crosby sings "The Horse" with Garry Owen, Candy Candido, and Merwyn "Ish Kabibble" Bogue, from Kay Kyser's band.
110. "I feel so smoochie, Nat, but where were you tonight? You promised to be home right after the last show at Bop City — How dare you come boppin' in at this hour of the morning! Listen nature boy if you don't straighten up and fly right and stop leading this lush life, we'll have to save the bones for Henry Jones, and brother that's the beginning of the end, that's what!" The voice returns at the coda to henpeck the poor husband even further, "You think you have a way with women, but don't blame me if I get on Route 66 and head for California. And by the way, can you look me in the eyes and tell me about this Lillian? *Harumph!* Now he tells me."
111. Bob Pondillo, "Saving Nat King Cole," *Television Quarterly* (Journal of the National Academy of Television Arts and Sciences), Spring–Summer 2005.
112. Information courtesy of Mark Cantor.
113. Cole would record "All Aboard" for Capitol Transcriptions with the four-man Trio in March, and he would recycle the melody in 1957 as the Rheingold jingle in his NBC TV series.
114. "Roses and Wine" was credited to Elise Bretton, Don Meyer, and Sherman Edwards. Edwards went on to a rather unique songwriting career that including several pop hits ("Broken Hearted Melody," "See You in September"), one jazz standard ("For Heaven's Sake"), and one all-time classic Broadway musical (*1776*).
115. Cole also performed "Jet" on an early TV variety show, *Showtime USA,* March 4, 1951, hosted by the veteran Broadway producer Vinton Freedley.
116. KW.
117. The Carnegie show was later issued by Hep Records, but the Shrine concert tracks still have been circulated only privately among collectors.
118. KW.

119. There also were parody versions of mule train by Mickey Katz and Spike Jones, but the funniest recording of "Mule Train" may be the apparently unintentionally hysterical performance by Nelson Eddy.
120. KW.
121. Toki Schalk Johnson, "Talking It Over with Mrs. King Cole," *Pittsburgh Courier*, July 16, 1949, 8.
122. Maria, 32.
123. Not to be confused with "Every Day I Have the Blues," although Joe Williams recorded both songs with Count Basie.
124. Johnson, "Talking It Over with Mrs. King Cole," 8.
125. ". . . And Baby Makes Three . . . Nat (King) Coles Will Adopt Niece," *Pittsburgh Courier*, June 18, 1949, 1.
126. DME, 186.
127. KW.
128. Cole and Rugolo had already recorded in May 1950 what was then known as a "race pride" song, the somewhat bombastic and sanctimonious "My Brother," which has lines like "My brother doesn't ask what church you may prefer." It's not nearly as effective as Sinatra's "The House I Live in" or Cole's own later "We Are Americans Too."
129. Nat Shapiro and Bruce Pollock, *Popular Music 1920–1979: A Revised Cumulation*, 3 vols. (Detroit: Gale, 1985), Vol. 1, 582. Four writers are credited altogether, Marcia Neil, Philip F. Broughton, Bob Merrill, and Hughie Prince, although it should be noted that Merrill's name does not appear in any connection to the song until well after Cole's death. (However, there are examples of songs in which the actual authors weren't credited to begin with because of publishing contractual reasons.)
130. *The Unreleased Nat King Cole* (Capitol Records EMS 1279, UK, 1987), sold only as part of a 20-LP boxed set.
131. The title of "Ooh, Kickeroonie" was clearly inspired by Slim Gailliard; Cole wrote it with two former Glenn Miller-ites, Billy May and Hal Dickinson of the Modernaires. Cole recorded it for Capitol in an unissued master from 1947, then performed it that fall in the feature *Killer Diller*. He brought it back in the Costanzo era, in the Universal short *King Cole and His Trio*, filmed in January 1950, and then last on the March 1950 transcription session. Both of the 1950 versions include the foreshadowing of "Rough Ridin'."
132. John Bustin, "Nat King Cole and His Trio Here Tuesday," *Austin American*, July 3, 1949, 14.
133. The best general history of the Snader project is a 12-minute short documentary entitled *History of the Snader Telescriptions*, produced by GS Musical Moments, featuring Gene Norman and Duke Goldstone. All quotes from them come from here.
134. By comparison, a low budget, pre-filmed TV series, like *The Adventures of Superman*, cost $15,000 per episode in 1951.

135. Charles Emge, "Top Producer of Musical Shorts to Use Color," *Down Beat*, May 1951.
136. Ollie Stewart, "European Glamour Fails to Lure King Over—Conditions Too Shaky Abroad—Will Marry Marie Ellington in March," *Afro-American*, January 31, 1948, 36.
137. *Down Beat*, October 20, 1950, 15; Quoted in KT, 263. Derek Boulton, then *Down Beat*'s London correspondent, later became one of Tony Bennett's managers.

CHAPTER 6

Epigraph: Quoted in BBC documentary on Nat King Cole, 1988, part of Arena series.

1. *Federal Bureau of Investigation Freedom of Information/Privacy Acts Section. Subject: Nat King Cole*. Retrieved from Archive.org, February 18, 2020.
2. "How to Make and Lose Money," *Down Beat*, April 20, 1951. All details concerning this incident are from a combination of this source and DME, 217.
3. "Timmie Rogers Joins Nat King Cole on Apollo Bill" (Norfolk, VA) *New Journal and Guide*, March 15, 1952, 22.
4. "I Can't See for Lookin'" (1943) became an early Trio classic, not least because it was the flip side of "Straighten Up and Fly Right." Later Dok Stanford songs for Cole include "I'll Always Be Remembering" (1954) and "Too Much" (1958). He also served in Sinatra's songwriting stable, resulting in "You'll Get Yours," "Take a Chance," and "Johnny Concho's Theme (Wait for Me)."
5. And yes, it's true: wise-ass kids of that time and since couldn't help but go around singing it as "The Old Masturbator." Likewise, when "Too Young" became a hit in 1951, wise-ass kids went around singing, "They try to sell us egg foo young."
6. Jay Livingston, interview with the author, 1993.
7. Ray Evans, interview with the author, circa 2005.
8. Maria Cole remembered that Paramount Pictures originally intended to put Cole on-screen, singing the song in a cameo role; by the time they abandoned that idea, Cole had already been paid for this performance, even though they never actually recorded or filmed it. Needless to say, this account conflicts with everyone else's. Maria, 53.
9. Alan Livingston, interview with the author 1990.
10. KW.
11. Very young indeed—this was probably late February 1950, only a week or two after Maria and baby Natalie, born on February 6, came back from the hospital. One can hardly blame her for making a lot of noise, even though it seems improbable that she was "running around." More likely it was the older daughter, Cookie (then six), who was causing the disturbance.
12. http://livingstonandevans.com/mona-lisa/—retrieved October 18, 2017.

13. Author's conversation with Debbie Whiting, daughter of Lou Busch (and Margaret Whiting), October 2017. When Mosaic Records issued *The Complete Capitol Recordings of The Nat King Cole Trio* in 1991, as many as 25 percent of the tracks therein had not been previously issued.
14. Nelson Riddle interviewed by Robert Windeler of NPR, circa 1984–85. All quotes from Riddle are from this interview, unless otherwise noted.
15. Recording contract for March 11, 1950, excavated by Jordan Taylor. .
16. Also quoted in Robert Windeler's NPR profile of Nelson Riddle.
17. KW.
18. Gordon, 86.
19. This is from the Wikipedia entry on the song, https://en.wikipedia.org/wiki/Unforgettable_(Nat_King_Cole_song)—retrieved October 31, 2017, but it doesn't seem to be backed up by any other source, including the composer's wife or son.
20. William Gordon, email to author, September 9, 2018.
21. Claire Phillips Gordon (83) distinctly remembered Cole playing piano on "Unforgettable"; however, AFM records indicate Buddy Cole as the keyboardist on the date. However, it's at least possible that Buddy is playing celesta and Nat is playing piano, at least on the intro, since both keyboards are heard at once. The most likely scenario is that Buddy is playing both, with different hands, simultaneously.
22. Nelson Riddle was never one to repeat himself, but he employs a variation on that idea with similarly voiced block chords on the 1954, "It Happens to Be Me." For his part, Gordon tried to make that same magic recur with a song called "Unbelievable," also in 1954. There was also "How (Do I Go about It)?" from 1952, but that never gained any traction either.
23. The best source of basic information on Lee Gillette (1912–1981) is Rich Kienzle's *Southwest Shuffle: Pioneers of Honky-Tonky, Western Swing, and Country Jazz* (New York: Routledge, 2003). Additional details are from Gillette's obituary in *Billboard*, by Dave Dexter Jr., September 5, 1981.
24. The song, written by Williams and fellow Capitol country and western pioneer Merle Travis, is one of the first to protest the dangers of nicotine addiction, albeit more social than healthwise, and in an exaggerated, comic fashion. (Of course, one wishes that Cole himself had not necessarily sung the song but had taken note of its message.)
25. The legendary jazz tenor saxophonist Sonny Rollins, who doubtlessly learned the song from Cole, recorded a contrafact variation titled "Here's to the People," in 1991.
26. Lee Young, phone conservation with the author, circa 1990.
27. KW.
28. *Star of the Family* was unearthed and preserved by Jane Klain of the Paley Center, and may be viewed there.

29. Considering that Freedley famously produced the original *Girl Crazy*, one wishes that Cole had taken the opportunity to also play either "Embraceable You" or his perennial favorite, "I Got Rhythm."
30. "King Cole Breaks Up His Trio—'Nat' Will Now Specialize as Lone Vocalist," *New York Amsterdam News*, September 1, 1951, 21.
31. John Collins, phone interview with the author, circa 1990. Collins, Harris, and Costanzo played with Cole on one "pure trio" session on January 2, 1952, when they cut six songs—all of which were well known King Cole hits—in a special recording issued as a special radio transcription to raise funds and awareness for the Sister Kenny Fund. The six cuts were issued as bonus tracks on the 1998 CD of Cole's piano album *Penthouse Serenade* in 1998.
32. John S. Wilson, "Nat Nominates Himself Advance Man for Bop," *Down Beat*, April 22, 1949, 1.
33. Don Freeman, "Critics to Blame for Confusion," *Down Beat*, October 5, 1951.
34. Don Freeman, "The Real Reason Nat Cole Cut His Piano-Only Album," *Down Beat*, January 28, 1953, 3.
35. KW.
36. Serene Dominic, *Burt Bacharach: Song by Song* (New York: Schirmer Trade Books, 2003). Making this track even more confusing, the 1923 Kern song also seems to be based on "Melody in F." In the end, it's hard to tell which parts of the track were written by Kern, Rubinstein, Bacharach, or Cole himself.
37. Don Freeman, "The Real Reason Nat Cole Cut His Piano-Only Album," *Down Beat*, January 28, 1953, 3.
38. Interview with Billy Strayhorn, March 1962 meeting at the Duke Ellington Jazz Society, New York, courtesy David Hajdu.
39. "Love You Madly" was recorded live at the University of Michigan, Ann Arbor, November 15, 1951. Available, among other places, on Vintage Jazz Classics CD VJC-1015-2.
40. Leonard Feather, "King Cole Trio Isn't Dead, Beams Feather," *Down Beat*, February 22, 1952.
41. https://www.imdb.com/title/tt0347610/plotsummary?ref_=tt_ov_pl, retrieved July 15, 2018.
42. Cole had recorded Russ Morgan's most famous song, "You're Nobody 'Til Somebody Loves You," in 1945.
43. Cole sang two other songs as part of *Small Town Girl*; he recorded "I Just Love You" for possible inclusion, but it wasn't used or even filmed. He also recorded "Small Towns Are Smile Towns" for Capitol, but that was sung in the movie by leading lady Jane Powell.
44. Source: email from Anthony Barnett, January 9, 2020.
45. However, the covers of Sinatra's saloon song albums such as *No One Cares* show that he was at least allowed to participate in the losing, if not the loving.

46. "Answer Me" was a hit in Great Britain for both the young British tenor David Whitfield and Cole's friend Frankie Laine; uniquely, both versions hit #1 on the UK chart in October 1953.
47. KW.
48. KW.
49. I've heard this from at least two people, Michael Feinstein and Andrew Lederer, who reported that Raksin, in casual conversation (never formally on the record), stated that he had written the melody that later became "Smile."
50. To get a tad more technically specific, the form of "Smile" is, more accurately, ABAB' and 30 bars rather than 32, in that the final B section is only six bars rather than eight.
51. Billy May, interview with the author, circa 1995.
52. On December 31, 1954, United Press International released a news photo of May and his new wife, with the following caption. "Los Angeles: Minutes after the court handed her the final divorce papers from her husband, Carlos, Mrs. Joan Gastel and her husband-to-be, Billy May, applied for a marriage license here (12/30). While this was going on, Carlos Gastel was in Los Angeles, celebrating his marriage to the ex-Mrs. Billy May." United Press Telephone.
53. Ironically, the hit version of "Teach Me Tonight" was by a now largely forgotten vocal group, the DeCastro Sisters, although few would associate the song with them today.
54. DME, 236.
55. "Nat Cole Hits 10-Year Mark," *Billboard*, December 26, 1953, 1.
56. Maria, 50–51.
57. From Nelson Riddle's personnel ledgers, as examined by Jordan Taylor.
58. By an apparent coincidence, "What to Do" was composed by Mark McIntyre, a former pianist for Sinatra who would become famous two years later as the force behind Patience and Prudence, the "tween" sister duo, his own daughters, who would land a huge hit with "Tonight You Belong to Me."
59. Crosby himself crossed a credible cadenza with Cole in 1951, when the artist guested on his radio show and took the place of Gary Crosby on the iconic father-son duet, "Sam's Song." Crosby, rather respectfully, addresses his guest as "King.")
60. Tommy Valando, phone conversation with the author, circa early 1990s.
61. According to the original AFM recording session contracts, as researched by Jordan Taylor.
62. "There Goes My Heart" was taken up by many R&B artists, like Julia Lee, Louis Jordan, and Dinah Washington, while "Little Street" was later sung by Tony Bennett.
63. *Radio Luxembourg: The Capitol Show*, Nat Cole, Guest, Show #94, Capitol Radio Broadcast 33 1/3 1 040-113341429. Produced by Dave Dexter and contained in the Dexter collection at the University of Missouri, Kansas City.

64. In 1987, Capitol issued a CD titled *Nat King Cole Sings for Two in Love (And More)*, which included all twelve tracks from the 1955 12" LP plus three completely unnecessary songs from the 1959 Cole-Riddle album *To Whom It May Concern*. Not only that, for some reason they used the cover photo from the 1962 album *Dear Lonely Hearts*.
65. *"'Biggest' Opens Big in Far West," Billboard*, February 14,1953, 47
66. "Nat Cole Is Hospitalized Just as Tour Takes Off," *Down Beat,* May 6, 1953.
67. Dick Nash, interview with the author, circa 1991

CHAPTER 7

Epigraph: Quoted in the *Chicago Daily Defender*, April 12, 1958.

1. Author's interview with Christopher Riddle, circa 1992.
2. In the years 1955 and '56, Como had thirteen chart hits, Sinatra twelve, and Cole eighteen. Source: *MusicVF.com* (retrieved February 10, 2019), which tracks both US and UK hit singles.
3. May Okon, "The Man Said 'Sing!" So Nat King Cole Sang Himself into the Big Time," *New York Sunday News*, April 4, 1954, 13.
4. Richard G. Hubler, "$12,000-a-Week Preacher's Boy," *Saturday Evening Post*, July 17, 1954, 30.
5. *Pop Chronicles*, 1969, hosted by John Gilliland. Available from the University of North Texas: https://digital.library.unt.edu/explore/collections/JGPC/.
6. *Kiss Me Deadly* begins with Cole singing "I'd Rather Have the Blues" (subtitled "The Blues from *Kiss Me Deadly*") over a car radio behind the main titles, but I'm including it here even though the song isn't titled "Kiss Me Deadly."
7. Cole is listed in most reference works as having sung the title theme of this 1964 feature, but I haven't been able to actually confirm this, or even be totally certain that the film was even released.
8. In *China Gate* and *Cat Ballou*, Cole technically doesn't sing over the actual main titles, but he does sing the theme song on-screen in the first scenes of these films.
9. Author interview with Monty Alexander, January 5, 2018. This Kingston appearance seems to have been one day only, March 29, 1955, probably with three shows beginning at about 3 p.m. (Additional details from *Kingston Gleaner*, March 30, 1955, 4,16.)
10. Alexander also distinctly remembers seeing Harry "Sweets" Edison on this show. This is possible, since Edison is known to have done some live dates in the Los Angeles area with Cole. However, it's unlikely that he traveled to Jamaica with Cole's group, since he's known to have been on several recording dates with Sinatra and others during this period. Edison later worked many times with Alexander in the 1980s and '90s, not least on Nat King Cole songbook shows.
11. Interview with Nat King Cole and family by Edward R. Murrow, *Person to Person*, CBS TV, November 1, 1957.

12. Don Freeman, "Nat Cole Cuts Piano Set: 'It's One I'm Happy About,'" *Down Beat*, November 2, 1955.
13. Gratitude is herewith expressed to the late pianist, composer, and educator Dick Katz for his help with these observations regarding *The Piano Style of Nat King Cole*. On one memorable afternoon circa 1992, I visited him at his apartment, and the two of us went through the album virtually bar-by-bar; he agreed with my overall contention that *Piano Style* is an overlooked Nat Cole masterpiece.
14. Don Freeman, "Nat Cole Cuts Piano Set: 'It's One I'm Happy About,'" *Down Beat*, November 2, 1955.
15. Interview on *The Howard Miller Show*, WBBM CBS Chicago, September 2, 1955.
16. *The Piano Style of Nat King Cole* came and went quickly both in the United States (as an LP and an EP set) and England (in both 10" and 12" LP editions); after Cole's death, Pickwick Records released half of the tracks on an eight-track budget LP entitled *The Piano Soul of Nat King Cole*, but the altered title didn't help sales.
17. This new take had been discovered by the British Cole collector and discographer Roy "Sherlock" Holmes, who found it on a US government transcription, and it was transferred by the world's most prominent sound restoration engineer, the now-late John R. T. Davies, at the request of reissue producer Michael Cuscuna.
18. http://www.nytimes.com/2001/02/09/us/bernard-asbell-77-professor-prolific-writer-and-folk-singer.html, retrieved November 6, 2017.
19. In 1964, *Billboard* published a tantalizing report that "a film [of Cole] taken at the Capitol studios will be shown in Italy," but no such film has ever surfaced. *Billboard*, November 21, 1964, 8.
20. From a review of his 1954 performance at the London Palladium, *The Performer*, March 25, 1954, quoted in DME, 242.
21. Bernard Asbell, "King Cole Cuts a Biscuit: Three Dozen Men Grind Out a Session of Song," *Playboy*, November 1956.
22. Doris Day's husband and manager, the infamous Marty Melcher, was forever trying to bring down costs of her sessions for this very reason. He even suggested that Columbia Records accompany Doris with an electric organ rather than an orchestra full of union musicians.
23. This information is from audio engineer Steve Hoffman, who has worked on many Cole reissues; he has been through copious session tapes and documentation, and has been able to reconstruct how they apparently worked together.
24. Information from scholar and producer Steve Hoffman, who has had the opportunity to listen to a lot of Cole's sessions from the actual master tapes. "Nat (I've discovered) was in the habit of looking through the window at Lee Gillette during recording to see if Lee was happy or not. Lee was careful not to have anyone else visible to Nat while the red light was on. Nat . . . totally relied on Lee Gillette and wouldn't have stopped a song on his own unless he really messed up. He trusted his producer and conductor."
25. John Fink, "Bowers Paces New 'Contact' Show on Vid," *Chicago Tribune*, July 10, 1955, N12.

26. Cole would sing "But Not for Me" many times from 1955 to 1959, beginning with his run at the Sands in Las Vegas in February 1955 (*Billboard*, March 5, 1955, 12) and also his NBC TV show, on the episode of February 4, 1957. This arrangement, which starts with the verse to the *Girl Crazy* song ("Old man sunshine, listen you . . ."), is probably similar to the lost Chicago master of 1955. Also, it's also believed that the late scholar, discographer, and archivist Roy G. Holmes apparently had at least a tape copy of the session in his possession. (As of this writing, September 2018, it's not known what will happen to Holmes's collection.)
27. George E. Pitts, "Rock 'n' Roll Department," *Pittsburgh Courier*, October 13, 1956, "Editor's Note." This column was written by Nat King Cole to his friend, Don Brown, the *Courier*'s West Coast theatrical writer.
28. Freddy Cole, informal conversation with the author, circa 2005.
29. Cole sang and played dozens of songs by McHugh over the decades, starting with "On the Sunny Side of the Street," which he recorded several times with the Trio. As we've seen, McHugh and Adams could have easily sued the composers of Cole's 1946 hit, "For Sentimental Reasons," since the bridge is virtually identical to their 1943 song for Sinatra, "A Lovely Way to Spend an Evening."
30. Information on *Strip for Action* from Alyn Shipton, *I Feel a Song Coming On: The Life of Jimmy McHugh* (Urbana: University of Illinois Press, 2009), 206–7.
31. Walter Winchell, *Daily Mirror*, April 25, 1956.
32. Both "I Promise You" and "The Way I Love You" also feature Juan Tizol on valve trombone.
33. The first song by either Sherman brother that Cole recorded was "Sweet William" in 1952, music by Joe Sherman and words by Sid Wayne, written while Noel was in the service.
34. Joe Sherman, phone interview with the author, 2005.
35. Author interview with Bill Miller, circa 1990.
36. George E. Pitts, "Rock 'n' Roll Department," *Pittsburgh Courier*, October 13, 1956, "Editor's Note." This column was written by Nat King Cole to his friend, Don Brown, the *Courier*'s West Coast theatrical writer.
37. Cole also recorded a lovely ballad for *Istanbul*, "I Waited So Long," that survives in two takes, but neither was used in the final film.
38. This may or may not be the same dancer named Patty Thomas who toured with Bob Hope during World War II.
39. "King Cole's Own Story—Tells How 6 Attacked Him in Dixie," by Nat King Cole, as told to Edward Newman, *New York Journal-American*, April 12, 1956.
40. Dana Rubin, "The Real Education of Little Tree: How the Author of a Current Best-Seller Conned the World into Believing He Was a Gentle Texas Novelist instead of a Vicious Alabama Klansman," *Texas Monthly*, February 1992. All facts regarding the life and career of Asa Earl Carter, also called "Ace Carter" and "Forrest Carter," are from this article.

41. "Continue Trials of Alabamans Who Attacked Nat Cole," Associated Negro Press, April 16, 1956. Kenneth Adams, thirty-five, of Anniston, and Willie (sometimes given as "Willis") R. Adams, twenty-three, also of Anniston, were both eventually charged with "assault with intent to murder."
42. "King Cole's Own Story—Tells How 6 Attacked Him in Dixie," by Nat King Cole, as told to Edward Newman, *New York Journal-American*, April 12, 1956.
43. KW, 6–1.
44. "Continue Trials of Alabamans Who Attacked Nat Cole," Associated Negro Press, April 16, 1956.
45. "The South—Unscheduled Appearance," *Time*, April 23, 1956.
46. DME, 256. In 1997, Maria Cole told Epstein that Sinatra was not only the one who first informed her of the attack but also arranged for the plane to transport Cole and his rhythm section from Birmingham to Chicago. Assuming this is true, it's kind of surprising she doesn't mention any of it in her own book, or mention Sinatra's name at all in connection with the incident.
47. KW, 6–1.
48. "Nat Cole Says He Saw 'Death,' "*Pittsburgh Courier*, April 14, 1956, 1.
49. Interview with Louis Armstrong by Willis Conover, Voice of America network, July 13, 1956. Also quoted in Ricky Riccardi, *What a Wonderful World: The Magic of Louis Armstrong's Later Years* (New York: Pantheon Books, 2011), 141.
50. "Nat Cole Ignores Critics, Continues Tour of South after Attack," Associated Negro Press, April 18, 1956.
51. "King Cole to Sing Again on Interrupted Dixie Tour," Associated Negro Press, circa April 15, 1956.
52. "White Disc Jockey Deplores Cole Attack, Loses Job," Associated Negro Press, April 16, 1956.
53. "White Disc Jockey Deplores Cole Attack, Loses Job," Associated Negro Press, April 16, 1956.
54. "Cole Tour Big Success," *Pittsburgh Courier*, April 21, 1956, A31.
55. "Arena Recap," *The Billboard*, May 12, 1958.
56. *The Papers of Martin Luther King, Jr.*, Volume III: *Birth of a New Age (December 1955–December 1956)*, Clayborne Carson, Senior Editor (Berkeley: University of California Press, 1997), 317.
57. Barry Singer, *Black and Blue: The Life and Lyrics of Andy Razaf* (New York: Schirmer Books, 1992), 307–9. All quotes from Blake are from this source.
58. Dolores Calvin, *Harlem to Broadway* (column), *Chicago Defender*, (Daily Edition, *Daily Defender*), August 29, 1956, 16.
59. "Inside Stuff—Music," *Variety*, August 29, 1956, 48.
60. "King Cole, Andy Razaf to Be Heard on Progress Show," *Los Angeles Sentinel*, June 7, 1956.
61. "We Are Americans Too" was first issued in the German-produced boxed set, *Stardust: The Complete Capitol Recordings 1955–1959*, Bear Family Records.

62. Lawrence Laurent, "Presidential Encounter Can Awe Even a 'King,'" *Washington Post and Times Herald*, May 26, 1956, 24.
63. *Norfolk VA Journal and Guide*, May 26, 1956, 1.
64. Tony Bennett, interviews with the author circa 1998.
65. KW, 6–1.
66. There are several sources that place Cole at the 1956 Republican Convention, including "GOP Convention to Be 'Brisk, Clear, Interesting,'" *Los Angeles Times*, August 17, 1956, 17.
67. Cole, interview with Willis Conover, for the Voice of America, Washington DC, May 1, 1956. The primary purpose of the VOA was to celebrate democracy and the American way of life for listeners mostly behind the Iron Curtain; obviously they weren't going to even mention an incident such as the Birmingham assault.
68. *Down Beat*, May 2, 1957, John Tynan, profile of Nat King Cole, "First Part of a Story about a Pianist Who Turned Singer to Find a Kingdom."
69. Interview with Stuff Smith by Anthony Barnett, 1965. Shared with the author via email.
70. The song that Smith mentions, "Miracles," was his setting of a poem by Suzanne Hester, the ten-year-old daughter of two friends of the violinist.
71. Robert W. Dana, "Tips on Tables: Nat Cole Cheers Souls at Copa," *New York Herald and Sun*, January 10, 1958.
72. *The Nat King Cole Show*, NBC TV, February 18, 1957.
73. Various details re *The Nat King Cole Show* on NBC from DME, starting on page 269. Although he gets a few facts wrong, including the name of pianist Frankie Carle, this is overall the best source of information on the series. Additional information from Bob Pondillo, "Saving Nat King Cole," *Television Quarterly* (Journal of the National Academy of Television Arts and Sciences), Spring-Summer 2005.
74. "TV Roundup," *Philadelphia Inquirer*, October 5, 1956.
75. "Nat King Cole Gets TV Spot!" *Pittsburgh Courier*, October 13, 1956, 3.
76. Maria, 18.
77. Cole and Jenkins would later perform at least one number from *Manhattan Tower* together, "Repeat after Me" (which is from the expanded 1956 version of the work), on the December 10, 1956, telecast of *The Nat King Cole Show* on NBC.
78. George E. Pitts, "Rock 'n' Roll Department," *Pittsburgh Courier*, October 13, 1956, "Editor's Note: This column was written by Nat King Cole to his friend, Don Brown, the *Courier*'s West Coast theatrical writer." Cole also talks about how his younger daughter, "Sweetie" (Natalie), is about to record a children's Christmas album.
79. Well, mostly. At the start of the first session, the engineering crew apparently had some difficulty with the new equipment, and the first two tracks, "Maybe It's Because I Love You Too Much" and "Love Letters" were only recorded in mono. From the third number, "I Thought about Marie," onward, everything was running smoothly.
80. Jack Cave, who played French horn with Jenkins on many sessions (including his albums with Sinatra), told me how much Jenkins "loved horns," but they don't

appear on any of his work with Cole, undoubtedly because Cole and Gillette wanted to focus on strings, and, in Gillette's perspective, the strings were expensive enough.

81. KW.
82. Radio interview of Gordon Jenkins by Wink Martindale, from KMPC Los Angeles, 1974.
83. Bruce Jenkins, in his biography of his father (*Goodbye: In Search of Gordon Jenkins* (Berkeley CA: Frog Ltd., 2005), 187–88), feels that Cole might have played in the band that Jenkins was leading for NBC on the radio series *Swing Soiree* in late 1938–early 1939. This seems unlikely, but hardly impossible. There are two tunes that the Trio recorded for Standard Transcriptions in 1940 and '41 that might be his work ("1, 2, 3, 4," credited to "Jenkins and Gabler," probably Milt Gabler, and "Ode to a Wild Clam," credited to Cole and Jenkins) which supports the notion and Cole and Jenkins worked together very early in both of their careers. Info regarding the Trio and Jenkins on NBC together in spring 1939 from *Swing: The Guide to Modern Music*, May 1939, 32.
84. Radio interview of Gordon Jenkins by Wink Martindale, from KMPC Los Angeles, 1974.
85. Radio interview of Gordon Jenkins by Wink Martindale, from KMPC Los Angeles, 1974.
86. Dick Kleiner, "Dick Kleiner's Pop Record Report," *Buffalo Evening News*, May 8, 1957.
87. "I Thought about Marie," copyright May 17, 1951.
88. Dorothy Kilgallen, *Voice of Broadway*, syndicated in many papers, including the *Jamestown* (New York) *Post-Journal*, November 7, 1956.
89. Earl Wilson, "Gisele Moves On," *New York Post*, May 14, 1957. For the record (pun intended), *Love Is the Thing* was Wilson's top pick, and the other two were *Miss Calypso* by Maya Angelou (yes, she was a calypso singer decades before she became poet laureate), and *Morgana King Sings the Blues*.
90. Walter Winchell, *Walter Winchell Writes of New York—Broadway Spotlight* (column), syndicated in many papers, including the *Buffalo Courier-Express*, March 20, 1957.
91. Richard Hubler, "$12,000-a-week Preacher's Boy," *Saturday Evening Post*, July 17, 1954, 106.
92. KW, 6–1.
93. There are at least two newspaper stories referring to the album as *Love Is the Thing* from well before the recording sessions; George E. Pitts, "Rock 'n' Roll Department," *Pittsburgh Courier*, October 13, 1956, A23; and Dorothy Kilgallen's column, *Voice of Broadway*, syndicated in many papers, including the *Jamestown* (New York) *Post-Journal*, November 7, 1956.
94. Radio interview of Gordon Jenkins by Wink Martindale, from KMPC Los Angeles, 1974.
95. KW, 6–1. When Gillette quotes Cole as saying he had no "eyes to do 'Stardust,'" he's employing vintage jazz musician slang usage associated with Lester Young: having

"eyes for" something means to like something or be attracted to it, "I had no eyes to play the clarinet" would mean, "I never wanted to play the clarinet." In 2001, David Meltzer published *No Eyes*, a book of poetry inspired by Lester Young.

96. Jonson painted dozens if not hundreds of covers for Capitol, mostly in the 1950s, including *Something Cool* and *Off Beat* by June Christy, *Where Are You?* and *All the Way* by Frank Sinatra, *Dino Latino* by Dean Martin, and *Politely!* by Keely Smith, among many others.

CHAPTER 8

1. Samuel Fuller, *A Third Face: My Tale of Writing, Fighting and Filmmaking* (New York: Alfred A. Knopf, 2002).
2. John Tynan, "Nat Cole—Story about a Pianist Who Turned Singer to Find a Kingdom," *Down Beat*, May 2, 1957.
3. "Gelt" or "Goldie" was Yiddish slang, used by Jewish New Yorkers in the 1950s, for black people; somehow they felt it was kinder than "schwartzer," the term used by Germans (and Nazis).
4. Two separate live recordings exist of Nat King Cole and Nelson Riddle live in Seattle, one believed to be from May 1957 and the other from May 1958, and are both most likely the work of recording engineer Wally Heider. It is hoped that these will be issued sometime in the near future.
5. KW.
6. DME, 269; although the first writer-director of the show is named "Jim Johnson" in DME, he was actually named Jim Jordan. (Source: "Tele Follow-Up Comment: Nat King Cole," *Variety*, November 7, 1956, 33.)
7. Frankie Laine and Joseph F. Laredo, *That Lucky Old Son: The Autobiography of Frankie Laine* (Ventura, CA: Pathfinder Publishing, 1993), 53. The King Cole Trio recorded "It Only Happens Once" for Capitol in 1945.
8. Originally introduced by Dick Powell and Ruby Keeler in a spectacular Busby Berkeley production number in *Gold Diggers of 1933*, the song was later parodied in the Broadway pastiche *Dames at Sea* as "The Echo Waltz."
9. Billy May, interview with the author, circa 1995. All quotes from May from this interview.
10. John Tynan, "St. Louis Blues—George Garabedian and Nat Cole: The Story of a Hollywood Film," *Down Beat*, April 3, 1958. All details regarding the production "groundwork" for this movie are from this source.
11. "Handy, Cole Discussed Film on His Life 16 Years Ago," *Chicago* (Daily) *Defender*, Tuesday, January 28, 1958, 18.
12. "Handy to Present Award to Cole," (Baltimore) *Afro-American*, January 18, 1947.
13. Incidentally, this seems actually not to be true. According to the most basic information out there, both *Carmen Jones* and *Cabin in the Sky* turned a profit, and *Cabin* was a substantial hit.

14. Ironically or not, this was Cole's last appearance at the storied showplace, one of the last times that the New York Paramount Theater featured live entertainment, along with the film program, before it closed in 1966. Considering that Cole was headlining a bill with Count Basie and His Orchestra, Joe Williams, Ella Fitzgerald (who dropped out of the run early on because of illness), plus the comedy team of Marty Allen and Mitch DeWood, it's hardly surprising that the run was a sensation.
15. In later years, Garabedian ran a nostalgia-oriented "collector's" record label called Mark 56, which issued many vintage radio shows as well as a set of transcriptions that the King Cole Trio had made for the MacGregor corporation.
16. Interview with Nat King Cole and family by Edward R. Murrow, *Person to Person*, CBS TV, November 1, 1957.
17. Bob Pondillo, "Saving Nat King Cole," *Television Quarterly* (Journal of the National Academy of Television Arts and Sciences), Spring–Summer 2005.
18. Quoted in Murray Schumach, "TV Called 'Timid' on Negro Talent—Nat King Cole Attacks the 'Pressure' by Sponsors," *New York Times*, October 24, 1961.
19. Pondillo, "Saving Nat King Cole."
20. Quoted in Cole's obituary by Louie Robinson, "Death Stills Voice of World-Famous Master Balladeer at Age 45," *Ebony*, April 1965, 123.
21. This is mostly from the memories of Bob Henry, as quoted in DME.
22. Oscar Godbout, "Nat Cole Scores Ad Men," *New York Times*, November 22, 1957.
23. Hal Humphrey, *Los Angeles Mirror News*, July 9, 1957.
24. Cecil Smith, "Nat Keeps Movin' in Musical Experiment," *Los Angeles Times*, August 27, 1961, N10.
25. Cole's adaptation of "Yellow Dog" includes part of the verse the relocated lover writes his girl back home but leaves out Handy's original line "Uncle Sam has rural free delivery" (which Smith famously delivered as "Uncle Sam is the ruler of delivery").
26. "Nat Cole—J. Gale's Three Pubberies," *Variety*, March 12, 1958, 53.
27. Interview with Nat King Cole and family by Edward R. Murrow, *Person to Person*, CBS TV, November 1, 1957.
28. Followed by "Just as Much as Ever," "My Personal Possession," "One Sun," and "Take a Fool's Advice."
29. Freddy Cole, informal interview with the author, 2005.
30. Carole Cole, phone conversation with the author, 2005.
31. Ren Grevatt, "'King' Again Sells Charm & Good Taste," *Billboard*, March 3, 1958, 9.
32. On his NBC TV show, Cole performed "Send for Me" at least once (July 9, 1957) in the same rock-combo arrangement that he had used on the record, but Johnny Mercer performed the song in a big-band chart on the October 29, 1957, telecast. Freddy Cole has performed it in a romping stomping big-band arrangement similar to the best of the Count Basie-Joe Williams hits—one wishes Cole and May had done it this way instead of this spare doo-wop treatment.

33. Colin Escott, "Clyde Otis: Looking Back," *Goldmine*, October 1, 1993, 42–43.
34. Interview with Nat King Cole and family by Edward R. Murrow, *Person to Person*, CBS TV, November 1, 1957.
35. "Nat Cole, Gastel, End 20-Year Tie," *Variety*, June 12, 1963, 57.
36. "Hot King Cole Trio Gets Mexican Offers," *Pittsburgh Courier*, October 21, 1944, 13.
37. KW, 7–1
38. That, at least, is the reason they placed their special assignment songs for Sinatra, like "Come Dance with Me" and "Come Fly with Me," with that singer's own publishing firm.
39. Douglas Sirk later referenced Cole by getting singer-keyboardist Earl Grant to do his best imitation of Cole over the main titles of *Imitation of Life* (1959).
40. *The Unforgettable Nat King Cole,* Mutual Broadcasting Company, NK 91–35, 1991.
41. Bruce Jenkins, *Goodbye: In Search of Gordon Jenkins* (Berkeley, CA: Frog Ltd., 2005), 187–88.
42. KW.
43. As Cole acknowledges in *Radio Luxembourg: The Capitol Show*, Nat Cole, Guest, Show #94, Capitol Radio Broadcast 33 1/3 1 040-113341429. Produced by Dave Dexter and contained in the Dexter collection at University of Missouri, Kansas City.
44. "Miss Me" (1951), "I'm Willing to Share This with You" (1956), and "Thanks to You" (1964). He's also credited with the lyrics to Prez Prado's "Patricia." (The words to the latter—other than the leader's grunt—are rarely heard.)
45. In his career as a songwriter, Lorenzo Pack wrote, among others, "You Must Be Blind" for the King Cole Trio, "Petootie Pie" for the duo of Ella Fitzgerald and Louis Jordan, and "The Black Cat Has Nine Lives" for Louis Armstrong.
46. Not to be confused with "It's Impossible," more properly known as "Somos Novios," a classic Mexican song recorded beautifully by Freddy Cole. If Nat had lived a few years longer, this would have been a great song for him as well.
47. KW, 7–1. Steve Allen's "Impossible" was also interpreted meaningfully in 1965 by the young Aretha Franklin, who probably learned it from Cole.
48. Radio interview of Gordon Jenkins by Wink Martindale, from KMPC Los Angeles, 1974.
49. "The Nat King Cole Nobody Knows," *Ebony*, October 1956.
50. Doris Day, telephone interview with the author, March 11, 2011.
51. KW, 7.
52. *New York Post*, January 23 (ad), January 24, and February 8, 1957.
53. *Chris Sheridan, Count Basie: A Bio-Discography* (New York: Greenwood Press, 1986), 455.
54. That identification courtesy of Peggy Lee's daughter, the late Nicki Lee Barbour Foster.

55. Vic Abrams is otherwise best known for several lesser pop hits, such as Mitch Miller's "Napoleon" and Eddie Fisher's calypso "Tonight She Is Crying." In addition to "The Blues Don't Care," which had also been recorded three months earlier by trumpeter Jonah Jones and the Five Keys (both on Capitol), Abrams also composed the excellent title song to Natalie Cole's 2002 album *Ask a Woman Who Knows.*
56. This information from a conversation with Mitchell Parrish himself, circa 1990.
57. Meehan, who was nominated for a Tony Award for *Funny Girl,* wrote one other memorable tune for Cole, "Something Makes Me Want to Dance with You," in the 1964 release *Let's Face the Music.*
58. As a team, Sigman and Russell wrote "Ballerina" and "Come In Out of the Rain," both recorded by Cole.
59. That album was *The Talented Touch* (Capitol (S) T 1044, 1958), and it featured endorsement blurbs by the other two most famous pianists associated with Cavanaugh, Nat Cole and George Shearing.
60. Joe Bushkin, interview with the author, circa 1992.
61. Songwriter James Cavanaugh had already co-written the all-time Ratpack standard, "You're Nobody 'Til Somebody Loves You."
62. "To Whom It May Concern" was very much a family affair for Cole: as mentioned, his sister-in-law wrote it, and the only other artists of note to record it are his brother Freddy, and his daughter Natalie.
63. Although unfortunately left off the album, "As Far as I'm Concerned" is quite possibly the best song written by the team by Earl and Alden Shuman, who wrote a string of generally forgettable hits for Perry Como and others in the years of the pop-rock transition.
64. And also of the Andrews Sisters hit "Bella Bella Marie"—a German song pretending to be Italian.
65. McCarthy's son, Joseph Allan McCarthy Jr., wrote two songs recorded by Cole, "A Boy from Texas" and "I'm Gonna Laugh You Right Out of My Life."
66. Radio interview of Gordon Jenkins by Wink Martindale, from KMPC Los Angeles, 1974.
67. Ironically, within two years, Cole's regular musical director would be Ralph Carmichael, who built a career on finding new and interesting ways to arrange and sing Christian Music. If Carmichael had been put to work on the project, or even if Jenkins had been asked to actually write some arrangements in his engaging, extravagant style, with his trademark army of strings, doubtless Cole himself would have been more inspired as well.
68. "Metropolitan Spiritual Churches Expect 3000 Delegates Here Sept 1, *California Eagle,* August 6, 1959, 5.
69. Ibid. Also *Jet* magazine, October 8, 1959, 36.
70. Mahalia Jackson, who also appeared in the film *St. Louis Blues,* was a guest on the NBC *Nat King Cole Show* on November 12, 1957. Cole sang a few bars of "Sometimes I Feel Like a Motherless Child" on the *Dinah Shore Chevy Show* of

October 10, 1960, and he and Shore did "Everytime I Feel the Spirit" together on her show of December 19, 1961.

71. Both the cover and the title were trashed when Capitol reissued the album seven years later in 1966, a year or so after Cole's death—apparently this religious project seemed like an appropriate choice for a new posthumous release. Now called *Nat King Cole Sings Hymns and Spirituals*, the new cover showed the singer standing on a dock, apparently on the banks of the Mississippi (actually on Lake Tahoe) with a solemn look on his face, as if he were contemplating the ways of God and the universe, or getting ready to sing "Ol' Man River." For my part, I always wanted to hear Nat tackle an album of traditional Jewish liturgical songs, which would have, of course, been titled *Nat King Kol Nidre*.
72. *Best of Broadway*, column by Hy Gardner, *Philadelphia Inquirer*, November 11, 1959.
73. The NBC TV special, *Some of Manie's Friends*, was (mostly) videotaped on February 22, 1959, and aired on March 3. Cole sings "Mona Lisa."
74. Nat King Cole (as told to Lerone Bennett), "Why We Adopted Kelly," *Ebony* April, 1960, 35.
75. Some of these details are from the unsigned album notes to *A Mis Amigos* (Capitol W-1220 & SW-1220, stereo).
76. KW.
77. Cole did not use the American adaptation and therefore avoided having to pay those royalties; instead, he made his own adaptation. The song was also recorded for Capitol by Mickey Katz with Yiddish comedy lyrics as "Kiss of Meyer."
78. Incidentally, both "Nao Tenho Lagrimas" and "Capullito De Aleli" were outfitted with fine English lyrics by Ervin Drake, the latter as "You Can in Yucatan" (recorded by Desi Arnaz)—but neither of these texts made it onto either of Cole's albums. (Cole had recorded Drake's adaptation of Dvořák's "Humoresque," also called "Mabel, Mabel," in 1946.)
79. Cavanaugh was credited as "B. Schluger," which is the pseudonym (it was the name of his wife's uncle) he employed when he was working on an ASCAP publishing project, since "David Cavanaugh" was under contract to BMI. "Schluger" is the name under which Cavanaugh collaborated with Peggy Lee on his best-known song, "I Love Being Here with You."
80. Nat King Cole (as told to Lerone Bennett), "Why We Adopted Kelly," *Ebony* April, 1960, 35.
81. DME, 301.
82. "That's Alright, Mr. Alston, Our Sox Were Very Different, Too," *Chicago Daily Tribune*, October 3, 1959.
83. Natalie, 33. *This Is Your Life* with Nat King Cole aired on January 6, 1960. Additional details from "'This Is Your Life' Surprises Nat Cole," *Los Angeles Sentinel*, January 14, 1960, C1.
84. Nat King Cole (as told to Lerone Bennett), "Why We Adopted Kelly," *Ebony*, April, 1960, 35.

85. Richard G. Hubler, "$12,000-a-Week Preacher's Boy," *Saturday Evening Post*, July 17, 1954, 30.
86. Richard G. Hubler, "$12,000-a-Week Preacher's Boy," 30.

CHAPTER 9

1. DME, 319–20.
2. Lee Zhito, "Music as Written: Hollywood," *Billboard*, September 28, 1959, 28.
3. From a conversation with Ed Walters, who worked as a pit boss at the Sands Hotel and Casino during the late 1950s.
4. *Federal Bureau of Investigation Freedom of Information/Privacy Acts Section. Subject: Nat King Cole.* Retrieved from Archive.org, February 18, 2020.
5. Milt Bernhart, interview with the author, circa 1991.
6. Nat King Cole, *Live at the Sands: The Complete Lost Concert* was issued by Very Special Records as VRS 001 in 2013, the closest thing to a country ID is "Europe." It seems likely that the original Capitol Recording leaked out from the private holdings of either Lee Gillette or Dave Cavanaugh. This issue also includes five "bonus" rehearsal tracks, including Nat's rather remarkable parody of a blues singer on "Joe Turner Blues."
7. Allen (1922–2018) had worked with Cole at several intervals, with his first partner, Mitch DeWood, at the New York Paramount in 1957, and then later with his more famous partner, Steve Rossi. Allen said that it was Cole who brought Allen and Rossi together (this from an informal interview with Marty Allen in 2016), and the three of them shared the spotlight when Cole hosted *The Hollywood Palace* in 1964.
8. Freddy Cole would record his version of this arrangement, with a variation on Cavanaugh's intro, in 2005.
9. Joe Sherman, phone interview with the author, 2005.
10. Of course, he actually did—Cole had already made around 30 rock 'n' roll singles by 1960, including the hit "Send for Me," some of which were written by the Sherman Brothers.
11. We know (from a *Variety* review, January 17, 1962) that Cole was singing "Where Did Everyone Go?" and a newer piece of special material titled "I Won't Twist," by Cahn and Van Heusen at the 1962 Sands shows, and hopefully they'll turn up on a longer version of the tape.
12. Tony Bennett, interview with the author, circa 1998.
13. TV discussion/interview with Nat King Cole by Hugh Hefner and Lenny Bruce, *Playboy's Penthouse*, October 24, 1959.
14. William Glover, "Nat to Try New Show on Stage," *Indianapolis Star*, May 1, 1960.
15. Cecil Smith, "Nat Keeps Movin' in Musical Experiment," *Los Angeles Times*, August 27, 1961, N10.
16. Dorothy Wayne, interview with the author, 2006.
17. Apart from Rasch, Wayne would write the lyrics for "The Night Has a Thousand Eyes," not the Buddy Bernier classic but a 1962 kiddie pop hit by Bobby Vee, as well

as "Never Trust a Dream," one of the more obscure songs by Cole's close friend Jimmy McHugh.

18. Additional info on Ray Rasch and Dotty Wayne from the Capitol Records press release for *Wild Is Love*.
19. "Cole Album Carries 100G Price Tag," *Billboard*, September 12, 1960.
20. "Nat King Cole Says 'Go Slow' Out of Tune," *New Pittsburgh Courier*, April 23, 1960, 2.
21. William Glover, "Nat to Try New Show on Stage," *Indianapolis Star*, May 1, 1960.
22. Four years earlier, "You Are Mine," words and music by Doug Goodwin, was recorded by singer Kathy Lloyd for Capitol. Although a forgotten (though decent song) and a completely forgotten singer, this was, in fact, the first vocal to be recorded in the brand new Capitol Tower studio, and arranged by Nelson Riddle no less, on February 23, 1956. Somehow Ms. Lloyd beat both Cole and Sinatra to this particular punch.
23. *The Unforgettable Nat King Cole*, 1988 documentary.
24. All quotes from Ralph Carmichael from a 2005 phone interview with the author.
25. Elsewhere, Cole had sung three songs by Stock, "In the Heart of Jane Doe" and two considerably better-known standards, "Blueberry Hill" and "You're Nobody 'Til Somebody Loves You").
26. Dick LaPalm, informal phone interview with Jordan Taylor.
27. Interview with Leo Branton by his son, Leo Branton Jr., July 27, 2001.
28. Gourse, 206.
29. Cecil Smith, "Nat Keeps Movin' in Musical Experiment," *Los Angeles Times*, August 27, 1961, N10.
30. "Cole Album Carries 100G Price Tag," *Billboard*, September 12, 1960.
31. Cecil Smith, "Nat Keeps Movin' in Musical Experiment," *Los Angeles Times*, August 27, 1961, N10.
32. Cecil Smith, "Nat Keeps Movin' in Musical Experiment," *Los Angeles Times*, August 27, 1961, N10.
33. "Cole Stars on French Network," *Cleveland Call and Post*, January 21, 1961, 3.
34. Cole and Carmichael recorded it twice, on two different sessions, in two different keys.
35. Cole would sing at least three different songs by Frisch: "All Over the World," "How Did I Change?" and, on television, the superior "Two Different Worlds."
36. "Nat Cole Stands on Artist's Right to Plug New Disk in Sullivan Row," *Variety* February 1, 1961. Additional information on the "Sullivan incident" comes from "Cole Withdrawal from Sullivan TV Rings Phone," *Chicago Daily Defender*, January 31, 1961; Chuck Stone, "A Chat with Nat King Cole—A True Philosopher King," *Afro-American*, March 18, 1961; "Nostalgic, Nat Calls Sullivan," *Cincinnati Enquirer*, September 3, 1961; and Gerald Nachman, *Right Here on Our Stage Tonight: Ed Sullivan's America* (Berkeley: University of California Press, 2009), 217.

37. Chuck Stone, "A Chat with Nat King Cole—A True Philosopher King," *Afro-American*, March 18, 1961.
38. "El Bodeguero" was included in the original Japanese telecast but for some reason was omitted from the laserdisc edition thirty years later.
39. According to Niehaus's own testimony, in an interview with Jordan Taylor.
40. Details re the forming of Kell-Cole from *The Incomparable Nat King Cole,* A. S. "Doc" Young, editor (Fort Worth, TX: Sepia Publishing Company, 1965), 53, and "Nat King Cole Forms Production Company," *Los Angeles Sentinel*, June 30, 1960, C1.
41. Stanley G. Robertson, "L.A. Confidential: Leo Branton Defends Nat Cole Show," *Los Angeles Sentinel*, March 19, 1964, A7.
42. Maria, 99.
43. According to Rory Burke, Johnny's eldest child, Nat's original idea was to name the girls after Johnny and Bessie Burke's twin daughters, Rory and Regan, born in 1941.
44. Stanley G. Robertson, "L.A. Confidential: Leo Branton Defends Nat Cole Show," *Los Angeles Sentinel*, March 19, 1964, A7.
45. It was subsequently recorded by four singers who were all profoundly influenced by Cole, three of whom were also pianists: Bill Henderson (with Cole acolyte Oscar Peterson), Buddy Greco, Shirley Horn, and Freddy Cole. PS: It's hardly the fault of Freddy Cole that the credits on his album (*Rio De Janeiro Blue*, 2001) attributed the wrong composers to "Wild Is Love," and also suggested that Freddy learned the song from Shirley Horn.
46. "It's a Beautiful Evening" was also recorded early on by Dorothy Dandridge, as well as Buddy Greco, but the most important treatment was the instrumental by the celebrated jazz trumpeter Donald Byrd (on his 1961 album *Out of This World*). Forty years later, it was revived by the contemporary trumpeter and Byrd-watcher Jeremy Pelt, who continues to play it in concert.
47. "Television Reviews: Wild Is Love," *Variety*, November 15, 1961.
48. "Television Reviews: Wild Is Love," *Variety*, November 15, 1961. All production specific details from this source.
49. This is a very familiar phrase in Cole's piano work; it actually belongs to two traditional American themes, the first strain of "The British Grenadiers," which was made into a popular song in World War II titled "The Girl I Left behind Me" (recorded as such by Kay Kyser, Bob Wills, and many others) and "American Patrol," most famously recorded by Glenn Miller, which, with lyrics, became "We Must Be Vigilant" at roughly the same time.
50. Stanley G. Robertson, "L.A. Confidential: Leo Branton Defends Nat Cole Show," *Los Angeles Sentinel*, March 19, 1964, A7
51. Haskins, 155; Kert is mis-identified as being Canadian (he was born in California), and Stan Harris as being an employee of Kell-Cole (rather than the CBC), but otherwise the gist of Kelly Cole's account would seem to be, sadly, correct.

52. Stanley G. Robertson, "L.A. Confidential: Great Show, Mr. Cole, But . . .," *Los Angeles Sentinel*, January 23, 1964, A9.
53. Stanley G. Robertson, "L.A. Confidential: Leo Branton Defends Nat Cole Show," *Los Angeles Sentinel*, March 19, 1964, A7.
54. It's pleasing to be able to report that the *Wild Is Love* special is far from lost. It survives in an excellent copy video master (for which I thank the late archivist Michael B. Schnurr for sharing with me). One number ("Stay with It") was included on *Black Magic*, a commercially released DVD anthology of African American performers on the CBC.
55. Cole had already recorded her 1949 standard, "Again" and also the lesser known "When You Belong to Me," both in 1958.
56. Cole also recorded "What Have You Got in Those Eyes" by Raye and DePaul in 1949, and "Teach Me Tonight" by Sammy Cahn and DePaul in 1954.
57. George Shearing, interview with the author, circa 1990.
58. Steve Race, "We Had to Break the Monotony a Bit, so I Started Singing, Says Nat King Cole," *New Musical Express*, September 15, 1950.
59. Cole was in an Ivy-Duke mood in fall 1961; nearly a half dozen songs from *Let's Face the Music* and *Cole/Shearing* had been recorded twenty-five or so years earlier by the Anderson-Ellington combination.
60. Sullivan was and is infamous for mangling and forgetting dozens of names out of the thousands of introductions he made in the twenty-two seasons of the show. He famously announced The Supremes as "the girls" but my personal favorite moment is the time he introduced "Jim Henson's 'Muppets'" as "Jim Newsome's 'Puppets.'" Quotes from Cole from Chuck Stone, "A Chat with Nat King Cole, A True 'Philosopher-King,'" *Afro-American*, March 18, 1961. Carmen McRae was on the same Sullivan show that Cole missed, January 29, 1961.

CHAPTER 10

Epigraph: "A King of Song Dies, and a Friend Remembers Him," *Life* magazine, February 26, 1965.

1. "Radio Review," *Variety*, November 28, 1962.
2. Medics 'Optimistic' for Cancer-Stricken Nat 'King' Cole: Chain-Smoking Singer Tried to Quit for Two Years," *Philadelphia Tribune*, December 19, 1964, 1.
3. Medics 'Optimistic' for Cancer-Stricken Nat 'King' Cole: Chain-Smoking Singer Tried to Quit for Two Years," *Philadelphia Tribune*, December 19, 1964, 1.
4. DME, 336.
5. Ralph Carmichael, phone interview with the author, summer 2005.
6. And Cole never even sang "La Paloma (The Dove)."
7. *Silver Platter Service* (Catalog # PRO 2123), 1962.
8. Bill Steif, "Frisco Masonic Temple's Cryptic Nix of Cole, Who Shifts to Civic Aud.," *Variety*, February 2, 1960.

9. Rory Burke, phone interview with the author, March 10, 2019.
10. Joe Sherman, interview with the author, 2005. All quotes from Sherman are from this source.
11. Ren Gravatt, "25 Years in the Business, Nat Cole Finds There's No Rest for Talent," *Billboard*, November 16, 1962, 4, 49.
12. "When You're Smiling" was written by Larry Shay, Mark Fisher, and Joe Goodwin; this Fisher was a Chicago bandleader and apparently no relation to the family of Marvin Fisher (Marvin, Fred, Doris, Dan) who wrote so many classic songs for Cole.
13. Friend Tony Bennett had experienced the same phenomenon a few months earlier that year when he released a single of a promising new show tune called "Once Upon a Time," and the B-side became the megahit, "I Left My Heart in San Francisco."
14. Cole's usual radio promo man, Dick LaPalm, recused himself from this one, feeling that another promoter with more experience in the pop-country field could do a better job.
15. Ren Gravatt, "25 Years in the Business, Nat Cole Finds There's No Rest for Talent," *Billboard*, November 16, 1962, 4, 49.
16. Pete Bennett later reported that the song would have surely reached #1, but there was some sort of "deal" in place for whichever song did reach the top spot that week, thus "Ramblin' Rose" was stuck at #2. The number one that week was "Sherry," the breakthrough hit by the Four Seasons, surely a worthy and iconic pop record.
17. Cole also sang "Where Did Everyone Go?" on *The Jack Paar Show*, October 26, 1962.
18. I'm not including *Every Time I Feel the Spirit* in this list; that doesn't qualify as a full-on "proper" Cole-Jenkins project.
19. This information from Dick LaPalm, informal interview by Jordan Taylor.
20. Fuller is, ironically, perhaps better known in the 21st century as the long-suffering girlfriend of the infamously inept cinematic auteur Ed Wood, and as an actress in several of his films. She was portrayed by Sarah Jessica Parker, opposite Johnny Depp as Wood, in Tim Burton's 1994 film *Ed Wood*. Coincidentally, she and Cole were both in the same scene of the 1953 thriller *Blue Gardenia*; she is visible as was one of the dress extras at the bar while Cole is playing and singing the title song.
21. *Live at New Latin Quarter* was issued by NLQ Entertainments as CD: MMV-1002 (2013).
22. Translation courtesy Maria von Niccoli.
23. "Nat King Cole Open-End Interview," PRO 2386/2387, Capitol Promo 45 RPM disc, 1963, courtesy Jordan Taylor. This is a pre-recorded "interview" that Capitol distributed as a promo to radio stations in 1963.
24. Their first cousin was Ida Tobias, best known to a generation of radio listeners as the wife of Eddie Cantor and the mother of his famous quintet of daughters. Harry's son, Fred Tobias, wrote songs in the early rock and roll era.

25. There was one aspect of the song that Sherman wanted to change, however: the title. He reported that most people seem to remember the song by its first line, "If I had to choose," and, in his estimation, speaking in 2005, he thought that would have made a better title, or at least a subtitle. I personally disagree. "That Sunday, That Summer" is a perfect title.
26. Caroline, 61.
27. "Nat Cole, Gastel End 20-Year Tie, *Variety*, June 12, 1963.
28. Many more details on this incident in DME, 329–30.
29. Caroline, 136.
30. "Nat Cole Plans Big TV Show Here," *Disc*, June 8, 1963, 3.
31. "Television Reviews," *Variety*, October 2 and 16, 1963.
32. Cole's two major "television concerts," 1961 Tokyo and 1963 London, have been relatively easy to see, readily accessible on YouTube. For better or worse, the BBC show is generally only available in "Digital Color," prepared by a firm called CST Entertainment, Inc. The color on this version looks so good that one is tempted to believe that it's an actual color videotape, even though the BBC didn't start broadcasting in "colour" until 1965.
33. *Variety*, August 29, 1963.
34. Gunilla Hutton, phone interview with the author, February 10, 2019. All subsequent quotations from Hutton are from this interview.
35. Silver Platter Service 113/114, July 1964.
36. Liner notes to *Nat King Cole Sings Selections from Lerner & Loewe's My Fair Lady*.
37. Silver Platter Service 113/114, July 1964.
38. DME, 335.
39. *Nat King Cole: Afraid of the Dark* (Documentary, *2014)*.
40. DME, 334.
41. Author's conversation with Timolin and Casey Cole, March 16, 2019.
42. "Nat Cole Visits Johnson," *New York Times*, January 9, 1964, 19.
43. Art Seidenbaum, "It Ought to Be a Warm December: Nat Cole at the Music Center Has To . . ." *Los Angeles Times*, December 6, 1964, 84.
44. Tony Bennett, interview with the author, 1998.
45. Friars' Luncheon for Nat King Cole a Not Too Ribald Ribfest," *Variety*, January 29, 1964.
46. Myron Feinsilber, "You've Gotta Have Gall in Tin Pan Alley," *St. Louis Post-Dispatch*, July 2, 1964, 2D.
47. Letter from Don Robertson to Jordan Taylor, 2005.
48. The new background, with the choir singing in Japanese, was recorded in Los Angeles on August 26, 1964, and Cole taped his vocal sometime during his final run in Las Vegas in November. (The original composer, Charlotte McCarthy, shares credit with the Japanese librettist, Kenji Sazanami.)
49. Ren Gravatt, "25 Years in the Business, Nat Cole Finds There's No Rest for Talent," *Billboard*, November 16, 1962, 4, 49. As we know from earlier chapters, he could

have easily done this in 1959. Also, while the *Billboard* story gets the name of the label right—this is not counting the Eddie Cole sides from 1936 or the many Trio transcriptions of 1938 and '39—it gets the year wrong in saying the Ammor discs were from 1938 and not 1940.

50. Quoted in Robert DeRoos, an unpublished manuscript of a biography of James Van Heusen, courtesy of Brook Babcock and the Van Heusen estate.
51. As an interesting—hopefully—side-note, back in the 1990s, Capitol Records commissioned me to produce an anthology titled *Nat King Cole at the Movies*, and I chose to include "Autumn Leaves," since that song had originally come from a French film called *Les Portes de la Nuit*. However, I wanted to use the 1964 French language version, which had never been reissued in America, as opposed to the original 1955 recording. For the longest time, however, it looked like we wouldn't be able to use the French language recording, because no master could be located in the Capitol vault. They scoured the tape library over and over and still no trace of the French "Autumn Leaves" turned up. Then, at the last minute, I suggested that they look under "Les Feuilles Mortes" rather than "Autumn Leaves," and voila! There it was. Not bad for a guy who learned all his French from Cole Porter.
52. Cole had also sung "Autumn Leaves" in Japanese and English on his 1961 Tokyo TV concert.
53. Natalie, 48–49.
54. DME, 33.
55. Cecil Smith, "Nat Keeps Movin' in Musical Experiment," *Los Angeles Times*, August 27, 1961, N10.
56. Cecil Smith, "Nat Keeps Movin' in Musical Experiment," *Los Angeles Times*, August 27, 1961, N10.
57. "Nat Cole, Dolores Del Río Team in Mexican Comedy," *Boxoffice*, April 23, 1962.
58. "Nat King Cole Sought for Role in New Film," *Philadelphia Tribune*, August 28, 1962, 5.
59. Andrea Passafiume, "The Big Idea behind Cat Ballou," http://www.tcm.com/this-month/article/220461%7C0/The-Big-Idea-Cat-Ballou.html, retrieved July 31, 2018. All unattributed quotes are from this source.
60. The notion of an intoxicated cowboy was famously reused by Mel Brooks in his classic western spoof, *Blazing Saddles*.
61. Quotes from Silverstein and other details are from *The Legend of Cat Ballou* (produced and directed by Michael Gillas), a "making of" featurette included on the DVD of *Cat Ballou*.
62. In the 1955 film noir *Kiss Me Deadly*, Cole sang "I'd Rather Have the Blues," a song written by De Vol, but arranged by Nelson Riddle.
63. David and Livingston had considerably more familiar songs to their credit apart from each other: David had written lyrics to several exceptional songs performed by Cole, including "Candy," "Where Did Everyone Go?," and "Morning Star" (from *St. Louis Blues*); Livingston composed the jazz standards "It's the Talk of the Town," "When It's Darkness on the Delta," and the Sinatra favorite, "Close to You."

64. Some sources claim that Cole and Kaye participated in the location shooting in Colorado, but given what we know about his schedule and his physical condition, this seems unlikely. In the finished film, there are at least a few shots of the two singers in what appears to be the Colorado location shooting, but a close examination of the recent Blu-ray edition of *Cat Ballou* reveals that these are, in fact, process shots.
65. *Nat King Cole: Afraid of the Dark* (Documentary, 2014).
66. DME, 341.
67. Louie Robinson, "Death Stills Voice of World-Famous Master Balladeer at Age 45," *Ebony*, April 1965, 123.
68. "Wanderlust" is by Bill Olofson and Mark McIntyre. McIntyre started as a studio pianist and was an early accompanist for Sinatra, before he became a recording artist in his own right in the children's music genre, notably the hit "Tonight You Belong to Me." In 1954, the trio of Nat, Cookie, and Sweetie had recorded his "What to Do."
69. Dunstan was a rather diverse individual who seems to have tripled as saxophonist (with Stan Kenton, and on the *L-O-V-E* sessions), singer (with Cole's "Merry Young Souls"), and songwriter (here on "Your Love"). In addition, he also worked as a copyist on several Cole sessions.
70. In some sources, most notably the back cover of a later "pick-up" album titled *Sincerely*, George David Weiss is credited as a third songwriter of "No Other Heart." This is almost certainly an error; Kretzmer and Lee are most likely the only authors.

POSTSCRIPT: THE AFTERLIFE

1. Caroline, 243.
2. Caroline, 154.
3. Art Seidenbaum," It Ought to Be a Warm December: Nat Cole at the Music Center Has To . . ." *Los Angeles Times*, December 6, 1964, 84.
4. Cecil Smith, "Music Center Switches from Classics to Jazz," *Los Angeles Times*, December 12, 1964, A12.
5. Maria, 140.
6. DME, 531.
7. Both stories from *Nat King Cole: Afraid of the Dark* (Documentary, 2014).
8. Maria, 141.
9. Caroline, 222, confirmed by Freddy Cole in an informal interview with the author.
10. Maria, 141.
11. DME, 535.
12. *New York Amsterdam News*, March 13, 1965.
13. Leonard Feather, *Feather's Nest* (column), *Down Beat*, May 6, 1965.
14. Leonard Feather, *Feather's Nest* (column), *Down Beat*, May 6, 1965.

Index

For the benefit of digital users, indexed terms that span two pages (e.g., 52–53) may, on occasion, appear on only one of those pages.